NOT SO WILD A DREAM

Post proofs that brotherhood is not so wild a dream as those who profit by postponing it pretend.

—*from* "On a Note of Triumph"
by NORMAN CORWIN

NOT SO WILD
A DREAM

ERIC SEVAREID

With a New Introduction by the Author

UNIVERSITY OF MISSOURI PRESS

Columbia and London

Library of Congress Cataloging-in-Publication Data

Sevareid, Arnold Eric, 1912-
    Not so wild a dream.
    Autobiography.
    ISBN 0–8262–1014–7
    1. Sevareid, Arnold Eric, 1912- 2. Journalists—
Correspondence, reminiscences, etc.   3. World War,
1939-1945—Personal narratives, American. I. Title.
PN4874.S43A3   1976   070'.92'4 [B]   76-11538

∞™ This paper meets the requirements of the
American National Standard for Permanence of Paper
for Printed Library Materials, Z39.48, 1984.

NOT SO WILD A DREAM

To L. F. S.

Introduction
to the New Edition

MOST BOOKS should be self-explanatory and require no preparation of the reader. First-born books, at any rate. Rebirth, thirty years later, may strike the reader, if not the author, as an unnatural occurrence, and he is entitled to wonder what it is all about.

When *Not So Wild a Dream* was first published in 1946 I did not try to explain it with an introduction. It was sent out on its own, across the rough seas of publishers' estimations, sales and advertising decisions, the attention span of reviewers and the quick guesses of book merchants.

Save for the special efforts of its devoted publisher, Blanche Knopf, this book of youth, adventure and war and a troubled love of life had to find its own forward currents and its own level. It floated slowly to a position quite near the very top—around fifth place on the best seller lists, a place among the *New York Times*' "Ten Best Books of the Year"—but not on top. It slowly sank through eleven Alfred A. Knopf editions over twenty-eight years.

But in the last few years it began to rise again, in a different sense. It became a reference book, a source book for historians and other students of the Depression years, the first American "student movement," which developed then, and World War II itself. It has acquired the cachet of "original source" for those events to which I was an eyewitness. Americans turned the normal circle, and interest in those seminal years was heightened as the new generation searched for the modern origins of America's present achievements and failures and predicaments. The book was in the process of rediscovery by individuals. Letters, a freshet, then a steady stream, began to flow my way from new readers, many of them writing with genteel excitement at having found what they considered a rarity in the dusty back room of the antique shop.

The critical judgments about this book when it first appeared were often mystifying, but mostly gratifying. Lloyd Lewis presumed to compare it with *The Education of Henry Adams.* Some others thought it a fair match with James Vincent Sheean's *Personal History,* which pleased me even more since that seemed more reasonable, and because I loved Jimmy and his book which I read during my honeymoon in a north woods' shack, years before we became intimates. That book must have unconsciously affected my own attempt. But a war-dominated decade separated the two books and, as Joseph Barnes observed over the nightcap in William Shirer's apartment after Jimmy had left, "You both went into the world, but *you* came home again. You remained the hundred-proof American."

I was a news correspondent, first with newspapers and then radio; a worker in miniatures, quickly fashioned, quickly forgotten. My public image had already been established as such. Little wonder that various critics had trouble judging the book solely on its own merits and demerits. A first-book author is allowed to get off to a cleaner start if he comes from total obscurity. I suffered from what my friend Robert Ardrey called "category trouble," as he did himself, when he changed from play- and screenwriting to his extraordinary series of books about the animal nature of man, beginning with *African Genesis,* written when we were both living in Spain in 1959.

One cannot "see" his own book when it is finished; he cannot judge it as a whole or even notice the trivial mistakes. Ideally, a new manuscript should be set aside for months before the author looks at the smallest portion of it again. But that requires time and leisure that I have never possessed and that professional life today hardly accommodates.

I winced, later, to discover that on the very first page of the book I had transformed the hometown family name of "Muus" to "Moose" and in the Lisbon episode I had the Russian doctor pushing Rasputin into the Volga instead of the Neva. (Only Jimmy Sheean caught the error.) I alone, apparently, am bothered—to this day—by the use throughout the book of "which" where "that" would fall more gently on the ear. And I would feel more at ease, for the reader's sake, had I made finite the infinitude of detail about the hike out of the India-Burma mountains following what I have been told was the largest mass amateur parachute jump in aviation's annals.

No doubt the many wrongs of omission are more serious than those of commission. Friends have told me that since the story is cast in a personal mold I owed it to the reader to solidify the brief references to my own family. In particular, they thought, I had told them so little about my wife, Lois, who had accompanied me through much of the story, made many things possible and endured much, including my wartime absences. Yet I found, in the course of the writing, that I could not do that. I was too young to handle true intimacies in public view, too lacking in the skills required. I had been reared in a fairly severe Lutheran home too full of rules of behavior, too empty of expressed love— though the love was always there, much of it not well understood by me until I was considerably older. One did not impose his deepest emotions upon others and certainly not upon strangers. There is, therefore, I now know, a certain impersonality about this personal narrative. The breed from which I was sprung was condemned to demonstrate their love for each other not in words on paper or tongue, but in behavior. Yet, for want of the words, the behavior so often, so sadly, is not enough.

The book had to go the way it did because I was the way I was. Nothing was altered from edition to edition, no errors of fact corrected, no misapprehensions of the meaning of the events set right. Somehow, it seemed to me, self-protection of that kind would bear a touch of dishonesty, and this book could claim rather little if it could not claim honesty. Nothing is changed now, in the book's resurrection, made possible by Herman Gollob at Atheneum, who sustained his belief in *Not So Wild a Dream* through these thirty years and was determined that it not be allowed to sink to a final death. Atheneum was willing to launch it once more, on the far rougher seas of a new generation of readers who are bound to perceive it, its author, the great war and the war generation through very different lenses.

It was written—nearly a quarter million words of it until my own presubmission excisions—at one sitting, as it were, over a period of eight months with only a few days' leave from the typewriter. I am unable to work at a manuscript, let it cool a time, then return to it, or switch back and forth between two writing themes for mental relief. Once set upon a track, mine is a one-track mind. I was working almost entirely from memory, with few notes or diaries. But at the age of thirty-two the memory of an intense young man with an intense, if not always penetrating, vision is an overcharged storage battery, ready to loose its currents until depletion.

One learns a few things about oneself in a marathon of concentration. I confirmed what I had vaguely sensed: that I am one who learns more through the eye than through the ear, whether applied to words or the scene before me. Scenes, persons, ideas—these are the sharp imprints upon my brain. So there is not much conversation in these pages. I would be the poorest of fiction writers, and it occurs to me that these quirks of neurochemistry draw much of the dividing line between journalist and novelist.

At best the journalist may infuse scene, person and idea with a certain artistry, provided that some portion of his nerve endings have caught the subterranean murmurings of the English language. Words themselves become beings, sentences become, not structures, but natural vegetation to be guided by the gardener's hands. Often during those eight months of horticulture I would wake suddenly in the night because my subconscious knew I had done injury to the plant with a misplaced comma, a bathetic sentiment, a not-quite-accurate quotation. It was then impossible to sleep until the page was retrieved, the remedy applied.

But all writers, no doubt, are overly conscious of their peculiar agonies, or for that matter, their ecstasies. Perhaps that is what makes them writers. One cannot, with honesty, explain the presumption of a narration in autobiographical form by a very young and not very important journalist save by acknowledgment of an intense self-consciousness. The events, the scenes, the persons and ideas did not truly exist for me save in my own feelings about them. One is blessed—or cursed—with "double vision." One sees simultaneously the outward action and his inner self as actor. But to write is also to act, in the existentialist sense. Thought leads to actions but actions lead to thoughts. One's actions alter one. In the process of writing this long personal accounting I know that I was changed as a person, and for the better. Maturation is not a smooth and steady process; it occurs fitfully, the fits and starts far separated in time. By no means did I develop fully, even within my own natural limits as a human being, but certain of the spirit's muscles were loosened and came into play. Even though I could not write of the deepest intimacies, the writing process forced me to think more closely about them than I had ever done in my strenuous and self-concerned young life. One day perhaps, if life allows it, I will be able to reach bottom, to write without constriction of the persons and places I have loved and what they meant and did for me. A blessing of age is that one is so much less afraid of his loves as well as his hatreds. In truth, the enmities grow dim while the loves glow all the stronger. Perhaps this, too, is selfishness, an element in the universal craving for immortality, but the need is there to declare the love in the only way available to such as I, by writing it down on paper. So that my family may know, and the residual friends who have loved me in spite of myself through so many years and whose esteem helped so much to pull me across mid-life's deserts of despair.

My mother always knew. It was my father with whom I could not communicate because he could not communicate with his children. In my childhood I thought he was God. In my early youth I thought he was the Old Testament God, remote, stern, all-seeing, remorseless enforcer of commandments, laws and by-laws.

It was in the process of writing that I understood that he was the God of silent love. By then I had experienced just enough physical hardship, weariness, disappointment, failure, just enough responsibility for the lives of others. My father's life suddenly came clear to me. I remember the moment. I was nearing the end of this book, writing in a house on Forty-eighth Street ("halfway between Dorothy Thompson and the Third Avenue El," as my landlord, Jay Allen, described it) when it came over me—the enormous stamina he devoted to his family's protection, the pleasures renounced for our sakes, the disappointments swallowed, the self-pity denied.

It was then that there began for me a new appreciation of the strong—by which I do not mean the powerful or oppressive; a comprehension of how they make life possible for everyone else; a capacity to distinguish weakness from virtue and to understand with some clarity the weapons and tyrannies of the weak.

As my father's greatness as a person revealed itself to me, my own paucities were simultaneously revealed—my blindness to him and no doubt to others, behind the veil of self-concern. I could hope, desperately, that there was something of the father in the son, but I knew that I must act if further writing were to be possible at all. I sent him a letter, saying with restraint, but saying enough, that I understood at long last, and asking his pardon for my tardiness.

Save for one other sacred and not dissimiliar consequence, this matter I think of as the chief reward for the writing of this youthful book. I think this because of the epilogue to the story. Eight years later I sat by his deathbed, the only child present. My sister was away in North Africa with her soldier-husband, my two brothers away in the Korean War. It was as if it were commanded that I see my father's life with total clarity. The lines in his face vanished, his eyes were powerfully blue and play-ful, and I saw the young athlete my mother had fallen in love with. He spoke calmly, with restraint to the end, about the absence of the others and asked if I would mind taking care of his few personal papers and make the arrangements for my mother. At the very end he patted the hand nearest him and said, "It's all right. Everything is all right."

After the funeral I looked through his effects, including his wallet. In it, creased and yellowing, was the note I had written to him from New York. He had carried it on his person all those years.

It was the alchemy of the writing process, the remembering process, that also helped restore my wife and me to one another. The long partings were over; the war was over; we had all survived. Love had not survived, we thought. But it had only taken miserable refuge from the hammerings of history. She went to my desk one night as I slept and read the earlier chapters of the book.

It was she, not I, who found the courage to speak, and the second miracle of love occurred. The walls of glass between us dissolved. Her very face altered in my vision. The vibrant young college girl I had met at a party reappeared.

It was just in time and it was too late. Time had been work-ing, after all, in hidden ways unnoticed by me and unrecognized by her. Within weeks a new tone entered into her exuberant happiness. There developed a touch of dramatics, an exaggera-tion of voice and gesture, a fierce certainty to her opinions. She slept less and less, and I too, in consequence. Then, suddenly, she was tired and listless, but the doctors could find no physical cause. The pattern of her behavior repeated itself, over and over. It was the beginning of the doctors, the drugs, the psychiatrists, the sanatoria, the endlessly differing theories and conjectures and advisories. Much less was known in those days of the cause of this kind of "mental illness" which is, in fact, a chemical disorder of the glands and is seeded in the chromosomes. Much less of the cause but quite as much of cure, which does not exist.

One cannot accept the idea of incurability in relative youth. Far more readily accepted by one such as I, reared in the Puritan ethic, was the concept of guilt, and even that may well be a reflection of the ego. I indulged it through the many years of seeking her health and my own redemption until the first came to seem out of my reach and the second came to seem, with the help of doctors and friends, an unreality, sprung from a false bill of self-indictment. Strength dwindled to a kind of mindless endurance. But I was not my father, after all. I became in my own way as ill as she, still functioning but with only the exposed tip of the mind. Professional skills masqueraded as creativity. A claustrophobia possessed me. I could find no door and the walls of my life were closing in. It was then that I learned the penalty of the loss of one's childhood religious faith. I tried to revive it and could not. I could believe only in miracles because nothing else was left. The fantasy grew in me that her last chance for health lay in my own departure as well as my own last chance to feel again, to see again with the poet's eye and perhaps, one day, to write something that would be more whole than the writer.

I never did, in spite of departure, of course, and of course she never found health. She endured her own far greater tragedy for a quarter century in all and then died with merciful speed.

The year 1945, the break-point and watershed in my personal life, was the break-point, too, for the public arrangements of people everywhere on earth. The old empires were finished, a thousand tribes and races and collectivities were thrown upon their own. What the Greeks and Romans had begun came to its end and Europe was no longer chief repository and guardian of the Western culture of freedom. The power that had moved from the Mediterranean basin to the Anglo-Nordic races now moved out of Europe entirely to North America. Power has a way of accompanying culture and we would see now what my own people could do with both.

The public history of these last thirty years requires no rehearsal here. These are merely new words about old words. But I find, with some gratification, not too many of the old words that I would change. In the greater themes and projections the reader was not seriously misled; indeed, I suspect I had a deeper and truer intuition for what would come to the world than I have today. And it seems to me my youthful judgments on the individual movers and shakers have held up well.

By no means did I foresee every development; not the quick reemergence of Japan as an economic power; not the rapidity with which the Chinese Communists conquered that immensity of people; not the strange paralysis of Britain which I had implicitly assumed would lead Europe into a new way of life.

But my sense of the innate strength of the culture of the individual in its historic basin, the West, seems justified now. Ed Murrow had speculated, as the lights came on again in London, that the British would be critically torn between the Russian way and the Western way, but I could not believe that, even then. It was the Germans at the heart of Europe whom I did not trust. This was partly a matter of the stomach as it was with so many Americans who saw and smelled the horrors, and partly the feeling that there was, indeed, a special knot in their spirit, a simmering self-hatred. For years afterwards I could not visit Germany and feel at ease. But in the spring of 1975 I traveled to Bonn to talk with Willy Brandt, the chancellor who had dropped to his knees before the monument to the slaughtered Jews of Warsaw. He was the authentic "good German" I had known among the neighbors in my boyhood village. I found a freshness, a guiltlessness, even a rich humor in the new, young generation of Germans. I felt at ease among them. I believed in them, because there is a certain duty to believe, but the tiny remaining doubt will not go away.

I thought for many years that I must have been wrong about southern Asia and was relieved to be wrong; the British legacy had gone deeper in India than I had suspected and at many layers political life was conducted with openness and there were no midnight knocks at the doors. But now it appears that I was not wrong after all; the capacity to sustain freedom with order and material progress has given out, and I fear the century's first woman dictator is only the first of many dictators to follow. "That dust of people," as De Gaulle called India, is too dense. They will have to find a way to sustain life itself before the good life is possible. Their way could turn out to be the Chinese way; I wish there were another.

Much can be forgiven any Indian leadership but I find it hard to forgive what Nehru did to the Naga tribesmen with whom I lived an unforgettable month. I learned of this soon after the great war ended and a Hollywood studio set out to shoot a motion picture in the Naga Hills, based on the relevant chapter in this book. Philip Adams, the former British district commissioner, who had rescued us, went with the advance film party, but Nehru refused them permission to visit the Hills. He was making war upon the Nagas to hold them within the newly independent Indian state. This war went on for years and years and, I believe, still faintly flares. No one has reported it at first hand; no one has been allowed to. But now and then a letter came from a friend in the area and once the daughter of a famous headhunter I knew, she now a sari-draped Indian schoolteacher, came to visit me in Washington. The ancient, stone-age culture of those strong and cleanly people has been destroyed by the Indian civil servants, the soldiery, the money and the gunrunners, as the young Adams, sitting on his lonely Mokokchung hilltop, had sensed in advance could happen.

I had touched down only briefly in black Africa during the journeys herein described and then only at the bases swarming with American soldiers. Fifteen years later I went back and learned that Dag Hammarskjold's "century of Africa" notion was absurd; the State Department's yearning for "Pan Africanism" was absurd; "people's movements" had not wrested independence from European power—mostly, the power had simply fallen from palsied hands; with the white rulers gone, Africans would have nothing left to unite against save each other and they would run through the full cycle of the nationalism others taught them, including their own international wars. We did much to bring all this about, we Americans. In Nigeria an aging black barber-politician said to me as he cut my hair: "We found out from your GIs what our fathers had never found out from the godlike missionaries and the colonial officers in their white suits. We saw the GIs laughing and weeping and stealing and

squabbling and itching for our women, and we began to lose
our inferiority complex. White men were no better than we."
And so did the Indians find this out, and the Indo-Chinese and
the Arabs. We spread the idea of democratic equality that was
ours; what they did with it was theirs.

What is happening in all these places has essentially been
beyond our American powers to control or guide. But we have
had our influence. We did very much to give Europe another
chance, to push Japan and Germany and Italy off in new directions. We have touched a great many other places with economic
modernity and their ordinary people are not the worse for this,
and many are better. No great power ever tried harder or more
generously and it does not matter so much in the long run that
much of the effort was for private gain. I had been correct in
my wartime guess that our most forceful extensions into the
world would be those of military America and business America,
not those of the evangelical minded. Military America made the
greater blunders because business is flexible enough to take and
to give, to advance and retreat. It does not want people's souls,
as do the intellectuals; it does not want their obedience as does
the military; it only wants their money, the cheapest of all com-
modities. I incline to think now that among the underpinnings
of the world's interdependence, which we have desired and
which is unavoidable, the underpinning of business may be the
most solid of all and the least offensive.

Yet it remains uncertain that even this has much to do with
peace or with human freedom. Our basic premise has been, these
many years, that peace, democracy and material progress are
not only good, each in itself, but interdependent. The proof is
not in; evidence to the contrary accumulates, as the democratic
British impoverish themselves and the totalitarian East Germans
prosper; as the Greeks and the Brazilians, among others, alter-
nate between harsh rule with economic progress and free rule
with economic chaos.

The world is not America's sick oyster. John Kennedy pledged
that we, with their cooperation, would lift the load of poverty
from Latin America's people in ten years' time, yet we have not
lifted it from the people of Harlem, New York, nor from the
Puerto Ricans, our intimate wards. I have come to agree with
George Kennan: "To many this view may seem to smack of
cynicism and reaction," he said. "I cannot share these doubts.

Whatever is realistic in concept and founded in an endeavor to see both ourselves and others as we really are cannot be illiberal."

It was a lucky stroke of timing to have been born and to have lived as an American in this last generation. It was good fortune to be a journalist in Washington, D.C., now the greatest single news headquarters for the world since ancient Rome. But we are not Rome; the world is too big, too varied. The "American Century" concept of Henry Luce was an absurdity, too. We were not born to be imperialists; we never learned the style, and the time for this is gone. We understand the concept of citizen, not that of subject. There is only one true imperium now, that of the Soviet Union.

Our reach exceeded our grasp, as it was bound to do. I think it was John Adams who said: "Power always thinks it has a great soul and vast views beyond the comprehension of the weak." And, said a Greek: "Nothing that is vast enters into the affairs of mortals without a curse." The power of America is vast and so is that of Soviet Communism. But I observe that as between the curses, millions of human beings around this world prefer the American curse. They wish to come here; next to none wish to go there. It is so strange—these ordinary, unlettered people know in their bones what freedom is, even if their intellectuals do not. Freedom is the condition of feeling like one's self.

To find one's self—this is the deep drive behind the mass migrations and upheavals that we witness, here in our own land as well. One identifies self only in the eyes of others. We see, in the migrations from the interiors of Africa and Latin America to the great cities and in the "Negro revolution" of America, a flight, not so much from poverty as from anonymity. Modern communications have created an "in" world and an "out" world. For most people the "in" world is Europe and North America; for people anywhere, including here, it is the great cities. In southern Italy the government built modern factories, good housing, health centers, but also cinemas and television. To keep the people where they were. But the newly mature got up and went to Rome because, said my colleague Winston Burdett, that's where Sophia Loren lives. The head of the tiniest African state wants his yacht to go to Monte Carlo, too. Alas, not all can find themselves by their own efforts. It is much easier to find themselves by losing themselves—in the collective personality of some mass movement. This makes for very strong governments, as in Cuba or China, but big governments must keep persons small, and small persons cannot accomplish big things—not for themselves, and in the end not for their societies. Ten thousand committees could never produce the Sistine ceiling. How many they prevent we shall never know. There is nothing fundamentally new about Communism; only the techniques are new. It remains less impressive as a way of life than as a device for seizing power. The result is as old as time and as dull as death. I have now seen the new China. I am impressed because I saw the old. The people are fed and they are housed and only the children smile in the street. I could not endure six months living there. And there is no mystery in it. There is no mystery in the Orient. The most mysterious people in the world remain the unpredictable Americans.

In our time history moves in geometric ratio. In these past thirty years the life of men has probably changed more radically than in any single preceding generation, and individual men, including this one, have changed.

Maturity cannot really pass on the lessons of its experience to youth; that is nature's secret way of preserving the idealism of youth, as a source spring of human creativity through trial and error. And age cannot really relive the feelings of youth; that is nature's secret way of preserving the old. The young can measure in only one direction—from things as they are to their ideal of what things ought to be. The old must add two other measurements—things as they are compared to things as they used to be and things as they are compared to things in other societies the old have known. Otherwise life can teach very little. And so one becomes a relativist. One becomes a "moderate," understanding that the Greeks were right: The good life, for a person or a society, is not possible save in moderation. A loathing of this century's continuing "politics of hysteria" has come over me. I cannot bear the universal categorization of human beings: "Bourgeois," "Bolshevist," "Capitalist," "Nigger," "Honky," "Hippie," "Pig," "Imperialist." The one so labeled may be reviled, imprisoned, tortured, killed, or exiled because he is no longer a human being, but a symbol. He does not bleed when pricked; his heart does not cry in the night. By this conjuring trick conscience is made to disappear. It is, perhaps, the profoundest corruption of our time. Burke was right about the man of intemperate mind who cannot be free because his passions forge his fetters. Eric Hoffer is right when he says that "people in a hurry can neither grow nor decay; they are preserved in a state of perpetual puerility." I had always had a kind of reverence for brilliance, eloquence and physical bravery; I have come to have even more for that quality the Romans called *gravitas*—patience, stamina, weight of judgment. This is the essential quality of the truly strong, our preservers.

Travels in all the continents have not lessened my love and respect for America, but deepened both, in spite of the distressing spread of our vulgarities. There is a civilization of the heart, too, and the goodness in Americans, their evangelical strain, has not disappeared. We have often been innocents abroad and at times have done unintended harm, but no other great power has the confidence and stability to expose and face its own blunders. We are a turbulent society but a stable republic. The mind goes blank at the thought of a world without one such power. The dangers that hang over the world could then have no outcome but fatality.

Perhaps the role of the general journalist is fading out in this age of specialization; I am not sure. A society of generalists only could do nothing; but one of specialists only would be the final chaos. We may be jacks-of-all-trades and masters of none save the trade of being jack-of-all. Yet someone must do it; someone must try to pull together the threads of disparate thought and desire and need and actions, to conjecture at their meaning and weigh their worth in the scales of common sense, at least, when men are wary of grander measurements. There is such a thing as common sense; it is.an instinct for what is likely to harm and what is likely to help. It is born of experience; it takes some living.

The generalist has little more to offer. He is a horseback philosopher at best. He, too, has entered unchartered terrain: a world stiff with the ultimate weapons, the age of outer space, the time of the poisoning of our physical sources of life. No man's experience has prepared any of us for any of this. One knows only that the answers lie in inner space, terra firma and inner man. We have solved the composition of a lunar crater but we do not really grasp the inner mind of the Communist commissar or the heart of the delinquent child.

If a man's character is his fate then the fate of men generally will flow from the character of man. Less and less am I impressed with the governing effect of impersonal "social forces" and more and more with that of man's genetic forces. I spent much of my life trying to understand nurture, to discover how little I understood nature. Man's mind is the final, unlocked riddle.

Unable, myself, to see beyond it, I accept the formula that what men need and must have are three things: security, identity and stimulation, and not always in that order. I think I understood the compulsions of the first two even when young; I did not understand the powerful, sometimes creative, often violently destructive role of human boredom because I had so rarely been bored with my life. This is the fatal flaw in those concepts of brotherhood that mean total egalitarianism or total anything. All one knows is that these three drives in men must find expression and yet must be contained. In this lies the secret of the good life and the good society. It is a matter of balance. Man himself is a precarious balance between love and hate, generosity and selfishness, peaceableness and aggressiveness. He is not perfectable but he is improvable, and nothing in his history or his nature obliges one to abandon belief in him. He may indeed be forever "trapped between earth and a glimpse of heaven," but he will hold to the glimpse, as he must.

Mine has been a frightening and enthralling time of youth and middle age. The scriptures say that the glory of the young men is in their strength and the beauty of the old men is in their grey hair. The meaning is that there is a beauty in wisdom. Surely, the search for it is worth the costs of old age. One asks that courage will not diminish too much, for it is courage that makes the other virtues possible. One asks not only for the courage of his convictions but for the courage of his doubts in a world of dangerously passionate certainties.

One questions the usefulness of giving counsel to others, however long and varied and intense one's own exposures to life and history. But there is a counsel, of another, that finds favor with me.

In the year when I was born in a Dakota village, Professor Gilbert Murray at Columbia was writing of Greece and its fate when it lost its nerve, that is, its faith in reason. He said: "As far as knowledge and conscious reason will go, we should follow resolutely their austere guidance. When they reach their limits, as they do, then we must use as best we can those fainter powers of apprehension and surmise and sensitiveness by which, after all, most high truth has been reached as well as most high art and poetry. Careful always to seek for truth and not for our own emotional satisfaction, careful not to neglect the real needs of men and women through basing our life on dreams, and remembering above all to walk gently in a world where the lights are dim and the very stars wander."

ERIC SEVAREID
Washington, D.C. 1976

NOT SO WILD A DREAM

Chapter I

THE SMALL BROWN RIVER curved around the edge of our town. The farmers plowed close to its muddy banks and left their water jugs in the shade of the willows. There is not much shade in the northern sections of North Dakota, nor is there much shelter in the wintertime. Even as very small children we could sense the river's life-giving nature and meaning to the farmers, to us all. By December, despite the river's current, the men could cut ice blocks three feet square, to be stacked and layered with sawdust in the shed behind Moose's general trading store on Main Street, against midsummer when the hot winds came across the prairie, a time when the milk seemed to sour just a few minutes after you had milked the cow, when you couldn't even be sure of the butter kept in the well.

Velva (nobody seemed to know where the name came from; I suspect it made a pretty sound to the wife of some early settler) was only one of various villages strung upon the river's wandering length, but naturally we felt we exercised particular rights of possession over its flowing. On the red-painted wooden bridge, leading into the "city park" was mounted a large sign bearing a white star and the words in block letters: "Star City on the Mouse." This led also to the baseball diamond and the swimming hole just beyond. Sometimes the team from a village like Voltaire would come to play our men, and I can still remember my own feeling of proud generosity when, after the game, the Voltaire team would hurry to our swimming hole, strip off their overalls, and slide down our mud slide into the water, shouting, splashing, and shoving one another. Voltaire was only a few miles away, but it was bare and riverless. These men swam awkwardly with a great deal of thrashing and spitting. Only their forearms were burned a dark brown, and the face and neck down to the junction of the collarbone. The rest of their bodies was dead white in contrast. Grown men in those climates did not expose their bodies to the sun, and it was years before I saw adults with carefully nurtured "tans," acquired in leisure, not working, time.

Wheat. So far as Velva was concerned, wheat was the sole source and meaning of our lives, which were given in continuing hostage to the vagaries of this pewter-colored ocean that lapped to the thistle-covered roadbed of the Soo Line and receded in perpetually undulating billows as far as a child could see from the highest point, even from the top of the water tank. We were never its masters, but too frequently its victims. It was our setting and scenery. It was rarely long outside a conversation. On the mercy of the wheat depended the presence of new geography books in the red brick schoolhouse, a new Ranger bicycle from Montgomery Ward's, good humor in my father's face. Its favor or disfavor determined the size and mood of the crowd of farmers on Main Street Saturday nights, and was the reason Pastor Reishus in the Lutheran church prayed as frequently for rain as he did for our immortal souls. In good harvests it meant that hordes of itinerant workers, I.W.W.'s (which meant "I won't work," according to the businessmen of the town), hung around the poolroom and Eats Cafe, hunched like tattered crows on the hitching rails, spat tobacco juice at the grasshoppers in the dusty street, and frightened the nice women of the town so that they rarely ventured on Main Street in the evening time. Good harvest meant that my father would have to leave his office in the back of the little bank, remove his hard white collar, change to overalls, and, taking my older brother with him, go to help out on one of the bank's farms by driving the four-horse binder, while Paul, who was big for his age, would struggle with the shocks. Hired man or town banker, wheat was the common denominator of this democracy. It made all men equal, in prosperity or wretchedness. It meant that my father, the banker, was more of a confessor than the Catholic priest. His office was connected by a door to the town library for a time, and I could slip in among the bookshelves on days when the library was closed to everyone else. Sometimes I looked through the keyhole. I remember times when I would see a gaunt, unshaved Norwegian farmer sitting before my father's desk, staring down at his blackened nails, speaking to my father with painful difficulty about the locusts or the reaper which broke its axle on a rock, and sometimes, with more difficulty, about his wife who had gone sick again. Those were in the bad times. Those were the days when my father could not eat much at supper.

Those were the days when a buggy would drive up to our house after supper and my father and a wheat farmer would sit on the porch talking in low tones, with long periods of silence, until after we children fell asleep upstairs. Wheat was our solace and our challenge. My mother, who came from a green and pleasant city in the distant, mystical East—in Iowa—feared and hated it. My father simply met the challenge without emotion, as a man should, and grappled with it as well as a man knew how. In the end he lost. It ruined him.

North Dakota. Why have I not returned for so many years? Why have so few from those prairies ever returned? Where is its written chapter in the long and varied American story? In distant cities when someone would ask: "Where are you from?" and I would answer: "North Dakota," they would merely nod politely and change the subject, having no point of common reference. They knew no one else from there. It was a large, rectangular blank spot in the nation's mind. I was that kind of child who relates reality to books, and in the books I found so little about my native region. In the geography, among the pictures of Chicago's skyline, Florida's palms, and the redwoods of California, there was one small snapshot of North Dakota. It showed a waving wheatfield. I could see *that* simply by turning my head to the sixth-grade window. Was that all there was, all we had? Perhaps the feeling had been communicated from my mother, but very early I acquired a sense of having no identity in the world, of inhabiting, by some cruel mistake, an outland, a lost and forgotten place upon the far horizon of my country. Sometimes when galloping a bare backed horse across the pastures in pursuit of some neighbor's straying cattle, I had for a moment a sharp sense of the prairie's beauty, but it always died quickly away, and the unattainable places of the books were again more beautiful, more real.

2

My father was of the second generation of Norwegian pioneers who came with the Swedes, the Germans, and the Danes to this bleak and barren northwestern country, where the skyline offered nothing to soothe the senses, but where the soil was rich and lumpy in knowing fingers. He was of the second wave. The first, which carried in my grandfather, paused, in the fifties and sixties, among the pleasant rolling hills of Iowa and the southern counties of Minnesota, where one was always sure of rain. The land hunger did not die there. The railroads pushed out across the Dakotas, reaching for the fertile and already long-famous Oregon country, and the sons of the first, considering themselves very much American but still easily speaking their European tongues, followed soon after. The westering impulse was still strong in those men when my father went, in the first decade of this century, and those who penetrated North Dakota sought quick returns as well as permanent homes. For this was bonanza country. The soil was perfect for the crop. There were no hills to circumvent, no forests to clear. It required steadier purpose, harder work, and better men than the finding of gold; but the wheat was their gold. This was the Wheat Rush. So, recklessly they plowed and planted, the same crop year after year. They grew momentarily rich in the years of the First World War, but then the rains ceased. By now the original buffalo grass, which had preserved the soil, was long since plowed away, and without rain the earth lay dried and desolate, the color of old mud, and the hot prairie winds of summer, with nothing to stop them, simply transferred the top soil in the form of fine dust to faraway places. God knows how families survived those years, but they were tough and patient people and they always talked of "next year . . . next year," until even a child could grow sick of hearing it.

(And this, in the very years when the rest of the country flourished in the most extravagant prosperity it had ever known. Before Franklin Roosevelt presented the principle that Americans were one, obliged to care for one another. An idea, I must say, which would have seemed very strange out there in my father's day, when a man still believed that his preservation depended upon himself alone, so that he blamed only himself—and the elements—when he failed.)

Perhaps it was our common dependence upon the wheat that made all men essentially equal, but I do know now, having looked at society in many countries, that we were a true democracy in that huddled community of painted boards. A man might affect pretensions, but he could not pretend for long. We lived too closely together for that. There were, of course, differences in degree of material wealth. There were what was always referred to as the "well-to-do," and we had a few families "on the other side of the tracks." No doubt there was envy at times and small bitternesses here and there. But no man lived in fear of another. No man had the power to direct another to vote this way or that. No impenetrable combine could foist a candidate upon the people if they did not wish, and it would have been quite impossible to rig an election and get away with it. This was an agrarian democ-racy, which meant that there was no concentration of capital goods, which meant in turn, since we had no all-powerful land-lords, that no class society based upon birth or privilege had a chance to develop. Only a very thick-skinned, insensitive person would dare to "put on airs" in that intimate community. If Mother dressed my brothers and me too prettily for school one day, it was a moral and political necessity that we muddy our clothes as quickly as possible before showing up in the classroom. If this was a Christian democracy, still, no virtue was made of poverty; the Scandinavian is too hard-headed for that. But to be poor was no disgrace. If the man of the house in one of the families that lived close to the edge fell ill and could not work, my mother and other mothers carried them baskets of fresh things to eat. It was not charity, not condescension to ease the conscience; it was neighbor-liness, taken as such, and no one's pride was injured. The Horatio Alger tradition was strong even then, and the village boys really read those insufferable little books. One day when we were out picking wild plums by the river bank, another boy said to me: "Your father is a pretty good man, even if he is the richest man in town." I had no feeling of pride; far from it. I was shocked, and hurried home, close to tears. I demanded the truth of my father, for if this were true, I felt I would be in a highly compromised position; somehow my own worth would be at a discount. Pa-tiently, he demonstrated to me that the charge of possessing great wealth was a false accusation, and I relayed this gratifying in-formation to the proper place without delay.

Later, I read all the exalting literature of the great struggle for a classless society; later, I watched at first hand its manifestations in several countries. It occurred to me then that what men wanted was Velva, on a national, on a world, scale. For the thing was al-ready achieved, in miniature, out there, in a thousand miniatures scattered along the rivers and highways of all the West and Middle West. I was to hear the intelligentsia of eastern America, of Eng-land and France, speak often of our Middle West with a certain contempt, with a joke in their minds. They contemned its tightness, its dullness, its bedrock of intolerance. They have much to learn, these gentlemen. For we had, in those severely limited places, an intolerance also of snobbery, of callousness, of crookedness, of men who kicked other men around. The working of democracy is boring, most of the time, and dull compared with other systems, but that is a small price to pay for so great a thing.

I must have been very young when *Main Street* was first published. It is a title I remember along with the *Rover Boys*, Horatio Alger, and the Bible. Not that I read it, then, but my mother did and the neighbors up and down our street. I remember the local wrath, and remembering my mother's distress I know it came from being deeply hurt. Of course, in these little places originality was frowned upon, and genius would have been suspect. Of course, the pressure to conform was almost irresistible, and the boundaries of that conformity were appallingly narrow. Of course, art was at a discount and "niceness" the standard of taste. But this terrible indictment bewildered the citizens and made them wonder if all they had tried to do was wrong and had gone for nothing. For they had no other standard by which to measure except the past. And what had the past been? It had been sod huts, a diet of potatoes and gruel. It had been the hot winds in summer that shriveled the crops, and the blizzards of winter that killed the cattle, that brought the pneumonia and influenza that killed their women and children, while the stricken men turned the pages of a home medical guide and waited for the doctor who lived twenty miles away. It had been the gnarled men who sweated beside a kerosene lamp to learn the grammar of their new country's language. It had been the handing on from neighbor to neighbor of a few volumes of the classics, a few eastern newspapers three months old. It had been the one-room schoolhouse in a corner of my grandfather's homestead, where a "bright" aunt could occasionally be prevailed upon to teach the rudiments to tired boys and girls, who had risen before dawn to lug the slops because the family could not afford a hired man. They came together in villages and put paint on the boards of their houses. They planted green trees, made a park as best they could. They put their money together and hired for their children teachers who knew a little more. They sent some sons away to come back with the knowledge of medicine and the law. They built hospitals and colleges. The colleges were not Harvard nor Oxford, but they saw that the right books were there. They thought they had done well. Who, in his present comfort and easy knowledge, is now to sneer? They were of the

men who built America; they are now of the men who keep
America. They *are* America.

I was to become one of that small swarm of young American
journalists who, however deficient in scholarly background, infested foreign capitals, boldly bearded their great men, pugna-
ciously investigated their political movements, demanded the
unornamental truth at a thousand press meetings where our
French, British, or Portuguese colleagues approached the great
with timid genuflections and regarded us with a mixture of dis-
taste and awe. Instinctively, we looked at men for what they were
—as *men*. A title of office, or a "von" or a "de" before their names
was no kind of passport to our favor. Partly this was due to the
rigorous downrightness of our American journalistic training, but
partly to our beginnings in a hundred Velvas.

When "Duff" Aaker died prematurely, why did the whole town
mourn his death with such unfeigned sorrow? He was only a
country doctor with no wealth, no lineage, no power over them
but the power of his personality. I can still feel, when I remember,
the tapping of his strong fingers on my chest and the cigar smell
of his salt-and-pepper beard. He was one of the first in our town
to own an automobile, which he drove with savage speed. He
played the piano, the 'cello, and the violin and even *wrote* sym-
phonic music, which would have made anyone else suspect in respectable eyes. He understood my mother's longing for the green
and leafy places, and to him alone she could talk. He could denounce the Republican party and vote Nonpartisan League—
heresy among the businessmen—and get away with it. He could
drink in Prohibition days and get away with that. He could speak
so wisely with a dying octogenarian that the old man was happy in
dying. In his wrath he could refuse anesthesia to a drunken farm-
hand, terribly gashed in a pitchfork fight, make him sit upright
on a kitchen stool, pour in the iodine overgenerously, and rebuke
the man if he grunted.

He drove down one day from the new hospital at Minot to play
the organ at the funeral of the local shoemaker, and rushing out
of the church tripped, I think, on a croquet arch obscured in the
weeds. He was injured internally and died in great pain. My father
was a big, stern man, who made stern judgments, and I had never
actually heard him speak any praise of the doctor. The night Aaker
died my father went up to bed early, without saying goodnight.
When we children were going to sleep we could hear his bed shak-

ing. He was sobbing, and we listened in terror all night, for we had never known him to do such a thing. Duff Aaker was the first great man I ever knew about outside of books. No president or premier ever seemed greater to me.

Sometimes now it seems to me that my generation lived in preparation for nothing except this war that has ended and which involved my own life so profoundly; but the First World War, which was really the first phase of this one, must have been a very minor interlude for that generation. It surely did not affect our village much. I do remember my father lifting me to the window of a troop train as it halted beside the water tank, in order that we children could shake hands with Uncle Ephraim who was passing through on his way "over there." I remember scolding Arthur Renning, next door, for putting sugar on his bread, knowing that the government in Washington did not want us to put sugar on bread. That's all I remember about that war, except a dream, which is clearest of all. I dreamed the same dream many times. A column of "Huns" was marching down Main Street, past MacKnight's drugstore, and had reached Welo's department store, when I, lying artfully concealed on the roof of the bank, let go with my father's Winchester .22 and mowed them down. They seemed to make no effort to take cover, or to stop me, and they all died instantly. (In the winter when this war was ending in Europe, the British press printed pictures of two German youngsters who had tried to snipe at our men. The captions said: "Examine the faces of these killers, this spawn of the Nazi beasts. Can we treat them as innocent children?")

There were a good many Germans in town, but your parents never talked about them as *Germans*, never pointed them out and set them aside in your mind. Broad women with kindly faces who opened the doors to their clean, good-smelling kitchens and handed you a piece of limp, fragrant coffee-cake. They were just the neighbors. You knew they came from Germany, but you did not move them into that side of your mind which contained the Germany of the devilish Kaiser, the spiked helmets, and the savage men who cut the hands from Belgian children. The conception of Germans as a race, with racial (or, at least, national) characteristics of their own, was something that did not enter my mind for many years. There were no races with us, except the Negroes, and we saw only one specimen, who worked awhile around Johnson's barber shop, then drifted somewhere else. Undoubtedly, there were Jews among us, a few, but I didn't know what a Jew was until I was almost ready for college. A Jew is still just another person to me. If I do not experience any special reaction in the presence of a Jew, it is not due to broad-mindedness. I cannot. It just isn't there. The toxin was not injected into our bloodstream early enough, for which we give thanks to Velva.

For my father's generation, born in America though they were, the "old country," which they had never seen, still seemed close. He carried a faint Norwegian accent in his speech throughout his life, which came from his early boyhood when few around the farms spoke English. Christmas dinner was never right for him without *lutefisk* and *lefse*, and Pastor Reishus always preached first in Norwegian, then in English. But there came a break with my generation, the third. It happened throughout that northwest country. Talk with visitors in the parlor about the old country bored my brothers and me. I hated the sound of the Norwegian tongue and refused to try to learn it. It meant nothing to me that my grandfather on my mother's side was one of America's most distinguished scholars of Scandinavian literature and life. The books in my classroom dealt only with the United States, and there lay the sole magnet to our imaginations. The thread connecting these northwest people with Europe was thinning out, and with my generation it snapped.

There was another course which changed in that period. We were the first to grow up without the American West shining before the eye of the mind as the vision of the future. Instinctively we knew that the last of the frontiers had disappeared. From the time when the Indian tales lost their spell and we began to think, we wanted to go east. It was the East that was golden. My father did move his family east—a little way, to Minnesota—but not to seek more opportunity, more freedom; years of drought ruined his wheatlands and broke his bank.

3

The high-school period, in America anyway, is surely the worst period in a man's life—the most awkward, uncomfortable, inept and embarrassing of all times. And the most fruitless. It is astonishing how little one is taught in these schools, or, at least, how little one absorbs of what they must be trying to teach. They handle

this period much better in Europe, particularly in France. At least
they do something with a boy's mind. They fail, however, to do
anything at all about the boy's body, which is important at that
age, so that almost the only exercise the pale, skinny Paris kids of
seventeen obtain is in chasing girls—and, furthermore, catching
up with them. This probably explains some of the pallor, although
most of it is due to the hard, relentless grind over the books
through which the French boy of seventeen understands at least
as much of the world of ideas as the American youth beginning
his junior year of college. In high school we obediently went
through brief courses in elementary physics and chemistry, without the faintest glimmering ever percolating into our minds about
the rigor and the glories of the scientific method, the long heartbreaking struggle of men to establish it against institutionalized
superstition, or how and why it had made our age fundamentally
different, more wonderful and more terrible, than all preceding
ages. We learned "civics"—that is, we learned to repeat, like par-
rots, the Preamble to the Constitution and perhaps the Bill of
Rights. We acquired not the faintest understanding of the Age of
Reason, nor the long, slow loosening and freeing of men's minds in
their contemplation of society which resulted in a Jefferson or a
Tom Paine. We had no idea of the older, European sources of these
ideas, or what their fruition in the American Colonies did to the
establishments and the people of Europe and half the globe in the
generations that followed. So far as we were taught, the United
States came into being because the forefathers were "against
kings" and "wanted to worship as they pleased." We were not
taught these things, because our teachers, with few exceptions,
did not know them. If they understood the economic interpretation of history and the meaning of the great Bolshevik revolution
to the future world we children would live in, they certainly did
not share that understanding with us. They knew of George Washington, but few had ever heard of Simon Bolivar; they knew about
Napoleon, but not about Rousseau; they let us read the life of
Herbert Hoover, if we wished, but none of them ever suggested
we look into the ideas of Norman Thomas. America makes high-
school teaching a trade. We turn out the tradesmen and trades-
women, "certificates" in their hands, by the thousands every year
from the assembly belts of innumerable factories called teachers'
colleges and education courses. There are fine, devoted souls

among them, but they are likely to quit trying early in the game. The system is against them. It is an exhausting grind with far too many bobbed, shaggy, or brilliantined heads before them every hour, all of whom, the system demands, must be treated exactly alike. Chambers of Commerce and parents' organizations are looking over their shoulders constantly, and periodically down their throats. The system is designed to prevent challenging, revolutionary ideas, particularly political, from ever reaching a youngster, and at this stage, when most of them are more conservative than their fathers, more priggish than their preachers, the vast majority of American boys end forever their formal education.

The virtues of the system have little to do with the intellect, but they are real: By competitive sports (vastly overdone) a boy may acquire that invaluable easy confidence with his fellows which can last him the rest of his life, which is the basic touchstone among young men all over the world, for the relationship of most men during at least one half their lives has a physical basis. By living and working among girls he can acquire that peculiarly American thing—a natural approach to women as friends and even as comrades, not purely as sexual objects; a level unattained anywhere else in the world, except possibly in Russia. By the complete, leveling atmosphere of the public school, he becomes almost oblivious of social classes—for a time—and, while he acquires more respect for brawn than for brain, he acquires more for brain than for birth. Finally, by the team and committee system, so frequently ridiculed by foreign observers, he learns that the worst disgrace of all is to "let the team down." He learns the doing of things together as the natural method, and since the central problem of our times is the social problem, the instinct of working together is the most important instinct a man can learn. Intellectuals go through a phase when "the team spirit" is a joke. Later I saw it win a war for my country.

I finished Minneapolis Central High School in the summer of 1930, pale and skinny, having learned nothing except how to put the school paper to press, believing that the ability to write a two-column "A" headline was of a higher order than the ability to write a sonnet, believing that Herbert Hoover was a great man, that America was superior to all other countries in all possible ways, that labor strikes were caused by unkempt foreigners, that men saved their souls inside wooden or brick Protestant churches, that if men had no jobs it was due to personal laziness and vice—meaning liquor—and that sanity governed the affairs of mankind.

4

I then proceeded to an adventurous enterprise so heroic in its scope that I am staggered to this day when I recall it. It is practically devoid of meaning and implication. In any case, I am going to relate it.

All through the high-school years I was the slavishly devoted comrade of a boy two or three years older than I, a boy of solid physique and remarkable energy who was so popular that he became the president of our graduating class. Walter Port came from the Big Woods country in the northern part of the state, where his people had been fishermen and timber cruisers. He had a dark and swarthy face which would have been handsome except for the indentations left by early smallpox. He worked until midnight each night in a downtown drugstore, then walked two miles to his rooming house, rose at dawn to do his "home work," then walked to school, where he managed to be the highly successful "business manager" of student publications as well as performing on the swimming and gymnastic teams. He was the confidant of everyone from the principal to the janitors. The girls liked him, and to me he was the knight without fear, without reproach.

The idea for the enterprise originated with him. He may have acquired it from reading the story of the Kensington Rune Stone, an unresolved mystery in American and particularly Minnesota history about which surprisingly few Americans have ever heard. In 1898 a farmer in the western part of the state plowed up a flat stone bearing markings that resembled some kind of writing. It turned out to be Runic, the alphabet of the early Teutonic or Celtic tribes, and as translated by Scandinavian scholars it told a brief story of a party of men ("8 Gothe and 22 Norwegians") who had come from the sea inland by the rivers and were attacked by savages, with the result that the author of the tablet was almost alone among the survivors. The date 1362 was inscribed, placing the event several generations before the time of Columbus's voyage of discovery. If literally true, this meant that Vikings of some description had penetrated to the Middle West, to the very land heart of the North American continent. Their most natural route would have been into Hudson Bay, then through the inter-connecting rivers which lead south and west to Lake Winnipeg, then straight south along the Red River of the North to the area where the tablet was discovered. The authenticity of the tablet has been in dispute ever since it was found—one group of scholars quite convinced the thing is true, others believing that a certain young Scandinavian scholar at the University of Wisconsin, disgruntled by bitter quarrels with his teachers, had fabricated the tablet and planted it, knowing it would be uncovered, excite the world of historians, and, he hoped, show up his superiors to be the unmitigated asses he was convinced they were. Altogether, if the second theory is correct, it is the most elaborate delayed-action booby trap in academic history. But it was half-dud, the explosion was muffled; nobody agrees who has proved what.

The story of the Rune Stone confirmed what was obvious from a glance at the map—that one could go by water from the Red River area to the Atlantic Ocean in the north. By a more careful look at the map, Walter and I saw that it was also possible to prove something which, in our minds at least, was ignored by our con-temporaries and was of historical consequence. We would demon-strate that it was possible to travel, entirely by water, from ocean to ocean, straight through the heart of the continent. Everybody knew of course that the Mississippi connected the Gulf of Mexico with Minnesota, and we would show that you could continue from the Mississippi to the North Atlantic by branching off into the Minnesota River at Fort Snelling, mount its five hundred miles, push through a couple of small lakes at the Minnesota headwaters, go the thirty-mile length of the narrow Bois de Sioux river (really just a swamp), which is the beginning of the Red River of the North; then you would just descend its seven-hundred-mile length, debouch into Lake Winnipeg, skirt up its eastern shore and get into one of the rivers that drain the lake into Hudson Bay some five hundred miles farther on, and there you were. (Just *why* any-body would treasure the knowledge that you could thus cross the continent, especially since it would have to be done in a canoe small enough so that a man could carry it on his back over the necessary portages, is a question that never occurred to us. We were less than twenty. Forgive us.)

The harassed editor of the Minneapolis *Star*, looking for any device to increase circulation, even among adolescent readers, gruffly agreed to pay us one hundred dollars—all we dared ask—

in return for the weekly descriptive articles that I would provide. I fear he lost his investment—the articles seem inconceivably flat and tasteless now. Walter had been raised on the northern rivers and had practical talents. My understanding of watergoing craft you may judge by the fact that when my father dragged our newly purchased but second-hand canoe into the basement to get the thing out of his way, I expressed fear that the dampness might warp its shape. My method of preparation for the trial was to read books on "how to live in the forest," while Walter simply went ahead collecting the instruments, equipment, and clothing which his experience and natural instinct told him would be required. I hadn't the faintest conception of what we were really letting ourselves in for—nor, I suspect, had my parents, who let me go. I think Walter had, and I do know that with any other type of partner my parents would have seen no more of me in the living state.

But in the actual practice one learns rapidly, even a boy who cannot drive a nail straight nor chop wood for a fire without gashing his shins. At seventeen one's capacity to absorb physical suffering is almost unlimited. Indeed, instead of breaking you down and wearing you out, it builds you up, hardens and knits your flesh together, makes you impervious to blazing sun, ants, mosquitoes and ticks, adjusts the pulmonary system to any number of freezing nights spent upon the soaking ground, grows tough calluses where blisters ought to be, and teaches your stomach to accept with relish any amount of lard, raw dough, burned beans, or even the flesh of carp, aged turtle, maggoty perch, muskrat, and porcupine.

We paddled, that summer and fall, something more than twenty-two hundred miles. It was not so much a test of the body; the body takes care of itself at that age. It was a test of will and imagination, and they too, at seventeen, have a power and potency which rarely again return to a man in like measure. I would follow shock troops across a hundred invasion beaches before I would repeat that youthful experience of the rivers. I simply could not do it again. As it was, death came closer than we realized, not once but time after time. Undoubtedly we had pleasant days of keen delight; but the light strokes have nearly all vanished from the picture as my memory retains it, and I am conscious in recollection of a mood of emotional weariness, anxiety, and downright fear; there is a remembrance of endless dark days of dull plodding, on and on through an impenetrable veil of rain and forest. Mr. Hemingway can have the camping life. When you are lost, when you are hungry, when the rivers and woods become your enemy, waiting for you to die, none of the senses—not even the literary—discovers pleasure. For years afterwards a visit to the woods produced a moment of nausea.

We had overcome some thirteen hundred miles of the physical test when we encountered our first really serious obstacle, which was of course of a moral nature. It was a concerted attempt of older and wiser persons in Winnipeg, Canada, to dissuade us, "for our own good," from attempting the vast lake and the wilderness beyond. At the Winnipeg Canoe Club, impressively grown-up people took us aside and described the tendency of this body of water to develop sudden, unforeseeable squalls and storms, recounted the disturbing stories of canoeing friends who had disappeared forever along those rocky shores. As for the five hundred miles of (at that time) practically uncharted wilderness between the head of the lake and Hudson Bay, none of them had ever done that by canoe, and none, we were assured, would ever be foolish enough to try it. Neither Walter nor I was a particularly defiant or cocky youngster, and this offensive against our will caused us many heartsick hours. But in the preceding weeks we had been gradually learning, though we had never objectively analyzed it, a fundamental lesson; we learned it the hard, empiric way. We learned that nearly all human beings get along without exact knowledge—indeed, that they seem to prefer inexactness, no doubt, because, to find the precise truth of any question, no matter how ordinary or near at hand, requires serious effort. We had discovered that almost nobody along the way, farmer or fisherman or camper, knew the precise nature—the currents, the rapids, the portages, the distances from point to point—of the very stretches of river or lake upon which they had spent their lives and all the secrets of which they were quite convinced they knew by heart. We learned, in effect, to distinguish between hearsay and fact. With feelings more of apology than confidence, we rejected the theories, the arguments, and the conclusions of our very well-meaning friends. When we stumbled upon a wizened old prospector in the government map bureau who knew part of the country we intended to traverse and who said we could probably make it provided we were not complete damn fools, that was all we needed to transform hope into belief.

At the settlement of Norway House, at the northern end of the lake, we met exactly the same kind of moral offensive, this time of an even more serious nature. They pointed out to us that it was already the first of September. Our equipment, including our clothes, was summer equipment. The rivers in those latitudes freeze very early and very suddenly. If we knocked a hole in our canoe or overturned and lost it in the rapids, we would find it impossible to walk through the impenetrable brush along the river's edges. Precise charts and maps existed only for the first two hundred or so of the five hundred miles we would have to paddle, and none was available for us. Even though we did reach Hudson Bay at York Factory, that place had been abandoned as a railway head, and there was no telling how we would be able to make it back inland, along the Nelson River to the rail lines, ninety miles from the sea. It went on like this for two or three days, and at one point, I know, there was a conference with the Royal Canadian Mounted Police, who were responsible for human lives in that region, to decide whether they could or should forcibly prevent us from going on.

We had decided that we could not descend the mighty Nelson River, which drains off Lake Winnipeg's waters to the sea, because it was far too bewilderingly varied in its channels for anyone without a guide. (A guide was something our remaining fifteen dollars would scarcely pay for.) We could not take the old trading route of the Hayes River, because, as I remember, of the seasonal shallows. There was only one route remaining. This was to descend the Nelson a few miles, branch off into a long series of tiny lakes, some connected by channel, others only by overhill portages, navigate the twenty-five miles of God's Lake, descend the God's River until it became the Shamattawa and then the Hayes, and so into the Bay at York Factory. The crude maps we had with us covered only to a line halfway across God's Lake. Again we found the same situation we had encountered at Winnipeg. Nobody at Norway House, white man or Indian, had ever actually made the trip to the Bay via God's River. But again we found a man who believed it could be done. He was a young Danish trapper of clear intelligence and warm heart. He had no maps to give us, but he had been fifty miles or so down the length of God's River, where he still had a winter cabin, unvisited for a year. He was not certain, but he believed that the river reached the Shamattawa in a single channel, with no insurmountable obstacles. He was alone in his sentiment, but he thought we could do it, assuming we were not injured or overturned in the rapids. But he made it clear that once we were well into the God's River there was no turning back. We could never remount the savage current, and walking would be impossible until the icè froze thick—and we would probably not last that long.

We left with an understanding that if no telegram was received from us after three weeks had passed, our people in Minneapolis should be informed that we were missing, when, if my father could raise the money, a search would presumably be organized. At daybreak, in cold, drizzling rain, we pushed away from the wharf at Norway House. No one was about save an elderly Cree male who squatted under an upturned skiff on the rocks, chewed on a large bone, and regarded us with impassivity. We fell into our accustomed rhythm of paddling which had become an automatic reflex of the muscles. The current moved us rapidly and the curtain of spruce and tamarack closed around us. I had no sensations of bravado and derring-do. I was scared and I knew it. I was experiencing that indefinable feeling which comes to most soldiers at some unpredictable moment in war, the feeling of having pushed one's luck too far. It was our will that drove us on into this thing, and yet it was something else too—something akin to fear, which also has its propulsive and creative properties. (Ten years later someone under the London blitz—Ed Murrow, I think —said: "I have never gone down into a shelter, because I was afraid to. I was afraid of myself; I feared that if I did it once I could not stop doing it.") What I was entering upon at Norway House was a contest with myself. I knew instinctively that if I gave up now, no matter what the justification, it would become easier forever afterwards to justify compromise with any achievement.

A few days passed; the nights grew colder. We came upon a French Canadian priest from the mission at Island Lake, making his way by canoe in the other direction, "going out" after five years in the bush. His eyes were a watery blue, some of his teeth were gone, and his beard had dirty streaks of gray. He looked fifty and was thirty. We shot snipe and duck and got lost. Men who have experienced varieties of lostness tell me that the worst is to be lost on a large body of water, when the horizon is the same in every direction and you haven't the slightest idea which direction to select. They are probably right, but I would not care again to

go through a couple of back-breaking days of stumbling, dragging
a loaded canoe up one narrow stream channel, then another, then
another, to find them all eventually become mere seepage from
the rocky ground. The stomach becomes very undependable and
you want to vomit. After a while you would just like to sit and
cry. But you drag around and eventually, by the simple process
of elimination, you find the proper channel. Our maps proved
almost useless, and we would certainly have got lost time and again
in this series of small streams and miniature, rock-bound lakes
if it had not been our good fortune to be overtaken by a freight
canoe bound for the trading post on God's Lake. Two Indians
were taking in the new post manager. Most young men who enter
the fur-collecting service of the Hudson's Bay Company come
from Scotland, and they are all called Jock. All the Cree Indians
in this happy hunting ground of the missionary have biblical
names; these two were Moses and James. We were quite welcome
to trail along behind them. We were expert canoeists by this time,
and we had little trouble staying with them on the water, but on
the half-mile-long portages, which frequently led over ninety-
degree crags, it was a desperate business. Indians can take up to
two hundred and fifty pounds on their backs, secured with nothing
but a flat tump line around their foreheads. And they do not walk;
they run. By the time Walter and I had transported all our gear
to the far side and thrown our aching bodies to the ground, our
traveling companions would have finished their meal and pushed
off again. In fear of getting lost again, we would throw our things
into our craft and take out in pursuit, cramming handfuls of cold
beans into our mouths between strokes of the paddle.

This went on for five or six days. On the morning of the day
we expected to hit the lake, we lost them completely. God's Lake
contains some five thousand spruce-covered islands, all looking
exactly alike. If you can tell from hour to hour which is island
and which is the main shore, you are doing very well indeed. But
we knew the approximate location of the trading post, we had a
compass, and we had learned to paddle in such exact measure
that we knew precisely how many strokes of the paddle we required to cover a mile on still water. In the darkness, we eventually
glimpsed the light. Jock had his feet up on the table when we
entered, a little embarrassed. "Excuse me," he said. "You've got
a long way to go on your own, you know. I figured if you could get
through that stretch alone we could let you try for the Bay. A lot

of people at Norway House think you are crazy bastards, you know."

To cross the lake we used the same method of dead reckoning, logging by paddle stroke. We had one point of reference: Elk Island, not far from the outlet to the God's River, had recently been burned off. It was the largest island on the lake, some twelve miles long itself. We wound in and out among the maze of smaller islands, and at noon, on schedule, we reached this smoldering island. We worked around it all afternoon and camped on its eastern tip that night. (We were probably the first Americans ever to see this particular place. There are millions of islands in the Canadian lakes, but Elk Island on God's Lake has a rather special place in my mind for the reason that some two years after we had obtained a night of dreamless slumber on its granite ledges, a lot of other people obtained their fortunes in the quartz gold those ledges contained. It was the biggest gold strike Canada had experienced in years. I hope our Danish trapper friend was in on it. A village sprang up there, and no doubt the wild run down the God's River to Hudson Bay became a concession for excursionists —the portages, for all I know, paved with flagstones and marked with neon lights.)

In the morning we cut straight north until we hit what we were convinced was the main shore of the lake. We skirted about and finally noticed that the grasses on the bottom of the clear shallows were all bending in one direction. Very shortly we were into the unmistakable current and were sucked into the God's River at its source. The sun was shining that day and we were happy. It was the last time the sun shone, and the last time we felt happy until the whole enterprise was over. The intervening period was and is unsurpassed in my life for sheer, concentrated misery. We had not progressed a mile on this rushing surface before the river collapsed with a roar over a ten-foot ledge, very nearly carrying us with it. Ahead, on the bend, we could see spouting white spray that meant another waterfall. We knew we were in for a struggle. The second sickening discovery was that the portage trails, even in this first stretch where our Danish advisor had traveled, were so overgrown with brush, so cluttered with fallen trees, that the paths frequently were impossible to find. This meant slashing away brush with our knives until our knuckles bled, hacking at logs with an ax that was far too light for the job, then hoisting, dragging, and shoving an awkward, eighteen-foot canoe. We went through this performance innumerable times, always in freezing rain and fog. A half-day's labor to accomplish a two-hundred-yard portage was a normal requirement.

We had been warned of the time when the rains would come, but nothing in our experience had prepared us for this. Day and night, the drizzle did not cease for so much as an hour. With the rain, the water we shipped over the gunwales in the fast stretches, and the water that seeped through the many cuts in the bottom of the craft, our equipment sloshed about constantly, our clothing and food were soaked through. There was nothing to be done about it. Our blankets were equally soaked. The woods oozed with water, every leaf held a pond, every dead twig and log was rotten with wetness. In order to build a fire at night we would have to stop paddling in midafternoon, then spend two or three hours whittling out chunks of heart wood. Not even birchbark would burn. In our wet clothes we slept, wrapped in wet blankets, with only the edges of our rubber ponchos pulled over our faces. We began to notice, in the mornings, light trimmings of frost on the ponchos, and one morning Walter beckoned me to the edge of the river. There, in a quiet eddy, was a faint film of ice. Our daily progress was heartbreakingly slow, and we were becoming obsessed with the urge to get on, to get on. We did not stop at noon any more, but ate, as we worked, a few cold pancakes saved over from the night, and a few beans and dried prunes. We were falling far behind our expected schedule, and our food was giving out. We were forced to pause for fish. One cast of the hook, with a piece of white cloth as bait, would bring a three-pound speckled trout in these unfished waters. I remember Walter gripping one by the head in his teeth, his bleeding hands too stiff with cold to hold the slimy creature.

We passed each day in silent anxiety. We rarely spoke. Our fear of being caught by the ice or running entirely out of food before we reached a settlement overrode our fear of the rapids. We took greater and greater chances. Frequently, now, instead of getting out to reconnoiter a stretch of rock and flying white spray, whoever was in the stern would simply stand, as we drifted in, make a quick survey, a quick decision, and then we would drive in to our opening. You must move at greater speed than the current if you are to have leverage to throw your canoe about among the rocks. We had already lost our extra paddle, and now we shattered the tip of one of the two remaining. We got along with it, somehow;

it would have been a day's work to fashion a substitute, however crude. We ran into shallows and for two days waded, dragging and lifting the canoe and its load. Once we carried the canoe over our heads a quarter-mile along a six-inch ledge on a sheer bank of greasy clay, twenty feet above the water. Once, while we were crawling on our bellies over an enormous granite boulder, slipping the floating canoe along below us with a rope, Walter lost his grip. He fell backwards, executed a quick flip in midair, and landed on all fours in the bottom of the canoe without overturning it.

One day we heard again the dull roaring that signified a waterfall ahead. But this time it was something new: the river had suddenly narrowed to one third its width and plunged through a rocky gorge, corrugating into four-foot waves. That, we could manage. But after roaring through the gorge, the river struck, almost at right angles, a solid wall of rock before careening into its normal shape. We were beyond all prudence by this time. Walter's back and the canoe itself disappeared for a few seconds from my sight in a white world of spray. Dipping a paddle was like offering the torrent a toothpick. (Have you ever *heard* the blood pound in your head?) The next sight was the black wall rushing upon us. We flayed the water, attempting to swing the canoe, did swing it, then, together, at the same instant, flung up the paddle blades as if they were lances, and absorbed the numbing shock in our arms and shoulders.

The river reached junction with a creek which poured in at the right hand. This should have been the location of the Dane's cabin. We searched through a morass of blackened, falling spruce and sodden ash. Either the fire that had obviously swept through the area some weeks before had eliminated every log of the cabin, or this was not the place, and we were very far, perhaps fatally far, behind our schedule. We did not speak that day nor evening; we were reaching a danger point of the spirit, when something was certain to happen. Readers who have experienced a long period in the wilderness with only one other companion, no matter how intimate a friend, will have been waiting for this. The pattern is a common one. Walter and I had different natures; he was more healthily extrovert than I, and his emotions demanded a physical outlet. I would simply stifle mine and brood. He had French blood and I Norwegian, and perhaps that helps explain why my anger could be suppressed and his could not. As always, in these situations, a trifle becomes the occasion for the explosion, though the causes are far more complex. We had reached that point where one feels the sick bitterness in his heart even before he is fully awake in the morning.

The explosion came on the morning after our profound disappointment at missing the cabin of the Dane. His first words to me in twenty-four hours were: "Why don't you wash that goddam pan the way it ought to be washed?" I forget mine to him. He was walking toward me, and I knew this was it. When I reach a physical crisis, there is always a brief moment of panic succeeded by a cold period of abnormal mental clarity. I was conscious, not of his doubled fists, but of the forest, the river, the distance. This would be the end. I said: "Wait until we get out of here." But in a moment we were hammering and clawing, ripping one another's sodden clothing, rolling and kicking through the ashes of the campfire. Walter had the deep chest and heavy arms of an athlete, but I was taller and broader, and three months of exertion had done unsuspected things to my thin muscles. Neither of us could manage to defeat the other, which saved the situation, since the loser would very probably have been killed. We lay a long time, in the drizzling rain, quite spent. I began to break up; I thought about my mother, started to cry inside, and said over and over again to myself: "I'm too young to die." Eventually, our flesh became chilled, we entered the canoe, avoiding each other's eyes.

Within eight hours we overtook the first human beings we had seen for two weeks, a Cree family in a freight canoe; within nine we were upon the Shamattawa; within ten hours we were eating roasted duck before a great fire in a temporary trading shack, just opened by two young Scotsmen from York Factory. Rolled in dry blankets before the fire, the two of us discussed with excitement the approaching end of our trip. We were fast friends; we were less than twenty.

Having received bad advice—or, what was more likely, having misunderstood—we ran, on the wrong side, the two-mile-long Shamattawa Rapid, of local fame. Two Indians had just died in it, on the proper side. There was one bad moment when the canoe lodged on an underwater ledge and began, quite audibly, to crack apart. The forests fell away, we reached the wide Hayes River, tried to sleep on a bank of wet clay, which was exactly like reclining on a cake of ice, gave it up, and gulping six prunes and three raw potatoes, almost the last of our provisions, we set out in pitch darkness. We paddled, without pause, nearly sixty miles that day.

We smelled the sea all afternoon, struggled with a mysterious force which we did not realize was the incoming tide, and at darkness came abreast of the low huddle of white buildings which is the old trading establishment of the Hudson's Bay Company. A schooner rode at anchor. It was the first time I had ever seen the ocean.

Factor Harding of York Factory was a warm host and wise counselor. For weeks he had been keeping our mail, including a check for fifty dollars from the Minneapolis newspaper, wondering who we were and from what point of the compass we were expected to materialize. He very decently composed and signed a testimonial to the effect that we had indeed reached York Factory by canoe. He also gave us thirty dollars for the worthless canoe, inasmuch as we would need cash for guides to take us over to Port Nelson, on the far side of the Nelson River, which entered the sea here, just around the headlands. An Englishman was present, Colonel Reid, an official of the Company, who had just arrived on the schooner from London. I had never seen an Englishman before. He appeared, with his gray tweed sports clothing and pipe exactly as the movies had taught me to expect an Englishman to appear. His accent, also, was exactly right. He said: "Minneapolis? Where the deuce is Minneapolis?" He said: "Twenty-two hundred miles by canoe? But what on earth for?"

Being seventeen, the world fascinated me just the way it was, and I accepted it the way it was. The Cree Indians in these sprawling little settlements interested me as a people, as Persons. I certainly thought of this immense northern region as "their country," and if they were in rags, if their cabins and tepees were cesspools of stench and many of the Indians themselves rotten with disease, why, that was just the way they were. They must *like* it that way, it must be due to the charming laziness of their idyllic forest life. I thought the "bishops" and "deacons" brave self-sacrificing men to come to these lost places and teach the natives to mouth the words and chants of ritual which would of course preserve their immortal souls. It never occurred to me that there was a chain of causation and purpose uniting the deacons, the red-coated police, and Colonel Reid in one system, and that the nexus was the stack of mink, otter, and beaver skins in the wooden warehouse. When I observed Colonel Reid stroll straight through a group of Indians on the board walk, without the slightest hesitation in his deliberate stride, without the faintest suggestion in his countenance that he

was aware of their existence, it left an impression somewhere in
the back of my mind—but I did not know what I was really seeing,
what I was to see later in many parts of the world. I had never
heard of Imperialism. I did not know there were whole races and
classes of people living in the relationship of master and slave and
that this coexistence conditioned the members of each group in
their very bodies, the working of the eyes, the carrying of the
shoulders, the timbre of the voice box, the whole interfunctioning
of the nervous system.

With two Indian guides provided by Harding we remounted
the Hayes a few miles in a freight canoe, then struck across the
five-mile neck of land, floundering in the muskeg morass to our
knees for most of the hike, in the course of which Walter badly
wrenched a leg. We were paying the guides; had we been born
in the milieu of Colonel Reid, we would simply have ordered the
guides to take Walter's pack and slow down their killing pace.
That never occurred to us. We were the strangers, in their land, and
it was a point of honor and duty to live up to their standards. By
the time we had traversed the turbulent four-mile width of the
Nelson River estuary in another canoe and begun the walk against
driving rain into the settlement, each step for Walter was an agony.
We carried a letter from Harding to the Mounted Police of Port
Nelson, the only white men who lived in this abandoned railroad
terminal of scraggly shacks and rusted machinery. The policemen
were away on a hunting trip. There was no possibility, given
Walter's condition, of our being able to walk ninety miles up the
disused roadbed to the Hudson Bay Railway. A return to York
Factory would serve no purpose. We found, at length, an evil-
looking half-breed who was going "up to steel" with a compatriot,
in two motor-driven canoes. It was a three-day trip. There was a
heavy snowfall. There were many hours of poling up through the
rapids, of "tracking" the heavy canoes by rope and pole from
the shoreline. Walter's leg grew worse, and he subsided into silent
suffering. I lost the heels from my rotted boots and drove a boot
nail deeply into my foot during a long stretch of tracking when it
was impossible to halt.

For several days we rested in the shack of a lonely old Swede
whose duty it was to patrol and watch one section of the rail line.
He bathed and bound our injuries while we went through his
library, which consisted of the Bible, the Essays of Emerson, and
several small blue pamphlets on healthy sex relations. He wept

a little when we climbed aboard the next freight train to come through from Churchill, and wrote to us for months thereafter.

One long night of blinding snow we huddled on the tender of a freight locomotive as it whistled and clanked through the Saskatchewan forests. There were two roustabouts lying beside us that night, and when we reached our destination at dawn we had to hand them down from the tender as you would a frozen log. To a pockmarked Chinese we paid fifty cents for fried eggs and a bed, and at noon we were roughly shaken awake by a broad-faced Chinese girl who informed us other voyagers were waiting for the bed. She remained in the room, leaning on a mop, observing us with quiet deliberation as we dressed. A highway reached to this point, hitchhiking was easy and pleasant, and thus we went home.

A boy does not grow up so imperceptibly that there are not sudden moments when he is acutely conscious of change within him. I walked, carrying my pack and paddle, toward my father's house, past the castellated red-brick high school, scattering the drifts of dry autumn leaves with my broken boots. The boys and girls on the sidewalk seemed unprecedentedly young.

We had paddled a canoe twenty-two hundred miles, had survived, and had proved nothing except that we could paddle a canoe twenty-two hundred miles, a capacity of extraordinarily small value for the future. My chief return on this investment, outside of a fleeting local notoriety which got me a job on a newspaper —as office boy—was that for several months thereafter, until sedentary habits softened my flesh, my older brother could not lick me.

Chapter II

IF A YOUNG MAN goes directly from secondary school to the university, and completes the study of his profession in theory and principle before entering his first office, everything is quite different. The faces, the titles, the very arrangement of the desks and departments he sees as a functional pattern. He has his mind on the end product of the concern; he knows how and why his product came about in modern society; he knows its present status in terms of history, and he no doubt understands the relationship of himself and his work to the times in which he lives. It must be a great advantage to begin that way, but it also means missing a brief period of complete enchantment. The old Minneapolis *Journal*, no longer extant, was an imposing and venerable institution in that northwest country, identified with the permanent structures of the landscape—the original buildings of Fort Snelling, the first dam on the upper Mississippi, the first roadbed laid by Jim Hill, the Empire Builder. It spoke with authority in the land, if not with wisdom, and it was an interconnecting cog in the social machinery of a widely scattered civilization. I was unaware that its directors were in, hand and glove, with the potentates of railroad, timber, and milling who for a very long time dictated, as if by kingly right, the political and economic affairs of this civilization. I was unaware that the men who wrote its pages *were* aware, bitterly so, of the paper's true function. To me at eighteen it was that most remarkable, most fascinating of all human institutions, a daily newspaper, peopled with those glamorous, incomparable men known as reporters and editors, actually there, alive, touchable, knowable. The ceremony of the "ghost walking" with the pay envelopes on Saturday afternoon was merely one of the more delightful moments of the week, a necessary bit of the engrossing ritual that preceded the ceremony of drinking beer down below at the "Greasy Spoon." The pay check of course was not really essential, these superhuman creatures being above anything so prosaic as the need for food, but was merely a kind of token and badge to signify that one Belonged. There was a positive sensual pleasure when one hurried from below-zero weather, so early it was scarcely light, into the warmth and smells of the city room where the telegraph editor was already waiting for the first yellow strips from the press association machines, into the warmer, noisier, greasier composing room upstairs where the limp, moist galley proofs of overset matter were piled and waiting for distribution below. The movement and noise built up with every hour, with the ordered cacophony of improvised symphony to the thundering finale by the great presses below the street, followed by the quiet aftermath of triumph when I would stagger into the city room with fifty fresh, pungent copies in my arms for the relaxing virtuosi who waited there, feet upon their instruments, gifted fingers lighting cigarettes.

This was my entry into the world of private enterprise in which most Americans pass their earthly existence. Surely, this was the best of all possible systems of life, where one simply chose the thing he most wanted to do, and, because he loved it, worked as hard as he could, and, because he worked hard, steadily rose from position to position, until he had "arrived," when the world would hold no more secrets or problems, and life gracefully leveled out on a plane of confidence, security, and happiness. I was convinced of the truth of this when after only six weeks as a copy runner I was made a reporter, with a desk of my own, admission to the Saturday night poker game around the copy desk, and fifteen dollars a week. Up to that time I had never made an enemy, never known anyone to feel that I was a threat to him, nor felt that anyone else was a threat to me. When I broke the great news that I was to become a reporter, to a rewrite man I worshipped, I received the first shock and hurt and began to learn. I expected warm congratulations and perhaps admiring predictions of future greatness. Instead, the Godlike journalist looked at me coldly and said: "For Christ's sake. The bastards." It was some time before I realized that experienced reporters, family men who required more than fifteen dollars a week, were being rebuffed each day in their search for employment.

My one regular chore on the paper, the inescapable heritage of the newest and rawest cub, was to spend each Friday as "religious editor," which meant putting together a page of copy with a summed-up story of Sunday's events, followed by several columns of "church notices" in six-point type. It meant interviewing a few visiting clerics of distinction, who never turned down the request. One of these was Billy Sunday, the evangelist, then in his last days. In his case, no questions were needed. He bounded about the hotel room, now peering intently out the window with one foot on the sill, now grasping the dressing table firmly in both hands while lecturing his reflection in the mirror. I never opened my mouth after introducing myself and scarcely remembered a word of what he said. Suddenly he ceased talking and darted out of the room, whereupon "Ma" Sunday unhooked a half-dozen typewritten sheets from a loose-leaf folder and handed them to me. This was the interview, all prepared, his emphasis marked by capitalized words and phrases in red ink with many exclamation marks. When I first took over this task on the paper I mentioned it one day to a Protestant pastor I happened to know rather well. He clasped his hands together, cast a brief glance upwards, and said: "Thank God for that! I have been grieving over the lack of publicity for our little church." He gripped my shoulder in a brotherly manner and said: "I hope this will be the answer to my prayers." I was quickly to learn that of all the citizens who rang the newspaper or came to the lobby seeking publicity, the men of the church were the most demanding and insatiable. I was frequently embroiled in controversy with pastors who would demand why I had not run the photographs of themselves which they had just sent in, whereas Pastor X had had *his* picture in the paper twice in the last three months. The rabbis were equally desirous, but generally more clever about it, while the important Catholic priests simply let their assistants handle the publicity question and rarely entered the negotiations in person. I learned that the newspaper was frightened of the preachers. The city desk could tell a vaudeville press agent to go to hell when his demands overreached the decent limit, but nobody ever spoke anything but soft words to the press agent of a church. I could see why nobody else wanted my task, but no doubt it was good training in basic diplomacy.

I was firmly convinced that a newspaper reporter "saw life" as did no one else in current society. (He sees no more of life than the iceman does, but he is compelled to note down and comment and thus acquires some habit of observation, if not reflection. That's all the difference there is.) I wanted to observe "human nature" and for some reason did not believe preachers exhibited any manifestations of human nature. So I seized any other kind of assignment anybody else was too lazy or too wise to want: interviews with the drinkers of canned heat who lived, and often died, in the caves and shacks along the riverbed, with movie stars of more majestic condescension than any bishop. Once I dressed as a waiter and served Katherine Hepburn her breakfast in bed after she had kept the reporters waiting in bitter cold for two hours at the station, then refused to see them. I have a vivid memory of knocking at apartment doors in the dead of night, to inform a young wife that her husband had just been killed in an accident or a police shooting, and did she have a photograph of him? Usually she turned white and ran to grab up the baby from its crib. These experiences left me limp and shaking. But somehow these wretched people—if they were poor, with poor people's belief that newspapers are powerful things with unquestioned rights —would find a photograph, would, between sobs, answer my questions. It was a surprise to find that the rich did not react the same way. When I went to ask questions of the wife of a manufacturer who had killed a man in disgraceful circumstances, she waited until I had spoken, then coolly requested me to leave the premises before she called the police. I spent three weeks in police headquarters, in Washington Avenue saloons, in the parlors of innumerable citizens, trying to solve the celebrated local mystery of the missing baby, stolen from the bed of its fifteen-year-old "unwed mother" in the city hospital. I worked morning, noon, and night, uncovered various bits of evidence, and finally located a youthful suspect who the police were convinced was the kidnapper, but whom they were unable to convict. I had always had the normal citizen's respect for the police, but during this experience discovered to my surprise that we reporters were frequently hours and days ahead of them unraveling the mystery.

One became, at that age, aware of social structure but not of social forces. One knew that certain individuals represented certain levels of the structure, in the city and inside the office, but one was scarcely aware that these individuals themselves were pushed and pulled by invisible pressures of a class allegiance, in society and business. It took me a long time to understand that the publisher had far more in common with, far more loyalty to, the bankers or grain merchants with whom he lunched at the Minneapolis Club than to the editors and reporters who worked with him to produce the paper. I began work with an idealistic view of the newspaper as the mounted knight of society, pure in

heart, its strength as the strength of ten, owing no favor, fearing
no man. I did not know that, while many great organs had begun
that way (a few retained their integrity) with rugged, incorrupti-
ble founders, they had been handed down to sons and grandsons
who were less interested in the true social function of the institution than in its money-making capacities which secured their
position in the luxury class to which they, unlike their fathers and
grandfathers, were born. You learned. You learned by listening to
the servile voices of the women who wrote the society pages as
they asked the great ladies of Lowry Hill to be so very kind as to
give them the names of their reception guests. You learned by discovering that if you became involved in controversy with an important businessman about the handling of a given story, you were
always wrong and the businessman was always right. You learned
by finding that if a picture were published of a Negro, however
distinguished, and one of the great ladies, who happened to be
from Georgia, telephoned to protest that she was offended, profuse
apologies would be offered the sensitive creature.

With this general discovery of the structure of community life
came the simultaneous discovery that nearly all men, working in
a large American concern, did their daily work under the tyranny
of fear. It varied in intensity from man to man, from prosperity
to depression, but it was always there. The reporters were afraid
of the city editor, the assistant city editor was afraid of the city
editor, and the city editor, worried about his job, was afraid of
his assistant. All were afraid of the managing editor, who in turn
was afraid of the publisher. None of them wanted to feel that way,
few were really "after" another's position, but each understood
the pressures on the other which might at any moment cause the
latter in self-protection to bear down upon the former. I might
have learned all this much earlier, as most boys do from their
fathers, who come home at night and relate to their wives at dinner
the latest move in their "office politics." But my father had been
an independent operator most of his life, and even when he did
join a large establishment his sense of personal dignity and honor
forbade him to discuss his superiors or inferiors, even with his
family. And so I had begun working life in the simple faith that
one's rise or fall was a matter solely of one's own capacities.

There was a charming old man who lived like an office hermit
in a musty room in the interior labyrinths of the *Journal*. He was
a scholar of some distinction, in love with the history of the north-

west country, and he wrote graceful essays and homilies for the Sunday edition. I was charmed by his style and occasionally would take my portable lunch and bottle of milk at noon to eat with him. I assumed that with his literary attainments he was an important and respected person in the establishment. Once I stayed longer than usual; we were both spellbound with his own fascinating account of a vanished village. He looked suddenly at his watch. He became extremely agitated, grabbed up his copy in trembling fingers, and said: "Excuse me, excuse me. The editors. They will be very rough with me. I am very late." His bent figure shuffled rapidly from the room. He had spent his life on that newspaper.

The financial editor worked at a desk directly behind my own. One night when I was working exceptionally late, he came in slightly unsteady from drinking. He emptied into a suitcase the contents of his locker, a few books, a batch of clippings, a pair of golf shoes. I asked in surprise if he was leaving. He said: "I've been on this paper eighteen years, son. I've just been fired by a guy I used to teach where to put commas." He staggered out, leaving me with a sick, hollow feeling in the pit of my stomach and a dark light dawning in my head. Innocence departed. Life, it seemed, was a relentless, never-ending battle; one never "arrived"; loyalty, achievement, could be forgotten in a moment; a single man's whim could ruin one. I began to take stock of the situation and discovered that the men who got to the top, no matter how long they stayed there, were nearly all men who had studied in universities, who knew something besides the routine of their own desks. It was fear as much as anything else that drove me to college, purely personal ambition as much as curiosity about the world I lived in and what had made it the way I found it to be.

For months, college to me was only night school, in crowded classes made up of housewives who had married too young and wanted to catch up; middle-aged workers from the flour mills, white dust still lining the wrinkles of their coats; scores of young clerks, penniless like myself, less interested in "college credits" than in digging out from books the history and the theory of their various businesses, the principles and abstractions that governed the practice. They sought the missing keys, which their bosses possessed. In my case, it was somewhat different. A journalist is a jack-of-all-trades and master of none—except his own, which is being a jack-of-all. I had to know, not only how to write a sentence with beginning and end, but something of history, government,

economics, science, languages, and art in its various forms. I had
at least to grasp the rudiments of these, to know what was known
and established in these fields and what men still sought in them.
For it is this which is at the core of "news" and its understanding.
I began with everything and only later realized that two alone
were important to me, politics and economics. We had no gay
campus life. In the dusk, when we arrived for class, we passed
the fraternity boys in their slacks and sweat shirts lolling on the
verandas of their stuccoed houses. From our windows in Folwell
Hall we could see the lights burning in these places, faintly hear
the shouts and laughter and the phonograph music. It was a distant, impenetrable world of the specially chosen which I never
expected to enter. For a long time I felt myself to be an interloper,
a trespasser on others' property. I hated it, but we worked—God,
how they work in night school! And we learned.

My editor was a decent person, and eventually he allowed me,
without having my salary cut, to work only mornings and attend
regular university classes in the afternoon. One had to "take"
athletics as a freshman. In the winter it was boxing, at which I
reached the class finals for welterweight champion and was struck
conclusively unconscious in the third round—a surprisingly pain-
less experience. In the spring baseball I pitched four successful
innings, then went to pieces and walked every man who appeared
at bat until the cursing coach sent me to the showers. I had no
stamina, and in view of my daily grind it was little wonder. When
summer arrived, I was pale and ill, and further school or newspaper work was impossible until I had done something about my
health. I spent the summer as an amateur gold miner in the High
Sierra of northern California.

2

At twenty, the eye is sharp, perceptions are keen, and the heart
is never again so warm. Every man one meets, the lowliest tramp,
is alive and vibrant with personality, with meaning, with Self. The
colors of the sky are brilliant, there is extraordinary beauty in a
cowshed at sunrise, and in the warm night the clicking cadence
of the freight car's wheels sends one easily to confident sleep with
no more than an arm for pillow. I traveled alone; it is the right and
only way. You do not have to talk if you would rather be silent;

you can stop where you will, doze when you wish, and think your own thoughts. All that the eye sees, the mind registers, and the heart envelops is filtered by the screen of Yourself, untreated, unmodified by the conditioning presence of another being. There is no other way to find out the world and to touch the boundaries of your own limitations for finding out. I discovered all this—and America.

The grain was full and high in North Dakota, this place which I had never desired to see again. I had forgotten that the grain rose and settled with the undulating swell of the ocean, that the distant barn became a rising and falling ship on the rim of this sea, its cupola a mounted stack. I had forgotten that the clouds of summer were fat and laundered white and that small shadows moved over the surface of this inland ocean. I had forgotten the precision design of a furrowed field on a canvas so spacious that lines were long and clean and never crowded. I had forgotten how the rails were fixed to the earth, how they bent and fastened the world down at the far edge, where the curvature of the planet was apparent to the human eye. It was incredible, at first, to find that Velva was still there, every house intact. It had grown not older, but younger. The river had not yet reached the width I knew, and the great trees in our yard had begun all over again as saplings. All should have been in decay and ruin, dying and dead among weeds. Instead, all was green, pruned, and trimmed. There was concrete sidewalk over the coulee where there had been only a treacherous board; radio antennae had replaced the lightning rods upon the roofs; there were yellow parking signs where the hitching posts had stood, and gleaming Buicks had replaced the dusty buggies.

It was not by their faces that one knew them all, instantly and without mistake. Things fade from the retina of the eye's recollection, but there are sixth and seventh senses which retain it all. The faces were strange, but not what was *in* the faces. The special, strong, untransferable *feeling* of each was the same. It is by this that a child knows those around him, and through this mysterious medium it all comes back when he is grown.

A young man with whom I used to make a daily trade—his pony for my Ranger bicycle—drove me to Minot (the "Magic City") in his six-ton truck. He had a farm of his own now and he considered me with the faint condescension and suspicion with which men of property regard the unpropertied. I wandered into a park in the

darkness and slept in a clump of brush, to be wakened in fright
by fearful noises from what sounded like very large animals. They
were. I was sleeping next to the bears' cage in the zoo. A telephone
lineman drove me forty miles in his Ford half-truck, remained
silent the whole distance, and uttered his first words when he
invited me in to dinner with himself and his wife at his roadside
shack. A young traveling salesman picked me up and drove me
seven hundred miles into the heart of the vast Montana country,
in a long limousine, the back of which was stacked with cases containing samples of his wares, which were ladies' under clothing.
His extra suits, carefully pressed, hung on hangers in the car's
interior. He wore dark sun-glasses and small, stiff collars which
he changed twice a day. He worried about the manicured nails
of his soft, white hands and talked constantly and confidently.
He told me, repeatedly, that he had the world by the tail, and
I believed him. "What you want to be a newspaper reporter for?
Naw, naw, that's no good. I know some of them guys around the
Tribune in Chicago. I can buy and sell any two of them guys.
Naw, I got the racket. I can clean up two-three hundred a week,
commissions alone, not counting the bonus. You gotta know how
to go at these local yokels, gotta impress them—big car, swell
clothes—gotta breeze in on them, talk fast, give 'em the idea you're
in a rush and doing them a favor. Of course, my goods are straight,
best that money can buy. Don't want to get mixed up in any cheap
racket, then you can't go back a second time. I make it, but I spread
it around. I ain't tight with it. Take the girls to the best spot in
town, tip a lot. Never turned down a bum for a handout yet, pick
up guys all the time on the road. Here. Here's five bucks. Go on,
take it. Take it. I know you're broke. Take it. What's the diff?
Lots of guys are broke." Unable to resist his sales technique, I
took it, humbly.

He was an inland sailor, with a girl in every department store.
For hours he discussed them—intimately—and I was fascinated
and impressed by this insight into a life of irresponsible, sexual
freedom which I had scarcely suspected. The one in Fargo he
called "Silky," in homage to the texture of her skin, more particularly the skin of the small of her back. There was Margie in Minot,
and somebody else in Great Falls whose private qualities and
capacities are better left undetailed. He always wired ahead to
these ladies to give them time to prepare for his coming. It never

occurred to him that he might be disappointed, and, so far as I knew, he never was.

I watched him haggle with a granite-faced garage man for a tire. His complete, overriding confidence was remarkable, and I listened in mute, uneasy wonder. He got the tire at much below the asking price—something I knew I could never do. I felt sympathy for the garage man, but my friend and protector took the keenest pleasure in his victory. He hadn't cared about the price at all; it was the fun of the contest, the testing of his powers. I understood that here was a man who would never go hungry, who would always be able to take care of himself and his round little stomach at no matter what cost to those around him. It was my first acquaintance with the Wise Guy incarnate. I was to see them later, in many countries, where honest people starved, where honest men stole that their families might eat. But these, the Wise Guys of the world, the Slick Operators, never starved, never had to steal. War and the collapse of their countries, their society, scarcely touched them. They are an international breed, owing allegiance to no one, not even to one another. They manipulate currencies, they operate black markets; they live for money, and money seems to exist for them. It is the only reality in life to them, and they are contemptuous of anyone who does not share their knowledge, incredulous of those who do not share their belief. They are the outlaws of society, but they are not the hunted. They are, indeed, the hunters, the merciless hunters.

Helena was a sudden discovery, isolated, alone in a lost valley, connected with the world by the frail liaison of a highway, a thin white tape that disappeared in the distant hills, and a rail line, a silver wire that flashed its presence to the sun before vanishing in turn among the crags. Here I entered the Ford roadster of a pink, chubby man named Smith whose business it was to advertise the benefits of milk to the American people. He was on a leisurely survey of the American West, with an incidental aim. There was a girl living in Missoula. He had not seen her since their college days, eight years before. They had rarely corresponded. But he had decided, in those eight years of experience, that she was the only girl he wanted to marry. He wasn't sure, now, whether she was married or not. At Missoula I slept among the smells of unwashed bodies and disinfectant in the Salvation Army, while Smith went off to pay his visit of surprise. He picked me up in the morning and said, after a few miles: "She wasn't married—but she's going to be." He could not prevent happy smiles from breaking out on his cherubic face. "Like a goddam novel, isn't it?" he said. He drove me many hundreds of miles and we were briefly chagrined at parting, before the door of my uncle's house near Seattle. (My parents came from extremely large families, far scattered since, and I had the benefit of intimate staging points.)

For five dollars, one could ride a double-decker bus all the way from Seattle to northern California. I rode for twenty-four hours or more, stifled by day, shivering by night, sustained on the thick sandwiches prepared by a worried aunt. At Portland, a slim girl with unnatural blonde hair and greasy lipstick climbed into the seat beside me. She carried only a handbag and wore only a set of green pajamas. At least to me they were pajamas; they may have been what we now call slacks. She was bound for San Francisco, or maybe Los Angeles, or maybe San Diego. She wasn't quite sure; it didn't matter. She chewed her gum, fiddled with her handbag, examined her eyebrows in the little mirror a half-dozen times, then peered over my shoulder. "Whatcha reading?" I was trying, between headaches, to understand an erudite article in *The Atlantic Monthly* on science and religion. "Jesus," she said, "you're pretty young to be a dope." She fidgeted awhile and offered: "What's the difference between a mountain goat and a soda jerk?" I did not know. "The soda jerk mucks around the fountain." She was something new; I did not know how to talk with her, and very soon she abandoned me for gayer company in the lower deck, a party of sailors from the *Pennsylvania*, whom she assisted with guitar, song, and flask throughout the night despite the timid protests of other, less enduring travelers. Undoubtedly the sailors solved the problem of her destination. She was a plain, honest whore, operating on her own. The Ritz hotels of the world are full of them, not so plain nor so honest; they do not wear green pajamas in public, and their jokes are slightly more subtle, but they travel by the same means, with the same happy indifference to the next destination.

I bathed in the brown, thick waters of the Sacramento River, slept under its willows, followed on foot the macadam road that wound through the vineyards, and crossed over the dreary wastes of lava rock, making for the purple mountains in the distance. At seven in the morning sweat blinded my eyes, the soles of my feet were burning, my tongue was swollen and parched. The nearest

hummock shimmered and dissolved in a subaqueous world of re-
fracted light. I became half-faint, stumbled frequently, lost sight
of the mountains, and made my goal the next telephone pole, and
the next, in whose six-inch shaft of shade I could lay my face.
I was lying thus, when the first driver came along and took me on
to Oroville. The rural postman's truck traversed the Feather River,
where the gold had once been shoveled up like sand, mounted the
Sierra heights, skirted a great hole in the side of the roadbed where
a mountain lion had chosen to bury his kill, and deposited me a
mile high, at the cabin of a certain Fitzgerald, fair-weather prospector, who surveyed my skinny frame with disappointed doubts
in his narrowed eyes. But he kept me, all summer, and I earned
my keep.

In those depression years of the early 'thirties, many men had
drifted back into the high reaches of these mountains, and a minor
resurgence of placer mining began. We were more like scavengers;
some filtered and fingered through the piles of sand and stone, the
"tailings" from earlier boom days when pressure hoses had washed
away whole sides of mountains, leaving them bleached and scarified. Others, such as Fitzgerald and I, hopefully enlarged the
abandoned beds of precipitous streams, heaved out endless blobs
of the slabby clay in long-handled shovels, ran tons of the stuff
over the washboard riffles of our wooden sluices. But, like our
neighbors, we worked only four or five hours a day. The hope of
finding gold, which almost none of us ever did, was more of an
excuse to live in the hills where life was cheap, than anything
else. There was a kind of mutual understanding among the men
that they were there waiting until the unnatural economic troubles
in San Francisco or Sacramento blew themselves out. They brewed
beer and turned their sluice boxes into iceboxes where the bottles
stood all day in the running water. If Big Foots at the Buster
Brown Mine shot a deer one day, we would all gravitate over for
a venison feast and would aid, without asking questions, in burying the bones, hide, and antlers so the game warden would find
no evidence. Beer parties developed with spontaneity at this cabin,
then at another—loud parties, attended frequently by large, blowsy
middle-aged women who often arrived on the fenders of decrepit
Ford cars which somehow bumped over the rutted trails. They had
powerful voices, and an enormous capacity for beer, and spoke
the four-letter words simply because they were ignorant of the
politer synonyms. If one were not careful, he would experience a

heavy, flabby, red arm on his neck, dragging him with astonishing
power down upon a cot amid screams of delight from the assembly.
I was just "Slim," the newcomer, the tenderfoot, and fair game
for all pranks. When the news somehow got out that I had been to
college and had even written things for newspapers, the relationship became unnatural and they left me alone. In a way, it was
relief; in a way, I regretted it. Few of the couples were married,
which surprised me, since I believed "living in sin" was an exclusive indulgence of the rich.

It was mostly a world of men, of artisans. It did not seem to
matter what they had been before—shipyard workers, printers,
saloonkeepers—they all had an easy, instinctive comprehension of
wood and iron, dynamite and cement, air currents, water pressures,
the properties of ore, of soil and seed. They could make trees fall
precisely where they wished, transform a motorcycle engine into
a power saw, build a fireplace with no question of its failing to
draw, produce a complicated plumbing system from a creek and
a few lengths of pipe, worm a dog one hour, bake a chocolate
cake the next, install a carburetor the next, and repair a gold watch
in spare time. So easily, all this was done! None of them ever read
a book of directions, studied a blueprint, or consulted with a colleague. They just did it, with leisurely, natural system, and it
stayed done, it worked. None of them could have quoted a single
law of physics or chemistry, and the words would have sounded
like embarrassing nonsense to them anyway. Yet they understood,
they *knew*, their *hands* knew. The world of the knowing hands,
a world I could never enter—yet half my countrymen dwell in it
always. A world of its own, inside America, from which we were
to draw a host of sergeants and corporals to make an army work
in a manner that was the envy and despair of the others—the
British, the French, the Germans, the Russians, all the others.

I had to take these men on their own terms, try to communicate
in their language, because they could not in mine. "Fitz" would
bait me:

"Jesus H. Christ, don't hold that bit like it was a lily flower!
Now turn it, turn it every time you hit it. Keep turning it. Now
douse the rock, let the pieces run out. How far in does the dynamite have to go? How far in! Well, that beats me—and you one of
them college boys. Jesus H. Christ, when I was your age I was
bossing a gang of fourteen men. What in the name of Almighty
God do they teach you in them colleges!"

But there were private moments that came frequently during the fresh morning hours of work, moments that never return to one in later years, of pleasure keen to the point of anguish. Fog would vanish, the mountain was unveiled and cleansed, and sweet, dank odors flowed out like perfumed oils upon bright waters. The day sounds would begin: the shrill chippering of a squirrel overhead, the dull smacking of a woodpecker, and down in the valley the tinkle of a cowbell. Near the ditch, in a patch of saw grasses, little globules of dew gathered and dropped, gathered and dropped, like the ticking of sweat drops in the secret hair. The taste of salt was sharp in the corner of the mouth, and the wooden shovel had a good, grainy feel in the hand. In these moments the power of life exploded slowly through the veins, and one worked in a savage orgasm until exhaustion came.

By the end of summer Fitz noticed that I could swing up the leaden-heavy shovel with easier grace than he and could stand longer spells at the bucksaw than he. He said nothing, but the baiting ceased, and that was understood between us as the highest form of compliment. In September he drove me down to Quincy, still unable to make out a young man who offered to perform the most back-breaking labor for no return, even paying his share of the board. I left with a deeper chest, heavier shoulders, and a souvenir phial containing about eighty cents' worth of gold flecks in black dirt—all that our mine had produced.

3

I awoke before dawn from a bed among the damp weeds by the Union Pacific tracks at Sparks, the division point near Reno, and found an "empty" in the long freight train making up for the thirty-six-hour run across the Great American Desert to Salt Lake. I entered a new social dimension, the great underground world, peopled by tens of thousands of American men, women, and children, white, black, brown, and yellow, who inhabit the "jungle," eat from blackened tin cans, find warmth at night in the box cars, take the sun by day on the flatcars, steal one day, beg with cap in hand the next, fight with fists and often razors, hold sexual intercourse under a blanket in a dark corner of the crowded car, coagulate into pairs and gangs, then disintegrate again, wander from town to town, anxious for the next

place, tired of it in a day, fretting to be gone again, happy only
when the wheels are clicking under them, the telephone poles
slipping by. Some were in honest search of work, but many were
not. They had worked—once—but jobs did not last, pay was low,
they had had to move on and on for new jobs, until finally it became easier just to move, to move for the moving. Perhaps this
world has gone now; one never hears of it. Perhaps wartime prosperity has wiped it out; I do not know. In the 'thirties it was a vast,
submerged, secondary United States with its own categories of
cities, advertised by its own kind of chambers of commerce, its
own recognized leaders, its strong men and its recognized bad
men, its ragged dowagers and grimy debutantes, and its own laws
—such as they were—which dealt primarily with self-preservation.
The true world of private enterprise and individual initiative. It
will come back, unless America is very wise, but next time it may
have lost its "picturesque" quality; they may not beg cap in hand;
they may fight with something else but razors because they will
know other weapons, and they may not confine their fighting to
themselves.

There were strange men among them, remarkable men, unknown to the rest of America. No one has written the biography
of Tex, King of Tramps, for example. I never saw him, but I knew
there was an obsession in him not unlike Hitler's, a terrible straining of the ego to find expression—either that or he was a wandering
imbecile having a glorious time. At least fifty times in the course
of a couple of thousand miles I came across his insigne, his coat
of arms: Tex—KT. You would find it carved on the wooden seat of
a privy on the edge of a Nevada town, penciled on the wall of a
shower room in a Salvation Army flophouse in Idaho, chalked on
the iron side of a locomotive tender in South Dakota, painted in
six-foot letters of red on a white cliffside high up in a Montana
canyon. Men told me you found it from Maine to California, everywhere, printed, written, carved thousands of times in the course
of what must have been fifteen or twenty years of wandering.

In the jungle, cities were judged and rated on the basis of their
citizens' generosity with handouts and the temperament of the
railway "deeks" who guard the freight yards. You did not, for
example, attempt to travel through Cheyenne, Wyoming, if you
had any alternative. You were apt to be chased from the yards
there not only with clubs, which was fairly common, but with revolver shots, and it was a long walk to the next station. You

traveled through a certain Idaho town only at careful intervals to avoid the monthly raid by the sheriff, who filled his jail with indigents, fed them on nineteen cents a day, and collected a dollar a day from the local government for each occupant. There was no rancor against the sheriff—he had to have his dodge, his racket, like everybody else—but you just avoided him, unless, of course, the weather was rugged and handouts were not forthcoming and you desired a month indoors with steady meals.

One of the most renowned and fearsome characters to dwellers in the jungle was Humpy Davis, railway dick at Harvey, North Dakota. He, it appeared, was a bearlike hunchback, who took a fiendish pride in his ability to clean out a crowded box car, single-handed, in one minute flat. Normally he used a club, and the score of broken arms and heads was running extremely high, when a conclave of hoboes out in Vancouver decided that Humpy must be eliminated for the good of all concerned. They elected a tall Negro, famous for his marksmanship, to do the job. News travels fast by the jungle grapevine. Humpy knew, and waited. One day he observed a Negro, alone, walking steadily toward him between the tracks. This was it. Humpy stood still, letting him come on. Suddenly the Negro stopped, swung up his hand, and fired. The legend relates that Humpy did not move, did not raise his arm. Instead, he shouted: "Shoot at my head, you black bastard, shoot at my head!" The assassin fired again. Humpy, unmoving, repeated his instruction. The Negro fired his six shots, yelled in astonishment and terror and, as he began to run, was brought down by a single shot. Humpy walked across the yards to a beer parlor, unbuttoned his shirt, and exhibited his bulletproof vest with six indentations over the heart so closely grouped that a coffee mug could cover them all. It is a favorite story in the jungle. If one doubts it, he is wise not to express his doubt.

My empty box car at Sparks rapidly filled, the train operators having deliberately left it open and vacant in order to avoid having the inevitable load of hoboes clambering around on top of the cars or clinging to the tender. All were bums by choice save one weather-beaten couple of advanced age who came from New Mexico. They had just lost their small farm and were looking for new opportunities. The man carried a great pack with a washboard strapped on it, while his wizened little wife held their scabby hound dog by a length of frayed clothesline. They represented Respectability among us, were accorded a whole corner to themselves and not included in the unending argument, jeering, boasting, and scuffling.

I sat in the open doorway, swinging my legs in the sun, and listened to a youngster of sixteen. He was well built, with a remarkably attractive, open face, which had a way of slipping quickly into a sneer, becoming then almost sinister. He was boasting of his racket, and I was failing to understand. Finally he took out a crumpled sheet of paper. I read: "For services rendered, I have delivered the following articles to—— [the boy]." Then came a list including watch, fountain pen, set of evening clothes, silver-backed hairbrushes, and so on. "That was in Frisco last month," the boy explained. "I work fast. I find the café where the queers go, mix in with the bunch that looks richest, go home with one of them, and before I get through with him he's given me everything he owns and the written statement. I'm a minor. It's a criminal offense. But he can't do a thing about it, not a thing." He discussed it openly, casually, as if he were boasting of his prowess at baseball. I had only the vaguest notion of what homosexuality was all about, had never been acquainted with anyone I knew to be abnormal in this way, and rather imagined it was something confined to certain boys' schools in England and the bohemian quarters of Paris. Suddenly it was all around me. I noticed men with glazed, slightly bulging eyes and uncertain voices who traveled in company with boys in their teens. The men were referred to as "wolves" (long before that word became slang for Casanovas of normal physiology). A Negro boy named Freddie, no more than fourteen, joined our group one day. He was complaining loudly about the perfidy of a white man who had picked him up while he had been hitchhiking the evening before. "Offered me a quarter if he could ——, then he wouldn't give me the quarter, the skunk. Kicked me out of his car. But I slammed a rock through his back window, the bastard," Freddie finished boastfully, and was rewarded by general acknowledgment that it had served the so-and-so right. All this told so naturally, as if it were an open, common matter understood and accepted by everyone. Except for me, apparently it was.

Freddie was very nearly the cause of my death one night. We had reassembled in the box car after a brief foray through a bleak Nevada hamlet, and now, as the train rumbled through the night, we squatted around a small fire in the middle of the car floor, exchanging tidbits. Freddie was missing; somebody thought he

had caught the train at the other end, and when we heard a banging on the roof we knew he had, and that he had run over the
tops, leaping in the darkness from car to car. Somebody slid the
big door wide open, and we heard Freddie yell: "Grab my legs,
I'm coming down." We looked at one another. There was silence
for a moment. A man said: "How about you, Slim? You got long
arms." I had no choice of action. I stood by the door, while a
chain of three or four men fastened themselves to one of my legs.
The wind blew in my face. The train was racketing along a narrow
bridge over a dark canyon. Suddenly there were Freddie's dangling feet, then his legs, swinging in close, then away again as the
box car tilted, then close again. I grabbed them, felt myself being
torn out of the car, then was toppled over backwards, on top of
the human chain, Freddie on top of me. Except for a moment, ten
years later, when I found myself at the door of a plunging airplane, trying to jump, I have never known a greater terror. Freddie
had stolen a bottle of cherry brandy. He was the hero of the
evening, and we ate, drank, and sang to the accompaniment of a
harmonica until long after midnight.

I was traveling with two boys of seventeen, bound like myself
for Minneapolis where they had recently been suspended from
high school for unauthorized absences. We had made a secret
pact: they did the begging for food (at which they were expert)
and, whenever there was no time to beg or the fruits were meager,
I would buy food for the three of us from my store of six or eight
dollars which was tied in a handkerchief and secured out of sight
inside my belt. (Murder for much less than that was a commonplace in the jungle.) One night we sat by the rails of the "Oregon
Short Line," next the water tank on the outskirts of Ogden, Utah,
where we knew our train would pause. We were after the manifest, the "hot shot"—a sealed, nonstop freight train, representing to
this social dimension what the Century does to another. We became aware that an enormous Negro was standing a few feet
away. He said: "Good evening," sat down beside us, and chewed
on a straw. Eventually he said: "Catching the hot shot?" I said
we were. Finally: "Rode it once myself. Long, cold ride. Get
mighty hungry." More silence and then he said casually: "Tell you
what. One you boys want to walk over to my house, have my wife
fix up a few sandwiches for you." I got up and said that was kind
of him and that I would go along. My companions said nothing.

We walked along a narrow road, bordered by weeds and

ditches. He seemed to be in no hurry and said nothing. I was worried about missing the train and asked him where his house was. "See that light?" he answered. The light appeared to be at least a half-mile away. We walked on, and it began to seem very strange to me. Why should a Negro, obviously poor, go so much out of his way to aid three young white tramps? I was becoming very uneasy, trying to think of some way to withdraw, when the man turned abruptly, walked across a plank over the ditch, and halted by a clump of willows. "Come here a minute, Slim," he said.

My throat had become suddenly dry and I could not answer. He called in a soft tone two or three times: "Come here—got something to show you." All manner of ideas flashed through my head. Did he know about my money and intend to murder me for it? Had he some grisly object there he wanted me to carry away on the train?

He walked deliberately back and stood towering over me so close I could smell his breath. "Want to make a quarter, Slim?" he said softly, coaxingly.

My voice returned enough for me to say in what I hoped were even tones that I couldn't do anything for him. I turned and began to walk back down the dark roadway, the hair on the back of my neck tickling, expecting something to strike me at any moment. Then two figures stepped from the ditch and stood there, waiting, in my path. My heart beat faster, but my head got very cool. I had walked into a trap and was about to be "rolled." I kept on, approached them, lifted my hands over my head, and said in an abnormally confident voice: "All right. You can have anything I have on me."

One of them said: "For Christ sakes, Slim, what do you think you're doing?"

My two loyal, very wise companions had followed us. They got out their knives and wanted to attack the Negro, but let themselves be dissuaded. They scolded me at length for being so dumb that I hadn't recognized a queer, and I had nothing to say. My hands shook for an hour afterwards.

There were glorious days of sunshine, days when we stretched out nude on a flat car cooled by chunks of ice someone tossed down from the "reefer" adjoining, days when we swung our legs idly and yelled to the girls working in the passing fields, days when we abandoned the trains and swam naked in deep mountain pools of cold, clear water. In the night there was hazard and danger, always. There was a midnight halt while the train reorganized at a sleeping Montana division point on the Milwaukee line. The hoboes gathered in a hamburger shop, the only concern still open for business. It was a cold night. With their pennies and nickels the tramps provided themselves with thick mugs of coffee. I ordered sandwiches for myself and my companions. Then to my horror I discovered I had only a five-dollar bill. I passed it over the fake marble counter to the waiter as surreptitiously as I could, and no one noticed. But Montana is a silver state, and the waiter returned with four heavy, gleaming silver dollars in his hand. He did not put them in my anxiously outthrust palm but proceeded to drop them, ringing, clattering on the counter, one at a time. I was conscious that the sounds of eating and drinking around me had ceased and that every eye had turned in my direction. I stuffed them in my pocket and we rose, leaving our food unfinished, sauntered out the door and then ran with all our strength to the train. We hurried along from car to car, scrambling, panting, until we found one with the door unlocked. It was half-filled with lumber. We climbed in, shifted the boards until we had made a hole, then pulled them over us. As the train began its slow, jerking start we heard boots scuffling the boards above our heads. Later we could catch a few words. The voices we recognized as belonging to two of the more evil-looking tramps of the earlier evening. They were talking about the kids with the silver dollars. The voices ceased after a time, and we drifted to uneasy, uncomfortable sleep. In the morning the men were gone.

I arrived at my father's house with my face black from the coal dust of a locomotive tender—my berth during the final roaring, kaleidoscopic night of clinging to a passenger express. Those were my last deliberately sought adventures, but they were not my last adventures. In distant countries I had never seen, the whirlpool of our times was beginning to move in the increasingly rapid, spreading gyration which was to engulf my whole generation and throw its members upon a thousand reefs. I had seen heartbreak, violence, and death in their individual forms, but the dictionary had not yet included as a generic term the word Fascism.

Chapter III

THE UNIVERSITY OF MINNESOTA sprawls over its many acres between the cities of Minneapolis and Saint Paul. It is an excellent center of learning, as mass-production institutions go, and has produced in profusion football players and poets, scientists and embalmers, vast numbers of politicians, businessmen, farmers, dentists, and writers of advertising copy. It is a miniature of American life, faithfully accommodating the taxpayers of the state in all their ideas of what their children and their civilization should grow up to be. With a flick of the wrist you can turn the index of its catalogues and locate Plato or the latest manual on disassembling the Garand rifle. It is a city in itself, which like most American cities has grown by accretion without symmetry or plan, so that the visitor wanders in a kind of architectural Wonderland, passing in a few steps from a red-brick Victorian monstrosity to a functionally sleek structure of glass and steel. Some time back it became evident that the university would continue to grow, and some kind of pattern was required. The decision was obviously in favor of a compromise between factory and academic cloister, for the dominant theme is now that of massive, warehouselike buildings with Greek pillars attached to the front.

Students came from all the northwest states, and some came from distant nations seeking to profit by our excellence in special matters like dentistry or journalism. Regularly, once a week—on Thursday, as I remember—a noted speaker addressed thousands of students who sat with their books in their laps within the softly lighted Northrop Auditorium. Local political candidates stirred us up, and there were frequent academic or scientific conventions, but the highest pitch of general passion was generated by the Saturday afternoon football games. In my period at the school, our brawny Swedes and Poles and Germans developed a habit of winning every game, and our fame spread far and wide. These behe-

moths of the gridiron became national figures, and it was an honor
to sit beside one of them in a class and to awaken him when the
class was ended. This matter of sporting fame eventually began to
get out of hand—the "downtown" sports writers seemed to have
acquired as much authority over the university's policies as the
regents—and I well remember the university president confessing
that he prayed secretly for a football defeat.

There were a few pleasant knolls and bowers for the summer-
time, but the odor of automobile exhaust was likely to have pre-
dominance over that of lilacs; and in the winter students and professors alike were obliged to fortify themselves against the blasts
that blew across the adjacent Mississippi by resorting to long
underwear, stocking caps, mackinaws, and ski pants. One's eyes
streamed with the cold, and the powder on the faces of the girls
crystallized into ragged patches in a way that the editors of
Mademoiselle would have to politely ignore. A railroad ran along
the river's edge, and the tramps who established their "jungle"
there used frequently to lie in the bushes for hours, peering toward
the established nooks in the hope of observing a physical manifestation of undergraduate romance.

It was, all in all, an excellent school for those who were not
wealthy; and most of us certainly were not—the records then
showed that two thirds of the men were obliged to work part time
in order to pay the very reasonable charges. Most of us came with
firm and serious intent, and those who did not usually drifted out
after a few terms. I came, like others, in the quest for first principles. Like most, I did not possess the exceptional intuitive powers
by which some men can grasp the interrelation of contemporary
phenomena and thus construct an ordered view of society without the discipline of organized study. Like all average brains, mine
required the impulse that cannot be planned—a stray book, a disturbing remark, or the challenge of a great teacher who deliberately kicks at the self-starter with which every mental engine
is presumably equipped.

I was twenty and, like most of my classmates of twenty, knew
nothing. I strayed one day into a class on political first principles
conducted by a young man named Benjamin Lippincott, disciple
of the Greeks and of another, more articulate disciple, Harold
Laski of London. Lippincott would survey us with darting eyes, a
tinge of sardonic humor in his soft, mobile face. His method was

new to most of us. He would throw an idea into our midst and
watch us struggle with it. In the Socratic manner he would challenge and play one of us off against the other.

"What is the State?"

Somebody would grope for a definition.

"All right—if that's the State, then what is the Government?

"What is Freedom? Do you consider yourself a free man, Mr.
Smith? Suppose you are very tired and lie down on the sidewalk
in Nicollet avenue. A policeman makes you get up. Has he interfered with your freedom? All right, the law does say so, but you
didn't have a thing to do with making that law, did you? But you
obey the law anyway—a law somebody made without asking
whether you would agree. Does that make you a slave? And if
not, why not?

"Ah, Mr. Jones, if the government can't tell a man where and
how he has to work, that's freedom, is it? But suppose the man
has to work in Mr. Ford's factory because there's no other job to
be found and he doesn't want to starve. Is he still a free man?

"What is Equality? When everybody has an equal vote, you say?
Well, now, Mr. Adams, why *should* everybody have an equal vote?
Why should Mr. Ford, who employs thousands of people, who has
properties all over America, have no more vote than a tramp, who
has no responsibilities except to his own stomach?

"What is Anarchy? Is it the same thing as Socialism, or as Communism? Your answer, Mr. Smith, sounds as if Anarchy were more
like Capitalism. Would you say this is a country of Anarchy?

"What is democracy? A republican form of government? But
England does not have a republican form of government. Would
you say then that England is not a democracy?"

So he would begin. At first, most of us were not only confused,
but angry and resentful. Some did not come back to his classes.
For those of us who stayed it was not an easy time, but it was
wonderful. We were just discovering the exciting world of Ideas,
the world of Theory and of Principle. Not having the capacity to
work backward from phenomena and discover first principles, the
only way I could ever understand my times was by going back
to the political Genesis, the Greeks, and working my passage
home. It was a long trip. We sailed and tacked through the Romans, the Churchmen of the Middle Ages, through Locke, Hume,
Roger Williams, Jefferson, Tom Paine, Adam Smith, Rousseau,
Voltaire, Burke, Hegel, Marx, Spencer, Marshall, Lenin, and

Trotsk The wide channel dividing Washington from Lincoln became understandable; we were able to pin Woodrow Wilson and
Herbert Hoover to their proper points on the chart; we knew
where Norman Thomas was and how he got there, and it became
no trouble at all to distinguish between a Roosevelt and a Churchill
or a Chamberlain. (The last two are so much alike at bottom!)
Five thousand miles removed from it in space, we lived in angry
intimacy with Fascism because it is a thing, first of all, of the mind.
To change the metaphor, it was like learning a foreign language
after one is grown. For a long time the words and phrases beat
without effect upon the brain—then suddenly one day they all
drop into place; one can understand, and he can speak.

But he continues to make mistakes, sometimes very grave mistakes. We did, my very articulate college generation of political
liberals. We made some frightful mistakes, and the story of that
is an integral part of the story of those last, dwindling years in
America between the two great wars. The new war, when it came,
was for us not merely a crisis in our physical lives but an intellectual and moral purgatory.

2

Now, when I read a novel of American campus life, or see a Hollywood version with its fair maidens in lovers' lane, dreamy-eyed
youths in white flannels lolling under leafy boughs or lustily singing, arms about one another's shoulders, of their school's immortal
glories and their own undying loyalty—when I come across all this
I am astonished and unbelieving, or I have a faint twinge of nostalgia for a beautiful something I never knew. I remember only
struggle, not so much the struggle of "working my way through"
as the battle, in deadly earnest, with other students of different
persuasion or of no persuasion, with the university authorities, with
the American society of that time. I remember emotional exhaustion, not from singing about the "dear old college" but from
public debate. I remember exhilarating triumphs and the most
acute bitterness of my life. A class reunion is something I have
never experienced. I would know few of the members of my class.
Our loyalties were not defined by such simple categories. I remember only a small group of all the classes, of various ages, some from
the college of liberal arts, others from law or medicine or agri-

culture—the small, intense group of my friends, cohesive by political conviction and solidified by struggle.

It would be possible, no doubt, and in an accepted tradition, to write of this university period with the humorous superiority of tolerant adulthood, to regard it as a natural manifestation of the naïve idealism of youth. It would be easier, but it would be an error of judgment in considering the recent history of America, for with my college generation a new thing developed: the "student movement," long a serious political factor in China and many European countries, became for the first time a reality in American affairs. We had a definite effect upon our times.

We were in revolt. Not in the manner of many preceding academic generations, not in any bohemian, individualistic sense of hating the smugness of middle-class life and mores. We sought no escape for our personal souls in new art forms or in any new concepts of emotional or sexual freedom. Those were minor matters to us. We believed passionately in freedom for men and in the integrity of the human personality, but we sought these ends, not by changing the individual, but by changing his environment, the way society—meaning chiefly economic society—was organized. For us there was no question of seeking new geographical frontiers, as our struggling forebears had done in their revolt. Even were that physically possible, to us it would have been mere escapism. We sought neither wealth nor fame, nor did we expect security and serenity in the end. The key to life in our times, we thought, was the relationship of a man to society in general and what a man did about it. To be otherwise was to be only half alive. We reasoned in reverse, compared with our fathers—not from ourselves to society, but from society to ourselves. We had to help change society and let private life take care of itself, and we knew that what we sought, the "good life" of the philosophers, would hardly be found in our lifetime. Nevertheless, viewing our fellows who concentrated solely on the narrow technique of their chosen professions, we had no neurotic sense of martyrdom. We did not feel sorry for ourselves; we felt sorry for the others.

If we were reformers, it was not in the old-fashioned, Lincoln Steffens sense. The reformation of local government, the putting of "honesty" into public affairs, seemed an outdated, fruitless, and inconsequential matter to us. We were concerned with the whole underlying motivation of public affairs, on national and world scales, with the forces that produced the phenomena we observed.

The methods would have to be the methods of election and legislation, of large-scale organization, of mass meeting and strike and
protest parade. The methods of the Christian Church in worldly
matters we wrote off very early as ineffectual, and we had nothing
but contempt for approaches such as that of the Oxford Movement, which would deal with dictatorship by improving the dictators and with capitalism by making capitalists better men. No
one ever got our vote for a public-office holder by proving the
man's personal sincerity. Hitler was sincere enough. What mattered was the force, the movement, the set of ideas the man represented.

To a degree, no doubt, we were sentimentalists, as so many liberals are. The man who labored with his hands became in our
minds a more precious human entity, endowed—by us—with
greater personal virtues. Had we ourselves been born among industrial workers we would have escaped this illusion. Still, this
sensation showed that we had bridged a psychological gulf which
the great majority of people never cross, for it is generally true,
in all countries, that members of one social class are quite unable
to feel personal sympathy for the pains of members of another
class. This is true of capitalists toward workmen and vice versa.
As our small group began to have obvious effect on the life of this
enormous university, we were explained, our behavior was rationalized in various ways. To the psychologist it was a simple pattern
—we suffered from hidden inferiority complexes and were trying
to compensate by taking it out on a society that frightened us. This
would not serve, since nearly all of us, certainly all the members
of our exclusive "Jacobin Club," had won high academic laurels
in the competition of our classrooms, we had athletic heroes among
us, and we knew perfectly well that we could compete successfully in the professional worlds most of us were preparing to enter.
If anything, we suffered from a superiority complex. To a tolerant
businessman like my own father it was a simple phenomenon of
growth: "If a man isn't a socialist at twenty and a conservative at
forty, there's something wrong with him"—a phrase that particularly maddened me. To the conservative students of law who
dabbled in politics for reasons of professional advancement, we
were simply fellow-travelers of the university and downtown Communists and were really dancing on the end of their invisible wires.
But we knew the Communists well enough—much better than our
critics did—and understood their methods clearly; and, while we

frequently worked with them, we never worked under them. We disbelieved their methods and program because we understood far more about the peculiar nature of American society than they did. It just would not work in this country. Furthermore, with two or three exceptions it was hard to like them personally. They were —most of them—obvious examples of the inferiority complex. Either by nature or as a fetish, they were uncleanly. They were definitely antisocial in a personal sense, quite humorless, and com· plete bores. We did not adhere to the strict line of any party allegiance. Philosophically and in our contemplation of the economic riddle, we were socialists; in state politics, we would vote Farmer-Labor; and nationally we supported Roosevelt. We were opportunists in the sense that we would use any lawful means, however diverse, to achieve a cohesive end.

It was true that Minnesota, politically speaking, was an exceptional state. It had a long third-party tradition, antedating most of the Progressive movement next door in Wisconsin, beginning far back in Civil War times with that truly remarkable agrarian revolter and scholar, Ignatius Donnelly, who organized farmers' revolts against the railroad and milling trusts one year and lectured at Oxford and Cambridge on Shakespeare the next. One of the great personalities of American history, now buried in oblivion. In the tradition was the elder Lindbergh, who was hated by "the interests," persecuted by the St. Paul and Minneapolis press, and stoned by mobs when he attempted to speak against American entry into the First World War. The contemporary successor of these men, the inheritor of the mantle, was Floyd B. Olson, three times governor of the state, a towering, fearless, extraordinarily able man with a hard eye, a tough manner, and traces of bitterness remaining from an impoverished childhood, but a man who loved people and devoted his life to the defense of the poor. He was almost certainly America's greatest political orator of that time, not excepting Franklin Roosevelt. To his office we as students always had access. He hated the stuffed shirts of the university as much as he hated them anywhere, and he gave us public as well as private support. His conservative opponents, incapable of understanding that ideals are a reality with some men, accused him of lining his own pockets as governor. He died very young of cancer, quite penniless, just as he was about to go to the United States Senate. He was our particular hero.

Doubtless we had absorbed by propinquity some of this purely local nonconformism, but state affairs were really a secondary matter for us, merely an accessible theater in which to perform the roles we had learned in the great books and by our own analysis of economic society, then so clearly in a state of collapse all around us. We were part of a nationwide student revolt.

These were the years of the tragic Depression, produced in part by the first war and removed, as it was to happen, only by the imperatives of the next. We observed bread lines from the street car as we went to school carrying the books that described the good society. We duly listened to lectures on orthodox economics, which explained the "natural laws" of capitalist competition, which would, if not interfered with, ultimately produce the general good by permitting everyone to pursue his selfish ends unhindered. And every day the headlines spoke of riots, of millions thrown out of work, of mass migrations by the desperate. All this was happening in the richest country on earth, a country that possessed all the political rights and instruments by which free men could change their condition—and still they could not prevent this. Meanwhile the experts on orthodoxy droned away: "The mobility and immobility of labor"—"The price of labor." Labor, under the competitive conception, was merely a budgetary item, to be added and subtracted, moved around like machine tools or money capital. The whole fabrication had a dreamlike quality about it; it had no connection with the painful reality we could see out of the classroom windows.

Fellow Jacobin Sherman Dryer would raise an indignant finger. "But, sir, it wouldn't work, to do it that way. There would be revolution."

Professor Garver (co-author of *The Principles of Economics,* studied in all languages including the Scandinavian) would peer over his glasses. "We are not concerned with other forces, including the political, Mr. Dryer. We are concerned only with the basic laws of economics."

It simply made no sense to us. There were no immutable "laws"—or damned few—about it. Economics was not a "science" at all; it was fruitless to treat it as such, and to study it as a special, exclusive field. It was all mixed up with politics, with sociology, with geography and a good many other things. Clearly the "economic laws" of competition were a fantastic delusion, merely an elaborate effort to justify things as they were by the invention of supposedly unchangeable forces which men mustn't attempt to interfere with. It seemed to us as much of a hoax as the medieval scholars' explanation of kingly authority as something derived from God. The system did not work, and if it did not work in America it certainly would not work anywhere. We knew from the history books that even in the famously "prosperous" times of the Victorian era, millions in England and elsewhere labored under insecurity and the most abject conditions of life. We believed the system had worked with passable success in the United States partly because the frontiers were constantly expanding; but even in those days it had frequently collapsed, and once had been rescued by the invention of the automobile which made a basic change in our pattern of living. But the frontiers were gone, and it was senseless to rely on mere chance.

When a Republican candidate for governor spoke to the Student Forum and declared with pride: "Why, the United States has gone through *fifty-two* economic depressions!" we screamed with delight at his unintentional indictment of the system.

No, it was clear that the system contained a basic flaw which invalidated the whole thing. The matter of production, we could see, was solved. Capitalism could produce overwhelmingly; but periodically, at the height of its production, it collapsed because it provided no certain, continuing method for getting the product into the hands of the mass of people. It could not *direct* its efforts to any channel, nor switch its accumulation of capital investment toward anything except that which happened at the moment to be profitable. That might be the manufacture of "Rendezvous" perfume instead of shoes, regardless of the fact that millions needed shoes and didn't care how they smelled. And thus came periodically the drive for export markets, the sending of machinery and whole factories after consumer goods, the political control necessary to safeguard the capital investments—in other words, Imperialism as an escape from domestic crisis that the system could not solve. Then the collision of expanding and competing empires, and thus war—all wars, we thought.

At the moment crops were being plowed under, and millions suffered from malnutrition. Doctors were impoverished, and hundreds of thousands lacked proper medical care. Teachers were on the breadlines, and vast sections of the country were populated by illiterates. To us, it was all a mess. We refused to accept it as inevitable, untouchable. Men were *not*, regardless of all the determinists, the helpless victims of uncontrollable forces. We did not live in an age of superstition, worshipping the mysteries. Men could take hold of the system and direct it. But they had to be taught to understand it, encouraged to organize, and they had to be led. We didn't like the leaders we observed in political life, and we didn't like the university authorities, who we thought were merely serving the system and not the cause of truth. (I fear we did them a little less than justice.)

The university was in a state of intellectual ferment, and we were fortunate to be students at this particular moment. The gaunt brick structures with their fake Grecian façades did not even look like ivory towers on the outside. The place was a kind of fortress for us, and periodically we sallied forth to do battle with evil. We enjoyed the privilege of having little to lose. Before we had even studied much about the function of the American labor movement, many of us had trudged around factories bearing strike placards to the mystified annoyance of the employers who couldn't see what the hell we had to do with it. In the summer of 1934 the two cities were thrown into uproar by the famous truck drivers' strike, led by the Dunne brothers, Trotskyists, who organized the strike as none had been organized before in American labor history. They had patrol cars of their own, stopping trucks entering or leaving the city, a daily strike newspaper, loud-speaker broadcasts, a commissary, and medical and ambulance services for their wounded. When they put on a funeral procession for one of their fallen, the life of the business district came to a stop on the streets.

I went to work as reporter for the Minneapolis *Star* to cover the strike. Some of the boys from the Greek fraternities on the campus joined the police and Citizens' Alliance forces with baseball bats on their shoulders, in defense of what they regarded as law and order. Some of my little crowd joined the strikers, in noncombative functions. Most of us, be it confessed, were not of the type that is willing to fight for its beliefs with brickbat or club. Fellow Jacobin Dick Scammon, son of the medical dean, was different; he was of the stuff from which true leaders are made. He was six feet four, weighed two hundred and sixty pounds, ate, drank, and sang with rabelaisian gusto, and belonged to thirteen political organizations before he could vote; he had a prodigious memory and thought so much faster and more incisively than his classmates that he could sleep through most of his courses. (Harold Laski told me in

London during the blitz that he regarded Scammon as the ablest American student he ever had.) Dick could swing a club, if he were convinced there was no other resort. We were all morally courageous, but he had physical courage.

The whole city divided in its sympathies. The *Star* was reasonably fair in its running account of what became a minor civil war, but the other newspapers were not. The police chief also worked on behalf of the employers, believing with them that "order" meant tranquillity no matter what kind of order it was. So the police took measures more lawless than those of the strikers to enforce their conception of order. There were fights every day, and mostly the victims were strikers. When a prominent businessman, who had gone into the streets with a club, was himself struck down by a picketer's club, the conservative newspapers went wild. Strikers could get hurt, and so could policemen, but *this* could not happen. This extraordinary reaction disturbed me very much. Why was this man with his white collar a human reality to a big section of the community while the truck drivers in blue shirts were not? Had class allegiance got so deeply into the blood of democratic America?

The police set a deliberate trap one day. The truck drivers walked squarely into it, and fifty or more of them were shot down with buckshot. According to the *Journal* the police had been "literally fighting for their lives." The results showed that one policeman had been hurt, while the nurses at the city hospital that night demonstrated to me that nearly all the injured strikers had wounds in the backs of their heads, arms, legs, and shoulders: they had been shot while trying to run out of the ambush. Suddenly I knew, I understood deep in my bones and blood what Fascism was. I had learned the lesson in such a way that I could never forget it, and I had learned it in the precise area which is psychologically the most removed from the troubles of Europe—in the heart of the Middle West. I went home, as close to becoming a practising revolutionary as one of my noncombative instincts could ever get.

My father sat on the screened porch, staring at the newspaper headline. His face was pale. "This—this—is *revolution!*" he said to me.

"Well," I flung out recklessly, "if it is, maybe we'd better make the most of it."

To my consternation, he let the paper slip from his fingers, put his leonine head in his hands, and in a husky, uncertain voice said: "I did not ever think that one of my sons would become a revolutionary." I had never seen him so deeply shaken since the day, years before, when Duff Aaker died. I had not understood that to some people like my father, the institutions of public order, no matter what kind of social system they reinforced, were endowed with a religious sanctity.

<h1 style="text-align:center">3</h1>

Of all the instruments designed to uphold the existing order, I think we most hated the military establishment. We would still have opposed it on this ground, but with less personal revulsion had we not been forced against our will to "take" military training at the University of Minnesota, for there seemed to be a law hanging over from Civil War days which made it necessary for any boy striving for an education at the people's university to don a hand-me-down uniform and shoulder a 1905 unfireable Springfield rifle three times a week for a full two years. Most of us resented this as an unrecoverable loss of precious hours before we learned to look upon the whole proceeding as a harsh interference with our liberty and a humiliating affront to our personal dignity. To me there was something revoltingly ignoble about the process of jerking my arms and legs this way and that on the shouted orders of a beetle-browed sergeant toward whom I felt an infinite intellectual superiority. True, when marching at the flank of a column (I was usually the tallest in the platoon) on inspection parade, I had a thrilling feeling of being part of a living, irresistible force; but this was a fleeting sensation, despised later as part of the seductive paraphernalia of the plot, along with the flags and music and shining brass, to lure us into feeling that training for murder was really something else. It is possible we would have felt less animosity if we had known we were really learning something, however ignoble; but partly because the system was compulsory and the officers did not have to compete for customers, the ROTC duty had become for most of them merely a soporific sabbatical from real work, and in the basic two-year course they taught us nothing. We never once even fired a gun.

My first officer was a Major John Hester of West Point (to us a hideous barracks designed to make citizens of a democracy unlearn all they knew of man's right to freedom). I saw him merely as a type, not as an individual human being. "Look at those boring eyes, that severe jaw," I said to myself. "The human automata. The military caste. The negation of the free personality. Listen to this talk about 'discipline.' They don't think. They press a button and a mechanical device starts clicking. Well, they won't turn *me* into that." (Several years later I sat on a log in a fortified forest with General Hester, an intelligent, compassionate man.)

At the end of the basic course one of the officers tried to persuade me to continue and become a cadet officer, but I would have none of it. As time went on, the ROTC officers came to regard me as their enemy and listed me as one of the "campus reds" who were trying to undermine the republic. Jacobin Phil Potter, editor of the university daily, was carrying on a vigorous campaign to end the compulsory aspect of military training, and we all pitched in. When a brilliant philosophy student named Kaplan was suspended from school for skipping his military classes, I got hold of the story and we made an issue of it. This forced a "trial" for Kaplan before a tribunal of officers, with Dick Scammon as Kaplan's self-appointed defense attorney. The officers took their secret verdict of guilty to President Coffman, who overruled them and reinstated the student—much to their embarrassment, which was made acute when I learned the details and published the story. After that the officers detested me, and, although I did not realize it, I had made an unforgiving enemy of the cautious president, much to my loss later on.

There was a wild scene in the university recreation building one afternoon when two or three hundred students assembled to debate the "Oxford Oath," which in its American version (then going the rounds of the colleges) solemnly pledged: "I will not bear arms for flag or country." Dick smashed his gavel on the table and bellowed the shouting crowd into a semblance of order. We accepted the pledge overwhelmingly, and I voted for it along with the others. The only thing that disturbed my peace of mind was a lasting memory of a tall young man in uniform—I believe he was the Cadet Colonel—rising with simple dignity, facing the hostile crowd, and saying: "If we are to enjoy the privileges of democracy, as you are in this meeting, why should we not be willing to defend it?"

There seemed no immediate threat of war at that time, but our "peace strikes" and meetings were frequent and passionately sincere. The president refused us use of the big auditorium for these mass meetings, so we gathered on the steps. Jacobin Lee Loevinger, distinguished student in science and law, smacked fist upon palm and shouted: "And next time, when they come and tell us we must invade the land of some other, some equally innocent and misguided people, to 'defend our wives and sweethearts,' we know what we will do—we shall defend them by preserving our lives, by staying at home with them. We will not listen to the scream for slaughter." (Brilliant Lee Loevinger, who went as an officer with the first naval mission to England.) Governor Olson spoke from those same steps of the forbidden auditorium, delighting in the knowledge that the embarrassed university president was looking down from his adjoining office.

Very few of us were conscientious objectors to war in the true, religious sense. We had no thought of working for a violent overthrow of the government itself either by removing its internal military defense or by encouraging its defeat by a foreign power. We believed that "preparedness," as the history of warring countries proved, was no guarantee of peace—that it would be, in fact, a force for easier involvement. We refused to believe that *any* people in the world desired war, with us or with their neighbors In any case, modern war was a product of the collapsing capitalistic system and the collision of its imperialisms and was encouraged and desired only by the professional military, financiers, and munitions makers, who were associated in a kind of loose but real conspiracy against the innocent people of every land. The whole effort, the whole meaning of our own lives in our time must be to improve the material and spiritual condition of man in society, and war was the negation of all this. A new war would mean the end of all we believed we lived for, and perhaps destroy forever all that the great men of our books had envisioned, all the progress toward decency and a common brotherhood that the human mind had achieved throughout the painful centuries. So we passionately felt. Why, at this portentous moment of history, the early 'thirties, did we say what we said and thus help to mislead our people, do what we successfully did about military training, and thus help, however minutely, to disarm our country? We, along with college men and women all over America, were involved in an astonishing paradox.

Lessons of the past have greater power over the mind than any forecast of the future, even if the lessons be conceived in error. We came along at the peak of the intellectual revulsion against the First World War. We felt ashamed, ashamed for our fathers and uncles. We were revolted by the stories of the mass hysteria of 1917, the beating of German saloonkeepers, the weird spy hunts, the stoning of pacifists, the arrests of conscientious objectors. As enlightened scholars, we considered that the professors of 1917 had degraded themselves and their sacred function by inventing preposterous theories about the essential depravity of the German race, the worthlessness of their art, and the hidden evil of their music. We refused to believe that war was the responsibility of Germany or any single country. We plowed through the pages of Fay and were convinced that there were no basic issues involved and that with a little intelligence and forbearance war could easily have been averted. Britain and France had acted as stupidly as Germany; no country had had any serious designs to rule Europe, let alone the world. America had been driven into the war by hysteria over the *Lusitania* and other incidents, by the diabolical propaganda of the Allies, particularly the British, who, our studies proved, had controlled most of the means of world communications. Our teachers of journalism exhibited innumerable posters from that time, depicting the German soldier as a grinning ape. We laughed bitter laughter over the propaganda stories of the "crucified Canadian soldier" and the little Belgian children with their hands cut off by the Germans. Contemporary research had proved there was no evidence to support these stories. We read with eagerness the new books purporting to expose the munitions racket and accepted all their implications. We cheered Senator Nye in his fight for the Neutrality Act long and loudly. We were excited over the newly unearthed and published dispatches from the wartime American ambassador in London, who mentioned the risk to American loans and investments unless we came into the war.

The conduct of the war itself, with the years of stalemate, the meaningless, slaughterous attempts by bankrupt generals to hang on to their jobs a little longer by sending thousands to certain death in order to gain a hundred yards of mud—all this chilled our marrow and made us, we thought, very wise. We read *Three Soldiers,* and *All Quiet on the Western Front,* and *Death of a Hero* with compassion and a sick feeling in our stomachs. We were young, and to those just beginning to taste the wonderful flavors of life the idea of death is a stark tragedy of unutterable horror. "To make the world safe for democracy!" Where was democracy now? It had perished in Italy, and was now finding violent death in Germany—a direct result, we believed, of that incredibly useless war. Men talked about the ennobling effects of fighting as comrades, about what military discipline had done for the character. We despised the organized veterans we saw, with their greedy lobby, their beery, boisterous annual conventions. We had more scorn than pity for the Gold Star Mothers. As a grim jest we joined the "Veterans of Future Wars." We began to detest the very word "patriotism," which we considered to be debased, to be a synonym for chauvinism, a cheap medallion with which to decorate and justify a corpse.

We regarded the uniform as a convict suit, worn by inmates of the prison house of the human spirit, and we despised all those who voluntarily donned it. We could not swallow the pose adopted by professional military men—"We hate war even more than you because we know what it is like." When an aging American general came to speak in the auditorium, we reprinted an extract from his memoirs in which he related with pride how he had sent men into combat—where many died—a few hours before the Armistice he had known was due. They couldn't kid us. Men could not spend half a lifetime training for a particular job and not wish for the opportunity to do the job and cover themselves with glory in the doing. With all their pretenses, we knew that in their hearts the professional fighters wanted war, enjoyed war. We hated them for it.

In general, war came from the economic system, from the conspiratorial efforts of a few occult groups, and from ignorant distrust and fear between peoples. Therefore the duty of the enlightened citizen was to change the system, to expose the conspiracies, and to create trust, beginning at home by refusing to rearm ourselves and making contact with other student and antiwar groups and forces abroad.

The paradox grows more mysterious when one remembers that all this was going on in our heads simultaneously with the coming to power of Adolf Hitler. It is more unfathomable when one considers that we, who had a germinal sense of democracy and freedom, understood the real nature of Fascism much earlier than did the public authorities in our country and in Europe's democracies, much more clearly than did the conventional students around us who went in for voluntary military training as a matter of routine. The actions of Hitler were being justified on all sides by a lot of people who believed in capitalism, in preparedness, in all the conventional ideas, as merely a necessary attempt to bring "order" into German life, and to give the Germans, frustrated by the mistaken terms of the Versailles Treaty, a sense of dignity and place in the world. These people were inclined to approve the Nazis as a "stabilizing" force. But we who had learned from history what the long struggle toward an age of reason implied knew the moment the Nazis burned the books that Fascism wanted war. We knew it in our bones. Why did we not immediately go all out for preparedness? Were we short on facts? Did we feel that, because the French had the "greatest army in the world" and the British the greatest navy, Hitler could be cowed or contained? I think perhaps we did. We were quite ignorant of the true designs of Japan, as were our diplomatic authorities, and while we began to accept with dismay the probability of a European war, we remained desperately anxious to keep America out of it, to preserve at least one oasis of sanity in an insane world. We grasped the implications of Fascism, but we failed to comprehend the *scale* of the thing, to understand that a *world* conspiracy was under way. We kept on, with our kind of methods to insure peace and—we thought—to save our own lives.

We continued to hope against hope that Hitler could be killed by organized pressure from the democracies of Europe who must —but did not—unite. We put great hopes in the German Socialists and Communists, believing with naïveté that the truth is strong by itself and cannot lose in the end. From all that we had been taught about the first war, we still conceived of the Germans as unwilling victims of the imperatives of desperate capitalism. We still believed that the mass of ordinary men was the same in all countries, with the same basic desires and needs and the same repugnance for war. If the Germans marched and goose-stepped it was merely because they were directed into it; we could not conceive that a whole people *could* be different, that they could actually *like* to goose-step. Surely all men wanted security above all else. It did not occur to us for a moment that whole masses of men could grow tired of security and consciously desire another kind of life. Fascism meant war, but, instead of accepting war as inevitable, the thing to do was to stop Fascism this side of war. For America the task was to keep the ink fresh, the microphones hot. We did not think about keeping the powder dry. The smell of powder made us sick.

4

We tried to apply our general ideas about human society to the specific world of the university. I doubt if our families and the public ever realized the deadly earnestness of "campus politics" and the appalling amount of time and energy students put into its practice. As in most state universities the authorities encouraged a modicum of "student government" as a kind of harmless training, always making sure to retain final control themselves. Hitherto, the machinery of student elections to various organizations and the organizations themselves had been the special preserve of the permanent fraternities and sororities, whose real leaders were frequently found among senior students in the law school. A small group of these men usually controlled all nominations by the dominant "party," which was essentially conservative, never dreaming of seriously challenging the university authorities on any real issue. They parceled out the elective honors to the Greek houses as a reward for party loyalty, arbitrarily deciding the class officers, for example, and which girls would have the honors of which places in line for the "grand march" of the class proms and balls. The award of these prerogatives was cause for endless conniving, bitter animosities, and the most acute heartburning imaginable. The most successful exponent of campus politics in years was a law student named Harold Stassen, who had been graduated two or three years previously and whose name was still a byword for political skill. But the coming of the new academic era with its intense concern over economic reform, over the issue of military preparedness and peace, edged our wooden swords with steel, and the battle seemed very real indeed. The Greek houses suddenly discovered that while they had been immersed in such matters as the class proms, other students by some diabolical and mysterious means had overreached them and were controlling the really vital instruments—the daily newspaper, the literary review, the law review, the board of publications, the student council, and so on. At the bottom of all this was the Jacobin Club, formed by

ten or twelve of us who were in general revolt against things as
they were. The Greek houses first learned of our organized existence when we were included with the regular fraternities in the
quarterly list of academic standings, and they found us at the top
of the list with a scholastic average higher than any fraternity
had established in thirty years. We became suspect among the
conventional conformists and very quickly feared by the university
administration. We very nearly succeeded—we thought—in making
student government truly that, and did succeed in abolishing compulsory military training, the most important issue of all. In the
midst of this campaign, the authorities were forced to throw over
all pretense of being disinterested advisors of student affairs and
clamped a censorship on the daily newspaper. They sent their
young stooges from the publications board down to our printery,
and the editorial column of the paper carried the heading: "These
editorials have been approved by the board of publications." Then
followed a series of mock essays on the joys of springtime, the de-
sirability of sprinklers that would throw water in squares instead
of circles, and the like. The embarrassed president and the dean
of men gave up this form of control, and tried other means, including personal intimidation; but it was too late. We had the
Governor of the state on our side, he controlled some appoint-
ments to the board of regents, and sixty years of compulsory military training came to an end at that university.

This battle and many others went on, however, and the next
year the editor of the paper also was a member of the Jacobin Club.
I was to follow him, by right of seniority and general agreement,
as editor in my senior year. But the habit of success had relaxed
our vigilance. As the election to the editorship drew near, the
authorities worked steadily behind us. They had found a weak
spot in the wavering convictions of my fellow Jacobin, the in-
cumbent editor. They turned his head with a great deal of flatter-
ing attention—the president would call him in for "advice" very
frequently—and convinced him that it was his duty to stand again
for election and for the good of the university prevent Sevareid
from taking over the paper, even though this meant that the boy
would have to change his life plan and enter the law school in
order to remain on the campus. It was a miniature example of a
recognizable political pattern: the liberal, softened by success and
propinquity with the rich and powerful, renouncing his comrades

in revolt "for the good of all." When we discovered that this lad was "doing a Ramsay MacDonald" on us, the fight became intense and bitter. My friends pleaded with the boy for hours at a time, warning him that his victory would turn to ashes because not only would he lose all his friends but his sponsors would despise him as their tool. It was too late. The military officers, we found, had been working for months on two or three members of the publications board to prevent my election, and the president did something he had never stooped to before—he ordered his own faculty representative on the board to vote as he desired regardless of that gentleman's convictions. After all, he had to keep his job. In sum, the administration in its own behavior betrayed all the principles of political uprightness that it insisted we be taught in our classes. As I later learned from my friends, some of the men and women in the Greek houses, who saw their chance to begin breaking down the power of the Jacobins, deliberately spread a rumor that I needed the editor's salary because I was in trouble and "had to get married." (I was engaged to a girl in the law school, an influential nonconformist herself.) The ferocity and vindictiveness of the campaign reached unbelievable heights. In the election by the board I lost by one vote. Tammany methods, when thus applied, were unbeatable.

Loevinger, who was president of the publications board, broke the news to me in the law review office next morning, and I was stunned. I had worked three years for this position and honor, and by every rule was entitled to it. I had never hidden anything nor worked behind anyone's back. I had assumed the opposition felt as we did: that controversy was controversy, that a man's opinions were his own, and that, however anyone opposed them, he did not resort to calumny nor twist the very lives of his friendly enemies. I was the naïve liberal, still feeling somehow that truth could defeat a Hitler. Dimly I began to perceive the realities of political life. I was unable to speak and walked down the stairs. Sherman Dryer caught up with me, put his arm over my shoulder, and solemnly said: "This changes my whole philosophy."

When the news got out there was an uproar. Although I was doing my major studies in political science and not in the journalism department, all the members of the journalism faculty protested the decision, and about twenty-five of the thirty or so students on the newspaper staff signed an objection. They offered

to strike, to refuse to publish, but—still clinging to the liberal's
characteristic belief that the persuasion of truth would somehow
suffice—I refused this drastic move. A second election was forced,
but after an exhausting all-night battle, the board confirmed its
vote and we gave up. I became a minor hero and martyr; my
opponent was expelled from the Jacobin Club, formally censured
for "conduct unbecoming a gentleman" by the journalistic hon-
orary society of which I was president, and continued as editor, a
friendless, lonely boy. The pattern of power politics was carried
out to its final orthodox step: I was called into the dean's office
and with much flattery informed I had been chosen for membership in the senior honor society. This corresponded to a knighthood
for an influential but defeated opponent of the ruling system,
which uses the glamorous apparatus of royal orders as a political
weapon.

After that I buried myself in my books, earning bread and board
by rising at five each morning and working in the university post
office before classes, handling and distributing bundles of the
newspaper which I had cherished and lost. It was many months
before the pangs of bitterness left me. I had one last fling. Every
four years the students staged a mock political convention, of all
parties instead of one, to nominate their choice for the presidency
of the United States. As comic relief, I made a nominating speech
for one Bernarr MacFadden, elderly exponent of vitamins and
setting-up exercises, at that time (1936) seriously trying to get
the Republican nomination. I hired a bugler, a girl acrobatic
dancer with a fulsome bust, and a football hero with sizable biceps,
and paraded with them to the stand carrying a banner that depicted a muscular arm wielding a dumbbell. The speech began:
"Fellow Americans, are we men or mice?" and argued the need
for a Strong Man in the White House. I was making a sarcastic
attack on the preparedness program and warned with mock
rhetoric of the imminent danger of the Japanese "invading the
California coast in bathing suits." The mass of students in the
field house screamed their delight. Sherman, with glittering eye,
made an impassioned attack on Governor Landon, "who would
sacrifice the youth of the land on the altar of the balanced budget."
We nominated Floyd B. Olson. The downtown political writers
complimented us on our oratorical mastery and wondered in print
why this level of platform brilliance was unattained in state
politics.

With this speech, with this message to my fellow students, I ended my university career. It was one year before the battle of Shanghai, two years before the *Anschluss*.

5

There was a new atmosphere in the editorial rooms of the old *Journal*, to which I returned. Even the older men, men who had spent a working lifetime on the paper and had achieved important editorial positions, had come to realize with reluctance that neither their gray hairs nor their loyalty had given them security, and the Newspaper Guild, inspired by Heywood Broun, had won over nearly all the staff. The spirit of the place was tense, but more courageous, less craven. The lines were tightening all over the world, and in every American factory and office the terms "Fascist" and "Red" were being put fervently and carelessly to local application. To publishers, the Guild represented a threat to freedom of the press, and they said they did not see how its members could be trusted to give the public a fair report of controversial issues, such as a labor strike. This was surprising to the Guild, whose members had never before remarked any desire for fairness on such an issue burning in the hearts of the publishers. They knew the publishers had been organized, however informally, with the Citizens' Alliance and the antilabor elements in the business community, and the working press regarded *that* as a threat to freedom of the press. American publishers began in this period to reap the painful reward of having subverted their precious public trust to private, selfish purposes. The truth was—and is—that the lowly hired hands in these institutions had a deeper sense of their duties to democracy than did the directors themselves.

Fresh from the theoretical battles of the classrooms, I was acutely concerned with the developing ideological struggle in the country. When a couple of Communist acquaintances came to me with the information that a semisecret Fascist group, the Silver Shirts, were organizing widely in Minneapolis, I went to work. It was an unbelievably weird experience; it was like Alice going down the rabbit hole into the world of the Mad Hatter. I spent hair-raising evenings in the parlors of middle-class citizens who worshipped a man named William Dudley Pelley, organizer of what they called the "Christian Party," devoted to driving out the

Jews from America and countering the "Communist Revolution," the exact date for which they professed to know—a few weeks ahead. They sang the praises of Adolf Hitler and longed for the day when Pelley should come to power as the Hitler of the United States. They had secret signs and symbols, saw the "Mark of the Beast" on American coins, put there by the archcriminal, Henry Morgenthau, and avidly read the hoary "Protocols of the Learned Elders of Zion," which Hitler and Rosenberg had used. Governor Olson, of course, was a leader of the "Communist Plot," and harmless little Maurice Rose, the Governor's chauffeur, they designated an "international banker." One of the Silver Shirt leaders, a retired businessman, led me into his kitchen and opened his cupboards to show me the stocks of canned goods he had accumulated against the day of the Communist uprising, when he expected to barricade himself in his upper duplex. He raised a quivering finger and in a quavering voice informed me: "If it be God's will that I fall as a martyr to the cause at the hands of these beasts, I shall die here, in my Christian home, defending my dear wife to the end." They were quite mad.

My city editor refused to believe the story I brought back to the office until he himself had gained admittance to one of their seances. He returned to the office and said: "Get me a drink, quick! God, I feel I've been through the most fantastic nightmare of my life." The lunatic fringe in advanced, civilized America was a far more spacious crazy quilt than any of us had imagined. I took them seriously, as a cadre of Fascism, and we proposed to expose the organization in a series of articles. Then, to my surprise, opposition to this move developed from unexpected quarters, revealing a standard pattern with which I was to become familiar. My young Communist acquaintances wanted the story withheld. As Communists would be, they were convinced that the lunatics were merely the tools of a small cabal of leading businessmen in the city who were providing the money and directing the whole affair as part of a ruthless conspiracy to help establish capitalist Fascism in the country. We must wait until we proved this. The Communists, too, were living in a dream world, and their view of the local tycoons was as fantastic as the Silver Shirts' view of Morgenthau. I was realistic and experienced enough to know that. Then a group of liberal rabbis and wealthy Jews asked the editor to withhold the story. It would all be most painful to them, most undignified, and would merely drag out into the open and abet a virulent form of anti-Semitism. It would be better to ignore the madmen and pretend they didn't exist. But the managing editor was a man of courage, and the stories were published—not as I wanted them written, as a cry of alarm, but as a semihumorous exposé of ridiculous crackpots who were befuddling otherwise upright citizens.

When the first article appeared, the paper sold several thousand extra copies. My Communist acquaintances refused to speak to me; the ordinary, poor Jews of the community highly approved the exposé; Sherman Dryer, already a power in the Farmer-Labor state machine, deplored the frivolous tone of the articles but tried —unsuccessfully—to persuade the party to make the Silver Shirt menace the main issue of the state campaign. And my personal life became a torment.

I was threatened by telephone and letter every day to such a point that my family was alarmed for my safety and my brothers wanted to sleep, armed, in my apartment. I knew perfectly well that Fascists of this type, like certain types of liberals, were quite incapable of physical violence, but as the threats continued I became somewhat worried myself. Odd characters, fuming and bridling, would march to my desk in the city room and demand to know whether I was a Christian or a Bolshevik. "Lifelong subscribers" would lecture me over the telephone, and, when I lost patience and lectured them back, they would call the publisher and I, to my disgust and amazement, would then be lectured by my bosses for being rude to a client. I sat in the balcony of the biggest Baptist church and listened to the influential pastor denounce me as a "Red," a foolish young "cub reporter." The latter accusation offended me deeply, and my serene bride said: "After all, darling, you *are* a cub reporter, really." I felt a hero one moment and a complete ass the next.

One arid afternoon the people buried Floyd Olson under the trees by a lake. In the glass-covered coffin his broad, strong face seemed pitiably weak and shrunken. For years he had suffered great pain, though he had never betrayed it in his face; but after death it was there and you could see it. When the news hawkers shouted the announcement from their corners, the noises of the street died down, and their voices with the shocking sentence were unbearably loud and distinct in the unnatural stillness. I saw a streetcar motorman get down from his car and walk back from the newsstand with tears streaming down his cheeks. Many thousands had a feeling that someone in the family had died.

In the city room there was noisy activity, and I could observe an editor expostulating with a reporter, who seemed to be arguing back with a flushed face. It appeared that the editor was ordering the reporter to write a story which would show in effect that the Governor had had many drinking companions among the rich and powerful and had served their causes as much as he had befriended the poor and weak. The reporter stood before my desk shakily drinking water from the cooler and said: "Christ, do they have to throw in the hook even after he's dead?" I walked out into the parched, lifeless streets with a numb feeling of dismay. Could one never win? How weak we were, when so much had depended upon one human being! There was no one else. We had had to produce a genius before our side could win even a brief round. They could win with anybody now, with anybody, because they had a machine, they had something, everything on their side. This was the end of the party, the end of everything we had wanted it to become some day. Why was it always like this, everywhere in the world? Could common people be made to work for their own interests only if they had a great personality as their symbol? What was wrong?

Various "scoops" came my way during the year; I began to feel that I was a person of some consequence on the newspaper and vaguely to suspect that maybe I was different, too valuable an asset to require the support of my colleagues through the Guild organization—which, however, I ardently supported in the interests of weaker persons. I was brought down to earth abruptly. One day I was sent to get some facts from a local banker about a suburban camp that he and his friends were subsidizing to house and care for the unemployable, elderly panhandlers who were begging on the downtown streets. This was to be done under the aegis of a church, and the contribution of the businessmen was to be described in the paper as their voluntary assistance to a worthy charity. "Of course," confided the banker, "between you and me, we have a hardheaded motive. These filthy bums are edging too far up Nicollet avenue. They are begging in front of the better-class stores. If we don't get them away they will tarnish the high tone of these blocks and drive real-estate values down." He nudged me and winked. The potentate, letting the lowly scribbler into the secrets of power! I delayed writing the story, and when an editor inquired about it, I was foolish enough to blurt out my feelings on the matter. I was told to conform òr resign from the paper.

In the spring the Guild forced through a contract under which most of us would get something more than the subsistence wage we were receiving. Various oral promises to me of a salary raise had never been carried out, and by the new contract I would receive one of the biggest advances because of my previous years on the paper. But there was a loophole in the contract, unnoticed by the Guild but quickly spotted by the publisher's lawyer. One day I wrote a single paragraph "squib" about a veterans' meeting and called the organization the American Legion instead of the Veterans of Foreign Wars, which it was. I was instructed to get my pay and my hat. Others followed me onto the street in quick succession. I buried myself in the musty files of the state library for weeks, trying to piece together the history of the third-party revolt in the Northwest, to understand what had formed the local community into the pattern I observed and how it fitted into the whole American society. A year or two later, a letter reached me in France informing me that the publishers had sold the *Journal*, apprising the employees of this abrupt change in their lives by a brief note found one morning on the bulletin board. The paper was closed down, and hundreds found themselves on the street.

Chapter IV

MY FATHER and most of his contemporaries in that second generation of Americans grew up with a feeling of kinship with Europe, and yet they had little desire to go there when they were grown. In their boyhood they felt as close to Europe in a certain way as to America, but later the new country was their only interest. With me and many of my generation it was the opposite. We had not the slightest feeling about Europe as children and yet, when we were grown, Europe had a strong attraction. It was not the same *kind* of feeling, not a feeling of personal origins, not in the blood but entirely in the mind. It was a secondary growth, an intellectual development. It had to do with political and social cause and effect; so much in our heads had come from Europe. To a certain degree we felt ourselves to be—at least we wanted to be—citizens of the world. My father, when he first understood about the Declaration of Independence and the *Federalist* Papers, felt a longing to visit the old places in Virginia. We, with our new sense of the world's essential unity, the closed circle of events, desired to move, not back in time, but around in space on the contemporary level. Whatever was moving now on the distant segment of the circle was bound to come around to us sooner or later. One may as well meet it now as then, and anyway, the waiting would be an intolerable strain. In 1937 we knew it was to be war; we knew it with extraordinary clarity despite the soporific statements of the "experts," the columnists, the business leaders who were always being quoted in the papers as they returned to the docks of New York.

If one is not pressed for hours, there is no method for traveling across America that compares with the autobus. To go by airplane, of course, is not to travel at all—it is merely to be translated from one condition in space to another. All sense of changing face and costume is missed, the proportions and slow vastness of the earth are not felt, and there is no real acquaintanceship with companions in travel. In a train there are so many people that one is alone, and while you can understand the countryside from a train, you cannot really see the towns and cities, because American cities hide their trains and stations away, behind sooty walls and the blank barricades of endless freight cars. It is not so bad in Europe, at least in the small places; they grow geraniums around the neat station and there is always the main square of the town directly outside your window with the fountain and the sidewalk cafés. In America the autobus is perfect, because you are a small group together in travel and soon become intimate. The busses heave slowly around the bank where you can see the tellers working in their shirtsleeves, pause by the schoolhouse to let the children pass, and stop in front of the hotel where the drummers are sitting on the veranda with the garrulous local historian. On top of the mountain divides you get out at small inns, and you can see the boy of the house going around to the kitchen entrance with the trout he caught a few minutes before.

It was Sunday in Wisconsin. We could see the German farm boys, very straight in the blue serge suits they keep for Sunday, their simple broad faces ruddy and freshly scrubbed, their hair plastered down with water except for the cowlick in back, their hands clean save for the black fingernails which a lifetime of Saturday night tubs would never improve nor ever be expected to improve. They stood in little groups on the sidewalk outside the white churches, scuffling a little, straightening their colored neckties frequently. They were waiting for the girls to come out and pretending they weren't. I knew. Already part of my mind was somewhere else looking with objectivity at my own country. I knew all this. I must have looked exactly like these boys on a hundred Sunday mornings at eleven o'clock. How imperceptibly but how completely one enters a new personal dimension! What mine now was I did not know, but passing through Wisconsin on Sunday morning I knew that I had been cultivated out of my natural roots, that I really had no home in the sense that my father's generation understood the word. Could anyone make the world his home? The world grew disturbingly large with every mile. And, if not, what was there for me and for all my friends? (We merely felt it earlier than most. Many thousands now coming home to America are troubled to find it is no longer completely home.)

New York was terrifying, and there was neither time nor presumption enough to decide whether I liked it or not. The *directness* of everything was astonishing. A straight line is the shortest dis-

tance between two points; New York is full of straight lines, and
everybody seemed to be moving with rapidity and determination
from point to point. In nearly every other place I had been, I could
tell by looking at a person more or less who and what he was. He
carried his social identification in his clothing, his gait, his expression. Here, I could tell a taxi driver—if he was in his cab—but
that was about all. It is the most anonymous city on earth. Lee
Loevinger was there, working as lawyer for the Labor Board.
There was a nest of a few others, living in connecting apartments
at London Terrace. They were now advertising men, or reporters,
or other things, all of them wearing white collars and all of them
possessing an authoritative manner with taxi drivers and capable
of calling out, loudly and naturally, the names of buildings and
squares that I knew only from books and movies and Broadway
columnists. I was astonished and full of admiration that they had
so quickly taken the measure of this unknowable, unconquerable
place. I was only too glad to get away, feeling that this was a place
I would never really know or be able to cope with, a city I would
have to circumvent the rest of my life. Later I changed my mind,
discovering that it was this very thing of unknowableness, of in-
exhaustibleness, that gives a very few communities the special
quality of being true, irreplaceable cities, worthy of one's lifetime.
New York has it, Paris and London have it; but Rome does not,
nor Washington, nor Rio de Janeiro.

The dozen or so passengers on the plunging *Black Eagle,* to
whose crew the cargo of Virginia apples was much more important
than the paying guests, had a variety of reasons for going to Europe
in this autumn of 1937. The seasick young sculptor and his stout
wife wanted to see Chartres, La Sainte Chapelle, and Avignon
again before it might be too late. The bland young student from
Cornell, who wrote poetry in little magazines for other poets to
read, was in passionate love with French culture, which he had
never experienced, and thirsted to throw himself into the Bohemia
of the Latin Quarter. The middle-aged Frenchman who paced
a regular twenty turns about the deck house each morning, collar-
less and bearded (he was saving his American razors and celluloid
collars) was returning to France to take more orders for an electric-
icebox firm. There was a handsome, raven-haired German woman
of middle age, wife of a professor at the University of Chicago,
with her aged mother and her three adolescent children. She was
returning Grandmother to die in Munich, and the children would

go to German universities, where, she made it clear, their education would really begin. Each afternoon she read Schiller and Goethe aloud in German to Grandma, while one child scraped dutifully at her violin and the others worked at their language books. She was full of firm convictions and denunciations. She denounced America at every meal for the terrible things people were saying about Der Führer. I wondered why it was that so many naturalized citizens defended their country of origin so much more frequently than their chosen country. They accepted with no second thought their right to criticize the American government but rarely ventured to attack the one they had just left, and it occurred to me that America is really an extraordinarily stable entity in the minds of men, and this phenomenon was proof of our accepted strength. She railed and attacked me violently when I demurred from her authoritarian concept of how children should be educated. The sculptor and his wife could not bear the woman, and the dirty Frenchman could not bear the loutish young German boy for the way he strewed his clothes around their intimate cabin. The one was dirty in a personal, neat manner, the other in a loose, sprawling manner—which is, after all, the main difference between an unclean Latin and an unclean Teuton.

On the day of our arrival in Antwerp the Frenchman appeared on deck, startling in a crisply pressed suit, with clean-shaven face, stickpin, and gold-headed cane. His eyes were bulging with excitement as we came alongside the wharf. He whisked down the gangplank and disappeared. I ran into him in the main square later that night. His face was shining, he smelled of wine, he twitched my shoulder every five minutes and, pointing with his cane, would say: "Look, look! Street girls!" and eventually scuttled off in pursuit like an agitated black beetle.

2

This was the continent of Europe. It was something that I had known all my life, that everyone who reads, however distant he may be, has known forever. Every detail was fresh and strange and yet exactly as it should have been. There is a smell in the continental cities, a wonderful smell that excites the blood. It is composed of many odors, sharp and mellow and faintly sour—the odors of fresh bread, of people, of roasted coffee, of old leather,

and of urine. It is an interior smell; it is like the smell inside a
general store in a country town. There is an indoor feeling about
the large cities of Europe; it is because of the smell and because
the sky is close, the light translucent and not transparent. You
walk endlessly the first night, sleepless, tireless, every pore open,
and you do not have to think; you learn of Europe by simple
osmosis. How small the men were, and how dowdy the women!
So few were really pretty as one thought of pretty women. The
girls regarded you steadily as they approached to pass, but not like
American girls, not with that easy, relaxed, and independent look.
There was something different here; the whole relationship was
different.

In the night from the hotel window the cobbles glistened and
the tops of the chestnut trees were pale in the street light. Their
trunks below were lost in a pool of shadow. The old woman with
the newspapers beneath the window called out all night, it seemed,
calling what sounded like: "*Ses Swoir—Paree Swoir*," calling it in
rhythmic sing-song: "*Ses Swoir*"—three beats—"*Paree Swoir.*" It
sent you off to sleep by its very monotony, and remained a remembered cadence in the subconscious for years thereafter. In the cold,
very early morning much of the magic had disappeared, and it
was a little like the Midway of the state fairgrounds the morning
after. The buildings were bleak and shriveled in size, and of the
smells that of the garbage in the gutters alone remained. Men from
the country poured from the railway station, small bunchy creatures in blue denim or rusty black, clattering in wooden clogs.
From her Olympia of straight bones and milk-fed American health,
Lois looked down on them with compassion and said they hardly
seemed like human beings. A million of the young from the Middle
West had felt like this, and a million who came after.

One had the feeling in Belgium that the people were as curious
about you as you about them, that they felt a certain respect, and
all this was good for the shaken sense of confidence. At the English
port on the North Sea it was not the same. The immigration inspector wore a suit for his work no better than the kind my father
would wear for a game of horseshoes, yet there was an infinite
superiority in his manner. It was a quick, ruthless inspection of the
baggage, and when the inspector bade me sit down and search-
ingly inquired about my financial resources, I had a guilty,
criminal sense of being unworthy to enter this precious preserve.
The Belgians had shown obvious respect for the American dollar,

but to the British it appeared to be a suspicious medium which had to be translated into pounds sterling before acquiring reality.

If you are a product and a victim of the English romanticists —and what young American is not?—you stare fixedly at the unnatural bright green of the countryside and ask yourself: "Is this it? Is this what Wordsworth and all the others were talking about?" You want to get down and feel the soil with your hands to see if it is really different. London was as I had always known London would be, and yet it was disturbingly different. It was a little like coming home after a long absence to find everything changed and no recognition in the eyes of the family. Why, we belonged here, and yet the landlady was nervously reluctant to let us into our room until she had found her glasses to read the careful references over and over again. For a few days we wandered and saw London through the subconscious filter of Pepys and Dickens, Sherlock Holmes and a dozen others. But very quickly the conditioned mind of the present applies its new scale of values, the veil falls, and London is incredibly cramped and mean. You perceive that the people are thinly clad in the cold, and you realize that they too are in *your* present condition—bathing in an icy bathroom, unable to get warm by their miserable, mocking gas fires, plugging their wretched, ill-fitting windows to keep out the damp air. It had always been a mystery to me why Shelley and the others were forever getting "consumptive" and having to go south, away from the fogs. The rare fogs in Minnesota were clean and delightful things, but in this evil smoke they called a fog one choked and gasped all night and became sick and filthy with soot. Did the English, the remarkable English, masters of half the world, allow themselves to live like this?

It is not long before one perceives that the British, who have the homogeneous feeling of a large family, are yet a lonely people. Like Americans, they are a nation of extroverts, but with the crippling difference that they are unable to express themselves. They do not permit it among themselves because they do not know how to begin. They cannot talk to one another. When we entered our first Lyons restaurant, we were astonished to observe the rows of young clerks, shoveling in their food with appalling directness, treating it as something to be disposed of as rapidly as possible, unnoticing the nearest neighbor, eyes fixed upon the noon edition or a novel from the rental library. As years went by and I saw them under the glaring light of crisis, I had cause to change many

ideas about the English, but never to change the first impression
that they are afraid of one another. They are afraid of nothing on
earth except one another.

There is a limit to the passing of judgments on the basis of Midwestern American values, and one must scrutinize himself as well
as the object. I had known certain kinds of tyranny, the tyranny
of the capitalist business establishment most of all; but in that
there was a sense of struggle, an unexpressed conviction of essential equality, a certain nonacceptance. But this thing of class in
England, this was somehow worse—so rooted, so accepted, so unquestioned. What a long, deep conditioning was this! Those at the
bottom didn't even understand they were at the bottom, put there,
kept there with cool deliberation. By God, they were so conditioned they even took *pride* in their particular station! The whole
politicosocial struggle seemed quite different here. How can you
even begin to restore the patient to health when he doesn't even
know and won't admit that he is sick? It was no good for the young
English intellectual friends I made to repeat that "of course, we
are so far ahead of America in social legislation." Those worthy
things got on the statute books earlier only because the crisis came
earlier, only at the last moment, as in every capitalist regime. No
good for them to point out the size of America's unemployment
lists. To be unemployed in America was to live better, with more
dignity, than millions lived here in employment. This was different; this was appalling.

A young acquaintance, son of Tom Jones, who had been secretary to Lloyd George and his cabinet for years, asked us to attend
a political demonstration. It turned out to be Communist. We
went along anyway, I most incongruous among these shabby raincoats in my fawn-colored topcoat and wide-brimmed hat. We
walked with them through the dingy streets to the prison of Worm-
wood Scrubbs, where there was much fiery talk, and the raising
of clenched fists as a salute of solidarity with a group of their
imprisoned comrades. With all the talk, with all the fists, it just
wasn't convincing. I couldn't believe them, I couldn't believe they
would go through with anything abrupt that really challenged
the system. One day, at the opposite pole, I met and talked with
Sir Oswald Mosley, leader of the British Fascists. The open palm
meant the same as the clenched fist, but I just could not take them
very seriously, either; they would never go through with it. This
is the great weakness—and maybe the great strength—of Britain.

We wandered among the gray buildings of Oxford University, and now and then, when one caught a brief vista of ivy towers and a green expanse of peaceful park beyond, there was the rush of sentiment that comes to a pilgrim at the inner temple of his religion. But the depressing Thing was even here. On the wall of one of the colleges hung an engraved plaque of generations ago which the young bloods of that time had dedicated to a college servant who had served them well: a memorial to their own daring generosity and unconventional condescension. I wondered what they had paid him per week and in what garret he had lived out those faithful days. In the High Street we sat behind mullioned windows among workmen and watched the students defying the cold in tennis shorts. The workmen huddled over cups of a nasty bouillon substance. We looked from one group to the other, and it was clear that even health, straight limbs, and large lung capacity were the exclusive properties of the privileged. *They* had the strong, bold, confident faces. The faces of the workmen were anything but that; they looked like members of another race.

Like all young American liberals of my generation, I had a sense of allegiance to a long list of British minds: to Robert Owen, Dickens, Lord Shaftesbury, Shaw, Wells, the Webbs, Cole, Brailsford, Laski, and all the others. I knew what they had done. I knew how frightful life had been here in the days immediately after the Industrial Revolution, and about the long, slow improvement. I was aware that they were endowed with a great liberal tradition that my country had hardly begun to equal; yet it seemed to me that life in England remained grim and hopeless for far too many, that the world's greatest and most successful conspiracy of man against man was still in full control.

I wondered how they did it. They were anything but supermen. We stood in the crowd in Whitehall and watched the procession of royalty and nobility—the opening of Parliament, I believe. There were strong faces among them, but many were weak and vacuous and some merely stupid. The women in their robes were remarkably ungainly and dowdy, and I wondered at the pleasure and respect in the faces of the orderly crowd. (When I asked an English youth: "Why don't they let Hollywood show them how?" he answered, "Good heavens, No! If they were glamorous we would never get rid of them. We put great hope in their dowdiness.")

I came from the isolationist heart of the United States, and I

found here, in the headquarters of the "outside world," a mental
and spiritual isolationism among ordinary people which surpassed
anything I had known at home. Most of the everyday Americans
with whom I had been reared longed to travel. But the civil servant
at Saint Albans with whom we stayed awhile said to us: "Yes,
Paris would be interesting. I might like to nip over to Paris some
day, but we really don't care much for foreigners, you know." In
Minnesota we delighted in purchasing imported articles—somehow they seemed to have an extra value. But in London, butter
sold better if it was marked "British butter." I thought of all our
months spent in the study of English constitutional history, and
found that there were only three chairs in American history in all
the British universities. I thought of the many columns in the New
York press about British men and politics, and found almost
nothing in the London papers about my country save an occasional note on Hollywood divorces and Chicago gangsters. I found
very few who could name an American political leader besides the
President and a complete lack of curiosity about my immense
country which took me sharply aback.

Hitler was striding the periphery of Germany and uttering loud
cries. Why was it that we, far back in the Mississippi Valley, were
so much more conscious of this, so much more worried apparently
than these people who sat on the lid of steaming Europe? Was it
possible that they were as unconcerned about, as ignorant of,
events across the narrow channel as they were about those across
the wide Atlantic? They were. Most of them were; and their
leaders—not many of their political leaders, but their thinking
leaders, the ones who understood what the book-burning meant,
what Spain meant—knew that their countrymen were both unconcerned and ignorant. In this segment of leadership the British had
something better than we had in our counterpart. The sheer brilliance, the articulate, unanswerable logic, of the editorials and
essays in the liberal journals took one's breath away. They were
saying it better, more acutely than we—but to no more effect.

Some of these men I met, in Whitehall and Fleet Street. They
were gracious and complimentary enough to waste no time in small
talk. I was impressed by them. I was more sharply impressed, as
it happened, by a young American, a tall, thin man with a boyish
grin, extraordinary dark eyes that were alight and intense one
moment and somber and lost the next. He seemed to possess that
rare thing, an instinctive, intuitive recognition of truth. His name

was Edward R. Murrow. He talked about England through half the night, and, although he had been there only about a year, one went away with the impulse to write down what he had said, to recapture his phrases, so that one could recall them and think about them later. I knew I wanted to listen to this man again, and I had a strong feeling that many others ought to know him.

We went away across the Channel, thinking we knew England, feeling that we had seen through the impressive façade with which the English confront the world. So this was the source from which had come the innumerable witty lecturers, who had so frequently explained the world and with charming presumption had even explained America to us in the Middle West. From these endless stretches of drab "semidetached" brick houses had come these gentlemen who twitted American communities on their "standardization" and on the Americans' love for decent plumbing, which to their minds was somehow a sign of barbarism. How often they had rebuked us (charmingly, to be sure) for the political racketeering in America—and they themselves represented a political and social racket so breath-takingly widespread and successful that it was scarcely questioned. I thought of Velva, of the thousands of Velvas scattered over America. Yes, it was better, it was a step in advance of all this. So I thought; so one begins to understand his own country by leaving it; so one begins to cherish it with the result that wherever he is, however rootless, however far and long away, he is never entirely normal and free of nostalgia for his homeland.

Paris had the smell again, the smell that made the blood move faster. It was familiar too, but also strange and new. What one had not understood nor been prepared for was the spaciousness, the serenity, the grandeur. There is a certain grandeur to London, but only to London as a whole, only if seen from a high place. In Paris you can see it from the corner of a hundred avenues. You do not have to view it through the veil of a thousand poems and stories, through the inverted telescope of a thousand bloody years of human deeds. It is just Paris, forever new, and the fascination never leaves. True, the people had shrunk in size and prepossessiveness away from the pages of Flaubert and Balzac; they were much harder to understand when one looked at them from the outside in, rather than from the inside out. But they wanted to talk to you—and they talked to one another. They were curious about you, and yet you felt that, unlike the English, they just took you for what you were; they did not trouble themselves with the painful preliminaries of deciding whether they were your superiors or your inferiors. You had no worried sense of threading through a thousand taboos, as you had in England; you sensed at once, in fact, that nobody really cared a damn what you did, how you dressed, or what you said. You knew that, if you stood on your head in the middle of the boulevard, you would get only passing attention. There was a freedom here, something one had never known either in England or America. It is in Paris that people cease their traveling. It is the place to stop.

3

Our young poet friend from the boat had gone directly to the heart of the matter and was living at the Hotel Select, Number One, Place de la Sorbonne. We followed. Our room and breakfast cost us fifty cents a day, and if the room was at least as clammy and cheerless as the room in London, still it didn't seem to matter so much. Doubtless, poverty has no more charm for the French than for anybody else, but France is almost the only place on earth where poverty can have a certain charm for a foreigner, no doubt because the compensations are so many. I don't know why exactly, but one retains, in the most abject condition, the illusion of living well, and to the young and unburdened the illusion is more important than the reality.

Victims of the American system of teaching languages, we found that despite our years of classroom French we were almost totally deaf and dumb in Paris, and this meant an early morning pilgrimage each day to the language school across the Luxembourg Gardens. The instructors never spoke a sentence of any language but French, and indeed nothing else would have served the purpose, in those classes, since we were English, American, Czech, Polish, Spanish, Russian, and Chinese, and one is bound, by sheer necessity, to master the common denominator when there is no other. Our first friends of course, were not French, but our own young compatriots, and it was the same for the other foreigners. One could feel that student life in this Bohemia must have been a gay and careless existence—once. But only remnants, faint echoes of the past, remained. The drinking had not ceased, paintbrushes flourished behind every attic window, love was audibly free just down the corridor, and yet there was an unreality about it all. It was too obviously forced, too clearly a determined effort to retain by conscious striving a way and habit of life which the closing in of history was grinding away. The café conversations might begin with Cézanne or Picasso, but they would end with Hitler and the Cagoulards. It was too late, too late for all these men and women of my own age who were trying to renounce their century. I was living in my time and they were not.

At first one could not escape a certain twinge of envy of the other Americans who made this effort to find Bohemia; doubtless they had more fun than I. I was impressed at first by their bérets and beards and their careless way of tossing a French phrase into an English conversation (where no French phrase was needed), but very soon I felt a certain embarrassment on their behalf and the desire to escape them on the café terraces. And besides, I had little time for this. I was working.

These were the last interwar years of the old Paris *Herald,* that rather absurd little house organ for the diminishing American colony, which made ample room for the resort and fashion-house advertisements and as a kind of afterthought squeezed in the news. The core of its staff was a group of American soldiers from 1918 who had never found their way home again, who had married and raised large families. Mademoiselle from Armentières was now fat and full-jowled and frequently collected her husband's pay at the entrance to the building before he could escape to the café on the corner. Their children spoke French exclusively, and by some miracle of intuition understood their fathers, whose variety of French remained strictly A.E.F. The publisher of the paper, ill and aging Larry Hill, desperately played the game of pretending Europe was secure and serene and that war could not possibly come, and our daily editorial wisely looked on both sides of the Fascist question and saw many virtues in the works of Hitler and Mussolini. (We still took in ads from Germany and Italy.)

My immediate superior, the day city editor until he and I reversed positions, was a viciously ill-tempered Pernod drinker named Kospoth. He had the face of a Manx cat, and his eyes were small and full of glitter. He pretended to be American, but his true nationality was a subject for endless café debates. He was a complete misanthrope who loved but three things—his riding horse, the legend of Napoleon, and Adolf Hitler. When we were alone in the city room, he ceased all pretense of work and strode

about, flinging indignant oratory in my direction on the superhuman qualities of Der Führer. Each Saturday he filed a story for
the *Sunday Referee* in London. It was always a pure invention,
and frequently related the doings of a white slave gang of Argen-
tinians who were kidnaping innocent French maidens for shipment. To give it an air of reality he did not hesitate to invent
quotations purporting to come from the mouth of the Paris Prefect.
When he was not writing or making a speech, he rode me unmerci-
fully since I was the newest comer and the only one who had not
yet taken his measure. This continued until, quite beside myself,
I threatened to hit him; thereafter he subsided into baleful silence.

Another mysterious character was our elderly but spry "sports
editor," a wizened little American named "Sparrow" Robertson,
who had been there twenty years or more. His exact age and
origins were never discovered. He had a fantastic capacity for
alcohol and was never, to my knowledge, seen to take in food. He
lived only by night, either at Fred Payne's bar in Montmartre or
at Harry's New York Bar, and his daily "sports" column consisted
of the exploits and comments of "my old pal" Fred or Harry or
somebody else. Thus he never paid for a drink and never had in
living memory. It was firmly believed that Sparrow knew only
two phrases in French: *à droit* and *à gauche*. For the first five or
six years he had known only *à droit* and had a difficult time reaching his hotel in the early mornings because the taxi, naturally,
continued in circles. He was obliged to learn *à gauche* as well, but
that sufficed, and he ceased his efforts there.

Toward evening, Sparrow would enter, hat perched on the back
of his grizzled head. He would weave through the city room, pausing to poke the managing editor in the rib, and exclaim huskily:
"Ahh, get away with that STUFF!" Whereupon he made his way
to a tiny cubicle where we kept our threadbare clippings. There
he punched out his copy on a typewriter that resembled a child's
toy and weighed about one pound. Departing, he would carefully
insert a sheet bearing the scrawled words: "Do not disturb." It
was hard to make out these words, for he had been using this sheet
of paper every day for a full decade. There was a legend that in
one memorable year a young copy reader, who had studied journalism at Columbia, demanded that Sparrow put commas in his
articles. Sparrow tried for two or three days, but gave it up and
told the lad that if he wanted commas he would have to put them
in himself.

Sparrow was vaguely aware that somebody existed by the name of Hitler, but beyond that he was happily ignorant of events in the world at large. Eventually, when the Germans entered Paris, he took it all as just another parade that blocked traffic and made it difficult to get to his hangouts. He did not appear to notice, they told me later, that the *Herald* had ceased publication, and each day for more than a week after the paper stopped, he carried through his routine, desisting only when he found the door to his cubicle locked, whereupon he wandered out, indignant and perplexed. Sparrow regarded the German-imposed curfew as a personal insult, and when a Nazi officer stopped him on the street late one night, Sparrow pushed at him and said: "Ahhh, get away with that STUFF!" Whatever machinery it was that had kept him going so many years was disrupted by the enforced change of routine, and the machinery ticked to a stop one day. They found him, crumpled, looking very much like a fallen sparrow.

Our chief editorial writer was a learned, barrel-chested Maltese in his fifties, who belonged to one nudist camp and to another semi-nudist camp on a lovely island in the Seine opposite the ivy-covered country house where Zola once lived. He took me to the island one raw March day and appalled me by ripping off his clothes and diving headfirst into the freezing, dirty water. Then he would spring up and down on the grass and slap his hairy chest like an orangutan, uttering loud cries that signified Strength Through Joy. One war was enough for him, and when the new one first began he departed instantly for the Riviera. Kospoth stayed. Just before the Germans entered he rushed about frantically from embassy to embassy, trying to get diplomatic immunity—for his horse. The Germans put him in a concentration camp.

Since the paper was put together in such slapdash fashion, one could ignore most of the rigid formulas of newspaper composition and write to suit his fancy. I was fairly free to wander about Paris and write of whatever amused me. Gradually I acquired a certain following among the permanent English-reading residents and among some of the fortunate and envied American journalists who covered France for the home market—something I desperately wanted to do. My interviewees among arriving Americans ranged from business tycoons, whose sagely delivered comments upon the international scene had to be printed (and were usually nonsense), to barnstorming heavyweight wrestlers from Chicago, one of whom complained seven times during our talk that he had forgotten his dripolator coffeepot, could not stomach the French coffee, and refused to take an interest in life or wrestling until they found a substitute. One of the best-remembered stories concerned the self-styled "Vagabond Coed" from the University of Wisconsin. She had traveled the world around on nothing but her wits and the most unabashed nerve I have ever encountered. She called it, of course, a "goodwill tour" and carried a supply of small bronze medallions. On one side was the figure of a tall girl striding forward clutching a suitcase, and on the other the inscription: "With best wishes from the Vagabond Coed." She had pinned one of her medals upon the broad chest of the Cuban president at a dinner, and had presented others to heads of states throughout Latin America and the Indian principalities. At Number 10 Downing Street they had refused her permission to see Prime Minister Chamberlain, and she left only after having given them a frank lecture in which she made it clear that this surprising behavior was costing Chamberlain more than it was costing her. Occasionally, when broke, she modeled clothes or invented publicity stunts to sell perfume and jewelry, and frequently she worked in night clubs where her specialty was blowing "smoke bombs." Only after months of hard practice had she learned this trick, which consisted in taking a deep drag on a cigarette, then forming a bubble with saliva and blowing the smoke-filled bubble into the air. It would land and burst upon the most interesting object handy—which might be a dog's nose or the bald head of a night-club patron. She called at the Élysée Palace and asked to see President Lebrun of the Third Republic. She was duly escorted by relays of spear-bearing attendants to the reception salon of the President's *chef de cabinet civile,* who apologized: the President was so very busy. . . . She patted his arm and said: "Okay, okay. Don't take it so hard. Wanna see me blow a smoke bomb?" While the guards and tail-coated officials stood in respectful silence, the smoke bubble wafted lightly toward the great chandelier which had illumined the faces of Napoleon and Josephine, drifted down, and sent up its tiny plume from the deep plush Empire carpeting.

(It was frequently difficult to explain the American character to perplexed French friends.)

The permanent American colony in Paris in those days was divided quite sharply between those who worked for a living like the newspapermen and those who kept country chateaux and moved between Paris and the various spas. The latter, of course,

would have nothing to do with the former if they could possibly
help it, except on the occasions when they wished publicity for
their social doings. Such requests were commands, so far as the
Herald was concerned. The most inescapable of these creatures
was a certain dowager with a massive chest. In the colony's Who's
Who, *Americans in France*, the paragraph following her name was
twice as long as that for the American Ambassador, for she belonged not only to the Daughters of the American Revolution but
to every conceivable similar group including one that was new to
me: "Americans of Royal Descent." She gave innumerable tea·
concerts at which she herself was the star and sole performer. She
sang. Once, in the *Herald's* lobby, a new reporter made the mistake of asking about her singing. She threw back her head, inhaled
deeply, and loosed an aria upon the neighborhood which stopped
all work and caused a large number of startled persons to come
running. The Third Republic, which didn't care any more, gave
her the Grand Cross of the Legion of Honor.

Officials of the American Embassy also regarded the paper as a
mere house organ, and the lightest suggestion from Ambassador
Bullitt for an editorial along this line or that entailed unques-
tioning compliance. *Herald* reporters were expected to report
scrupulously all the Ambassador's remarks and ceremonial activities; but the Ambassador himself always feigned ignorance of the
existence of these assiduous note-takers. One day a wire story
from Moscow said that Bullitt had sent an order for special caviar
which had broken all records in the Moscow market. I asked a
sweet young girl reporter on the *Herald* to request a comment
from the Ambassador at a convenient moment during his visit that
afternoon to the American Legion headquarters. She asked him,
with a smile. His face contorted with rage, and in front of a startled
audience he scored her savagely for daring to ask such a question.
She returned to the office in tears.

I went to see Gertrude Stein one day, expecting to be amused,
and was not only amused but deeply impressed by the finest flow
of talk I had ever listened to with the possible exception of that
from Schnabel, the pianist. She has a remarkably lucid and
germinal mind and disguises a profound understanding by a simplicity of rapidly flowing speech that misleads the casual listener.
A conditioned mind like mine, trained to the conventional for·
mulae of expression, could retain her ideas clearly but was quite
unable, later, to reproduce her own words. They were too basic,

too simple. In written form her words seem bizarre and difficult to follow, but when she herself reads them aloud it is all perfectly lucid, natural, and exact. She had just then finished her own version of *Faust*. She walked heavily up and down her study in front of her dark Picassos and read the script aloud to me, carried away by her own words and breaking off into ringing laughter which so overcame her at times that she would stop to wipe her eyes. She was a warm and wonderful person. When I published the story of her rewritten *Faust*, it was reprinted all over the world, and she was delighted as a child. Like most artists she thought in terms of the human individual and was quite lost when she considered people in groups. She could not think politically at all. Thus she assured me: "Hitler will never really go to war. He is not the dangerous one. You see, he is the German romanticist. He wants the illusion of victory and power, the glory and glamour of it, but he could not stand the blood and fighting involved in getting it. No, Mussolini—there's the dangerous man, for he is an Italian realist. He won't stop at anything." She did not understand Fascism; she did not understand that the moods and imperatives of great mass movements are far stronger and more important than the individuals involved in them. She knew persons, but not people.

The world was growing nervous, and the stream of American tourists became a trickle. They were mostly the young, for the older were becoming cautious about leaving the American sanctuary. A few elderly couples did arrive, however, and with one retired Kansan and his wife some friends of ours had a unique experience. After our friends had shown them the traditional tourist sights of Paris, the spry couple confessed that before leaving Kansas they had taken a dare during their farewell party and pledged themselves to visit a French "fancy house." They were taken to one where the madame led them to the top chamber, in which *"les spectacles"* could be witnessed. The fascinated old couple watched while two girls lashed each other's skin with silken whips. After a time the representatives of Kansas seized the whips and enthusiastically lashed the girls themselves. My friends swore to the truth of this and added that the couple said the experience was very relaxing.

It was a bit startling how easily one could recognize other Americans in a crowded Paris street. There was no doubt of it: from the heterogeneity of the United States a definite type had evolved. It was not just their clothes, nor the way they wore their hats; it was something about the way they held their bodies, the way they walked, and—there could be no mistake—their very faces were different and exclusively their own. The feet of an American do not attack the ground like the feet of an Englishman, nor do they plod reluctantly like the feet of most Continentals; they are part of his legs, which swing naturally from the hips. Nobody else on earth walks so easily as the American. His body is neither rigid like an Englishman's nor compact and crowded like a Frenchman's, and his head turns very easily upon his neck. No one else on earth can approach a stranger without a subtle change and affectation in his manner, and no other faces are so readable and clear. Their voice and speech of course involved no problem whatever; all the world recognizes American talk. Living abroad, one not only sees his countrymen differently—he hears them with a far more sensitive ear, and we were suddenly aware of the slovenly impreciseness of Midwestern speech. It was more noticeable in the higher tones of the women. From a lovely, serene young countenance would come the disturbing nasal accents: "An' 'nen we wen' over there, an' I said yeah an' he said well wat we gon' do now, an' 'nen . . ."

The young Americans who came to Europe in the summers sought what adventure they could find, and for the girls this meant sexual adventure. Wholesome-looking sorority girls, who had always limited themselves to leading their college swains up the garden path, came over with the secret determination to have their first affairs anonymously in Paris, far away from home town and Mother. Many of them quailed at the last moment in the company of Frenchmen, and these baffled and disgusted gentlemen would ask their male American friends to be so kind as to explain the mysterious mental processes of the lovely, double-dealing ladies. The typical American girl arrived with the conviction that Frenchmen had much more finesse and sense of romance than the neighborhood boys she knew, but she quickly found herself embarrassed and ill at ease in the routine of hand-kissing and elaborate attention. She usually gravitated very soon to the natural and more familiar company of the young American bachelors she found. She simply had more fun with them, but anything more serious than fun would have seemed almost like incest.

One young American girl accepted an invitation from a quiet, darkly handsome German named Weidmann, who murdered her for the change in her purse as he had murdered five other persons He was called a second Landru, and Landru's lawyer, Moro Giafferi, conducted his defense in the three-week trial at the Versailles Cour d'Assize where Landru had been tried. The idle ladies of Paris fashion perched in the grim courtroom gallery like a rustling row of bright-colored birds. To wangle a pass and take in a session of the Weidmann trial became one of the "smart" things to do. For many days I lived and thought nothing but the trial and wrote columns about it for every issue of the *Herald,* which had not been blessed with a local event like this for a very long time. The personality of Weidmann became a minor obsession. He was a brutal, primitive animal who killed simply because it was a natural thing for him to do. And yet there was an intelligence in his brooding eyes, a certain nobility in the cast of his handsome head. He was equally fluent in German, French, and English, and inside his prison cell buried himself in books of philosophy. When he rose to speak, he dominated the courtroom with a commanding presence. He spoke slowly in a low but penetrating, resonant voice As he talked of his childhood and the struggles of his life, the mysterious impulses within him which drove him to his deeds, there was a hush over the crowded room. The listening women leaned forward, their eyes fixed on the handsome, gaunt figure at the rail, their parted mouths indicating some inner ecstasy. When he reached the climax of his confessional he crumpled over the rail sobbing, and the gallery was a bedlam of screaming, hysterical women. He was a far greater actor and performer than any of the famous criminal lawyers present.

At the guillotining of Weidmann in the clammy dawn outside the Versailles prison gate I learned a minor fact and a major lesson. The fact was that the grisly apparatus of the guillotine provides the quickest and the least horrible formal death one could possibly imagine. Suddenly his half-naked form appeared beside the machine and was thrown down upon the carriage. A block banged into position over his neck, the wedge-shaped blade fell, the carriage revolved, and the lid was slapped down upon the basket. All this happened so quickly that it was almost impossible to follow the sequence of movement. I stood no more than ten feet away, and I saw neither his severed head nor the torso. I possess an unerringly queasy stomach, yet I felt no nervous reaction whatsoever. It was all quite unreal. What upset me and made me a little bit ill was the witnessing mob of Frenchmen, and therein lay the lesson. Men, women, and children, they booed and chanted their impatience before the gates opened and the victim appeared, and as he was rushed to the knife they sent up a savage, blood-curdling scream like an animal pack's. France is a civilized nation with a tradition of respect for the dignity of the human personality, but there was also something here I had not rightly understood— a strain of sadism, a certain callous cruelty, a capacity for hatred which I had not known in England or in my own country (I had never seen a race riot).

4

How blind he can be to evil intentions, the liberal humanitarian, when the good which he consciously tries to see diverts his eyes. To be sure I had read the anti-Semitic fulminations of *Gringoire* and *Je Suis Partout*—but I remembered the harmless mouthings of the Silver Shirts. I read Maurras's cries in *L'Action Française* for direct action against the Socialists and Communists: "Blum and Thorez to the gallows!"—but I thought of Mosley's Fascists. I had listened to any number of French financiers and publishers at American businessmen's luncheons in Paris, warning that the French workmen were a more serious danger than the Germans— but I likened it to the Chamber of Commerce speeches that called the New Deal "Communistic." Now I understood. This was different; this was serious. This was not at all like the middle-class American temperament I understood, nor like the British. This was not Velva nor London. This was the same people who had taken ten thousand compatriots' lives in the Revolutionary Terror and many more than that in the Communard slaughter of 1871. France had come around again full circle, and every word, every threat and gesture, was in deadly earnest. The French were living in a miasma of hate, hatred of one another, something far different from their cold hostility toward the Germans, their indifference toward all other peoples. "The basis of Fascism is hate," wrote Harold Laski. I would have liked to believe that Fascism produced the hatred, rather than the other way around; but though the Fascist movements intensified the hate and brought it to a crisis, it had been there, dormant, always. It was akin to the "stranger hatred" of the psychologists, which no rational analysis can ever quite explain, and its framework now, in France as elsewhere, was composed not only of racial differences but also of the strictures of class society which made men truly strangers to one another. It was that in France, and it was also something else—not the hatred of strangers, but the more terrible hatred between brothers, between members of the same family who live too long too closely together.

From early university days we had understood that Fascism implied war, because a fair amount of training in the history of interlocking ideas and events had provided us with enough intellectual discipline to comprehend the logical imperatives of the movement, to know that a deliberate assault upon reason made inevitable an assault upon order. But now one left the rational view of irrationality and moved into the emotional heart of Fascism. Once having made this transfer, the atmosphere of Paris, of all Europe, became the atmosphere of Minneapolis during the bitter, excited days of the truck drivers' strike, but a hundred times intensified. Like the Minneapolis police, the Fascists of Europe were preparing a gigantic ambush, and, as their press made ready to call it self-defense, the buckshot was carefully loaded for the time when the people's backs would present the best target. The preliminary, practice ambush was almost over now, in Spain, and the bleeding, scattered victims were struggling toward sanctuary. The hatred and bitterness ran like a river straight from the Pyrenees to Paris. Americans that I knew—men with hearts and minds like Vincent Sheean—were returning from Spain hollow and sick from emotional exhaustion. One personal friend, the studious, stubborn, owl-like Jimmy Lardner, was already gone. He had said simply: "All you guys will have to meet this thing somewhere pretty soon. I just decided I'd like to meet it in Spain." He was killed, it appeared, by Moors, the last American volunteer to die in battle there, for the foreign volunteers were withdrawn from the lines the next day. Men like Edmond Taylor and Jay Allen had long since tried to tell Americans in Paris what was really going on; David Scott, the eminently civilized English journalist, tried again to tell the businessmen of the American Club that this was a struggle for liberty and was sneered at for his pains. France was sanctuary for the fighting men—of a kind. They retreated from the Fascism of Franco to find themselves victims of the Fascism of the French police. (What is there about policemen even in democracies that makes them partial to nonconformists of the right and enemies of those of the left? It was true of the Gardes Mobile under the democratic Daladier; it was true of the FBI under the liberal Roosevelt.) The Spanish refugees crossed the frontier and were herded into stinking camps, treated like unwanted animals.

In Paris we could do little more than try to help the Americans involved, to get sick and wounded American volunteers out of Spain, out of French jails, and back to their homes. Hemingway, I believe, began the effort while in Spain, and in Paris Louis Bromfield became titular head of the rescue organization; but most of the real work was accomplished by Frederick Thompson of San Francisco, assisted by my wife. Thompson was something new in my experience: a rich man with a conservative, Catholic background (his sister is Kathleen Norris, the novelist), who fought for the left, for the underdogs, not as an indulgent pose, but out of conviction and passionate belief. I had known no man who had so completely unfettered his mind from the compulsion of origin and environment, who had so thoroughly mastered his own mental processes and freed his soul against such odds. He was gay and generous—and devoted, determined, and tough. We loved him as much as the conservative Americans of Paris hated him. He is one of the truly original personalities of America, and legends about him have grown up among his friends. One (which he denies) is this: When he lay very ill in San Francisco and was expected to die, his sister pleaded with him, for the good of his soul, to make provision in his will for the Church. He said he would be delighted and altered his will to read: "I hereby bequeath the sum of ten thousand dollars to the Archbishopric of San Francisco on the condition that the funds be used to erect an equestrian statue of the Holy Ghost."

As a young man he had thrown up his job and properties in San Francisco and gone to Mexico to work with Pancho Villa. He had known Jack London and John Reed. His son fought with the Loyalists in Spain, and when Thompson was stopped by the French on the border of Spain, his nearly sixty years did not prevent him from crawling under the barrier in the night and walking over the hills toward Barcelona.

Thompson faced what seemed an impossible task: he had to raise money from those who had it, round up the scattered Americans in the south with the aid of American consuls, get train space from the French authorities for their removal, break into that fortress of snobbery, the American Hospital in Paris, make the State Department reverse its policy of regarding the volunteers as outcasts who had abandoned their rights as citizens, and then find shipping space to send them home. He bearded the Ambassador in his sanctum sanctorum, endlessly circled Paris, and went from Le Havre to the Pyrenees and back again over and over again, coaxing, cajoling, and bullying. The first citadel he broke into was the cautious Paris *Herald*, and I wrote a running account of the campaign. Thompson and the committee were attacked in innumerable letters to the paper for aiding "the dirty Reds," and verbally by Dean Beekman, the sententious head of the most fashionable American church. At this point Thompson digressed and took great delight in writing and distributing a pamphlet that abruptly reduced the mighty dean to the level of ordinary, compassionate Christianity. Only once did Thompson lose his temper. That was when the consul at Le Havre objected to returning one terribly maimed youngster to the states because "he would not be able to find gainful employment and might become a public charge." The ensuing scene in the consulate was described by witnesses for days thereafter.

All that he set out to do he accomplished, and many young Americans owe their life and freedom to this man. In the early mornings we would meet the sick and wounded at the Gare d'Austerlitz and help them off the trains. They were the first casualties of war I had ever seen, the first men who were victims of Fascism in their bodies. The sight left one numb and sick. They did not look or act like shining knights of liberty—but they were. They looked dirty and wrinkled, and their faces were gray and their eyes red from want of rest. They did not talk the language of Tom Paine; they muttered and swore with a subdued bitterness. One man of forty, a truck driver from Brooklyn, as I remember, shuffled to the curbing and vomited. When somebody tried to help him into the ambulance, he knocked the arms aside. He was going to die, and he was aware of it. Another younger man had been shot in the rectum, and his intestines hung out of a hole the doctors had cut in his belly. This was it; this was what was happening to men in Germany, Italy, Austria, Czechoslovakia, Spain, and China; this was what was going to happen to millions more, to your friends and perhaps to yourself. This was what the struggle, which began with ideas, came to in the end; and that which I had known—the contest by typewriter and tongue—now seemed a faint and mocking battle of the shadows.

The rivers of fear and hate ran also into Paris from the borders

of Austria and the Reich. The refugees came to France instinctively because France has always been the refuge of the politically
oppressed. They were welcomed by the government because it
was democratic, and their personal lives were made a misery by
the French police, because policemen are policemen. For a small
group of them our apartment became a central gathering place.
George Stoessler, a Czech, lived there for months, moved in and
out of French jails later on, and ended as a sergeant with the desert
forces of de Gaulle. There was Ernst Adam, once a socialist professor in Germany, who helped organize the defenses of Madrid
and was now morose and idle, one arm made useless by a Franco
bullet. In the months that followed I was involved in efforts for
his salvation—and so was Mrs. Roosevelt. There was the charming,
unembittered Hertha Pauli, pacifist and novelist from Vienna, who
lived to write delightful stories about the Christmas spirit for the
children of America. There was young "Karli" Frucht, who blushed
when anyone looked at him, a gentle boy with a tendency to
dreams of pastoral peace which the awful nights of hiding from
the Gestapo had not entirely made to vanish. In odd corners of the
earth, at unexpected moments, this boy was to appear and reap-
pear in my life for many months to come, until he came to represent my private, personal victory over Fascism.

Through many nights, over innumerable bottles of cognac, one
listened to the stories of what was happening in the central
fortress of the Fascists. You could not disbelieve—and you could
not quite believe. No effort of will or imagination could bring me
all the way into the world of the human spirit which they had
known. This was the basic motivating force for my generation,
perhaps for all my century, and I knew I did not really, truly understand. Perhaps I never would or could, but if I was not to
wander forever on the periphery of comprehension it was a clear
necessity to live inside the Reich, however briefly, and make the
effort.

For weeks all movement toward central Europe was frozen by
the crisis that culminated in the "treaty" of Munich. From hour
to hour, on the crucial days, Americans called the *Herald* office,
seeking advice as to whether or not they should move out of the
city. American tourists and students began to head for the western
ports; one American resident of Neuilly spread a large Stars and
Stripes over his rooftop. Now even the *poules* on the boulevards
altered the routine of the slow, suggestive walk, and stood by the

kiosks reading the late editions. On the day Daladier returned from Munich, I watched him in the almost hysterical, praying crowd on the Champs Élysées—a dumpy, bent little man carrying his black hat in one hand, looking bewildered and uncertain. The crowd pushed him along toward the great Arc, where searchlights played through an immense diaphanous drapery in the colors of France, producing a sudden, eerie effect of the sun's having risen again in the west. Letters came in suggesting that the Rue de la Paix be renamed the Rue Neville Chamberlain; *Paris-Soir* began collecting money to build a "house of peace" for Chamberlain somewhere in France where he could resume his eternal fishing; one of the men on the copy desk came in with flushed face—a woman on the bus, learning he was American, had kissed him on both cheeks. She thought Roosevelt had saved the peace.

5

I should like to know what happened in the end to the Chicago Jew who shared the third-class compartment that carried us toward the Rhine. Surely there was never a conspirator in the anti-Fascist underground who had such contempt for the Gestapo and who made so little a secret of his work. Born in Karlsruhe, he had run a haberdashery in Chicago until he volunteered to fight in Spain. He was now coming directly from Spain and with no qualms at all was proceeding to Karlsruhe to see his mother. "Best country in the world—Germany," he said. "Place I want to live, once we get these goddam Nazis out." He carried in his coat pocket a thick wad of anti-Nazi pamphlets of the most inflammatory type, which if found would most certainly bring his immediate arrest. He hadn't the slightest fear. "When you know Germans," he said, "you know how dumb they can be. I'll go right across the border with this stuff, I'll get it into the right hands over there, and I'll be back in Paris two weeks from now. Tell you all about it then." He stuck a few of the incriminating sheets under the carriage seat just for luck, hoping they would be carried as far as Munich. He got off at Strasbourg. When the train started up again and we headed across for the German customs inspection, our nerve gave way and we quickly transferred to another compartment.

The train crawled across the German fields and tunneled slowly through the dark, oppressive forests. In the garish light of the drab compartment the heavy, white German faces, no longer showing hostile interest in the American strangers, nodded in sleep, their heavy chins settling into the cheap fur collars of their ugly half-coats. We had been observing the boy across from us, a boy of eighteen or so with an extremely handsome, open, and sensitive face. His face was ruddy, his hair blond, and his clear eyes a remarkable blue. He had spoken to the conductor in perfect French. For a long time he regarded the opaque darkness beyond the window, and suddenly we observed that he was crying. He had lived all his life in Marseille. He spoke French, thought French, considered himself a Frenchman—but his dead parents had been Polish, and the Poles in this time were mobilizing into their army anyone upon whom they had a legal claim. He had returned to his rooms a few days ago after a holiday on the beaches with his sweetheart and found an envelope. A slip of paper had made its way unerringly across the heart of Europe and was now dragging him through the darkness of Germany to fight and perhaps to die for a country he had never seen, with men whose language he could not speak, whose cause he did not understand. There was a warmth and glow about this boy, a simple decency and innocence, a vital love of life that made one feel a helpless love for him at once. In him was all the unutterable tragedy of the European night; he was all the innocent hearts and clean bodies of the guiltless youth of Europe, unwilling but unable to protest, pulled and shoved to the unfamiliar sentry posts and barricades along the unreal frontiers everywhere upon this forever unhappy, eternal continent of Europe.

People talk again of "good Germans" and "bad Germans" in a vague and blundering attempt to organize their conflicting impressions of these extraordinary people. The elderly Junker sisters, spinsters, and all the household in that highly respectable Ohmstrasse pension in Munich, were not good Germans—they were good human beings. How many others like them exist in Germany I have no idea; for all I know, none. I do know their house seemed more like home to us than any other we had known in Europe. They were dear old ladies of education, understanding, and compassion. In this house there was no sign or symbol of the Nazis; the radio remained silent when the party leaders spoke. It was just after the terrible November pogrom against the remaining Jews, and at this dinner table one could express indignation and horror without restraint or fear. Indeed, there was a note of belligerency here, provided chiefly by Anna, the raw-boned cook, who understood little of politics but who knew that what the old sisters thought and felt was right and who therefore thought and felt as they did. In the night, she had heard the shuffling of feet, the tapping of hammers, as the block leader and his minions went from house to house tacking up the placards against the Jews on every door. When it came to her, she flung open the door, wrenched off the poster, and threw it in the face of the astonished block leader, who never attempted thereafter to replace it. When orders were given that the corner grocery must no longer sell to the single Jewish family in the block, it was Anna who marched into the store and delivered an indignant oration in the name of Christianity to the bewildered grocer. But in the end he proved, of course, to be more frightened of the party than of the cook, and this meant that the Jews' food was purchased by Anna on the sisters' account. The next move was to dispossess the Jewish family. They moved into the spare room of the pension. The next move after that, and the final one, was to send a gang of ruffians to take them bodily away. They were never heard from again.

We knew Germany and the Germans—or at least Bavaria and the Bavarians. It was not as we knew France, through books. It was because of childhood and youth in the Nordic civilization of the American Northwest. It was the same, and we understood Germany as we now realized we would never understand France or any Latin country. There is little difference between the makeup of Munich and that of Minneapolis. We understood wide, clean streets like this, the clean smells—or absence of smells. These houses were as houses should be, well defined, set apart, numbered in the orderly way that houses should be numbered. We were familiar with the clothes, we could read the faces and could place in the structure of society everyone we saw, the bathrooms were like bathrooms at home, the kitchens were large and warm and clean as kitchens should be, and the food was the kind of food we had always eaten. Christmas day was like Christmas day at home, the cookies with colored frosting, the mashed potatoes and gravy and the turkey with the proper stuffing, the Christmas tree by the parlor window where its lights would reflect on the sidewalk snow, the strains of "Silent Night, Holy Night" from the phonograph on which hung the red paper wreath and the holly.

Because Germany was part of our intimate lives, we knew well how it should have been, and therefore we could see very clearly how, in this December of 1938, it was utterly warped and changed. The place had been poisoned; the place was sick, heavy with a fog of unhappiness that was composed of suspicion and hostility, private shame and self-reproach—and public, belligerent, and arrogant justification. You could feel it in the hesitant manner of the shopkeeper whose eyes wavered before he spoke to you. You could feel it in the beer halls like the Hofbrau Haus, where there was no longer the careless clinking of mugs, no longer any song. The customers came there merely out of habit, silently drank from their foaming steins as a matter of ritual, and over them, ever present, more vibrantly alive than any living man in the great hall, was the painted portrait of Der Führer—the burning eyes looking straight into your face, into the back of your head when you turned away, the stiff, upraised arm pronouncing its inescapable curse upon the assembly.

In an apartment overlooking the Englischer Garten we stayed an hour with the family of Chicago Germans we had known on the boat from New York. An hour was enough. These people, who had America somewhere in the subconscious, were more aware that the poison was in them and, like drug addicts in the earlier stages, defied and forestalled the unspoken rebuke of their normal friends. The raven-haired mother with the firm jaw now spoke very little and avoided any discussion of Hitler's Germany, but we knew that her words would have been more violently righteous than before. The boy was no longer the easygoing lout; he had hardened into a Nazi bully, and there was a metallic ring in his tones when he mentioned the Jews. The girls remained silent. One was engaged to a young Nazi who sat beside her at tea, kept his eyes on the table, and never ventured a word to us. It was clear: they had discovered there was no middle ground, no possible compromise, and they had chosen.

We seemed to be almost the only foreign "tourists" in Munich, and in the mountain resort of Garmisch-Partenkirchen we were quite exclusive and alone. Heads always turned to watch us in any public place. The adults looked at us in silence, but our appearance caused the more expressive young boys to gather in a group and covertly point. We were American; obviously there must be something inferior about us, something they could understand as bizarre and wrong. When they saw us walking through the snow with arms about one another's waists, they found it in that, and jeered this exhibition of shameful sentimentality. They too were sick and poisoned.

On every charming Bavarian building were the pastel paintings of the Bible scenes, the painted messages of brotherly love—and on the door of every house beneath the holly and the wreath was the stark and ugly placard, black print upon blood-red paper, which carried the same words, everywhere: "Jüden Unerwünscht." If you opened a menu in the little restaurants, the red and black paper fell out upon your plate like a living scorpion. It was everywhere.

There were two other guests in the small pension we had chosen, a morose salesman from Munich and a female schoolteacher, angular and thin with bulging eyes and a knobby Adam's apple. On New Year's Eve, the exhortations and imprecations of Joseph Goebbels poured from the radio in the corner just behind our dinner chairs. The salesman and the teacher leaped to their feet and stood rigid, eyes closed tight in an agony of bliss, their arms outstretched toward the Voice, and their wavering fingertips almost touching our noses as we sat facing in the opposite direction, transfixed, frozen in fascination before them as they were before the Voice. So all the rational world was transfixed, watching Germany, hypnotized and unable to move.

On the slopes around the Kreutzighaus, a mile high in the frontier Alps, many of the skiers were young, ruddy men in gray army cloth. In long, patient lines they stood in the snow, listening to their barking officer instructors, then executing the maneuvers, falling, getting up and falling again, training, training, training day after day, never lifting their voices, never laughing or playing, working at it grimly. We lunched on the glassed-in terrace, and one day—the day we noticed the Nazi flag on the pole—the noises of clattering dishes and talk abruptly died. At the next table Rudolf Hess was just taking his seat. The people looked at him quietly, with no expression, and the dark, deep-set eyes in the heavy, carved face moved slowly over all their faces, very coolly, very steadily. It was the face of a man who had mastered himself completely, and everything around him—a powerful face and a little frightening. With him were a young man called Goebbels (a younger brother, they said) and two lovely wheat-colored Rhenish girls not yet twenty years old. We never saw any of the other people speak to Hess, except once at the top of the ski run when a fervent young girl made bold to approach him with a sharp Nazi salute which he solemnly returned.

My professional conscience nagged me, telling me it was my duty to try to get an "interview" with Hess. But reason told me it was silly; that if he deigned to speak with me it would only be to repeat a few of the stereotyped phrases with which the readers of the world were but too familiar. It was a disservice now, not a service, to present the Nazi argument again. Besides, the attempt would mark me out in that place and take away what anonymity remained to us; and I had no desire for anything more intimate with the police than the routine inspections we had already undergone. My passport still bore the identifying word "student." It was better just to watch. Hess skied very well, with determination if not with grace, jerking his heavy body this way and that to maintain his solid balance. Once he rested on his poles to observe in silence the training of the future ski troops, and once, when a plane circled low, he halted and watched it intently for so long as it remained overhead.

On the last day I almost became more intimate with Hess than I would ever have desired. I was rushing down óne slope of a miniature valley when I looked up to see the bulky, unmistakable figure of the Deputy Führer rushing down the opposite slope directly in my path. My legs were too weary or too inexpert to make a sharp turn, and in a panic I let myself fall to the side as he came upon me. The sleeves of our jackets just ticked in passing. The twisting fall I took wrenched an ankle and neatly split one of the rented skis. It looked as if Hess had ended my Alpine skiing career. Lois, at this moment, trudged up and plaintively said: "I'm awfully cold." I asked: "Where?" She said: "Here." It was not surprising; there was nothing between her and the snow. Carefully, I backed her away from the other skiers, around the hillock, where a large safety pin re-established propriety. It would hardly have done to mock a leader of the master race with such an impudent, barefaced gesture from one of the lower races. Simultaneously unhorsed and unharnessed we decided to give it up.

All the seats on the little intervillage bus were occupied by one or two persons, mostly boys and girls in their late 'teens, dressed in bright sweaters and scarves and bound for neighboring ski runs. At the first crossroads stop outside Garmisch a tall man with heavy, bent shoulders mounted the front step and stood beside the motorman, fumbling for his coin. The patter of adolescent conversation ceased. The man was a Jew, of obvious culture—a doctor, one would say at first glance. In a week's stay at this populous resort center this was the first Jew we had seen. He took overlong to find and place his coin, and one understood at once that this distinguished man of dignity and character was stalling, putting off the moment when he would have to turn toward the faces of the company and somehow, without betrayal, without loss of dignity, find a seat beside one of them. Slowly he turned. I had a feeling of paralysis in my body. Lois's fingers tightened hard over mine. His head remained half bent, his eyes over the top of his spectacles wavering rapidly from one side of the aisle to the other. If only there had been no space at all; if only there had been one completely empty seat. But here and there was a seat occupied by a single person; it was up to one of these to shift toward the window. The newcomer had to move; he took one step forward. Nothing happened. He took another. It was unbearable, the excruciation of this timeless moment. A girl slipped quickly on her seat and turned her head to the window pane. He sat down on the edge of the seat and rode with his head bent forward, his shoulders hunched. He never lifted his head until we approached the next village. When he descended it was again at a crossroads stop outside the village.

(What has been done to this man? What has been done to these boys and girls? My God, it affects me too! I am looking at him as if he were something strange and special!)

It could not be true, yet it was true. Beside the road, at the entrance to Oberammergau, the holy village, the inviolate temple of German Christianity, there was a large, octagonal metal sign that bore the words: "Jüden Unerwünscht." The village seemed chill and lifeless under the low-hanging winter clouds. We walked the small winding streets alone. In the shop windows remained the blue and green pottery, the biblical figures carved in wood, and on the door of each shop was the black and red sign bearing the two words. On the Passion Theater itself—yes, on the Passion Theater—in a window between the glass and the wire screen stood the little sign announcing that here, too, Jews were not wanted. There was just one more place to go, and at length we found the shop and home of the late Anton Lang, who had played the Christus for thirty years. His door was clean and bare. I was looking at the pottery on the shelves when Lois pulled at my sleeve and pointed. It was a smaller sign than usual, tacked to the counter just below the cash register. The sweet-looking girl with corn-colored hair who stood behind the counter observed our glances, and a faint blush began to rise in her neck.

She hesitated, then volunteered: "You see, we have nothing to say about it. They just come and put it up, and we have nothing to say about it."

"Why is it necessary? Are there any Jews here anyway? We have seen none."

"There was one," she said. "He was a Catholic, too. They took him away."

It was beginning to snow in the gathering twilight as we waited for the bus. By the bus sign was a neatly painted hoarding fronted with glass. We brushed away the soft snow and saw that the hoarding presented an opened copy of *Der Stürmer*. In the center of the page was a large drawing illustrating the state of civilization in the United States. It showed Uncle Sam, endowed with a hooked nose and a cigar in his mouth, dancing in a night club, his arms around two bawdy-looking, semi-naked women. When the bus rounded the corner, the sticky snowdrops were feathering over the glass and had obscured all but the cigar and the feet of the dancing women. On the mountain peak, the great cross that stands above Oberammergau was only faintly to be seen. We boarded the bus and headed for Garmisch and the way out of Germany.

From Munich to Nürnberg, from Nürnberg to Cologne, it was the same—soldiers in the trains, in cars, in the innumerable planes on the fields, in the restaurants and hotels and city streets. Every day they sat across from us in the narrow train compartments, the fresh-faced, simple, polite German boys in field gray. The faces I had known all my life, the faces from the churchyard in the Wisconsin town, the honest, dumb, German youth. Youth was innocent, yet it was the youth of Europe that was so frightening, so terrible.

The people of Germany were sick, neurotically sick, their nerves on edge. They hated the world, and they hated themselves. The suspense could not very long be borne; something had to happen. We picked up copies of the Paris *Herald* and the words simply made no sense. "Appeals for peace" were still being made to Hitler; the "experts" were still analyzing the speeches of the Fascist leaders and trying to find clues to their coming moves; debates went on over whether Hitler had achieved his "aims" for his people and was now stable and satisfied, or not. It was all absurd and

stupid, maddeningly stupid. No number of statements or statistical
facts could have any bearing on the matter. You had only to experience the *spirit* of the Reich, and you knew there was no way
to halt and to go about the peaceful business of men. The German
leaders were riding a motorcycle downhill, and there was no way
to stop without a voluntary fall that would break them apart.
Desperately they clung to this machine whose motor they themselves had started, screaming their excitement, more confident
every moment that there would be no wall to stop them.

At the station in Aachen, the sacred city of German history, we
looked out of the train window into the crowded public square,
not caring very much that the hard-eyed young S.S. man was over-
insolent as he ripped through the contents of our bags—we were
too relieved to be getting out. The public square of Aachen was
my last sight of Germany before all Europe blew up. It was also
my first sight when the concussion had subsided.

This came five years later on a chill spring day. The solid buildings of the square were by then obscene heaps of rubble. Standing
in the debris, looking at the place where the station had been,
was my younger brother, the gentle one of my family, the one
who had wished to be a geologist and was not much concerned
with the transient affairs of men. He stood easily with his hands
in his pocket, looking as if he had worn a heavy pistol all his life.

6

Nineteen thirty-nine wore on into the hot, nervous days of summer. I was now working at the Paris *Herald* by day and the United
Press by night. Writing for one of the great news agencies was a
new experience, an uneasy one. There were good men in that office,
and they worked very hard for very little return. On them and
their colleagues in the other agencies lay the heaviest responsibility: to provide the public minute by minute with the basic, factual news of the day. They did the spade work, while the other,
"special" writers for individual papers had time and leisure to
select their material and to take the long view—or the jocular view,
depending upon their characters. The agency men were able, but
they were in the grip of an unrelenting system that had evil results.
The insistent demand was for speed and "exclusives," not for
accuracy or quality of composition. New York headquarters de-

manded new "leads" for every edition on a running story, and if there was no really fresh news when the demand came, new leads would be invented, by a turn of a phrase, by a bolder interpretation of somebody's statement, by a reckless guess as to what would happen next in the affair. Each week reports came from New York comparing our success with that of the opposition. Success was always measured on the basis of which agency's story had received "top billing" in the headlines, not on the writing quality or the factual accuracy. It was like two or three competing merchants, each watching the others like a hawk and putting gaudier and gaudier displays in his window to attract passing customers.

One night Hugh Baillie, the president of United Press, arrived from New York. After a brief talk he offered me a job that was excellent for agency work. I sat alone in the office, trying to think it out. War was coming; I must be in a position to write for the people at home. I had waited nearly two years for the chance. But I was worried about the agency system, uncertain whether I could perform this way or whether I wanted to. The 'phone rang; it was a call from London, with Edward Murrow at the other end, asking if I would like to try reporting by radio. "I don't know very much about your experience," he said. "But I like the way you write and I like your ideas. There's only Shirer and Grandin and myself now, but I think this thing may develop into something. There won't be pressure on you to provide scoops or anything sensational. Just provide the honest news, and when there isn't any news, why, just say so. I have an idea people might like that." I was flattered and scared, but willing to try. He set up a period the following night for me to speak on a closed circuit, for the various executives in New York alone to hear and judge. It didn't matter what I wrote, so I composed a piece about the Weidmann execution in phraseology I trusted was suitable for speech. Two hours before the talk was to begin I learned that there had been a misunderstanding, and my words would be carried over the entire Columbia Broadcasting System network. Hastily I wrote a new speech on contemporary affairs and delivered it before the microphone with my hands shaking so violently that listeners must have heard the paper rattling. It appeared that New York did not think I would do. The material was good, they had said but the manner of speaking was very bad. "That's all right," Murrow said. "I'll fix it. Quit your other jobs anyway and don't worry about it." My friends told me I was crazy to follow his advice, given the circumstances. It was true that I knew Murrow only slightly, and that I risked falling between two stools; but there was something about him that evoked a feeling of trust. H. V. Kaltenborn, then in Europe for Columbia on a quick trip, gave me fatherly advice after I had accepted the job, then overran his time on a joint broadcast with me so that I was forced to condense my script as I read it. I committed terrible slurs, pauses, and stumbles, and would have resigned then and there had it not been that I lacked the courage to inform Murrow.

I faced the prospect of speaking each night to a new and frighteningly large audience, through a new and frighteningly personal medium about the event we had known would happen, which had obsessed our minds for years, which came now, almost as a relief after so much tortured suspense, at the beginning of September

Chapter V

THE HAWKER OF SHOELACES was standing where he always stood, pulling at the passers-by and calling his wares in the same cracked voice of yesterday and the day before that. Snoelaces go on forever. The young fellow who worked for the department of sanitation opened the conduit on the corner as usual and let the piped water from the Seine gurgle down the gutter, washing away the accumulation of paper wads, cigarette butts and dog droppings. Sewage systems never stop. The girl behind the show window of the beauty shop was polishing the metal gadget that fits over the heads of the women clients, getting ready for the day's business. Nothing more permanent than permanent waves. I don't know what I had expected; perhaps I expected the life of the city to come to a dead stop. Didn't they understand that everything now was changed, that it could never be the same again? They continued to go through their ritualistic motion; it was absurd. They were characters moving on a cinema screen, and I was alone in the audience.

On all the morning newspapers the fat black letters formed the phrase: "*C'est la Guerre.*" That didn't really translate into "War!" It was still just "*C'est la Guerre,*" which you flipped off your tongue every day like "the first hundred years are the hardest, chum," or "it never rains but it pours."

We hung around the Gare de l'Est waiting for the café across the street to open up. Our driver, the one we used in the daytime, who wore walrus mustaches and had been a farmer in Normandy, had never been loquacious, but suddenly he started talking, and it poured out: how it was at Verdun with him in la dernière, the way the farm went to pieces, the trouble he had keeping the son out of jail after the mother died, speculation about what sector the son would be moving toward today and the quality of the son's regimental commander compared with his own in the last. All his life he lived over in front of me, the only accessible ac quaintance of the moment, as though I were the priest who came at the final moment, just before he let go of the threads.

You could see that it was very bad for the older ones. They did not know if they could start up again and remake lives that were already over the middle divide; and mostly it seemed to be the older ones walking into the station on this September morning. They were coming from the slums and tenements around the east side, and they still had on their soft, powdery denim, their working clothes. From the elbows of some hung the oval helmets they had kept in the back closet since 1918. They did not look like soldiers beginning a war; they looked like soldiers at the end of a war, when soldiers resemble any other tired men. Their wives had come with them to the station, hanging to their arms, shuffling rapidly in their felt slippers to keep up with their men. Their hair was pinned carelessly in place, and their eyes had the dry glaze and coloring that signified all-night weeping. They waited for the trains, standing facing one another, oblivious of anyone else, the husband staring over his wife's head at the floor, the wife staring at his chest, and neither speaking. A tall, handsome young officer with shiny dark straps was grinning at his fashionable wife, pretending to sock her in the jaw, kidding her. Form. A behavior pattern. Noblesse oblige. The poor, who struggle for daily bread, have time for reality only.

No bands played, there were no flags, and nobody made a speech about "la gloire." Nobody shouted any orders. They moved to the trains of endless length as though it were a weary routine they had practised for twenty years. As far as you could see there were the clusters of faces, expressionless faces in the compartment windows. Another journalist who saw it—Miss Dorothy Thompson, I think—said, "Not one replaceable face." No more needed to be said. This was the spirit of France on the day it began, the conviction that no human body, no single face, was expendable for any cause. The knowledge, which only a civilized people could have, that the last one had really been a defeat for them, regardless of what the words in the peace treaties said. But wisdom, like peace, is indivisible; and even the Christians in the grove will throw an arm across the face to ward off the swords of Caesar's men.

Neutrals are privileged; and one of the questionable privileges was to become more obsessed with the personal problem of describing the tragedy than with the tragedy itself. The first year of war in France was a year of fighting with censors and military press authorities, who, like the American Embassy, did not regard radio journalists as legitimate journalists, with beating my colleagues, and with being beaten. It began the first day. A government censor, who, perhaps, was merely careless, had passed my script saying that France would be officially at war beginning at five o'clock in the afternoon. (Great Britain began at eleven in the morning.) No other reporter, it appeared, had been able to clear this momentous story for filing. My broadcast was set for noon. I paced up and down the studio in a cold sweat, looking at the clock every two minutes. Just before air time the studio engineer, a gray, troubled man in his forties, put his head out from his compartment and informed me New York had just cancelled the Paris broadcast because they wanted more from London. They were ignorant, of course, of the scoop I held in my hands. I struggled with the telephones and cable circuits to London for thirty frantic, despairing minutes, trying to make contact, shouting orders to the engineer, who did his best. Suddenly he burst into tears and yelled at me to get out, to get out. What did it matter, my little news item? What did any of this nonsense matter? He was a family man, who had spent four years in the last war, one year in a German prison camp, and he had suffered three wounds. He had just received his call-up notice that morning. I sat in the café outside with the useless script in my pocket, feeling as I had felt those nights on the old Minneapolis *Journal* when I had gone to demand photographs in families where a death had just occurred. My neutrality, my personal inviolability, was precious and a little indecent.

Apparently all America was sitting beside the radio; New York could not get its fill. Tom Grandin and I were on a relentless treadmill for the first two or three days. I would rise at two or three in the morning, never having removed my clothes, stumble into the car and go to the studio. When I returned, he would repeat my performance; then I again and then he again, around the clock. America seemed to be in an emotional state, but we were warned over and over again to speak calmly, dispassionately; we must not display a tenth of the emotion that a broadcaster does when describing a prize fight. America was neutral; our company at least was determined that it would never be guilty of propagandizing Americans into war. This was right, it was the only legitimate way to perform our function—but it was very hard. Once, through sheer exhaustion and not emotion, my voice cracked, and

I received a polite reminder. Once the windows happened to be
open to the street when Grandin was speaking, and the eerie wail
of the air-raid siren sounded in a million American parlors; after
that we checked the windows before we spoke.

Long lines of Americans and others with American visas besieged the shipping-line offices of neutral countries. Some left for
the south of France. Our Austrian, Czech, and Spanish refugee
friends suddenly disappeared, Karli among them. We guessed that
the police had them somewhere, but inquiries produced no results.
Each night we expected Paris to be devastated from the air. No
one knew what a serious bombing would be like, and imaginations
worked overtime. When the siren sounded at midnight the first
time, a French colonel banged at our door in the Continental Hotel.
"Les avions! les avions!" His voice shook with fright as he ran
from door to door. In the underground hotel kitchen, which was
like a whitewashed cave, we huddled in our bathrobes. An American waiting for passage home tore his gas mask out of its case,
put it on with trembling hands, and wore it for hours; so did thousands of others during these first, uncertain nights. A fat, greasy
man named Knecht, a director of one of the reactionary papers,
sat in his flowered bathrobe with his elbows on the kitchen table,
his head in his hands. I remembered his assuring an American businessmen's club in Paris that it was the French workmen who were
to be feared, not the Nazis, that Hitler was no threat to France.
No news came back from the western front along the Rhine, only
rumors, new ones every day of gigantic battles. Word had gone
out to the neutral journalists that none of them would be allowed
at the front until formal arrangements for a tour were completed
with the embassies. One man in an American news agency in Paris
sent a sensational account of the Germans crossing the Rhine in
force near the border of Switzerland. The story was not denied.

The old pattern was sure to repeat itself: the British would send
an expeditionary force and take up positions at the front somewhere on the northeastern sector. Geoffrey Cox, the agile and able
New Zealander, correspondent for the London *Daily Express,* had
received a hint that Cherbourg would be the debarkation point.
On the tenth of September we made the long run by automobile
to the port and were the only journalists to observe the landing
in France of the new B.E.F., twenty-five years after the first. They
were sharply different from the French troops we had seen; they
acted out a ritual they had been taught. They stamped the earth

with their hard heels when they turned in march formation, swung
their arms in vigorous unison, chorused back the barking orders of
their officer. You did not see on their ruddy, shaven faces the
knowledge of what was happening as you saw it in the French.
It seemed impossible that these men in their shining straps were
men who had known the last time, or the sons of men who had
known the last. They were as fresh and new as the German soldiers
skiing in the Bavarian Alps. But they were eternally British: The
aristocratic officer with the slim face, the quiet voice, the inoffensive swagger stick, and the careless handkerchief in the sleeve;
the young stockbroker reservist imitating as best he could with his
carefully cultivated mustache and a swagger stick which, unfor·
tunately, swaggered; the kid Cockney we picked up who wanted
to know where he could find a pint of beer, who said: "Promised
the old woman, Oi did, that Oi'd bring her little old 'Itler's mustache." French poilus in their formless uniforms sipped their drinks
at the zinc bars and watched the British march and turn and stamp
the ground. They looked at one another, said nothing, and continued to drink.

At midnight in Paris the censor passed my script, but I could
not indicate whether they had arrived by ship, by plane, or by
walking on the water. It was a remarkable censorship in those days.
It was either so ruthless that it cut out the most harmless observa-
tions, or so inefficient that one could pass the most sensational
news. It operated entirely by whim and caprice, and one never
knew from day to day how his dispatches would fare.

One week later, Geoffrey, Walter Kerr of the New York *Herald
Tribune,* Charles Findley, a news-reel executive, and I drove out
of Paris in the very early morning, heading for the western front
of World War Number Two. There was merely an "understanding" that no journalists were to go; we had received no specific
orders. And the intolerable delay on the part of the authorities
and the press attaché in the American Embassy had, we considered, made the whole arrangement null and void. We had no idea
how far we would get, whether we would be welcomed or returned
in chains. At Château-Thierry the military policeman in the middle
of the road looked at our press cards, shrugged his shoulders, and
said it wasn't his responsibility to stop us but that we would probably not get through Rheims. At Rheims they shrugged their
shoulders and said they'd probably stop us at Verdun. At Verdun
they said we would surely be stopped at Metz, and at Metz nobody

paid us any attention. All the photographs and books of boyhood came to life around me; I was living in the exact world of 1914. Camouflaged busses—the busses of Paris—were loaded with infantry and writhed in long lines over the rolling hills, past the overgrown bunkers which had been the old trenches, past a rusted tank which had been left by the road as a souvenir these twenty years. In the barrels of their old rifles some of the French conscripts had stuck long-stemmed purple flowers. They had done that too, before. Decrepit trucks bumped along pulling the seventy-fives, and plodding horses were still drawing the old-fashioned soup kitchens, the steam rising from the stew inside. It was all the same; the projector had stopped in 1918 and now was turning again.

It was damp and chill in the twilight when we reached a point near the Luxembourg border. The front was just over the low hills, three or four miles away. In the village, everything seemed normal and at peace. The old people wearing their stiff black Sunday clothes and their high white collars were walking sedately from the church; children played in the puddle beside the village pump. Only when a short column of Moroccan troops, muddy and caked from the front-line dugouts, passed through the village was there any suggestion of the great new war. It grew dark, and we had to turn back. We paused at a quiet crossroads and listened; we heard one gun and that was all. It was quite incredible. We were just behind the front lines, and all was quiet; there were no wounded, no new cemeteries; the civilians had not been moved away. In the night at the hotel in Metz, Findley suffered an attack of appendicitis, and we returned as rapidly as we could to Paris. We had the most important story in the world in our hands, the answer to the question all the world was asking. As I was writing in the Continental, Geoffrey rang me up and said: "Meet me out in front of the hotel. Better hold your story—we're in trouble." But when he came he wore a sheepish grin. Somehow the news of our trip had reached other reporters in Paris, and Kenneth Downs of the International News Service instructed one of his French speaking assistants to impersonate a Quai d'Orsay official in a telephoned threat to Cox that he would be ordered out of the country if he tried to send his story. An hour later, apparently feeling remorse, Downs called Cox and said it was all a joke. The delay, however, was long enough for Cox to miss the important edition of his paper. My story and Walter's were passed by the censors, to our great surprise. General Gamelin, as we later learned, was furious and demanded that we be expelled, but the wise and diplomatic André Morize of Harvard, then chief of the American section of the French information ministry, talked the general out of it, and we received nothing more than a stern but inoffensive lecture. We reported our findings to the embassy military people, who had not been permitted to go to the front. Three days later, another group of journalists including Downs made essentially the same trip. Either they wrote their stories better or they "needled" them more sharply; in any case, their exploit and revelations got most of the attention in America, and they are down in the history of American reportage as the first reporters to see the western front. But the truth was out; there were no great battles, there was no fighting of any consequence at all. After a while, the American editors grew bored with it, and ordered their Paris correspondents to file the daily communiqué and nothing more, American wits dubbed it the "phony war," and there seemed to be general resentment back home that the contestants were not putting on a more exciting show to titillate the neutrals.

2

No wartime broadcasts had been done from the tripartite neutral corner of Holland, Belgium, and Luxembourg, and with Geoffrey, rarest and most lovable of companions, I went to see what was happening in these little countries, which occupied no man's land and stubbornly pretended they were somewhere else. The fact that they were trying to play the neutral game, to seek treaties and "assurances," simply meant that the ruling majorities in their governments still failed to understand what the Nazis really were. Leopold had proclaimed the neutral status for Belgium two or three years before, and the British and French general staffs got nowhere in their pleas for bases and fields. The Dutch were even more obtuse, and the strong-minded Queen herself bore a great deal of the responsibility. Much as I liked and admired her when I met her later, she was one of the principal obstacles to a united front when there still was time. We wandered the Ardennes in a long limousine lent by Ambassador Joseph Davies and found the Belgians had fortified this land frontier with a few logs across the narrow roads and very little more. Two Belgian soldiers, a forest frontier patrol, stopped us—to ask if we carried any liquor. They were already drunk and hung on our necks, beseeching us for a joy ride in the limousine. When we went on, their parting words translated about like this: "Post's jush down nex' turn. Don' tell captain we're already drunk." A colonel informed us one Saturday night that fifty percent of his regiment was AWOL in Antwerp, and there was nothing in the world he could do about it. We should have known, but the pillboxes along the Meuse and the Albert Canal made us think Belgium was efficiently preparing to defend herself—made us think so, no doubt, because we wanted to think so. (The latest volume of Liddell Hart still spoke of the Ardennes as a natural defense.) In both Belgium and Holland we found the Nazi propaganda machine, directed by their embassies, working at full blast; the French and British were doing nothing, beyond issuing prosy little "information" sheets occasionally. Geoffrey wrote a stinging report for the *Express* about this and caused a minor crisis in the British information headquarters in London.

In Amsterdam the American consul was pleased that I wished to do a broadcast about Holland. He fished in his desk and brought out a sheaf of printed papers. "Here is lots of information about the tulip industry; doubtless you will wish to describe the canals and the winter skating, and perhaps you know about President Roosevelt's Dutch antecedents." He was surprised when he learned that I intended to broadcast about the news of the day; all previous broadcasts from Holland to America had dealt with the windmills and the tulips. Broadcasting was entertainment, and he could not quite comprehend this unprecedented incursion into the realm of the newspapermen. The Dutch officials were polite, formal, and very tough. Baron Tindahl of Radio Hilversum was obliged to escort me by train down to The Hague in order that a cabinet member might personally peruse the fairly harmless words I intended to breathe into their radio antennae. I was starchily told that the authorities would be listening over a special wire, and that if I deviated by so much as one word from the approved script, my broadcast would be cut off the air. The lovely little town of Hilversum made me suddenly, overpoweringly homesick. Here again were clean, tree-lined streets, individual homes of brick and stucco, set well back in the shrubbery, showing in the soft evening the colored lights of reading lamps. Young boys and girls with clean white shirts, open understandable faces, strolled arm in arm

under the street lights. I felt again how foreign Paris really was to
me, how impenetrably alien. No amount of mobilization for war
could alter the essential peace of Hilversum and Holland. I hardly
guessed that less than a year later I would be sitting in London,
hearing a snarling Nazi voice from this same Hilversum studio
attacking with venom the leaders and the journalists of America,
including myself.

To be in the Grand Duchy of Luxembourg at that time was to
have an orchestra seat at the spectacle of war; the press box was
the veranda of Monsieur Ropp's café at Remisch on the vineyard
slopes that overlook the Moselle. We sat there in wicker chairs, feet
on the balustrade, the yellow wine at our elbows. You could almost
reach out and touch the hills across, the hills upon which lay the
Germans and the French. We would hear the dull boom of the big
guns, the shuttling whistle of the arching shell and the muffled
explosion of its arrival. Now and then an airplane would twist
crazily along the river and black puffs of smoke from antiaircraft
shells would mushroom around it. Neither side cared or sent regrets if the fragments occasionally rained down upon the Luxembourg side, but the reporters, scuttling for cover, one hand
balancing a wine glass, were indignantly resentful. Walter Kerr
and Bob Casey obtained German visas and rode a taxicab through
the Siegfried Line into Trier, and the story became a joke in the
press bars of New York. It was a pleasant, entertaining war, at
least to the neutral journalists, who did not have to share the
soldiers' mud and who ran small risk of injury.

In the city of Luxembourg we lived in the hotel where Luden-
dorff and his staff had lived in 1914, and sat in their special, high-
backed chairs at the corner table in the dining-room. The new
German consul lived there with his charming Austrian wife. He
was polite and would talk—carefully—but never tried to share the
hallowed corner table. He was a tall, thin, dish-faced man with
courtly manners, who had arrived from the Paris embassy after
the declaration of war. His name was Count von Something-Thun
and in his bearing, his soft regrets for the civilization of France,
he gave a convincing impression of the old-line, non-Nazi German
diplomat of the traditional school.

The American diplomatic representative was George Platt Waller of Alabama, as original an ornament of the State Department
as one could hope to find. He knew the complete history of every
crumbled castle in the land, kissed the hand of the Grand Duchess

with a stately flourish, and could discuss her latest gown with the
avidity of a gallant at the court of Louis Quatorze. All he lacked
was a powdered wig and snuff box. He bowed us into his parlor,
prayed that we be seated, clapped his hands sharply, and, when a
scared little country girl in maid's uniform popped in at the door,
said: "I must apologize for my unfortunate lack of attendants, but
the times are bad, and I am left with only this little creet-chah."
All of us, I fear, drank too much of his excellent wines, and when
we gathered to admire an ancestral portrait he discoursed upon
the South. Delicately balancing his glass, he said with emotion:
"One never knows, in these wretched and violent times, when
one's span may be abruptly terminated. I have been giving thought
to my tombstone. Like Jefferson's, it shall be the utmost in simplicity and modesty. The inscription will merely read: 'George
Platt Waller, born on such-and-such, died on such-and-such, alum-
nus, University cf Virginia.' Nothing about the Order of the
Grecian Thorn—with crown. Nothing about the Royal Order of
the Luxembourg Aspen—also with crown. Just the words: 'He
aided his countrymen in every clime. He walked with princes and
gave counsel unto kings.'" Bob Casey, eyes bulging with rapture
and champagne, exclaimed: "True! You done it!"

Mr. Waller took me to the tapestried office of Dr. Joseph Bech,
the Foreign Minister, whom he never failed to address as "Your
Excellency," accompanied by a deep bow. Bech was the grand old
man of this charming Ruritania, foreign minister or prime minister—
he alternated—for twenty years or more. He would have been, I
think, a leader of his people in any country, however large. He was
wise and tolerant, humorous and compassionate, a man with the
mind of a Briand and a kindly face not unlike that of the eminent
French internationalist. Bech would censor my broadcast scripts
himself, and he was the best censor of my extensive acquaintance.
He never suggested a single change, ever, but would read out
loud to himself, breaking into chuckles, then pat my arm and say:
"Excellent, my boy, excellent! The Nazis won't like it, but, after all,
we are still masters in our own house, you know." He would get
down one of the books from the massive shelves and read to me in
French of the days when the Duke of Marlborough's army opposed
the French, the British occupying the very hills where Hitler's men
were now dug in, the French on the very hillocks Gamelin had
made his front line. Marlborough got no farther and eventually

pulled back to Trier. "Let's hope history will repeat itself," said Bech, a little sadly; "but I have my doubts."

Bech was having his daily troubles with the German Minister to Luxembourg, who came to him one morning during this period and complained stiffly that the villagers along the Moselle were in the habit of shouting insulting remarks about the Führer to the German soldiers across the narrow stream. "Come, come," said Bech, "surely so small a matter does not disturb the government of the great Reich?" The Minister said: "Sir, it is a serious matter, I assure you, and if it should come to the ears of the people in Berlin, we shall all suffer for it."

"Well, do you know precisely what the insults are?" inquired the Foreign Minister.

To his astonishment, the German envoy pulled a sheet of paper from his briefcase and read out: "Hitler is a pig. Hitler is the south end of a horse going north," etc., etc.

Bech gravely asked to be given the list and promised that immediate official steps would be taken. That afternoon he called in an old schoolmate who was commissioner for the region lying along the river. Two days later, the criers in all the river villages rang their handbells and assembled the people. The criers held up an official document and said: "Hear ye, hear ye! From this day forward it is forbidden for any citizen of the Grand Duchy to publicly utter the following remarks [raising his voice to a shout]: 'Hitler is a pig.' [Delighted screams from the people.] 'Hitler is the south end of a horse going north.' [Louder screams from the people.] 'Etc., etc.' " The result was, of course, that the people's vocabulary was considerably enlarged.

(When the avalanche fell upon Luxembourg on the morning of May 10, the gracious Thun, who had disappeared into Germany a few days before, was the first Nazi into the city of Luxembourg, rushing to government offices with a band of Nazi gangsters, confiscating official files. He had been Gestapo chief for the Grand Duchy. Bech got away with his wife before dawn, missing capture by Thun by a scant ten minutes. I saw him next, five years later, at the San Francisco conference, helping to draw the document intended to make wars impossible. George Platt Waller, to everyone's surprise, proved that he too had been wearing a disguise. He was tough and defiant with the Nazis, hid away intended victims in his quarters, saved some of the Luxembourg youngsters from forced labor in Germany, and even went into Germany to find and aid some of those who had not escaped. The Duchy's quota of ruins, unfortunately, was increased in appalling numbers, square miles of the yellow vineyards were uprooted, and Ropp's café terrace collapsed upon the hillside.)

3

The French government did not refer to their detention camps for German nationals and political refugees as concentration camps. They called them "assembly centers" and justified the round-up of refugees on the ground that there was no alternative. They could not use the refugees as soldiers and rely on them to fight other Germans and Austrians, by whom they would be executed if captured. They could not be left in the cafés of Paris, where French soldiers returning from the front would see them and take offense. By December various unverified reports were appearing in the liberal and leftist American journals suggesting that the camps for refugees, which no foreign journalists had been able to enter, were not much different from the Gestapo camps inside the Reich. Pointing to the bad impression these articles were making in the States, I obtained permission from Sarraut, Minister of the Interior, to go to the camps, after Robert de Saint Jean of the Information Ministry had interceded with him. From Le Mans, a school teacher in the uniform of a lieutenant, a sad-eyed young man with limp mustaches, drove me to a camp for German nationals, as distinct from refugees. These prisoners had to be incarcerated, of course; it was far too risky to allow them to remain at liberty, for there could be spies and saboteurs among them. Commander of this barbed-wire enclosure was a professional French officer, a major of colonial troops, with all the habits of mind and action that the North African service breeds in a French military man. With me at his heels, he flung open the door of one of the long barrack buildings and shouted: *"Attention!"* In the moment before my eyes got accustomed to the dimness, I heard the quick rustling of straw, the muttering of many voices, and the scraping of boots on boards. Then the major cracked his riding crop against his leather puttees and we began the inspection parade. They stood beside their double-decker wire pallets, their eyes fixed upon my face, their eyes peering out of their long, matted hair from dead faces white as chalk. One or two could not have been more than sixteen years old; several were men of sixty or seventy who brushed back their white hair with trembling, blue-veined hands or clutched blankets around their shoulders. It was clammy and very cold inside; there was one round-bellied wood stove in the center of the barracks, which was at least a hundred feet long. After the first few steps, I had to drop my glance; I, with my warm coat and gloves, was under inspection, not they. After what seemed an eternity of running this terrible gauntlet, we reached the exit. In the center of the yard was a pile of stove wood, encircled by a high barbed-wire fence. When I pointed to it, the commandant said: "They're thieves, the Boche bastards, every one of them. They were stealing the wood at night."

The following day was a day I shall not soon forget. I was taken, as the first foreign observer—and, I think, the last—to inspect a camp for central European political refugees. My memory retains now but a poor picture of the physical setting. I am conscious of the eyes and faces of men, their voices and their hands.

The lieutenant led me through the wire gate and indicated the bare, muddy grounds. "You should have seen it before. Just a swamp. There was nothing. Now they even have entertainment facilities." I noticed one sagging volley-ball net, suspended over a puddle. We climbed broken steps into what had been the hayloft of a great barn. Men of all sizes and ages, in shapeless coats and trousers, lay on their backs, their sides and stomachs on low pallets made of chicken wire. For pillows they had rolled bundles of old clothes, and I could observe two or three lifting the bundles to extract a dirty deck of cards, a soiled book, or a cracked photograph. Their personal treasures. The lieutenant prattled on about how hard he and his men had worked to provide these facilities, how terrible it had been at the beginning when hundreds had to sleep on the swampy ground, quite unprotected. He had the pious, ingratiating tones of a professional benefactor. He sounded like the Salvation Army official in a stinking flophouse in an Idaho town.

Heads turned to look at me. They regarded my war correspondent's uniform, which was of the French type, and I knew they were trying to make me out. I do not know how it was that one of them learned I was an American journalist. I noticed a man of about forty, a stout, pale man wearing only corduroy trousers and a filthy undershirt, who appeared at my elbow trying to catch my

eye. The lieutenant said something and I turned. The man was at
my other side. Now I looked at him frankly and saw that his jaw
was quavering, as he tried desperately to find courage to speak.
I asked my guide to excuse me for a moment and bent closer. The
man said: "Please, sir, can you give me a moment? I am —— —— I—"
Tears suddenly poured from his eyes. He forced out the words. He
was —— ——, an Austrian, who had been Vienna correspondent for
the Amsterdam *Telegram*. His name was familiar; he was a journalist of some distinction. Suddenly he stepped to his pallet, found a
stub of pencil and a piece of paper. He scribbled the name and
address of a friend in Paris and put it into my hands. His fingers
closed over mine for a moment, and he tried to say something
more, but could not, and broke into sobs and turned away.

News travels fast in a place where news rarely comes. When I
stepped from the barn into the yard, I was immediately surrounded
by dirty and bearded men. They all began talking at once, in
English, French and German. I was the first man from the outside
they had seen since their arrest, nearly four months before. Each
was desperate to be heard, and in a moment they were trying to
outshout one another, and then two or three would begin shouting
to make the others stop. They shoved and wrestled one another to
get in front of me, pulled and jerked at my raincoat until the buttons tore away. The lieutenant, thinking to rescue me from unpleasant embarrassment, urged me on with him to continue the
tour. I tried to walk away, and they clung to my coat skirt like children. Some began to cry, and others, red with anxiety and rage, demanded that I stop. They had the appearance of human animals,
and they were: a cinema producer from Prague, a well-known
novelist from Vienna, the leading tenor of the Vienna Opera; they
were journalists and poets, doctors and lawyers and university
students. They were all the things that civilized, aspiring men
become in civilized Europe.

When the lieutenant got me to the last barracks barn, my coat
pockets bulged with scraps of paper, playing cards, and torn bits
of handkerchief on which they had written the names of friends in
Paris, London, New York, and Washington—friends who could
help them. And I had heard a fairly coherent account of the situation: arrested without a chance to get in touch with friends; not
allowed to bring extra clothes with them; herded into a sporting
coliseum, sleeping on the ground, men. women, and children; raw

barn floors and the ground as bed in this camp for many weeks; one water spigot for seven hundred men; two hours in line to get a meal; no toilet facilities until they made their own; some with visas to America and unable to get out to make use of them; their requests to fight with the French army ignored; their requests to be formed into labor battalions for the army equally ignored; their money stolen by the guards. They had never been beaten or kicked or stoned, but that was the extent of their blessings. They were lost and forgotten. Victims of the special French kind of cruelty—the cruelty of neglect.

No words of mine were worth expression. I could promise them nothing, except that I would try to report the story. I could give them no hint of their fate. When I stepped into the last barracks, merely as a gesture for the benefit of the lieutenant, who by now was silent and resentful, I ached in every bone as though I had been undergoing a severe physical trial. It was growing dark in the winter afternoon. As I began to make out more figures on the wire cots, I heard a choking voice call "Sevareid! Sevareid!" In the short, fat and ragged body before me I recognized Kurt Dosmar, a journalist from the Saar, who had covered the Weidmann trial with me for the Chicago *Tribune*. The sound of his voice brought hurrying footsteps on the board floor, and in a moment Karli Frucht was beside me.

It was his beard, I suppose, which gave him a certain Christlike appearance. The beard somehow made his soft and gentle eyes more noticeable than ever. His cheeks were drawn in a little, and his wrists were very thin. It was curious; he could utter only polite formalities, and I knew my voice was sounding cold and strange. French officers were waiting in their car for me at the gate. We had a date for dinner in the best place in the village, the tavern where they served duck with orange—which, they assured me, was rather remarkable considering the town. Karli walked toward the gate with me, and there was nothing we could say. When we were a few yards from the group of officers, he slipped one arm over my shoulder, and I turned away from him and began to cry. I was filled with shame and self-loathing. But I could not help it; I stood still in the mud, dressed in my fake French uniform, before my officer hosts, and cried in my handkerchief.

I got back to my squalid hotel room in Le Mans and fell asleep in my clothes and boots. I had bad dreams and awoke just before dawn. I was sweating and my side hurt, where I had been lying on the thick bulge in my coat pocket—their wadded-up words, their silent cries for help.

The tragedy of war is not in the dead nor in the living; it is in the living dead.

4

Many things are clear now, of course, which we did not understand during that first year of war; many phenomena we then observed without recognition now form a pattern; it is easier to understand why things happened as they did—or, perhaps, why things did *not* happen. After the defeat that came in the summer, the experts said: The French should have taken the offensive at the very beginning of the war, but did not because they suffered from the "Maginot complex"—or because they had not built offensive weapons such as tanks—or because their military leaders were Fascists who felt a basic sympathy with Hitler and would rather have got at the Russians—or because their military leaders were pure defeatists, traitors who sought a defeat so that they could take over the country. In all these simple explanations at which men groped there is a portion of truth; but there was something else, something far deeper and more universal, which concerned the *spirit* of men, the kind of thing that really governs men's behavior in war and which the experts rarely understand because they rarely live with the common soldier, who is, after all, merely an ordinary man wearing a different suit of clothes.

It was not that the French were not brave; all soldiers in the mass are brave. (The adjective should be dropped from the military vocabulary.) They were not *afraid of* death; they were *unprepared for* death. It was not true that they did not think their country worth fighting for; they wished to avoid defeat, but they had no particular wish to win a war. Their last experience had taught them that there is no such thing as true victory for civilized men who have no desire to conquer others. Their tragedy was that they had reached a high point of human progress too soon; they were living before their time. They were the last people on earth who should have had Germany for a neighbor. Experts now may say that the French generals should have attacked into Germany in those first few months. But purely rational considerations do not govern an army if they are contrary to the spirits of men. I am inclined to be-

lieve it would have been impossible then to make the French army
go into a serious, bloody offensive. They were no more capable of
taking preventive action based on a rational analysis of the facts
than the American people were of attacking Japan prior to Pearl
Harbor or than the British were of getting down to serious business
prior to Dunkirk. They were as sickened by the chauvinist's mis-
use of "la gloire" as we, as university students, were of "patriotism,"
and they were unable or unwilling to believe that their personal
lives and the life of their country were mutually incompatible, until their own patriotism was put to the test. Because of their geographic fate, when the test came for the French, it was too late.

So the French remained inside their forts along the Maginot
Line and stood in the shin-deep clay mud of their dugouts on the
banks of the Rhine. It was cold and miserable, the dark nights were
long, and the snow and rain seemed never to end. They shivered
in their eternally wet clothing and coughed, and the hospitals
filled up with the sick. But they were staying alive, nearly all of
them, and nothing counted but that. I remember a night spent in
a bare, cement pillbox on the flats near the Rhine. That morning a
young corporal working with a spade on the outside had been
killed by a sniper's bullet from across the river. Just one man, one
soldier out of millions of soldiers who presumably were expected
to die. The lieutenant in charge was close to tears as he described
the terrible tragedy—how the boy had fallen, what he had told
them to write to his parents before he died. The other men in the
pillbox scarcely spoke all evening, but stared at the floor, thinking of the frightful thing that had just happened. It was awful; it
was murder.

As the weeks wore on, all feeling that this was really war seemed
to pass out of the minds of the men. It became merely a wretched,
dull routine, a sublife unworthy of the dignity of men. In this un-
bloody life ridiculous and amusing things could happen. A war of
words developed, between the French and German propagandists,
and this war came to seem more real than the sporadic, long-range
fighting. People in Paris and at the front grew anxious about propaganda "victories" and "defeats." Once, when President Lebrun
arrived at the Strasbourg barricades and, keeping his head down,
peered through a loophole at the German positions across the river,
the Germans raised a great banner that read: *"Bienvenu, Monsieur
le Président."* In one division command post, French officers heard
the Stuttgart radio blithely announce changes in the command of

their division which had been made only the day before. They
were astounded and should have been uneasy, but they laughed it
off. I entered a pillbox on the river one dark night, to find the small
garrison roaring with laughter at the German radio, which had just
read the names and addresses of French soldiers taken prisoner
that day—including the name of one boy listening in on this station.
I drove along the line of fortifications in the woods all one night
with a lieutenant who grew so sleepy he forgot everything including the password. A young sentry stopped us at one road block and
put his frosty face in the car window. *"Le mot?"* he asked. The
lieutenant stirred from sleep and said: *"Ah—ah, Bonaparte."* The
sentry dropped the butt of his rifle and in disgusted tones said:
"Idiot! C'est Bordeaux!"

The greatest and most famous victory scored over the Germans
that winter occurred on Christmas Eve at the Strasbourg-Kehl
bridge. I arrived the next day, and they told me the story. The
French had built a small pillbox at their end of the bridge, and the
Germans had one at theirs, each with an artillery piece pointing
along the span. The guns were never fired, nor the bridge disturbed.
Early on Christmas Eve the Germans set a small Christmas tree,
glowing with lights, on top of their pillbox. It was done, of course,
to mock the French and was so understood by them. Around midnight the young French private on guard duty could stand it no
longer. He slipped off his boots, crawled over the seventy-five gun,
and crept along the bridge, alone and unarmed, with only the
moon above him and the glistening water below. In the morning
the German garrison noticed that their tree was missing and observed it at the other end of the bridge, perched on top of the
French barricade. No other incident along the front was discussed
so much that winter.

I had spent Christmas Eve inside one of the major forts of the
Maginot Line to handle a "live" broadcast to America of the
soldiers' Christmas service, their singing and their prayer, from a
munitions room turned into a chapel. These underground cities
were quite unbelievable with their miniature trains, their complicated ventilation systems, their barracks rooms for hundreds of men,
their dispensaries, commissaries, and immense stores. All the professional soldiers were quite proud of these engineering marvels,
but sometimes the ignorant amateur, like an open-minded child,
will spot the essential weakness at once. The fort, like the iceberg,

was nine tenths below the surface. There were two protuberances, the two concrete-and-steel gun turrets, each of which contained within its cylindrical interior one seventy-five cannon, an extra barrel, a couple of machine guns, a platform for the loaders to stand on, and an automatic hoist that brought up fresh ammunition. The turrets were the eyes, ears, and teeth of the whole enormous body. Obviously these guns would make it almost impossible for any large body of enemy troops to mount the valley which the guns directly covered. But where a regiment could not take such a fort, a single daring man could. It seemed to me that all he had to do was to land beside the turrets by parachute or slip there by night, and that with one hand grenade or one gas bomb he could put the turret completely out of action, rendering useless the rest of the complex establishment. The more I thought about it the more preposterous the whole fortress conception seemed to me. The elaborate underground installation, designed to hold hundreds of men, could serve no more useful purpose than a self-contained turret manned by a dozen or so. Quite aside from the weakness of the strategy of static defense—which I certainly did not understand at the time—the constructions themselves were conceived in fatal error. The French taxpayer had surely been sold the greatest white elephant in modern history. The Maginot Line, as it happened, was never seriously put to the test by the Germans, but I think there can be little doubt that it would have proved but a momentary handicap to the aggressors.

Grandin and I had labored for weeks to unravel official red tape and organize this Christmas Eve broadcast. For this purpose we had traveled hundreds of miles in all. When the moment came the men sang with moving effect, my script was read without a hitch, and I relaxed with the good feeling of hard work well done, thinking that all America must have been deeply stirred by this vivid voice picture of front-line life. A call from Grandin in Paris informed me that an engineer either in Paris or in New York had misunderstood, had thrown the wrong switch, and that nothing whatsoever had been heard on the network. It appeared that William L. White had been scheduled to go on during the same program with a piece from the Mannerheim Line in Finland, and that the engineer got "Mannerheim" and "Maginot" mixed up somehow. White's broadcast got through and was so effective that it resulted in Robert Sherwood's play, *There Shall Be No Night*—so perhaps it was just as well in the long run. Such are the hazards of radio. This was not the last of these minor tragedies for me.

French officers were unfailingly courteous and hospitable to the neutral correspondents who traveled around the front in those days. They were too hospitable—almost every visit to a command, however small, became something of a ceremony. You would arrive tired and dirty, seeking only a quiet corner for a nap, and find the regimental band drawn up in the farmyard, ready to play a salute to you and your country. If you called upon a corps commander intending to spend a quarter-hour questioning him, he would invite his staff in for luncheon with you, which involved at least two solid hours of eating, drinking, and often extemporaneous speeches. Divisions and regiments seemed to be judged on the basis of the officers' *popote*, on the quality of the conversation and the atmosphere of bantering camaraderie. General Dentz in his farmhouse at Paffenhofen took great pride in his overpowering cigars, and whenever I think of him now I feel slightly queasy, on account of the cigars as much as his Fascist behavior after the defeat, for which he was accused of treason by De Gaulle. At the *popote* it was generally a rule that no one must talk about the war; to do so meant a small fine, dropped in the "kitty." In this kind of atmosphere, with these daily habits, it is clear that very little hard work could have been accomplished, and very little was.

In the absence of real news, purely ceremonial affairs such as a visit by Chamberlain or King George were welcomed by the journalists, who felt that their editors had forgotten their existence. It was always the same: the gentle, rather empty face of General Gamelin next to the mustached red face of General Georges, the French equivalent of Colonel Blimp; the presenting of arms by the guards of honor; the playing of the national anthems; then that rapid meaningless gesture, the "tour of inspection" around the fort or along the ranks of the stiffly saluting troops. Journalists were always allotted their small patch of mud on which we stood in an attitude of respectful attention while the great men came and went, until our feet grew cold and our minds wandered. I always rather wanted to hear what these superhuman figures said to one another, what profundities issued from their exalted minds. Once, as Gamelin and King George passed right beside us while "inspecting" a line of small French tanks, we heard His Majesty comment: *"Eel sont lay-jay, ness-pas?" "Oui,"* replied the commander in chief, *"c'est celà."*

Did we, the journalists whose duty it was to inform you of the truth, understand the serious weaknesses of the French and British army line-up on the continent, the strategic errors of their system of defense? Very, very few of us did; I certainly did not. Purely journalistic scruples rather than wisdom prevented me from referring to the French as "the world's greatest land army," as so many of my colleagues did every day, or of the Maginot Line as "impregnable," which was the common adjective. But I did not understand the truth of the situation any more than did the political and military leaders in Paris and London, simply because I was ignorant of the *facts* about the German army and its new tank tactics, despite the lesson of Poland. I was troubled about the spirit of the French soldiers, and there I was right; but I was not competent to judge the efficiency of their arrangements, and so I just assumed that they knew what they were doing in that mechanical realm. Tom Grandin had glimmerings of the real situation, despite his purely amateur standing, and I know that George Millar of the *Daily Express* (a remarkable boy of whom you will hear again) and David Scott were appalled after their first trip around the whole front. De Gaulle knew, and a few others like Richard Casey, Australian Minister to Washington, who protested the whole defense scheme to the unbelieving Chamberlain after a visit; but of these fateful forecasts we did not hear until later. In the office of the American Ambassador in Paris or the office of his military attachés, we heard no suggestion that the allied military giant on the continent had feet of purest clay. Bullitt, in fact, had convinced the President that the French would put up a magnificent fight, so that the President's concern was over the quality of the British.

5

In the freezing dugouts at the front, the Parisians talked and dreamed of their city, while their hands grew rèd and numb, and lice made the nights a torment. They came to Paris on leave, their hearts beating faster as their train drew into the station. Within a week, saddened, sick and resentful, they wanted to get back to their comrades and the filthy life at the front which somehow made them feel cleaner inside. Since I had lived at the front somewhat, I could understand a little of what they felt. It was my first understanding of something that was to be reaffirmed many times: that

in war, the world of the front and the world of the rear are separated by such a wide gulf of the spirit that they can never under
any circumstances come together, and that all the efforts of tongue
and pen and photograph can never even faintly bridge the chasm.
The men came back and heard their Paris friends say: "Well, *mon
vieux,* not like last time, is it? You should have seen how it was at
Verdun, when we . . ." It was impossible to make anybody understand that there are forms of war that are harder on the mind
and soul than battle is.

There was something shameful about Paris to anyone who knew
what millions of other Frenchmen were going through. Yet the
Parisians could not see it that way—they thought they were being
very brave and "carrying on." That's what the American fashion
writers said about the Paris couturiers when they arrived to report
the latest fashion shows. That's what the theatrical reviews said
about music halls like the Casino, where Maurice Chevalier sang
with much feeling *"Paris sera toujours Paris."* The keepers of the
expensive shops in the Rue de la Paix believed they were doing
their bit when they sold silk scarves embroidered with the Tri-
color and the Union Jack—at a price. The Paris press had not
changed. The filthy little anti-Semitic sheets were still hawked on
the café terraces, the big, pro-Fascist organs like *Le Journal* and
Le Matin continued to speak lightly of Hitler, if at all, and to ful-
minate against the Russians in an effort to convince France that
Russia was the real enemy. The high political circles of Paris are
loose-tongued places, and the difference between political gossip in
Paris and in other capitals is that in Paris the gossip is more often
true than not. Few officers from the front remained long in ignorance of the fact that a cabal led by Pierre Laval was even then,
behind the government's back, trying to reach an understanding
with Adolf Hitler. Men from the front felt lost and bewildered,
angry and depressed; they preferred the front, where, if tomorrow
was always uncertain, one's duty was clear, and the task of pulling
a trigger or lanyard was understood.

There was less and less to report to America about the war from
France. There were "feature" broadcasts to be done, of course,
which usually bore little or no relation to the state of Europe. I
was asked to get the Duchess of Windsor to broadcast—something
she had never consented to do. This required endless pulling of
wires, visits to the Duke's aide in their Boulevard Suchet home,
and efforts to get intercession from their good friend, Lady Mendl.

I went to one high French authority who turned out to be a member of one of France's oldest families; he did not wish to have anything to do with it—on the surprising ground that the people concerned were not of true society but only of what he contemptuously referred to as "circus society." The excuse for the broadcast was to be the Duchess's particular war work, which, I believe, was the collection of woolens for the men at the front. Lady Mendl interceded, after many hints that she ought to broadcast herself, since she was really assuming heavy responsibility in the charity group; but in the end it came to nothing. The Duke just wouldn't let his lady talk for the public.

Ripley's "Believe It or Not" program wanted three minutes from Philippe Bunau-Varilla, the aged French engineer, one of the world's most amazing adventurers and agile brains. When he was less than thirty he had been chief engineer of the De Lesseps company in the first attempt at a Panama Canal. For years, after this attempt had been abandoned, he, almost single-handed, kept up the campaign for a canal through Panama, and on the merest hint of assent from Theodore Roosevelt, himself organized the Panamanian "revolution," which resulted in American intervention and our lease on the canal area in the treaty which Bunau-Varilla chiefly wrote and which he negotiated with Hay, since he had had himself, through a French citizen, appointed Panamanian diplomatic envoy to America. He was involved in the Dreyfus affair and was one of the men, if not the man, who discovered that it was not Dreyfus's handwriting after all on the famous *bordereau*. In the siege of Verdun he was a colonel in charge of the sanitation system, and, although he lost a leg there, he invented a new system of water purification which he called "*Verdunisation*" and which is today installed in many French municipalities. He was a remarkable product of the French genius, and I spent many long afternoons with him. Despite his eighty years, his wooden leg, and an extraordinary six-inch snowfall, he made his way to my apartment to await the three A.M. program hour, He fell asleep over his coffee, my watch stopped, and with only five minutes remaining to salvage the broadcast, all our hard work, and his personal dignity, we got across the street to the P.T.T., and he performed, excellently. It was the last time the public ever heard from him; he died before France attained liberation.

One night, by a talk of ninety seconds over the air, I was the cause (without really intending to be) of a world sensation and a diplomatic crisis. I had been slowly growing aware, through conversations in what political and military circles I had access to, and through assiduous reading of the press, that a group of French reactionaries were trying to make the government take the view that the way to get at Germany was to get at her "ally," Soviet Russia. These gentlemen, Weygand among them, thought the Finnish war was proof that the Russians would fold up at the first bold thrust. One day my eye roved through a long, rather obscurely written editorial in the semiofficial *Le Temps,* and a single sentence caught my attention. It turned a key. I read it over and over to myself and to Lois. It could only mean, if language meant anything, that the decision had been made, that the French were going to send arms and troops to Finland. I was sure of my interpretation, as sure as one could be without actual proof, and a bolder broadcaster no doubt would have made the flat prediction. But I wrote my script carefully, qualifying my conclusion, supporting it by corroborative evidence. (New York had warned us often enough about foisting opinion upon listeners in the guise of news.) It went through the careless censorship all right. When New York came through on the circuit I was nervously ready with a three-minute talk, which would follow immediately after Bill White's report from Holland, and would end the program. That meant I had to get off the air exactly on the second, or I would be cut off. White talked on—and on, running over my beginning time. When I got my cue to go ahead, ninety seconds remained. I could do one of two things—remain silent and let them give up Paris, or cut my script, as I read it, in half.

I chose to read it, which meant eliminating as I read all the qualifying phrases, all the corroboration. It amounted to a bald prediction—my own personal prediction—that France was going to send troops. I went to bed, worried but certain that I was right. In the morning a cable arrived from Paul White, the CBS news director, reminding me that I had gotten myself "furtherest limbward," which meant that I was as far out on the limb as anybody could get. The story was reprinted and rebroadcast all over America and flared around the world, resulting in a violent warning to the western allies from the Russian government through an editorial in *Pravda.* I was in a bad spot for a time; I could prove nothing. But some weeks later the French officially admitted the whole plan. (Eventually they explained that these troops were intended chiefly for the seizure of the Swedish ore in the north, to keep it away from the Germans; even so, the risk of a clash with the Russians would, given the existing relations with that power, have been acute.)

The dark days lengthened and lightened, and as the people of France emerged from the long tunnel of winter, they felt the tension increasing in the spring air of Europe, and they made disturbing discoveries in their own house. With the shock of tremendous events expected at any time, they learned for the first time how frighteningly disunited and uncertain their leaders really were. Daladier went down, in a snarling boil of recriminations, and Paul Reynaud was chosen premier—by a majority in the Chamber of just one vote. From the gallery I watched and listened, and for the first time began to feel a sense of panic. They were Frenchmen, facing a great physical crisis in the life of their ancient and civilized country, and yet their behavior was that of petulant, quarreling children. They shouted, called one another names, and debated every conceivable minor issue; they talked the language of party, of special interest, of regional concerns—but no voice rose above the clamor to speak for France. The lion-hearted Herriot tried; he smashed his gavel and shouted, *"Faites l'union National!"* It was like a bus conductor saying to a selfish mob: "Do not shove, gentlemen." But Reynaud was in; he was neither extreme left nor extreme right. I knew from some slight personal acquaintance that he was a man of exceptionally keen mind. But when he reached the podium and began to read his acceptance speech as Premier, my heart sank. He was terribly nervous, he seemed to have lost all self-possession, he spoke in terms of cautious conciliation, not in terms of national duty. A great man, a moral hero was required in this moment of history, and all that they had been able to find was a compromise candidate, an intellectual with none of the rugged qualities of leadership. Reynaud would have gone down soon, replaced by God knows whom, had it not been that the Germans invaded Norway and Denmark, and even the most irresponsible party politicians were sobered. Reynaud continued in office; France continued leaderless.

World affairs and intimate personal affairs were converging to bring my own life to a crisis. Nearly all French doctors had been taken into the army, and, no matter how much they were willing to pay, few pregnant women in Paris could get much medical attention. Dr. Vigne, colonel, with a large military hospital to run, would stop by each Sunday noon to give Lois a quick examination and measurement. Her pregnancy was of heroic proportions. Dr. Vigne, still France's foremost obstetrician despite his sixty-some years, seemed to take professional pride in the fact that the increase in her girth exceeded by two centimeters anything he had known in forty years of practice. X-rays showed twins, unprecedented in our families. The chance of losing them was considerable, and Lois, with iron determination to keep them, remained three months flat on her back. On the morning of April 25 the dash to the Clinique St. Pierre in Neuilly was obviously in order. A broadcast was also due. William L. White, whom I had never met, and whose voice had come into my professional life at various critical moments, suddenly arrived from the Low Countries and took over the broadcast without hesitation, while a knowing taxi driver got us to the clinic in record time. There was a bad moment in the night, when Dr. Vigne came out of the delivery room for a respite, looked at me, said nothing and went back in. After a while he came out again, covered with blood. He leaned against the door of my room, lighted a cigarette, and said, "I think it will go. For a time I was not so sure." A few minutes later a nurse, the young one who prided herself on speaking English, burst into the room, and, forgetting she was bilingual, exclaimed almost hysterically: "*Deux beaux garçons!*" Lois was all right, considering that she had just been delivered of thirteen and a half pounds of children. At three in the morning, Dr. Vigne got out of my car at his apartment, moving slowly, looking suddenly bent and old and incongruous in his uniform and shiny straps. He was France, weary in the unceasing struggle for humanity and life, revealing in an unguarded moment that she did not fit and did not wish to fit the trappings of rationalized evil and justified death.

A few days went by, and, believing that Italy might come into the war before Hitler moved, I left Paris for the Riviera mountain frontier and for Algiers and Tunis, where I expected to line up correspondents and radio facilities in case of an Italian attack in that direction. I said goodbye to Lois in the clinic. As I was about to mount my train in the Gare de Lyon my name was called. Karli ran up to me, looking slightly ridiculous in my old topcoat, which was much too large for him. The refugee prisoners had finally been taken under command of the British army and given paid labor on military installations. Self-respect had returned to his face and dignity to his bearing. We had a brief, happy talk before the train began to move. Feeling confident in life in general, I settled into my seat, facing a group of French officers bound for the south, on leave from their regiments at the front.

It was the night of May 9, 1940.

Chapter VI

I HAD BEEN SLEEPING an hour in the little hotel by the station in the Provençal town of Valence when the siren woke me. Ordinarily one would not rise merely because of the siren, but there came the heavy sound of airplane motors unusually close by. I peered from the window and saw in the thin dawn sky two bombers side by side, coming from the direction of Lyon, flying in a leisurely, confident manner. I could make out the black crosses on their wings very clearly as they passed over the town. In their lazy flight they seemed singularly unhostile. I went back to bed and was dozing off again when I became conscious of a sharp sound that somehow was more alarming than the siren and the motors: the sound of a man running in hard boots—just one man's footsteps, echoing in an empty street. From the window I saw him, a French enlisted man, running heavily toward the station while struggling to don his coat. A hundred men marching in the street at any hour one would accept. But one man? The pressing sense of urgency this phenomenon communicated prevented further sleep despite the exhaustion of an all-night train ride. I dressed and went down.

Next door, before a little shop, stood a silent group of people: the hotel night clerk, still in shawl and slippers, the butcher with his blood-spotted apron held in his hand, a policeman holding his bicycle by the handlebars. The shopkeeper was chalking large words in capital letters upon a blackboard. Slowly they formed a sentence: "The Germans—this morning—have invaded—Holland—Luxembourg—Belgium—They bombed—the Lyon airport."

One could not even get near the telegraph office, and the telephone operators refused to take any more calls for Paris. At noon the northbound train was filled with officers and men, called by the general radio announcements back to their units. The bulbous-nosed regimental colonel who sat across the dining table from me was heartily military. "We've been expecting them," he asserted. "We were not surprised for a moment." It seemed to me a little strange that he should have been sent south on leave from his front-line infantry outfit just two days before if the high command had known the Germans were going to strike. In the train load of men about to meet the shock of invasion there was an air of restrained excitement; there was also a discernible sense of relief that at last the intolerable waiting was over and that a decision would soon be achieved. Since I was a Paris correspondent many of them assumed I knew the real story of what was happening, and they asked many questions. I hardly dared admit that I had been on my way in the opposite direction at the hour the Germans struck. At Lyon and Dijon we picked up rumors that Paris had been heavily bombed. I cross-examined all the rumor carriers, demanding to know *where* the bombs had struck, whether any had landed in the suburb of Neuilly. Nobody had any precise information.

It was midnight before the taxi-driver got me to the Clinique St. Pierre. Cars in the courtyard were taking away bundled-up women patients and their babies. The corridors were dark and deserted, and I had to feel my way to the room upstairs where I had left Lois and the twins. A faint light burned in her room; she was lying on her back, looking at the door with wide eyes when I came in. She knew I would come back, and the sirens and distant explosions had not disturbed her very much, but all day nurses and patients had been leaving the clinic. No one had been in to see her for hours, and sometimes, when she did not hear footsteps, she had the panicky feeling that she had been left all alone in the building. She was quite helpless, unable as yet to walk.

Now the terrible pressure began, the pressure of crisis which was never to relent for many weeks. Telegrams were pouring in from New York; the broadcast schedule was going full blast, around the clock; the army press office was on the 'phone demanding to know if I was to be included in the party of correspondents leaving for press headquarters in Cambrai; I had to find a nurse and an ambulance and a place outside of Paris for my family, and get them to it. It is remarkable how long one can go without sleep if the impulse to action is strong enough. Even immediately afterwards I could not retrace the sequence of my own movements, but a Danish nurse materialized, and a hearselike ambulance, and there was a minor parade, weaving in and out of the scrambled traffic, through Versailles and Saint-Cyr to a little inn at Pontchartrain. I cannot remember how I had persuaded Madame Exiane, earlier that day, to harbor my complicated ménage. The thousand-franc notes, I suppose. In any case, the peroxide-blonde lady, retired from the night-club choruses of Montmartre, ran about wringing her hands from the moment the family was settled. The Danish nurse was all right, except for the small black cigars she smoked and her accent which convinced the nervous villagers that she was a German spy. The mayor, thank God, was a calm and rational man. It was midnight when I fell into a bed in the railroad station hotel at Cambrai, toward the Belgian border.

It was three in the morning when I stumbled, half-dressed, to the cellar basement. The whole building was shaking from the roar of airplane motors, from the concussion of bombs and defense cannon which were tearing with livid gashes the velvet fabric of the night. The grandmother slept upright on a kitchen chair, and the blue-eyed girl who had checked me in lay curled on a packing box with the old tomcat sleeping in the curve of her body. The building continued to quaver, and the dust slipped down on the rows of wine bottles, leaving naked their glass necks. This was something I had never known; this was *it*. I remembered the devastated little railway stations on the trip up from Paris, and there was no more sleep—only brief blackouts when the mind became unconscious, the body remaining alert. The sleep of wartime, which the minds and bodies of millions were to learn and practice for years to come.

In the morning long freight trains moved slowly through Cambrai, every car packed with refugee families from French towns farther north, from Belgium and from Holland. They came on foot, in oxcarts, in automobiles, on hay wagons through the public square, and some stopped to tell terrible stories of what the Blitzkrieg had done to their homes and families. Rumors of German spies and saboteurs in French uniforms and in civilian clothes obsessed the people. A fifteen-year-old boy spoke with careful pleasantness to me on the street; then, as I later discovered, ran immediately to the police to announce that he had spotted a German saboteur in a fake French uniform, speaking with a foreign accent. Before the Cambrai episode was over for the press, the dignified P. J. Philip, British-born chief New York *Times* correspondent in Paris, a man who had spent his life in the country, was seized by hysterical peasants who believed he was a German spy because he spoke *without* an accent. They lined him up against a farm wall with their pistols ready. He stalled for time by asking permission to sit down and put his boots back on—"At least permit an

Englishman to die with his boots on," he had said; and at that moment the gendarmes rescued him. Essentially the same thing happened to David Scott. We became almost more nervous about the French people than about the Germans.

All the careful arrangements made over a period of months by the army press officers now fell to pieces. At first we were denied transportation and told it could not be spared to go to this battleground or that. Each time the information liaison officer came to report events to the foreign press, he confessed with much sweating and apology that he had nothing to tell us. Gradually we began to suspect the truth: that they did not want us near the fighting because the fighting was going so badly for them. We did get a few miles away, over to General Corap's headquarters; he refused to see us and took away our car. We returned by bus to Cambrai having seen nothing of the enemy beyond two German fliers who had been shot down and rescued by French soldiers from a screaming mob of farm women with pitchforks, and another German flier who lay with a broken shoulder on the floor in Corap's headquarters, moaning for hours before anybody paid him attention. We made another short trip to the Belgian border and flung ourselves into a ditch when one British fighter plane and two German planes in a dogfight shot over us just above the treetops. One German plane went down, and so did the British plane, the pilot of the latter maneuvering the falling craft until he got it away from the innocent roofs of the next village. In the pasture back of the churchyard the cows were browsing peacefully when we arrived. There was a great blackened hole containing smoking parts of the plane, and one of the pilot's trim black boots was standing upright, unsoiled, beside the cavity. Two Frenchmen with gunny sacks moved slowly around in the grass picking up with sticks small pieces of red meat which they buried as the village people watched and wept. We found the plane's serial number and returned to Cambrai, a little sick, very sobered, wondering what was happening to France. A correspondent who had made the rush toward Brussels with the British arrived full of pride and confidence over the way the British and French striking force had driven north toward Holland with no opposition. "With no opposition?" one of the wiser ones among us asked. No opposition, no real opposition, even from the mighty German air fleet? This was very, very strange, and the first faint suggestion that perhaps the Germans wanted it that way appeared in our brains. But we brushed

the idea aside. It couldn't be possible that the Allies had rushed
into a trap; it just couldn't be possible.

We gave up the attempt to learn the course of the war at the
advance headquarters and decided to return to Paris and try to
find out what was really happening. With Kenneth Downs and
Ralph Heinzen I climbed into a third-class compartment of a
mile-long refugee train, to begin a journey I shall remember forever. (About one hour after our train left Cambrai dive bombers
killed fifty people waiting on the platform for the next train, and
demolished the station. The old grandmother and the girl who
slept on the packing box were killed. Of the tomcat I received no
news.) It should have been a four-hour trip; it took us eighteen
hours, and for most of those eighteen hours we stood. There was
a Belgian family in the compartment—a burly blacksmith of fifty,
his massive wife with great red arms, and two small children. They
had been sitting upright on the straight, hard benches for twenty-
four hours, most of the time without food or water. The man slept,
his big head rolling from side to side as the train jerked along.
The woman held the young daughter. After a time we noticed that
she was beginning to breathe rapidly, and her wide, honest face
began to contort in anguish. She rocked her body rapidly from
side to side, moaning now, her lip beginning to bleed where her
teeth were fastened into the flesh. Downs and I took the child and
held her in our arms. At this the woman said: "Ah, the Americans,
they are nice people," and the tears, so long restrained, flowed
unattended. The Americans were so nice; all the neutrals, whose
children were not crying with hunger, whose homes were not in
ashes, the neutrals had so much generosity to spend.

The night came, and there were long halts on the dark prairie.
We were puzzled, for the train was not continuing on the straight
run for Paris but was being shifted constantly westward. Obviously, things were wrong somewhere; events unprovided for
were causing sudden changes in the routeing of all the trains.
There was the drumming of planes overhead every few minutes
and the dull crumping sound of bombs ahead of us and to the
rear. Seeking a brief surcease for our aching bones we got down
during one long halt and stretched out on the damp prairie grass.
For a few minutes it was still outside, and then we became aware
of a curious sound. It sounded at first like tiny squeals from some
horde of small animals at a distance. It was the children; it was
the children crying, the hundreds of children inside the train whose

dark bulk stretched away in both directions, a solider line of blackness in the black night. To the northeast, we noticed small flarings of flame which flickered in regular groups. Then as we strained our ears we caught the faint echo of their dull, rumbling roar. It was not bombing; it was artillery fire. For a time this conveyed no meaning to us. Heinzen peered at his watch and counted the seconds between the sight of the flashes and the sound of the guns. He estimated the distance and the approximate location of the guns. There could be no doubt—a battle was going on well inside the French frontier line, somewhere in the direction of Sédan. The Germans had broken through!

It was a strange manner in which to learn that the impossible had happened; to peer at a watch in the night, count the seconds, and thus to know by the silent, uncompromising intelligence of mathematics that the defenses of France, the barricades of western humanity, had been breached. It was so; and we had many hours, standing in the press of stinking bodies to think about it, to understand what it meant.

In the Paris station the homeless covered the platforms. The refugees stumbled out of our train, some falling flat as their feet touched the platform, some handed down from one pair of arms to another. Women of Paris in white starched gowns ran among us with spilling pails of milk and long-handled dippers, pouring it into the outstretched cups, shouting: "Only for the children, please —only for the children!"

I reached our apartment office and got my blackened fingers upon the telephone dial. I talked to the embassy people and to some informed French friends, and it was all confirmed: the French line had broken at Sédan again, and German tanks by the thousand were pouring onto French soil, on the *flank* of the mobile army which had hurried north toward Holland. But nobody had got the news to the press and radio of the outside world; the censors were stopping everything. I wrote out a one-line telegram and sent it, hoping that a little scheme which I had all but forgotten was going to work. The telegraphed sentence was a code sentence to my New York office. On general principles, the use of a private code to send news from a friendly country engaged in crisis is a dubious procedure; this was the first and last time I resorted to the practice. But it was warranted: no military security was involved, and the censorship (as we had known would happen on great stories the world was entitled to learn) was withholding the

news without any justification. Some weeks before, I had composed a series of code sentences for such events as a Rhine crossing
by either side, a German breakthrough of the French line, or
victories by one side or the other in a great battle. Bill White had
taken one copy of the amateur code back to New York with him.
I learned later that when my mysterious telegram of this day
reached the New York news office it lay on the editor's desk for
some hours, meaning nothing to him, until he suddenly remembered the paper White had deposited. They dug it out of the
files, deciphered my sentence, and Elmer Davis went on the air to
say that, "according to a usually well-informed source," the Germans had made a major breach of the French frontier defenses.

The days succeeded one another, the hot, bright, dry days of
the finest spring France had known in years, perfect for the German tanks and planes—"Hitler weather." Each morning at the
Ministry of War the good Colonel Thomas indicated with a schoolteacher's pointer the outlines of the German "pocket" which flowed
ever farther with protozoan movement toward the sea. He never
failed to mention "terrible German losses," and each day newspapers like the London *Daily Mail* carried great headlines: "1,000
German Tanks Lost," "Germans Suffer Immense Casualties." But
the pocket grew, and the people did not know what to think. The
British and thousands of French with them were pressed back
toward Dunkirk; French attempts to cut north across the German
salient failed, and each night the heavy, jeering voice of "Lord
Haw-Haw" mocked us and numbered our days. Weygand was
recalled from Syria with great fanfare; the French people were
being offered a name, a legend. We should have known this was
a last resort, but we continued trying to disbelieve the truth.
Leopold capitulated; and Belgians in Paris laid a black wreath at
the base of King Albert's new statue by the Place de la Concorde.
Geoffrey, Walter, and I circled the Paris outskirts and found a few
soldiers at a crossroads here and there, one gun pointing down
the road at Le Bourget airfield. Perhaps they planned to put in real
defenses as they fell back upon the city; we could not accept what
our eyes plainly told us: that there was no intention to defend the
capital. We talked to everyone we could find who returned from
a sector of the atomized "front." No two stories, no two conclusions
or predictions were alike. Accurate, consistent reporting of developments was an impossibility. I went to see the remarkable poet
and flier, Antoine de Saint-Exupéry, who had just returned from

an observation flight around Arras. He, we thought, would have the bird's-eye view, the overall picture in his mind. He sat at a café table on the Boulevard Saint-Germain, writing in a large ledger. I was taken aback by his appearance. I had expected a face identifiable as that of a poet; his was tough and scarred, and his big eyes were hard and cold. He would say nothing except: "From the air, the war is a frieze. You see the black dots which are the tanks and the trucks and the veil of dust. There is no movement when you see it from 20,000 feet. It is a still life."

One day when we were walking out of the embassy, Walter stopped and looked hard at me. "Now, God damn it," he said with startling vehemence, "let's be honest about this. Are we kidding ourselves? Do *you* honestly think the French can stop them?" Before I had time to think I said: "No." Had I thought I would not have said that; I would have rationalized, as I now realized I had been doing for a long time. But the "no" had always been there. We were all victims of "wishful thinking," true, but of something else too: the effects of our professional compulsions. For what was a journalist's duty? Suppose he was clear in the knowledge that France was going down, that the game was up—had he the right to say this to the world and thus to the French themselves, to join, in effect, the Nazi propagandists, so long as even one chance in a thousand remained, so long as the miracle of military accident might still come about? It was the first time I had been confronted with the basic problem of reconciling the conflict of professional duty and my duty to a universal cause. "The truth is its own justification," I had always been taught and always believed. But was it? Was this always so, at all times? I was unable to decide.

2

Most of us, like most of our French friends, were beset by indecision on many counts; everyone seemed mesmerized by the specter bearing down upon us, and few found it possible to do more than carry out their accustomed habits, including the hour of sunning and drinking on the terraces. One of the weapons of Blitzkrieg is the technique of certain reptiles that fix their victims with a stare before they hit. Lifelong habits of security simply could not generate the energy of imagination required to visualize Paris in ruins or an actual flesh-and-blood German soldier upon these

streets. (Even months later the photographs of German goose-
steppers in the Place de la Concorde seemed unreal and faked to
me—a superimposed piece of montage.) The government was
under the same hypnosis, unable to make decisions, unable to tell
the people what to do, except to *"rester tranquille."*

I made one decision: to send Lois and the babies to the United
States. Reluctantly she agreed, on the babies' account. An American ship might be putting in to Bordeaux to pick up American
refugees—or it might not. The State Department could not seem
to make up its mind. I could not send Lois down there with two
infants a few weeks old and take the chance of their having to travel
back across France again if the ship did not come. The Italian
liner *Rex* was taking bookings, for a sailing from Genoa, and the
embassy people thought Italy would not come into the war for
a while anyway. I paid nineteen thousand francs to the Italian
Line and received an apologetic call from them next day: Mussolini had ordered the *Rex* not to sail. This meant that Italy *was*
coming into the war soon, but I had no choice other than a cabin
on the *Manhattan* due to sail from Genoa about June 1. It took a
special plea to the manager of the United States Line office, beset
and harried man that he was. Lois carried each baby in a basket
into the Gare de Lyon while I checked the berths. I had a bad
scare when, as they began to call the train, I could not find my
family in the crowd. It was merely that so many French papas
and mamans had gathered around to regard my twins that Lois
and her large summer hat had disappeared from sight. Cecil
Brown had made arrangements in Genoa by telephone from Rome,
and Byron Price, the Associated Press executive, who happened
to be on the train, calmed me with assurances that he would keep
his eye on the family. Returning with Lois was Charles Findley's
wife who was going back because she was pregnant.

(I know nothing about prenatal influences, but she produced
twins upon arrival in Omaha. Lois, reaching New York the day I
fled Paris, to her astonishment found news-reel cameras and reporters following her from the cabin to the deck, and from the ship
to the hotel bathroom where she hung up the diapers to dry.
Neither of us had had any conception of American high-pressure
publicity methods or of the homespun curiosity of the American
public; at every airplane stop from New York to Minnesota she
found crowds of complete strangers at the gates, well-meaning,
friendly people who just wanted to gaze. Her indignant mother

promptly put her to bed for a week, barred the doors, and unhooked the telephone. To this day I meet sweet old ladies who want to ask about the voyage of my refugee infants.)

The spell was broken on the fourth of June when the Germans made their first serious bombing raid on the city of Paris. They hit the new Air Ministry building and the Citroën works on the Seine, and odd bombs landed around the Avenue de Versailles. It was noon, and in the ministry the French Minister for Air, many high military and political officers, and foreign diplomats including Ambassador Bullitt were standing about holding cocktail glasses at a buffet luncheon. One bomb came through the roof, pierced each successive floor, and rolled at their feet. The discipline of social poise has its advantages in warfare: nobody so much as dropped his glass, and the bomb did not go off.

Paris knew, now. Paris knew what the northern cities knew: how it is to sit in the corridor or the dank cellar holding tight to the children who cry with fright at the look in their parents' eyes while droning like that of a million bees fills the sky; how it is to feel the old house quiver, to see the plaster peel itself from the wall, the wine glasses roll crazily on the table, and dust fill the room; how it is to walk over powdered glass on the sidewalks, thick as drifted sand, to have the acrid smell of cordite in the nostrils, to see an old woman on her hands and knees at the doorstep, mopping up the blood of her husband with the parlor curtain. The exhausted refugees from the north got up from the curbing and plodded on, out of the city by the southern gates; thousands of Paris cars emerged from their garages and courtyards, with mattresses tied to their tops; and the families of Paris swelled to a river the stream of human particles flowing to the south.

My orders were to move out, if and when the French government moved; our correspondent with the German army, William L. Shirer, would be able to work in Paris under the Nazis. The tenth of June arrived, and I learned that the Paris radio station would be demobilized that night, but they promised to remain open until after my midnight broadcast. By noon dark smoke obscured the sun and crept in streamers along the Champs-Élysées. It came from the army's smoke screen down the Seine, and it hung like a giant shroud over the dying city. I drove up the great boulevard and saw that the cadres of wicker chairs on the café terraces were empty. The waiters had removed their aprons and were shuttering the doors. One last client sat alone at his little round table, finishing a drink while the waiter stood patiently beside him waiting for his glass. Inside their offices and homes people sat by their radios, hoping for advice and counsel from their leaders. They were not told what was to happen to Paris—whether it would be defended or not; they were not told to go or to stay, what to do if they remained, where to take their families if they went. They waited for words that would give them strength and courage and defiance, and they heard only the funereal voice of Premier Reynaud, sealing their doom, informing them that Mussolini had broken his pledges and had that day declared war upon France. I wrote a broadcast on Walter's desk in the New York *Herald Tribune* office, saying that if listeners in America were again to hear a radio voice from Paris "it would be under jurisdiction other than the French." I was trying to make it clear that the capital was abandoned, that the government was leaving, and that the Germans were on the verge of entry. I was afraid of the censors, so I wrote obliquely, a good deal in the past tense, about what Paris had been, what it had stood for in the minds of millions of all races and peoples. News reporting by broadcast has its severe limitations, but sometimes it can convey meaning merely by tone and inflection in a way the printed word cannot. I do not know what the press correspondents succeeded in getting out that day —nearly all wireless and cable facilities were closing down—but many people were to tell me later that they learned for the first time from my sad talk that Paris was finished.

I had been wrong about the censors. Pierre Comert himself looked at my script, spreading it out upon a packing box in the empty information offices while the lovely, saddened Mme. de Vogué looked on. Comert had no heart to delete anything. At nightfall I went back to the apartment and sent the tearful Bulgarian maidservant away, promising to convey her love to "Madame" when next I saw her. The concierge and her daughter sat on the floor of their kitchen, surrounded by suitcases and boxes. They had tried to take the subway to the Gare Montparnasse and had discovered that the Metro was no longer running. They had walked all the way, carrying their heavy bags; then found that no trains were running, and so had struggled home again. I could see that both had been weeping. I offered to take one of them in the car to Tours where they had friends; but they decided to stay behind and take their chances.

Toward midnight, Edmond Taylor (he had replaced Grandin

as my associate) and I got to the broadcast station and were involved at once in a maddening controversy. The studio officials had received no notification, they said, that I was to have the microphone. I showed them the certified script and tried to impress upon them the importance of the occasion. "Ah, but it is not regular. See, the proper form has not been filled out on our schedule." A girl employee sat by the microphone, playing her regular program of recorded dance music, designed to help the jaded pass their boring hours. All France was tuned to Paris Radio, all the shortwave listeners in many anxious lands. They heard the nasal voice of a moaning crooner who wailed of unrequited love. Indignantly, the girl refused to give up the studio to my use. A series of telephone calls traced the station manager to his Right Bank apartment, where, he informed me brusquely, he was having dinner with his fiancée. Eventually he came to the station, profoundly annoyed, and the broadcast went through on time. Then the station staff drifted out to their loaded cars and trucks. This was the end; the voices of free men, speaking of the fight for freedom in their many tongues, were to be heard no more from the traditional capital of liberty.

We drove the little Citroën past the railway stations where the trains lead to the south, and found the gaunt buildings banked with masses of people, quietly waiting for cars to carry them—where? They did not know where they were going, or exactly what they were fleeing; but the ganglia of their nerves, the blood cells of their brains, demanded that the body take action, and flight was the only action possible for them now. We nosed into the silent, ghostly caravan on the Avenue de Versailles and inched forward at torturously slow pace, our front bumper tucked under the van of an army ambulance, our rear one under the darkened headlights of a truck. Occasionally an auto lamp flickered briefly far ahead or far behind; the line of the homeless stretched for many miles, but we never saw its beginning or its end. Clouds gathered overhead to obscure the stars; it grew very dark, and for long hours it was only by their coughing and the scraping of their boots on the stones that we were aware of the pilgrims who walked beside us. Paris lay inert, her breathing scarcely audible, her limbs relaxed, and the blood flowed remorselessly from her manifold veins. Paris was dying, like a beautiful woman in coma, not knowing nor asking why. The night wore on; a single plane sounded overhead, and then we heard a quick murmuring on the roadside, the sound of hurrying feet as the walkers went into the ditches. No one blessed with an automobile would leave his precious vehicle for any cause now. Someone in a car scratched a match, and an old village woman screamed and hysterically beat at the car with a stick. It grew faintly light, and the houses of the villages appeared beside us. They were tightly shuttered, their curtains drawn. Sometimes the hostile, frightened face of a villager appeared in a window, watching the stream of lava flowing past, the unstoppable river which came from the unimaginable eruption somewhere to the north and, defying all natural laws, crept up hill as well as down, made sharp turnings in the streets as though directed by some living instinct or intelligence.

I fell asleep at the wheel and awoke two hours later to find my face pressed against the glass on the other side and Taylor driving the car. I had no memory of shifting places. The unlike spires of Chartres Cathedral were going down below the rise behind us, and now in the clear morning the spectacle before us took the breath away. A broad, black hand lay upon France, the massed palm covering the plateau, and a hundred twisting claws stretched toward the south, their points invisible, sunk below the surface of the green earth. Beside our road, on the dewy and sweet-smelling grass were many cars, casualties of the night, lying obscenely on their backs, their wheels still turning in the reactive motions of after-death. Horses had been dragged to the edge of the road, their heads hanging limply in the ditches, little pools of blood drying up to their noses. Whole families slept in the ditches where they had fallen, sprawled in careless heaps like bundles of rags tied with strings. In each little town those on foot swarmed into the bakeries and dairies seeking sustenance for the aged and the children. The show windows of these establishments were empty; some had the glass broken, and from within came the angry sounds of hysterical argument, shrill pleas, and shouted rebukes. And part of each little town was drawn into the magnet of the caravan as the contagion spread, as the horde of locusts moved through, stripping each place of all that could be eaten.

3

We had seen the physical establishment of a great nation breaking apart, and now, when we came to the fair city of Tours on the Loire where the refugee government had paused, we had the first news of the moral breakup. The rapid disease had spread to the brain. The government had caught the fever and could not think nor act. And we soon learned that it was the men of action themselves, the military leaders, not the despised politicians, who had lost their heads completely and desired to quit. Rumors spread everywhere: reports that the Russians had declared war, that the United States had declared war, that Paris was being victoriously defended—spread, in part, by Nazi agents who counted upon the demoralizing letdown when the truth should be known. In the Hotel Univers, the bearded old Senators sat three hours at lunch, as they had always done, chatting with their mistresses while their country was perishing. It was the time for defiance, for rally now, for embattled brotherhood, and yet the old tight habits prevailed. When a filthy, exhausted family from the tenements of Paris stretched out upon the velour-covered sofas in the hotel lobby, removing the shoes from their stinking, bleeding feet, the hotel manager ran about wringing his hands in despair, not for the sufferings of his fellow countrymen, but for the injury to the name of his bourgeois establishment. The American and British journalists drank in the bar and compared their notes. A small, fat Jewish journalist of Paris burst suddenly into tears, bit his knuckles, then beat upon the bar until his fingers bled, moaning: "France is finished! France is finished!"—which meant "I am finished."

A short wave transmitter in central France was still manned and functioning, connected by a line with Tours, where a makeshift studio had been set up in a dismantled perfume factory next to the railway yards. The problem was to cable advance word to New York that I would be broadcasting at such-and-such an hour. With the other broadcasters I stood in line at the cable office and filled out the form. Ah, no, it could not be accepted. We were foreigners, therefore the cable must be visaed by the commissariat of police. It was the regulation. So we stood in line at the commissariat while an aged bureaucrat with walrus mustaches went through his accustomed motions and with painful slowness duly inscribed the pertinent facts with green ink in a vast, soiled ledger, which would of course be stacked one day in the corner along with the other soiled and meaningless ledgers, destined for no other function than collecting dust. The French bureaucracy, which was helping to strangle the country, never relaxed its grip for an instant. I realized the cable would never reach New York. A remarkably efficient young American named Louis Huot had moved his portable Press Wireless machines down from Paris and was now handling all written matter describing the death of France for the outside world. I saw his teletype operators collapse, fainting, over their machines. Huot took my message and threw it down on top of the pile of press cables in front of an operator whose fingers clicked automatically on, and it was in New York in a matter of seconds. That is why my company was able to put broadcasts from Tours on its network.

Paul Reynaud was to speak to the country and the world by radio in the night. I stood in a corner of the "studio" and watched. The time for his speech had been previously announced over the air, and all France was waiting. The studio timepiece was a decrepit kitchen alarm clock, which an operator now shook to see if it was running. They had recorded his speech, and now, as they were carrying the historic wax document to the turntable, a careless operator dropped it. He caught it with one hand just before it hit the floor and flipped it nonchalantly into place. There was the sound of scratching and then the doleful Reynaud voice. He was calling upon the President of the United States to send airplanes, clouds of airplanes, which would fill the skies and blot out the sun from the German faces. (Careless news stories from America had frequently announced that Henry Ford and others could turn out a thousand planes a day—if and when. The French, like all Europeans except the German Fascists, still thought of America as the land of miracles, where one simply turned a screw and the miraculous was accomplished.) The government uprooted itself and carried its violent arguments to Bordeaux. With Taylor and his slim, cool Swiss wife, I followed, leaving Tours very early in the morning, an hour before German bombs smashed into the center of the city.

If Tours had been confusion, Bordeaux was confusion confounded. One night I slept in the back seat of the car, another night in an old woman's attic. I do not remember how we found food; we must have had a few meals, at least, during those four or five days which one lived as though in a waking dream. I do remember Edmond sitting on a fender, with the typewriter propped up on the hood of the car, typing a broadcast script in the middle of the crowded city square. I slept at least one night in my clothes in the top room of a tall, sagging hotel, stretched out under the bed on which the Taylors slept. There was an alert that night and hys-

terical voices in the hallway, the sound of panicky persons bumping
and falling down the precipitous stairway in the darkness.

One could still broadcast. The studio was far out on the edge of
the city, but our extra *bidons* of gasoline, carried from Paris, were
not yet depleted. The Germans were getting closer to the transmitter in the center of France, and every few hours the transmitter
crew 'phoned in to Bordeaux to report the enemy's position and
to ask how long they should remain on duty. They were told to
remain at their post until the Germans walked in; and they did not
desert. A combination of fortuitous circumstances now meshed
in a fashion which, combined with abnormally strenuous leg work,
permitted Taylor and me to perform a series of broadcasts which
in the American world of radio remain something of a minor
legend. It has been my general experience as a journalist that
eighty percent of so-called "scoops" result from pure chance; the
other twenty percent are the result of correct thinking (or guessing), leg work, and intimate knowledge of communication facilities. Since radio reporters, technical amateurs though all of us be,
are obliged to know the communication situation, we frequently
find ourselves at an advantage over our press competitors in abnormal times. The latter are accustomed to the easy habit of writing
out a telegram and handing it to someone, never having to worry
about what happens from then on. The press reporters knew
nothing about the shortwave transmitter, yet they had as much
right to use it as I did. I went to the government radio officials
and asked them to turn over the microphone to me at any hour of
the day or night when I should appear, no matter what other program was in progress, and to beam the transmitter toward the
Western Hemisphere. This time I found myself dealing with officials of imagination, and they agreed at once.

The crowd of press reporters, representing the great agencies
and newspapers all over Britain and the neutral world, were entirely dependent upon Press Wireless, all the regular French
overseas cable facilities having broken down in the confusion. The
Press Wireless transmitter was an hour's drive outside Bordeaux.
The copy could not be telephoned and had to be carried there in
a courier car which departed from our headquarters in the labor
exchange building every two hours. Late one night I sat on the
concrete floor of the labor exchange, in the midst of the reporters,
some of whom slept and others typed. I was talking with Meyer

Handler, an able representative of United Press. We had been working together in a kind of friendly partnership since leaving Paris. One of his French "tipsters" ran in, sobbing from want of breath. He was the first man back from the prefecture building, where the carefully guarded cabinet, we knew, was in crucial session. He whispered hoarsely in our ears: "Reynaud has resigned. Pétain has become president of the Council. Here is the list of new cabinet members." We looked at the scribbled list of names—Weygand, Darlan, and Colson among the military, and civilians we knew to be partisans of Pierre Laval. There was no doubt: this meant capitulation. Somebody else burst in, and the news began to spread, reporters leaping to their feet and grabbing for their typewriters. But the Press Wireless courier had left not five minutes before, and not for an hour or so at the earliest would they be able to send a word of this, the most momentous story in the world. Handler had the news and he had received it first.

I grabbed him by the arm, dragged him out of the reportorial maelstrom, and told him the secret of the shortwave transmitter. We careened through the streets, nearly murdering sleepwalking refugees who did not yet know what we knew—that everything, the fighting, their own physical torture of flight had been without meaning. As we rushed up the steps toward the studio, my principal competitor, an English-speaking Frenchman who worked for another American company, emerged from the studio and regarded me with a self-satisfied smile. He had got word from Havas, and had already spoken. Since it was I who had made all the arrangements with the radio officials from which he benefited, I was savagely angry and upset. I questioned him briefly, and he said: "Why, I told America, of course, that this is a war cabinet, to carry on the fight. Look at all the generals and admirals." I must confess, to my eternal shame, that I was overjoyed that he had so misinformed the public. We would still be the first to announce to the world that the great French Republic had quit and intended to sue for armistice. I spoke without script, emphasizing my words, repeating: "Regardless of what you may have heard, this is *not* a cabinet designed to carry on the war." Handler went on, calling the United Press listening post in New York, and spelled out all the names of the cabinet members, which must have sounded strange to millions of listeners as it came out of their parlor radios. A white-faced radio engineer caught my arm as we were leaving. "Do you mean it? Is it really capitulation?" The radio staff were stunned; all work ceased and they gathered in the corridor, staring at us and at one another, unable to speak their thoughts.

Then I became frightened. In my excitement, I had forgotten about the official censors, who still functioned by candlelight in a building on the main square. We could be jailed for this; anything could happen to us. I looked at the list of cabinet posts again and noticed that it did not contain a Ministry of Information; I could claim, if arrested, that the old ministry under which the censors functioned had no legal existence. So Taylor and I ignored the censorship, the studio officials never raised the question, and we broadcast thenceforth day and night, for long stretches every hour on the hour.

At noon on the following day, the old Marshal of France, dressed in a carefully belted raincoat, mounted the steps to the radio studio with portentous dignity and informed Frenchmen everywhere, including those still fighting, still willing to die, that "*il faut cesser la guerre*," telling them solemnly that he had "made France the gift of his person." He seemed to regard it as a fair bargain for the nation: defeat, shame, and torture to be made palatable by this precious "gift"—a vain, doddering old man. He baldly informed the German army and all the French soldiers still resisting that the fight was over, even before he had made the slightest attempt to see what armistice terms Hitler might give. (The afternoon Bordeaux papers, under orders, changed his phrase to read: "It is necessary to *attempt* to end the war.") Even the elements seemed to protest. When Pétain finished speaking, the sky exploded in a violent thunderstorm, sheets of water lashed the windows, and sparks crackled out of the radio control panels.

The paroxysm of elemental rage subsided as quickly as it had begun, and I drove down to the center of the washed and sunny capital of vestigial France. I should have been thinking pertinent, human thoughts about the fate of my French friends, or, at the least, about the effect on the outcome of the war. But I was thinking in terms of history as if this were something I was reading in some future, objective volume. At long last the balance of military power in Europe had been radically shifted. It was comparable to what? Perhaps to the defeat of the Spanish Armada which established British sea power for centuries to come.

I stopped in the square and realized that something had happened to the city. It was uncannily quiet; its life seemed to have come to an abrupt halt. The clamor of the dense traffic was stilled, and the hubbub of talk from the jammed sidewalks and outdoor cafés had died away. They had heard the high priest, intoning the confessional of France and pleading the shameful supplication. Those who were walking stood still; those who were talking fell silent; those who were drinking regarded the glasses on the table. I met a party of French friends, good human beings, who wore with ease the dignity of intelligence and pride. "Sascha" de Manziarly, *grand blessé* of the last war, a man of wit and sparkling charm; Mme. de Vogué, who had beauty and sympathy. Sascha was tapping his cane absently and looking across the street at nothing. Mme. de Vogué's eyes caught mine for an instant and looked away. Nobody said anything; there was nothing to say. Our worlds had parted, and this side of the resurrection they could never come together again. It was the same thing once more: Karli in the concentration camp, the Belgian woman in the Cambrai train. Their integrity had been mortified and stripped bare, and I, the neutral, was again somehow dishonored.

An American journalist, a fat, Buddhalike man noted for his erudition, appeared before us, chubby fingers linked together over his round stomach. In his solemn, nasal tones, he inquired: "Ah, um, what is the reaction of the mass of people to this development? Has anyone attempted to assay public opinion?" The beautiful woman flinched slightly. It was unbearable: I turned away and walked across the square.

The quiet was broken by a French bomber plane, a single plane that dived toward the square, pulled up and dived again, then roared in circles over the rooftops. A strange act. What did it mean? The private protest of one maddened, suffering man who wished to fight? Somebody said: "It is Saint Exupéry." I never found out.

4

Broadcasting from France was finished for me. The Germans, I knew, were only a few miles from the transmitter and would have it within a few hours; and, in any case, I had no heart to carry on reporting from the kind of France this would be. I could join the caravan of neutrals already making for the Spanish border and Lisbon and listen to their endless postmortems and complaints about personal losses, on the way to America; or I could go to England. We knew, somehow, without inquiring, that England would continue to fight. I thought I had reasoned myself away from all youthful feelings of kinship with England, but now England seemed intimate, understandable, and terribly important.

The boats for England, most of them, had already left from the estuary, and now the British journalists were driving out of the city to catch the last one available. Geoffrey and George Millar leaned out of their car to say goodbye. With them, too, I sensed a subtle change in relationship. They seemed almost happy; they were British, and their course was clear. They were sticking together now; all the British were together. I wandered alone toward the Hotel Splendide, caught sight of a caniche that looked familiar, and following the long leash recognized an American couple, Dan and Claire Slawson, whom I had known at a ski resort in Savoy. They wished to go to New York and wanted help, which I could not provide. I wished to go to London, and they thought they had the answer to that. With female directness, Claire had simply hunted through the waterfront bars until she found a ship captain about to sail for the States. But he had just received orders to take his ship to Liverpool instead, and they had no wish to go to England. We searched the waterfront again, and found Captain Jorgenson, a stocky young Norwegian-American, downing a glass of beer. His brief case stood on the table, bearing the name *Ville de Liége*. Claire was prepared to employ her feminine wiles on my behalf, but they were not required. He simply looked me over and said: "American? All right. Meet me down the river at midnight tonight at this place." He scribbled it out on a piece of paper. "I don't care whether you've got passports or visas or any of that red-tape nonsense."

At midnight, the Taylors and I sat in our car beside a little shack, fifty miles down the Garonne, toward the sea. Twelve-thirty came, and Jorgenson had not arrived. An air-raid siren began to wail somewhere; we heard distant planes and then saw the orange flashes in the direction of Bordeaux. It began to pour. Through the blurred windshield we saw headlights of a car, and in a moment Jorgenson was there, to tell us he could not sail tonight, that we should get out to the ship somehow in the morning. "It looks like I've got to pick up a lot of refugees. The Belgians, anyway. This ship is under Belgian registry. But you people are first. I'll see you get whatever quarters are available."

The *Ville de Liége* rode high at anchor in the middle of the immense river; she was a big ship of sixteen thousand tons. The

grizzled old Frenchman who operated the motorboat said he was
sorry, but it was against the law to take a woman out. Five hundred francs altered the law, so far as he was concerned. They
pulled up our few bags by ropes and we sprawled over the rail, I
somewhat discommoded by my bulging pockets, which contained
around fifty thousand francs in notes, the remainder of Columbia
Broadcasting's French bank account. The ship was really the old
American Farmer, which had carried her share of Europe-
bound American students, tourists, and professors on sabbatical.
Her American owners were still managing the ship, but the flag we
flew was Belgian. (We also possessed Panamanian and other neutral insignia to hoist as the emergency might require.) The deck
cabins had all been knocked down before she had left New York,
to carry guns, airplane motors, ammunition, and five hundred
horses to the French army. The horses had been unloaded, and
their leavings were drying on the boards of the makeshift shelters,
giving the ship the faintly pleasant smell of a disused barn. The
war materials Jorgenson had refused to unload when he heard
what had happened in Bordeaux; those things we would take to
the British, who could put them to use. Jorgenson was no disinterested mercantile bureaucrat. He had a wife still in Oslo, under
the Germans.

Now, along both far banks of the estuary we saw a thick black
line on the sands, which extended for miles toward the sea. It was
composed of living human beings, thousands upon thousands of
them—Poles, Czechs, Austrians for the most part, men and women
who had reached the end, the place where French sanctuary came
to a stop. They were people who could not live under Nazi occupation. They were the hunted, who would be as wise to walk into
the water, leading their children by the hand until they perished,
as wait until the Germans found them. The Germans were almost
in to Bordeaux.

The crew was composed of Scandinavians, Armenians, Englishmen, Belgians, Italians, a Lascar or two, and even a couple of
native-born Americans who carried faked passports of other countries, which permitted them, like the ship itself, to evade the American neutrality laws and sail into belligerent waters. They came
up from the bowels of the ship and gathered at the rail to watch.
Small black objects were floating out from the shoreline. They
came on, grew in size, and were distinguishable as rafts and boats
loaded to the waterline with men, women, and children. The first

raft 'jumped along the ship's side and Jorgenson called down, asking their nationality. "Belgian!" they screamed. "We are Belgian!" Men began to hoist themselves up the rope ladder, some carrying small children who clung to their necks. They fell on deck and lay spent. One husky crew member suddenly broke from his silent group, slid down, and came up again with an old, crumpled woman in black, whom he had secured on his shoulders with a piece of rope.

I heard violent talk from the top deck. Jorgenson was standing there, feet planted apart, a pink flush in his face, looking down at a man before him. The man was enormous, with a hairy chest and great hairy hands. He was on his knees, alternately clasping his hands in supplication and beating them in anguish upon the deck plates. Tears were dripping from his chin, and he pleaded and wailed in Polish, French, and German. The German Jorgenson could understand. He shouted: *"Nein! Nein!"*—caught my glance and swore. The man was a Pole, and Jorgenson had said he could take only the Belgians. It was a shameful and repulsive scene; but the man was saying no more than the truth when he cried that his life and the life of his compatriots were at stake. Eventually he collapsed and stretched out sobbing into his hands. There was nothing to say; it was up to Jorgenson. He could be executioner or savior. Jorgenson stared at me, his Adam's apple working up and down. Then he nudged the body with his toe and said: "All right. They can come on. Then you go to the galley and don't let me see your face again."

The Poles came on; they all came on, until we had three hundred or more on board a ship equipped with very little food and fresh water, with lifeboats that would handle no more than a third their number. A young Pole doffed his hat and asked me if I spoke French. "My general," he said. "He is sick; he was wounded. Could he be shown to his quarters?" He indicated a tall, spare, very pale man of distinguished features who was dressed in ill-fitting civilian clothes and was sitting apart from the crowd on one of the hatches. "His quarters" did not exist, but Jorgenson had the general taken to the ship's hospital, one whitewashed room with a narrow cot. The general's aide was not the only man aboard who could not comprehend that the comfortable routine of their private lives was now over, that this was impromptu, catch-as-catch-can, an unplanned, desperate attempt to save their lives at the risk of all our lives. The poor—yes, *they* understood at once. They immediately set about making themselves comfortable on a coat, a single blanket, a bundle of old clothes in a corner. They never complained; few did, one must grant, but those who did were always those who had been rich or important, or both. Several men attached to the Polish exile government were on board with their wives. While I was standing with Jorgenson, one of these men approached to protest in French that there appeared to be no arrangement for meals or service. Jorgenson said: "Tell him we are very low on food. We will try to share it out equally, but the children and the crew come first. I have got to get this ship to England." The gentleman seemed to take offense at this. I asked him to wait and got from my cabin a gunny sack partly filled with canned foods I had brought from Paris. He spread out the tins and asked: "Is that *all*?" It is just as well that he could not understand what Jorgenson then expressed in English. But some of them were wonderful. There was a Polish couple with beautiful twin boys who slept each night on deck next to the warm ventilator, their arms clasped about one another for the greater comfort of their bodies and their hearts. Each morning they were covered with soot. When, from embarrassment more than compassion, I offered them my little cabin, they politely declined.

Most of the refugees went aft, scrubbed the flimsy wooden stables as well as they could, hung blankets for privacy, and spent their days there in endless conversation. There were several dozen French, Czech, and Polish soldiers with their rifles. The Czechs and Poles were bitter toward each other; both were bitter toward the French, and the French were bitter toward the world. It was a solemn cargo on an anxious voyage, and none among them found it pleasurable, unless it was the rubicund wife of a minor Czech diplomat and the greasy-haired guitar player with whom she spent the nights rolled in a blanket. The soldiers in khaki we had to try to keep on the lower deck. Once they were seen by a German submarine, the U-boat was bound to shoot first and ask questions later.

The first night, before we got out of the estuary, it was the planes. Shipping choked the river, and it seemed that bombs could hardly miss. But they did miss, and no doubt the cascading streamers of antiaircraft fire from the British cruiser next to us helped them to miss. As we neared the sea, wreckage began to float by on the tide: an overturned lifeboat, an oar, a couple of wooden chairs. The radio reported six ships sunk just outside the estuary and a large pack of U-boats in the neighborhood. The refugees never knew what we knew—that each time the radio operator came out of his cabin and hurried in to the captain with a slip of paper, it meant another ship had been attacked near by. One of the first was our sister ship, the *Ville de Namur*, I believe. We could not make for her and try to help; our own position was far too precarious. We had only one chance: to strike straight out for deep water and make a great circle, coming round to the British Isles from the north.

I sat in Jorgenson's cabin with him and the awkward daughters of two long-bearded Amsterdam diamond merchants who, everybody was aware, kept their jewels wrapped in rags under their heads at night. Somebody flipped the radio on, and a calm, collected, and very familiar voice was speaking very slowly and clearly. It was Bill Shirer, speaking from the forest at Compiègne. The high priest of abnegation had sent his elderly votaries to accept the new Cross of the anti-Christ from which there was no resurrection.

5

I found that I was lying hours every day in my bunk, scarcely possessing the energy to get up for meals, overcome with exhaustion of the body and lassitude of the spirit, feeling that I was part of the defeat. Everything was cut adrift; I no longer had a home, my family was scattered, all my books and possessions were gone, and I did not even know whether I had a job. I could not be sure that my people in New York had received a single one of the many broadcasts Taylor and I had delivered from Tours and Bordeaux; there had been no way to get confirmation. I had left France abruptly, on my own initiative, without orders. Perhaps it would be considered desertion, and, as England drew near, I felt disturbed at the prospect of confronting Murrow, who had put his trust in me.

There was something else: I knew, if I were honest with myself, that I was physically afraid of the violence of war. To be sure, others were, too, but I had hoped I would be different, that under bombing and shelling I would be able to remain poised, at least on the surface. I didn't think I had ever betrayed panic, but I had certainly betrayed fear. It was clear that for journalists this war was a different proposition from anything that had gone before I searched my memory of the history of war corresponding, beginning with the London *Times* man in the American Civil War and the Crimean War. I couldn't remember any of them being killed or huddling in ditches under sustained fire; somehow I had had the idea that war correspondents were a privileged, unhittable species. Well, this war was different; no house, no field, no function could guarantee personal safety. And God! the terrifying violence of bombs near by, how they stunned the mind, ripped the nerves, and turned one's limbs to water! I knew that I was going back into it, that I would continue going into it until it was over, for nothing else now seemed important; but I knew also that it would represent for me an internal struggle, a crisis of the will every time I did it. I could frequently hear the radio operator scraping back his chair on the other side of my cabin wall, hear his quick footsteps going toward the captain's quarters. Each time it happened, my stomach reacted. I wanted terribly much not to die; and yet in calmer moments I realized that on the rational, philosophical plane I was less afraid of death than I had been when I was younger, when death appeared only in the imagination. It was, I think, because I was just beginning to understand that there are forms of life that are worse than death, that there *are* causes in whose behalf it is worth while to die, almost a privilege to die. And for me, the idea seemed a little easier to confront because of the children. I suppose most men feel that way when their first children are born—that death is not the complete end for them.

I could hear some of the refugees outside the cabin, arguing in some incomprehensible tongue. Ever since Paris I had been witnessing a spectacle of mass human suffering such as I had never imagined, but the truth was, I now realized, that except for a single, special case here and there I had felt no conscious compassion toward them. I, who had stopped hunting years ago because I hated to injure an animal, had looked on these people coldly, and at moments—such as the moment when they invaded this ship—with downright hostility. I knew that almost everybody else, the village people, the shopkeepers, the hotel keepers—nearly everybody—had been the same way. Was it, then, that the instinct of self-preservation was so much stronger than that of pity, that only when they have security and comfort themselves can men feel sympathy for the insecurity and pain of other men? Suffering *en masse* was no longer suffering; it was only a phenomenon that one observed as he observes the working of the tide or the erosion of the soil.

On the floor by my bunk lay a pair of shoes wrapped in a late copy of *Le Figaro,* published in Bordeaux. I could read it from my pillow. A line caught my attention: "France was like one of those majestic old mansions which look so strong and imposing from the outside, but which are in reality riddled with termites." What were the termites? Were they individual men, a few weak politicians, a few stupid generals, a few traitors and defeatists? That was what they were saying when I left Bordeaux. They were finding the answer in certain evil men. There were such termites; there could be no doubt of it. But suppose there had been no traitors on the extreme political Right; suppose the Communist party had not opposed the war and divided the working class after the Russian-German treaty; suppose the French generals had done all the right things instead of all the wrong things. The battle would have been prolonged, but I could not believe that the outcome would have been much different. There just happened to be twice as many Germans as Frenchmen, and Germany was totally organized for war, every man, every wheel directed to war in a way that had no equal in modern times. France could not have survived in the First World War without massive British, Russian, Italian, and, in the end, American aid. This time a vast Russian army was not there to draw off the Germans; this time British aid was a minor item, Italy was an enemy, and America was totally absent. The only difference now was that the instruments of war moved with greater speed, and so the inevitable had come about more quickly. We knew that the strategy, first of static defense, then of rushing northward, had been abysmally stupid— we knew it now. We knew the French had hundreds of tanks and planes that had never gone into battle, because we had seen them during the flight to the south. We knew all about the Bolshevik bogies of Pétain, Weygand, and the others which made them prefer defeat at the hand of what, in their ignorance, they believed to be enemy soldiers who would give their country an honorable, soldierly peace. We knew they had not the faintest understanding of Fascism.

Already the radio voices were saying that France was "decadent." I thought of all my intelligent, devoted French friends in Paris, the heroic patience and endurance of the men in the

freezing trenches, the rugged capacities of the workmen and
farmers, people who worked terribly hard. It was an error, an
insult, to dismiss this whole nation as decadent. But it was true—
to whatever extent this contributed to defeat—that there were
many gaping lacunae in the moral armament of France. There was
a lack of trust by the people in their leadership, and among the
leaders a lack of faith in themselves to a disastrous degree. It was
not, regardless of what the Fascists said, an excess of democracy
that government was conducted on the front pages of the Paris
press; it was an excess of inefficiency in the machine, which democracy, like all systems, must have. Large groups of Frenchmen
hated other large groups. The French army staff had degenerated
again into the miasma of political hatreds that had ruined it in
the Dreyfus era and from which it had been purged only just in
time for the First World War. All men were troubled and unsatisfied with life. They repudiated the old ways, or they feared the
new and unfamiliar ways. The economic class structure of bourgeois society had made men more distant strangers to one another
than ever before; it was as if they inhabited different countries.
The French suffered from what all the world suffered from: the
pangs of fundamental change, the labor pains of a new order of
life, a transition potentially as fundamental and drastic as that
of the French Revolution period. Those who clung blindly to the
old order feared the defeat of that order more than the nation's
defeat by an exterior enemy. Those who welcomed the coming
order had done better in the crisis. They, at least, had understood
that defeat by Fascist arms would mean that all would be set
back; but they had been led to the fight by men who offered them
not the slightest guarantee that, if victorious, they would also
welcome the future. The Communists were a special case. They
had been abysmally wrong, not because they failed to understand
Fascism, but because in their blind devotion to the Soviet Union,
they tried to believe that despite defeat it would all somehow
work itself out through Russia.

The *Ville de Liége* plowed due west, halfway to the United
States, then swung to the north and touched at Belfast before
crossing the Irish Channel in the cold northern night. In fear, the
Czechs, Poles, and French aboard had not been on speaking
terms; in safety, the ice was broken, and the last night at sea they
gathered in the ship's dining-room, even the general honoring

them with his presence, and applauded warmly the Polish and Czech peasant songs and songs of their fighting men. They forgot about the scanty food they had had, and the stench of the waterless lavatories, and they anointed with beaming glances the harassed little Belgian steward who had found means and strength in his body to feed them. (Devoted, honest little man—he was to die months later in the freezing North Atlantic when, with some of the others, he mistook an American destroyer in the winter fog for a German submarine and put out in an open boat. Soon thereafter, the *Ville de Liége* went down after carrying arms to Britain, but Jorgenson was not then aboard.) The refugees were taken off at Liverpool in a large tender, and before they pulled away they raised a mighty cheer for the captain.

It was a little more complicated for the Taylors and me. Jorgenson had put us on the crew list as apprentice seamen—even Mrs. Taylor. The British immigration inspector fixed us with a stern glance and asked the embarrassed captain: "Are these people ready to swear that they intend to follow a seafaring life?" Jorgenson said: "Well—ah, you know—they got to begin some time." The inspector snapped his brief case shut and said with finality: "I doubt very much if that is their intention." After a day's delay they let us on shore, and from the consulate I got Murrow in London by telephone. I announced my presence in England and with some anxiety awaited his reaction. "This is the best news I've had for a long time," he said with a chuckle. "We've all been in a sweat about you people. You know, you and Taylor have pulled off one of the greatest broadcasting feats there ever was. Come on to London—there's work to be done here." He "fixed" the Home Office in London, the Home Office fixed the immigration inspector, and as honest refugees we walked off the boat and into the railway station. In the train, we talked about England and tried to gear our minds to the new situation. We tried to understand what we had seen in the Liverpool docks: a liner about to leave, packed to the rails with British soldiers in tropical uniform. They were *leaving* England at the supreme moment of England's danger. What was going on? (It was only later that we learned that Churchill had taken one of the most courageous, reckless, and fruitful decisions of the war—the decision to reinforce the Middle East.)

The conductor reached in and pulled our shades. "Air raids, ye know." We rolled toward London on the first of July, 1940.

Chapter VII

WAR HAS MANY FACES; or, rather, in war men and nations wear many faces. Now, in this English summer which no man there will ever forget, although he cannot recall to what dimensions the cultured rose attained or the fullness of the streams, a new face appeared to the world. There was anger in it, yes, and this the world had seen; there was defiance, which was not unfamiliar—but there the resemblance ceased. The anger bore no ferocity nor the defiance bravado, and, if the eyes were slightly darkened, it was by reason of pain and not because of fear. The world had never seen pain in this face before, and the sight was more than a little disturbing.

London was again familiar when I returned there in the midst of a crisis bearing the imprint of finality which one could accept for any place in the world except this one. If I had found strangeness in intimacy three years before, there were mysteries now which no rational analysis could possibly align in logic. Being civilized people like the French, they shared with the French a basic disbelief in the old kind of victory, the victory of conquest, and with the French believed only in preservation. No people in history had conquered more, and yet they had permitted history to close over their conquests until these had no meaning to the Englishman except as a fixed and accepted part of his mental landscape. Perhaps it was because he had arrived at this point that a defeat charmed and excited him more than a victory, and he became so fascinated with the defeat of Dunkirk that, finding no other name for so wondrous a spectacle, he dubbed it "victory." (Perhaps *that* was the victory: that he called it victory.) In all rationality, the English should have been appalled by the loss of France, and yet only a few with cosmopolitan imaginations understood what a loss it had been. Churchill understood, but his romantic gesture of offering common citizenship to the failing French rather annoyed the mass of his countrymen. Certainly it surprised them. If you spoke to the man in the pub about the defeat of France, he would say, yes, wasn't it too bad—for the French. He didn't feel that it concerned him very much because the British are twice as egocentric in their bones and marrow as the American Middle West has ever been, and to them the neighboring French were merely part of that vague outside world of "foreigners" who are not really very important to the real world—that is, the British Isles.

Since the Londoner had never thought of London as anything but the world's center, it did not surprise him that the world's attention was now fixed upon London, when upon occasion he observed that this was so. British leaders with imagination and the rest of the world were overwhelmed by the stark drama of a situation in which Britain stood alone. The average Londoner, however, though he realized he was engaged in drama, found nothing particularly novel about the alignment of forces; he was hardly conscious that it had ever been anything but himself against the Boche. Still, he did not think of himself as a hero—not at the beginning of that summer's trial by fire. However self-contained and self-satisfied, he was not self-conscious, and he had to be taught, by Churchill's stirring speeches, by the turgid leaders in his daily paper, by the somewhat hysterical adulation showered upon him from the other side of the Atlantic, frequently in broadcasts from such declamatory persons as Miss Dorothy Thompson. He had to be told that he was indeed a hero, and he found the role to his liking; but it is doubtful if he would have behaved less well without the knowledge.

It is for history to decide what the outcome of the war would have been if Britain had succumbed. Certainly most of us felt at that time that the war would be irretrievably lost, although men in Moscow may have had other ideas on the subject. Today most British people are firmly convinced they saved the world by their summer stand against the bombs; all Russians are convinced that *they* saved the world at Moscow and Stalingrad; nearly all Americans are convinced that *they* saved the world by entering the war at Pearl Harbor. However the facts may balance the scales, historians are likely to be ignorant of the moods and the spirit of the moment with which they deal, and men are motivated by their spirits. It was Pitt, in another crisis, who said: "England will save herself by her exertions and Europe by her example." But in this

modern war her exertions could guard England for a time only;
her ultimate salvation lay in the salvation of Europe, and so, in
a very real measure, it was by her own example that she saved
herself. For therein lay the difference between the contribution
of Britain then and the contributions of Russia and of America
later on—she gave the world its first example; she showed the world
a face it had not seen before in this war. During those bright days
and livid nights of 1940 the spirit of the British called up from
despair the spirit of other men, and, wearing the borrowed armor
of Britain's example, men assembled in this bright, beleaguered
citadel of courage from France, from Czechoslovakia, from Poland,
from Belgium, Holland, and Norway, and backed by the spiritual
credit of Britain and that alone, they scattered their promissory
notes everywhere in their own lands until they stopped the run
on the bank of faith, and their countrymen—first by tens, then by
thousands, and then by hundreds of thousands—put their separate
funds of courage together again. Thus new armies were called up
in uniform and mufti, and the Germans found that, despite their
killings and captures, the number of their opponents only increased. They buried ten, and a hundred sprouted from their seed.

And it was this spirit and example which tipped the scale in
America, which overbore the defeatists in the United States and
won there a momentous battle for the minds of the citizens. Americans thought they were saving Britain—and they were; but the
spirit and example of Britain also were saving America, from the
Wheelers and abnegation, for the President and a positive faith.

Almost certainly, the historians will misinform posterity. In the
tables of military statistics, the heading "Britain" may mark a short
column. In the war's full, terrible scale, the bombs that fell upon
us that endless summer were few and paltry, and several acres
would contain the broken bodies of those who died. But who can
compute the whole result when each such fall pulled unnamed,
unregistered others up from their knees? What instruments will
history possess to recapture the echoing of Churchill's voice in the
empty places of the world, to measure its decibels in the eardrums
of millions who until then had thought that they would never hear
again?

2

Anyone coming from the scene of a great collapse was bound to be acutely conscious of the mechanics of defeat. I looked for the revealing signs, which now we understood. I listened to the talk of the British Communists, who still spoke of this as an "imperialist war." So far as I could see they weakened the government on nothing more than the issue of providing stronger shelters than the flimsy brick structures in the center of the streets. I could not see that they were dividing any accountable section of the working class. I listened to the debates in Parliament and found no major champions of minor issues. I talked with many of the rich and powerful and, even after the bombs began falling on Mayfair, found no appeasers among them. If any there were, they remained decently silent. If the old-fashioned generals with whom Britain had begun the war remained in the hierarchy, at least they had been shifted to stations where they could do little harm, and fresher minds were brought to the fore. The people trusted the government, and the men of the government had faith in themselves. Britain possessed all the virtues under trial which had been absent in France. Yet even so France might have survived with a twenty-mile moat; even so, her virtues might not save England if the moat were to fail. Often we sat on Shakespeare Cliff at Dover and looked across at the narrow dark film on the water which was the coast of France, where the enemy was looking across at us. We watched the planes come over, tiny white feathers most of the time against the stratosphere. We grabbed our hats as the concussion of the defense guns flapped our clothes, and yelled in excitement at the brief, bright speckle in the blue, like a match lighted a mile away, which meant one plane down in flames. The photographers—hoping, almost, for the chance to film the end of our world—dozed on the warm clay, beside a mock headstone that bore the words: "Here lies a British photographer, who died of boredom waiting for Adolf Hitler." From down below on the waterfront, where the deck chairs stood in empty rows upon the verandas of the shuttered resort hotels, we could hear the calliope's strains of "Annie Doesn't Live Here Any More," to which the young boys and girls swung in circles on their roller skates. Such was the world's front line in those days. It was only as the weeks wore on that we all understood, every man and child, that it was not the water in the moat which contained our fate, but the space above it.

In the crowds in Piccadilly, I caught sight of familiar French faces, men who had been fortunate enough to escape the high priest's tyranny and who had not required the British example to make them what they were. Pierre Comert had come over and was gathering the French journalists together; a brilliant group of broadcasters ducked the bombs each night to reach the BBC fortress and repeat over and over again into the ears of their countrymen that France was not finished and would rise again. Eve Curie was there and generated faith by her presence alone to all those near her. They were ashamed of some among their countrymen; never for a moment were they ashamed of being French. They absorbed and gave out the spirit of the place and moment, but they remained French in every pore. When we sat that day in the House of Commons, gripping the edges of our seats, and heard the Prime Minister describe the terrible naval transaction at Oran, French friends accepted it, but said, a little sadly: "I wish they had not cheered."

On the Quatorze Juillet I wandered idly into Whitehall to observe the French parade and was fascinated by what I saw. I had been spectator at a hundred parades of military might, and they were all essentially the same: merely a perfunctory display of organized, faceless bodies. Now I saw a couple of lines of French sailors, airmen, and soldiers, stretching for no more than a city block. Just a handful—but one was aware of every single face. They were men who could have remained in France or returned to France after the collapse. It would have been a familiar, French thing to see the inspecting officer smile benignly into their faces, pat one or two, and address them with *tu* and *toi*. But the towering general with the improbable nose, whose name was only then becoming a standard, strode stiffly along the ranks, never opening his tightly compressed lips, glaring, almost, into every pair of rigid eyes. He had the portentous air of a general surveying a great army. Somehow, you could not feel sentimental, nor could you smile. You had the impulse to remove your hat and stand rigidly at attention yourself. This was impressive; it gave one to think. Every man there bore the conviction of consequence. There was a sense of strength in this handful that I had never felt in a demonstration by a hundred times their number.

British colleagues from Paris turned up in uniform, and a few,

I was aware, had disappeared into France again on more hazardous enterprises than the journalistic. George Millar, who had the physique of a guardsman and the rosy face of a beautiful girl, wrote from somewhere in Scotland: "I have joined the army. You should see my motorcycle. If your country ever gets itself against the wall like mine, I think you'll be happier if you do what I have done." Geoffrey Cox made the decision too, and freely admitted that he was frightened. He has the quickest mind I had known, but he is a small man and the sheep ranches of New Zealand and the rugby fields of Oxford could do nothing to give him bulk. The day before he was to report for duty, we were looking at a picture of six-foot Nazi paratroopers who had captured Ebaen Emael. "Oh, God," Cox moaned, "it will be the old business again. Like grammar school, when I had to play against the big guys, and I used to wake up in the night in a sweat, sick at my stomach." He went ahead and became happy. He and Millar were next to meet under a broiling sun, on a dusty road outside of Cairo.

On every hand, friends were going. The nerves could not abide inaction then. For most of us there could be no action. Even for most of the British this was true, for now the war had taken a new turn backward into the history of combat, and it was only a small group of the semiprofessional, the élite who seemed to us like shining knights—the airmen—who could come to grips with the enemy. The others could only take it and resist with their hearts and minds, not their hands. One night Ed Murrow stood on his rooftop with a young British bomber pilot who had flown over Berlin many times but had never before been under bombing. The boy was appalled and shaken, said he had never dreamed it was like this, and wanted only to get away from London and into what he regarded as the safety of his machine.

For the men who fought the fires, rescued the wounded, and herded the shelterers, it was not so bad. Their hands and feet had pertinent functions to perform, and so their nervous imaginations remained quiescent. For me and others like me, cursed with both imaginations and idle hands, it was very bad. The time came when I found myself unable to tolerate the shaking room, and when there was no broadcast errand to be run I found myself going down to the basement shelter, which seemed somehow ignoble. There were days when even in the quiet I could not align my thoughts nor summon energy for the most trivial tasks. At times I felt myself the victim of an incomprehensible trance, and the high historic meaning of fierce events could not break through the corroded consciousness. I rode across London Bridge one night, and Vincent Sheean, pointing to the flames in the heart of the city, turned to me and demanded sharply: "Do you understand what that *means*—London *burning?*" I didn't know what he meant and had the impulse to beat my head to make something jar loose. One morning I couldn't make it to the bathroom, and the doctor who thumped and peered said: "You've been sick for weeks, I think." I suppose I had been sick since before Bordeaux. The gyroscopic motion of violent events has a way of keeping one upon his feet long after all tangible supports have given way.

I learned about this matter of the hands one night when, above the throbbing of the bomber motors, I caught an unfamiliar clicking sound. An incendiary had landed on the roof of the building directly across the street, and the flames were already high. The auxiliary fireman in my building turned out, at this moment of need, to be stone deaf, and I had to drag him to the door and point. I can't remember how we got to the rooftop, but I know that I flung the sand and then pumped while he played the nozzle. There was a moon, and the planes were directly overhead, but all fear had miraculously dropped away, and those were the most serene twenty minutes I spent in the Battle of Britain.

After a while most of us came to feel that our margin of protective behavior was so small as to be almost nonexistent, that whether we lived or died was a matter that we could do very little about. A few strong souls like Murrow found a certain release in that, I think; on me it had a depressive effect for some time. I remained obsessed with the notion that one's luck could run out, that his chances narrowed with each escape. (This is absurd, of course; your chance is always fifty-fifty—you get hit or you do not.) You never knew. You could as easily die in the shelter as on the roof. You would step inside a hotel to light a cigarette, and the sidewalk outside would disintegrate to sand. You would break a date for dinner and learn next morning that the restaurant had been reduced to ruins in the night. I do not know whether there is an extra, mysterious sense that detects danger without benefit of sight or hearing, but at times it seemed so. One night, Ed, Larry Lesueur, and I filed out of the BBC and around to the side. We heard nothing, but Murrow suddenly stepped into a doorway, and Larry and I immediately followed suit. At that moment a jagged casing from an antiaircraft shell crashed precisely where we had been. The nerves established a fairly definite behavior pattern for the muscles. If you were walking in the street when you heard the shriek of a descending bomb, you would stop; if you had been standing still, you would begin to walk. If you were sitting down in a room, you would rise, and if you were standing you were likely to sit down. In the *Herald Tribune* office one night a whistler was coming very close. Every person in the room quietly changed his position. Tania Long stretched out on the floor, rose when it was over, and said simply: "I just thought I'd try it that way, once." Nobody thought her action peculiar.

Some persons found refuge in rapid talk when the shriek began. A tin hat on your head made you feel far more secure, and it was good when you were with someone else in the exploding streets. If you were with a person less brave than yourself, you were braver than you would have been alone; if he were braver than you, you tried to emulate his behavior. To be alone was sometimes awful. To get to the underground broadcasting studio meant a walk of several blocks for me. I would shuffle cautiously through the inky blackness to each curbing where the guns would make the crossing street a tunnel of sudden, blinding light. When the shrieking came near I would plaster myself upon the nearest wall, and, however sternly I lectured myself, I not infrequently found myself doing the last fifty yards at a dead run. One felt horribly defenseless if caught in the bathtub when the whistlers came down; once while I was floating in a pool at Roehampton the planes came over, and I could not get out of the water fast enough. There was no logic in living during those days.

In a sudden crisis one did things bizarre to the highest degree. Stories of bombed householders who ran out of their blasted homes having salvaged the dishpan instead of the jewels were heard every day. Ed returned to his flat once from the studio before dawn and awakened Larry Lesueur, informing him that the building was on fire. For reasons known at the time only to Larry and God (and now only to God), Larry gathered up his clothes and shut himself in the dark and crowded closet to put them on. I relate these incidents, not because what happened to me and my friends is of any particular consequence, but only to illustrate what daily life was like for tens of thousands of ordinary persons, whose bodies, however weary, carried through the daily routine of work, but whose minds, however alert, obeyed the conscious will only at times, at other times being twisted and tossed by mysterious forces that defied explanation. Modern war has become altogether too much for the delicate anatomy of the mammalian brain and nerve cells. A sight, a sound, a hot breath of blast can turn men's minds to water within the untouched bone and leave them incoherent idiots ever after.

You in America were told each day by your press and radio that the people of Britain were brave and heroic in their endurance through those frightful weeks—and so they were. But it would be to make them more than human and thus to do them less than justice to suggest that none of them at any time betrayed stark fear or that there were no individual cases of panic and hysteria. And the wounded *did* cry, very frequently. The British may not be a hot-blooded or excitable people, but they are still people. I was drinking at a lobby table in a large hotel one night with a British girl when the table described a slow parabola. We had not heard that one coming down; the first sound was a giant cracking as though the back of the building were being broken; then came the cascading water from burst pipes and a falling curtain of powdered plaster that partitioned the lobby. My companion screamed at the top of her lungs and was halfway to the basement shelter before anyone else had moved. An hour or so later, I left her there in comfort and quiet safety to run through the pattering hail of shrapnel pieces to the BBC, where her cousin, with blazing eyes, screamed imprecations at me for "deserting" the girl.

One witnessed terror at times in West End and East, and I do not think class was a working differential in the matter of courage. The poor took the hardships better, true, but the nerves of the upper class were equally sound. Whatever the faults of the British ruling class, they are not a very "soft" people; the tradition of physical courage, however poor a substitute for intellect, is with them still, and it has its uses in preserving empire as well as in building it. The day the Germans raided the docks, the first great daylight raid on London, Larry and I saw terror in the eyes of hundreds as they moved in a great migration away from the awesome pillars of black oil smoke, trudging through snowpiles of powdered glass, pushing their prams, heads turned over shoulders, staring eyes fixed upon the quiet and mocking sky. I saw it again at Tilbury in the estuary of the Thames. I thought I could stick out the raid in the tall wooden inn, even after the building began to sway back and forth, the window glass exploding in the casements. Ultimately it was the insupportable realization that I was completely alone in the dark building which brought me downstairs. The docks were only about three hundred yards away; there was shipping right in front. The sputterir.g flares began to descend—they seemed to hang in space forever—and the world was turned a ghastly surgical white. To know that you have to deal with random bombs is one thing; to realize that you are *on* the target they are aiming at is something else. I burst into the covered trench shelter in the garden, my head well in advance of my feet. This night I understood terror if I never had before. Through the long hours we crouched in candlelight, felt the convulsions through the dirt walls as the large *crump*ing bombs were crat*er*ing the earth around us, and listened to the sharp knocking of snrapnel chunks on the thin, curved metal roof of our cave. A woman employee of the inn with her hair done up foolishly in curlers wept throughout the night into her apron and murmured over and over: "How's it going to end? How's it going to end?" I think few among us in that cave really expected to live through the night. Yet dawn did come; I stepped over the soiled and sleeping bodies and lifted up the entrance flap to see the world intact, gray and stiff under the lifting fog, a tree down in splinters a few yards away, smoke idling from the nearest wharf. The inn remained, and a tugboat was drifting easily with the tide.

There was terror—but not panic. One could panic in his heart, but two together could not show it, nor a hundred in a group. They neutralize one another, and therein lies the thing that makes the British slightly different. They have laid manifold restraints upon themselves in their mutual intercourse. The British were still afraid of one another.

3

And yet, as the crisis mounted, as the realization deepened that they were all together now in the same boat, regardless of accent or income, cap or Homburg, some of the restraints were wearing down, and they became less afraid and easier in company. They began to discover one another, to talk together in train compartments and in the shelters. Diverse minds made common contact, and hearts that suffered identical requirements could not long remain closed and without means of communication. We would talk about this, Ed and I, Scotty Reston and others, when sleep was

not to be had for the trying, and we thought that perhaps a wonderful thing was happening to the British people: some kind of
moral revolution was underway, and out of it would come regeneration of a great people who had been strangling their greatness
with a thousand invisible cords of restraint. One observed the
first and most obvious manifestations in the visible establishments.
The leaders of labor were taken into the Government; the small
core of élite in the army and air force began to be overborne by
thousands of officers from the ranks, and even the ultratight naval
hierarchy had to give way to some extent. Men who could accomplish with their hands—firemen, first-aid volunteers, bomb ex-
tractors—now became not only important but honored citizens;
and the wide level of professional technicians—the engineers,
chemists, metallurgists—were elevated in the nation's crisis to a
position no aristocrat could claim by birthright alone. The country
realized abruptly that a broker in the city was of scant value compared with the man who could fashion an airplane propeller.

And so it was at this point that a new conception of the war
began to take root in the minds of the imaginative and articulate:
the idea that Hitler's pressure was accomplishing rapidly what the
long struggle of organized working-class British people had been
approaching only very slowly. Perhaps we confused the wish with
the fact, but we caught sight of a new England: men who had so
suffered and achieved in common would no longer fear one another's clothes, accents, or manners but would regard one another
in terms of true worth; under the imperatives of mass struggle
England was discovering the latent genius and brains of her submerged working classes, and the doors to higher education could
no longer remain closed to them; men and women who sacrificed
their chill and ugly dwellings for the absorption of the enemy's
explosives would demand to return to something better than the
slums; people who had fought the flames all night and urged their
weary bodies into the factories in the morning so that England
might have weapons would demand and get something better than
a diet among the worst in the civilized world; soldiers who fought
together in the foxholes would think and vote together when it
was over, and the young men who came back browned and stal-
wart from the deserts, conscious of having saved an empire, would
insist that the fruits of empire begin to reach more than a handful
of the overrich who sat in the City. In this extremity the fox-hunt
lands were spaded for food; the income of the very wealthy was

taxed to confiscation; trades-union workers were called in to help
plan factory production; food distribution, railroad traffic, financial investments—all these things and more were being *directed*
to the widest and most efficient use, in the interests of the nation,
not of private profit, by government officials representing all
classes of the people, not by a few men around a directors' table.
All that men of social conscience and vision had always insisted
could be done was now being done. It was being done to make the
nation safe; it could—and would, we thought—be done later to
make the people happy.

For the first time the war seemed to have taken on a positive
meaning.

We had put on new lenses to view the phenomena before us.
I saw a strange and unprecedented sight on the heath of a great
estate near London and placed it in my new category. Two or
three young Spanish Republican refugees and a handful of Englishmen who had fought Franco and Fascism in Spain were running a continuous outdoor course in guerrilla tactics. These men
had been denounced, had been pilloried by the conservative press
and the Colonel Blimps as "Reds" or criminals at worst, adventurers at best, had found the same official obstacles in returning
to their homeland as the American boys we had pushed through
Paris. Very few had honored them for what they were—the advance guard of volunteers, prepared to die on one of the first
barricades, which if lost would allow the tide to pour upon later
barricades in whose defense volunteers would be indistinguishable. Now here they stood, handing out wooden practice grenades,
barking orders at a group of civilian men that included bankers,
brokers, and landlords—and once Sir Nevile Henderson, one of
those who had tried diplomatic argument with evil. These gentlemen threw grenades, strung hidden wires, crawled on their bellies
along the ditches, and gathered around their instructors, perspiring, eager for advice and praise. A stumpy, gnarled little Cockney
Communist said very casually: "Now I personally like to take my
tank from a little bit to the rear—like this . . . " I wondered:
Would the Hendersons do this if the tanks came? I was convinced
they would.

4

Three years before, 1 had been an American stranger in London.
Now I was an American neutral there, but, I learned to feel, no
longer a stranger. It was true, as Ed remarked, that London had
developed a certain small-town atmosphere, and in the new intimacy I with my compatriots was included. The people knew no
more about America than before, although now for the first time
the British press and radio began to do a decent job of explaining
the most powerful country in the world; basically, they were no
more interested in strangers than before—but here were strangers
living with them in their time of trial. Only a few of the better
informed, who understood Britain's almost hopeless position, began to drop hints to us that America had better wake up before
it was too late for her, too. The shopkeepers, the people in the
buses, and the porters simply reasoned that we were there when
we did not have to be, and they liked us for it.

I was asked, to my surprise and momentary anxiety, to deliver
a lecture on the French defeat before the Royal Institute of International Affairs at Chatham House. I gave it as well and as
honestly as I knew how. Before me sat professional army officers,
stiff dowagers whose limousines waited outside, high-ranking civil
servants, an undersecretary or two—the very people who had so
discomfited and, I had thought, rebuffed me three years before.
What they gave me was far more than polite and perfunctory
attention, and, when I had finished, some of them crowded around
to ask more questions and seek my interpretation of this uncertain
point and that. It was both gratifying and illuminating. I felt that
I had smoothed out a wrinkle in my own perceptions and that
never again could the Colonel Reids of this world give me a sense
of inadequacy by manifestation alone or by anything short of a
true superiority lying behind the bold face and the manner.

Of the American journalists who did more than their technical
duty none reached the stature of Murrow, whose physical, intellectual, and moral performance in those deadly weeks is not likely
to be equaled by any reportorial voice or pen in this generation.
He is a complex of strong, simple faiths and refined, sophisticated
intellectual processes—poet and preacher, sensitive artist and hard-
bitten, poker-playing diplomat, an engaging boy one moment and
an unknowable recluse the next, a man who liked people in gen-

eral and loved a few whom he held off at arm's length. He is elastic and pliable and yet remarkably stubborn, with a hard core of integrity which the impact of no man however powerful or persuasive has ever chipped. He could absorb and reflect the thought and emotions of day laborers, airplane pilots, or cabinet ministers and report with exact truth what they were; yet he never gave an inch of himself away. His whole being was enmeshed in the circumstances of those days and events, yet he held his mind above them always. One can read his broadcasts now, years later, in the printed form for which they were never intended and find London all around—its sights and sounds, its very smells and feeling through the changing hours, all brought back; yet in the works of this Boswell-to-a-great-city one will never find a case of sentiment becoming sentimentality, of blundering excused, of people high or low colored and transformed into something they were not. It may be because I shared his basic beliefs (though perhaps with more confusion), but I rarely knew him to be wrong to any serious degree in his analysis and judgment of a public man or issue.

It was not his perfect poise, his magnetic face, or even his compelling voice that made him the first great literary artist of a new medium of communication. No practice, training, or artifice made him the greatest broadcaster by far in the English tongue. He was simply born to the new art. It is his and—I sometimes think—his alone, never to be shared. A perfect artistic creation can rarely be delivered by radio, no matter how flawless the words or the conception, unless the personality and being of the artist himself approaches the stature of the product—because he is a part of the product, mixed up irretrievably in its essence. It makes the art of radio literature infinitely more difficult for nearly everyone who tries it, and natural and much easier for the rare few whose personal presence matches its requirements. Of these, Ed Murrow is first and foremost, and almost alone. Franklin Roosevelt and Winston Churchill could use the medium with profound effect, upon occasion and for a special cause. They could never use it day after day and night after night, as Murrow did, and still make their message live.

The generality of British people will probably never know what Murrow did for them in those days. A few in Whitehall and Fleet Street knew quite well, and their honoring of him was done, not out of calculation, but out of simple gratitude for his understanding. Murrow was not trying to "sell" the British cause to America;

he was trying to explain the universal human cause of men who
were showing a noble face to the world. In so doing he made the
British and their behavior human and thus compelling to his countrymen at home. He was of far greater influence than the American
Ambassador to London. *He* was the ambassador, in a double role,
representing Britain in America as well as America in Britain.
There is no doubt of his immense aid to the President in awakening the American people to the issue before them. And when he
returned home a year later, very tired, it is not to be wondered
that Roosevelt gave him a warm personal welcome and that the
assembled great in New York rose to their feet in a reception to a
reporter unequaled since Stanley returned from the relatively
simpler task of finding Dr. Livingstone.

Ed Murrow selected most of the men who formed that original
Columbia foreign staff; and through his influence and example,
backed by the organizational and editorial genius of Paul White in
New York, a kind of daily journalism quite new in its form rapidly
developed. Familiar, very American voices now brought faraway
scenes and issues into millions of living-rooms at regular hours in
precise succession, giving, not just the bones of the news, not an
editorial by itself, nor a descriptive "color" story by itself, but in
a very few minutes putting it all in one package—the "hard news"
of the day, the feel of the scene, the quality of the big or little men
involved, and the meaning and implications of whatever had
happened. All the rigid, traditional formulae of news writing had
to be thrown out of the window, and a new kind of pertinent,
contemporary essay became the standard form. Columbia had
begun it when the war began, relying on its own small staff from
whom it required honesty and judgment rather than flamboyance
or dramatics. Very soon the other radio companies, who until then
had put politicians and acknowledged public thinkers on the air,
or unco-ordinated series of newspaper journalists, found themselves outstripped and obliged to imitate our example as best they
could.

If Ed was a radio "natural," nearly all the rest of us—like myself, trained in writing for print—had to attack the matter consciously. I had to write my broadcasts down on paper myself and
could judge their effectiveness only if they looked right on paper.
Ed never did that if he could help it, but would walk up and
down the studio or office, dictating to someone else. Sometimes
his words and phrases didn't look right to me in the script. But

I always discovered, as I listened, that they *were* right for the medium and that my changes would have been ruinous.

5

The Germans gave up their mass daylight raiding when, in the middle of September, they lost around two hundred planes on one day. They did not know that on that day which broke their courage, the back of the Royal Air Force was also broken and that hardly a complete squadron remained in reserve in all the British Isles. Had they been able to continue mass raiding a few more days, it is quite possible that they would have torn an irreparable breach in the barricade of the sky which would have laid England open for successful invasion, altering, perhaps fatally, the outcome of the war. But the Germans lost their nerve; the British did not, and so they won out.

It was time for me to return to America. I was both ill and homesick and of no great use in the postcrisis days of pure endurance which were coming. I had been away for three years and knew little of what my people were thinking, of whether I was doing this unfamiliar work properly or not. On the eve of departure I said something in conversation which struck Ed, and he asked me to do a final broadcast about London. I gave it, three years to the day on which I had sailed out of New York to a war I knew was coming but of whose nature and scope I was totally ignorant. I talked a little about France, about Paris dying in her coma, about the cities which had broken in spirit, about London which had not—London, which "is not England" but which is Britain, which had become a city-state in the old Greek sense—and about a peaceable people who had gone to war in their aprons and bowlers, with their old fowling pieces, with their ketchup bottles filled with gasoline and standing ready on the pantry shelves. I quoted someone there who had written: "When this is all over, in the days to come, men will speak of this war, and they will say: I was a soldier, or I was a sailor, or I was a pilot; and others will say with equal pride: I was a citizen of London." I could not hold my voice quite steady and I felt ashamed of it; I felt that the broadcast was filled with bathos, mawkish, and embarrassing to all who heard it. When I reached home a businessman told me he had listened while driving and had had to stop his car for a moment. A professor of English history told me he had heard it in his bedroom and had had to bathe his eyes before he went down to dinner. In contribution it was a mite, but apparently it helped, and that was reward enough for any man among so many who did so much.

Ed drove me to Waterloo Station where the people hastened. It was the evening hour, the hour which in other London summers had been the only peaceful time, golden in the streets of mirrored windows. Now it was the hour of dread and the constricting heart, for it brought the night. I wondered how long it would take before I could watch the sun approach the rim of darkness and think of the day that had passed instead of the night that would come.

The Atlantic was slate-gray below, and in the cabin of the fast flying boat there was the sweetish smell of vomit throughout the eleven endless hours from Poole to Lisbon. We had made two false starts, and out of exasperation rather than calculation the pilot determined to keep on and buck the headwinds even though they reduced our average speed to something like ninety-seven miles an hour. We had thirty minutes' gasoline remaining when we churned the water of the Tagus between the rows of burning flares in the first night landing there that this passenger service had ever had to make. Gentle, sardonic Henry Buckley of the *Daily Express* stood on the pier and said: "What bad news bringeth thee now? The last time I heard your voice you told me Paris was doomed. What of my countrymen's city?"

A strange and nervous place, Lisbon. An oasis and an escape hatch for Europe. British planes bound for London, German planes bound for Berlin, passed each other in the sky over the city. British spies watched the German spies and vice versa, and both watched the Lisbon docks. At Estoril, wise old Joseph Bech of Luxembourg paused on his way to London; Camille Chautemps, once premier of France, and not untainted with the armistice guilt, was there on his way to Washington for Pétain. In the lobby of my hotel, the Palacio, the American Ambassador to London, Joseph Kennedy, strolled past the outstretched legs of Sieburg, prime intellectual saboteur for the Nazis; Biefurn, just arrived from Berlin on behalf of Heinrich Himmler; a morose Russian doctor who they said had helped push Rasputin to the Volga's edge; and following Kennedy, shuffling painfully between this gauntlet of his country's foes, came Paderewski, once Poland's premier, now on his way to America, there to die in freedom. The sun was good, the flowers had nothing to fear, and there was only soft music in the night.

I had forgotten the unfathomable peace of children in the sun, the children who squat in the sand and look at you with grave and steady eyes.

I was happy to be going home and unhappy to be leaving Europe, the struggle, and excellent friends. I was not sure whether it really would be home that I would find. Home must be both right and real; and I was not sure that any place away from the war could now be either. I had some roots in America, but I had others elsewhere now, fastened to the soil of diverse human hearts and minds to whom I owed allegiance. My university had not been a home to me, but the Jacobin Club had been, and I had now found and attached myself to new members speaking other tongues. "Internationalist" is not a good word, but there is a confraternity with branches in many lands of men of goodwill, and I was beginning to understand that it was this club which would be my home hereafter—the only one, I thought, proper and possible for the times in which my life was lived.

The tweed coat by the Casino door covered familiar shoulders. It was Ernst Adam, and when he turned I gave no immediate sign of recognition, uncertain of his status here. Later we talked by the water's edge, and he turned abruptly when he asked: "Sieburg here? That is a bad sign. I think I will investigate the friendship of some of the men with fishing boats tomorrow." For a time we watched in silence a group of children who played mumblety-peg with a sliver of metal under the lamplight. Then Adam said: "No, I won't. Some time or other you have to stop this running and turn around. It may as well be here. There is no longer any room to be a neutral or a refugee."

I knew what he meant. I knew that I myself had come to a crossroads and was taking a turning which I had never expected to take, that the thing had come for which my education and my basic beliefs had not prepared me. I knew that the change had been subtly working in me all through the terrible days of London, when I had continued essentially to retreat and hide. The course was quite clear now, and perhaps it was not too late. The duty was to fight with every means available, even though the better future of men was not guaranteed by success in the fighting. But success in the fight would give the future a chance at least; and failure meant the end, perhaps for a great many generations. Truly, in Fascism the "underworld has risen," and reason itself

was under assault. The victory of Fascism meant the victory of a
new world barbarism among men; it meant the end for a very
long time, if not forever, of the long, long struggle toward truth
and justice.

Now, for the first time, really, I acknowledged to myself that
all my hesitations, all my blind hopes that my own people could
somehow stay out and avoid this fearful business were foolish and
impossible hopes. I had clung to them even through this last year
in a hundred arguments until I didn't try to argue any more but
guarded them to myself. My more acute colleagues and friends
had been right all the time. There was no possible living with
Fascism, even for a strong America; neutrality was quite impossible. The Fascists could not halt now any more than they could
halt after they had gotten Spain, Austria, and Czechoslovakia.
Europe was small, and with Europe gone the world was very
small. They could not let go of their speeding motorcycle even
now. They could not live even in their kind of peace so long as
one strong democracy remained. Now they stood upon the Atlantic coast of Europe. The Middle East might go, and India
with it. England might go, and they would possess all the incal-
culable mechanical resources of Europe. This would mean that,
even though America were not directly attacked, we should have
to live forever under arms as conscripts. All our wealth and work
must go toward preparation for war which could come at any
moment. If we took the opposite course and tried to appease, it
would mean that every Fascist-minded man and group inside my
country would rise in power and prestige; it would mean the end
of education in freedom as I had known it; would mean that the
Silver Shirts and all men of darkness like them would move out of
the dim parlors and into the city halls. It was all clear: this *was*
a world conspiracy, as capable of attaining success in the shrunken
condition of the modern world as any conspiracy in a small Ruritania once had been. The Nazis meant it when their legions sang
that tomorrow the world was theirs. They could do it; and they
could do it either by arms or by the defeat of men's minds. They
had allies everywhere, in Minneapolis as well as Tokio or Buenos
Aires.

I wondered what people thought back in Minneapolis, what
the scattered brethren of the Jacobin Club were thinking now. I
felt that I had just run a tortuous, bewildering course, and was
breathing hard. But I was satisfied. It was something to come to—

to desire your own people to take up arms and join the killing. But there it was; nothing could be done about it. There was no other way.

In the morning Karli, a bit shabby in such pretentious surroundings, broke into a run when he saw me at the end of the lobby. It had been a bad time for him, the running down to the South of France to hide. But the underground railway had been quickly organized, and he found himself before the right trails that led through the Pyrenees. He felt he could not just go like that, and so he had stayed for weeks, leading many parties of the hunted on foot through the passes into Spain. In the last party was his sister, carrying her baby in her arms. We sat on the beach a time, discomfited by our common realization that I could leave and he could not. He said: "If it was the mountain, then I could make to America; but with only these water, no, I cannot." There were a few lines in his face I had not remembered, and his expressive eyes bore a somber cast. He said: "There is nothing more to love in Europe, only nature, only the geography."

The Clipper flew carefully westward with its burden of the fortunate who were so comfortable and so safe. In my pocket was Karli's note in his own brand of English: "I send you thankfulness for the money, but I will not believe you won it with the cards. You are too lucky in the love." I knew he was watching the Clipper, and I was rather glad I could not see his eyes. I was too lucky in a lot of ways.

Chapter VIII

In the first days, it was not unlike a dream. From vaguely familiar faces came loud, unnatural accents; handshakes were buffeting attacks; to the minutiae of commonplace remarks, complete with subject and predicate, no ready answers could be given. One felt weakly mute in the thralldom of this dream, and when one spoke with serious intent there was, as there is in dreams, the uneasy feeling that the others were not listening, that the words were alien to them and conveyed no meaning. The suburban houses appeared out of shape; even on Long Island they seemed crudely contrived shelters, unfinished and apart from one another, as in some settlement of pioneers just staking out their claims to new soil. It disturbed me that the houses were of wood, and for a long time the sight of crowded wooden tenements brought an automatic mental calculation of the havoc incendiaries would cause among them. The buffalo five-cent piece was strangely small in the palm; none of the long-forgotten coins seemed quite valid, and there was a foolish sense of relief when the first shopkeeper accepted them. The visored caps of the hulking policemen were almost brutally crude, and no officers of the law had ever seemed so solid and undeniable. The fat letter-boxes on the corner were a new discovery in their green paint, and the milk bottles were wondrously thick and heavy.

New York remained a phantasmagoria the first week, devoid of all meaning in my sight which now, like a fixed prism, sought to identify every scene within the spectrum of the world struggle. If a newspaper headline shouted of the battle abroad, another one beside it shouted equally loudly of a train wreck; if friends listened intently to the broadcasts from Europe, it was the federal election that really stirred up their enthusiasm or their anger, which I simply could not share. I marveled at this city which seemed so integrated, intact, oblivious, and I could find no purpose in the ceaseless rushing to and fro upon the streets, in and out of the great fortress buildings, up and down the clicking elevators. When I noticed a husky, grown man on a bus top deeply absorbed in the page of comic strips, I felt astonished. In time I began to apply moral judgments to all this, as did the others who came back from Europe; but at first there was no feeling save the purest wonder. After dark the glare of lights produced uneasiness rather than delight, and sometimes the shrieking wail of an ambulance or fire engine passing my Park Avenue hotel brought me from my bed with a bound. I experienced an involuntary tightening in the stomach, sweat would break out on my cold flesh, and I would slam down the windows with an hysterical impulse to scream out and order them not to make that terrible sound when there was no need.

The bustling, efficient offices of the broadcasting company were a little overwhelming at first, and I felt conscience-stricken in the realization that so many men, so much complicated machinery, had been devoted so often to processing the brief, hesitant little speeches I had been giving from the areas of war. To stand on a street corner and hear Larry's words, spoken that moment in the curtained underground London studio, blaring now from the passing cars, to walk through a hotel lobby and hear Ed drawing in his breath three thousand miles away—these were experiences thrilling beyond compare. I wanted to write to them that the whole thing was real after all, and not pantomime in an empty room.

This was the city through which I had passed three years before, lost and without identity; I found now that a measure of fame or notoriety had attached to me and that whenever I gave my name there was immediate recognition and the most genuine and friendly interest. It was a heart-warming experience, but it always came as a surprise, and often after these impromptu conversations I had a feeling almost of guilt—that I ought to have said something more or something better, and that, measured by this reputation they seemed to have accorded me, I was not living up to it. Americans, I learned, love a "name," a celebrity, even so minor a one as I; they clothe a "name" in a personality of their own construction, and when people said: "Why, you don't look at all as I had imagined," I had again this guilty feeling of being somehow an impostor under my own name. Now and then I felt it was a kind of duty to these generous people to look and act in accordance with the role they seemed to expect, but I had neither the histrionic instinct nor the ability for it. It was a relief to find common ground with serious friends whose own hearts were in what was happening to the world; it was a relief when I gave a short talk to a small group of worried Jews in Brooklyn, men and women who were interested, not in me, but only in what I had to tell them. I could not help liking direct interest in myself, but I was too self-conscious or immature to bear its weight gracefully and found I could relax and freely talk only within the terms of the common concern. Frequently newspaper and magazine people came to interview me—something that never happens to reporters in other countries, and that I suspect ought not happen to any journalist. For it tends to give him later too much sympathy with the interviewee when he should have none. I found it an awkward experience, and if I was misquoted, on however unimportant a point, I felt I had been made to look ridiculous—although of course no one really noticed.

The techniques of deliberately contrived publicity were a fascinating revelation. The company employed one man whose exclusive duty was to obtain "plugs" in the gossip columns of Broadway writers. I was informed in reverent tones that I was to meet the great Walter Winchell. No, I was not to go to his office, nor he to come to mine, and the telephone would not suffice; it was all much more subtle than that. I was to be present in a certain night club at midnight, when, as if by chance, the meeting would occur. I sat in the ultra chic establishment, submerged in the murmuring flood tide of small talk on matters beyond my comprehension, watching the confident men with glistening hair who smiled brief, measured smiles at one another in passing, and the amazing girls, no more than twenty, with chalk-white faces and scarlet, weary mouths, who sat with their thin elbows on the tables, the white petals of their fingers drooping under the burden of a cigarette. The young publicity man with me drank his highballs with a flourish and said "Hi-yah!" with a flip of the hand to many who passed our table. He held his chest in his hands, stretched his legs, and said: "What a country! You know what? Two years ago I was driving a truck around the slums of Boston. Now look at me." He held up two fingers, crossed together. "I'm like that, see, with Winchell, Lyons, Runyon, all these guys. Took me just two years. What a country!" Various unfamiliar men sat a moment at our table, including one of middle age with whitish hair and white, soft flesh. My guide and mentor would poke me and say: "Tell him about London. Give him the lowdown on that Bordeaux thing you was.in." But the visitor's eyes revolved constantly about the establishment. He was clearly not interested in me and suddenly rose to his feet and said: "Send the dope to my office." I asked: "When does this Winchell character arrive?" He straightened abruptly, the smile vanished, his eyes widened, and he exclaimed in a whisper: "For Chris' sakes, *that* was Winchell you was just talking to! You mean to tell me you didn't even know that was *him?*" He was quite unnerved, his evening ruined. By other mysterious processes, however, a few items about London that I wrote the next day appeared in the great man's newspaper space all over the country. I was his "guest columnist," although I am sure he scarcely remembered our brief meeting.

Three years constitute a long time when they pass in the period of one's twenties. The innumerable influences beating upon me in these years had been a thousand times intensified beyond the norm, and I had been stretched all out of shape upon the Procrustean bed of widening events until I could not fit the "normalcy" of America and home. When old friends, reporters, came to see me at the Minneapolis airport, I could think of little to say to them, and no doubt they were hurt and attributed to vanity the strangeness they found within me. When my father, slightly grayer now, made a remark soon after our greeting about the alarming government debt, I could not repress a laugh, partly because these matters now seemed so absurd and pointless, partly because of the affectionate family memories the well-worn complaint brought back. I lay long awake in my parents' house, listening to the soft thudding of the snow clumps as they fell from the familiar lilac trees beneath the window, watching the moonlight on the shaft of the carefully polished floor lamp, on my mother's best "doilies" upon the dressing table. I thought of the evening's conversation about children and school and relatives, the weather and the cost of living, and my mother's anxious glances when I remained silent through the talk. I felt miserable in the knowledge that I had given them cause to feel they were boring me. It was not that; it was just that a chasm had grown between my life and theirs of a width I had not anticipated and that I was a little sick over the confirmation of what I had hitherto only suspected: that home was no longer home, that I could not stay here ever again for long, that something had happened to me so that, outside the family, friends were no longer friends unless they thought as I did about the only things that mattered. I was beginning to understand that in neutral-minded America, I was going to be involved in a fight, would make enemies, perhaps of old friends, a struggle that would not be professionally confined to the public places but would enter the hearts and homes of everyone and leave its rancor everywhere.

Doubtless, I was in a hypersensitized, neurotic state of mind. When I saw the university football team, the hulking Finns, Swedes, and Poles in their ungainly costumes run out upon the field, they reminded me of Nazi Storm Troopers, and the precision and crushing power of their play was so much of a piece with the Nazi's Blitzkrieg manner that I felt an absurd resentment toward them. When a doctor ran out to a writhing boy, I wished to see no more.

There were compensations—too many for a man still very young. When I gave my first real "lecture," in Evanston, the sense of self-importance that lies in every man was enlarged by the realization that so many competent persons had arranged their children for the evening, dressed carefully in their formal clothes, and driven or walked some distance to pay a dollar and listen exclusively to me. Perhaps it was simply because I was so intent and intense and unpossessed of any professional platform techniques; at any rate, few later talks I made were ever accorded the rising ovation these people gave me when I finished, exhausted and dripping. I began a short series of lectures with the belief that people wanted to be informed, and soon learned that they wanted to be entertained as well; I was expected to compete with the cinema for the evening. I was soon disabused of the notion that they wished me to talk and nothing more. There was always a reception committee, largely composed of local society women, for whom the big moment of the evening was not the talk but the cocktail party beforehand or the "little supper—just a few of us" which came after. Clearly, the social prestige of various ladies was involved in these matters, and if I failed to be affable at the little supper, the whole affair was a failure to them no matter how brilliantly I might have spoken on the stage. It was an exhausting business, and there were disturbing adventures. Once when snowstorms grounded all planes, I was obliged to ride a sleepless train for thirty hours to Boston, changing clothes in the smoking room and then being driven at full speed from a suburban station. to be thrust before the impatient crowd of leading citizens, twenty minutes overdue. There was no loud-speaker system—which Boston apparently regarded as demeaning to true orators—and in my condition my voice simply could not carry through the hall. Toward the end of this nightmarish hour I saw only dancing specks before my eyes and felt myself staggering. Some persons were wise enough to leave before it was over; the lecture manager in New York reproved me. In the high school auditorium at Flint, Michigan, the amplifier in the rear was connected with another microphone in the superintendent's office, and for some minutes my account of France's fall was mingled chaotically with the obscenities of two janitors who did not know the office microphone was open but who did know each other's canine ancestry.

America was just entering in earnest the quest for rapid knowledge, feeling the first irritations, then the tortures of trying to make up her mind. I knew the answer. I was sure I knew it as I had never been sure of anything in my life, but distance confined this to a battle of words, and words are blunt weapons at the best. As did others who came back from Europe then, I used the words with all the precision and frequently all the passion at my command. There were inspiring moments, when I felt myself in a true communion of understanding with an attentive, eager audience, but there were too many times when I finished my peroration only to observe expressions of distrust on stolid faces, when I stepped down to hear departing women already placidly chatting of the terrible problem of getting kitchen help. I learned to understand a fundamental suspicion in the American character, a Yankee trait which I had to admit was an outgrowth of the democratic habit, part of its bulwark in normal times, but now a downright menace as precious time rushed by. It was an American trait, not so much to avoid action, but to avoid the humiliation of being "taken in." America was terribly afraid of losing its fancied status as the "wise guy," of being a "sucker." I wondered: Do these people disbelieve by nature, or have the press and radio completely lost the people's faith? For, time after time, I would find an imposing man—generally a businessman—approaching me after a lecture, patting my arm, and saying: "That was mighty interesting. Now let's you and me have a little drink with some friends of mine and suppose you give us the real low-down?" They could not believe that I had already told them all I knew, that their press and radio each day was telling the whole truth to the best of their abilities.

After a time I began to think that this was a special trait of the middle classes, and I felt that perhaps I had made a great mistake

in speaking so much before the women's clubs and "town halls."
Perhaps it would have been wiser to speak exclusively to the working people or the children. Yet my country was predominantly a
middle-class society; whatever the sluggishness that supposedly
appertains to this class in general, still the nation could and would
take no action without its consent.

Many of us tried our best in our various ways; none, I think,
performed the heroic work in the interests of the truth that was
accomplished by a slip of a girl I had known in Paris, a foreigner
at that, whose English was not perfected. This was Gitta Sereny,
daughter of one of the great landed families of Hungary, hardly
past adolescence but matured by the suffering she had witnessed,
childlike in appearance with a rosebud face. There was a flame
in this youngster which no defeat or discouragement could ever
quench. She had gone as a nurse with the French army to the
beaches of Dunkirk, and, when all was lost, she suffered through
the freezing winter in a dank château caring for the orphaned
children of French families separated in the melee. More than
once she risked her young life to aid the escape of RAF pilots who
had crashed in France. When she came to America she turned
down opportunities in Hollywood (she was a promising actress)
and refused lucrative offers to speak before the wealthier organizations. Instead, she toured the schools, driving or riding the day
coaches from town to town, sleeping in the cheapest inns, speaking two and three times a day to the children of all ages about
what she had seen in Europe, what was happening to the world
of decent people, and the terrible danger that confronted the
society in which they had been born. She was tireless; she made
hundreds of speeches in a year and, judging from the thousands
of letters the excited children wrote to her, there was no doubt
that she had stirred something in them untouched before and had
left new seeds in their aspiring minds. The experience left new
seeds, too, within her own understanding, for something happened
to this "refugee" which happened to few of her social compatriots
who were content to view and judge America from the bar of the
Hotel Pierre: she came to understand and love this country, to
know the mighty strength behind the flaccid talk, to recognize its
courage and its decent instincts despite the defeatism of its lunatic
fringe and would-be Fascist leaders. She grew apart from the
tight, condescending little crowd of expatriates in New York, and
for her contribution to America's understanding she received in

turn something of the unalterable American spirit. It was a good exchange; the misfortune is that the transaction was not often repeated with others.

For a few days I was in Mexico City broadcasting the inauguration of President Camacho and acquiring a rapid infatuation with that vivid land. This was my first experience with that special Latin American brand of democracy, which in its gaudy crazy quilt exhibits some of the patterns of Fascism and yet—at least in the case of Mexico—is not really Fascist. Cardenas had long since taken back the oil lands from foreign exploiters, giving his people a self-confidence they had not known before; Roosevelt had offered convincing proofs that he was quite sincere in his desire to be a good neighbor; yet Mexican supernationalists could still make capital out of the dormant suspicion of the Yanqui, as our own isolationists did with our feeling about the British Lion. An hour before Vice President-elect Henry Wallace, who bore them anything but ill will, was due to arrive at the American Embassy, partisans of the defeated Almazan rioted before the embassy buildings. I was caught for a moment between the tear-gas pistols of the police and the crowd armed with stones. Only the most undignified ducking and running saved me. I managed to scribble out several press telegrams on my knee in an alleyway and sent my driver off to dispatch them; and, when the other reporters arrived and dashed about to collect the story, I relaxed with that tolerant, superior feeling a reporter has when he knows he is far ahead with his scoop. But it was their stories, not mine, that commanded the top headlines next day in the States. Mine never appeared. This time I paid a penalty for being first: the panicky Mexican censors had held up my telegrams. Only the succeeding wires went through.

Here was political practice where human bodies and direct action counted for everything and abstract principles for very little. A palace guard of resplendent, tough-looking generals surrounded Camacho on the Senate rostrum where, from the balustrade, I was broadcasting. When Camacho descended the steps, the generals, jealous of their very physical position vis-à-vis the leader, scrambled down in hot haste, knocking over my microphone stand and jamming me against the railing. My arms were pinned, and the remorseless crush of sweating official bodies bent me over sideways until I thought I could hear my ribs cracking, and the gilt and velvet décor began to whirl in my dizzy sight. Nor had my

troubles ended—later we discovered that a union of telephone
workers, piqued by the election results, had snipped the broadcast line up near Monterrey and only half of Camacho's inaugural
speech was heard abroad.

The well-fed Americans of the business colony sat in their exclusive tearooms, sipped cool drinks, and sneered at the Mexican
people whom they had been milking for so long that they had
come to believe they were there by some divine right of economics.
To them Mexico was not a democracy, and to prove it they used
contradictory arguments without distinction: that a clique of generals dictated to the people, or that the people ("the mob," in
their words) dictated to business. One could indeed see many
secondary characteristics of gang rule: election bribery and corruption, vassal newspapers, feudalistic landlords, quick fortunes
side by side with slow starvation. And yet democracy was not dead
in Mexico; it was just struggling to be born. Its true spirit and
fervor were there and had been since the revolution. They welcomed the oppressed who came from Fascist lands abroad; men
were not persecuted by official fiat because of race or religion or
political belief; workers' and peasants' organizations grew and
could not be denied; and on every hand—in the publications, the
schools, among the artists and writers—one was aware of a fierce
aspiration toward the freeing of men's minds from the long, dark
oppression and the freeing of their bodies from the ancient bond-
age of their animal labors on behalf of others. The revolution was
still revolving. Counterrevolution dared not make a frontal attack
and was obliged to limit itself to indirect measures. Yet the coun-
terrevolutionists could not, I felt, do the people down—not unless
the rest of us lost the present battle elsewhere and their neighbors
joined the Fascist world and overwhelmed these struggling people
with their pressure. It seemed to me all so simple, so terribly clear,
that the world was one, that no barricades of water or desert or
mountain range could fence away ideas, that if the present fight
were lost, all the little, beginning peoples like the Mexicans would
be swept away in the same tide that would engulf the big and
numerous peoples. Here, too, we had allies as well as mortal
enemies, as they had among ourselves, and somehow our action
must be concerted before it should all be too late.

The year of defeat, 1940, sputtered out to its end, inglorious
and abject save in the green islands of Britain. At the beginning
of the next year, whose direction no living being could foretell, I

was sent to Washington, the tribunal of last resort, where the final
testimony for and against civilized, decent man was about to be
heard and judged.

2

Here was the brain center which was to decide the immediate
fate of the most powerful people in the world; here was the command post destined to rally the free men of earth. A strange and
disarming place. A quiet collection of lofty stone museums, a leafy,
dreaming park. It seemed unreal and quite unto itself as a campus
town is unreal and withdrawn from the world. A city within a
capital, rather than, like London or Paris, a capital within a city.
An orderly repository for the records of past deeds and of men
long since passed away. Here was no turbid flow of toiling men
and women with factory sweat upon their faces. The drive and
clangor of a mighty, working nation could not be felt nor heard.
This was the clean and well-hedged suburb to the nation, connected with the nation only by the hourly train, the smooth highway, and the telegraph line. The white collar was its insigne, the
brief case and the mimeograph machine were its tools, and the
common cold was its occupational disease. The climate was mild,
the food ran to starches, and long before midnight the lights were
put out. There was no market place for public demonstration; sin
was unprovided for; its most vigorous indulgence was conversation, and its deepest passions were engendered and spent across
the bridge tables on the screened verandas. One watched a care-
taker trimming a hedge and a party of respectful tourists gathering before a portal, and one thought that this place could never
sense the agitation of the world, that it would remain forever the
dead center of the whirlpool.

Churchill had said: "Give us the tools and we will finish the job,"
and the President argued that the grant of the tools would be the
cheapest way to buy our own salvation. Neither one, it was certain
even then, believed in his heart that either proposition was the
truth. Their opponents knew this and taunted them, daring them
to tell the people the truth of their conviction that America must
enter the war. This bothered me; I wondered whether there was
not something fundamentally undemocratic and dishonest in this
gradual procedure of moving from one objective to the next—

from lend-lease to the taking of bases in the Atlantic, to the arming of merchant ships, and so on. I had much to learn about the practical workings of democracy. We were in a race; it was the rate of America's growing understanding versus the rate of the Fascists' physical advance. What was the President to do? Was he to withhold action until a clear majority of his countrymen had made up their minds, and so risk arriving too late when the few remaining bastions of the shrinking world would already lie in enemy hands? Was it his duty to lead or to follow the people? As I watched this extraordinary personality from week to week I began to understand why he was a very great man. I realized that he possessed, as we as college students had possessed, a sense of history in its inevitable course, but that he, far more clearly than any of us, understood the modern workings of a democracy. He knew America as we did not. He knew its vastness, its countless pockets of diverse tongues and cultures and habits of thought; he knew the conflicting varieties of its moral allegiances and material interests. He knew, in effect, that we were still a federation, divided by deeper things than artificial state boundaries, united only by the buried thread of a common spirit that must be touched now and awakened. He knew that he must act and that only in the test of action would the people rally and this democracy become more than a debating society in a world of violent action. He was running enormous risk; but he was living now only for history and his country's preservation. Therein lay his courage and his greatness.

It was this matter of understanding the swift movement of history which in my eyes divided the people in Washington—the men in Congress and my colleagues of the radio and press. To those who had the key, everything was clear. The others wandered lost in a pathless forest of "facts." They measured the oceans in miles and found them comfortably vast; they estimated the millions of men we would require to assist our friends abroad and said we could not do it; and yet by a curious distortion of geography they believed that Argentina was closer than Europe and quite defendable. Failing to understand that this was a war for men's minds, not understanding that ideas overleap all barricades, they limited our duty to the armed protection of this "hemisphere." And these were the better, decenter men among the President's opponents; the British-hating, pro-Hitler pseudo Fascists were a different case. For days I sat in Congress and at the lend-lease hearings, impressed by the brilliant legal minds of the Vandenbergs and Tafts as they tore the President's bills apart, and marveled that such men lacked the imaginative power to sense the quick drift of history. With the best will in the world, they would have let American democracy destroy itself. Those were bitter, heart-burning days, when a vast country was trying to understand itself and the world in which it lived, when the Wheelers and Nyes and Lindberghs almost took the nation away from its chosen leader.

For the first time I began to comprehend the importance and power of the "observers," all those who speak and write. The nation had entered full into a war of words, and words were my business. I learned a new respect for my profession—and a new fear of it. It was not an easy position I was in, along with colleagues who shared my anxiety and my basic beliefs. Save when I was speaking around the country in lecture halls, completely on my own, I was supposed to be doing an "objective" job of reporting the crisis in the Capital. No matter how much I tried to be objective, I could never be neutral in my mind, and neutrality is a different thing. The pressures were immediate and relentless; almost every broadcast, no matter how cautious, brought some manner of protest from an angry Congressman or a worried radio-station director somewhere on the network. My immediate superior for some months was an older man, a journalist of long experience and manifest goodwill. He was often praised as a "stable" and "objective" reporter in the same communications that denounced me as a "prejudiced propagandist." The difference between us was that he was neutral in his mind and I was not; I had come to a conclusion on the basic matter and he had not. (Apparently if one thinks through a problem, comes to a conclusion, and thus holds an opinion, he is prejudiced.) Our relationship was always polite but often awkward. I became somewhat obsessed with a fundamental problem: every journalist, since time and space are limited, must select the facts he will present, the quotations he will emphasize. He is not a machine, and he does not work in a vacuum. Now, in these critical days, his daily selections were helping to decide the mind and thus the fate of his people. After it became evident which way the country was going, but when the vociferous minority could still fatally slow down action, I wondered how much time and space one should give to their remarks. During one morning broadcast I wondered out loud about this problem into the microphone, for I could not

forget the stifling role played by the press in France when it was
a distinct force for defeat. I was denounced by some isolationists,
my superior was shocked, and I received a letter of expostulation
from New York. I was given to understand that the opposition was
entitled to equal time and equal space, and that I had no business
even raising the question.

There was honor among journalists in Washington, but it was
often accorded on a basis that I could not understand. I found
I was not easily welcomed into all their circles. To many of the
regulars, the old hands, who had spent years in the Capital running to press conferences, rewriting hand-outs and amassing major
and minor facts, I and those like me were somehow suspect. Most
of them still gave only grudging acceptance to the radio men, and
I was doubly suspect because I was a broadcaster and because I
was far more interested in presenting and clarifying the major
issues than in filling a notebook with secondary facts and figures.
I had had enough of that procedure in other years; someone had
to do it, but I had no wish to spend my time in such a manner at
this moment in history. So it was not unusual to enter the press
room of the White House, for example (dominated by a clique
of reporters who prided themselves on how close they could stand
to the President or how fast they could rush from his conferences),
and be greeted thus: "Make way for the com-men-ta-*tor!* Make
way for the ideology boy who sees all, knows all, and don't say
nuthin'!" There were little Peglers among them—small, bitter men
who compensated for their lack of background by a sneering contempt for those who understood ideas and believed and fought
for them. One could stand high with them, no matter what his
beliefs, if he rushed about vigorously enough with notebook in
hand, or patronized the Press Club bar enough—if he was, in effect,
a "regular guy." Among the regular guys were Chicago *Tribune*
and New York *Daily News* "hatchet men" whose false and almost
treasonable writings never impaired their standing in this curious
club. Many were sickened by them, but there were no organized
ethical standards among the reporters which could be broken only
at the peril of fraternal penalty. As a result, journalists who had
worked in Europe and understood what was going on tended to
drift together, a little defiant and contemptuous of the others. We
divided, as the whole people was dividing.

I continued hypersensitive to the point where an afternoon
spent in the halls of Congress would leave me with a physical

revulsion. I could not stand many performances by tobacco-chewing, gravy-stained, overstuffed gila monsters who, nestled in their bed of chins, would doze through other speeches, then haul up their torpid bodies and mouth the old, evil shibboleths about King George III, the war debts, "Uncle Sap," and "decadent France." At times, I must admit, I felt a wild surge of the sensations that the young Nazis and the young Croix de Feu felt when for other reasons they wanted to sweep away their parliaments which "did nothing but talk." It was a Fascist impulse and I knew it, but now and then I could not help it. Scotty Reston, who had also come to Washington, would frown benignly and admonish me: "Take it easy, Eric. They're slow, but don't forget—they *are* democracy. Maybe they would also be slow in giving in to a man on a white horse. They're torpid, but some day maybe you'll thank God they are." Scotty was right, as he was always right, but swift-moving time and shocking events obsessed me. My subconscious was always somewhere else. I wouldn't walk around the block to see a streetcar accident, no matter how unprecedentedly awful, but when the battleship *Hood* went down, a thousand miles distant, I suffered indigestion half the day.

One did indeed lose friends. With the few American Communists whom I knew, I could not carry on a conversation for long without losing my temper. They still spoke glibly of the "imperialist war" which could somehow be miraculously stopped and Hitler made to step gracefully back if only America would "get together" with the Soviet Union. If you suggested that the Russians themselves were in danger and would be mortally so if Britain went down, they returned a wise, tolerant smile that suggested: "There are things you do not understand, my simple friend." Even with dear old Frederick Thompson, one of the first to oppose the Nazis in Europe, it was a little awkward. But he could understand that my feeling about the British under bombing was the same as his about the Spaniards under bombing, and our friendship did not break. When, on that June day, the Russians found themselves in the war—they, too, stupidly surprised and minus seven thousand front-line planes thereby—I felt no particular pleasure at the sudden conversion of the American and British Communists. They had forfeited all respect.

With some young liberals—decent, intelligent men and women with whom I had always identified myself—I now felt a curious lack of unity, almost a repugnance. One would drop into the taste-

ful apartment of friends, both Jewish and Gentile, able young
"New Dealers," and find a company sitting cross-legged on the
floor, listening to Bach or fervently discussing a new book on, for
example, "Freudianism in the American literary tradition." Copies
of *The New Republic* or *The Nation* would be strewn around.
They would argue about Fascism, Diego Rivera, the Dunkirk
beaches, and the philosophical conception of esthetics with equal
ease and equal vigor. They were the true intellectuals, not I, for
they believed in knowledge for its own sake, while for me it had
no meaning beyond its application to the mortal crisis of my time.
I could only fall silent in their presence. I felt that, for all their
rightness, they understood the war only in their minds and did
not feel it in their bones.

Old idols became new enemies in this upheaval of the nation.
Men I had worshipped in college days, leaders of the Populist
tradition in which I was bred, who had taught me once to hate
war more than anything else, whose devotion to the cause of common people could not be questioned—these men now suddenly
appeared upon the scene as the most dangerous misleaders of the
very people they had fought so long to aid. The "good, grey"
Norman Thomas, the LaFollette brothers, Burton Wheeler, and,
to a lesser degree, Nye and Senator Shipstead, a family friend. I
remember Floyd Olson saying to us once: "I would rather have
Burton Wheeler head a third-party ticket; I'd be his manager." I
wondered where Olson would stand now; I could not believe he
would be with them still. From my northwest country had come
only one leader who had renounced our native tradition and seen
that it was too late—Senator Ball, whom I remembered as a shaggy,
fierce-eyed reporter around the state house in Minnesota. Two—
with Governor Stassen, whom as students we had glibly written
off as a simple "power politician" and who was doing more for the
intelligent cause now than the rest of us put together. But what
had happened to the others? Or, rather, what had not happened?

They had not altered; they automatically applied the lessons (or
the supposed lessons) of the first war to this new crisis. They
believed that making war to save democracy would be the surest
way of losing it. They believed that the struggle itself was the
greatest of all evils—not the results if the struggle were lost. They
could not see that a society can become *more* democratic by
reason of the struggle, as the British had proved. They could not
see, as I had seen in France, that the alternatives to fighting can

be worse than the fighting, that men who have known the alternatives would, of their free will, fight again rather than submit to those. The deep suspicion of all things European, native to our northwest soil, inherited from our forebears, still dominated their minds, and they would not understand that the world had drawn together and was one. But one could not repress a certain admiration for their stubbornness; they clung to their beliefs by a deep conviction and not by reason of political party alignment as did so many others. Yet a sincere man in the wrong is the most dangerous of opponents; they were very dangerous men. One could meet their old, familiar arguments. It was harder to contest the far more modern objections of men like Robert Hutchins of Chicago, who broadcast his cogent warning that the American people were "intellectually unprepared" for war, that they would enter it, if they did, not knowing precisely why they fought and unlikely therefore to make fruitful the victory they would win. His speech shook me deeply. His premise was correct, his conclusion wrong. It didn't matter; it didn't matter now whether we fought blindly or with understanding. We had to fight and there was no time to stand upon enlightenment. (I was to see at first hand as victory approached in other lands how right his premise had been, how badly we misused our triumph—but still there had been no other real choice.)

In the leafy outskirts of the Capital azaleas flamed beside the quiet doors. The dogwood clothed its branches in the tender white of first communion, and cherry blossoms fattened by the placid waters. In the early morning, even at the city's center, one caught the perfumes in the downy southern air. The city toward which all the world looked in hope or fear lay nestled in its scented couch of spring. News came that the bloodied band of New Zealand soldiers was staggering, beaten, toward the southern shores of Crete. Somewhere among them, I knew, was Geoffrey, a steel helmet tilted over his mobile, sensitive face. How was he faring under the "physical thing" that he had feared so frankly and dared to face? What had been the transaction between him and those six-foot paratroopers of Ebaen Emael? In the early morning a young man with a slim face walked with slow dignity back and forth before the White House gates, bearing a sign that asked: "Do you want your sons eaten by sharks?" He, too, feared the physical thing and did not wish to face it; there, but for the grace of God and a cheap ticket to Europe, I walked myself. From the radio in my living-room came the grandiloquent words of the Senator from North Dakota, the man with the dark, tight face who had once been a hero: "If we can marry freedom to the conquest of poverty, we can kindle the light which ultimately will put to flight even the darkness of the lands under dictatorship, as the morning sun puts to flight the shadows of the night. This is our true and glorious destiny." He was saying that we need not face the physical thing, that by purifying our own souls we would cause the great brutes of Ebaen Emael to steal away in shame. Private news arrived from Egypt: Geoffrey was missing on Crete.

Public speakers were using the word "patriotism." It occurred to me suddenly that I had never heard nor seen it used in England.

Somehow, many of those who had been uprooted by the streams of hate in Europe made good their escapes. Hertha Pauli was already in America, unembittered by what she had seen, writing for children of the Christmas spirit and of Nobel who had tried to endow with money the spirit of peace. I did what I could for Ernst Adam, but he had honestly told the Lisbon consul that he had once been a Communist. (Some who lied got to the States.) The British ultimately took him in. Fat little Kurt Dosmar of the prison camp at Le Mans walked into my office one afternoon. Nineteen times the Vichy police of Marseille had thrown him in and out of their jail; how he had existed he could scarcely remember. On the Spanish boat he and his fellow refugees had been cursed and half-starved by the Fascist crew. Sick and despondent they remained aboard for weeks, not allowed to disembark at Havana. Some took their own lives. They passed close to Miami, and the sight of the gleaming, luxurious lights made them tremble and weep. In New York harbor Dosmar, with sharpened cunning, got his first and last revenge. He whispered to a port official that there was typhus among the crew, and none of the Spaniards was allowed on shore while the ship remained. A telegram arrived from a Jewish rescue committee in Norfolk, Virginia, informing me that a refugee named Karli Frucht required a further endorsement before he could land; he had been held aboard by immigration authorities unsatisfied as to his political beliefs. All the others had disembarked. The ship was due to put about for Europe within a few hours. I ran the two blocks to the telegraph office. He appeared one day with a wide smile, held out a soiled roll of khaki cloth, and said rather shyly: "You see, I have returned your sleeping bag to you. I think in America there will be no need." He thrashed wheat in Indiana, labored as a machinist in a New York defense factory, then joined the army as a private and became a citizen of the United States. Others came. All felt constrained to public silence in the great American debate, but now and then, after vociferous guests who believed it was "none of our business" had departed, hesitant remarks, dry as alum, escaped their unsteady lips.

The members of the original Jacobin Club were scattered now into their various professions. I found a few. The old, heady feeling of comradeship had been dissipated with absence and maturity, but it was a distinct relief to find them thinking now as I did. They were teaching, practicing the kind of law that counted, editing papers, or serving in government in capacities where government touched the people. Loevinger remained with the Labor Board; Fritz Rarig was with the Justice Department; Dryer was each week collecting the best brains of the country to expound for millions some fateful issue at the University of Chicago "Round Table." Scammon was with him, but he remained a direct actionist and was following his convictions out to their logical conclusion; long before he could join the army as a private, he was organizing home guards in Chicago and drilling with wooden weapons in the evening. Bill Costello had returned from Japan and was beating the warning drum wherever he had the chance. All of them knew. I had had to see the thing at first hand, to feel it, in order to comprehend. They were blessed with the courage of their reasoning powers.

Slowly the President was gathering together a reluctant, bewildered, and resentful army. No civil leaders dared call them "soldiers"—as though there were something shameful in the word. They were "draftees" and "selectees." An impression was given that they were herded together for wholesome reasons that had to do with their moral upbringing and physical training; few made so bold as to suggest that their job was to learn to kill. The War Department spoke soothing words to their parents, to whom it was pointed out that the food was just like the food at home and that movie actors and actresses were taking a personal interest in "the boys." There was a great deal of talk at official cocktail parties about "morale." No one seemed to understand that morale is a matter of the spirits of men, that it is a word left unspoken when men know clearly what they do and why they must do it. How could they know, these civilians in khaki, when they read the Hearst and McCormick press, when they listened to the contentions of congressmen that the nation had no need for soldiers? What could there be of morale when in August 1941 the House of Representatives, dividing on party lines, decided not to disband the army—by a margin of just one vote?

A national magazine solemnly declared that the new army was breaking up, that the men would desert when their first year's term was ended. OHIO was furtively printed on barrack walls—it meant: "Over the hill in October." I went out to the nearest army camp, ate with the men, and watched them. I thought, with rather smug self-satisfaction: "I have learned something about soldiers in Europe. These men will not desert." They bickered, complained, and cussed—but they did it out loud. They slammed the baseball around in the evening, whistled at the few girls who passed on the board walks, chased one another with buckets of water. The solemn warning was absurd. It is when men say nothing to one another, when they bend silently over their food, when they lie listlessly on their bunks in the evening, that spirits are breaking, that the danger point is reached.

In the fall it was a relief to get away from the queasy atmosphere of the Capital and work for a month as a correspondent with the new army on its first—and last—big maneuvers, beginning among the steaming Louisiana bayous and then on the frosty red earth of the Carolinas. There was immense release in dealing again with things that one could see and feel: the rumpled, red-eyed men humped together in their trucks in the foggy half-light of dawn, their talk and laughter, their vibrant curses, and their silences through the changing hours of zest and utter weariness. The Negro boy who sat silhouetted on the hillock each night as the fires died, playing a guitar and singing a little off key a song about Georgia with an unspeakable pathos and love. It was glorious to ride a lead dive bomber through the splendid world of blue and white, to look to the right and the left and see the wing planes steadily there, so close one could almost touch them, the brown faces of the pilots turned at the same precision angle, arrowing in toward me. (It was my last affair of love with an airplane.) We correspondents were very military indeed. Some, including me, wore riding boots; we had conducting officers, press conferences, and technical sessions over the maps. Sometimes, when they would rout us out of bed at three in the morning for a hundred-mile drive, we felt they were carrying the simulated war a little too far; but for the most part it was all an enjoyable camping trip—at least for the reporters. Some of the colleagues had long, abstruse discussions about the strategy involved; the "military experts" from leading newspapers were concerned with the technical excellences and the more evident deficiencies: the bad intelligence work, the indecision shown by junior officers, the failure of troops on the road to appreciate the menace of strafing planes, the timidity of tank drivers who were reluctant to break off the highways. Visiting British officers were impressed by the native American genius in handling the convoys—and indeed I was rapidly coming to the conclusion that half the art of handling a modern army in combat is the purely mathematical business of controlling traffic. For the most part, however, I found that these matters left me cold and that I was truly concerned only with the men themselves and their state of mind and heart. I clung to my intuitive belief that the true test of any army is a matter of the spirits of men, which alone could not be improvised by American ingenuity or purchased by American wealth.

One saw the answer in quick little moments of revealing action. A fighter pilot of the "Blue" army had engine trouble and was obliged to make a forced landing in "Red" territory. He was really in trouble—no "practice" was involved; yet when he stumbled out of his half-wrecked plane an excited "Red" sentryman was already upon him, fiercely thrusting his gun in the pilot's direction even before inquiring whether the "enemy" was injured. One frosty Carolina evening a slow line of fat transport planes passed before the russet, sinking sun like lazy fish, emitting rows of great, white bubbles from their gills. In the night the electric lights of our headquarters camp went out and the 'phone was dead. Under a strategic bridge, where all our traffic was stopped, we came upon the dark, nimble figures of the paratroopers. They were gathered around an umpire who doubted that they had properly wired the bridge for blowing. They behaved like tense high-school basketball players contesting a close decision. They cursed, pleaded, expostulated, slammed their leather caps on the ground in their frustration, and one trembling young sergeant burst into angry tears. Some of the reporters decried it as a "mess"; I was elated and astonished. What gave them this fierce drive and spirit? I could not imagine French troops behaving thus in any kind of "practice" war. For the French *knew* war—they knew it in their souls, even the very young who had missed the First World War It was true that these American boys were ignorant of what they were training for, but did it matter? When the blank cartridges became real and their comrades began to die beside them, would they draw back in revulsion and fright, or would they, challenged and angry, fight the harder? No one could tell for certain. Now they were striving so hard out of "team spirit," out of pride in their particular outfits, out of the pure American sense of competition and a certain pride in competence which seemed to me also a special American trait.

I sat on a log in the command post of Brigadier General Hester, who had been my first commanding officer in the military training of college days. I wondered that I had failed to notice the kindly wrinkles around his eyes, the paternalistic, affectionate manner in which he spoke to the youngsters under his charge. He joked a little about the activities of my undergraduate crowd. There was very little I could say on this autumn day of 1941, surrounded by men in uniform, by a world in uniform, myself clothed in khaki. Yet I was thinking: Even so, even so. We, at least for one short, holy moment in our lives, tried to renounce all this in the only way we knew how to. At least once we were touched by the purest of passions against all this. I still do not believe you who deliberately chose this profession have ever really felt the exalted thing we felt. You pity me, perhaps; I still feel a little sorry for you.

As we sat there two of the maneuver directors walked in. One I knew—General Mark Clark. The other, who answered my questions with quiet precision and looked at me with remarkably steady eyes in a relaxed face, was introduced as Eisenhower; he had just been made a general officer. (I recalled that in the preceding maneuvers Robert Sherrod had urged me to see a Colonel Eisenhower—"he makes more sense than any of the rest of them." I hadn't bothered.) Two generals. Two men with the same training and beliefs. As the succeeding years passed, my own daily life and the life and death of countless others were to become mixed up with the thought processes and instincts of these two personalities. I was to see one of them become the victim of the natural pressures of his position and fame, while the other became their master, his heart expanding rather than contracting under duress until he was more than a mere leader of men.

A few days later, on a Sunday afternoon, I was sitting in my own living-room talking with Phil Potter, who had been editor of our university paper and now was a news editor of the Baltimore *Sun*. I had not seen him for several years, and we were speaking of our college activities, trying to puzzle out what had happened to us. A neighbor, hatless and in a hurry, tapped on my window, shouted: "Turn on your radio," and dashed to the next house in the street. With the others I worked many hours that night of December 7 in the White House press room. Ed Murrow, on this night of all nights in a lifetime, was dining inside with the Roosevelts, they having declined to cancel the invitations despite the sudden events. He came into the office around midnight and said: "It's pretty bad." He looked in my direction and continued: "What did you think when you saw that crowd of people staring through the White House fence?" I replied: "They reminded me of the crowds around the Quai d'Orsay a couple of years ago." "That's what I was thinking," he replied; "the same look on their faces that they had in Downing Street."

The stunned and anxious nation slept badly that night, I have no doubt. For me there was a feeling of enormous relief; the feeling that we had won, even before the fight began, had survived, even before the onslaught. I slept like a baby.

3

There was growing danger that the British would be thrown out of Africa, that Hitler with the connivance of the Vichy French would control all of northwest Africa and Dakar. The Japanese were sniping at our ships along the western coastlines; all of Latin America lay defenseless and exposed on the Pacific; and inside these uncertain countries, as all the world knew, tens of thousands of enemy aliens were waiting, willing subjects of orders from Tokio and Berlin. Somehow their governments must be held in line, their people made to understand the Allied cause, their ports kept open for us and closed to the enemy, their immense resources of food and rubber and ore made to flow in our exclusive direction. A vast continent had to be organized quickly, by diplomacy, by money, by promises, by the gift of guns, and, if need be, by the threat of guns. The foreign ministers were called in conclave at Rio for the third Pan American Conference, and I flew down to watch Sumner Welles—a stiff, correct, reserved product of Anglo-

Saxon life—try to make common cause with the voluble, excitable, fickle leaders of the totally different Latin culture.

Heretofore, the compulsion of events and cultural inheritance had confined my movements in thought and space almost entirely along the axis of East and West. The "top" of the world, north of the equator, had been the only world of palpable reality; all that "down below" was a kind of vague, grassy suburb of civilization, peopled by a curious mixture of black, brown, and white human beings of diverse and obscure origins, of interest to anthropologists and amateur explorers with cameras and plenty of time to waste. I possessed but the vaguest notion of the material advancement of each South American land, their regimes and their aspirations. The stream of history, as I knew it, had passed them by. I took it for granted that they were acutely aware of us; but I had little sense of embarrassment in asking them questions about Bolívar and exactly what it was that he had done. However I may have accepted myself as a citizen of the world, I was a natural product of the North American-North European segment of the world's culture, with all its limitations. Now I made the disturbing discovery that, despite my peregrinations, I had never really broken across native frontiers, that in terms of the whole world I remained provincial.

It was disturbing to find Brazil so vast, so tranquilly at ease in her spaciousness upon the earth of crowded frontiers and shoving peoples. Even from a speeding plane, one could take the measure of her unending forests and limitless plains not in hours but only in days and nights. It was a discovery to look down upon scarred, interior mountain ranges and to realize that great movements of men had surged into these areas in a gold-seeking rush comparable to that of California before my ancestors had even heard of the Northwest Territories. It was a revelation to walk the mosaic pavements of an Amazon city—until then a meaningless dot upon the map—to see a stately opera house now drowning in jungle growth, to read a forgotten plaque that read: "Pavlova danced here," and thus to know that a highly cultivated life had flourished briefly in this fetid jungle, then died away while its symbols in mortar and stone turned yellow in decay and sank back into the damp, suffocating tentacles of the forest. All this had occurred in a shorter span than the one in which my forebears had won and temporarily lost the prairie country. *They* had won back their civilization with the simple aid of rain; the men of the Amazon were receiving back

their life now as a curious gift of war. The whole story was one
of the superbly ironic and tragic jests of history. Shortly after the
turn of the century an Englishman had smuggled out through the
rigid Amazon control a few of the precious rubber seeds, and
from them was developed in a short space of time the whole
rubber economy of the Malay Straits. As a result the industry
and civilization of the Amazon decayed and perished. It was a
monumental example of the fatal anarchy that ruled the unplanned
world of commercial license which operated without heed of the
deliberate plans of other men and the inevitable course of politics.
The industry so basic to power and security, removed from this
safe geographic center, was inherited intact by Japanese expansion, and now the desperate Allies were being obliged to pour
men, machinery, and money back into the Amazon jungle in a
frantic attempt to recreate a dead economy and bring the ghosts to
life.

The plane issued from the Brazilian hinterland through a tunnel
of purple storm cloud and passed through the narrow gate formed
by two soaring mountain peaks, and Rio lay spread below, inert
and gleaming white beside azure waters. It is at once a majestic
and a gentle vista, this dreaming city on the underside of the world,
painted with sunny colors into the great dark scar in the continent's
side. It seemed to me at first that I had returned to Paris, a Paris
shifted to the Riviera shores. The impression soon passes. It is not
that the Brazilians are slow and warm to strangers while the
Parisians are quick and self-contained, nor that the one is curious
and the other indifferent. The difference is that Paris has an inner
life and Rio has almost none. The life of Rio is there, on the surface, simple, comfortable and lazy, in one dimension, quite flat,
with no deepening perspectives of art, philosophy, or social aspiration. In time it becomes merely a pleasant, painted backdrop to
a sunny, caressing, and sensual life, the dullest and emptiest of
cities. Here I found a few familiar faces I had last seen, white and
drawn, in the cafés of Lisbon and Estoril. A journalist from Paris,
a Dutch photographer I knew well, a humorless Austrian woman
and her terrier which had nipped my heels in Portugal. They had
all grown brown and healthy and slowly desperate. They rose
late, ate slowly, dozed hours on the beaches, and in the cool evenings grew a little hysterical over their drinks as they were stabbed
by the pain of our presence into an acute awareness of their arid,
emptying lives. They had leaped from the frying pan into the warm

bed of ashes where they slowly suffocated in their comfort. They
had found sanctuary for their bodies and a desert prison for their
minds.

Brazil was a bizarre exhibit in the South American hall of political wonders. It did not fit into any of the categories with which
I was familiar. It was praised as a true democracy by some who
pointed out that whites and blacks lived, if not in complete economic equality, at least in easy tolerance, that no one was penalized
by reason of race or religion, that there was no vast apparatus of
ruthless state police. Indeed, one saw none of the usual trappings
of Fascist rule. When President Vargas felt the impulse he simply
walked out of his government palace to the café on the corner
and had a coffee while chatting with the clients, without benefit
of armed protection. Others who admitted that this midget, kewpie-doll of a man had taken power by force and abolished the
parliament maintained that he was a "benevolent dictator," that
the people were manifestly happy, and therefore what did the
label matter? Why should I concern myself that the people did
not truly rule when the people seemed quite content to let him
do the ruling for them?

Many of our embassy officials argued thus; and surely the Roosevelt administration was happy in the arrangement—so long as the
regime remained on our side. When I said I preferred Mexico,
however unruly, they snorted in derision. What was the end of
social life? To them it was tranquillity and order. To me, despite
this offensive, it remained freedom—the freedom of the individual
to develop his own personality to the fullest within his personal
limitations, and the security to make that possible. They said: "You
mean that black man carrying the hod at the corner must be guaranteed the opportunity to find out whether he is another Tolstoy
or Picasso?" I thought that this *was* what I meant, and they smiled.
It was a rude test of all that I had learned in my earlier life—and
somehow, in these surroundings, those precepts were made to
seem naïve, childish, and quite inapplicable. I told myself
that the basic strivings of men remain universal, and that there
must somewhere be evidence that this kind of system is stultifying,
a negation of all that democracy ought to mean. The evidence
was not, after all, so hard to find. Students would come furtively
to the hotel at night with fat dossiers, small dark young men with
anxious eyes who ticked off the names of their fellows, their
teachers, who had been squeezed out or driven away and im-

prisoned because their spirits were too liberal for the government. Political hostages still decayed in their cells back in the hills or on barren islands. With bitterness they acknowledged that the people were torpid, that intellectual and artistic life was scarcely breathing—but how could their people ever begin to know that a rich life could be theirs for the effort, when a half-dozen men controlled all that was written and spoken in the name of "order"? Only Brazil's rulers needed order; Brazil needed a little disorder that would touch the heart.

It seemed quite incredible that this enormous section of the earth, and these millions of human beings, were firmly under the control of these few men who pumped our hands, bared gleaming teeth in the warmest of smiles, toasted us and one another at innumerable receptions, danced with one another's wives, and moved constantly between two or three government buildings, to the Copacabana, to the Urca casino, and around again in a circumscribed circle. This was Ruritania, this was Luxembourg City planted in a country bigger in extent than the United States. One could walk into Vargas's palace with only a smile from the guard as a barrier; one could gamble with Vargas's son and learn to dance the samba with his attractive daughter; one could chat for two hours with the army chief of staff, look over his most secret document—a Nazi map showing all their enclaves in the country—and be admonished only thus: "Now you mustn't tell about this map. But of course you will not, you are our good North American friend." In the presidential summer palace at Petropolis I did a broadcast seated at the cabinet desk while the most powerful dictator in the hemisphere, his shirt open at the neck, looked over my shoulder, puffed on a cigar, and balanced his newest grandchild on his arm.

It was indeed personal government in more ways than one. The whole psychology was personal. One did not discuss political programs or principles; one discussed the predilections of individuals. There was the same thing I was to encounter in China, the matter of "face." If you criticized the methods of the propaganda ministry, you were insulting the minister himself; you were not a "friend." If they said that the United States and Brazil were close allies, they meant that Vargas and Roosevelt got along well in their occasional telephone conversations. When, some time later, I wrote in a *Saturday Evening Post* article that it was significant that a gambling casino was the only new piece of construction the ministry showed reporters (meaning only that the country was far distant in spirit from the war), officials protested to my company that I had accused the propaganda minister of personal corruption, and all copies of the issue were confiscated in Brazil.

If these gentlemen were Fascists in a soft, chrysalis stage, the Argentine leaders who came to Rio were a matured variety, but with their own special characteristics. They were not back-alley gangsters of the Hitler or Himmler type; they were sleek, social snobs like Franz von Papen, but less assured, less adept. They were beautifully dressed, glossily finished to the last hair in their eyebrows. They carried themselves with an air of ostentatious superiority and expressed by the very angle of their aristocratic noses their contempt for the "primitive" Brazilians whose white suits were carelessly rumpled, and for the "vulgar" North Americans who chewed gum and mixed their drinks. They clung to their French cultural tradition and affected to despise the crass materialism of the United States. They were quite absurd, more vulgar themselves than anyone present. Visibly tense and touchy they were undoubtedly the world's worst diplomats. Instead of cleverly playing upon the susceptibilities of the Northern journalists, their foreign minister, Ruiz Guinazu—an insufferable, pompous man with pince-nez and a haughty abdomen—would cancel press conferences, then call them again and keep reporters waiting in a suffocating corridor for an hour. The result was that only a few of the meeker spirits among the journalists ever saw the man, and his ultimate statements were quite worthless.

The Argentine upper class clearly resented and disapproved of the rest of the world. One of them, an honest friend whose horizons had widened through residence in the States, was complaining to me about the Hollywood characterization of his country as a land of fandango dancers and gauchos, and about John Gunther's comments on Argentina in his latest book. I said: "I don't understand you people. You can write or say anything you please about the United States and its culture. Our people may be a bit amused by it, but they don't get their feelings hurt and they don't get angry." He showed the most remarkable reaction; he was like a man struck in the breast by a sudden arrow. He looked at me with a suffering expression. "My God," he said, "you are right! We've just got a terrific inferiority complex. That's the answer. Oh, my God!"

As I came to know him with growing intimacy, I developed a

respect for Sumner Welles, who was often written off by many Washington observers and by the public as merely another "old school tie" professional diplomat, more interested in the form than the substance of his work, intellectually rigid and sheltered from the sweating realities of common people. In truth he could not help his formal manner and his Harvard accent any more than I could help my soft felt hat and my Middle Western speech. If he was rigid in manner, he was equally so in his integrity, and if he was unrelaxing in social intercourse he was that way also in devotion to his tasks. He possessed a Jacksonian sense of duty, which I was to find in a few other Americans such as General Marshall and Henry L. Stimson—the thing that had been so fatally lacking among leaders of the French. One was awed to witness the daily labors these men accomplished. After war began, Welles rigorously followed a routine that involved rising at six, riding horseback for a precise forty-five minutes to keep his body toned, then some ten hours at his desk, uninterrupted by lunch, which he ruled out as a waste of time. Except for a cabinet session or a White House function he never went out at night but worked through most of the evening.

I was beginning to understand what it took to master the responsibilities of public life, and my own work habits appeared in contrast as the spasmodic gestures of an adolescent.

It was wiltingly humid in the auditorium of the Tiradentes Palace as one of the general sessions droned toward a fretful close. Rio's midsummer heat weighed like a heavy sleeping gas upon the rows of worn-out delegates. We wiped the rivulets of sweat from our faces for the hundredth time, plucked our sticking shirts away from our prickly skin. Welles had spoken; Aranha had spoken. God pity the orator who would try now, and God pity us. Now Padilla, the foreign minister of Mexico, quietly rose, walked with slow easy steps to the podium, and lifted up his tall, broad body with a catlike grace. I found myself straightening up and watching with slow fascination the handsomest man I had ever seen in public life. There was something almost noble about the leonine cast of his head, crowned with soft, curling black hair; there was strength in the breadth of his bronzed Indian countenance and a tender serenity in the big, dark eyes that moved leisurely across the assembly and came frequently to rest with an almost yearning regard upon the Argentine and Chilean delegates, who alone were spoiling the unanimity of this historic meeting. I cannot remember his words now, though they were printed in a million copies. I know that he spoke in a low, compelling voice of the brotherhood of men and the dreams of freedom and liberty which had lived in the breasts of those who came to settle this new world and to struggle for its survival. There was a quiet, throbbing passion in his words which could not have been simulated by the greatest actor in the world. I knew Spanish only very poorly, yet the simplicity and power of his words seemed to burst all barriers of communication and one could not help understanding him clearly. Cynics in the press gallery were scribbling madly; Ruiz Guinazu was removing and replacing his pince-nez with agitated fingers; and Welles, the "frozen Boston cod," was bolt upright, his austere face aglow. There was pandemonium when Padilla finished and stepped slowly down. In the women's gallery there were tears. Frank Gervasi of *Collier's*, next to me, breathed a long "Jee-zus!" and said: "Eric, my friend, you and I have just had the uncommon privilege of seeing the debut of one of the great men on earth. Or a great personality. Anyway, by God, a great *something!*"

Traffic stopped wherever he went. The women threw flowers in his path. Rio was at his feet. He was something of a mystic, but more than that: he was also an extremely shrewd practical politician, and—as leftist Mexican friends sometimes complained—he frequently compromised and turned with the tides. But for that matter, so did Roosevelt, or any man seeking full power. He cherished a concept of the free Americas as a new and powerful entity, as a self-sustaining, protected garden in which democracy could flower. He thought in terms of the combined spirits and personalities of the Western countries—the United States, which meant liberty most of all, Brazil, which stood for equality—"the land of cordial men"—and Mexico, which had a particular passion for social justice. I could not quite share his enthusiasm for this Western association of nations for I believed the world was already too small and crowded for anything but the union of the whole; but, despite the later attacks upon him, I could never quite lose faith in Padilla himself. I could not forget that he had accomplished at least one big thing at one crucial moment and had proved again for me, as Churchill had proved, that words can affect the course of state affairs and that the personality of a man

can be a weight in the balance of institutions, however impersonal
and vast.

In the soft evening the stars were close, and the Southern Cross
glowed faintly in a far corner of the blue-black sky. A thousand
guests in summer white drifted through the perfumed, seductive
gardens of the Guanabara Palace, more serenely lovely than the
Bagatelle. The kewpie-doll master of the land smiled benignly
from the top of the marble stairway. Colored fountains were playing, soft music floated out from orchestras hidden in the waving
palms, and a graceful ballet group was dancing in filmy white.
High on the mountain peak the majestic lighted figure of the
Christus soared over the city with outspread arms. This was Versailles under Louis Quatorze; this was no part of my world of
crisis. A cocktail glass fell with a tinkling crash. A sleek Brazilian
with brilliantined hair was saying: "Brazil doesn't want war.
Brazil doesn't want peace. Brazil just wants to have fun."

In the morning, the white sand of the Copacabana beach was
warm against the drowsing body. A cannon went off on the island
fortress that guards the bay. It was only a salute, another toast to
somebody or something. A friend dropped the morning paper
beside me. The leading story related how an American division,
the first to go overseas, had just landed in Ireland after a cold
passage on the blustering North Atlantic. It was a National Guard
division, the Thirty-fourth, composed of the Scandinavians, the
Germans, and Irish from Minnesota, Iowa, and parts of the Da·
kotas.

4

Rommel's legions reappeared at Tobruk, and the whole Middle
East was again under mortal threat; enemy torpedoes sucked
American ships below the surface of the crystal Caribbean, so
close that a chorus girl in a Miami penthouse could see men die
in flaming oil, and all the work to mobilize the southern continent
faced humiliating failure; Englishmen, the lords of the East, were
stripped and beaten on the streets of Singapore; all of Australia
lay exposed, and on a rock in Manila Bay exhausted, ragged men,
suffering too deeply for tears, hoisted a white flag in the first real

American surrender in more than a hundred years of secure existence.

And in the crowded night clubs of New York men and women danced slowly to the saccharine melody of a song called "Remember-r-r Pearl Harbor-r-r," and rapidly to the frenzied strains of the latest jive hit. There was money to burn, and it was burned in a bright, gay flame. Fifth Avenue shops sold handkerchiefs embroidered with patriotic monograms for ten dollars apiece, news reels pointed out the "military motif" in the latest fashions, and the expanded society pages gave convincing proof that the Junior League had indeed gone into uniform. Resort hotels ran out of space, and gasoline and rubber bootleggers became our richest citizens. Six-column headlines blared the good news every time that three Jap planes went down; full-page advertisements announced the inspiring news that Lucky Strikes had gone to war; street placards in three colors advised the nation that its war production would be increased if everyone masticated a few extra sticks of Wrigley's per day, and a hundred local radio stations offered the virtues of laxative and liver pills along with the news of humanity's crisis and in the same fulsome tones. The cuffs were eliminated from men's trousers, and it made front-page news; coffee and sugar were rationed to the accompaniment of loud complaints, and neighbors were encouraged to spy upon one another's pantries.

In Washington the Office of Civilian Defense held solemn conferences about the problem of leisure hours and considered folk dancing as one solution. "Ten per centers" made a hundred thousand dollars by introducing a manufacturer to a Navy purchasing agent at lunch in the Hotel Carlton. The McCormick-Patterson press continued to revile the Russians and suspect the British as if America had allies to spare. New Dealers worried more about social gains than about society's life or death, and anti-New Dealers saw their chance to smash the New Deal and tried their best to do it. The South remained reluctant to use the latent powers of several million Negroes. Coal miners' unions thought they saw their chance to consolidate themselves and struck the mines, while antiunion businessmen believed their hour had come to smash the unions. The Hearst press warned that to give the President power to run the war would be to sell the country into slavery. The President set up three agencies to do the work of one, so that no one could tell who was doing what, and did not fire anybody, however incompetent. War agencies sought the aid of the radio and press while the Justice Department and the courts ordered the radio networks and the greatest news agency to alter their basic system of organization. Mr. Donald Nelson wanted to organize production by industrial committees, but there was always the threat of Mr. Thurman Arnold, who still fought monopolies. The President said that no man should earn more than twenty-five thousand dollars a year after taxes; the head of the National Chamber of Commerce said that this would cause "dislocations," and the chairman of Cleveland's Chamber said it would force men to work for nothing and that few men were *that* patriotic.

The Congress alternately dozed and shouted, and its members sought to make debating points rather than to find the truth. They seemed to believe that wars are won exclusively on the fighting fronts, and did their best to emasculate the Offices of War Information and Price Control. They refused to streamline themselves for war and abolish their fatal seniority system; they refused to face down the lobbyists in the name of the whole people, and in the name of politics they gave the farmers everything their insatiable self-appointed spokesmen demanded, while sleepy-eyed Ed O'Neal of the reactionary Farm Bureau Federation watched from the gallery and for days at a time controlled the Senate of the United States.

The nation was encouraged to believe that it could produce its way to victory, or buy its victory by the simple measure of writing a check. Life was easy and getting more prosperous every week, and nobody believed in death. In the interests of "civilian morale" the War Department refused to permit publication of pictures showing dead American soldiers; and when I wrote a broadcast about the broken young bodies and trembling hands already to be seen in Walter Reed Hospital and the faceless boys whose airplanes had exploded, a War Department censor tried to make me write about the splendid new drugs and instruments instead.

No one would understand that the war was also a social revolution and a civil war between one old form of life and one trying to be born. Little men sniggered at the Four Freedoms, and the great vision of the century of the common man was sneered at as "globaloney." The New York *Daily News* consulted with its soul and discovered that the aim and end of our bloody struggle was to get back to the baseball game and the full tank of gas. In a dozen allied countries liberal and progressive thinkers bled in

Gestapo jails and died of unmentionable tortures because they wanted to remake the world in the people's name, and in Washington kid lawyers of the FBI, lately out of Delta Upsilon, gumshoed about in federal agencies hunting for "subversive elements" —frequently defined as anybody who wrote for *The New Republic,* or had supported the Republican cause in martyred Spain, or had entertained Negroes in his home.

One felt bewildered and at sea. Those who had known France during the "phony war" and Britain before the iron of Dunkirk had entered its soul were anguished and ashamed before their Allied friends. No doubt one wrote and spoke more than once in a tone that bordered on pious preaching. One lost his temper and his serener friends and was often told that the people were all right at bottom and to please stop nagging them. But this was not the America of Tom Paine and Valley Forge; this looked like the France of 1940 when major men were champions of minor issues. We had the greatest potential apparatus in the world for waging war and the best possible reservoir of healthy soldiers, but did we have the *will?* We had the freest discussion in the world and the greatest fund of information, but did we have the *faith?* What had happened to the passion of Sam Adams, the vision of Jefferson, the unshakable courage of Abraham Lincoln? Where, indeed, were the stark proposals of a Churchill who offered nothing but blood and tears, so great were the issue and the gain? If the battle news was good one day, people relaxed; if it was bad the next, they fretted and were gloomy—as though we were the helpless victims of mileage and tonnage and the alternating proportions of steel and iron gadgets, with faith and will of no account in the settlements of human destiny.

We argued these things on a hundred evenings while the azaleas flamed again and another spring approached. Out of our talk and agitation, Scotty produced a book he called *Prelude to Victory,* in words that burned the pages and electrified the spirit. It was perhaps the finest statement of our troubles and the issues written throughout the war. Few read it. "People won't pay money to be lectured," the publisher said.

Robert Ardrey, playwright of the magnificent *Thunder Rock,* said: "Maybe we cannot blame the people too much for what appears complacency to us. In playwriting terms, we've had no 'inciting moment,' when all the threads draw together in the second act and the dénouement becomes inevitable. The people have

been living in the second act for too many years. This generation
has never known a period when it was not in crisis. Not even
Pearl Harbor was our inciting moment. The action has gone on
so long that people cease identifying themselves with the actors
and remain the audience."

Either we had had so many minor crises that we could not
recognize the great and final one, or else the last great crisis calling
for true national faith was so long past in time that in our diversi-
ties of origins, work, and space we had come to think of ourselves
as laborers or managers or Easterners or Westerners, and only
last as Americans. Certain it was in these months that thousands
vented their spleen upon compatriots instead of upon the nation's
enemies. Justice Brandeis, before he died, confessed to a feeling
that perhaps Americans needed a war to resurrect their common
faith and unity.

Yet America was not a moral bankrupt. There were great men
around who required neither profit nor adulation to hold them
to their duty. There was first and foremost the President, who
alternately irritated, disappointed, and enraptured one, and yet
one was obliged in the end to recognize him as a man who would
surely stand near Washington and Lincoln, who was a great man
in historic terms despite his failure to cast his thoughts in historic
utterance. There was General Marshall, the Chief of Staff, a hulking, homely man of towering intellect, the memory of an unnatural
genius, and the integrity of a Christian saint. The atmosphere of
controlled power he exuded made one feel oneself a physical
weakling, and his selfless devotion to duty—beyond all influences
of public pressure or personal friendship—made one feel oneself
as will-less as a weathercock. To stand in the presence of men like
this, to question them and listen, was to me a kind of recommence-
ment of basic moral education; it was the thing one felt as a school-
boy in opening one of the great books for the first time.

And if one looked behind the headlines and the squabbles, one
did find common, everyday men into whose souls the iron had
most certainly entered. I went to a Navy shipyard where, in docks
begun under John Quincy Adams, Americans had once built the
Clippers that made them famous seamen in all the oceans. Rivers
of men and women moved in and out of the great portals in a
flood so wide that, when the whistles blew and shifts changed,
all traffic was forbidden to move. They slept in trailers, in filthy
tenements, four and five to a room, under conditions more Spartan

than any we imposed on our soldiers outside of battle. Thousands
worked, not a forty-hour week, but a fifty-six-hour week at labor
that blackened the hands and bent the shoulders. There were no
Sundays or holidays, and sometimes men would have to ask each
other what day it was. I stayed with Navy production officers who
had not passed through the gates and seen the outside world for
six long months. There were proud men there who were responding to incentives that had nothing to do with the "profit motive."
There was the oldtime boat-maker who had devised a system to
turn out, in his little shed, several more wooden lifeboats a day
than they had ever produced before. There was the construction
officer who launched a modern destroyer sixty days after the keel
was laid. He was a hero, not to a board of directors, but to his men
—and that was reward enough.

In the evening a thousand shop superintendents and master
mechanics, who had already labored ten hours that day, crowded
into an unpainted hall to hear me talk about the war in other lands.
Here was no audience in evening clothes who came partly to be
informed and partly to be entertained. They wanted to know the
realities, for they were men who had to meet them. There was
something in their solid, attentive bodies, something in their serious
eyes, that had a curious effect on me. I felt a communion with
them I had never known with any other audience, and very soon
I found I was ignoring my notes and saying things that crowded
my head and tongue, about this country, these eastern shores
where the first ones had come, about the others who had pushed
inland, and what it all meant and why it was wonderful and must
never be lost. Ending, I felt a stab of fear lest I had transgressed,
lest they would not and could not be expected to take this from
anyone with my soft hands. But they came to their feet in one,
rippling motion, cheered at the top of their powerful lungs, and
crowded to the platform to shake hands with me. When they sang
the national anthem in a mighty voice and the Admiral presented
me with a ship's clock in their name, I was extremely close to
tears. As I walked out I asked about a huge painting that hung
over the door; obviously home-made, it depicted the burning
of the Cavite naval base. A shop foreman had done it in his spare
time, because he "didn't want anybody to forget." I went to bed
with a blessed feeling to the sound of riveting by midnight.

I began to see America as a composite picture, in its paradoxical
complexities, its frivolity, and its dignity, its generosity and its

meanness, and to realize that it is almost impossible to generalize about this country, harder than with any other I had known. I saw now, in Alabama, that part of the picture which I, like so many liberals, had instinctively confined to the subconscious, pretending it really did not exist. The Deep South seemed almost another country, not really an integral part of the American homeland, a backward spiritual wasteland—the soiled, airless basement of the house. The auditorium in which I was to speak was connected with the police station, and, as my hosts showed me through, a good-looking young Negro woman in a torn sweater and jumper was led in by an officer. Rather, she was dragged in, as one tugs along a reluctant dog on a leash without looking back. As the other officials bent to their work, not bothering to look, her captor held the woman with one hand up against the high desk and with the other rummaged over her body, looking for some article she was accused of stealing. It was a methodical, deliberate, and quite sexless act—like a man carefully looking through the hair of a hound for ticks. He pulled open her blouse front, felt under her breasts, carefully patted her waist, pulled out the sweater, and thrust his hand down into the front of her skirt. All through this performance she remained inert, her expressionless eyes blankly regarding a wall. It was not inhuman but *un*human, and therein lay the immeasurable brutality, not of man to man but of species to species. This was the permanent matter of rabbit and ferret, frog and snake. The brief transaction gave me a sense of helplessness, of utter frustration. It seemed not a social problem but a condition of nature. I felt that none of the keys to society's troubles with which I was familiar could possibly fit, and for the heroic men and women I met who did try to grapple with the matter I had more feeling of awe than of admiration. My contribution could never be more than a lip-service, and I knew this was something from which I would probably always run away, weaponless, unable to face it.

Colleagues returned now and then from the fronts seeking rest for their bodies and nerves, but finding inevitably that they could not rest in an area that seemed to be no part of the war, however vast its work for war. Leigh White returned on a stretcher from German-occupied Greece, to begin an exhausting series of surgical operations on his thigh which had caught an explosive shell from a Messerschmidt that strafed his refugee train. Few escaped some manner of injury to their spirits. Leigh developed spells of black despondency, alternately lost his temper and felt ashamed of losing it.

Larry Lesueur came back from Russia and the Middle East with a serious stomach ailment, aged suddenly by years, minus much of his natural exuberance. I took him to the White House press con ference, and when the others had left we remained for a private talk with the President. The feeling of relaxed ease he gave one at once was remarkable; one became so absorbed in the man, the friend, that it required effort to remember that he was the President. Indeed, one experienced a curious feeling that this could not be the throne, the final repository of decision, that it must be elsewhere, austere and obvious. This man was another citizen, more effective than most, but still subservient to some other, indefinable authority. I was catching sight of the basic pattern of organized democracy, which is not linear but circular, which has no top or bottom and no beginning or end. He asked a few questions of Larry about the Moscow press and what the Russian people were being told of our Far Eastern battle. But it seemed obvious that he asked the questions more as a genial formality than from a desire to know the answers. When Larry began to answer —and he had some items of significance to impart—the President slid at once into an anecdote from Chinese folklore about how the Japanese had first acquired the epithet "monkey people." His technique was clear: this was his defense against the further burden of another man's ideas. The pressure from an unending stream of information and ideas, often in conflict, was too much, and he held off as far as he could by this instinctive method. Only thus could he preserve an area of freedom within his own mind which permitted decision. And yet, considering his behavior soberly, one was forced to the conclusion that it was proof that his burdens were becoming too much for him, that he was no longer the confident master of himself.

From this visit sprang a bizarre episode. As we were about to leave, Larry pulled from his pocket a German Iron Cross on its ribbon. He said: "I know you like souvenirs, Mr. President. I'd like to give this to you."

Quickly Mr. Roosevelt asked, with an edge in his voice: "It didn't come from a body, did it?"

Larry said it did not, that it was one of those which the German

High Command had planned to award after their troops had taken
Moscow. The President placed it on his desk and immediately
told a story from the First World War about similar Iron Crosses
he had seen which were to have been awarded when the Germans
entered Paris. As we left the White House, Larry suddenly laughed
and said: "Damn it, I really wanted to keep that medal. I don't
know why I gave it to him."

At the press conference a few days later, the President astonished
everyone by handing the Iron Cross to Earl Godwin, a broadcaster,
with instructions to award it to John O'Donnell, the bitter anti-
Roosevelt columnist of the New York *Daily News,* for something
he had written that offended the President. The public took the
gesture badly, and Larry had no idea just what to think.

On a warm holiday afternoon I was trimming bushes in the
garden when the telephone rang and a well-remembered voice
crisply said: "Geoffrey Cox, here," with that quick British lilt. He
had flown directly from the desert front in response to a summons
to become *chargé* of the New Zealand legation in Washington.
After a minor difference of opinion with the taxi driver while
Geoffrey tried to establish which American coin was which, he
flopped into a deck chair with his arms dangling, surveyed the
flowers, the rows of white brick homes, the badminton court, and
the brown children, began to chuckle, and said: "Oh, my God, this
is it all right! This is exactly the way I thought of America."

We talked far into the lilac-scented night, and it was evident
that Geoffrey had mastered the "physical thing" and was a better
man for it. He seemed living proof that what war can sometimes
do for societies it can also do for some individuals. He had been
reported missing in Crete by error, but it had been a near thing
at that. When the paratroopers and glider planes began descending without warning, he and a few others grabbed up the nearest
rifles and jumped into a trench. A glider was settling directly
toward them, so close that they could see the staring eyes of the
Germans inside. At this moment they discovered that all their
rifles were packed with cosmoline and incapable of being fired.
With that curious detachment that some men possess, he was alternately cursing and laughing at the absurdity of his fate while
struggling feverishly with the weapon. The glider was upon them,
almost touched down, when a sudden gust of wind or a pilot's

mistake caused it to buck sharply upwards, skid forward a hundred yards, and crash into a great boulder. Every German inside was killed.

It was not long before Geoffrey was sitting in the weekly White House conferences of the Pacific War Council with Halifax, the President, Soong, and others. Diplomacy, like everything else, he took in his stride. "An overrated profession," he decided. "It's mostly just accurate reporting, separating the wheat from the chaff. Any decent journalist can do it. You know how we reporters used to hang round outside Downing Street or the Quai d'Orsay, waiting for the diplomats to come out of a conference, and how they would usually tell us: 'I haven't a thing to say.' We would never believe them. Well, they were right! They *hadn't!*"

The invasion of North Africa excited me beyond words—almost literally, for when the "flash" came from the White House my voice trembled so that I made complete hash of the broadcast. For days I suffered from a sense of frustration, and as the inadequate, contradictory, and frequently stupid news dispatches about the French situation came back (surely one of American journalism's worst performances) I pulled wires, without success, in an effort to get there.

It was the appointment of Admiral Darlan in Algiers that really shook one, that changed the whole nature of the war, or rather that first revealed that the meaning of the war for me and those like me did not correspond to the meaning it had for many who were directing it. The British, in 1940, were the first to give the struggle a positive, idealistic meaning; the Americans, to the world's surprise, were the first to take this away, with an abrupt, almost cynical gesture. The shock was profound, and it gave one a long, frightening glance into the future. It was all clear: American military men, however truly nonpolitical themselves, would nevertheless exert a profound political influence upon the world, simply because of their neutrality. They were fighting against bodies, not ideas, against Germans instead of Nazis; they would use any means, including individual Fascists and Fascist institutions to aid them in their specific task, regardless of how the basic issues were muddied and the future placed in jeopardy. The American contribution to the world would be men and guns—not the powerful cleansing breath of the great American democratic tradition. They could always argue that they were "saving time" or "saving lives," and it would be terribly hard to meet their arguments. Perhaps Hutchins had been more right than he knew. In any case, one had no choice but to fight the battle of ideas with increased vigor, using all possible weapons—which, alas, were limited to words and very little more.

It was a hard time. One was frequently accused of being "more interested in preserving an ideology than in preserving American lives." And there were other shocks. It was a shock to me to learn from indisputable authority that the State Department's reasoning behind their De Gaulle policy was this: De Gaulle was merely a British "puppet," and therefore his entry into France as the head of government would outrage the French and intensify the danger of Communist revolt, backed by Russia. At the bottom of all their devious reasoning was, even then, the fear of Russian influence in western Europe. It appeared that already the war was degenerating into mere jockeying for balance of power. And this, it seemed to me, without giving the ordinary people of Europe a chance to make it something else, without really trying to understand what was going on in their hearts. The misjudgment of the De Gaulle movement exhibited a fantastic obtuseness. One could only cling to his instincts again and try to withstand the barrage of official "facts." Among even American diplomats there had been a drying up of common feeling for the natural desires of the mass of men. These gentlemen were living in a withered world where nothing, however simple, was ever what it appeared. True wisdom had departed, and cleverness had taken its place.

But the clever suffer the disadvantage of never being quite sure of themselves, and in this queasy period the highest authorities were acutely sensitive. I did a broadcast, saying merely that Britain and America differed widely in their interpretation of the methods to be used in restoring France. The next day there was a call from the office of the British Ambassador, who sought a copy of my talk. Later I found out what had happened. Secretary Hull, already most uneasy, had exploded. He called in Halifax and protested that the British press was carrying on an inspired campaign against him, which was spreading over here—"Look at that broadcast by Sevareid last night." Hull asked Halifax to request Churchill to halt the press campaign in Britain. Churchill promptly wired back that the British press was free and that if it spoke as it did it was because the feelings of the British people were outraged by the actions in North Africa. However, Brendan Bracken, British Information Minister, issued a public denial that there were any differences between the State Department and the Foreign Office on this matter. This was a palpable lie but, because of the confidences involved, I could not publicly prove it. At this point Murrow, to my profound relief, declared over the air that if there *were* no differences, then that was a "new development." Hull continued angry and lectured Leigh White for twenty minutes on the behavior of the CBS broadcasters, who regarded him as a "Fascist"—a vast exaggeration by an honorable but very thin-skinned gentleman.

The time had come now when I could no longer postpone what was bound to be a personal moral crisis that I could resolve only by myself. It was, of course, the matter of becoming a soldier. I believed that we had to fight the war and help kill the Fascists. I had believed this since 1940, and in my small way had urged this course upon my countrymen, so many of whom would have to die themselves in the performance. Many of my friends, including the Jacobins, were already in uniform. I had come to the point where I knew I could kill if placed in the position where killing was required. Although I had seen war, I do not think the experience had given me an exaggerated fear of injury and death. While such fear was undoubtedly present, still I was no different from anybody else in feeling that I would somehow not be hit. In trying to analyze my hesitation, I knew I feared something. I feared somewhat the physical competition, not with the enemy, but with fellow soldiers, much younger than my thirty years, beside whom I would have to march and fight. I had the fortune (or misfortune) to know something of army organization and the deadening blind alleys into which one can so easily be turned by a vast, impersonal organization. Some friends in uniform, already disgruntled, said: "Don't do it. You will find yourself cranking a mimeograph machine in the public relations section of some Nebraska army camp for the next three years." But they might be wrong. Ultimately I realized that what I feared more than anything else was the psychological trial of living constantly with soldiers—the matter of eating, sleeping, talking in relentless intimacy with young, boisterous, back-slapping, hard-drinking men, the utter lack of privacy day or night, the cramping impossibility of self-expression. I understood now that too many youthful years of reading books instead of playing football had distorted me somewhat out of a healthy, extroverted relationship with other men. I simply was not a "regular guy" in the barracks-room sense of the term. I understood the paradox and the tragedy of so many liberals and radicals on the "intellectual" side, who believe that men must work in groups, yet who cannot bear a committee meeting themselves. We were social by conviction, but intensely individualist by nature. We are mocked for it, perhaps with justice, but there it is.

A thousand times I longed for someone or something to make the decision for me. Voluntary enlistments were now stopped, and it was not likely, since I was the only support of several persons, that I would be drafted. Still, there were ways of getting in, of course. At length I went to the Army Chief of Public Relations. That was the only kind of job I knew I could do with some expertness. He said abruptly: "Keep on with what you're doing. It's much more useful to us than anything you could do in uniform." Yet.this was not a true solution; it was merely a false balm to the conscience. The days dragged on, and the mental torture increased. Washington was becoming unbearable; I felt I was drowning in a flood of words. I was earning far more money than I had ever expected to have and, as self-respect dwindled away, I felt that I was no more than a war profiteer. I had a desperate desire to see the war, to be in the war, to know what the men of my generation were going through, to share their experience, and yet I could not face the prospect of ceasing to express myself about it. Ultimately I concluded I could do both by returning to the army as a war correspondent. I think I really believed I could truly share their experience. It was a long time before I understood that it could not be done this way, and by then it was too late. The basic mistake had been made. All those who made it can try to convince themselves that they did not make it; society sees their badges and emblems, notes that they were there, and asks no questions. But one must live forever afterwards with oneself, and there are children who grow up.

But this was my decision, with whatever elements of courage or cowardice it contained. After long wrangling, I managed to break away from various radio and other contractual obligations, disestablish my home, and prepare to return to the war in Europe. At a late date events intervened to change my itinerary in such a manner that I would arrive in Europe by way of China.

Chapter IX

ALL IN ALL, the circumstances surrounding my little mission to China were rather extraordinary, and they raised a fundamental question: does it *ever* pay to suppress the truth?

In this summer of 1943 there was extreme worry about China in the highest political and military circles in Washington. By all reports, the Chinese army had fallen into a state of worthless desuetude; they were not fighting the Japanese, even when the opportunity arose; Chiang Kai-shek was keeping a high percentage of his best troops as a blockade against the Chinese Communists in northcentral China. The Chungking government seemed to have lost all serious interest in fighting the common enemy and was concerned chiefly with the Communists and the inflation. A flourishing trade had developed between Japanese-occupied and free China, by which the Japanese were profiting as well as a growing number of free China's generals and war lords, politicians and businessmen, who were thus more interested in maintaining the status quo than in opening warfare against the Japanese. Unless some kind of union, political and military, could be formed between Chungking and the Communists, it appeared an almost hopeless task to try to align an effective Chinese fighting force against the Japanese for large-scale operations in Burma and for campaigns on China's soil, when and if the Americans landed in force on the east coast. It was quite possible that we could not defeat Japan without massive battles on the soil of China, and it was neither to our interest nor to China's that these be conducted by American troops exclusively or primarily.

The first and most acute problem was that of public opinion in the United States. Professional lovers of China had instilled in the American mind a vision of Chiang's China as an organized nation of idealistic democrats, fighting tooth and nail to stem a great tide of Japanese. Present reports indicated that the Japanese had taken about as much of China as they could effectively make use of *for*

some time, and the almost daily communiqués out of Chungking
which spoke of great battles, generally victories for the Chinese,
were pure inventions. The American government had not sought
to correct these impressions in the public mind because it had a
bad conscience about our own furbishing of the Japanese military
machine up until Pearl Harbor, because it was quite true that we
were able to get pitiably few supplies into China over the Burma
air route, and because there had been a belief in Washington that
unless Chiang received every possible encouragement he might
throw in the sponge to the appeasers around him and end his technical state of warfare—which would have the immediate effect of
knocking out our small air establishment on Chinese soil and also
a profound effect on future operations. Up to now, Chungking
had been the hero and Washington the villain, and we had been
trying to make up for it.

But now the whole situation was altered. The problem was to
force Chiang's regime into honest action, to make it reorganize
and really train the army, try to come to grips with the inflation,
clean out the corruption, come to terms with the Communists, who
(according to what fragmentary reports were available) *did* have
spirit and *were* fighting the Japanese. America was China's only
real friend remaining in the diplomatic world, since we honestly
desired China to be independent, free, and strong, whereas the
Churchill British did not and the Russians had not yet shown
their hand. In this position, and since we alone were furnishing
China with material help, we should have had great diplomatic
power over Chungking. We did, but the Chungking crowd had
acquired a powerful weapon to counteract it—American public
feeling. How could we begin to get tough with Chiang's regime
when the American people was profoundly convinced that they
were all heroes? A stalemate had been reached, and nothing was
developing save bitter feelings among the diplomats and army
people on both sides.

Our government did not have the support of an enlightened
public opinion, partly because it had let the situation drift blindly
along, partly because independent journalists were not telling the
people the truth. It was not entirely their fault. American reporters
in Chungking were stopped by the most stupidly severe official
censorship existing anywhere in the world. Many of them had
their families, their careers, their future invested there, and when
occasionally one came out he was in no position to be very frank.

One or two journalists such as Leland Stowe and Vincent Sheean
had gone in for short visits and come out with much of the truth,
but their storm warnings had been all but drowned in the floodtide
of propaganda by the Chinese and by the "old China hands." It
was a clear necessity to get more American reporters who were
not old China hands into China and out again and let them tell
the whole story. Not only in the interests of implementing government policy, but for another reason: to prevent a sudden strong
anti-Chinese reaction in the public mind, when, through military
reverses in Burma or China or some other inevitable scandal, the
full story of Chinese inadequacy would surely burst through, and
American public opinion, which always moves in sudden, emotional gusts, would become as blindly anti-Chinese as it now was
blindly pro-Chinese. The dam was certain to break sooner or
later; the wise policy was to let out the water little by little.

Madame Chiang Kai-shek had just made her propaganda tour
of the United States. Congress and the people had fallen in love
with this brilliant and beautiful woman, and in everybody's mind
she personified China. She had accomplished an incredible diplomatic feat: she had done nothing less than marshal an emotional
army of Americans and was leading it against the President and
the American government, openly, brazenly, while they were
forced to silence for the duration of her visit. The duration of her
visit was overlong, from her point of view as well, for stories about
the less admirable sides of her character were already leaking out;
such as her treatment of distinguished American personalities she
was too bored at the moment to see, and her lavish purchases of
gowns and furs while others were collecting funds to aid her starving countrymen. Many of the American journalists who followed
her entourage about the country returned east and reported privately that they had been treated like the lowest of coolies. I had
stood with the other correspondents in front of the President's
desk the day she shared in his press conference. To his remark
that we were supplying China as rapidly as the good Lord would
let us, she had replied: "The Lord helps those who help themselves." The reporters roared, and the President turned red. Some
of the correspondents thought of it as merely a *bon mot;* others
considered it an outrageous insult to the greatest friend China
possessed in the world.

It was at this point, when the situation had become both dangerous and ridiculous, that a close friend of the President's, a

man I had never met, asked me to come and see him. He put it
bluntly: Could I go to China, see as many people as possible, and
come back to write and broadcast what I had learned? I said I
felt I could go only as an independent reporter with freedom to
report the story as I saw it, whether it agreed with his conception
or not. He assured me that there was no other idea in mind, that
it was a simple case of the need to get honest observers into
China and out again, and that he believed I would do an honest
job. I explained that my knowledge of China was confined to
university studies of Far Eastern political history and the journalist's normal checking on contemporary events; he made it clear
that this was preferable to preconceived personal notions.

I talked it over with the staff of the *Reader's Digest* and described the Chinese situation as it then appeared to people in
Washington. They accepted the idea at once in the belief that a
complete and balanced story of China at war would be a public
service. But it might take six months before my material, whatever
it turned out to be, would be ready; in the meantime, there might
be a campaign in north Burma, and the public ought to have some
preliminary idea of what the situation was. I refused to write anything then, based purely on information in Washington, but since
they still thought some kind of moderate ice-breaker was required,
we agreed that Hanson Baldwin, the New York *Times* military
analyst, would be a good person to produce one, and we left it
at that.

2

Again I found myself in a war correspondent's uniform, under an
army's jurisdiction, enjoying its very real privileges and, like
countless other men doing a civilian job in army disguise, suffering
from the baffling complexities and red tape of a mass military establishment. In our antimilitary college days we had read a good
many books and articles on the general subject of "stupidities of the
military" and had believed there was something essentially obtuse
about the "military mind." As time went on, I learned that, while
there definitely are a military point of view and military methods,
often maddeningly rigid and unimaginative, there is no such thing
as a military "mind." Armies must operate by formulae; the
formulae reach innumerable individuals and situations where their

application is impossible, and so the whole secret of getting anything done in the army, of avoiding early nervous collapse, is to
√ learn the art of breaking the letter of the rule while preserving
its spirit. Orientals must save the "face" of individuals; Anglo-
Saxons must save the face of institutions. The institutional formula
said that only highly essential persons could have air priority for
flights over the route I had to follow. The public relations officers
therefore delayed a respectable time, then gave me my travel
ticket. An officer somewhere, who had been ordered to get army
cooks to Assam, India, delayed a respectable time, then put two
sergeant cooks on the plane. The highest-ranking officers of the
Pentagon Building, who wanted their Fort Meyer mess improved,
respected the formula by issuing a low air-travel priority for their
mess officer so that he could study the excellent officers' mess at
Belem on the Amazon. All of us came together on the same plane
though not one of us was truly essential to military operations. The
sacred rule was rudely violated on all counts, and everybody was
satisfied.

Madame Chiang's party in a preceding plane had left a well-
marked trail behind them. In one place, air-base soldiers exhibited
with pride her signature on their "short snorter" notes; in another,
one boy asked: "What kind of dame is she? She wouldn't sign a
bill I handed her because it had the picture of a Negro girl on
it. I never heard of a Chinese being anti-Negro." At one base the
official army greeter had been charmed by her graciousness; in
another he cursed at the mention of her name and complained
that he had been treated like a porter.

I entered now upon a new scene and began to watch a new manifestation in history—the average American boy away from home,
thrust upon the outside world, the world thrust upon him. Our
men had suddenly invaded the world; they accepted the world
without trying to understand it, and the bewildered world accepted
them perforce, tried to understand them, but for the most part
soon gave it up. In their ignorance of foreign peoples, our men
were the same as the British, but their behavior was different. As
somebody said: "The British walk the earth as if they owned it;
the Americans walk the earth as if they didn't give a damn who
owned it." The British were self-conscious in their superiority; our
men were even more breath-taking in theirs because they were
perfectly natural about it. It never occurred to them that anybody
questioned it. The various peoples of the world, particularly the

peoples of other colors, were astounded by what they saw. From the United States, the hope of the world, the one great reservoir of democracy and goodwill, the melting pot of equality, came this swarm of noisy, rowdy, hard-working, hard-fighting youngsters who called them all "Wogs," laughed at their dress and customs, shouted abuse when they couldn't figure out how to change the tire on the jeep—and then invited them to have a drink and join the poker game.

Day and night I lived with youngsters who flew the world for the transport command. They measured the far horizons and calculated the heavens with their stubby schoolroom pencils. They peered through the majestic avenues of castellated cloud and wiped their dime-store colored spectacles. Their young eyes looked into the depths of mysterious seas and regarded the unfolding of the vast continents which showed on their faces the laboring of God's time and the hands of men, while they munched a wad of Wrigley's Spearmint, fingered the newly sprouted mustache, and wondered about its effect in Lauterbach's drugstore back in Des Moines. They knew the lines and corrugations of the ancient earth as they knew the palm of their hands, and took them equally for granted. They followed with a flick of the controls the mountainous roadways that generations of men had carved out with their nails, and ticked off on a cellophane-covered chart the cities that centuries of human sweat and dreams had caused to grow upon the dusty plains. In all recorded history men had dreamed of the magic carpet from which to view their earth as it appeared to the eagle and their various gods; now the magic carpet had come, but the earth was belittled, and of mysteries and dreams there was no sign. Watching these boys, listening to their talk, I felt old; I felt myself a foreigner upon a new planet. We were separated by no more than ten years in time, but in those few years something fundamental, something disturbing and strange, had occurred. Either they were living life in a vital new dimension from which I was forever barred, or I alone among them was alive and they were stillborn and dead.

They had girdled the earth in a span of weeks, walked among strange peoples of long histories and diverse cultures, and they delivered their judgments to me: "Australia? Yeah, good drugstore joint in Melbourne. New Caledonia? Governor's daughter was all right." In Brazil it was the Swiss watches and mosquito boots you buy; Cairo was remembered, not even for the obvious Sphinx but for the shimmy dancer at Dahl's; there was a soda fountain among the soaring crags of Eritrea, a swimming pool in New Delhi, steaks at Firpo's in Calcutta, and at Agra, not that exquisite jewel the Taj Mahal, but the great Halliburton swindle. "That guy wrote he swam in the pool, and the water's only eighteen inches deep, by God! We measured it!" Nearly all the rest—mid-Africa, the Persian Gulf, the Punjab—were lumped together as heat, flies, stink, and Wogs. The realities of life were reduced to the well-loved plane which gave the narcotic of motion and Lauterbach's drugstore in Des Moines.

The earthbound soldiers were not essentially different in their imperviousness to new peoples and places, but they fought the extra enemy of boredom and sameness. The pattern was the same everywhere: bored with Des Moines and Peoria, the boys arrived in Brazil, or Africa, or India anxious to know about this mysterious place which Hollywood and the pulp magazines had told them was exotic and exciting. Within a few days their shallow fund of curiosity was spent, and they began to hate the place and its people and wanted only to be back in Des Moines and Peoria. The army tried. Language classes were organized, and lectures and tours to study native culture. At first attendance was large, then it quickly fell off. In one immense African air base containing two thousand men, the class managed to hold exactly seven students. They were in these places, of course, to work for the war, not for cultural reasons, and they lived under the hard and restrictive rules of army life. With many individuals among them it might have been different under different circumstances—if they wandered as free men with American Express checks in their wallet; though with only a few, I fear. They wanted, they said, only to get home again, but the conviction grew upon me that, once they returned, home too would seem more flat and tasteless than ever before. And, as time and civilian life went on, they would forget that they had deliberately cultivated their ignorance of the far-off places. They would read with interest newspaper accounts of current events in those areas and would profess expert knowledge: "I was there, brother."

If acquaintance with the world was not changing them very much, acquaintance with them was surely changing the world. Their presence was enlarging the mental horizons of many peoples; their talk was depositing new words in foreign tongues; their habits were teaching cleanliness to thousands who worked closely with them; their freely spent money was lifting standards of material aspiration; their machines were teaching the rudiments of the mechanical age—and their rowdy behavior was debasing ancient conceptions of reserve and politeness. American materials and American "know-how" were altering the face of the earth. Dense, creeping, unstoppable jungles had been fought back by the bulldozer and pinned down by acres of cement, leaving cleared and habitable islands of space in the green seas of vegetation. Cities of tin and wood sprang up over night in desert places that men had avoided for centuries, water was made to flow, and human life became possible.

On Ascension Island—lonely, lost steppingstone in the South Atlantic—they had knocked down mountains that grew straight out of the sea and made it possible for their great transport planes, their bombers and fighters, to swoop in level with the waves and course flat ground for a mile without obstruction. The Allies needed this island; a British survey party of engineers said it could not be done, that no landing level could be created on this precipitous crag of pumice stone. Our men did it, because it had to be done and because they were the children of men who had tamed and settled the mountains, deserts, and forests of North America, after which nothing was impossible. They had the minds of simple children, perhaps, but their hands were wizards' hands. They knew not where they were nor why, and they cared not what came after; they did not understand peoples or tongues or modes of life, but they understood the soil and the subsoil and the vein of granite, the drill, the scraper, and the acetylene torch, and with their hands and magical gadgets they so worked upon the earth that the fates of whole peoples were radically changed. The American army—a blind Gulliver, sweeping masses of Lilliputians around with the gusts of his breath, idly scooping up the sand with his giant fingers into piles which would be wondrous monuments forever after, leaving footprints as mysterious valleys, to be regarded with awe.

There was a green coxcomb of foliage atop the highest peak on Ascension Island; elsewhere there was not a single growing tree nor blade of grass save one weary palm by the water's edge; Coconut Grove, they called it. There were many flies. The air was fine and always clear, but that was the extent of their blessings. The Quartermaster Corps in Washington had convinced the country that the diet of the American soldier was passing fine; here,

although ships could come, the food was unspeakable. The menu
was reinforced daily with terns' eggs picked from the reefs, most
of them rotten, their odor stinking up the mess establishments.
"Ascension Island morale" had already become a byword, and
young suicides lay in the tiny cemetery. Yet they did their work
and did it well. They had no books save bound copies of the un-
comical "comics," and had it not been for the nightly movies
shown in the natural rock arenas there would surely have been
many more casualties of the soul.

We reached the Gold Coast of Africa, a continent outside my
previous experience, and my first sight was a great, gleaming
Bush Negro in white shorts, bending down and, with a whisk
broom, dusting off home plate.

Here I was delayed a week with my traveling companions—a
couple of Hindu scientists, British civil servants from India, and
officers and airplane technicians of "project seven" bound for
Assam to help keep the planes going "over the Hump" into China.
At the great air base near Accra, a new American city had come
into being. There was heat, malaria, and hard work; but there was
a regular bus run down to the swimming beach, and there were
movies every night, tennis, and baseball. But the real war was
still as far off as home, and, worst of all, there were no girls. There
may be isolated groups of men in the world who can do their work
and omit any reference to women for hours at a stretch; but
American men certainly cannot. One could not decide whether
the rows of "pin-up girls" made them happier or more miserable; in
any case, the pictures were omnipresent. One found Red Cross
girls in many places. Some were devoted workers who had come
with a high, selfless cause in their hearts; but more were homespun
adventuresses on the "good girl" level, who wanted, not men, but
a man, and who worked for and smiled at the enlisted men by day
and gave their personal company to officers by night. To some of
these lost and forgotten boys in the faraway places, sex became a
serious reality devoid of humor. Beside me one night at the Accra
open-air theater sat a Brooklyn boy who followed the antics of
Lana Turner and Robert Young with a rigid gaze. The heroine
sat up in bed. In the bathroom, the hero began to remove his tie,
paused, asked himself: "Am I a man or a mouse?", concluded he
was a mouse, and put his tie on again. At this point the Brooklyn
boy commanded my attention. He sat back, snorted: "Wat a dope!",

and abruptly left the performance. No middle-class, Anglo-Saxon country would consider it, of course, but the intelligent procedure would have been to keep at home the Red Cross girls—who could stand just so much pursuit and jitterbugging—and to ship out large numbers of young and carefully regulated prostitutes. A few successful romances for the decent girls made a poor exchange for the countless cases of disease and twisted nerves that one came upon in every army area.

The Gold Coast seemed to me an example of imperialism at its worst. The British called it the white man's grave, and said it was hard to get Englishmen to stay there and work on the natives' behalf. This was true; but it was also true that white men were willing to stay and work in their own behalf and had succeeded in taking many hundreds of millions of dollars in gold, palm oil, and other products out of the region. What they had done for the natives in return did not impress me, though my stay was a short one and I did not see everything there was to see. The Negroes were filthy, illiterate, and ridden with frightful diseases. You saw a few well-scrubbed Negro children in clean, starched clothes marching in brisk groups with books under their arms; but missionaries had done that. Dr. Eric Don, chief surgeon and director of the government hospital, took me through his wards. The ravages of venereal diseases, tropical ulcers, and elephantiasis were a horror to behold. Every morning, two overworked internes struggled with the ailments of two or three hundred native out-patients who sat patiently on the benches. The chief surgeon himself performed an average of three hundred operations a month, besides managing the place. He was a strong man, but malaria was in his blood as it was in the blood of everyone else, and he could not stick it out much longer. Treatment after disease had begun was merely to fight against the tide; what was required was a vast project of prevention. Imperialism will sometimes attempt this if the monetary return is thereby augmented. But here there was plenty of labor for mine and plantation; a few thousand needless deaths each month made little difference. "Psychological warfare" men, both British and American, were here as everywhere else, trying to show the natives why it was to their interest that the Allies win the war. The natives were fascinated by the motion pictures shown from itinerant trucks, but if the Four Freedoms had any reality for them nobody could prove it. One weary young English propagandist said: "We try to explain how bad it would be for them if the Germans came. But, you know, they remember the German rule in Togoland, and they don't seem to think it was so terrible."

To anyone who would test his powers of endurance, I recommend a trip across mid-Africa in July on a "bucket seat" army plane flown by half-trained pilots of tender years. You take your seat on the uncompromising ledge of aluminum; the doors are shut. You wait, sealed in the metal tube that becomes so hot you cannot touch it. Your shirt turns black with sweat, and the cooking aluminum gives off a sickening smell. The pilot, of course, has forgotten something in the barracks, so you continue to wait. Eventually he is ready, and you are tossed abruptly upwards. A precious stream of cool air saves you from unconsciousness, but purgatory has only begun. You then start to freeze, the sweat congealing on your clothes. Your bones ache, and you discover you cannot lean either backward or forward, and you cannot lie down because the aisle is piled high with baggage. At each desert stop you are again sealed within and the frozen sweat begins to run again. You are released from the death cell to be dealt a crashing blow across the eyes by the African sun and to find that your happy-go-lucky pilot has skidded the plane off the runway into deep sand, so that every man will have to help push. Far away across the field you see little brown buildings, where there ought to be food and drink. It may be only a mirage, of course, but you stagger the distance, and by the time you have found the commissary the crew is finishing off the last bottles of Coca Cola and announcing that departure is imminent. Late at night, when you have journeyed for eighteen hours with no sustenance save one chocolate bar turned to mud, you are disinterred and driven fifteen miles in a gaseous enclosed truck over a washboard road to an inhabited place. Here an army corporal who, having been routed out of bed is justifiably surly, hands you an aluminum tray containing a lump of sour bread, a piece of fat bacon swimming in grease, and a cup of coffee suitable for tarring roads. At midnight you collapse fully clothed onto an army cot, and at three in the morning are awakened. This does not mean that you are leaving; it means you *might* be leaving, and they want you on hand. You do not leave, of course, until around nine in the morning. In the meantime the cots are occupied by others near the point of death, so you sit in what shade you can find and fight the flies.

It was again midnight when we stood for thirty minutes in a line at Khartoum to get our billeting tickets. As I received mine and shouldered my bags, a cheery voice announced that our plane would go on at once. Though it happened to be one of the rare periods in my life when I have been in rugged health, this was too much. I sat down, determined to remain in Khartoum that night if it meant a week's delay. Then, for some mysterious reason, they changed their minds and showed us to our cots, where I found some sleep despite the flies, a roaring ventilator fan three feet from my head, the light which went on and off, the constantly banging door, and the unending parade of new arrivals, each and every one of whom with unerring accuracy managed to bump my frail, shuddering bed.

A new passenger squatted tailor-fashion in the narrow shaft of shade under the wing of the waiting plane on the baking Khartoum field. He was a man of medium size, with thinning, sandy hair, an obvious civilian, hatless, and dressed in khaki trousers and a cotton army shirt open at the neck. With complete self-possession he continued to sit there, reading a book, oblivious to the activity around him. Here, I thought, is a superior man, who has mastered this nerve-shredding business of doing a civilian job under army routines. I noticed that the book was Laski's *Reflections*, and then I recognized the face. He was John Davies of the State Department, political advisor to General Stilwell; when I had seen him last it was in the salon of a wealthy Washington publisher, and he was dressed in a summer dinner jacket with a bright flower in his buttonhole. I was traveling in good company, with Davies and Lieut. Col. Dick Heppner. The latter was from the Office of Strategic Services—one of the "cloak and dagger boys"; and a time was coming when Davies's intelligence, humor, and coolheadedness were to be important factors for personal salvation in a common crisis.

We slept well that night, high in the cool mountains of Eritrea. In the morning the crew were red-eyed, somewhat subdued, and as abashed before one another as young boys would be after an evening spent in the "House of Mirrors" in Asmara, constructed by the Duke of Aosta during the Ethiopian invasion. We contested violent air currents above the stark knife-edges of the coastal mountains, issued from the motionless cloud formations over the Red Sea, and settled into a new world again near Aden. Here it was flatter, hotter, more barren than anywhere else in Africa, the end of the earth for white men, a place where men's spirits drain out of their pores along with their perspiration. Among the young American boys stationed in these places, I saw none smile, I noticed none of the universal American banter and horseplay; something very bad was happening to them here. There was a saying in these places that went something like this: "After a year you start talking to the lizards; after eighteen months you start talking to yourself; after two years you don't talk at all—and then you've had it." As we would re-enter our plane to leave, we were conscious of their unsmiling eyes upon us, and no gesture to them, no remark, was possible.

By the time the great red pile of the Viceroy's palace showed Delhi on the plains ahead, the hardiest among us had about reached the limit of endurance. In these last few hours, while the pilot got himself lost and pretended he hadn't, Heppner and I whiled away the fretting delay by drawing up a charter for "The American Society of Airplane Haters." Under the rules no one would be eligible unless he had spent so many hours on "bucket seats," with extra points for those who had passed their hours over Africa or Asia in midsummer. We envisioned our coat of arms: Locomotives Rampant on a field of Crestfallen Airplanes, and our motto would be: "We travel by train, as God intended man to travel." At New Delhi a very proper young officer entered the plane, described the city as a tourist guide would, and announced: "You will now leave the aircraft in the order of your rank." (In the name of justice, let history do honor to my friend Turner Catledge of the New York *Times,* who on another occasion heard this same speech at New Delhi while he stood by the plane exit, loaded with heavy bags. When the officer had finished his announcement, Catledge loudly said: "I assume that means American taxpayers first"—and stepped down.)

3

The perfumed, luxurious city of New Delhi is an oasis and a fortress; it is an oasis for Westerners such as I, who flee to it from the misery of Indian India, and a fortress for the uncertain, unnerved officers of British officialdom, who pass their diminishing moral ammunition from one to the other at their clubs and their ceaseless cocktail parties, where they proclaim in voices that grow ever more shrill and hysterical that they are still right and India still wrong.

I arrived at a moment when the miasma of hatred, bitterness, and distrust was at its thickest. Gandhi and Nehru—that eminently civilized and lofty soul—had been in prison for a year, and every day the papers carried long lists of men, women, and even small children who had been imprisoned for attending the wrong kind of meeting in somebody's parlor. The atmosphere was not unlike what I had experienced in Nazi Germany after the pogrom against the Jews; imperialism here had accepted, as was inevitable in its extremity, the mechanisms of Fascism. The endless debates over the "complex facts" of India, the Hindu-Moslem differences, the various interpretations of the Cripps proposals, seemed to me minor matters. The moral climate was poisoned; the place was neurotic and sick, and it seemed to me that no compromise within the framework of imperialism could ever put this country upon the road to health and unity. Whatever the acrimonious differences among groups of Indians themselves, their deep detestation of the British overrode all else; whatever the British had done in the way of national defense or irrigation or public services, there was a fundamental failure here that one could never understand at a distance, through books or statistics, but only through living here —hearing and watching and feeling it. There simply was no common ground; no true meeting of minds between Anglo-Saxon and Indian was possible save by the nexus of mutual respect and dignity, and this had been broken down.

I found here a kind of Englishman who was new to me. I had the impression that most of these civil officials were essentially second-rate men who in India had found position, income, and personal importance they could never have achieved at home. In London they would have been earning a small salary, commuting each day by tube between dim, chilly offices in Whitehall and a semidetached bungalow in the suburbs. Here, each had a lovely white home surrounded by sweeping tropical gardens and maintained by a half dozen white-clad, whispering, obsequious servants. Whatever the wishes of Parliament or the people at home, these men would fight to the bitter end to remain as masters of India. They dealt in the lives of millions upon millions of people, and yet they regarded this as their private business. One must admit that a few, young magistrates in country districts among them, were not only intelligent but generous-hearted men—social missionaries, in a sense. A censorship official with whom I had close dealings was more typical. I had expected that if he took issue with what I wrote about Indian affairs, it would be in the manner of his London colleagues; he would be friendly, offer me civil respect, and argue dispassionately the merits of the matter. But an astonishing scene ensued. As soon as he saw the word Gandhi in my script, his face contorted with anger and he delivered a tirade about Gandhi—not about his party or policies, but Gandhi as an individual. I doubt if he had ever met Gandhi, but he spoke as though a personal feud existed between them. There were no definite censorship rules here—there was no rule of law in India at all so far as I could see, save martial law. This man haggled and fumed over every line of my copy, and ten minutes after I had accepted and written in a substitute line (in words that he himself proposed) he went back to it and exclaimed: "That will never do!" It was quite impossible to send out the truth from India; and inside India it was impossible for Indian editors to print the truth without risk of immediate arrest.

Either these British officials were small men to begin with or something had happened inside of them during their years in India. Rational discussion with most of them was out of the question. In their minds a world issue, involving a large section of the human race, had shriveled to an intimate sore, painful to the touch. Next to Indian politicians they hated liberal British journalists or Labor Party parliamentarians who came out from England to study the problem. The traditional British façade of suave politeness with political opponents had disappeared. If a student of the problem, like Bill Fisher of *Time* magazine, became a sincere partisan of Nehru, the British press boss would do his best to "cut" him socially, and when press parties were arranged would see that he did not receive an invitation. I went to a charming dinner party at the lovely home of an important public health official. That is—it was charming until the conversation got around to Indian politics. If, in my questions, there appeared the slightest hint of criticism of British policy, my hearty host would grow redder, would fume and splutter and finally roar at me, beating the table with his massive fist. Next to me sat a younger man who was government whip in the legislative assembly. He explained that at Oxford, where he had been president of the Union, he had led mass meetings in favor of Indian freedom. But nine years in India, he said, had opened his eyes. He had acquired a vivid hatred of Indian leaders. "Turn India over to them? My dear boy, you don't know what that means. Why—why, these villains would

stab us in the back before we could get our families to the boat!"
He meant it; like most of the others he was no longer rational.

Imperialist rule produces clean hatred; it also requires patroniz-
ing, falseness, and hypocrisy to sustain it. Inevitably, the rulers
become either brutal or intellectual frauds and the ruled martyrs
or sycophants. Poise becomes pose, and inner pride becomes an
outward, conscious armor. The dignity of men is crippled within
them, and they become something less than men. Many of these
British men and women (who loved to remind Americans of the
cruel position of American Negroes) would cut off a hand before
they would mix socially with dark-skinned Indians—unless these
happened to be rich and powerful Indians like the Princes. In
this land, where the contrasts of material wealth are as extreme
as they ever were in America, wealth was worshipped as abjectly
as it ever was in America. A large crowd of the political and military "four hundred" gathered in the gardens of a Hindu indus-
trialist, where overstuffed sofas for the guests had been placed
among the tropical bushes to surrealist effect. Our host had just
donated two lakhs of rupees—a large sum—to the Delhi poorhouse, and with proper modesty he bowed right and left as the
guests toasted his health and generosity and consumed his cakes
and ices. Officials who were capable of casting the Christlike
Nehru into jail fawned upon this man and murmured: "Hear,
Hear!" to the humorous speech of the Jam Saheb of Nawanager,
a kind of superwealthy Irvin Cobb, who jested with our host
about his money in the traditional banter of rich men anywhere,
while the pure emerald buttons twinkled on his enormous, shaking
belly. A few more withered bodies, stupefied by hunger and disease, had been shoveled out of sight into the poorhouse and, with
this as an excuse, fat and powerful men gathered to congratulate
one another upon their fat and their power. I had seen essentially
the same thing in Minneapolis; it was no less indecent here.

The enormous red pile of the Viceregal palace was itself an
affront. Built at great expense, it loomed over vistas of human
wretchedness. It was a pure symbol of power, designed purposely
to further intimidate the fearful. It represented, not British justice,
but British might. Even the legislature seemed to me a cruel
mockery of free expression and self-determination. Inside the imposing legislative building, purporting to house a true congress
of the people, Indian politicians, like intellectual puppets, debated
in the manner of the House of Commons, said "Mr. Speakah,"

waved their spectacles like an orator at the Treasury Bench, carelessly dropped careful Latin allusions—all in the Whitehall manner, while the men who held the real power sat politely by and listened and dozed. It had no more reality than the political congresses we went through as college students.

Indian soldiers of the British army were periodically decorated with medals and publicity, and formal praise was accorded them at regular intervals; but none of them at this time could rise above lieutenant colonel, the bulk were simple mercenaries, and the sincere among them were embittered and without spirit.

In a way, torpid climate, disease, and fatalistic religion were greater enemies to Indian freedom and unity than police rule. Perhaps most of the men of spirit were in jail, but one found a terrible defeatism among many Indian thinkers who were still free to talk—privately. They had come to pin great hopes on Roosevelt and America, and when they saw that America had no implemented policy toward India, when they learned that Churchill had squarely rebuffed the President in all discussions of India and shouted down the cautious protests of Ambassador Phillips, they began to lose all heart and spoke as if it were America's duty to secure their independence for them. At times one wanted to shake them, to remind them sharply that political salvation was never handed to any people—that they had to fight and dare and die themselves to get it. In time one became convinced of two things: that whatever the risks of internal civil war between Indians (anyway, that was their privilege), the British *had* to go; and second, that no matter what happened here, the British would not leave unless Conservative rule was broken in London. The Indians' fate was to a large degree in the hands of the British voter—that little man with the bowler in the corner pub, that well-meaning man so ignorant of India and of the kind of Englishmen who represented him there.

New Delhi was headquarters for both British and American military staffs; here the planning for the Southeast Asia campaigns went on. But it seemed at times that the hectic social life was a more important matter than military operations. In spirit New Delhi was farther from the war than Hollywood. The competition among officers for the few attractive white women was very serious, and schemes for dancing and drinking parties were laid many days in advance. British residents were kind enough to open their clubs to American officers, but as the Americans swarmed all over the place and monopolized many of the more desirable women, animosity rapidly developed. Inequalities in pay between the two armies became here, too, a point of bitterness, and the influx of dollars meant that servants' wages rose two and three hundred percent, to the profound annoyance of the old-time residents. The traditional social fabric of the ruling class was torn apart. The magistrate's wife at the club—the one who had always been pointed out because she owned an electric icebox—now slipped into obscurity because electric iceboxes appeared everywhere. These people felt little real concern over the war, and had one overriding desire: to have it all end so that these newcomers, both British and American, would depart. For the working Indians, servants and shopkeepers, the presence of the Americans meant greater income, of course, and to Indians in general it brought the first realization that there were other powerful, efficient people in the world besides the British. But Indians of any class are not a jocular, brash, back-slapping people, and there was no doubt that here too American rowdiness and bad manners caused offense. I remember dining with a party that included an American colonel of considerable military achievement. He had always been a poor man, and a part-time "hired girl" was the only servant he had known at home. Yet here he commanded the waiters in ringing tones and, as he grew more intoxicated, yelled at them and menaced them with his fists. There was agony in the eyes of the bewildered waiters, and one noticed the cool glances of the British couples near by. In a way, the colonel was paying the Indian servants a compliment: he recognized their existence as human beings, as his British opposite numbers did not—though I doubt if the servants took it that way.

Here too one saw the paradoxical, self-defeating effects of the Americans' presence, the thing I had seen in other places and was to see in still others: Among the masses, an excitement over new faces and over the material aid in more work and more money, followed by resentment at rowdy behavior and almost brutal treatment; among the thinking classes, elation over the arrival of Americans, symbols of democracy and freedom, who would aid their own cause of freedom, followed by a bitter realization that few of the Americans gave a damn about their cause and that those Americans who did were backed by no positive government policy. America as a material power became a reality; America as the world's hope of freedom was turning to myth. In the case of India,

our soldiers arrived with a vague feeling of sympathy for the
Indian cause and animosity toward the British. Within a week,
exhausted by the climate, appalled by the disease and poverty,
maddened by the inefficiency and lassitude of Indian workers,
most of them sided with the British and said: "If the British want
this horrible place, they can have it. I want no part of it."

American Office of War Information people did what they could.
They did not join American policy toward India with the present
Fascist British policy, but, since they could offer no positive program, the Indians made the connection for them. They could do
nothing to give the Indians a sense of having a stake in the war
worthy of their efforts, when the British had themselves destroyed
all such feeling. All they could do was issue pictures and information to show the enormous part that America was playing in the
Far Eastern as well as in the European war, and on this score they
found they had to fight the British government in India. The London agency, Reuters, had a virtual monopoly on news distribution
in the country, and American news agencies were severely crippled
in their attempts to operate. In this period (it improved later,
owing partly to protests in Washington) exploits by American
bombers became in the Indian press the deeds of "Allied" bombers;
stories of America's prodigious war production would be placed
obscurely in the papers, but a race riot in Harlem received top
billing.

Co-operation among the Allies here, even for military plans and
operations, suffered from mutual hostility and suspicion, and it
soon became clear that long-range political policy was the cause.
Our people, led by Stilwell, wanted to free northern Burma in
order to get into China with supplies on a large scale. The British
obviously had no wish for this campaign. Churchill had little interest in strengthening independent China, for obvious reasons of
future effects on the politics of British areas in the Far East. The
British had no desire to have Chinese troops in Burma, which they
wanted to free by themselves, later on, or by-pass and let fall, in
order to keep the British title uncompromised. For these various
reasons they were giving us little help in building air bases in
Assam or in the heartbreaking task of pushing through the Ledo
Road toward China. There was plenty of native labor available
on the tea gardens of Assam, which we could have had if the
British government had insisted upon it. They did not, and it was
a constant struggle to get more labor released; in large degree we

were left at the mercy of the planters themselves. On the face of it, it was rather astonishing that Americans should be operating in India and Burma at all. It was a British area, and in India there stood an army of around two million armed men who should have been able to push through to China, or clear Burma, or accomplish anything they wanted to in that part of the world. But Wavell had made one half-hearted attempt to take Arakan and had suffered humiliating defeat at the hands of the Japanese, who outthought and outfought him, as he himself admitted. Clearly, the main purpose of the great Indian army was to maintain martial law over the Indian people. When one thought of the excellent co-operation between the Allies in England and in North Africa, this appeared a shocking, intolerable, and dangerous situation. New policy, new minds, and new methods had to come if this shameful stalemate was to be broken.

4

Flown by Dick Theisen, Stilwell's personal pilot, I headed southeast in company with John Davies and Captain Duncan Lee, a boyish, highly intelligent agent of the OSS, a man who like Davies had been born in China, and who had been a Rhodes Scholar at Oxford and later a lawyer in General Donovan's Wall Street firm. We flew into the green, wet valley at Ramgargh where American officers were training Chinese troops for future fighting. Here was an example of American daring and efficiency that made one proud again of his countrymen. Thousands of Chiang's ill-fed, ill-trained infantry troops had been packed, thirty and forty at a time, into American transport planes and flown over the Hump into India—"Operation Vomit" it was called by the boys who flew the planes and had to clean them out. It had taken Stilwell six months of negotiating before the Generalissimo would consent to appoint the Chinese general whom Stilwell wanted to lead these men, for the reason that most Chinese generals are politicians whose power depends entirely on the number of armed men they command. These men, now husky, well fed, imbued with fighting spirit by the Americans and their own young and able officers, would one day re-enter Kuomintang China. They would make a startling contrast with the rest of Chiang's starved and spiritless army, and no man could prejudge the result. These troops in train-

ing were proving what had been proved at Shanghai in 1937 and
not witnessed since: that with arms and, above all, spirit, the
Chinese were fighting men at least the equal of the Japanese.
They found a new life at Ramgargh, and it took them awhile to
adjust to a situation in which they were treated as human beings.
One day one of them said to the American paymaster: "We have
concluded that you are the cleverest man we have ever seen. You
give us our exact pay each month, and how you get your squeeze
from it we can't quite figure out."

The three of us flew then to Chabua in Assam, the vital corner
of northeast India facing Burma and Tibet where, within easy
sight of the towering, white Himalayas, we were building our air-
bases and beginning the highway lifeline into China. I stayed with
a British couple, tea planters, in their restful bungalow under a
roof of thatch-covered tin, sat on the wide verandas and drank
cooling beverages brought by soft-footed servants. Here were the
colonists come to life from the pages of Somerset Maugham. In
this forbidding country, where one had to struggle with the elements, there was genuine hospitality but no easy camaraderie be
tween planters, none of the togetherness in hard work that my
father had known in pioneering North Dakota. Capitalism and
class had reached out from distant London and clamped their
curse upon men and women even here. The plantations were operated by great combines in London working through agencies in
Calcutta. The planter couples came out under very long-term
agreements, most of them expecting to remain twenty years or
more. The rigid social hierarchy followed the lines of the business
hierarchy, and when the wife of the regional superintendent entered a room, the wives of managers and submanagers were expected to rise. Wherever you find Englishmen you find their clubs,
and Assam was not different. Each year, before the war, the planters would gather at a large club for a week of what was supposed
to be drilling as armed militia. It generally became a great house
party, largely because the uniforms upset the hierarchy. A superintendent would discover that a mere submanager held the King's
commission as lieutenant, which put him above the superintendent
—which was just too painful and intolerable to be continued. It
was an iron tradition that their children be sent back to England
at a certain age for schooling, no matter how miserable this made
them or how lonesome their parents. None would dream of send-

ing the children to an Anglo-Indian school, however fine its teachers and educational standards. The fate of them all was the same
—a yearning loneliness at first; then compromise and adjustment
with brief moments of happiness stealing in around the edges;
then, when their best years were gone, retirement to a cottage
somewhere in the south of England, where they found nothing in
common with anybody except others like themselves. All their
active life was spent in lonely and correct preparation for a lonely
and correct death.

When I saw the American establishment at Chabua, where
hundreds of Americans and thousands of natives slaved in scorch-
ing sun or dismal rain to get supplies into China, I could not help
feeling a certain resentment of the Chinese resentment over the
inadequacy of these supplies. Our men were killing themselves
and being killed every day in the effort. Save for a few officers who
could enjoy the comfort of tea-garden bungalows, they were living
in shocking conditions. There were at this time absolutely no
amenities of life—no lounging places, no Red Cross girls, nothing
cool and refreshing to eat and drink, no near-by rest resort to visit
on leave. It was a dread and dismal place where dysentery was
frequent and malaria certain, where haggard, sweating men
dragged their feverish bodies through the day, ate execrable food,
and shivered on cramped cots through nights often made unbearable by the mosquitoes. Men collapsed under the strain, and
officers were frequently broken by distant superiors when the
statistics of their performance fell short. They were trying to do
too much with far too little. Pilots were overworked, and when
they had made the perilous flight to China and back the same day,
having fought storm and fog and ice, they simply fell into their
cots as they were, unshaved and unwashed, to catch a few hours
of unrefreshing sleep before repeating the venture next day. Hardly
a day passed that the operations radio did not hear the distress
signal of a crew going down in the jungle valleys or among the
forbidding peaks. Few at that time were ever found again, and
there was a saying among the pilots that they could plot their
course to China by the line of smoking wrecks upon the hillsides.
It is not often that one sees fear in the faces of fliers, but I saw it
here. Each one reckoned that it was only a matter of time before
his turn would come; they had the feeling of men who know they
have been condemned. Assam was "the end of the run" for new

equipment from the United States, and there was never enough of anything. So communications were bad, maintenance was bad, and good planes had to be "cannibalized" to provide parts for other planes. At the moment they were having a desperate struggle with a new large transport plane, the C-46, fifty or sixty of which had just arrived from the States. These planes, sound in principle and design, were not ready for anything like the Hump operation. There remained, it was estimated, a hundred and ninety-six alterations that should be made in them before they were really safe. But they had been sent out by the President prematurely because of the Chinese pressure coincident with the visit to America of Madame Chiang Kai-shek. I met technical experts in Chabua from the airplane company who were afraid to fly the Hump in their own craft, and a legend was rapidly growing up about these "flying coffins."

Davies, Lee, and I spent a day up on the Ledo Road, skidding and pitching through the slimy red clay in a jeep driven by General Hayden Boatner, who commanded the Chinese and American combat troops charged with the defense of the road. Swarms of Nepalese and Chin tribesmen, barefooted and wearing wide straw hats to shed the constant rain, clawed at rocks and shoveled away the muck while the white labor contractors who had produced them squatted by the roadside in their raincoats, leaning on their walking sticks and smoking their pipes. And in the advance party which then was just reaching the Burma border, we came upon the American engineers, both Negro and white, driving their rearing bulldozers into the side of the mountains or huddling under the dripping tropical trees as they swallowed strong black coffee. Many were boys from Minnesota, lost and homesick, but doing their job as it had to be done. And the job itself was breathtaking in its implications and its majestic proportions. They were simply tunneling their way to China, driving an incredible shaft through an enormous mountain barrier to a vast country cut off from the rest of the world; with their bulldozers, their shovels, and their tireless hands they were connecting two worlds. Before they had won, a thousand of them died in those jungles, in order to give another chance of national life to a country most of them would never see.

We made our tortuous way back to Chabua, and after midnight drifted to sleep on cots set up in the high wet grasses. I was thinking: before noon tomorrow I shall be in China, among still another new and strange people. As it happened, before noon the next day I was sitting by a waterfall on a high mountain. Where I was I did not know; but it was not China. The naked brown men who stood in a semicircle around me, holding long spears and swordlike knives, were certainly not Chinese. Who they were I did not know; what they would do with me I had no idea.

Chapter X

.IT WAS the second of August, 1943. I find that I cannot now recall what the early morning was like, whether misty or bright, when we gathered with the other passengers. I remember a severe examination of our baggage by a young major who was under strictest orders to stop the smuggling of saleable articles into China, a practice for which a number of American soldiers were then facing courts-martial. Even Davies seemed to be stripped of all diplomatic immunity, and I remember his expression of resentment. I had to fight for all my smallest possessions, even the lipsticks destined for the wives of press colleagues in Chungking, and I nearly lost my large bottle of real quinine capsules—which could, of course, fetch thousands of dollars in the Chinese black market if I chose to sell them. Davies introduced me to a man named William Stanton of the Board of Economic Warfare, a tall American of forty with close-cropped hair and a lilting British accent. We were seventeen passengers in the truck that backed up to the door of the waiting plane. There were two smiling, silent Chinese officers; the others were American soldiers, all making their first trip "over the Hump." Of one of them I asked: "Isn't this a C-46?" He nodded. I thought to myself: Now if I had any real moral courage I would refuse to get aboard. But that's something one just doesn't do.

We took our places on the aluminum bucket seats, facing one another in two long rows. From the truck a soldier tossed in parachutes with a weary, automatic gesture as though he were heaving sacks of potatoes. They were the earlier type, very heavy, with a pack at the back and a thicker one, containing the folded 'chute, that hung over the buttocks and provided a seat. The crew went up forward, dropping their parachutes into a careless pile by the radio operator's little desk. Nearly everyone else had chosen his when I decided to pick one up, remembering that they sometimes did not fit without a great deal of adjustment of the difficult straps.

This one seemed to fit perfectly, and I sat with it on, leaving the buckles unclasped for greater comfort.

We took off smoothly and rose into a downy lather of mist and delicate streamers of white cloud. The intensely green earth dropped slowly away, and the tea gardens assumed precise, geometric formations. To the northwest I caught a glimpse of snow-covered Himalaya peaks and wondered if one of them was Everest. Now the cloud streamers appeared below us, sheltering the depths of the valleys, and we were in a world of blue. The plane turned slightly, and quick shafts of sunlight flashed across the interior, burnishing the metal and briefly illuminating the row of brown faces. The men looked at one another as strangers in confinement will, in a state of relaxed suspension. Their bodies had nothing to do; it was too noisy for conversation. Duncan Lee, beside me, settled back and opened a book. I reached into my brief case for a notebook and began jotting down a few items for an article I had vaguely in mind. There was the faintest tremor in the drumming of the motors, and I looked up sharply, realizing that my subconscious mind had been listening intently. I wrote some more, looking about now and then. We were over mountains now, and the valleys were very deep, thick with green vegetation. Obviously we were taking the more southerly route across the Hump, a little longer, as I remembered, but the peaks were not so high. Somewhere ahead, I realized, we would pass over the Chindwin river where the Japs were. I noticed a heavy-set corporal with a mustache sitting upright on the floor by the door, his parachute completely buckled.

We had been flying an hour, when somebody stumbled over my legs, and a corporal, no more than a boy, leaned toward my ear. "Know what?" he shouted. "Left engine has gone out." He was grinning broadly and apparently took some kind of perverse pleasure in the situation. I felt a tightening in my stomach, the thing that had come when the London sirens sounded. Duncan looked at me without expression. So far as I could tell, the plane was still flying smoothly. I wondered why the kid had chosen me to hear the news; probably because of my correspondent's insignia. Americans instinctively want to tell all they know to a reporter. I noticed the two Chinese officers, sitting with their eyes closed. Obviously their first airplane trip and probably they were feeling a little sick. Apparently they remained in happy ignorance of the mechanical situation. I tried to continue writing, but found it im-

possible and snapped the brief case shut. I was on the left side of
the plane, and I squeezed my cheek against the window to look at
the engine. I rather expected to see the propeller blades hanging
motionless. They seemed to be going around all right, though I
knew that didn't mean anything. Sunlight flashed in from another
angle, and I realized that we had turned, which must mean that the
pilot was making back for India. A day wasted, at least, and I was
already long overdue in Chungking. The door to the pilots' compartment opened and shut, and I caught a glimpse of one black-
headed boy and another, a tall fellow with thick brown hair seated
at the controls. It occurred to me that I had never seen their faces
and had no idea of their ages or experience.

A sudden blare of noise and light filled the plane. The crew
chief, a sergeant of about forty, had torn the door from its hinges.
As I leaped to my feet, he knelt by the aperture, reached for a
suitcase, and shoved it through the opening. Now a cry came
rippling back from somewhere: "All passenger baggage out! All
passenger baggage out!" Men were shoving and pushing around
me, and I stumbled over a barracks bag. I was breathing hard,
and my stomach was hurting. My beautiful new bags! The perfect
outfit that it had taken me weeks to gather in Washington! Somebody grabbed my suitcase and I wrenched it angrily out of his
hand, then abruptly shoved it out of the door myself. It disappeared with a whistle. I found myself perilously close to the door.
It was like standing on the edge of a fantastically high cliff, looking down on the rest of the world. Heavy barracks bags were
crashing against my feet as the others slid them down, and I kicked
and shoved them toward the kneeling crew chief. The elder Chinese officer was hugging his bag with a desperate expression, and
an American youngster, his face contorted in rage, tore it from him.
My brief case! Hell, that didn't weigh more than ten pounds, and
it contained all my voluminous notes of weeks past; I jammed it
under a seat. A small bag containing toilet articles and a few odd
gifts I tied to my belt by its strings. I noticed Davies thrusting
various articles into his shirt front.

The baggage was out and the metal floor bare save for bits of
rubbish, cigarette stubs, and a few candy wrappers and pieces
of string. Everyone was on his feet, gathered near the door, until
someone began shoving us forward to distribute the weight more
evenly. The plane seemed to be circling again and I shouted angrily
at Davies that it was madness to try to continue to China, that

none of us could exist there without our equipment. He looked at me with a tense frown, then shouted: "Have you got a map?" I shook my head, and he stumbled forward toward the pilots' compartment. I noticed the radio operator on his feet, bending over his instruments, quickly turning the dials. John came back and shouted: "Can't get any information. I don't know where we are. No goddam organization here." His fear, like mine, was taking the form of anger. We stood about, saying nothing, all of us looking at one another as if for a sign of what was to happen. Two or three were pale. The younger Chinese was staring at the door, his jaw muscles pulsing rapidly. Several minutes passed, and the plane seemed to be flying much lower. I thought we were following a valley, but then a peak or ridge would pass very close beneath. More minutes went by, and the suspense was unbearable. I found myself opening the notebook again and absurdly scrawling sentences: "Nine fifteen A.M. Baggage out. Left engine not working," etc. I closed the notebook, carefully inserted it in the brief case, snapped it shut—and threw it out of the door. Then I realized that I had not buckled my 'chute.

There was no announcement, no orders of any kind.

The decision was made known to us all by a brief, bustling scene forward. Members of the crew were scrambling in and out of their compartment, grabbing up their parachutes from the pile. I felt all my body stiffen, and a great weight pressed on my lungs. Blood was pounding in my head, and it was hard to breathe. For a moment there was utter suspension of thought, and I existed in a vacuum. There were no articulated thoughts, only emotional protest. "Oh, no, no! Oh, no! This can't happen to me, not to *me!*" The mind did not accept it, but the numb body moved toward the door. There was a jam of bodies around the door, and somebody was shoving from behind.

Under the crust of panic a small kernel of the brain was ticking rapidly. "Wait! Wait! Plane is still flying level. Don't be a fool! We must be heading back toward India. We *must* be! Every mile counts—every mile away from the Japs." A heavy boot cracked against my ankle. Several men were shouting above the engine's roar. I found myself shoved to the periphery of the semicircle of bodies. I recognized Duncan beside me, his eyes large and white. He had a pistol. I yelled in his ear: "I want to jump near you!" Over a shoulder I caught sight of John Davies and watched him in frozen fascination as he crouched by the door staring down

into space. There was a curious half-smile on his face just before
he leaped, froglike, and vanished with a whistling sound. I felt a
twinge of human emotion, a feeling of affection for him and regret.
I said to myself: "Goodbye, John." The impasse of general fear
was broken a little by his act, and one or two others went over.
The young Chinese tugged at my arm and pointed to his parachute ring. The lower part had come out of its pocket, and there
was a terrible question in his eyes. A glance told me that the effective part of it was quite intact and I yelled: "Okay!" He understood and nodded. I looked for Duncan. He was gone. I was
buffeted away several feet. The tall civilian, Stanton, was screaming in a high-pitched voice at somebody: "For Christ's sake, if
you're not going to jump, get out of the way!" He shoved two men
aside and went over.

Suddenly I was aware that only two or three passengers remained in the plane, and with a sneaking feeling of reassurance
I thought: "We're still flying level. She'll stay up, she'll stay up!"
For a moment I had the ignoble feeling of having put something
over on the others. But then the black-haired pilot was running
at me, his mouth wide open, though I could not hear what he was
shouting. I leaned out to let myself go, but a peak was passing
directly under us, so close that I could distinguish the branches,
and I pulled back. At the same instant I felt my knees buckle
slightly as the plane tipped abruptly to the left. There was no
interval between the realization that the pilotless plane was going
into a dive and the action of my body. I closed my eyes and leapt
head first into space. The mind ceased to operate, and I have no
recollection of thought. I do not know whether the air felt cold or
warm, but instantly there was a terrific rush of wind. Some part of
me was calculating, for I waited a long second before pulling the
ring with both hands. A terrible blow struck my body, and my
eyes opened.

The silence. The crushing silence.

I heard a loud voice saying: "My God, I'm going to live!"—and
realized it was my own voice. A green mountain seemed to be
rising up in front of me, and from its side spurted a geyser of
orange flame. The plane had gone in almost at the moment my
eyes had opened. Two or three 'chutes were settling toward the
trees, and one seemed to be heading directly for the flames. I
noticed that my thin mosquito boots were still on my feet. My eyes
printed a precise map on the brain: a brown river at the bottom of

the valley. No visible trails or roads. A small village of grass huts two miles to the west, halfway up this side of the mountain. The silent, inert mountain was closing in on me. Nothing lived save the twisting flames that seemed to be advancing toward me. I heard the voice again, saying: "Dear God, don't let the fire get me. Please!" I became aware that I was suspended in a canvas seat and began twisting frantically. I could distinguish leaves on the bushes, and then the hillside moved around behind me. Everything went dark, branches were slashing at me, and I knew I was rolling head over heels.

2

When my eyes opened again I was staring through a screen of leaves at a blue sky. I felt no pain and knew I was quite unhurt. For a moment there was a warm, relaxing sensation of sheer comfort, and I closed my eyes again, feeling an impulse to rest in my quiet bower.

But an instant later I was on my feet jerking savagely at the clasps of the harness. Panic took full possession of me. The harness was a strait jacket and the thick brush a dark, suffocating prison. My nerves behaved as if this were the mortal struggle. With my bare hands I beat at the thorny brush and the cutting sword grasses and plunged uphill where, my instincts told me, the wreckage lay. The fire alone lived and made a connection with the world I had just left. I was hysterical, and this earth was no refuge, but a maddeningly impassive barrier between me and the other world I frantically sought. I slipped and fell heavily, tried again and fell once more. Each time I rose and plunged forward the brush closed in again and beat me to my knees. I tried to shout, but there was vomit in my throat and I could make no sounds. A few coherent thoughts began to take racing form: "I have no food. There are berries here. Where are the Japs? Who lives in that grass village? I have no weapons. I have a penknife. A razor. No, the little bag is not on my belt. This is one of those things you read about. That boy from Minnesota. He lived forty days in the New Guinea jungles. Maybe I can, too. No, this is too bad—no, I cannot do it." I floundered on through the brush and realized that blood covered my hands and was seeping through my trouser legs. I tried to shout again, and a small wail resulted.

I lay for a minute, exhausted, listening intently, but there was no sound of any other living presence. It was at about this moment that I accepted the idea of death. My body struggled on, but my mind seemed for a time to be existing quite independently. It examined the idea quickly and was almost at once reconciled. There was no particularization of the act of dying, whether by hunger or exposure or an enemy bullet. That was of no consequence. I remembered my wife and my baby boys. No picture of them took form; there was only the warm, intimate *feeling* of them deep within, followed then by a profound wave of regret. At such a moment conscious concern with oneself vanishes completely, and I found myself, as I fell and got up again, calculating the total of my savings and insurance and estimating the prospects of comfort or poverty facing my family.

I heard a shout near at hand, and a wonderful feeling of relief came welling up with the knowledge that I would not die alone, anonymously in the jungle prison. The undergrowth thinned a little, bushes near by shuddered violently, and two men were crawling towards me. One was the crew chief, the other a tall, thin young sergeant with blond, almost white hair, whom I did not remember from the plane. Their faces were bleeding, and they were breathing hard. We sat together for a time, saying nothing, regarding our feet, and waiting for our pounding blood to calm. We heard a faint cry of "Help!" from farther up the hill toward the wreck, now clearly indicated by a pillar of black smoke which formed a tall stem for a giant mushroom spreading over the sky.

We came within sight of a parachute tangled in a tree top, and below it an enormous man was sitting upright, holding one foot crossed over the other thigh. It was the radio operator, who had stuck to his instruments in the plane, repeating our position until the very last moment. He greeted us simply. "God damn it—biggest man in the outfit and I have to get hurt." His ankle was red and badly swollen. As we sat there looking at it, the black-haired pilot crawled out of the brush. He crawled awkwardly, one hand pressed against his chest. He said: "I sure am sorry." For a moment I did not know what he meant: he was feeling personal guilt for the crash. He informed us that he had broken a rib. The men seemed curiously inert, and as confidence returned rapidly to me, I felt an impulse to take a lead. I ripped off a piece of the radio man's parachute and bound his ankle as best I could. The crew chief asked me: "Where's your 'chute? Did you get the jungle kit out of the back pack?" I had not even been told that such a thing existed, though I probably would have neglected it in my panic, anyway. Now I stumbled back through the brush until, after what seemed an endless search punctuated by brief flashes of fear lest I get lost again, I came upon the 'chute and pulled it down. The zipper-operated pack was quite empty. The knife, rations, mosquito netting, and first-aid kit were gone. (Another illustration of the state of discipline at the Chabua air base.)

At length we climbed toward the wreck, the crew chief going ahead, slashing at the undergrowth with a Gurkha knife, two of us trying to support the radio operator. Sweat poured down his broad face, and he bit his lips until the blood ran over his chin. When we reached the blackened mass of twisted, smoking metal, he sank to the ground and buried his head in his arms. The plane had dug a great pit, and the wet black earth lay heaped in mounds. About a half-acre of undergrowth had been cleared by the explosion. The pilot, a very young boy with the rank of Flight Officer, stared blankly at the obscene, twisted entrails of what had been his beautiful machine. He seemed overwhelmed with depression and muttered: "I don't know about Felix. I don't know if Felix got out." Lieutenant Felix had been the co-pilot, the tall brown-haired boy whose back I had observed in the pilots' compartment. I undertook to search the wreckage for human remains, but was unable to approach too closely. I climbed up and down the steep slope, peering into the mess, but could see nothing of a pertinent nature, save one small lump of melted metal that had a vaguely familiar outline: my portable typewriter, which I had completely forgotten about on the plane. Something stirred by my boot. It was a small jungle bird, trying to hop away from me, most of its feathers seared off. I killed it with a stick, the effort requiring all my courage. It seemed sickeningly brutal now to bring death to any living thing.

We sat for a time, wondering what to do, wondering about all the others who had jumped. We could see no parachutes along the expanse of mountainside. My trouser legs were stiff with blood, and I found a fat, blood-swollen leech on each leg. I shuddered as I brushed them away. We contemplated the river and wondered whether we should try to descend to it in hope of finding a trail that would lead to the village. No—Oswalt, the radio operator, would never make it; clearly, his leg was broken. We doubted if we could make it, ourselves. It was nearly a half-mile down, and fifty yards through this jungle required an exhausting effort.

One of the men jumped to his feet and in a hoarse whisper said: "Listen!"

The glorious sound of airplane motors drummed through the wide valley, growing louder, louder, louder until suddenly there it was—the familiar Douglas transport nosing steadily over a ridge, dipping its wing for a wide circle around the pillar of smoke. Now it cut in and roared directly over us, its wings rocking in recognition, while we ran back and forth, stumbling, rising again, frantically waving our bundled 'chutes and absurdly shouting at the top of our lungs. This was quite unbelievable. Although it had seemed a lifetime, we had not been down more than an hour. This was Oswalt's work—the man who had repeated our distress signal and our position over and over again and who now lay on his back trying painfully to wave. It was his work and that of a relenting God who had provided us with a clear, sunny day in the midst of the monsoon season, so that the rescue plane had spotted the column of smoke. One hour! Surely, we had won on a thousand-to-one chance, for we all knew too well that very few crews who went down on the Hump run were ever found at all.

The plane flew back and forth over us several times. Finally the pilot said: "I know! They want us out in a clear area so they can drop a bale. See—they've got the door open."

Leaving Signor, the thin, white-haired boy, with Oswalt, the three of us charged at the brush again, fighting our way uphill in desperate hope that we would find an open space. Within minutes we had stumbled out onto a narrow footpath. We jammed a stick upright into the ground to mark the spot and hurried along the path. For a moment we caught sight of the distant grass village; then it disappeared as we descended a ridge. We had to slow down—we were too far gone for strenuous effort. A small stream issued from a nest of rocks, and we observed a length of split bamboo sticking out horizontally from the rock, forming a crude spigot. Some human being had done that. Farther on in a muddy stretch of the trail we noticed the prints of bare feet. I wondered vaguely if natives had been close by, watching us, at the wreck. Next we saw a shoe print. *That* had been made by someone from the plane—or else, I thought, by a Jap.

We reached a clear slope covered only by low grasses, and in a few moments the plane had spotted us again and was drumming

over very low. Obviously, we were the only survivors they had
seen. A fat bale tumbled from the plane's door and swung wildly
under its parachute to crash within a few yards of where we stood.
We dragged it to the trail and hastily tore it apart to find an axe,
a couple of long jungle knives, two blankets, cigarettes, army
rations, mosquito netting, and two old-style Springfield rifles, one
of which had a broken stock. It was comforting merely to handle
these familiar things. The plane came over again, and now a small
gray sack attached to a bright cloth streamer plummeted down
like an arrow. Inside was a typewritten note:

*Remain at wreckage until rescue party reaches you. You are
safe from enemy action there. Give some sign of life to searching
aircraft by building a fire or displaying unusual signs by parachute
panels. Further provisions coming by air tomorrow including a
radio. Your location: 26° 25' N.–95° 20' E.*

But they were not waiting until tomorrow to bring the radio.
Two bright orange 'chutes billowed out on the next run, and we
knew that they brought radio equipment. We retrieved one and
found a receiver, intact. The other 'chute had closed together
during the brief fall. Miller, the crew chief, and I descended into
the brush to search for it while the pilot remained on the trail with
our precious belongings. As we searched, we heard yelling from
the farther side of the slope. We straightened up and listened intently. It grew louder; it was from many human throats, and it
rose and fell in rhythmical sing-song. We would know in a moment whether we had to fight again for our lives. In quick whispers,
Miller agreed to crouch, hidden, in the brush, while I, who had
no weapon, scrambled up to the pilot and the pile of equipment.
I had time to grab up a jungle knife and whirl to take my stand
beside the pilot when they poured over the ridge.

They were fifteen or twenty in number: short men with deep
chests and muscular legs, coffee-brown in color and quite naked
save for narrow black breechcloths pulled up tightly under the
crotch. They had straight black hair, cut short around the head so
that the effect was that of a tuft of trimmed thatch. Some had faded
blue tattoo markings on their chests and arms. All carried long
spears with splayed metal points, and some also held wide-bladed
knives a couple of feet long, heavy and slightly curved, almost like
a butcher's cleaver.

All this one absorbed in a moment. We were really looking intc each other's eyes. I felt myself abnormally calm and kept the knife hanging at my side. The pilot remained still and did not move his hand toward his pistol holster. The psychological advantage lay with us; they had to continue their trotting advance or halt, and either way we would know the answer. The leaders slowed up, the chanting yell ceased, and the others pushed up beside the leaders, forming a semicircle. Some instinct, born no doubt of the Wild West novels of childhood, prompted me to step a pace forward, raise my palm, and say: "How!" However comical, it seemed to be taken as a clear gesture of friendship. They stuck their spears into the ground, reached back over their shoulders and slipped the big blades into a sheath at the small of their backs, and came up chattering, their mongoloid faces breaking into smiles. Some squatted down and felt of our shoes. Two older men picked up the axe, felt its edge and awkwardly tested its balance. They were obviously deeply impressed by our belongings. (Many months later, on the Anzio beachhead, John Vandercook, the explorer and broadcaster, explained to me that primitive tribesmen are often awed by white men because they think that the white man's marvelous tools and weapons are fashioned by his own hands as the savages must fashion their crude instruments.)

One of the men offered us a closed section of bamboo from which a hollow pipe extruded. I sucked, and the liquid tasted like a very raw, very alcoholic wine. Another held out a shallow gourd filled with a sticky substance that smelled something like the mash farmers feed to pigs. The pilot shook his head, but when I nudged him he pretended to eat the sickening stuff. They rubbed the parachute silk through their hands and over their faces, chattering loudly. A young boy pointed to the piece of silk I had tied around my head and then to himself. I gave it to him and was besieged by clamoring others. They were getting into everything, and it was necessary to wrap up our possessions in the bale and sternly motion them away. But none had attempted to steal anything at all.

Miller crawled cautiously out of the brush, and with gestures I indicated that a bale that had fallen from the plane was lost in the bushes. Instantly a dozen of them dived into the brush and almost at once came triumphantly back with the packaged radio transmitter, which proved to be smashed. Neveu, the pilot, suddenly reached into his jacket and pulled out a cardboard list of "Useful Phrases in Kachin and Burmese," provided by the army

to Hump fliers who might go down. I tried some phrases: "Naiy
gaw American—I am an American," and "Kurrum oo—Help me,"
and "Ante nah aiy shara peh-kum sun oo?—Where are the Japs?"
They smiled and shook their heads. Nothing worked. This must
be a race or tribe the army had not provided for. Neveu had a
map, and showed us where he thought we were. If he was correct,
we were on the very ridge which marks the theoretical boundary
between Burma and India, farther from the Indian plains than
the Chindwin River, where we knew the Japs were garrisoned.
Undoubtedly they must send patrols in our general direction from
time to time. Neveu indicated our position at a point just between
two large blank, white blotches on the map bearing the stark
word "Unsurveyed." We must be far back into little-known country, and from the map it was clear that many ranges of mountains
lay between us and inhabited, British territory. I knew then that
if we survived, it would be a matter of weeks before we got out.

By this time several more men from the plane had come hobbling up the trail to us. Their clothes were torn and all appeared
exhausted. They squatted or stretched full-length on the grass,
too tired to take much interest in the savages.

Suddenly most of the natives stood up, looking past me, their
smiles vanishing. I turned around to confront another spear-
bearing savage trotting toward us from the direction of the wrecked
plane. He was a beautiful specimen of manhood with long, rippling
legs. But he was different. His hair was long and tied in a knot
behind his head. His face was longer, and his appearance was
very much that of a Sioux Indian of the American plains. He hesitated, looked nervously from one of us to the other, then extended
his hand toward me, in it a folded slip of paper. I opened it and
made out a scrawl: *Those who bailed out this morning should
join the rest of the party at the village. The bearer will lead you.
This means you, too, Eric.* It was signed *John & Duncan.* I tore
out a blank page from my correspondent's pass book to scribble a
disjointed reply with trembling fingers: *Dear John. Eleven men
here—2 have bad legs—supplies dropped here, plane will return
here—rescue party on way—please come here—we about one mile
south of wreck. Eric."*

I took the small orange parachute and put it over the messenger's shoulders and then, as an added measure, gave him a half-
dollar, the only bright thing I had in my pockets. He looked at

the coin curiously, turning it over and over, then stuck it with my note into his breechcloth, turned abruptly, and ran down the path.

Now six or eight savages, chanting in unison, appeared over the rise, staggering together as they carried something very heavy. It was Oswalt, stretched on a litter fashioned from two army jackets. Despite his broken leg he had climbed from the wreck up to the trail, but there he had collapsed. He must have been in great pain, but he smiled broadly at us and lay on the ground absorbed in testing the radio receiver.

We all sat for a while, most of us, I think, beginning to ache in every muscle. Two or three men had canteens, and we all found that we were suffering from unquenchable thirst, the nervous ordeal apparently having completely dehydrated our systems.

Miller, the forty-year-old sergeant, said quietly: "I, ah, used to hear you on the radio from London and Washington. Used to listen around suppertime." He said it almost shyly. It was absurd that, even on this mountain in this lost section of Asia, the old pattern of familiar human relationships should already begin to take form. He was a "member of the public." I was the "celebrity." It gave me a small, sinking feeling of disappointment, but also of reassurance.

Obviously we must try to get Oswalt and the equipment to the village about a mile farther on. The natives seemed willing to obey the orders we gave them by gestures and readily loaded up their backs, and thus our improvised safari moved up and down the grassy wadis, the white men limping slowly and stopping at each little spring to drink some more. I found that I was taking the leadership in organizing the movement—rather to my surprise, upon reflection, for this was not my normal reaction, either by instinct or by reason of habit as an "observer" of other men's action. But all feeling of civilian-soldier distinction between us had disappeared in me. One quickly takes the measure of other men, and I felt somehow older and more responsible than the others, while the pilot, who technically should have been in command, continued to appear stupefied by events. It may have been because I was quite uninjured, but I sensed immediately that my mind worked faster than theirs, and it seemed natural to make suggestions.

The trail passed around patches of millet, roughly terraced on the steep slopes, intersticed here and there with crude fences made of sticks. More men and boys from the village appeared, and our bearers shouted at them, ordering them out of the way in self-important tones. The huts of palm-covered bamboo nestled in a planless huddle along a ravine halfway up the mountain ridge. We could see perhaps fifty or sixty huts, some of them mounted on stilts, with flat, uncovered platforms or porches at one end; across a deep gorge, thick with jungle growth, we caught sight of more huts with what appeared to be roofs of dark tiles. As we approached, Stanton, the elder of the Chinese officers, and three enlisted men came running out. Now we understood what one of the savages had meant when he held up five fingers and gestured in the direction of the village. One of the enlisted men, a grinning youngster, was licking his fingers as he came on. "Come on in," he shouted; "the chicken and eggs are swell!"

We crossed a narrow bridge of logs, sliced level for surer footing, passed an ingenious system of drain-piping made by connected lengths of hollow bamboo to form what must have been the village pump, and found ourselves in the muddy, filthy center of the community. Small pigs ran squealing away from us, and every few moments we observed women, naked save for a very brief apronlike skirt in front, ducking out of sight inside the huts, pulling the small children with them. The bearers did not hesitate, but carried Oswalt directly to the largest house, which had a wide-opened front, the two sides rising like an inverted V to form a high-pointed gable supported by a tall main post of bamboo. Beside the entrance stood some manner of totem pole with crude layers of carvings upon it. The building was about forty feet long, with a wooden platform covering the ground at the entrance and long woven mats stretched along the sides in the dim interior. In the center was a ring of stones encircling the dying embers of a fire.

Oswalt was carefully stretched on the platform, while most of us ran back out of the village to the edge of the incline that sloped steeply down toward the river, for we had heard the sound of airplane motors once more. A dozen big bales were swinging down, and we simply could not get to them fast enough. The natives were upon them in a moment, grabbing at the cotton cloth and the ropes, shoving one another about in a frenzy of greed, and yelling at the top of their lungs. Some had their cleavers out and were waving them menacingly. Yet somehow every fight was settled, and they would bring each bale to the central pile we were trying to organize—minus the cloth and rope.

Another small sack plummeted down and the message said:

*The most important thing is for you to remain where you are.
This is absolutely imperative for several reasons. Do not go to the
native village, as they probably are not friendly. Also be on guard
for any natives that may approach you, as they may or may not be
friendly. An effort is being made to inform the village chief that
you are friendly, but this information will take some time to reach
him. Do not antagonize any natives. We will drop you anything
you may need, and if it is not in the code-groups of the air-ground
liaison code we dropped with the panels, use the alphabet code-
groups. . . . Again, do not leave the area you are now in, and
keep the party together. If you follow instructions we will get you
back to the base much quicker. Be assured the entire wing is working on your rescue. Enclosed is a more complete air-ground liaison
code.*

Well, we were already in the village and, so far as we could
see, the natives were friendly. Anyway, we had to have shelter;
already the ominous rain clouds of late afternoon were beginning
to form on the surrounding peaks.

Some of the men made a quick study of the air-ground liaison
code and spread out the white cloth strips they had dropped to
form the code for "medical assistance needed." Oswalt's ankle had
turned purple and was swollen to enormous proportions. We directed the natives and ourselves carried the heavy bales into the
village and stacked them inside the large hut. I caught sight now
and then of old men, men who had not yet approached us, wearing
fancy headdresses crowned by bright red feathers. They were
chiefs of some kind, and they were gathering in another house
some distance from ours. I was too tired to do more than vaguely
wonder what it was all about.

We had just stretched out to ease the misery of our muscles when
the plane came back again. We all groaned, but three or four of
us limped to the edge of the village to watch, determined to let
the savages do whatever work was in store, no matter how much
equipment might disappear as a result. Twilight was approaching,
and the plane was black against the storm clouds. It seemed to be
flying a little higher than before. Three bales tumbled out, and
three 'chutes opened. I wondered what could be so important as
to necessitate this late trip. Somebody let out a yell—the bales were
growing legs!

For a moment my own legs simply would not function; everything inside my chest seemed to be melting. I began to run, digging at the tears in my eyes with my fist, like a child. This was wonderful—and impossible. Of their own free will, men were coming to help us, voluntarily casting their fate with ours. I got to the crest of the steep slope as the first jumper floated past, missing the summit by a scant few yards. I could see the insignia of a lieutenant colonel on his jacket shoulders. He grinned at me and I shouted foolishly: "Here! We're here in the village!" He held up a finger in a crisp gesture, like a man strolling past on a sidewalk, and said in a conversational tone: "Be with you in a minute." Half weeping, half laughing over the wonderful absurdity of the meeting, I scrambled down the slope and slid to a halt before him as he was brushing dirt from his clothes and beginning to unwrap protective bandage from his knees. He was a slim, closely knit man of about thirty-five, with cropped hair, and vivid dark eyes in a brown, taut face. He smiled easily as we introduced ourselves. "I'm Don Flickinger," he said. "I'm the wing surgeon. Saw you needed a little help."

While the other two jumpers were extricating themselves from a picket fence farther down the hill, Colonel Flickinger and I climbed toward the village. I was feeling profound relief at his presence—due not so much to his medical kit, I realized, as to his quiet air of competent authority. The problem of discipline and organization for our conglomerate party was solved. I knew now that the responsibility of leadership would not rest with me, that I had not wished it despite my amateurish gestures, and that I could not have sustained it. I had a sense of comfort at falling back into my familiar niche as a participating witness without the responsibility of decision.

The Colonel casually remarked, as we crossed the footbridge: "By the way. Friend of yours in the plane sent you his best wishes. St. Clair McKelway." This was too much; I could not repress a giggle. McKelway, the owlish, sophisticated essayist, I had last seen leaning against the bar of "21" on Fifty-second Street. He was now a major, wing information officer in the air forces.

While Flickinger was examining Oswalt's leg, his two assistants limped into the "town hall": Sergeant Harold Passey and Corporal William MacKenzie. Neither one had ever made a jump before. The Colonel had not ordered them to jump, but had simply told them that if they wished to follow him down he would be pleased

to have their aid. MacKenzie admitted to me later that his knees
had trembled so that he could scarcely stand upright at the door.
Gallant is a precious word; they deserve it. They had followed
the Colonel without a moment's hesitation, and one knew at once
that it was not from a sense of personal heroics, but simply because
of faith in their leader. Flickinger was a regular army officer who
already held the Distinguished Flying Cross for his work at Pearl
Harbor and in the Philippines, where he had bailed out to save a
crew. He had not been under orders to jump to us. Indeed, he had
been annoyed at our panel signal, which merely said "Medical
assistance needed." Apparently there was another sign for "Expert
medical assistance needed," and he had been in doubt as to the
necessity of jumping. At the last moment he decided he could not
take the chance.

He had guessed right. Oswalt's leg was in frightful condition. I
shall not soon forget the scene in the central *basha* that night.
Naked bodies of curious savages choked the doorway, a hundred
pairs of eyes peered in through the cracks along the walls. Several
native citizens squatted around the fire, chewing on roast pig or
goat. Most of us lay stretched out in exhaustion, or sat about
digging food from the ration cans with our fingers, while Flickinger set Oswalt's leg in bamboo splints by the beam of a flashlight.
The big sergeant simply held his knee, and regarded the painful
operation in silence, with no show of suffering on his face. Then
Flickinger sterilized the point of a hunting knife in the flame of
a cigarette lighter and attended to us all, digging out leech and
tick bites. He had quinine and mosquito lotion for us and gave us
something for the sore throats of which we all complained. (Later
we realized that this was purely muscular, due to the jerk when
our parachutes had opened.) There were several sprained ankles,
and one youngster, Waterbury, had ugly abrasions on his chin
and cheekbones. He had jumped with his steel helmet on, the
heavy strap fastened around his chin. Fortunately, the strap broke
before his neck did, and he got only cuts. All of us had black-
and-blue stripes across the shoulders and around the upper thighs
from the parachute straps.

A wrinkled old man squatted behind the Colonel as he worked.
He had a whimpering baby tied to his back, and he tried patiently
to get the doctor's attention. When he succeeded, he pointed to
a large abscess under the child's ear, then opened his fingers to

disclose an egg, which he had brought for the doctor's fee. Flickinger took a pill and demonstrated how the father should chew it in his own mouth, then spit it down the baby's throat. The man got the idea immediately and retreated with grateful smiles.

The fire died, and it grew dark inside the *basha* which quivered and bent under the flood of a tropical cloudburst. Icy drafts blew in along the ground and froze our dew- and sweat-soaked clothing. I tried to sleep, exposed and shivering, with my head jammed against another man's boots. Some began to snore, and one young boy cried out in his dreams. It had been the most strenuous day of my life, and I ached in every fiber, but I could not sleep. I was beginning to doze when I caught a faint and ominous sound. It was the distant yelling of many human voices. It grew steadily louder and I sat upright, my heart beating wildly. Through the cracks I saw the glowing lights of many torches bouncing up and down in the blackness. I had scarcely time to get to my feet when two savages of the long-haired type burst in at the door, leaping over the sleeping bodies at the entrance. For an instant I was paralyzed. But they did no more than squat by the dead fire in the center.

From the entrance a cultivated, musical voice called: "Doctor Sevareid, I presume?"

It was Davies, with Duncan Lee and three others including the young Chinese officer. They stood in the doorway, their hair plastered down and water streaming from nose and chin. Davies was chuckling as he surveyed the weird scene, an amused smile on his face.

We talked until midnight while they tried to dry their clothing. The five of them had come to earth not far apart, in a millet field just outside a native village on the other side of the range, seven or eight miles from our village. John said he got to his feet and cursed as he saw the plane proceed steadily over the range, making for India. Until he saw the gathering mushroom of smoke in the sky he had no reason to believe the plane had gone down. A native chief came out to greet them, holding out a sword with a beaten silver handle as a gesture of friendship. Acting on the hunch that the ceremonial gestures of Chinese "form" would be understood, John bowed and scraped and otherwise gave the chief to understand that the visitors acknowledged a lordly presence. The chief fingered the parachute with curiosity, so Davies slipped it over his shoulders, and the old man hopped about like a boy with the seat pack flapping at his buttocks. Then they were led into the village and seated at a fire. A tiny, wailing goat was produced along with a heavy knife. Sergeant Evan Wilder, a silent Texan, was chosen as ceremonial butcher. He closed his eyes and hacked off the goat's head, as the savages indicated. The chief lifted the body and drank the spouting blood as one would drink wine from a skin. It was then handed to the visitors. With admirable courage they drank, retained their solemn expressions, and managed not to vomit.

Davies sent the note to us, making it as cryptic as possible in order not to let any important information about himself or the party fall into the hands of any Japanese who might be near. (He could not afford to assume that the Japanese would not recognize his name as that of General Stilwell's political advisor.) When my reply arrived, they set out with guides for a tortuous hike over the hills in darkness and drenching rain. One or two men wanted to give up halfway and simply sleep exposed on the trail, but with the help of young Colonel Kwoh Li, despite his own badly sprained ankle, they managed to keep everyone together.

When he had finished his account, we checked the roll call against the complete list of names Colonel Flickinger had been given by the agitated officers at the air base. Two were missing: Co-Pilot Charles Felix and Corporal Basil Lemmon. Nothing further could be done until the next day dawned. I lay down on the wet matting and instantly passed out.

3

In the chill dawn we were a painfully stiff and blear-eyed company. The faithful plane was over us again when we had scarcely finished a clammy breakfast of cold army rations, eaten with fingers and pocket knives. More bales, mostly containing food, were dropped. The excitement of the operation had worn off for us, but not for the savages, and we found ourselves occasionally fighting them off. I remember shoving two or three evil-looking men aside in an outburst of bad temper. They did not smile, but let go of the bale reluctantly, muttering among themselves. We had already come to feel that we could dominate them without trouble, but another note from the plane, signed by McKelway, was most disturbing:

The British political agent is with us this morning, trying to identify your position from the air. The land party will start out as soon as we know where you are. Important that you stay where you are until we get to you. The agent is sure there are unfriendly Nagas all round you. They will have to be fixed before you can go through them safely. It may take a week or more to get to you. Let us know your needs.

So these were the famous Nagas! They were quite another story from the Kachins and the other familiar tribes who worked in loose alliance with the British of India. None of us had ever seen a Naga before, but it was well known that many of them were merciless head-hunters. If the British agent was having trouble identifying our position, then surely we were far back in unfamiliar territory, perhaps among an unknown tribe, almost certainly a tribe which recognized no exterior authority.

As we gathered the bales on the crest, a chief in a gaudy red blanket and headdress indicated by signs that he wished us all to move out of the village. I believed that this was because the bales were smashing down their stands of maize. Colonel Flickinger believed (though he did not mention his fears then) that they had decided to attack us or wanted us away from the village in case they did decide on a fight. They indicated a grassy shelf a half-mile out, toward the wreck, and immediately the chiefs organized the men and boys, who began trotting in with bamboo lengths and piles of palm leaves to throw up three *bashas* with incredible rapidity. We wanted one for the officers and civilians, one for the enlisted men, and a small one to hold our supplies.

A small party of "long hairs" arrived. One of them approached us and made signs to indicate a man lying down. He struck his knee several times with the edge of his hand, and we thought at once: "It's Felix or Lemmon, down somewhere with a broken leg." MacKenzie and Passey took one of the army stretchers the plane had dropped and, with Sergeant Kittleson, a husky, reserved boy from Montana, I went along on the party. Our camp disappeared behind us and we walked in single file between heavy walls of thick grass. Glancing over my shoulder, I could see that one of the savages, a man wearing a heavy ring of solid brass around his neck, was keeping close to me, his spear swinging with the movement of his arm. As the minutes passed and they gave no sign, I had an uneasy feeling that we might be the victims of a crude plot to divide our company for violent purposes. Then suddenly they called a halt. I recognized the spot—directly above the plane wreck—and knew then that we had come to see a dead man.

The plane was now a sodden, steaming mess, with only a faint tendril of white smoke rising from the blackened metal. Several savages were squatted in the midst of it, banging on a crumpled strip of aluminum. MacKenzie stiffened and pointed. Somewhere under the wreckage the natives had found the body of Felix, had dragged it to one side, and partly covered it with strips of aluminum. One leg was severed at the knee. I recognized the back of his head, because I had seen it through the door of the pilots' compartment; I had never seen his face. He appeared to be stripped of all clothing, and his identification disks were gone. I returned to the camp to inform the Colonel, while MacKenzie and Passey set about their difficult task. Later I found Mackenzie, a quiet, sensitive boy, sitting alone outside the camp. He and Passey had dug a grave and buried Felix. Then, while the natives, through some instinct of reverence, ceased their banging, he had erected a cross of bamboo and read the Lord's Prayer at the grave, from the army pocket Bible he carried in his shirt. He had said "Amen" —then stepped aside into the brush and was sick.

What had happened on the plane during the last few seconds was not clear. Though Felix had been superior in rank to Flight Officer Neveu, the latter was pilot for the trip because he was more familiar with the Hump run. When they realized that the scuttling of the baggage was not going to keep the plane at the required altitude, Neveu had sent Felix back to get his parachute on. Then Felix had replaced him while he did the same. They had clung to the controls as long as possible, until the remaining engine heated up to the explosion point. Then they had set the controls and dashed back for the door. Why Felix had not been able to jump successfully nobody was sure; it had all happened too quickly. He may have jumped but been caught in the tail assembly as the plane turned on its side, though it seemed more likely that this movement of the plane had caused him to slip momentarily on the slippery flooring and that the moment's hesitation had prevented his leap. If there had not been two or three

of us still trying to get out when the crew arrived at the door, the
few seconds saved would perhaps have meant the saving of his
life. One could, if he wished, move the point of responsibility
farther back: If there had been definite orders for and organization
of the passengers, all of them amateurs; if the passengers had
been briefed on the ground; if the C-46 had not been used for passengers in the first place; if Washington had not ordered these
planes to the Hump run before they were perfected . . . There
was a long chain of errors and happenstance, and no one could
determine that this or that was the fatal link. So far as we could
see, both pilots had done their duty to the utmost and had got
us away from enemy territory. Neveu felt very badly, but it never
occurred to any of us to hold him responsible; indeed, we were
more inclined to be grateful that he had kept us in the air as long
as he had.

The supply plane dropped a .30-caliber army carbine for each
member of our company. A grinning savage imitated the action
of a rifle going off, which told us that this tribe knew perfectly
well what firearms were, but it was clear they possessed none
themselves. Unless we walked some distance away from our camp,
we did not carry the arms but kept them out of sight in the *bashas*,
each man under orders to keep his rifle by his own bedroll, loaded
and ready for immediate use.

Colonel Flickinger called us together and read off a list cf our
individual duties. Davies was to handle the organization of natives
for the retrieving of the bales and all barter with them, which was
already a thriving affair—pieces of string, cloth, and empty ration
cans exchanged for their scrawny chickens, generally rotten eggs,
ears of maize, and occasional fresh meat. Captain Duncan Lee had
charge of all our supplies; Bill Stanton would take care of the
signal panels whenever the plane came; Oswalt would take messages over our receiver, which lay by his side; Neveu would delegate guard duty at night; Sergeant Joseph Gigure would be cook
(hardest task of all)—and so on down the list. I, with Davies and
the Colonel, was on the "general planning committee" and was
delegated to keep the daily log and preserve all messages and documents. The Colonel said: "Sevareid, I think you'll also be our
chaplain." This startled me, but he went on firmly: "You're probably the only man here who ever made a speech." It was an order,
and in our situation it would not do for any man of us to set a
precedent by trying to disobey an order.

By a payment of tin cans, which they prized highly, we got a dozen savages to clear away the long grasses with their knives. We needed space for many reasons, not the least of which was the added advantage it would provide in case of a surprise attack. The only angle from which attackers could creep within spear-throwing distance without being detected was on the downhill side—unless, of course, they chose to attack at night.

The two-hour watch in the middle of the night was a lonesome affair. If one strolled away, too near the brush, he ran the risk of silent disappearance with no chance to warn the company. If he stayed by the fire he could not see well and was clearly outlined himself. I walked slowly back and forth about midway, holding the carbine in stiff fingers, trying vainly to huddle some warmth out of a thin army jacket. As the fire died to glowing embers, the rounded hills were sharply outlined in the moonlight. That was Burma just over the ridge on whose slope we were camped, and the plains of India were somewhere in the distant west. I started at every cracking twig, every chattering yell from the gibbons in the brush. Every cloud that passed before the face of the moon patched the gloom with blackness in which a dozen fancied human forms took shape. It was with distinct relief that I shook awake the next sentry and rolled into my blanket on the unrelenting ground. During his tour of guard duty, Colonel Flickinger heard something at the corner of the enlisted men's *basha*. The beam of his flashlight revealed a leopard clawing up at a chunk of fresh meat suspended from a small tree and covered in mosquito netting. With good sense, Flickinger refrained from trying a shot which might have merely wounded the creature, and it leaped noise-lessly away.

I attempted to keep as complete a diary as one could in the blank pages of my pass book, borrowing fountain pens until all our ink was exhausted. (Ink was one of the things, along with cameras, soap, and eating utensils, which we could not seem to get from the aerial supply service, no matter how often we signaled for them.) Following are some excerpts from my log, which was quite unprofessional and included remarks intended only for myself:

August 4—Duncan has collected everyone's cigarettes and has rationed them out. Came to twelve apiece. Seems to rain every night and the *bashas* leak rather badly. MacKenzie is better; he suffered from fever and continuous vomiting after the burial of Felix. We have driven a fence of bamboo stakes around the camp as a psychological barrier to keep the curious crowds out. At earliest dawn, small children shivering outside in rain, holding fistfuls of firewood they want to trade for tin cans. McKelway seems to sense our information needs. Another note from him:

> *You are within eight miles of what is called British control territory, some sixty miles southeast of Mokokchung.* [Must mean as crow flies according our map.] *There is British subdivisional officer there. Try to get word to him by the natives, but don't leave the place you are in now. He is known to the natives as the Sahib of Mokokchung. Our land party will start from there tomorrow or next day according to present plans. British political officer flying with us advises you to be as friendly as possible with natives but not to relax vigilance. To stay together as much as possible and not to wander about singly. You know best, being on spot, but he thinks display of arms will make them suspicious and perhaps cause them to attack you. . . . Reason you shouldn't start out before we give the word is that there are savage Nagas between you and Mokokchung who have to be fixed by the British first. . . . Try to contact the head man of Chingmei, six miles due west of you. He is said to be a good fellow, loyal to British.*

Dug latrine downhill, another one near by for Oswalt's private use. Short on cellulose products. Davies contributed sheets from mimeographed memorandum by some Washington thinkers on future world league. Trust fate of memorandum no portent. Colonel has sent messenger to Mok. giving details our state. Our transmitter unworkable. Tried flying kite for aerial. No wind. Went with six men down to river try get fish. No luck, no troubles. Caught in drenching downpour trying to climb back up. Surroundings most desolate, forbidding when no sun.

Chief of Chingmei seems already be with us. Old man, slightly bent, not unkindly, rather intelligent face. Red blanket, white cowrie shells as ear ornaments (how did they get up here from sea?). Ornate red-feather headdress and heavy chest tattooing. Name appears to be Chingmak. Squats and smiles by hour, pleased to puff cigarettes. Doesn't seem to have any suggestions. We gather his village about twenty-five-mile march away. Another newcomer, name of Sangbah. About thirty-five, has red blanket too. Extremely intelligent, pleasant. Seems understand few words of English and speaks of Mokokchung frequently, so he must know the British there. He gets the men of Pangsha (village we are near) to do whatever we want by few soft words and gestures, but seems to speak different dialect. Carries some authority obviously, and we gather he is some kind of representative of British control. Wandering amateur diplomat—kind of native Bill Bullitt. Points to Pangsha men, makes gesture of head being lopped off, and smiles. We get the idea. One or two of enlisted men treat natives as bothersome children, shove them about occasionally. They *are* like children, but these lapses must be stopped. Guns or no guns, there are far too many of them. Ponyo is name of village on Burma side where Davies party dropped. "Ponyo brothers" are two warriors who show up each day. Most magnificent physical specimens I have ever seen. They stand apart, by themselves, refuse do any work, consider work demeaning. They are obviously of élite warrior caste.

August 5—Natives brought pig, which strung up by hind legs, and Corporal Cherrill stuck it while natives caught blood in segment of hollow bamboo. Have made benches for fireside eating. Also kind of sidewalk in mud, of sticks and stones. Danger of tin-can inflation, ruining their value. Davies says he has put ceiling prices on firewood, bamboo, and eggs. Relates example of reverse lend-lease: a native offered *him* a silver rupee for some silk. Where did he get the coin? Plane over at noon, catching brief period clear sky. Natives ran wild, almost riot among them, fighting for 'chutes and cords. Chiefs beat them with sticks, some law-abiding ones threw dirt at them until quelled. Heavy rice bags came down without 'chutes, just missed killing several savages. Pilots flying so low we can glimpse their grins. But must be more careful with bags, can't afford any deaths here. Plane dropped list all our names with code signal for each name to indicate whether he all right, injured slightly, injured seriously, missing, or dead. Laid out panels according instructions as plane circled over slope twenty times, getting dope, one name at a time, dipping nose when got it okay. This breath-taking flying. Twice we certain plane would not be able to turn in time to avoid crashing on opposite side valley. Since I complained not having enough work to do, I am now "apprenticed" to Davies as assistant bargainer. For this retrieving job we picked out fifteen or twenty men, tied cords around their arms so could identify them and make sure right men got paid, and no others. When everything carried in, we sat them all down in row while the Chinese officers cut out strips of cotton parachute cloth as reward. Then as each worker got to his feet and came forward, Davies handed him a roll of white cloth. Looked not unlike Commencement Day. Some of savages laughed at process, others scowled. Suppose they never been regimented in any such manner before. To one or two bad ones, Davies said: "You are a low, common, lazy, evil-looking, wife-beating, murdering scoundrel, and I hope you roast in Hell," all the time smiling and bowing.

Great luck today. Natives arrived with Davies' brief case which had been whipped out of his arms when his parachute opened. Everything was in it. Important documents for Stilwell, several hundred dollars, Lee's traveler's checks, some of my own letters to people in Chungking, and my notes from Washington. Natives had broken locks and had slit inner leather case with knife, unknowing how to work the zipper. John's extra wrist watch had crystal and back intact, but insides were separate. Another savage brought in a 'chute with blood on it. Thought it was a sign of Lemmon's fate, but apparently belongs to Waterbury, whose helmet straps cut his chin. Crazy proportion of supplies dropped today: two enormous boxes of tea, which we are spreading down as bedding; three and a half pair of socks; two pair underpants; and a hundred and ten *undershirts!*

Another note dropped. Carbon copy of army instructions to somebody concerning the rescue party:

. . . *Party, led by Lieutenant LaBonte of radio air-warning station, will proceed to Mokokchung. Here large party will form and start for scene of wreck. Porters and guards will be ready and have been arranged for. Mr. Adams, accompanied by Lt. LaBonte, will lead rescue party. Meantime, thirty guards have started to stranded party for protective purposes if necessary. Coolies to carry stretcher cases, if any, will be available. Trip in and out from Mokokchung will require between two and three weeks. Advisable to put a plane or two a day over the stranded party for moral effect on natives and to pick up messages. Two thousand silver rupees have been furnished Mr. Adams. One half-ton of salt should be dropped on village where stranded party is as reward to Nagas.*

August 6—Pouring rain this morning, holds up searching party ready to make effort find Lemmon. Fright of my life at noon. Crest of hill direction village suddenly filled hundreds Nagas, running

down trail toward us, yelling top their voices. Several of us excitable ones grabbed rifles, I certain attack had come. From distance looked like wobbling line of crawling butterflies, due to fact
each savage held palm branch over head. They were pulling young
bull tied by vine rope. Outside camp they lassoed each hoof and
threw him down. Then one man held point of spear against animal's side while reciting long, chanting speech. Seemed repeat
many sing-song phrases. Occasionally cleared throat and looked
embarrassed like any banquet orator. Thrust spear in and blood
caught in gourd. While bull dying, one boy jabbed his bare toe
in bull's eye repeatedly. One hacked off animal's tail. Apparently
feel no sympathy for suffering. Flick stripped off shirt and skinned
bull expertly. Our camp given two quarters. Vast audience, festive
spirit. Natives bring in two bamboo poles, tie bull's hoof to one
pole, and after another long speech thrust it upright in ground.
Then Colonel asked plant second pole, tying one our hoofs to it.
Flick tries make speech: "We who came to you from skies . . . oh,
hell, let's sing them a song." We gathered and sang "I Been Working
on the Railroad," "He's a Jolly Good Fellow," and as afterthought
the national anthem. They listened solemnly, much impressed. A
gaudy ceremonial spear with dyed clusters of bright red hair on
shaft stuck upright before camp. We now appear to be officially
friends by treaty. Feel much more secure.

No plane today. I went into jungle, with much difficulty cut
down bamboo tree. Dragged it out and fashioned large cross
which erected in clearing above *bashas*. Made no sense to natives,
who laughed.

Lemmon is here, alive. Two Ponyos arrived midst festivities,
very excited, indicated man somewhere down trail staggering this
way. Passey, MacKenzie, couple others, and I took stretchers and
hurried down trail. Came upon Lemmon who stumbling along
arms over shoulders two savages. Put him on stretcher. Recognized him as the boy with mustache who had sat so closely by the
door of plane when took off from Chabua. I threw my jacket over
him, put cigarette in his mouth. He tried smile, said nothing. As
carried in through crowd, kept his arm over his eyes. Think he was
weeping. Colonel requests boys keep away from him awhile. Later
said Lemmon suffering fatigue, shock mostly, and will recover all
right. Clothes soaked and in rags. Shoes almost gone and his feet
look terrible, white, bloated, and wrinkled. Between sips of coffee
he whispered story: Someone on plane had told him we were over

enemy territory. After rising in brush he saw no other 'chutes, and each time caught sight of a native on trails he hid himself, fearing they might be Japs. Had no idea what Japanese looked like. Abandoned parachute and wandered in thick brush. Found that he was going in circles. Four nights he lay exposed in freezing downpour, being consumed by leeches and other insects. Would try to cover himself with large palm leaves, but soon rain broke them up, so just lay with rain directly on him. Found nothing to eat, so chewed his wet cigarettes for stimulation. Early this morning he crawled into a small thatch hut standing in a field of maize and collapsed, praying he would die quickly. Apparently he was observed entering the hut, for natives soon followed him in. He was too far gone to be frightened. They squatted down, built him fire, gave him rice to eat, then took him to us, distance of about three miles. He had heard planes but never saw them. "One guy carried me on his back for at least a mile," he said. "Guy half my size."

August 7—Another note indicates rescue party will be here around fifteenth. No sign of any "guards" arriving. Who they supposed to be—Assam Rifles? Ponyos discovered we desirous of their spears, so brought five tasseled ones for trade. Can't get their business spears for any price, however. Noticed one spear had five notches on it. Flick running daily clinic for them as well as for us now. One man is definitely a leper we think. Makes me nervous. They take iodine on open cuts without a quiver. Chinese explain to John that they wish to take their share of guard duty. He explains they left out only because of language difficulty, which might be serious matter if had to give alarm. (Actually, we bit afraid they might get panicky, shoot when no need.) Kwoh Li is grand soldier. Made retreat out of Burma with Stilwell. Peasant type, up from ranks. Wang on other hand was Burma road-profiteer-desk-officer of high birth. Nobody likes him. He scolds at natives as if they were Chinese coolies. Always seems to be fresh-shaven and washed. Where does he get the soap? Beginning to take fancy to my beard. Bronze-red color to my surprise. Kwoh Li tells John he deeply impressed with gallantry of Flickinger in jumping out to us. Says no officer in Chinese army would think of such a thing. Men in this predicament would simply be left to die.

Some of our leavings showing up as native ornaments. Noticed pieces bloody bandage and ration-can-opener keys stuck through ear lobes. Fashioned spoons from bamboo; stir coffee with bayonet; eat out of ration cans. Chinese officers expert at cooking rice, delighted to take over the job. Native kids hang around Oswalt all day, listening radio. Wonder what they think of Benny Goodman's music coming from San Francisco. Kids never seem to play among themselves. Oswalt teaching them English phrases. Like this: "Cherrill is a chow hound!" They repeat it accurately, and Oswalt roars like a bull. Nearly every day we catch distress call some plane going down in jungle. Suppose the Washington columnists still bleeding into their typewriters about our not trying get supplies to Chinese. Endless recapitulation of everybody's jump story around fire at night. Fair song sessions. Lemmon reveals baggage belonging to Harmon, the football player, was on the plane. For some reason boys scream with laughter at this. I feel surprisingly well here, about five-thousand-foot altitude. Very few mosquitoes, thank God. No signs malaria yet.

Some kind of chief named "Poom" showed up wearing Scotch plaid midriff. Has rupees given him by Japs at Singkaling. Apparently Japs eight days' march from here. Sangbah says if Japs come close, natives will warn us. Plane over two P.M. Inform them about Lemmon. We signal required shoe size for each of us. Took hour for plane to get them all, circling in low for each number. I asked size twelve. Pilot's voice on receiver asks: "Who 'n Christ got the big feet?"

August 8—I assembled party for "church" this Sunday morning at eleven, which used to be hour for services at home. Men formed up before cross. I felt very nervous, uncertain. Think my conscience was objecting that I had no business doing this; I not been inside church in years. I said this was memorial service for Co-Pilot Felix. Made few impromptu remarks about his death while doing duty, our regrets and gratitude his part saving our lives. Read 107th and 23rd Psalms and Lord's Prayer, then tried to lead men singing Doxology which I seemed remember all right. Ragged results. Felt embarrassed with men afterwards. Somehow this tends set me bit apart from them, don't like that feeling. Yet sensed they all been feeling drama their salvation and instinctively wishing some kind of formalized notice of it, beyond flippant conversational remarks. Colonel congratulates me privately, says some of boys comforted by ceremony. If so I feel better. Davies said: "Eric, you know I was really moved." In evening heard Bob Hope and Glen Miller band. Middle of night Duncan and I sit long time by fire, holding rifles, drinking coffee to keep awake. Find we think alike, have friends in common, such as Sheeans. He's been desk officer in Washington. Scholarly, reflective type, but felt same need partake action of war that I felt. Both confessed we rather glad this happened to us, even if is just stupid accident. In backhanded way it helps narrow gap between us and fighting men.

August 9—Shoes and socks this time. We itching to get started on hike out. Stanton urges we not wait for rescue party, but have no other choice. Four strangers among savages. One wears leopard skin and carries crossbow. Sangbah directs building of new *basha* fifty yards away for those who coming. Becoming aware distinct personalities among natives now. Some are lazy, some humorless, some shy. But most very friendly, laugh loudly, love practical jokes. Certainly have nothing in common with Indians of the plains. Some have fine, almost cultivated faces, expressive, intelligent eyes. One of these is "Moon-sang," whose baby Flick been treating. He has magnetic charm. One shyster we call "the mayor of Pangsha" though no evidence he is leading chief. Ward-heeler type. Does no work, but shrewdly guesses our desires, so brings in spears and knives for trading to get his cans and cloth. Hard bargainer. Brought Flick knife holster made of two fitted slabs bamboo. On each side he'd drawn pictures with hot knife. Line drawing, very crude, showing plane, parachute, and man dangling from its ropes. I most excited about it and now he's making one for me.

Fleas dreadful at night. Flick sleeps next to me and never gets a bite. Nor does Davies. These competent, self-possessed men—even have immunity from fleas. My original leech bites ulcerated. Shouldn't have brushed them off, should touch with burning cigarette or iodine, then they depart pulling head out with them.

Flick's authority never questioned. He's very human, not stiff army-officer type, so occasionally gets into wrangling argument with some lazy lad (have one or two) but he so obviously competent, intelligent, and likable we willingly defer to him including civilians. Cherrill is our clown—every outfit has one. I find his silly humor delightful, some others don't. Beneath silliness is gay and brave spirit. Signor, cross-eyed solemn lad, is another clown, quiet type. Tried his new shoes and reported: "Caress my feet somep'n awful." This now byword for anything: if have uncomfortable night, "ground caressed my back somep'n awful," etc. Evan Wilder is steady, stocky Texan, good soldier, rarely opens mouth. Not pleased at going China. "Ah'm too fur from Lubbock, awready." Sergeant Clay, Georgia farm boy, very skinny, sits cross-legged in supply room all day wearing white silk headdress, looks like Hindu fakir. Never says a word. Get impression he regards whole scene as suspiciously improbable. Lieut. Roland Lee, Chinese-American from New York, bit mischievous, has positive ideas in manner of very young boy, occasionally irritates Colonel, but good lad at heart.

August 10—Rain all day, heard plane but he could not get in. Natives huddle all day on "grandstand" like crows at roost. Leopard Skin put on crossbow exhibition. Cocks bow with feet, it so strong. Small arrow about foot long. Fantastic accuracy. Seven of us hiked through farther suburb of Pangsha which uninspected so far. Village is miserable place in mud. Saw almost no one, save couple desiccated old women, flat, pendulous breasts, smoking pipes. Discovered enormous drums made hollowed log, resembling dugout canoe almost. Long discussions around fire at night. Talk about kinds women we have known (no names), how different movie stars look in flesh, Winston Churchill, Clare Luce, restaurants and dishes and drinks, socialized medicine, democracy. Flick thinks democracy expensive luxury, I think it basic necessity. Typical locker-room talk. Passes the time.

August 11—Out of latrine paper again. So went back to Davies' world organization plan, working through the Whereases. Started daily calisthenics in group, led by Colonel. His idea, to get us in some kind of shape for hike out. Natives doubled up with laughter, especially at our "running in place" while chanting count. One hour of sun late afternoon and plane was there. Kwoh Li fixed lunch of rice and some greens Sangbah found in woods, like turnip greens. Stars, full moon at night. We sang for hours. At such moments I love it here, wouldn't be elsewhere.

August 12—Finest weather. Jap plane over very high, probably photographic observation. Several bathed in stream, rubbing gravel over bodies, no soap yet. Hard time keeping kids out of our "compound." They seem to regard it as game, scurry away, then ooze back in. One old fellow whom Davies had frequently shooed away shooed *him* away from the new *basha*, crying:

"Ow'side, ow'side!" For once Davies taken aback. He obeyed. Oswalt getting fatter, growing wide beard. Remarkable resemblance to Holbein's Henry the Eighth. Many visitors, some apparently from villages several days' march distant. Spear-throwing contest developed. Natives wanted use cross as target, but dissuaded. Our star is Passey, six-foot, natural athlete, who beat many savages their own game, but squat, grinning little guy finally beat Passey with last throw and won the prize—three tin cans. Ran off with cans clutched to chest, shrieking his delight. Got excellent waterproofed map from plane, with another injunction not to move.

August 13—Very early plane today. Message from General Alexander at Chabua for Flick:

You are to put your party under cover at all times that aircraft are heard until you positively identify them as being friendly. Reports reached wing headquarters that some enemy reconnaissance been carried out near your position. Believe it advisable for you to dig slit trenches in unexposed area. Do not permit your party to congregate or expose themselves even during dropping operations. Do not lay out panels until you are certain plane overhead is ours. Do not worry, our fighters are covering the area. Have you any information to convey pertaining to enemy activity air or ground?

Colonel decides necessary to dig slit trench only for Oswalt, which three savages eagerly do under my direction. Ravine gives us good natural protection against strafing. Paratroopers would be another problem. Colonel orders each man to take his rifle soon as hear sound motors, to take off our white undershirts, pull down white clothes from the drying line, and disperse into brush. We practice, I clock men as run for brush after Colonel yells "battle stations." Takes full minute before last man hidden. Much too long. Colonel gives orders that in case Jap patrol or paratroopers, the three civilians—Davies, Stanton and I—are to take our rifles and hit down trail, try to get to Mokokchung. In other words, we not to fight. Technically, he may be correct, but we protest. He insists, but we three talk it over, agree impossible do such a thing, every man, every rifle would count too much. I hate having this out. Suppose I afraid I might take advantage of it in test. Davies sick, touch of fever; Stanton has bad ulcer on ankle.

Dropped us copy of the Calcutta *Statesman*, only three days

old. Had page one account of the "stranded party" and gave names
of us three civilians. For once I am on censors' side. This dangerous
mistake. Means Japs know Davies here, and unquestionably they
hear plane talking with us every day and must be aware our position. All very disturbing.

Dropped us a few books and magazines, bless them. I just reading first line of Agatha Christie: "As the butler handed round the
soufflé, Lord Mayfield leaned confidentially toward his neighbor
on the right . . ."—when somebody yelled "airplanes!" We were
hidden in brush in few moments, but most of clothes on line were
tied tightly. Six fighter planes going southwest. Thunderheads
piled up in late afternoon. Mountains appear distant, forbidding
and dark. Late at night a good moon, streamers of white mist move
down mountain slopes like fairy glaciers in motion. We have seen
a sight few men ever see—a perfect rainbow by moonlight, arched
across our valley, like a good omen, a benediction and blessing
upon us.

4

Fog hung over the camp, drizzled down the palm thatching and
smothered out the valley. The miserable day moved past on slow
and sodden feet; the men huddled unspeaking by the fire or lay
rolled in their blankets staring at the roof, now decayed and
brown. The camp looked old and spent, sagging like the spirits
of the young men within, whose minds had exhausted the variety
of their surroundings and were now turning over and over warm
morsels of thoughts of home. The heart sickness was beginning
among us, and I vaguely wondered who would be the first man
to be found missing one night if the time passed and no relief
arrived.

They came as the light was dimming away. The mist was spread
below us, and we seemed to be alone, on the summit of the world.
A low chanting sound came from beneath the cloud layer, growing louder and louder until it seemed that a subterranean forest
of voices was rising to engulf us. Dark, glistening bodies appeared
from the ravine, more and more of them, flooding among us and
surrounding our space of habitation. A tall, slim young man wearing a halo of shining fair hair, carrying the mystery of civilization
in his casual posture and soft blue eyes, materialized from the

void. He was standing at our gate, smiling gently, like a stranger in the countryside, out for a stroll and dropping in with an air almost of apology. He was garbed in a soft blue polo shirt, blue shorts, and low walking shoes. His legs were bronzed and firm. From his smiling lips drooped a long cigarette holder. He was Philip Adams, the Sahib of Mokokchung, king of these dark and savage hills.

The young man from Sussex had come to us with a mighty company. With him were two American soldiers, Lieutenant Andrew LaBonte of Boston, radio officer, and Sergeant John DeChain of San Francisco, a burly, bearded man, so long in the jungles that he lived and moved as if this were his natural habitat. With him were many coolies from below and sixty Naga guards, naked as the men of Pangsha and Ponyo, loyal to Adams and to his "foreman" and interpreter, the potbellied, powerful Em-long who wore a leopard skin, spoke a few words of English, and was a famous tiger hunter. The guards were tough, belligerent, and contemptuous of "our" natives in their shotgun-carrying superiority. The shotguns were mostly for moral effect—on themselves as well as on the enemy—for they relied mostly upon the spears and knives that never left their sides.

Adams took quarters in one of the new *bashas* with Shouba, his shy aide and cook, with the hand-crank radio transmitter, his peppermints, his jug of rum, and his chess set. While his men drove a fence of sharpened bamboo stakes all the way around the camp for protection against any sudden attack, Adams dangled his bare legs before our fire. He bore a striking resemblance in face and manner to the actor Leslie Howard. In his hesitant Oxford speech he answered our innumerable questions and enlightened us on our predicament and our native hosts. We were indeed on the Patkoi range, marking the boundary between Burma and India. We had come down with precision at a remarkably precarious spot. This range marked the end of even theoretical British control; the effective boundary of his administration was at Chingmei village, two days' march to the west. I gathered that he had never been to Ponyo village, where Davies landed, over the ridge, and that, so far as anybody knew, no other white men had ever seen that place. But the Ponyos were well known by reputation. Last year they were said to have taken a hundred and six heads from neighboring villages. One reason why Adams had made the eighty-five-mile march over the peaks from his Mokokchung headquarters in the record time of five days was that a runner had arrived there with news that some of Ponyo's younger hotheads were urging a general attack upon our camp.

The Pangsha men had been reluctant. (Undoubtedly the meeting of chiefs we had observed on the first day had to do with this debate.) Adams had guessed they would think carefully before attacking us, but he could never be sure, so he was anxious that we give them no provocation. His reasons were several: Six years before, the Pangshas were a very powerful village and terrorized the region. When they started raiding villages too far into controlled territory, Adams's predecessor had led a company of Assam rifles to Pangsha—virgin territory then—and burned down the village after a brief battle. Then the Pangsha men had stayed subdued, until three years ago when Adams was obliged to repeat this grisly performance. He had returned here a year ago and made a formal peace with the Pangsha warriors. Six months before we had landed here, he had sent word through the hills that any parachutists were not to be killed, but were to be helped. We were the first test case in this region, and he could not be sure what the results would be. The Nagas possess a well-developed sense of revenge.

Sangbah, as we had guessed, was Adams's friend. In his childhood he had briefly attended a school at Mokokchung. He had great prestige in the villages for his wisdom and his good nature and because of his relationship with the Sahib of Mokokchung. He had organized the thirty gun-guards of which our various messages had spoken. They had been hidden miles down the trail on either side of us, without our knowledge, and would have given us warning of any attack by natives or Japanese. The leader of these guards was Tang-bang, the leopard-skin wearer with the crossbow. He was a brother of Sangbah, their father being chief Chingmak. Tang-bang was quite different from his brother. He was something of a gangster and had once been driven from Chingmei because he got his fellow citizens into too much trouble. He had taken seventeen heads and was feared as the most powerful man in the region. Some tribes used the crossbow, firing a poisoned arrow. The poison, unknown to chemists in India, had a paralyzing effect upon the respiratory organs. Adams himself, while leading an attack on a village in the preceding year, had been struck in the shoulder by such an arrow. The poison, fortunately, was old; he was very sick for a time but recovered, and of course his godlike prestige was increased thereby. "I should have liked to meet the man who shot me," he said sincerely. "He took a great risk to do it. He must be a very brave man." On his last expedition to Pangsha, Adams had camped on the very site where we were now, to which the chiefs had directed us. He believed they had wished us away from the village to avoid any troubles over their women. If, he explained, the women and girls were hidden away when you entered a village, it was a sure sign that the men did not trust you and expected a battle might ensue. (We had rarely seen a woman in Pangsha.)

The British first came into contact with the Nagas in the middle of the nineteenth century, and many punitive expeditions into the foothills were necessary before the Indians of the Brahmaputra plain were secure from Naga raiders. But in a century, according to what I could learn, no white men had ever pushed as far as Pangsha until six years ago. That expedition came very close to disappearing forever. Five to six hundred Pangsha men charged the fifty gun-bearing Sepoys from the summit of this slope and drove them helter-skelter through the tall millet stalks to the river bottom. But in the melee five Pangsha men were killed by bullets and a number wounded; the head-hunters accepted the result as a defeat for themselves (their homes, after all, were burned out) and sent emissaries to the British force two days later at Chingmei to make peace, the symbol of which was their giving up of a slave child they had captured from another village. The leader of the emissaries on that occasion was a famous Pangsha fighter named Mongsen. This was the man of charm and intelligence we called "Moon-song." Despite a badly burned foot, he had led the charge against bayonets and bullets.

We talked long into the night with Adams and learned much of the Naga methods of war. They rarely make an attack by night, but prefer to wait for the first light of dawn, and their usual method is the ambush, to which the dense patches of jungle lend themselves perfectly. Unless in overwhelming numbers it is difficult to attack a village successfully, since nearly all the villages are built on the peaks and are defended by stout stockades of sharpened stakes set into the ground at an angle. Thus large battles are not the normal thing; most heads are taken in surprise attacks upon individuals who stray too far from home. If a man returns with the head of an enemy woman or child, he is credited with great courage, rather than the contrary, because this means he crept perilously close to the enemy village. Some villages lost so many women and children at the streams outside the compounds that they were obliged to pipe in the water via bamboo aqueducts. Where paths thread through heavy undergrowth, strange forms of ambush are often encountered. In one, the victim's legs bump a taut string which releases a poisoned arrow into his breast. Another trick is the concealed pit on the trail, into which the victim falls, impaling himself on pointed stakes in the bottom. One devilish instrument is the *panji*—a short bamboo stick sharpened to a razor edge and dropped on the ground to be stepped on by the barefoot natives. It will thrust entirely through the human foot and is quite impossible to detect until too late.

The Nagas fight one another for all the reasons that motivate civilized peoples—for slaves (very infrequently), for security, for aggrandizement, for pure self-preservation, for revenge, or by reason of fear. They do not often keep prisoners until they die of starvation as do civilized peoples, nor do they often torture their captives. They give enemies due warning by a declaration of war more often than not, and they respect treaties of peace and friendship at least as scrupulously as do modern peoples, if not more so. In battle they try to kill quickly and cleanly and do not deliberately employ weapons that deal slow, lingering deaths. Like civilized races, they have fought for centuries, and if in recent years the peace has been well kept among them over large areas it has been due not to having waited for any "change in human nature," greater "education," or any kind of "spiritual regeneration," but entirely to a rule of understood law, backed when required by force which is applied only against aggressors. In microcosm, the problem of the Nagas is the problem of humanity.

All Nagas possess a highly developed sense of personal honor and integrity. Stealing is almost unknown among them, and no doors are ever locked. Adams related how he had once dropped an automatic pencil on the trail and a Naga lad had run twenty-five miles to return it to him. When at Mokokchung it happens that he, as prosecutor and judge, must sentence a Naga to jail for some crime, he merely informs the culprit of his fate, whereupon the convicted man walks unaccompanied to the jail and requests admittance. Of the Nagas' keen intelligence there could be no doubt; it was one's first impression. While they seem rather insensitive to bodily suffering, especially by animals, they are anything but insensitive to personal dignity. A Naga thinks a long time before he delivers a calculated insult to another man, for it would "make his mind hurt."

They are instinctively democratic. Their chieftains are chosen not only for their capacities as warriors but also for their wisdom and common sense. A would-be dictator does not usually retain power very long; chief Chingmak himself had once been stripped of authority for growing too arrogant and absolutist, but was permitted to continue with his lordly ornaments as a kind of elder statesman and counselor. It may be, as both Fascists and Communists declare, that liberal democracy is possible only in economically secure societies—the Nagas were secure in that respect—but centuries of equalitarianism among them helps disprove the contention that democracy is the exclusive privilege of highly advanced and educated peoples. It seemed to me that they give clear evidence that the sense of equality and tolerance is as deeply rooted in human instincts as the contrary impulses. What would happen to their society if accumulation of capital goods or a medium of exchange were economically possible, I do not know. Perhaps they, too, would then find classes developing, followed by concentration of political power, and thus the death of their true democracy.

Philip Adams, this young man of culture from the quiet lanes of Sussex, had acquired a deep admiration and an honest love for these naked "savages." With him as medium, I myself learned both a greater fear and a greater respect for the Nagas. To most of our company, I have no doubt, they continued to be merely "Wogs," both fearsome and absurd. Adams they learned to respect for his physical prowess and his commanding prestige among the natives. For me, he takes a place among the few rare men I have known, of limitless courage, unfettered mind, and controlled compassion for others—the great, lonely men, some in the spotlight, others in obscurity, who are everywhere and always the same, devoted coworkers in the difficult and dangerous conspiracy of goodwill.

The appearance and atmosphere of the camp now radically altered, with the building of new *bashas* and the accretion of Adams's retinue of a hundred men. The presence of the "great sahib" brought hundreds of visitors, who were frequently shoved out beyond the bamboo enclosure by Adams's guerrilla fighters with kicks and blows. Several times we thought individual knife-fights to the death would begin, but the visitors always retired, muttering and scowling. Our company was a little disturbed by the new state of affairs; we felt we had gotten along extremely well with the Pangsha people, and we wanted to continue our little sessions around the fire with some of their likable leaders. Everything except the internal management of our own company was now in Adams's hands, and he did not have a simple problem. His guerrillas were newly recruited guards, without discipline beyond their fear and respect for the white administrator himself. They would have loved a battle—with anyone, it seemed, and the Englishman was obliged to use an iron hand with them. The first crisis occurred when two of the guards snatched away a couple of tin cans from Corporal Waterbury, who had been washing them at the stream. When he demanded their return, they made menacing gestures with their knives. The Pangshas had never done anything like this. Adams regarded this as a serious matter of principle and immediately ordered Em-long to line up all the sixty guerrillas. They squatted in two rows before our *basha* while Adams and Em-long walked back and forth before them, demanding that the culprits come forward. They chattered together; some looked defiant, others worried. No one came forward. Then Adams took a great risk. He collected every man's *dah* (knife), carted them away into a pile, and informed the men that none would get his indispensable weapon back until the culprits were produced. This was a mortal insult and, if they had so wished, they could have taken over the whole camp and left us stranded. The guards retired into their big *basha*, from which the sounds of acrimonious debate issued for an hour. Adams won; the guilty men finally confessed. The knives were returned to all but these two, who were sentenced to become coolies for the first two days of the march out. In addition to that, their colleagues were entitled to collect a fine from them, in the form of pigs or goats.

We were now able to speak by voice or code directly with the American army in the plains by means of the hand-crank wireless set operated by Lieutenant LaBonte, while relays of us took turns whirling the crank, which proved to be exhausting work. We ordered more shoes, khaki shorts, army cots, medical supplies, and a hundred other items necessary for the long march, besides a ton and a half of rock salt as payment to Pangsha. The salt came down in forty-pound sacks, without benefit of parachute. They hit with the force of bombs, frequently just missing the native crowds and once bashing in one end of the gun guard's shelter. After long powwows, Adams turned the salt over to the Pangsha chiefs for proper division among their people. He asked that the people return to the village before the allotment was made, and when they did not move, he said: "Perhaps the people of Pangsha do not trust their chiefs." This brought a roar of laughter from the crowd and many scowls from the chiefs, who thereupon saw to it that the villagers retired.

On Sunday I conducted another brief religious service before the cross, and this was followed by an afternoon of festivities which included the slaughter of another *mithun* bull, dispatched this time by a rifle in the hands of Sergeant DeChain. The Colonel experimented with the problem of carrying Sergeant Oswalt by having several of us try moving him on an army stretcher to the stream and back. The total load was around two hundred and fifty pounds, and the stretcher was just too difficult to manage on the muddy slopes; he was bound to roll off it sooner or later. Then Davies had an idea: with the help of our two Chinese officers, he fashioned a crude Chinese sedan chair of bamboo and ropes, in which the sergeant could sit half upright. With its long poles it was extremely heavy, but eight Naga coolies working together could manage it. Adams explained the organization of our march, Sergeant DeChain showed us how to pack our cots into our bedrolls, we spent hours driving hobnails into our new boots, and by the night of the seventeenth, we were ready and waiting only for the dawn.

The Ponyo chiefs from the Burma side asked for a final meeting with Adams. It appeared that the inhabitants of some other village over the range had been spreading libelous stories about Ponyo through the valleys. Would Adams make objection or inflict punishment upon them if they were to avenge these insults by a massacre of the loose-tongued ones? He thought rapidly: They were out of his jurisdiction, which he had neither legal right, nor time, nor adequate forces to expand. If he asked them not to do it, they would very probably go ahead anyway, and his authority on this side would be seriously weakened, which could lead to another series of bloody raids in administered territory. He shrugged his shoulders and said it was for them, as responsible men, to decide. They departed in good humor. How many men and women died in the next few days I did not learn.

As we sat on our blankets for a last smoke before retiring, a visitor came in to see Colonel Flickinger. It was Mongsen, the warrior with the gentle eyes, whose baby the Colonel had saved from death. At the Colonel's feet he laid a beautiful crossbow of polished red wood inlaid with pieces of yellowing ivory. It was without doubt his most precious possession.

It is difficult to decipher my own handwriting in the diary entries for the days that followed. They were written at moments of paralyzing exhaustion, and the sheets became soiled and sweat-stained.

August 18—Writing this in Noklak, end of first day's hike. Broke camp this morning in rain and fog. Most of convoy started down to river when serious crisis arose over junk we leaving. Nearest we have come, I think, to general massacre. Suddenly natives were yelling, threatening us and one another with knives, one old man brandishing knife and leaping up and down exhorting others to attack. I stood by nervously holding rifle and umbrella, could see Adams gravely worried. He moved like lightning, snatching head-hunters by the hair, tossing them right and left without looking back, got guard around junk until passions cooled and he could share it out to the chiefs. A near thing, I am sure. Think if he had shown indecision or fear we would have had bad fight. Believe Adams sore at us for leaving so much stuff. Column stretched out nearly two miles. I first minor casualty, nail in these stiff British boots drove through into my foot. Adams and guards into camp hours ahead of us. Colonel, who was near end of convoy, slowly drew past us, looking pale, jaws clenched, muttering to himself —sheer triumph of will, he determined come in ahead of party, preserve his leadership. Colonel Wang collapsed two miles from Noklak, was carried rest of way. He now having coolies build him bamboo chair, seems have plenty rupees besides jewels for payment. Colonel Kwoh ashamed, feels this great loss of face for Chinese. Flick sitting head in hands when I pulled in, said: "This will separate the sheep from the goats." Try tell myself foolish have juvenile pride over hiking abilities, but still have deep fear being one of goats myself. Skinny Sergeant Clay breezed in early to astonishment everyone. Some Panso villagers here to see Adams with offerings of eggs, pig, hens. Unless a trick, this good sign, for we must go through dark pass in couple days which famous ambush place, and he afraid Panso people might attack us there. He held court, ordered Panso men to get out of piece of arable land Noklak men say belonged to them for generations. Unsure how Pansos taking this decision. Noklak big village, hundreds *bashas* on stilts, covered by whole population sitting packed rows watching parade. Sleeping on cots tonight. Adams had camps built for us on way in. Have blister large as silver dollar on ball of each foot. Changing to American shoes, but damage been done. I have ordeal ahead, but so do others.

August 19—Chingmei. Camping in middle village this time in natives' *bashas*, full of rats and fleas. Last two miles up steep mountain. Two or three youngsters, despite youth and muscular legs, were pushed and pulled by natives over the hard spots. See now that this is a *moral* problem as much as physical, a test of the will. It is the Manitoba canoe thing all over again. Damn this phony Norwegian pride and dignity complex, causes me extra suffering. The two men on litters are carried by eight or ten coolies, besides 20 or 30 who pull on long attached vine ropes in steep places. Marvelous cataracts today, real Metro-Goldwyn-Mayer jungle in low spots. Some drank too much water, including me I fear. Were to rest a day here but Adams apparently thinks we doing bettern expected so will push another fifteen miles tomorrow.

August 20—We at place called Kuthurr. Last night in Chingmei, Flick, Adams, Passey, and I visited Sangbah in his large, clean *basha*. Sangbah been there several days ill with fever. Apologized being unable go to Mok. with us. Flick thanked him for all he has done for us. Sangbah shook head, said he not done enough, gave Colonel his brass head-hunter ornament, highest gift his possession. His wife had really lovely face, air of refinement. We drank much *zu*. Both Flick and Sangbah deeply touched at parting, both close to tears. We shall send him gifts from Mok. Then crowd of chiefs from other villages in powwow with Adams on platform of Tang-bang's *basha*, bringing gifts livestock. Adams said: "Afraid we are in for an evening of pub-crawling." Drank much *zu* in Tang-bang's place which much dirtier, his young wife much coarser, behaved like gangster's gun-moll trying do well before the quality. Wore dozens brass arm rings. Each time she served us, breasts hung in front of our faces, embarrassing Passey, who is proper, religious type. Then, all somewhat drunk, we climb to Wang-do's *basha* in upper *kehl*. His wife giggled constantly, filled cups every sixty seconds. Wang-do is Arabic-looking, very strong face, gather he has rather supplanted chief Chingmak. Adams mischievously tells Wang-do he disappointed that Wang-do has but one child, means he been on trail too much, neglecting his household duties. All laugh, find keenest pleasure in jest. Flick gives his wife his silk parachute scarf, and Adams says this will insure twins and that the "Colonel Sahib" will be part father. More giggling. Flick gets bit sentimental under influence of *zu* and tells Sergeant Passey how much he admires him, to further embarrassment of Passey, but Passey much pleased. Horrible night, almost no sleep, fleas maddening, pigs rooting under cots, rat runs over my chest, squawking hen lands my face. Adams says we won't sleep inside villages any more.

Came to ambush pass in midmorning. Guards went through first, very carefully, cutting back some of banana-tree clusters close to trail to make attack more difficult. Thick jungle, great trees, hanging vines, very dim with occasional pools sunlight, all rather awesome. We carried our carbines in hand, coolies kept their *dahs* out and ready. Immense feeling relief when emerged onto open hillside.

Most of us limping badly tonight. Legs burned from hot sun. DeChain gave me his floppy fatigue hat. Strong sunlight affects my eyes considerably. Davies and I limp along, rifle one hand, spear as walking stick in other, discussing State Department and U.S. foreign policy as though strolling down F Street. John has great reserves moral courage. On toughest part of hills, when I almost collapsing, he will do loud, very funny variation on natives' chant which amuses them greatly, or sing out: "Onward and upward with the arts—Excelsior!" Duncan seems take pleasure whole affair, looks rather like cultured, bespectacled pirate with bandanna around head, knife and pistol on hips. John kids him ruthlessly, groans with mock annoyance when Duncan leaps out of bed before anyone else. Plane drops note from General Alexander: "Good luck and good going. I will send you everything you ask for except pianos and violins. I take it the morale is good. We are much relieved at the safety of your party. Let us know if you need anything." Need nothing except new pair of feet.

August 21—This was the worst. I could not do it again, I am sure. First went down hill to river, then three-hour climb so steep at times had to grab grass and branches to pull ourselves. How they got litters up I have no idea. Sun hit us directly. Sword grass higher than our heads on both sides trail, no air could get through. Sun began to get me, Davies went on, left me half-pint water which helped. Began to get dizzy, seeing veil of specks in front of me, was thinking why it was ice cream tasted better in a cone than in a dish and apparently commenced debating this matter out loud. Anyway, Flick caught me as I caved; he had been sticking close to me, realizing I going out. Sunstroke, I guess. Ordered natives cut away grass for some air and dragged me off trail for rest. But we out of water and no streams on hill. Got up to a resting coolie (several of them knocked out, their loads too much). This man's back mass of blood. Flick broke rules, opened two cans apricots, sugar content giving me bit of energy. Coolie came down a half-mile from summit with water. Neveu's left leg went bad, had to be helped along. Fortunately for American prestige, Gigure and Passey had caught Adams's party and reached top along with them. They our best hikers and best workers, have that extra something which makes a man superior—in addition to powerful legs. Passey was a ski champion, I believe. A Mormon, direct descendant of Joseph Smith. I wonder if deep religious faith has anything to do with his capacities. Yet Bill Stanton has quite different background, was financier or something in Hong Kong for years, and despite forty years of age can outclimb nearly all of us. His country-club, polo-playing life has something to do with it.

This small village called Helipong. Sits on bare, rocky peak nearly eight thousand feet high. Clouds level with us. It is very cold. Magnificent view of ranges and believe we can see Brahmaputra plains. This village really an outpost colony, occupied as sort of advance post to prevent surprise attack on main village.

Plane over several times, while I helping furiously crank wireless set as LaBonte shouts into mike. Shower bags salt all over village, causing cattle to stampede, women to run for lives with babies in arms. Couple *bashas* hit and Adams furious, but by grace of God nobody killed. LaBonte screams protests into mike and pilot says: "All right, God damn it, tomorrow we'll use a Norden bomb sight." Fusillade of bags hit our own *bashas* off on spur, three times out of three. Place a mess, natives now rebuilding it. My cot knocked over, Flick's beautiful crossbow smashed. Pilot also said: "We are going to drop you ice cream and fried chicken soon." We asked repeat and he says: "No joke, no joke!" Boys talking of nothing else now. Dropped us copy of *CBI Roundup* containing story about us and review of John's book, *Here's How*, designed to teach G.I.'s how to get along in China. Can hear enlisted men in their *basha* having violent argument about which year Detroit Tigers won the series, if ever. We shaking with laughter in here. Overhear voice of Oswalt: "Tell you who can hike—that correspondent guy can hike." Voice of Corporal Holland: "Oh —, he gets just as pooped as anybody else." Still, I guess I am doing all right despite today's embarrassment. Sure the others ache as much as I do tonight, but find have little positive sympathy for others' suffering. The Bordeaux phenomenon again.

August 22—Shortest, easiest hike of all so far. Boys helped me send four-hundred-word dispatch out to Ravenholt of United Press who will forward it to CBS, which apparently been screaming for my story. Took three hours of hard cranking, last few minutes in downpour. Crank handle flew off, gave Cherrill deep gash on head. Flick excused me from holding any church service today, on account of rain. He gathered company and severely lectured some of boys who been saying that only reason air force men at Chabua giving us all this attention is presence of three civilian "big shots." Also ordered boys not to try to keep up with Adams and guards, not to run downhill. Wants no more injuries.

August 23—Fifteen miles today, mostly in lashing rain, used the umbrellas, which look pretty ludicrous in these surroundings but prove very useful as protection or as walking sticks. Now at village of Chare. Trail slimy with mud, I slipping, breaking my spear in half (damn it, it was the "official friendship" spear from Pangshas). Severely wrenched my shoulder in the clumsy fall. In midafternoon, washed off in stream. Colonel arrives, bawls out some, including Duncan, for "trying to keep up with Adams" on downhill run. Really in a rage, informs Duncan doesn't care who he is, whether has direct pipeline to General Marshall, he is responsible for wellbeing of party and goddam well determined see we come in with whole skin. Up from stream hit a "bridle path," clear, broad, fairly level roadway.

Now suddenly all feeling of wilderness, of danger, has gone. Many villages, and many natives have bits of Western clothing, some salute us. Natives smaller, even their *dahs* are smaller. In a way, rather a disappointment.

Now in tiger country, also herd of eighty wild elephants near here. Wonderful jungle, waterfalls, ferns in Rousseau style. While bathing under bamboo spout, native man points to my privates and shakes head with frown. This bewilders me until Adams ex-

plains they never expose private organs; it is regarded as an insult
to other men for some reason obscure to me. Plane dropped case
of canned beer, Pabst Blue Ribbon. Some of boys fondle cans
long time before opening, others pocket them against moment of
greater need. Ravenholt contacted me from plane, says censors
won't pass my story with word "head-hunter" in it, since would
indicate general area we been in. Fear I lost my temper. Two
Nagas have just come in from Helipong with the white panel
cloths we left behind, having no use for them. Means about 45-
mile round trip for them! Colonel publicly apologizes for the lecture, saying he was wrong on his facts. Only a courageous, decent
man would do that.

Colonel Kwoh is not accustomed to boots. His feet are a mass
of blisters and blood. He comes into camp hours after everyone
else, plugging along, leaning heavily on a stick, frowning to himself. Soon as he meets anyone he smiles brightly. John says he is
China; example of why China is never beaten. The three of us
resting in glade today, they speaking Chinese. John grins, says to
me: "Colonel Kwoh presents you his compliments. He says it is
remarkable to see a literary man who is such a good soldier. I explained to him that in America literary men do not sit in tea houses
all day with long fingernails and soft feet." I said: "Tell him American literary men have no pride; they are not content with literature.
They try to imitate soldiers and explorers and bullfighters. It is a
bad thing." No idea what Kwoh makes of this. We can glimpse
Mokokchung from here, across lovely valley. Tomorrow, easily.
Tonight one of the guards said to Private Schrandt: "India *there*"
—and pointed west. "China *there*"—and pointed east. "America
there"—and pointed *up*.

5

The garrison village of Mokokchung sprawls over spurs and ravines of well-trod earth some forty miles into the Naga hills from
the plains of India. For the men of British India it is a lonely,
primitive outpost, connected with civilization by a single strand
of telegraph line and a broad foot trail. For us it was civilization
itself.

An American corporal stood at a bend of our trail as we limped
up the hill toward the town. Two days back, there would have

been a round of handshaking and much talk. He merely smiled, snapped innumerable pictures, and said nothing as we passed. He was freshly shaved and his shirt was clean and pressed. We moved along a lane of carefully planted trees and noticed moss-covered headstones in a cemetery, the mark of the Christian missionaries. At the first cluster of *bashas,* a native welcoming delegation awaited us, the chiefs wearing khaki shorts and red blankets, the women shamelessly crowding around us. They had lined up bamboo benches on the trail for us to sit and rest while they plied us with *zu.* A group of them began singing "God Save the King" in native dialect. It made no sense, but one could not help being somewhat awed. There were sandbags in the chill gloom around Buckingham Palace, and London was brazen with stiff upper lips; here, on the other side of the world, brown men with tattooed faces and spears smiled in the sun and suggested to the white men's great spirit, wherever he was, that he take care of their Great Sahib —wherever *he* was. The British Empire makes no sense, but there it is, an imposing, ubiquitous fact which will not be denied.

Its immediate representative, the unbelievable Philip Adams, reigned in English comfort from a neat bungalow that one reached by climbing several hundred steps. The lawn looked English, and the tea bushes did very well as a Sussex hedge. The "view" from the veranda had been provided for, the library was extensive and very Anglo-Saxon. Altogether, Adams's predecessors had faithfully obeyed the unwritten law of empire that Englishmen, regardless of where they are, shall live, speak, and eat like civilized men—that is, like Englishmen. A few of us dined with Adams (we said "dined" instinctively). We listened to a radio crooner named Frank Sinatra from somewhere, talked over the brandy about London, about New York, which Adams had never seen, and about the Naga hills and tribesmen—his city and his people. This lonely young bachelor faced a question that only a Solomon could answer: Are the benefits of civilization really benefits for the tribesmen, and how far should civilization be allowed to penetrate the hills? It was a nice point for debate on the ultimate goal of human life and the constituent elements of happiness.

I do not believe Adams shared the simple philosophy of Jean Jacques Rousseau on the "happy savage" in his "perfect" natural state; he had no fake bohemian contempt for modern civilization. I think he did have a certain sentimental liking for the Nagas' primitive costumes, their colorful rites and ceremonies. But governing all his tormenting concern for them was his realization that the savages back in the hills were happy people. They were strong, cheerful, keenly intelligent, more straightforward and healthy both in mind and in body than the Indians of the tepid plains. They were men of honor and instinctive dignity. What frightened him was that up to now, wherever "civilization" and its ways had crept in among the Nagas, it had harmed and debased them. The forerunner of civilization was the Christian Church, represented by a group of fundamentalist American Baptist missionaries who had come direct from the small towns of the Middle West. They had won over many of the Nagas—that is, had got them to believing that seminudity was shameful, that drinking *zu* was debauching. They had taught them to murmur the tuneless hymns of the church rather than their stirring tribal chants, and to leave off their brass and ivory ornaments, replacing these with ugly skirts and trousers. They were told that their totems were vain idols, insulting to God, and that members of the church must be solemn and grave rather than smiling and gay. And the impressionable Nagas, eager to please and to be like the all-powerful white men, tried their best. The only result was that they fell between two stools. They lost their roots. They became confused and felt ashamed of their origins. Their dignity was impaired, and they became sick in their minds. The old basis of personal honor was destroyed, and one found that it was only here, in the mission areas, that they lied and stole and told tales on one another. They became men and women without a home, without identity and rootless, they lapsed into a debauchery and criminality which would be unthinkable in the primitive villages. Adams felt there was room for missionaries with a social sense and for men who could teach the Nagas modern medicine to prevent their jungle maladies. But although British policy was to leave them alone in their primitive state, it could not very well forbid American churchmen to enter the hills. Adams had only one concern if India went back to the Indians: what would Hindu politicians and traders do to the innocent Nagas?

We rested for a day in Mokokchung. We bound up our wounds, tried in vain to scrub clean our stinking clothes, sent telegrams, received messages from the outside, made a few purchases in the crude stores, and held a feast on the grass of our "inspection bungalow" after the pilots had fulfilled their pledge and dropped us fried chicken, ice cream, and mashed potatoes, all done up beau-

tifully in aluminum containers. Colonel Flickinger and I had tea
with Em-long, the tiger hunter, in his rummage store, where we
inspected with a shudder the photographs he proudly exhibited,
showing himself after the last battle of Pangsha, smilingly posing
with a cluster of severed, bleeding Pangsha heads. Flickinger felt
of his own head and looked at me with an effort at a comic smile;
it was a poor effort. We civilians and the officers among us each
contributed a blanket to be sent back into the hills for the convalescent and well-remembered Sangbah. I sat up until midnight
typing out a story for the United Press and my own office which
Corporal Ted Kenez of the radio post worked at, tapping on his
key until the dawn arrived.

Again we organized our convoy and the next day walked eighteen miles in the rain. Some of us were lost for a short time. Duncan
Lee and his group nearly stepped on a tiger which crashed away
in the brush. I caught a chill, Neveu fainted quietly away on the
trail, and Lieutenant Roland Lee, who suffered from a foot infec-
tion, was carried the last few miles to the inspection bungalow
which was our resting place for the night. Then another day of
fourteen miles to a second bungalow, where the advance guard of
civilized men from the plains arrived to join us. The American
tradition of adventurous journalism has not entirely died away—
these men were Ravenholt and my friends Jim Shepley of *Time*
and Frank Martin of the Associated Press. Later in the evening
the ineffable St. Clair McKelway plodded up the hill, collapsed
onto a cot, and mustered up strength for a wan, embarrassed grin.
For some years, Mac's physical exercise had consisted in walking
from the door of "21" to a taxi at the curb. On the trail this day he
had made the mistake of carrying a heavy pack. It was all uphill,
and the sun was very hot. Gradually, the others drew away from
him. As he leaned against a tree for the tenth time, wondering
whether he would survive the leeches if he slept on the ground
that night, an adolescent Naga boy in a white shirt came trotting
by. The meticulous master of English prose gestured eagerly and
said: "You—coolie. Carry pack. Carry pack. Five mile. Give much
rupee—much rupee. [Jingling of coins in pocket.] You help um
white man, no?" The boy regarded him gravely and replied: "No.
I am on my way to the Christian high school and I'm just as
fatigued as you are."

The trail wound along the edge of the descending hills, and to
our left across a few miles of dense forest lay the flat plains of

civilized India, shimmering in the August heat. I looked back many times at the jagged blue lines of the mysterious mountains in which we had lived, felt a pang of unreasonable regret, and said to myself, as men do: "I will go back one day," knowing, as men do, that I never would. We heard the muttering of automotive engines ahead, rounded a bend in military formation with the colonel walking at our head, and came upon a line of parked jeeps and command cars and a small crowd of smiling officers and men and newsreel photographers. The sun was crushing, and after an hour of posing with the others and trying to speak into a micro-phone for the film sound track, I felt as limp and exhausted as I had on any day of the long march. Within two minutes my command car had slid off the trail. After another half-hour of back-breaking work I rode on, bouncing from side to side, clinging to my seat, becoming violently sick at my stomach, feeling that my head would split. The road flattened out, there were water wheels and tired buffalo, drooping, torpid Hindus, soiled houses and heavy smells. One sweated, and the muggy air was hard to breathe. We were back in India, the India the world knows.

A smiling Texas army nurse stood by the steps of the hospital plane as we climbed into the cabin. We sat again in the two rows of aluminum seats, mopping our scraggly beards with our filthy bits of silk, looking again across the narrow space at one another. The same bad joke occurred to everyone: "This is where I came in." Neveu, the pilot, looked around with a pale face and suddenly got very sick and was made to lie down on one of the suspended stretchers. I listened nervously to the engines and sweated despite the cool rush of air.

At Chabua—the base from which we had begun our trip to China one month before—General Alexander met us on the field, much relieved that we had survived. It seemed that never before in aviation history had so many passengers, amateurs at that, suc-cessfully bailed out of a stricken plane. Several of the army men in our party were sent at once to hospital. Doctors who examined my feet ordered me there as well, but Flickinger saved me this loss of time by overruling them. Coincident with our return to Chabua, a group of touring United States Senators arrived there from China, including a friend of mine, Cabot Lodge. Senator "Happy" Chandler of Kentucky, whom I had never personally met, grabbed my hands in his fat, moist fingers. His round, ruddy countenance was beaming with evangelical joy. "Eric, my dear

boy, I *prayed* for you every night! Yessiree, got right down and
prayed for you!" I introduced him to Colonel Flickinger, who had
done a little more than pray. He pumped Flickinger's hands up
and down, turned the beam on him, and exclaimed: "Greater love
hath no man! Nosirree! Greater love hath *no* man!" The colonel's
countenance was varicolored, and when the statesman turned
away Flickinger muttered to himself and did not look at me.

6

There must always be anticlimax:

Because of our crash, Sergeant Oswalt missed being sent home
to the States with his outfit. Soon after he was released from hospital he managed, despite Flickinger's orders to the contrary, to
join the crew of a bomber plane doing daily searches through the
jungle valleys for other lost Americans. The plane was attacked
by Jap fighters. The magnificent Oswalt met a sudden death in
the mountains he had so painfully survived with us.

Corporal MacKenzie, who had jumped out to us with Flickinger,
found his unarmed plane under Japanese attack, a few weeks
after our return to Chabua. He jumped and was one of only a few
who made it out of the jungles.

Several of the boys with us, who had been perfectly well while
in the hills, now came down suddenly with malaria and spent as
long a time in the hospital as they had in the jungles.

A dish-faced American major sneered and said: "Them Nagas
ain't nothing. Now you take the natives up the Amazon. Why,
let me tell you . . ."

A young American reporter knowingly said over his lunch in
Calcutta: "Oh, Sevareid and those guys, they had a picnic. All it
was—a picnic."

At a dozen army bases: "Hear they dropped you guys hot meals
every day you were up there." And: "What about them two Red
Cross girls that bailed out with you? Give us the lowdown." No
denials were sufficient.

To my astonishment a story was spread widely (by pilots, I
suspect, trying to find an answer to Felix's death beyond the
simple answer) that "most of them including Sevareid had to be
shoved out of the plane—bastards too scared to jump."

To Flickinger's astonishment fellow officers in Delhi and Washington greeted him thus: "What's your next publicity stunt? Who's your press agent now?"

My own story was stopped by the War Department and not released until many weeks later when I returned to America.

In Calcutta, the people were dying. All over Bengal they were dying by hundreds of thousands because there was no rice and the authorities couldn't or wouldn't do anything about it. In the Calcutta stock exchange, enormously fat brokers dozed in their deep leather chairs, surfeited with their heavy lunches; they sprawled out with their feet apart, their snoring mouths wide open. You went down the stairs and sidestepped to avoid a totally naked Hindu who was foraging with his head in the garbage pail. You stepped over the frail, white-swathed bodies of women who lay on the sidewalk in front of your hotel, dying quietly with their babies clutched to their breasts.

I gathered new equipment, to go to China, to get away from this place. I did not know what I would find in China, but on the way the air would be cool, a man could breathe, and he could look down through the clean clouds at the lofty, unblemished Naga Hills.

Chapter XI

THE PASSAGE had not been a journey so much as a transmigration. We were patients passing through the stages of anesthesia from depressive reality through the misty nether-world of delirium, awakening to a new reality, cold and hard, with sharpened forms and solid colors, a high plateau firm to the touch and suggestive of health and permanence. We had climbed into the apparatus in the torpid, fevered land of India. We observed the oil-blackened hands of the surgeons doing incomprehensible things with their gleaming instruments. The attendant placed a rubber breathing mask over our mouth and nose. We breathed and moved our eyes and looked through a panel of glass conveniently placed so that we could observe the approach of the nether world. Tufts of greenery appeared in the panel, then the ghostly white shapes of prodigious mountain peaks that guard the entrance to the dream-space. 'Then these too slipped away below the frame, and we were conscious only of a dull throbbing pain somewhere, which was identity; all surrounding existence was a transparent blueing, flickering at last with streamers of white that twisted and curled into grotesque shapes of animals and trees, eventually fusing together until there was only a depthless void, wet and grayish white.

Reality returned with the grind of the landing gear being lowered into place, which made the machine shudder. The patients sat up, stripped off masks and rubbed aching heads. The glass panel presented China; all one had to do was to turn his head, and there it was. It could only be China. It was green and russet, and the blood-red earth was rounded, molded by a million human hands and feet into the timeless terracing which I knew at once, which I had always known since childhood. It was true, again. It was the experience of Antwerp and of Norfolk, and the same old excitement returned. It is not the excitement of the strange, the undiscovered; it is the excitement of rediscovering the old, forgotten treasures of earliest years. It is this that men seek, rather than the new, and it is this that really touches the heart of any who moves and explores his earth.

I lay on a cot, shivering in my inadequate summer clothing, suffering a feverish, postoperational relapse from the transition, which had been too abrupt for the body to stand. Jumbled thoughts were trying to sort it all out and to comprehend this astonishing change of scene and actors. We had suddenly moved from the spiritual swamp of India's hopeless, sorrowing, fetid earth, onto this high shelf of Yunnan, where the breath came easily and clean, where the white cliffs and the blue lake stood out in bright distinctness, where men trotted crisply on muscled legs. Here one did not look into somber, fathomless, and despairing eyes but into hard, bright eyes that smiled and had a surface to them. In India I had seen proud buildings and sad faces; here I saw only sad buildings and proud faces. One had the feeling of having been lifted out of the cloying underbrush, up onto a dry plateau where men could find firm footing, shout if they wished, regird themselves and fight if there was challenge. What made the difference? A different religion? Climate only? Political independence? All these together? Yes—but something indefinable in addition; exactly what it was I did not know.

The atmosphere of my daily life immediately following the elemental struggle with the Naga jungles was indeed different. The company in which I found myself provided the sharpest of contrasts. Their conversation was magnificently preposterous and frequently exhausting, but it was never dull. McKelway and I fell in with two of the zaniest merry-andrews ever to bring Fifty-second Street overseas. In a Calcutta hotel room we found Colonel Rex Smith, the ex-editor, a beety man with the perpetual grin of a small boy caught with his hand in the jam, and Major Charles MacArthur, the playwright, a corpulent elf from whose mischievous lips no commonplace remark was ever heard from the hour of rising (very early) to the hour of retiring (very, very late). Of those few days in Calcutta I retain memories of bottles, empty and full, of bewildered taxi drivers unsure whether they were being insulted or not, of bemedaled generals drooped over the back of their chairs, too weak to laugh any more. I had not seen this pair for a year or two. When I walked into their room, still soiled from the jungle, still wearing a piratical beard, the eminent playwright stepped fat and naked from the shower, wordlessly handed me an advertisement for the "El Morocco" night club, and retired again to his bath.

Having explored all my resources until I was no longer fair or interesting prey, Smith and MacArthur turned to McKelway, who was better briefed by previous acquaintance. As we drove to the airport, MacArthur would tap McKelway on the shoulder and in a tone of polite gravity inquire: "Major, sir, from what era or shall we say epoch does that religious temple or temple of religion derive? Could you list briefly the major industries of Bengal and the approximate percentage of output in terms of 1939, that is, antebellum?" Or, cocking his head back in the manner of a tourist guide, the eminent journalist would say to the eminent playwright: "Now those dish-shaped hats you observe on the heads of the soldiers are known as steel helmets because they are helmets made of steel. They are worn with a view to the possibility of a bullet, or let us say a piece of shrapnel, striking in the region of the head." This continued endlessly, exhaustingly.

The affair of the snakes took place on the screened-in veranda of Flickinger's dispensary at the Chabua base. The general effect upon the spectators was aggravated by their physiological condition, which was the one normally consequent on an evening of gentlemanly indulgence. Attached to the Colonel's medical staff was one Corporal Dickinson, an enthusiastic herpetologist from a New York museum. There was nothing abnormal about this thin, stoop-shouldered young scholar who peered through thick spectacles, except perhaps that he felt for venomous snakes the same kind of affection an Albert Terhune feels for dogs. He believed that all snakes are fundamentally harmless and indeed friendly creatures, and was prepared at the drop of a hat to prove this to visitors. Undoubtedly, he was worth his weight in rupees to the air force command and the tea agencies, since whenever a poisonous snake was encountered, it was customary for the native workers to flee the region and not return for days. These periods of idleness were materially reduced by the example of Dickinson, who would gather the large-eyed natives behind him, approach the cobra or banded krait, squat down in front of it and utter soothing, purring sounds. After some minutes of this, he would know —by whatever means of communication there is between snakes and snake-lovers—that the creature was in a trusting mood. He would then tenderly gather it in his hands and gently deposit it in a box, explaining to the astonished Indians that a snake bites people only because it is afraid. By assiduous quoting of statistics he had convinced a few in the neighborhood that cobra bites, like the bites of other poisonous snakes, are not necessarily fatal, but that many victims die of sheer fright. By agreement with Flickinger, Dickinson himself would receive no treatment beyond local incisions, if he were bitten.

The demonstration for our benefit was under way almost before we were aware it was coming, and we had no opportunity to take up advantageous positions. True, I was near the door and could make it in one jump; but MacArthur and Smith were caught with the screen wall at their backs and with the snake boxes between them and the exit. Dickinson opened a box, began stroking the slimy monster within, and recited as if addressing a class: "This is the common Indian python or *molurus*. He does not kill by the secretion of venom but will subdue his victim by constriction of his very powerful body. Kindly observe, if you will, how he raises his body in a hump when I stroke him—thus. Now, he does not behave in this fashion in an effort to ward me off—he merely humps his back as will a housecat, in order to feel the caress more keenly, for it gives him bodily pleasure. Observe his strength. Try as I will, with all my weight, I cannot force down the hump." (Colonel Smith's eyes were abnormally large by this time, and MacArthur was visibly fretting.)

"Now this," the corporal went on as he lifted out a black, hooded reptile and moved closer to his distinguished guests, "is the king cobra or hamadryad—*naja hannah bungarus*. He is rarer than the common cobra. He is kindly disposed, as are most of his kind, and indeed exercises more parental care over his young than is customary. Observe, if you will, how I hold him in my hands—very loosely. One must not clench him tightly, since that would frighten him and perhaps cause him to strike the holder. You see how he likes to wriggle through my hands and curl himself about my neck." The solemn corporal then thrust his thumb into the cobra's mouth, turning up its lip to exhibit the fangs, which were still capable of injecting the poison. "You may observe the structure of his graceful fangs and their keenness of point if you look closely," he said, stretching out his hands toward Smith and MacArthur. The former had lost his ruddy coloring; the latter's mischievous lips were compressed in a firm line, and small clucking noises came from his throat.

We emerged at length from the porch clinging tightly to what

ragged shreds of dignity remained to us, and for some hours thereafter the conversation was rather weirdly normal and free from
witticisms.

While MacArthur and McKelway remained behind with Flickinger to make the flight in a succeeding plane, I joined the
party of General Harold George, chief of the ATC, with General
Alexander and Colonel Tom Hardin (who had come to replace
Alexander), and we made the Hump flight over the northern
route, piloted by Major Klotz and Colonel Dick Kight, the men
who had flown Wendell Willkie around the world. For two hours
we circled in the dense fog over Kunming, close to some twenty-
two other planes unable to land and unable to go back to Assam.
Smith noticed that my eyes frequently strayed to the parachute
compartment. He leaned forward and yelled: "You CAN'T jump!
Everybody in New York will be DISGUSTED! They will think
you are in a RUT!"

Somewhere on the ground a cool youngster on the radio was
trying to save the precious planes by rapid mental calculations,
staging them one by one down below the low fog ceiling. The
calm voice would say: "All right, Number Seven Four Three, you
can go down to nine thousand now. Two Four Eight, you can go
to ten." Two pilots of C-46's were in trouble—they could send but
could not receive on their radio. As we circled in the impenetrable
mist at seventeen thousand feet, expecting a collision at any moment, we could hear them calling for a formation to come up so
they could follow it down. One found it, the other did not. The
pilot's voice: "Only ten minutes' gas left." Then: "Only five minutes' gas left." Then: "Sure like to save this ship, but I guess we'll
have to bail out. See you on the ground." Then silence again.

At length we came in. Thanks to the cool-headed boy in the
operations room, all the planes came in, except the one, whose
crew floated down well beyond the airport, caught a ride in with
a Chinese truck, saw an idle C-46 on the field, and demanded
permission to fly it back to Assam then and there because they
were scheduled to take part in a poker game that night.

Many hours later, there was a banging at the door of my sickroom, and a freezing gust of wind blew in the playwright, a gleam
in his eye and bustling portent in his manner. I held my feverish
head with one hand and tried to wave him away with the other.
It was quite useless. He burst out: "Eric, wake up! It happened!

Yessir, it happened! *Corporal Dickinson got bit!* Right on that gentle hand. The king cobra did it. But he didn't mean to. Oh, no! He didn't mean to do it at all. You see Dickinson was feeding him a frog. It was dark. The cobra smelled the frog and he struck— and got Dickinson's hand instead of the frog. It was merely an unfortunate mistake, and the cobra felt terrible about it—just terrible. He curled up [business of the narrator cowering back, face nestled into arm, remorseful eyes pleading for forgiveness] and he *looked* at Dickinson and he just felt *awful* about what he had done!" Dickinson, it appeared, stuck to his bargain, took no treatment except local incisions, and enhanced his prestige by staying alive. He did, however, get pretty sick. Though his audience of the day before tried not to, they couldn't help having a sneaking sensation of perverse pleasure.

Top American generals had come together that day in Kunming from all parts of the CBI theater of war—Stilwell, Davidson, Stratemeyer, George, Glen, and Alexander among others—and I dined with some of them in Chennault's simple, austere house, while others among them came and went as the conferences continued. Stilwell was boss in the China theater, but the great American hero to the Chinese was Chennault, whose very face in its grim, scarred belligerence had come to be a symbol of China's resistance. In the room were some books of history and philosophy, including *The Laws of Civilization and Decay,* a few simple chairs, and a pile of tennis and baseball things; and on the walls were Chinese scrolls and mottoes. In the dining-room a gleaming white Frigidaire shared honors with an oil portrait of Chennault. Anyone who is considered a hero by a people and their government is not likely to regard them with objectivity, and no underling of Chennault's ever dared criticize the Chinese leaders in his presence. The remarkably efficient air tactician had been in the Orient a long time; his life was invested in China to a far greater degree than is generally true of American officers in foreign lands, and one had the instant impression, reinforced by later experience, that for Chennault the war was not so much a matter of America against the Japanese as China against the Japanese.

Every man in the room wore military uniform, but there were a few of them—such as McKelway and MacArthur—whom I could not associate with the professional soldiers. Instead I identified them with myself, though they bore army rank and I was strictly civilian. In general terms of education and intellect these two were the superiors of most of the high-ranking commanders, yet in their hesitant speech and occasionally fumbling manner they betrayed an acute sense of inferiority. It was not just because they were majors and the others were general officers; it was the old matter of the complicated "intellectual" up against the streamlined man of action, intensified because the environment belonged to the latter. I shared the feeling myself perforce, but discovered now that my civilian status was an advantage rather than otherwise: that I could talk with the generals on fairly even terms, that if I took my function seriously they did the same, and that no question from me was regarded as presumptuous.

I learned admiration for McKelway, whose cast of mind was like my own but whose skill was developed to a greater degree of artistry. Where I had drawn back, he had taken the plunge, despite all the same forebodings, into the army life. The struggle had been tortuous, but gradually the "know how" was coming to him. There were still times when he would trail down the hall to the washroom only to find he had left half his shaving equipment behind; times when he would hold up a jeep party while he rushed madly about searching for his glasses and then discover them in his pocket. But this sort of thing happened less and less often. He had learned that he really could contend with the dismaying problem of "arranging about the general's baggage," do it correctly and on schedule. "I think it has all been to the good," he said thoughtfully. "I don't think it will mean that I can no longer write a good sentence; I suspect that maybe now I'll be able to do it quicker."

For months it had seemed to McKelway that among the men he was encountering there was absolutely no one with whom he was able to talk. Gradually he was finding out how to. He had learned not to have a rush of blood to the head and slam down a mental trap door when one neighbor at mess damned the labor unions, or another dismissed the Jews with a savage curse. "They are people," he said; "they have other things to think about all day, and they just haven't got time to be logical and articulate on such matters. So what you do is just relax and say: 'Well, look, Butch, here's the way that business looks to some of us. . . .'"

Men like Flickinger and Dick Kight, we agreed, were perfectly normal, integrated men, who did all practical things automatically and did them right. *They* never forgot their razors and they always knew where their glasses were if they carried glasses. They never

wrestled with their souls or worried half the night about something they had said or hadn't said at dinner. Long ago they had
had sense enough to decide they couldn't solve all the issues of
human existence, so they had just dismissed these from their
minds. They live, they act, and then they die—in other words they
are adjusted to this earthly existence. Once in a while the neurotics
produce something fine, but so do the normal men of action. With
them, one could see, the drive for perfection took the form of
efficiency in their jobs—having that medical kit always exactly
ready, checking every item on the airplane an hour ahead of time.
They are the leaders of other men, they are bound to be, and this
time of war was their particular moment, for the duration of which
we willingly delivered ourselves into their hands.

Of all the men of action with whom one lived, the Texans
seemed the highest, or anyhow the most extreme, examples. Men
like Colonel Hardin, or like Colonel Gentry, Chennault's medical
officer, seemed to McKelway and me a very special group, quite
distinct from others in the air force or navy or infantry. You could
always tell them. There was a certain easy bravado about them;
even their uniforms were worn with a special jaunty ease. They
were a little more self-conscious about such matters as manliness
and physical courage. I thought perhaps they were a hangover
from an era of old-fashioned chivalry and gallantry which most
of the rest of us have progressed beyond. McKelway was not so
sure; he was inclined to think they were not retarded but were
just healthier and sounder than the rest of us. Certain it is that
they are different and rather refreshingly so.

(At this point it may be worth while to insert a brief item in
further explanation of McKelway's seeming nervousness among
the generals that day in Kunming. A few minutes after General
George's plane (in which I rode) had taken off from Chabua,
McKelway suffered a lapse somewhat more serious than the mis-
placing of a razor blade. It had been up to him to "lay on" a second
plane for the following party. He called another field on the shortwave radio and said: "Need a plane in a hurry to get over to Kunming. Party of generals including General George himself has
just left for there. Big confab of generals from whole theater
beginning in Kunming tomorrow. Need aircraft urgently." As he
walked away from the transmitter, he stopped suddenly and asked
God to strike him dead. He had used the wrong means of communication, and the Japanese, if they had been listening, must

have heaid the whole thing. Their fighter planes could pick off
the unprotected transports on the Hump run any time they chose,
and they frequently bombed Kunming. Mac suffered feverish
visions of court-martial, disgrace, firing squad, and an unmarked
grave. However, if the Japs did hear the message they did nothing
about it—probably suspecting it as a crudely obvious trick. None
of the enlisted men gave him away and I did not hear the story
myself until McKelway, by then in civilian clothes, confessed it
in New York when the war was over.)

2

Chungking. Ugly beyond words. Sometimes in the daylight hours
a scorched and battered fortress, indestructible and proud, bearing its wounds with fortitude, clinging with grim determination to
its scarified hills which preside over the titanic confluence of the
two mighty rivers. Sometimes, when the streets were empty of
life and the endless mud-and-wood shops were shuttered, it was
a façade, hollow and without depth, a bodiless, flimsy stage set.
The colors were all gone, and the tones of Chungking were gray
and black. Once the walls had been white, but when the bombing began they had camouflaged the city by simply painting each
building black as one would paint his windows if he had no shutters. I walked with John Davies for hours the first day, pushing
through the sweating mobs on the sidewalks, trying to breathe in
the haze of grayish dust. In the steep, curving streets were a few
rickshas, a few boxlike horse carriages with four prim chairs inside to supplement the public busses, and heavy carts with rubber
tires, loaded with a crushing weight of bags and pulled by men
with rigid muscles in their legs. It was cool, but rivulets of sweat
trickled down their chins and fell in the soft dust of the pavement.
There were barred gates at the entrances to the famous caves in
the reddish cliffs where thousands took shelter from the bombs,
and in the dim interiors one saw whole families eating or sleeping.
They were still digging out the caves; a tired boy shuffled from
one carrying a stone in each small hand. Miles of jerry-built shops
were rising from the old rubble, and here and there one saw again
the familiar trademark of the world's present trouble—fallen
rafters sticking foolishly from a pile of broken masonry.

It was staggering when you comprehended what had happened

to China: the immense country had wheeled around and no longer faced to the east. It was as if the United States were walled in on the east and south, with New York and Charleston, New Orleans and Galveston blocked up and all travelers from the other side of the world obliged to filter in through the Alaskan mountains and arrive at Helena, Montana, to find that this little city had taken the place of Washington, all the great men and great affairs gathered there. A few sick-looking soldiers on straw sandals limped through the streets; beyond that, there was no immediate sign of war. As I stood with John on the high terrace over the boiling river, as we watched the immense panorama of this pulsating hive of people, I could not escape the feeling that for the uncounted Chinese this war was only an episode in their ancient story, a brief distraction in their unquenchable life.

While it was yet dark, the lonesome soldier with the fake steel helmet of chocolate brown would bang on the door to my cubbyhole in the press hostel compound. I would roll out of the hard bed, careful of the shoulder I had wrenched in the Naga Hills, and trudge through the empty streets to the radio station near by. A sleepy attendant would bring me a cup of lukewarm water with a few bloated tea leaves floating on the top. The faithful Mike Peng, who loved America, would sometimes be asleep in his hard chair. (Thieves had stolen his cot and another one was impossible to obtain.) Like most civil servants he was half-starved, and there were holes in his shoes. But he was always there, at whatever hour, ready to try once more to make contact with San Francisco, undiscouraged by an almost unbroken series of recent failures. I would sit at a high dais, peering in the fitful light at my script, well scratched by the censors, and try to explain to my countrymen at home about this backwoods capital city:

". . . The climate is bad, the diet is far from balanced, and foreigners are often ill. You need a strong pair of legs to do your work in Chungking now; except for the fortunate few there are no cars, and a bus ride is an experience the average mortal will stand not more than once a week. So you must walk, and that means up and down, for Chungking is built on the hillsides. It has been hot and humid, and the perpetual dust settles in your pores and coats your shoes. A strange, unpleasant odor hangs in the air; it comes from the thick black exhaust of the alcohol-driven busses and from the interior of a thousand little shops; it is something like the smell of paint gone rancid. There is no ebb and flow in the streets; the movement is spasmodic and jerky—the sudden, swerving busses, the sprinting rickshas, the trotting coolies bearing unbelievable weights. Sprinkled among the half-naked, whose bodies gleam with sweat, are those in white and modern clothes, who hold cloths to their faces when the dust swirls up or they pass an odorous corner.

"There is little talk of war. After six years, even that topic loses much of its fascination, especially when there is so little action. What people talk about at the bus stops and in the tea shops is, if my interpreter interprets correctly, wages and prices and the high cost of everything under the sun. For the Chinese inflation there is no parallel anywhere in the world today. One's small possessions are worth their weight in gold. The other night a long arm reached in at my window and took my watch. It had cost seventy-five dollars in New York; to replace it here would cost five hundred American dollars. The American Embassy residence has no meat platters any more. It did have two, but the other day a messenger appeared at the door asking for them. Ambassador Nelson Johnson had borrowed them from Standard Oil two or three years ago, and Standard Oil wanted them back.

"Recreation is a problem. The narrow parks are bare and transparent. There is no grass, and dust turns the struggling leaves a dirty gray. Privacy is unknown in Chungking, and where young lovers go I have never discovered. Social life is at a minimum, and the restaurants are not supposed to serve wine under the new government rules for puritanical living, so they change their names and become cultural associations where wine may be had. For foreigners, recreation is dinner and talk. The talk is good, although Chungking lives on rumor and gossip about those in high places —wherein it is little different from Washington-on-the-Potomac. When you are deciding between invitations to two foreign embassies, you try to recall which one possesses that glorious invention, an ice-cream freezer. There is no whisky whatsoever, and no Western wines. There is only a local vodka, which is best used as rubbing alcohol, and a white wine that works extremely well in a cigarette lighter.

"You see a few American jeeps and a few shiny Buicks of the year 1941, but apparently you must be a general to rate one of these. Everywhere there is hammering and building going on, for the city is bursting out of its well-patched seams, and the new structures are nearly all of bamboo and mud. One good bomb blast, and they would disappear like straw in the wind. But the bombs no longer fall here—they have not fallen for two years; and it is something to realize that this great city, once smashed to the ground, rebuilt its houses and took up its multitudinous life again because of the appearance of a few adventurous American fliers in a handful of patched-up American planes.

"There is no color except at sunset, when the two great rivers that enfold the city flow red and golden with a million tiny flames dancing on their rushing currents, and then the bare mountain peaks near by soften and purple as the day grows misty with night. Suddenly it is dark, and the lights come on. There is no soft lamplight in the homes of Chungking because a lampshade is almost unknown. You work or you dine by the glare of naked bulbs, and because the city power is weak your eyes are tired by nine and by ten you are in bed.

"At five in the morning you are shocked from your sleep by the clamor of bugles; by six the babies in the alleyway are wailing, and your room-boy is clattering the screen door as he brings the kettle of freshly boiled water which alone is safe to drink. Another day begins in this city of Chungking, which was old when Christ was born. . . ."

The little shops were filled with "luxury articles"—thermos bottles, imitation Kleenex, cigarette lighters, packaged candies, and dried fruits. For years the enemy had held the eastern cities, yet if you turned over the packages you saw labels on the bottom proving that they all came directly from Shanghai or Hong Kong and sometimes Tokyo itself. The trade across the "fighting lines" was not a matter of spasmodic, illegal smuggling; it was an established, tolerated industry by which tens of thousands made their living. Friends received letters every day from acquaintances in Hong Kong or Shanghai, and if one wished to send a letter there all he did was drop it in the Chungking post office, and it would be promptly received in the Japanese area.

I began to go about my professional business of trying to understand this capital and these people in their functional relationship to the world of war I knew. For days I was haunted and depressed by a sense of uncertainty, of a need for caution, such as I had rarely known. Always before, a knowledge of national history and institutions had been an unquestioned key, had given me confidence in my assay of the evidence my eyes and ears arranged before me. It was not that I was ignorant of the long background which had produced these people, but China's experience in modern "Westernized" political and social forms had been but a brief moment in the scale of her millennia. How valid, then, was praise or criticism of her present leaders, their achievements and shortcomings? Did one judge the character of her regime against the concepts of four thousand years, or against the ideals and goals introduced just thirty years before? I discovered that the foreign observers in China were themselves divided and measured the country by two quite different sets of scales:

The hardheaded American newspaper correspondent: "High government officials are grafters; they are making immense profits out of the inflation misery."

The English scholar, in love with old China: "Squeeze is part of the true Chinese tradition, as old as China, and the people expect it."

The correspondent: "They are bold-faced liars. They manufacture military victories where no action whatsoever has taken place."

The scholar: "What we call hypocrisy is merely form and face-saving to the Chinese. The tradition of conveniently forgetting evil and speaking only good helps to hold society together and preserve men's dignity with one another."

The correspondent: "Chiang's gang are tyrants. They have cast thousands of decent, liberal opponents into prison and have slaughtered other thousands."

The scholar: "China's history is the story of one tyranny succeeding another. The people hope the next one will be a little better, but they know that the more things change the more they are the same. And they know they will go on forever, whoever rules them."

The correspondent: "The government speaks of its democratic fighting army. Actually Chiang's soldiers are recruited by force. They raid a village, tie a farmer's thumbs behind him, and he becomes a slave-soldier. The universal conscription law is a fraud; no man with any money would dream of becoming a soldier—he pays somebody else to go in his stead if need be."

The scholar: "The Chinese are truly civilized people. They have an abhorrence of war, and soldiering has always been regarded as a bestial pursuit. Their ideal has always been the scholar in his

robes, not the soldier in his uniform. They place the military life
where it truly belongs. It proves their wisdom."

The correspondent: "The Kuomintang people are traitors to
their own proclaimed principles. Many of the leaders and generals
in the border regions deal openly with the Japanese, and if trade
is good across the lines they forbid any fighting. You watch—the
puppet Chinese bosses in the Jap areas will be welcomed back
into the fold when the war is over. Collaboration is condoned
everywhere."

The scholar: "In the course of centuries, many invaders have
swarmed over China. Many stayed much longer than the Japanese
will stay. The people know this, and they know that now as in
the past they will absorb their conquerors, or they will outwait
them and in time the conquerors will go away. It proves their
patience."

The correspondent: "They are making no effort. The big men
sit back here in the safe hinterland acquiring fat, money, and
concubines. They mouth the old mottoes of Sun Yat-sen but smile
at them in their cynical hearts."

The scholar: "It does not matter. The spirit of the true China
remains with the young, the students. Remember how they carried
their universities on their backs over hundreds of miles from the
coastal cities. Nightly they pore over their books until they faint
with exhaustion, but their great dreams do not die. *They* are
China."

And so it went, interminably, indecisively, the two sides advancing from completely different starting points. And both were right,
in everything they said. Chungking, it seemed to me, was made
up of the Colonel Kwohs and the Colonel Wangs in fairly equal
proportions. Many of the high government officials with whom I
talked were Wangs: The one who assured me with a straight face
that there were no landlords in China. The one who said the people
must not be told the truth about the war's progress because they
were not to be trusted with bad news. The one who said we must
not publicize the fact that tens of thousands were dying of famine
in the Toishan area near Canton because it didn't really matter;
those things were always happening, and what were a few more
thousand lives to China, anyway? The Wangs would say these
things, then clap their hands to order their Buicks brought around

while they prepared to go off to another dinner party. But there were also the Colonel Kwohs, like Mike Peng, like the young censors in the Ministry who would slash your copy with lowered eyes, then come to your room at night and beg forgiveness, almost in tears—they wanted to be honest men, but they feared for their freedom and their food. Another was little Miss Tang Sheng, smiling and cherubic, who came up about to my fourth rib as we roamed the streets and she explained everything we saw. Though the rule—on paper—said that the young and able-bodied were not to ride the rickshas, the rickshas seemed to be occupied almost exclusively by the young and able-bodied. But Miss Tang would frown as she watched them and would never have dreamed of doing it herself. She did not agree that Chungking was ugly and mean. To her it was beautiful and thrilling, though she had been reared in the eastern cities in conditions of luxury. "It is beautiful," she said, "because we are at war, and this is our war capital. I do not regard the bomb holes as ugly sores. I am *glad* there is no comfort."

I made my decision. Chiang's China could not be interpreted in terms of ancient history, for his regime sprang from Dr. Sun's great modern revolution, claimed that it was the true descendant, and justified itself in accordance with the categories of Sun's ideals. One had to accept China's rulers as they saw themselves, and decide how they measured up to China's present and future, not to China's past. They claimed membership in the modern world and participation in that world's present crisis, and so they were to be viewed with the naked living eye, not with the inverted telescope. However distant Chinese governments had been from the mass of people, still the government was China in the eyes of the world; what China did in the world was decided by the government, not by the masses. Even here, politics was life, as it was wherever I had been in space and in my time on earth. And, seen with the naked eye, the spectacle was an evil one.

I had some familiarity with dictatorships which used the complex apparatus of propaganda, censorship, and secret-police terror to hide what they were really doing; but this was the first one I had seen that used that machinery to hide the fact that they were really doing nothing. Worse: they had no *intention* of doing anything. They were simply sitting out the war, making a gesture here and there for the benefit of their allies. No one was fooled, except of course the sentimental American public, including those of its members who took seriously the books of Lin Yutang. There was nothing positive in Chungking except the "statements." The nakedness was covered by successive layers of official statements, but the statements were wearily the same, and those who had learned to see through the tissues kept their eyes on the shocking nudity. So many statements were given out that sometimes the statements themselves exposed those who gave them out. On my first working day in Chungking the official military spokesman made two supposedly unrelated remarks in the course of his speech. One was that the Japanese would be finished within a year. (Sometimes in a dull week the Generalissimo would say "six months" to add a spot of color.) The other was that no offensive by the Chinese army could be expected for at least a year. I put the two remarks together in my script and added them up to mean that the Chinese army did not expect to play any positive role in the Pacific war. Agitated censors padded from room to room, telephones rang, and I was solemnly informed that what the spokesman had really said was that the Chinese army "might not" be able to begin an offensive. Even those reporters who understood the original Chinese and had not relied on the interpreter agreed that I had heard correctly. But it did not matter—I couldn't say it.

Official, printed "orders" from the War Department directed that henceforth officers must give their men on the march some kind of medical attention, must provide hay for their rest, must not lock them in at night, must not put sand in their rice, must not withhold their pay, must not beat or whip them, and must not use them for labor from which the officers made profits. This innocent attempt to soothe foreign opinion backfired with a loud report when we quoted the orders verbatim in our dispatches. The censors had a difficult time justifying the use of the blue pencil on this story, but they managed it in the end.

Like the Brazilians, the Chinese officials were extraordinarily sensitive to the slightest criticism. It was, of course, the attitude of men who take everything personally; but it was more than that: the reaction of nervous, cornered men who must announce each day that they are right because they know they are wrong. They protested too much, and even those foreign critics who suffered through the execrable winters and summers in their flimsy rooms because at heart they were in love with China and its people grew sickened by it and then completely cynical. They became so distrustful that even when the officials had truth on their side the

critics could not believe them. It was a condition of complete
moral stalemate, and very little could be done about it.

It seemed to be a place of mockery and make-believe, solemnly
repeated day after day. The correspondents would sit about on the
dusty grass of their compound, one playing with his baby, another
reading a novel, another absently chucking twigs at a squawking
chicken. At the appointed hour, they would shuffle along in their
shirtsleeves to the press conference room and sit on stools at the
long table. The dapper Minister of Information would read some
Kuomintang resolution, or announce that within a year after the
war the government would convene a national congress to adopt
a new constitution. In any other big capital this would be front-
page news of consequence. But the jaded reporters would listen,
draw faces on their scratch pads, whisper a wisecrack in your ear.
There would be a few of the usual loaded questions, which as
usual got no satisfactory answers, and then all would shuffle out
again—and nobody, except the agency men who had to file everything, would bother to send a line about it. They had all heard it
far too many times before.

There were true democrats in and around the government on
secondary levels who looked to America and Britain for their political ideals. (The "returned students" were replacing the robed
scholars as the élite.) But it was the mechanics of Fascist Italy
or Germany that one saw in operation. On the thirteenth of September it was officially announced at four o'clock that the Generalissimo had been elected President, succeeding the late Lin
Sen. Precisely at four o'clock newspaper extras were in the streets
with the news. Precisely at four o'clock red slips of paper were
stuck in every single shop window hailing the G'issimo. Precisely
at four o'clock martial music blared out from loud speakers beside
the radio building, and clusters of firecrackers on the ends of
bamboo poles popped and spluttered at every street corner in the
city. The Nazi "block system" prevailed here, and all "spontaneous"
demonstrations—like the one for Wendell Willkie—went off with a
nice precision.

They loaded us into cars one morning and took us to the opening
of the People's Political Council in a long, low, whitewashed hall
in the lower part of the city. This annual session of chosen Kuomintang members was the nearest thing that remained to a free legislature in modern China. There were the inevitable portraits of
Sun Yat-sen and Chiang Kai-shek (the American G. I.'s who find

their own words for everything, called them Sunset Sam and Shanker Jack), flanked by the national and party flags and a great banner bearing the Generalissimo's words, "Love and Sincerity." A brass band occupied the rear seats just behind us. The members entered, some in Western dress, some in robes, some in uniform, some clean-shaven and others with long chin whiskers, and all wearing the pink and yellow ribbons pinned to their clothing. This was the one occasion on which everyone present did not have to stand throughout the Generalissimo's discourse. He turned and bowed to Sun Yat-sen's portrait, joined the singing of the party song which had become the national anthem (more shades of Nazi Germany), laid his army cap on the stand, and, taking his manuscript in both hands, read it in a high, sing-song voice. He was smaller than one expected, slim and neat, a man of dignified precision, quite at ease in his consciousness of authority. The speech was the usual one of high-sounding phrases, devoid of new facts or suggestions. When he had finished, he was "answered" by a tiny, whiskered man in a blue gown. This set-piece was the formal concession to "free speech," and in it the member politely asked the government to do more about solving the inflation and alleviating the suffering of the people. He droned on, chairs became uncomfortable, many members began to doze or to read their papers, and the foreign reporters began to lay bets on how long the speech would last. This was not the conclave of a fighting, besieged, and democratic people. This was the familiar atmosphere of Tammany Hall, the routine of party hacks wearily familiar with all that was said and with one another.

The party members were all army officers or teachers or landlords or bankers or civil servants. There was no single representative of workingmen or farmers among them—and eighty percent of the Chinese people are farmers. Nobody expected any real words of opposition, and none was heard. Of the tiny and ineffectual political groups other than the Kuomintang, I believe six men attended the meeting; the Communist delegate, representing sixty or seventy million Chinese in the North, walked out after the first few days. It was all very polite throughout the week it continued. Nobody had forgotten that the last time a member had raised his voice in genuine criticism of the regime he had abruptly disappeared from his chair at one of the universities.

I carefully went over the translated proceedings of the week's performance, and it was all too clear what the Kuomintang were

concerned about. It was certainly not the war against Japan. Their
interests were obviously in this order: the inflation first, the Communist problem second, postwar reconstruction third, and the war
last. Indeed, on the eve of the final session it had become so embarrassing that the American chargé gently suggested that it might
look better abroad if the PPC said something about the war.
Hastily a fulsome statement about China's determination to bear
her full share of the struggle was drawn up and issued over the
Generalissimo's name. General Stilwell seized it, and exclaimed to
a visitor: "I shall wave this under the G'issimo's nose every chance
I get!"—so helpless were the American military in getting commit-
ments from the Chinese.

Though it was customary for the Generalissimo to grant to each
visiting correspondent a brief, formalized interview (in which
nothing was said), mine was postponed until too late. But through
reading his speeches and writings, and through endless conversations with those who knew him, one could acquire a fair estimate
of the man himself and of his present role. That he was a great
figure, both in the historical sense of power and in the personal
sense of character, one could have very little doubt. If he was a
dictator, he was as sincere and honest a one as Stalin; there was
no Mussolini cynicism about the man. But was he a dictator? In an
absolute sense, he was not. He was the Strong Man, but he was
more a symbol for Nationalist China than its boss. He was the
symbol of unity, the substance of which had withered away, and
it was he who had maintained the resistance, however technical,
against the Japanese and preserved a geographical enclave where
resistance could be marshaled, however weak. For these reasons
he was irreplaceable for the moment and must be maintained in
power. But he was more of a balance wheel among contending
generals, war lords, and banker-politicians than a boss. His power
was by no means absolute, but he managed to keep the rickety
state edifice together, to prevent the mercenary war lords from
fighting one another. His staff and his own central troops were
gradually winning a controlling position over the local armies of
the provincial governors. But if he was the man of the hour, he was
not, in political and social terms, the man *for* the hour. He was a
curious anachronism, ignorant of the Western world, quite ignorant of modern political and economic thought. He seemed to
have a sentimental vision of the old China of "order" and "dignity"
and respect for the elders. Like Hitler he spoke of the "one leader,

one party, one nation" principle, of "blood ties," and of the "original virtues" of the race. He, too, was a mystic in considerable degree, antiintellectual, antiscientific. Like Pétain he seemed to want to go backward in time and did not understand that this is the one move it is always impossible to make. Like Pétain he talked of the old "golden world" of family authority and discipline and wished to return to an outdated, feudal society (exactly what the Japanese wanted for China). Some of the Generalissimo's speeches could have been uttered by Pétain at Vichy word for word: "I think of the army as a family. I look upon the soldiers under me as a father regards his children. If his children behave well, the father feels they reflect honor upon him; if they behave badly, they disgrace him." This man could perhaps hold stationary China together, but he could never move it forward.

A large house with a sparse garden of dusty plants on the flat roof served as aerie for the grizzled American eagle whose job it was to rally the Chinese soldiers and make them fight the common enemy. I walked along the river bank to his house as the Chialing shimmered in the dust-refracted light of sunset. The sampans were drawn together in neat clusters by the shore, a river steamer was hooting somewhere upstream, and tendrils of the evening fog were creeping down the dark ravines on the steep hillside of the north bank. General Stilwell crouched at his desk, his thin shoulders bent as he peered through steel-rimmed spectacles at a Chinese document. His hair was closely cropped; he wore a simple khaki shirt open at the neck, devoid of ribbons or medals, and his clothes somehow resembled a private's outfit, just issued from the quartermaster store. The room was almost bare, save for the littered desk and enlarged photographs on the walls showing the Chinese troops in training at Ramgarh, his pride and joy. He looked up at me without raising his head and smiled that dry, grim smile with the corners of the lips bent down. His eyes shifted around the room as I sat down and he said wryly: "I guess we're not wired for sound in here." (Tai Li's secret agents had been discovered in nearly every foreign office in Chungking, and twice Stilwell had caught servants looking over his private papers.)

We talked until it was quite dark outside and only the bobbing lights of the ferries marked the great river. As he spoke, jerkily, emphatically, pulling at a cigarette or popping peanuts into his mouth, I began to have the same feeling I had had at the desks of

General Marshall and a few—very few—others. Here was another man with the same tremendous drive, the same soul-absorbing sense of duty. There was a white flame in this man, a kind of dry passion and a biting impatience to get on with the job. One had the impression, not that he was "driving himself," but that he was always spurting to keep up with himself. He had a loathing of inefficiency and slackness that was almost physiological. He was dry and supple as an old-fashioned buggy whip; he was like a leathery Oklahoma farmer in the drought years, and he seemed driven to a crackling frenzy by the slow pace of events in the Orient. He had an exalted concept of true soldiering and an impossible ideal of what the true soldier should be. He snapped his fingernail against the little blue can of "Planter's Peanuts" which somebody had ordered flown over the Hump by the hundred-weight and snarled: "Luxuries! That's what they think makes morale, do they! Peanuts and cookies and chocolate! Fighting men must fight. But if they can't fight, then by God, they must bear their boredom like soldiers, because that's part of it, too." He was damned if he would return men to the States simply because they had been out in the Orient for such-and-such a number of months. He would not tolerate unfitness even in his officers; he had led them all in the walk out of Burma and had been contemptuous of younger officers who could not maintain the pace.

I knew how this man behaved when he was with his troops, American or Chinese. There was then a magical change in him and he became radiant as he strode among them. During a mock battle at Ramgarh, when real bullets were used to condition the men, he had run from one to the other, throwing himself down beside each Chinese private to see what he was doing, how he was taking it, while the leading Chinese visitor, a general, stood off at a safe distance and observed the explosions through binoculars held in his spotless white gloves.

This fighting man was an anomaly in the queasy, gossipy atmosphere of Chungking politics; he made all the Chinese politicians miserable, and he was miserable himself. He had no graces, he could not be subtle, "form" held no interest for him; yet he had to try to work in a place where form was all-important. His official mission, as defined by President Roosevelt and accepted by the Generalissimo, was "to increase the efficiency of the Chinese armies." He was trying, desperately, but his worst enemies were the Chinese leaders themselves. Chiang had been very skeptical about the whole idea of flying thousands of his miserable soldiers to India for genuine training. For what would be the political effect when they returned after the war, healthy, well-paid, fine fighting men with a real esprit de corps? He had delayed six months before he would give his consent to the appointment of a young, devoted general whom Stilwell wanted as leader of these new troops in India. Why? Simply because the general—like any Chinese general—would then be a political factor in the uneasy balance of Chinese affairs.

"Vinegar Joe"—or "Uncle Joe" (what they called him depended upon his mood at the moment)—held two basic beliefs that governed all he did: that Japan had become a continental power and that it would therefore be necessary to begin, some day, a massive campaign by infantry on Chinese soil, for which many Chinese divisions must be trained quickly; and that the Chinese man had fought well in the past, was essentially brave and intelligent, and could be made to fight well again. In the meantime, there was North Burma to be cleared to let the new road go through, and there was the matter of protecting the American bases, chiefly at Kunming and Kweilin, which he felt the Japanese might try to take by an overland campaign.

In America everyone believed that the problem of the Chinese fighting was merely the problem of giving them enough guns and planes. I had always believed this myself, and had undoubtedly added to public misinformation in two or three broadcasts on the subject. The point was that the men were generally so diseased, so spiritless, so badly led, so utterly devoid of any technical training, that it was criminal waste to give weapons to any but those we had taken in hand and trained from the basic rudiments on up. There were other troubles. Much of the material we had delivered to them, before Stilwell insisted that all lend-lease goods be billed to him and distributed carefully by him, had disappeared. It was found stored up by private profiteers and drained off into the illegal trade with the enemy, and some of it was used by the quarter-million of Chiang's troops who were doing nothing but standing guard over the Chinese Communists in the North. The same things had happened to medical supplies, the disposition of which had become a great scandal. It even happened to trained men who were not under our strict control. When Ambassador Gauss (a not-so-bad diplomat who was unfairly condemned by Willkie and others) last saw the President he made only one recommendation on military matters: that unless greater control could be exercised over the Chinese aviation cadets we were training in America, the whole program ought to be discontinued. One large batch of them had returned to China and ended up serving the allied cause by being used to bomb and strafe Chinese peasants in Szechwan who were revolting against their oppressive taxes. Stilwell was absolutely certain that the Communists *were* fighting the Japanese, but the Generalissimo was stopping all Stilwell's efforts to get material up to them.

That, in brief, was the situation. I could not doubt the facts; the evidence on all sides was simply too overwhelming. I remained somewhat skeptical about the performances of the Communists, not from any political bias against them, but merely out of reportorial caution, for there was very little concrete evidence available in Chungking, and the last reputable eyewitness had come from the "Red area" a long time before. But all my instincts told me that the high praise of the Communists was probably fully justified.

Stilwell had tried so hard and so long that it seemed to me a point had been reached where his very vigor, his very passion for helping China, had become a handicap in the effort. Utterly without the instincts of a diplomat, he had become so obsessed with the goal in view that he had given up all effort to use the secondary methods of personal relationships, of handling each Chinese personality with the strategic care that each separately required. From too much intimacy he had come to regard them almost as children. He wasted no time on ceremony, and they had come to resent his manner so deeply that they instinctively reacted negatively, even where their interests were the same. The Generalissimo knew perfectly well what Stilwell thought of him and said about him. They were hardly on speaking terms, and both were such proud and unforgiving men that the deadlock could not be broken. When the general had been last in Washington, he had greeted Mme. Chiang at a party with the sharp words: "Your husband wants you home." She had abruptly turned her back on him. It was hard to imagine another American who could have the same drive and the same grasp of the problem; but it was also hard to see how this shocking psychological stalemate could be permitted to continue. In lesser degree, the same thing was true of the relationship among all our diplomatic officials in Chungking. Beneath the polite formalities, there was a clear antagonism between the embassy and the ministries, and the tragedy of it was that this was the ablest group of young diplomats I had ever seen in a single American mission abroad. They were the best-informed foreigners in China, many of them had been born there and truly loved the country and the people, and it was indeed largely because of this feeling of intimacy that they had developed an attitude of paternalism toward the Chinese which became, in the time of trial, offensive to the Chinese and destructive of its high purpose.

A Chinese lady of famous name and gallant heart was living out these miserable years in a fake-modern house within a dusty, ramshackle courtyard littered with broken-down, rusting trucks, squawking chickens, and naked neighbor children. To Mme. Sun Yat-sen, who had established the famous liaison of the Soong family with political power, thus bringing her sister to world renown, I took letters from American friends—letters salvaged from the jungle by our Nagas. Everyone who could or dared went to see her and took courage from her. Her position was most curious: she was a kind of hostage of Fascism and at the same time a rallying point for the spirit of democracy. She remained on friendly enough terms with her sisters and their powerful husbands, Chiang and Kung, yet she would denounce the regime as a cruel Fascist betrayal of Dr. Sun and all his highest hopes. She had escaped to Chungking from Hong Kong with nothing but her handbag, and her present rooms were filled with a kind of cheap modern Grand Rapids furniture. A black-enameled export radio set stood over a few worn English books of philosophy. Flowers and some lovely modern oil landscapes brightened an otherwise austere parlor. Coffee was waiting on the cocktail table along with a rich, sweet cake and an opened tin of English cigarettes, gifts from the countless admirers who brought her things from all parts of the outside world.

She came downstairs dressed in a blue flowered print dress which left her plump arms bare. Her hair was done severely and there was just a touch of rouge on her lips. Much of the beauty had faded, and the face at first seemed heavy and the expression frozen. But as one talked and watched the clear, black eyes, the same thing happened that occurred in conversation with Mrs. Roosevelt: the eyes seemed to mellow, the features softened until the whole impression was of a patient countenance, rather lovely, with an inexpressible sweetness about it.

We talked a long time, and even before me, a stranger, she was unsparing of the present policies. I mentioned the Bengal famine. She immediately replied: "There is terrible famine here. The government talks about the rich crops, and in Honan the people are eating bark and leaves and mud." Local gentry and the military were taking all that the farmers grew, as taxes, and sometimes they took for thirty years in advance. (As I later discovered, relief funds raised in America were frequently used to buy back from the officials and give to the peasants the very food the peasants themselves had raised.) She spoke with bitterness of the starvation among the students and teachers, the government spies that infested the classrooms, the liberal professors and poets who were slowly dying of malnutrition while generals and businessmen were making fabulous profits out of the wartime inflation. It was their spirit that dominated the place. Men who spoke too passionately about resisting the Japanese were regarded with suspicion; it was not good form. Mme. Sun was a member of the Kuomintang's Central Executive Committee, then in session, but she had long since given up the fruitless formality of taking part. She was regarded as a Red. She looked favorably upon the Communists in the North simply because she believed they had given new spirit to the common people and because they fought the common enemy. Believing this, she had tried to send a shipment of painfully gathered medical supplies to their army; it was all confiscated by Chiang's men. I asked: "Will they declare the period of tutelage officially ended, and will democracy then begin one morning at six o'clock?" She said: "Somehow, the clock always stops." The essential difference between her and her brilliant sister was simple: Mme. Chiang thought and spoke of China in terms of independence, nationalist power, and position in the world; Mme. Sun thought of China in terms of the ordinary people. She was humanitarian, with respect for human life, among countrymen who would not turn their head to look at a corpse in the streets.

For several days I carried on negotiations with Mme. Sun through an intermediary for a broadcast by her to the United States in which she would break her long silence and speak out of her heart and mind of China's problem. At length she agreed to take the plunge, and I got everything ready. This would be front-page news everywhere in the world. Twenty-four hours before the broadcast time, a note arrived, scribbled with red ink in her large, firm script. She had changed her mind. She had decided that this was not the moment for it, and she did not wish to speak at all unless she could say everything she wanted to say. Even for this great woman, I thought, the psychology of prison outlasts its walls.

With Brooks Atkinson I walked one day past the ugly black villa where the Generalissimo lived, through a narrow, incredibly crowded alleyway, filled with fly-covered meat, decaying fish, fruit, sewage, children, and old hags hobbling on bound feet. We turned in at No. 50 and went down a few steps. A small block had been sawed out of the wall through which visitors could be scrutinized. This was the headquarters of the Communist representatives in the capital, whose presence there kept up the formal pretense of unity, who published a heavily censored newspaper, and who were followed by Tai Li's police everywhere they walked. Tai Li lived just a few steps away, and his men noted down our arrival as they did that of every stranger who appeared at this door. The few Communists present worked on the ground floor and slept on the third, passing through members of the Kuomintang's executive Yuan, who slept on the second floor. The chief Communist delegate, General Chou En-lai, had recently gone back to Yenan, where he had just given a speech in bitter tones which indicated that even the fictive unity might not last much longer.

In his absence, the leading spirit of the headquarters was a girl of twenty-seven, of whom I had heard a great deal and whom we had really come to see. We stood in a large, bare room of soiled white walls on which hung old portraits of Dr. Sun, Stalin, Lenin, and the Generalissimo. Miss Kung Peng came in so softly that we did not hear her arrival. I am afraid I cannot adequately describe her nor convincingly explain why it was that I lost my tongue and forgot the questions I had wished to ask. One can describe the externals: She was tall and slim, of willowy figure, her glossy black hair was piled high on her head, and she was dressed with extreme simplicity in a gray cotton gown on which the only ornamentation was an exquisite circular brooch clasping the dress at the neck. The picture of this tall-stemmed flower in the damp and soiled cellar was a quick sketch contrast that will remain in the memory always. She was graciousness, urbanity, but she was also the fresh, trusting decency of open-faced youth. She was a beautiful woman, but in her presence the male-female feeling all but disappeared, replaced by a sexless awe and admiration.

Kung Peng had grown up in Canton and Shanghai, the daughter of a man of wealth who had been an early collaborator with Sun

Yat-sen. She was in Shanghai at the time of the famous May 30
incident in 1925 and became impressed with the revolution as a
child. But she went through the usual routine of the Chinese
bourgeoisie, attending Saint Mary's Hall and Yenching University
in Peiping, and it was not until her father suddenly lost all his
money and their friends deserted them overnight that she fully
understood her society. Turning down a chance to study abroad,
she went to Yenan to help lead the student movement. She married
a Communist and became a peasant organizer for two years in the
guerrilla area. When he was captured by the Japanese and died,
she came to Chungking in 1941 as secretary and assistant to General Chou.

More than a few foreign correspondents and diplomats fancied
themselves in love with her—but it was a little too much like being
in love with Joan of Arc. She was often invited to social affairs at
the foreign embassies in a kind of pleasurable defiance of Kuomintang officials, and sometimes she accepted; mostly, she remained
in this miserable hole ceaselessly working. There was a silent conspiracy among the correspondents and foreign diplomats; her full
story was filed away in various drawers, and if ever she were to
disappear, or if ever her life were threatened, at that moment the
cables to America and England would have become overactive
and something like a diplomatic incident would surely have occurred. Tai Li undoubtedly knew all this; Kung Peng knew it herself, and it was probably this conspiracy of admirers that made her
life possible in Chungking.

It was a heartbreaking life at best, and only a woman of soul and
exalted vision could have maintained it. Even so, at the time I
first saw her, she felt herself weakening a little, and it caused her
worry and a touch of shame. She was then a little wan, convalescent from a severe stomach illness, and she had recovered only
because Brooks had taken matters in hand and got her into the
care of Dr. Herrington. This was an American Marine medic, a
morose man of conscience and tender patience who eventually
made daily rounds, treating Chinese friends, correspondents, army
officers, or whoever was suffering, expending his time and precious
store of medicines regardless of what his superiors or the rule book
said. Without this man, God knows what would have happened
to many of us.

The long, long effort to come to an understanding with the Kuomintang and the poisonous atmosphere of concealed terrorism in

Chungking were gradually wearing the girl down. Endlessly, we debated schemes to get her away to America under a scholarship plan or something of the sort—provided she would really leave which we doubted. During the last evening I spent with her she was unusually silent and depressed. "The same old thing," she said wearily. "I went to call upon a dear friend across the river. After I had left, the secret police came to their door and warned them never to see me again under threat of imprisonment." She pressed her hand against her breast and went on: "Sometimes I feel I can hardly breathe any more in this place. It is like being sick, when you feel the walls of your room closing in on you. If only I could be for a little while in a place where there is freedom, just to see what it is like again for a little while!"

Again I had the old feeling of uselessness, the crushing sense of ineffectualness that comes to the vacillating liberal, who contests only with words, in the presence of a truly strong, dedicated person who has accepted the perils of action, made his decision, and cast his personal life into the account as a thing of value only in terms of the future he himself will never see—the "tomorrows that sing."

I spent several weeks in Chungking, suffering more frequent bouts of dysentery, growing steadily thinner, until a time came when I realized that my thick stack of notes already contained all the pertinent political, military and economic facts that I could garner in the capital. There was just so much journalistic information of the moment available there, and with the aid of unusually free access to its sources I had it all.

On the night before leaving I said goodbye to friends in the lower city and at midnight climbed the long mile up the curving street toward my billet. A light, cold rain was falling. It made a dry, rustling sound on my waxed paper parasol. In the pool of fitful light at the crossings the top of each wet cobblestone was burnished in faint reflection. All the little shops, the endless shops, were shuttered and were again a frail façade. I heard a woman coughing, and somewhere at an upper window a man was trying to vomit; the sounds were loud and harsh. Behind that curtain of painted paper were huddled masses of human arms and legs and closed faces, touching through the thin strips in endless tiers. There were no homes; nobody had a home. Even in the night of rain the fetid smells of day pressed upon the nostrils. One could close his eyes and see at once this street by day—raucous and noisy, the river of sweating humanity, walking, running, shouting, laughing, and wailing, the arguing men, the hobbling women, the serene children quietly pissing in the gutter.

My great boots made echoing noises on the stones; I felt a dull, intrusive Gulliver in a land of little ones I would never understand, a land where I was not meant to be. At a dark corner a child was standing motionless, the rain dripping from his peaked hat of straw—an orphan with no nest of bodies in which to worm his own. He was China, of mysterious origin and incomprehensible destination, timeless, old and young, suffering and saying nothing, patient in the rain, with straw and the sky between him and eternity.

You heard yourself muttering: "Oh Christ, this land of China!" But to what God did you pray for such a land as this? The bosom of no Jehovah was massive enough to bring all these to rest; the ear of no omniscience could gather this oceanic murmuring of pain and all the soft lappings of little hopes. As well pray for the mountains that never crumble, for the rivers without end or beginning which spring forever. It would be better, perhaps, if we prayed *to* China, not for her.

3

At Kunming, the sun again warmed the earth of ripening fields, the lake was still blue and calm, there was dignity in the bent forms of the peasants who tended the moist rootlings, and the clouds kept a decent distance, banked in high tiers of lapis lazuli over the far, rounded hills. In the night from the barracks yard one watched the arching red bulb of a plane, aiming toward the translucent moon, a hole in the sky. There was the sound of billiard balls clicking through the opened window, and casual American cursing. A Chinese boy was singing in a shack near by. One slept deeply and awoke like a convalescent, feeling whole and well again. In the early morning the lungs remembered the sharp edge of clean air. The sky was mottled with high clouds like gray patches sewn upon blue silk. Rows of well-mannered poplars and pines escorted the diminishing highway toward the old, walled city, and blue morning-glories nodded under their burden of dew next to the gravel path outside the barracks. As the sun rose and the colors gathered in the mountain pockets, you could hear the sound of motors from the field. A few more boys in brown leather jackets

were taking a last deep drag on a cigarette, working a succulent
bit of breakfast bacon loose from their teeth. They were slamming
the metal doors, shutting out the fragrance, enclosing themselves
in the oil-smelling tube. In a few minutes, or an hour, doubtless
one or two of them would careen down from the blue and violate
a peaceful, anonymous jungle acre on some mountainside to the
west. But it was not good to think of that; there was too much war
ahead for everyone. Meanwhile there was morning in China.

Among the pilots in the mess hall there was less banter, less
horseplay. Those who sat at table with their parachutes beside
their chairs, ate with more deliberate concentration than usual.
The day before, the Japanese had commenced fighter attacks on
the unescorted transports across the Hump. This was something
new, and nothing could be done about it. Nine planes had been
attacked, and three or four were missing, including one that carried fourteen passengers. Perhaps they had been after the various
"loads of brass" that were coming through. But they were fooled.
Mountbatten, bound for Chungking to pay his respects to the
Generalissimo, had arrived by night; Stilwell, Somervell, Wheeler,
and others came with a fighter escort. The bouncing young British
lord and admiral jumped out of his car and came over to speak
with Atkinson and me, but he heard few of our questions—he
wanted to know all about my "jungle jump" of August. No distrust was deeper than that between the Chinese and the British,
but the ebullient Mountbatten captivated the Chiangs, male and
female. To the Generalissimo he said: "Sir, I have come directly
to see you. I have not even paused in Delhi to collect my staff.
I realize you have been fighting this enemy much longer than any
of us, and I know how heavily I shall have to rely upon your
counsel." Witnesses reported that the Generalissimo was almost
speechless. No Englishmen had spoken to him in such terms of
respect before. He blew a blast of fresh air into the stale British
military hierarchy in New Delhi, packing many torpid pukka
sahibs off to England at once. He refused to allow the traditional
summer pilgrimage to Simla to escape the heat, refused to believe
that "nothing can be done" in the monsoon season, and called
special meteorologists, psychologists, and medical experts from
England to find a scientific answer to the problems of fighting in
wetness and jungle heat. The pukka sahibs frowned upon him as
an amateur salt-water sailor who did not understand; but events
proved that he and his methods were long overdue.

Mountbatten was irrepressible, formidable, and immensely charming. One night while downing cocktails, he was describing the plans for the invasion of Sicily which had surprised the Italians. "But it was quite obvious that Sicily would be next," I remarked in a knowing tone. He took a long sip of his drink, then wheeled upon me and with a wide grin exclaimed: "Quite. But you know— we *almost* went to Sardinia!"

When I entered Chennault's office for a private hour with him, empty chairs were still arranged in a semicircle before his desk; his morning talk to his staff had just ended, maps were still unfurled, and the place had a little of the atmosphere of a schoolroom. I was sharply impressed by this legendary figure, but afterwards I wondered whether the legend was not more impressive than the figure. He was a man who did not smile easily; he was a little deaf and like many deaf persons gave the impression of being somewhat humorless. With a pointer he showed me on the maps his whole system of triangular defense by interlocking airfields, and I was surprised to find that he had so many alternative locations from which to work. (So, one may add, were the Japanese.) If his opinion of the Chinese was much higher than that of so many other American officers it was not only because they worshipped him almost as a god, but also because the secret telephone and short-wave warning system by which they reported enemy planes almost as soon as they took off from Hong Kong really did work. Chennault was a hard driver, and all his men respected him, but except for a few close to him there was no feeling of affection; he did not "inspire" the mass of his men in the Stilwell way. It seemed to me that he was a man who had developed the arts of combat tactics almost to perfection. But he was a limited technician—not, I thought, a man of expansive imagination, capable of handling the immense strategic and political problems which American officers were contending with in all parts of the world. It would have been only human perhaps if he resented Stilwell's superior position in China, since the only American fighting forces there were his fliers, but it was widely known that he did not accept the arrangement with grace. Frequently he was reluctant to carry out orders, and he permitted the Chiangs and other Chinese authorities with whom he was on good personal terms to play him off against General Stilwell. It was frequently reported that he had gone directly to the President, through Mme. Chiang or Soong, and that they had done the same through Chennault. Here again was an unfortunate problem of personalities among able and devoted individuals, as unfortunate as the problem in Chungking. In a cabled dispatch I wrote that despite his great efforts to build up his force, the big clashes with the Japanese would probably occur in other theaters, and that, if so, Chennault would never have a chance to really come to grips with the enemy. But it never occurred to me for a moment that Chennault himself would be taken out of his position as air chief within China.

I stood one sunny day at a bend of the road on a promontory which gave a view of the lovely valley and watched a scene close at hand. It was heartbreaking, but it filled cne again with wonder at the endurance of the human body and respect for the unconquerable human spirit. A group of young Chinese men—mere boys, most of them—wearing tattered remains of khaki were moving slowly on the dusty road toward a group of sprawling buildings up the hill over which the American flag flipped in the breeze. They seemed to be creeping as slowly as a man could possibly move. All of them were limping, and their eyes were stones. Most were barefoot, and some hobbled with the aid of sticks, their feet swathed in dirty rags. I had seen men in like condition before, but they had always been men going away from war, refugees seeking haven. But these were men bound *into* war. They were Chinese soldiers for the American infantry training school on the hill. They had walked—I do not exaggerate—five hundred miles from their divisions in the Northeast. This is the way they arrived, a new batch of them every few weeks. A third to a half of them had died on the march.

When the Generalissimo had first agreed to the training scheme, men were pulled from the ranks and ordered to go, often under threats of being whipped or beaten. Hundreds deserted on the way or were shot by their overseers. But the thing had gradually taken hold, for the men had seen those who returned healthy and eager and proud of their new accomplishments. These that I saw were volunteers, selected by competition. According to the routine they would all be hospitalized until they were fit for the classes. With the camp director, Colonel Harry Buckley of Plattsburg, New York, I went through the school. If I had never understood why lend-lease weapons could not be handed over to the Generalissimo outright, I understood now. Not by any stretch of the imagination were they soldiers, save in the quality of their spirits. Our officers began by teaching them the things an American Boy

Scout knows at the age of fourteen: how to build a simple log bridge, how to find the Big Dipper and the North Star, how to apply a simple tourniquet. They had to be taught to aim their rifles before pulling the trigger, instead of closing their eyes and firing in the enemy's general direction. In a large room equipped with field telephones in the four corners, boys of fifteen and sixteen were learning to use the instruments, and they chattered at one another with delighted expressions on their innocent faces. In another room a hundred of them sat at long tables with radio head-sets over their ears. They were learning code, and the record showed that they learned it more quickly than American soldiers. It was almost impossible to think of these children as soldiers. They looked like eager orphans in a public institution. They were pitifully anxious to own something for once in their lives, and they were constantly chewing their pencils in half or tearing out sheets from their notebooks to secrete under their straw pillows at night.

On the hillside, among the rice paddies and the burial mounds, they fired at target butts. One morning a village woman was bending in the rice stalks directly in their line of fire. They shouted at her to move or she would die. She straightened up and said simply: "If we have no rice we shall die, anyway," and went back to her work. Another range was staked out somewhere else. Colonel Buckley had just had a startling experience; he shook his head in regret as he discussed it. He noticed one day that several young officers were sound asleep in their class in the pine grove. This had happened too many times, and so, although he knew this would be a terrible loss of face for them, he ordered the offenders sent back to the barracks. In the morning he learned from a casual remark from one of the Chinese instructors that the men had been taken down the road in the night and shot.

We were bound for Kweilin, far down in southeastern China, close to the Japanese holdings on the coast, but my reputation among the pilots as a Jonah held good (taking off at Chungking, my plane had almost fallen into the river), and we circled for hours in the fog before making it down on a fighter field at Lingling with very little petrol remaining. Here we lived with a handful of lonesome American youngsters who were farther from home than any others in the war. They had a small field, bad food, frequent peril, water buffalo, rice paddies, the endless rain—and one another. Leader of this outfit was Captain Elsner of Missouri, just twenty-three years of age. While the rain blinded the windows, we sat for hours in his room, covering the floor with cigarette ends and burnt matches. A brilliant figured-silk cloth hung on the wall, and a picture of Elsner's lovely young wife. A can of precious coffee was shared out and a bottle of Shanghai beer, bought for 250 Chinese dollars. Men stamped in and out, and we all talked. There was an effervescent, collegiate humor and love of life in the hearts of these decent, open-faced youngsters. There was no mistaking it—they were a physical and mental élite in the armed forces, gladiators who hated their dull, confined days upon the earth and loved their exalting hours in the air. One of them said to me: "I don't know just what it is, but when I get up there in that fighter and feel all that power responding to the touch of my hands, I almost go out of my mind. Sometimes I just yell out loud in the cockpit. I lose all fear, I feel I can do anything. I just want to speed, smash, fight. I guess I go mad for a while."

One of the squadron members was the husky football player of renown, Tommy Harmon. He was in a difficult position owing entirely to his fame. Day and night he had to listen to snickering remarks: "When are we getting that film *Harmon of Michigan?* I can hardly wait." Or, "Send me in, Coach, send me in." Or, "Come on, Harmon, tell us some more about Hollywood." At first I felt sorry for him, but there was no need for it. It became clear that he was taking the chaffing with a grin, and they liked him for it and accepted him as one of themselves despite the handicap of fame.

These fliers. Their full, firm faces, the clear skin and white teeth and steady eyes. Unblinkingly they regard one another and offer the most scathing, obscene insults, the steady smile unshadowed. "Why, this jerk—know what he did? He went down alone and strafed a Jap battleship. Jerk." "Aw, hell, how'd I know it was a battleship?" "This screwball with the dishmop he calls a beard. He's downstairs, see, and he yells: 'Come on down, you guys, I got six of the bastards trapped!' "

They thought of death, yes, and—contrary to general belief—they talked about it. They did not speak of it "casually," either. They spoke seriously, but a quick remark was all that was required: "When Smitty got his" . . . "If I get mine I'd rather get it this way . . . " It was there, in the front of their minds, all the time.

When we got up to go, one said: "Hey, why don't you two guys come in again tonight? This is the first time we haven't talked about women."

When the weather cleared and they had put on an exhibition for us, "buzzing" the field at three hundred miles an hour and causing the panic-stricken Chinese workers to fall flat on their faces, we sat in the operations shack cracking peanuts and peeling tangerines. A long, lean, tow-headed youngster bumped his head entering the room, and there was a yell of greeting. This blushing lad was Captain James "Willy" Williams of Texas, once of the AVG, who now commanded another squadron and had not been seen at Lingling since before he had been shot down near the Jap lines several weeks before. He stood with legs spread wide apart, gulped tangerines, and blew the seeds across the room as he described what had happened:

"Well, sir, Ah was just finishing this strafing job—it was a purty day—when Ah caught a twenty-millimeter shell in the engine and the smoke began to pour back over me. Boy, Ah felt awful. Ah turned around to get out of there and Ah *talked* to that airplane, Ah did. Ah said, you just *got* to get me a little piece further on. Purty soon my engine just froze, so Ah got out of there. Ah came down right gentle in the 'chute. Ah just hit for the hills and hid there. Then a Chinese boy came along the road and Ah ran down to him and showed him my identification in Chinese. Ah tried to get him to help me and take me along with him, but Ah guess he was plumb scared. He was trembling-like, and Ah guess Ah was too. But purty soon some men came along looking like they was hunting for me. Ah took a chance and they smiled and raised their thumb up like this and said 'Dinghow' and boy, Ah felt a whole lot better. Well, sir, we walked and walked until Ah got a bit sick and they carried me in a *see*-dan chair." Blushing at this confession Willy went on: "Ah didn't really care for that, much. You know, a feller sort of likes to do things for himself. Well, we came to an army headquarters and from then on we went in trucks, and you know there was a banquet in purty near every blame town we came to, with a lot of long speeches in Chinese. Ah never *did* find out what they was saying about me, but then Ah'd get up and make a speech myself." I asked Willy what he had said. "Well, you know, Ah said we was mighty grateful for all their *co*-operation and all that stuff. You know—just stuff."

In the evening we had a "dinner party" in a bamboo shack by the field. They were like college freshmen on a Saturday night binge after a winning game. They gulped down raw red wine and tough, burned steaks, shouted and flipped exploding firecrackers

into one another's faces. One after another they would spring to
their feet to make a speech, filled with a declamatory, innocent
obscenity, and each time the speaker sat down, his chair was gone
and he sprawled on the ground. I felt a complete stranger in the
midst of something I could never share. I felt sad over this, and
because the thought kept coming back: Some of them are going
to die. Captain Elsner responded to their pleas and rose to speak.
He was a quiet, thoughtful boy with his decent heart in his eyes.
They worshipped him, and they were silent while he was on his
feet. He made a little halting speech and said he didn't care what
they did tonight so long as they didn't wreck the whole shack the
way they did at the last party. He spoke like a grave, liberal parent
admonishing well-loved sons. They were a blood brotherhood;
it was a thing to see and never to be forgotten.

(Two weeks later, news reached me in New Delhi that both
Harmon and Elsner were missing in action. Harmon parachuted
safely down and made it back. Elsner was killed, a noble boy
among so many others to go, and nothing—no peace among men,
no freedom—can quite make up for this.)

We broke through the clouds and circled to land at Kweilin.
The landscape was something beyond all reference; we seemed to
be landing among the mountains of the moon. Tall, straight spires
of green mountains jutted up from the plain like rows of immense
Gothic spires, each one quite separate from the next, spiking the
sky as far as the eye could see. On the ground the air was cool,
heavy, and liquid. Everything was green with the consistency of
wet moss, and one seemed to be walking on the bottom of a translucent pond. I had never seen anything like this in my life, and
yet it was faintly familiar. This was the mystical Chinese land-
scaping I had seen since childhood on a thousand silk scrolls and
watercolors. This was the enchanted temple where sky and sea-
bottom came together, to which centuries of Chinese artists and
poets made pilgrimage in their hearts.

The half-modernized city of Kweilin remained, so far as Americans were concerned, the "sex capital" of Free China. The struc-
tural barrenness of Chungking and Mme. Chiang's impossible
"New Life Movement" had driven sex underground along with
free expression, but in Kweilin it was a flourishing trade. The city
was miles from the American airbase, so an old AVG hostel had
been turned into a combination night club and brothel beside the
highway, where the fliers ate bad steaks, drank poisonous liquor,

danced with the girls, and retired with them to the little cubicle bedrooms constructed in two wings beside the main building. It was a good arrangement; officers came one night and enlisted men another, and everybody was happy.

But Kweilin, first major stop for refugees out of Hong Kong, was also the spy capital of Free China, and, as our harassed security officers knew, too many of the girls were doubling in brass. There was Betty, who was setting up a new night club for American officers. Her boy friend in Hong Kong was believed to be a Japanese agent. Our security people had no authority to make arrests, and the Chinese police refused to do anything about it. There was Fatima Ismail, half-caste, who welcomed company at the "Ledo Club." She had been intimate with Endo, head of the Japanese-sponsored Indian Independence League. All we could do was to warn the air-force personnel about her. There was "Eddy" from Hong Kong, an ugly-looking thug. He frankly admitted upon questioning that he had been sent in by the Japanese. But, he said, he had decided to make a clean breast of the matter and would like to work for the Americans. An old dodge. The American security officer never succeeded in having him arrested and was tempted more than once to shoot him in a dark alley some night. Eddy roamed the streets, smiling upon one and all, and asked the Americans if they would mind if he opened a cozy little hamburger shop for the fliers, who were "such nice, lonely boys, so far from home." The Chinese police would say: "Let us not arrest him. Let us follow him, and maybe we will find more spies," while the security officer tore his hair. As in Chungking and Kunming, the Japanese had a transmitter right in the middle of Kweilin. Our men had listened to it during a Jap bombing raid, as the operator spoke confidentially to the pilots and directed them where to drop their bombs. We knew within a few blocks where the transmitter was, but it could not be found.

"Some day," the security chief said to me, "there's going to be a miniature Pearl Harbor right here. I'm scared. Somebody is protecting these spies, and I can't break the system."

It was because of experiences like this and a thousand others—such as the attempt of profiteers to sell lend-lease trucks back to the army—that innumerable American soldiers were learning to despise the Chinese rather than respect them. Each man's own little experience would represent all of China in his mind forever. If he had a similar experience in his own country, he would not condemn the whoie country, but, because he was ignorant of the Chinese beyond those he dealt with himself, their behavior was all China's behavior. The hopeful theory that international brotherhood is increased by personal contact was certainly not working in this part of the world.

Now and then an American soldier would fall in love with a Chinese girl, but it was a rare occurrence. There was the well-substantiated story of the sergeant at the Kweilin airfield, who saw a lovely peasant girl working in the rice paddies. He walked over to her, held out money in his hand, and said: "Come, come." He took her to a café in the village and ordered a rich meal of meats. She would touch none of it, and later, when they had found a room, she ate curds and beans, which was all she had ever known. He sequestered a shack near the field, where he would go during off-duty hours. She washed and pressed his clothes, sewed his buttons, and kept the place neat. Then she disappeared, and his frantic searching produced no trace. Two or three months later he was spending a night in a hotel within the city and sent a boy out for a prostitute. The girl who came to his room was his sweetheart, who had been living in the city after her parents had driven her away from the village in disgrace because of her affair with him. They were occasionally to be seen walking hand in hand about the city, and at last report the boy was still pestering his officers, demanding permission to marry her and bring her to America.

In a hotel I found a dark, sallow man of misfortune, a German doctor, who represented another little tragedy of Chinese Fascism. He had fled from Hitler and had served with the Spanish Republicans until all foreign volunteers there were obliged to leave. He could have sought haven after years of striving to help democracy, but like others he could not rest. The general European war had not yet begun; so with a group of other doctors from Spain he had made the long journey to China, hoping to aid there in the fight against Fascism. Soon they found that their medicines were not arriving—were instead falling into the hands of private profiteers. They learned that they were suspect because of their liberal ideas. They were shunted aside, ignored, and left to live as best they could, while they grew older and their talents withered—and while thousands of Chinese soldiers died for want of their talents. The American army had rescued a few and taken them to the Ramgarh training camp in India. For this man and the others there was no prospect save that of living from day to day, doing nothing to excite the attention of the secret police, ministering to a sick Chinese friend here and there, and hoping.

With Graham Peck, who directed the Kweilin outpost for the Office of War Information, I walked across the wide green river and climbed the hill to sit on the balcony of a Buddhist temple of gilded lattice work. We cracked peanuts, looked at the clusters of sampans in the river, and talked about the Asiatic world. Graham was perplexed and wondering. Through our broadcasts and leaflets we were convincing the Indians, the Burmese, the Thais, the Malayans, the Javanese, and the Indo-Chinese that the Allies were bound to win the war. Perhaps that helped a little. Perhaps it meant that a few more of these men would take the deadly risks of underground work against the Japanese. But what could we promise them as reward? They put no faith at all in the word of the British, the French, or the Dutch, and believed only America, which had guaranteed outright independence to the Philippines. So America was taking the lead as spokesman for all the Allies. And what could we say of the future? We talked about the rights of small nations, and about the Four Freedoms; but nothing specific was offered, no guarantee of outright political independence or international trusteeship could be given. For the Allies had not agreed on any concrete policy of generous postwar treatment, and America seemed to have no policy of her own. The people of those colonial areas were sick of fine words and promises, just as the people of Chiang's China were sick of them. What would happen when the fighting ended? Would the colonial administrators move right back into their former posts with their former hardhanded policies? Would the native groups who had learned to organize and resist under the Japanese accept them back? Neither of us could believe they would. A fire of resistance had been started in East Asia, and it would not stop at the Japanese. World wars usher in new epochs; the long era of unquestioned rule by white men over brown men was most surely breaking up under our eyes.

For the Chinese and Indians, at least, political independence seemed almost a certainty. What methods, then, should they follow to give their people life and happiness? Like myself, so many of those from the Western democracies who advised them and hoped for them were products of a Jeffersonian liberalism. We would like them to use the methods of the free ballot and free assembly. Russia's methods of a ruthless dictatorship, even though the aim

was good, were repugnant to us; to many they were more repugnant than the frightful conditions of life they were designed to
end. But my basic beliefs in the liberal approaches were deeply
shaken by what I had seen in this part of the world. I began to
doubt whether, in any case, they were universally applicable.
Could men apply the methods of literate nineteenth- and twen-
tieth-century societies bred in the tradition of tolerance to societies
that were centuries behind us in social advance? The great aim
of freedom in security for the individual seemed to me universal
and eternally right. As for the methods, however, it seemed clear
that there was a time-space equation involved which could not be
ignored. The basic economic problems of India, for example,
could be largely solved by a ruthless collectivization of the land.
Thousands, even millions, of men might suffer liquidation and
death in the process; but millions were dying every year under
the present conditions, and would continue to die every year until
the matter is solved. Half the human race was barefoot, filthy,
sick, and worried from morning till night, from birth until death,
over no other problem than simply finding food for their bellies.
The truth was that, no matter how ruthless the effort might be,
nothing could be worse than the present condition. And maybe in
ten years, or twenty, or fifty, these hundreds of millions *would* be
able to live, to be clean and whole, to rise above their animal
state and walk as men. True, there was danger that the means
would become the end. But it seemed to me that the risk was worth
the taking.

Under these circumstances, what had the Western democracies
to offer these peoples in comparison with the Russians? We could
offer a ballot box and education in tolerance. This was slow
medicine, to be taken voluntarily by the patients, as rapidly as
they learned to understand it. Russia offered a forcible surgical
operation without anesthesia, but with a quicker, more certain
cure. For the Western peoples, I had serious doubts that the future
belonged to Communism; for those of the East I was not so sure.

4

There was not a cloud in the sky over the Hump, and that was bad.
Once a Jap fighter pilot spotted our lone Dakota transport, our
chances would be very small. Lieutenant Hannah, the Knoxville

boy with the drawn face, was making his ninety-fifth run over the Hump as pilot. He was keeping low in the hope that the plane would be blurred against the brown-green landscape, skimming over the ridges with only a few yards to spare, dipping down the valleys. I was the sole passenger, walking back and forth in the empty cabin, trying to fight back the phobia that had been with me since the second of August. I was beyond all feelings of personal pride and kept the parachute on my back, not caring what the crew might think of me. The radio was sounding: four Zeros reported in our neighborhood. We took turns, standing on an upturned ration box, peering into the sun through the glass bulge at the top. We dipped into a valley and flew directly over a Japanese army camp no more than a thousand feet below us. We arrived and departed too quickly for them to do anything about us. Sometimes they had let fly with a machine gun, and sometimes our unarmed pilots retaliated by dropping a few hand grenades among them, just to soothe the nerves. One engine sounded queer to my over sensitive ears, and I asked Hannah what was the matter with it. He merely looked at me from the corner of his eyes and said: "Nothing, chum. Except it insists on going around and around and around." A crawling white gash in the green mountains came into view. It was the Ledo Road, now miles into the Burma side. We were safe.

The next night, ill and tired, thinner by thirty pounds than I had been three months before, I sank into the cushions of a limousine that drove me into the city of New Delhi. For this night it did not seem a preposterous, pretentious place. The car purred smoothly over the washed pavements, the cool, healing night draughts carried the perfume of the gardens, and as I relaxed between clean, white sheets I thought: However mistaken and cruel it is, for this one night I am grateful for the white man's rule.

. Between sessions at the army hospital I wrote out the articles on China intended for publication in the United States. I determined not to submit them to any censorship in the Far East. (By an unprecedented arrangement, anything one wrote in India about China would be submitted to the Chinese commissioner there; and the scheme worked in reverse if one were in China, writing about British India. The same sort of arrangement was working in Cairo, I discovered, among the British, Egyptian, Greek, and Yugoslav regimes. Shaky regimes everywhere, agreeing

on little else, were uniting in a spreading plot to stifle criticism.)
General Stratemeyer kindly offered to let me fly home on a returning bomber. I was to carry a few documents to the War Department, so I knew I could get my writings safely to Washington.

What was the matter in China? The people had strength and
daring, imagination, intelligence, and a smiling courage in the
face of bitter odds that made one want to cry. And God! the things
they had done—the Communists who had made the epochal five-
thousand-mile march to create their new life in the interior reaches;
the students and factory workers who had carried their universities
and machines on their backs up the long, weary road to Szechwan.
You cannot indict a whole people for anything—indolence, apathy,
corruption, or anything else. Certainly you could indict the Chinese
last of all. They had fought valiantly at Shanghai only a few years
before; they had been magnificent when Chungking was battered to the ground, rebuilt, smashed, and again rebuilt. Why,
then, were they not trying to fight now? True, they had lost the
great ports and Burma, and the Japs held the best industrial and
food-producing regions. There was sheer physical weariness after
years of war. But others had fought on—the British, the Russians,
the Greeks, the Yugoslav Partisans, however starved and weary.
Often they too had had no weapons, but when they didn't they
fought and worked anyway, with their bare hands if necessary. It
seemed to me that the answer was clear: It was not a matter of
materials—it was a matter of the human spirit.

What I had been seeing in China was the present consequence
of a great, slow betrayal of the spirit, of the aspirations of the
common people. The answer was that for several years the people
had been given nothing to fight for except the vaguest promises,
and these had been repudiated so often that they no longer
believed them. Every day they heard their government talk about
new industries after the war, new ways of encouraging foreign
capital. But they were farmers, eighty percent of them, and nothing, absolutely nothing, had been done to solve the ancient, the
basic problem of the soil: getting the land into the possession of
those who toiled upon it, quelling the arbitrary power of the landlords, relieving the peasants of their unbelievably crushing taxes.
Chiang would talk about a constitution after the war, complete
with parliament. They did not believe him, for they had no civil
rights whatsoever, and though the regime might be called a
"republic," they still struggled in the old, old morass of "fate, face,

and favor." They saw corruption in high places undiminished.
They saw their generals and political leaders grown dyspeptic
with overeating while famine was striking again and again and
thousands were dying by the roadsides.

In their controlled press they read over and over again glowing
praises of the leaders, written by starveling scribblers. They read
only of Japanese defeats and rarely of Japanese victories, and they
knew that the truth was withheld from them. They went to the
movies and saw over and over again pictures of the Generalissimo
receiving a medal or pinning a medal on somebody else. They saw
nothing, they read nothing, that was real and vital about their own
terrible problems of daily life. They heard day in and day out
the Three People's Principles of Sun Yat-sen, but it was a poor
substitute for food and clothing and freedom from Tai Li's brutal
secret police. The old slogans of the Kuomintang were fading
from the fence and farmhouse walls, and the Kuomintang didn't
even bother to think up new ones. It was all gone sterile. It was
simply the old story of Chinese leaders grown secure and fat and
callous. Chiang was not the heir of Sun Yat-sen. He was not a
Washington, nor a Juarez. He was not even a Vargas. He was a
Franco. This was counterrevolution, the betrayal and debasement
of a great movement for the freeing of men—the saddest spectacle
that history knows.

No wonder he feared and hated the Chinese Communists with
an unimaginable bitterness. They could not threaten his regime
physically, because they were too weak and few in number. But
even Kuomintang officials had admitted to me that the Communists had done great things for the people. There was spirit up
there, and enthusiasm; men worked and studied together in a
spirit of union and hope, and they faced the future with high
faith. This would spread eventually throughout awakening China
—unless Chiang stopped it. He could stop it by offering his people
something better. But the miserable truth was that up to now
he seemed intent on stopping it by force of arms. America had
great diplomatic authority in Chungking, and the Communists
looked kindly upon us. It was our duty to do our desperate best to
bring the two factions together in a coalition regime in which
each could learn from the other, save the people from civil blood-
shed, and together build a new China. It was my personal duty
to make Americans understand the true situation. I started for
home with high expectations, feeling that I had done my work

in fairness and as thoroughly as possible. I would have liked a
little more time—but events were pressing close and Americans
must have the background before something went wrong in the
Burma campaign or somewhere else.

My home for nine days was the tail section of the *Rangoon Ram-
bler*, which the public relations handout described as a "venerable
Liberator with fifty-six combat missions to her credit." The tail
section was a disordered nest of parachutes, sweaters, barracks
bags, and bedrolls. After Karachi the Sind desert faded behind
with its chasing that resembled the effect of a child's dragging
his careless fingers through the dust. The returning crew of air
warriors could not suppress their feeling, and a grin spread from
face to face. Sergeant Paak said: "I'm just going to watch India
fa-a-a-de away." Lieutenant Currie peered out of the window and
said: "And so we bid goodbye to bee-utiful, exotic India, land of
mystery and dys'ntery." All of these boys had had too much, over
Rangoon and the Car Nicobar Islands. Currie affected an easygoing manner, but sometimes he spoke fiercely in his sleep. Wilson
frankly wanted to be grounded and was trying to talk it out of
his system; that was his way. Once a bombardier had died in the
arms of Spotts, the navigator, and now Spotts on his last trip
navigated with relentless concentration, needling himself to get
it safely over. At the airbase near Basra, American boys in greasy
shorts were putting planes together for the Russians on a veritable
assembly line. They would carefully remove the cigarette butts to
avoid getting grease on their mouths, flip them away, and stare
a moment at us without saying anything. There is no breed exactly
like them; they can do anything. While we tried to sleep under
the hum of an air conditioner, an intense-looking pilot with dark
eyebrows that grew together was talking bitterly about the South
Atlantic jump. His buddy had gone down, and he didn't think
the search party had taken it seriously enough. Another boy who
was just discovering the awful gap between the war as the advertisements and the radio programs said it was, and the reality of it.
He had a phobia that somebody was trying to kill him by neglect.
Some never make the adjustment.

We rose over the beige-colored, serrated hills of the Holy Land.
There were all the Bible places, close together, neighborly, just
as they had seemed on the colored cards in my Sunday school
classes at Velva. The Dead Sea, Jericno without its walls, Galilee

and Jerusalem straight ahead. We circled over Jerusalem and
Bethlehem, and Spotts said that Jesus would look like an ant from
this high. The press agent lieutenant drove his elbow into my
ribs and pointed: "Mount of Olives! See the dome! Got footprint
of Christ there. FOOTPRINT OF CHRIST!" Salley went back
to the sleeping bag, and Knechtel was already immersed again in
a *Doc Savage* magazine. Around Cairo the buff-colored British
armored cars, the old tanks and rusted barbed wire, seemed like
props from an old film I had seen many times, getting yellow now
with age. From the rear the head of the Sphinx resembled a round
haystack the cows had rubbed. I caught a ride around the Pyramids
with some American soldiers in a jeep, and when a guide ran
flapping after us, the driver deliberately slowed down to encourage him and then speeded up whenever he drew near. They
knew the guide—too well. "Let's get the bastard good and tired
out," the driver said. There were crisscross marks on the desert
floor, but the desert had obviously borne the battle lightly. Mersa
Matruh, Salum, and Bardia passed by, looking from our distance
quite whole. Geoffrey had fought at Sidi Rezegh; now there were
only little squares and rectangles of dark brown; binoculars showed
them as masses of rusted planes, tanks, and trucks. None of the
boys slept through this. It caught their imaginations more than
anything else; this was something within their adult memories.
They had read about this when they were in high school, and my
friends were dying here. Here the blushing George Millar had
disappeared; where was he now?

At Tripoli, Wilson asked: "What is this state—Tripolania?" Captain Rote corrected him, and Wilson went on: "What are these
Halls of Montezuma?" Spotts said he thought they were in Peru
or Ecuador, and when I explained Wilson said: "Goddam, when
the war is over I want to get me a history book and just *read*. Be a
lot more interesting than it was in high school, now I've been
to all these places." Tripoli was blacked out, but the lovely white
buildings along the quay were gleaming under the full moon.
The hard heels of British patrols on the pavement sounded sharp
and loud. From cracks in the doors we could hear low, Italian
speech. There were lights on the black hulls of ships in the harbor,
and Currie said: "Baby, how'd you like to low-level that bunch?"
In the RAF club Rote looked at his watch and said the boys would
be getting briefed, just about now, for the trip to Rangoon.

At Marrakech Arabs pulled us into town in a cart behind a

tandem bike. We chewed almonds and drank good beer, and I could see that the Frenchmen looked shabby but that the women had somehow managed to remain neat and attractive, as French-women nearly always do. Currie carefully examined all the ped-dler's brocaded shoes and leather wallets, but in the end he handed them back and said: "That there ain't worth a diddlee-doo." He wanted one, but suffered from the American fear of being gypped.

The first half-hour over the water, out from Dakar, there were strong gasoline fumes even in the tail, and we could not smoke. I wore my yellow life vest, but the others didn't bother. By the time we sighted Natal I was halfway through Churchill's *Early Life*, observing that in all his pages about India he had never once mentioned the Indian people, how they lived, or what he thought about them. Obviously he didn't think about them at all.

Americans were wandering about the softly lighted city streets. I leaned against a fender with a corporal. Two girls about sixteen with arms interlocked swung to a stop in front of us and said something in Portuguese. The corporal replied with a contemp-tuous stare, and one said: "C'mere, dammit," which I imagined was the only English phrase they knew, and then flounced away. A dreamy Brazilian in a felt hat and torn sweater of barber-pole colors leaned over the plaster wall. "Senhorita bon," he informed us. The corporal said firmly: "Senhorita no bon." "Sí! Sí!" the man sadly protested. "They're all right," the corporal explained to me, "if they weren't all syphed up."

Over Devil's Island Salley and Paak and Scolovina were scrib-bling in their diaries, trying to catch up. Paak asked me to point out Dakar on the map, and then Marrakech. "Oh," he said in sur-prise, "I thought Marrakech was way back there in the middle." Salley told me he had kind of thought of writing a book about his experiences but supposed there would be too many guys writing about theirs. Knechtel said he wished he could write; he wished he were an intellectual, he said, like President Roosevelt.

Over the Caribbean toward Miami, Paak and Salley wadded up their greasy coveralls, flung them out of the hatch, and watched them flop foolishly toward the blue sea. Even in their new uni-forms the fliers still resembled mechanics, technicians, not really soldiers. Over the long white curve of Miami Beach, a United Airlines plane came along at our level. Scolovina, who had been standing stiffly at the hatch to avoid creasing his uniform, sud-denly shouted: "Zero at nine o'clock!" He bent his arms at the elbow, cocked his thumbs, pointed his forefingers at the transport, and went: "Ah-ah-ah-ah-ah," making a sound like a machine gun firing.

When I came down to the hotel lobby at four in the morning, the heavy-set Wilson, who had been feverish during most of the trip, was still sitting on the clerk's counter, trying to get his call through to Kentucky. It came. At the end of the conversation, he said: "I love you," his voice breaking in the middle of the sentence, so that the last word was merely a whisper.

5

It was almost exactly three years since my first return to America from the war zones. Then I had been filled with wonder, followed by a nagging indignation at the luxury, the easy living, the complacency. This time I stood in the soft lights of Fifth Avenue, listened to the polite murmur of small talk, watched the cool, lovely women in their smart clothes, and experienced a stealing sense of sensual pleasure and delight. The thing itself was not wicked; the wickedness lay only in the fact that others who deserved it did not have it. Again, one could not indict a whole people—not even for this. We alone of the great Allies were fighting a war a long distance from our home land; we alone were enjoying an economic boom in the midst of war, though we would one day pay for that. The truth was that, for the time being, most people at home were *better* off because of the war, and if hardships do things to the mind, so do comforts.

But there were little things that irritated sharply. Men's faces seemed so white and soft, the color and texture of bread, and clean jowls folded over white collars were somehow a repulsive sight. In the parlor cars between Washington and New York the faces of the businessmen seemed exactly alike. Fat, well-manicured fingers turned over the white pages of production documents, and the monotone went on—taxes, profits, taxes, profits. In the halls of Congress the brass spittoons remained where they had been, and the cigar-smoking men of the lobbies were again conniving for subsidies; everybody was trying to get his share of the pot. When people spoke of the war they seemed to think it would all be over in Europe by Christmas, because of the great headlines announcing the daily bombings of Berlin and Germany. Still seeking a quick, easy way out of it all.

The magazine advertisements made one laugh or made one furious. They always showed a clean-cut American youth with a movie star's face and a spotless uniform fighting in the Solomon Islands or Italy. Then followed a few crocodile tears in chic type about "our boys," a few gratuitous remarks about how we must all do our bit. And finally the coy little "plug" for whatever gadget it was—naturally the best obtainable, far better than anything the enemy had, which was also doing its bit for our boys. No blood, no eyeless faces. One got the impression that the little gadgets were doing it all and that only oil was being spilled. A nice, clean, streamlined, plastic, superheterodyne world-struggle, fought with spark-plugs and carburetors and directed by smartly dressed men with hair graying at the temples who manipulated the forces of democracy by tapping with sharp pencils on neat graphs hung around the walls of tastefully furnished, indirectly lighted offices. One gathered that the war had been taken over from Marshall, MacArthur, Eisenhower, & King by Batten, Barton, Durstine, & Osborn.

The reality and the suffering were there, but they were out of sight, back in the inside pages, within the curtained parlors of a growing number of families. Every day the letters came from mothers and wives: "The War Department reported John missing on August tenth somewhere in India. . . . I have been trying desperately to get more information. . . . I am sure you would remember him. He was five foot ten, with curly black hair. . . . His father is very much upset and has taken to his bed. . . . Please tell us what you can about John."

At Christmas time I was writing in my father's house in Minneapolis when a husky, almost inaudible voice on the telephone announced the speaker as the father of Lieutenant Charles Felix, who lay buried by the scorched piece of earth on the Patkoi Range. The father had not received my long letter from Chungking, but somehow he had followed my movements to Minnesota and had come up from Iowa in the night. His train had been stalled in a prairie blizzard for many hours without heat, and he had caught a terrible cold. He came directly from the station, his clothes wrinkled and his eyes bloodshot from weariness and worry. He had a wooden leg, the result of wounds in the last war. Charles had been his only child, and the snapshots showed him as a tall, handsome boy with an easy smile. (I had never seen the face before.) The father had been half-mad with sorrow and the torturing question: Why was my son the only one to die? I showed him the maps and tried to explain it all, so that he could set his mind a little at rest in the knowledge that his son had not been at fault himself, nor had anyone else, and that his son's courage and devotion to duty had helped to save us all from the Japanese. He breathed rapidly as he leaned over the maps and pictures and coughed into his handkerchief, his whole body racked with the effort. He rubbed his eyes with his fist, but I could not tell whether it was because of tears or of illness. I convinced him, I think, that his son had died instantly and had not suffered. When he understood this, his tense face relaxed a little and his body slumped back. He looked at his hands for a long time and said he knew what it was like from the first war. He knew that some boys had to go, but he had been praying that his son could get through it safely. He didn't mind about the unperfected C-46 airplanes, which these innocent boys had been ordered to fly. "No," he said, "I have no resentment about that. I know from the other war how those things happen. It is just a part of war." At the door he pressed my hand and said that I had no idea how much better he felt now. He could not stay, but must get back at once to his job, and he clumped heavily down the stairs, coughing into his handkerchief.

There was a faint carpet of fresh snow over the roofs and gardens on Christmas Eve. In all the windows down the street one could see the colored lights on the Christmas trees in the living-rooms and the sun porches. From my window I heard the tremulous voices of small girls singing "O Little Town of Bethlehem." The old custom: the children and the Christmas carols before each house. I heard a door open and the greetings: "Hi, Nancy! Hi, Lorraine!" There was peace here, and trust and love. There were clear eyes and firm bodies, gay voices and a welcoming of life. This was happiness; I had forgotten it existed. I had a deep desire to let go, to sink back to childhood beginnings, to recapture, if I could, something I had lost. But one can never do it; there is no going back. One can only go on with those of his own generation, living in his own time. It may not be forward; it may only be a wandering which will lead in the end to some way station that is not a home. And there is always the danger that one may so lose acquaintanceship with happiness that it can never be re-gained, even if a home is found. But there is no choice. Mine is a time without choices.

6

Now, I discovered, a reporter must not only travel, study, and risk his life to find the truth; he must also be a politician and a wire-puller before he is allowed to tell the truth. Important men in Washington had helped to get me to China to find the truth; now it appeared that equally important men in Washington had decided that the truth should not be`told. Men of the type who assayed Chinese-American relations on the basis of how well they themselves got along with the Chinese Ambassador over the teacups found that the truth caused them personal embarrassment. Let the public get along with half-truths; it was more comfortable that way.

A curious thing had happened. The article on China by Hanson Baldwin, which we had agreed upon before I left for China, was more than an "icebreaker." Baldwin had gone all out on the basis of local information only, and condemned China's war effort in general terms, without the concrete evidence. Chinese officials had created a diplomatic incident over this piece, and somebody in the State Department requested War Department censors to pass nothing on China by war correspondents without the sanction of State. My original article was killed outright. I rewrote it slightly, in view of the Cairo conference, which had occurred in the meantime. The piece had the support of the War Department's intelligence officer in charge of Chinese affairs; it had the support of nearly all the men in the Far Eastern division of the State Department; but the head of the division, who had not visited China for years, was against it. I trudged back and forth and saw a dozen influential men in their offices and homes. All agreed I was right; almost none of them was willing to "go out on a limb" in the interests of truth. I tried to convince the State Department press chief that the War Department was bound to let them down one day, for there would be setbacks in China and for the War Department's own self-defense it would have to let people know why these occurred. He agreed with me, but nothing happened. Just before I was to sail in a convoy for Algiers, I had the promised support of an Assistant Secretary of War: he would put pressure on the Secretary. Two other friends would take the matter to the Secretary of State. Confident that the article would be passed, I departed from Washington. Weeks later in Italy I learned that the whole thing had been suppressed.

The aftermath is history now:

Stilwell's American-trained Chinese did an excellent job in helping to reconquer northern Burma, while the Japanese crossed through the southern regions of the Naga Hills all the way to the Brahmaputra, to be liquidated by a British army which, at long last, moved with aggressive efficiency. The Nagas performed beautifully as agents and informers for the Allies.

Kweilin, Lingling, and the other advanced bases in southeastern China were lost, just as Stilwell had feared they might be—something that Chennault had discounted. Chiang's troops put up a poor show.

Stilwell's tenuous relations with Chiang broke down, partly over the issue of arming the Communist forces who wanted to fight the Japanese, and Stilwell was recalled. Ambassador Gauss resigned. The back-slapping Patrick Hurley arrived as Ambassador, dismissed John Davies, Jack Service, and the other young men who really loved and understood China, and tried to settle the deep-rooted Kuomintang-Communist troubles with a twist of his own hand. He failed, and then threw all support to Chiang with no questions asked. This support encouraged Chiang to resort to outright warfare, and, as this is written,* internal peace for China is still in doubt.

And, of course, the very thing we had all tried to prevent came quickly to pass with the recall of Stilwell: the swollen bladder of hypocrisy broke, and American public opinion swung to the opposite extreme of condemning Chungking with all the vigor with which it had praised before.

For me there was small satisfaction in having been right and my opponents wrong. There was a little more satisfaction when I learned later that my fight in Washington had weakened the opposition to the extent that when Teddy White of *Life* and others returned they *were* able to tell the truth.

It is rather extraordinary how men must plot and combine and negotiate merely to tell the truth. It always comes out somewhere, some time. Always. But sometimes it comes too late.

* January, 1946.

Chapter XII

In January it seemed clear that 1944 would be the year of climax in Europe. The Russians were pressing the Germans steadily back over the longest front in the history of warfare; Rome lay under threat of becoming the first enemy capital to fall; in England a tremendous force was gathering for one of the most dangerous direct assaults ever contemplated, which could not possibly be delayed. It was likely that this would also be the year of decision in Europe. I obeyed a strong emotional compulsion to return and see the end, to find out what had happened in the middle acts, and to try to gain a clue to the future of the European civilization, whose contemporary condition and meaning I had just begun to understand when I departed from Lisbon in that autumn of continental collapse and degradation.

The Pennsylvania Station was crowded with uniforms and encumbered with barrack bags and foot lockers bearing the stenciled identifications of innocent American boys—the names and the numbers. They were born as names and would die as numbers. Their destiny was neatly stated, without a smudge. There were long, crushing kisses with the women and fumbling, embarrassed handshakes with the fathers and brothers. In the train for the Virginia port they looked straight ahead into the necks in front, seeing nothing, or stared out of the window at the fields and hamlets, seeing nothing. In this moment they were possessed by vivid recollections of the past and vague imaginings of a climactic future. I was thinking only of this night's trip, of how I would manage to sleep upright in the seat, of the exact process by which I would get out to my ship; I realized how different I had become from these others, how easily I accepted departures and distant arrivals.

The Liberty ship *Thomas B. Reed* was standing well off shore in the vast gathering of other vessels which would be formed into a convoy for Casablanca, Algiers, Sicily, and Naples. When the

Coast Guard boat drew alongside, the first assistant engineer was still working on the motor of the captain's lifeboat, still sweating and cursing over it as he had been when I first saw the ship at the Brooklyn pier. They were rather surprised to see me reboard the *Reed*, and took it as a good omen. For the *Reed* seemed to be a ship under evil auspices, marked for more than its quota of troubles. These had already begun when I first boarded the ship in Brooklyn. Stevedores had loaded part of the cargo quite wrong; several crew members had violated the captain's orders and slipped ashore, hand over hand on a rope, for a last spree, which angered and frustrated those who had obeyed instructions. Various vital pieces of machinery would not work properly, although this was a new ship. The lifeboat engine was hopeless. The chief engineer had been fired on the eve of sailing for being drunk. Every one of the youthful deckhands was merely an apprentice seaman (some had never been to sea before), except the twenty-one-year-old bo'sun who tried to discipline the boys but couldn't quite make it. At the first lowering drill with the lifeboats the Coast Guard inspector had thrown up his hands in disgust. They simply didn't know how. Then, ten minutes after putting out from the pier, the *Reed* ran onto a submerged mud bank just off Staten Island and remained there three exasperating days, unresponsive to the tugs' efforts until the wind changed. Thus she missed connections with her convoy and was obliged to wait for the next to form up. So delayed, she was ordered to Caven Point, where we took on some thirty tons of TNT, causing one of the assistant engineers to jump ship, while I went ashore to live in comfort in New York until I was sure the vessel really would sail from somewhere.

The skipper was a husky, intense, and ambitious man of twenty-seven, and the *Reed*, which he had bossed on two or three previous trips, was his first command. The fifty or so Navy boys on the guns, most of whom were making their first trip to sea, were under the command of a young ensign, an income-tax collector just emerged from the Navy training school. One of the engineers, a charming, snow-haired man, was sixty-six, making his first trip since he had retired from the sea twenty years before. Altogether it was a not unusual collection for the American Merchant Marine in the third year of war. The cargo fleet had undergone a rapid, forced expansion, and too many thousands of the old veterans had already been drowned. The convoys did move, the materials of war did arrive where they were needed, and perhaps the end results justified the means. But the arrangement set up a poisonous relationship between the Navy men and the merchant sailois. The Navy boys, no younger and no older, no different in any respect from the merchant sailors, were under strict discipline and received a static income of fifty dollars a month. The other lads got two hundred a month including their "war bonus," received an extra five dollars for every day their ship was in the Mediterranean "danger zone," and had more pay every time a bomb dropped anywhere near, to say nothing of their "overtime." When the ship reached port they were free to go ashore and carouse as they wished and to jump the ship for a better one when they returned home with hundreds of dollars in their pockets. Most of them in both groups were well-meaning youngsters; their task was essentially the same. But since few were able to grasp the war's great meaning, there was no union among them, no comradeship, and the small matters of their personal conditions drove them apart until they became almost like enemies. What the consequences of organizational disunity could be I was to learn quickly and in extraordinary fashion.

I was put into the radio operator's cabin on the bridge deck while "Sparks" was moved in to share the deck cadet's room next door. I arranged my books and effects and looked forward to a pleasant cruise in the Gulf Stream, determined not to think about the TNT in the hold near me or the fact that our torpedo nets could not be lowered because of the landing craft we carried as deck cargo. Shortly before twilight on what was to be our last day before sailing, a small launch drew alongside, and the captain and the Navy ensign returned from the final convoy conference on shore. I had become friends with Matthews, the young skipper, but I noticed that, as he handed me a roll of charts to free his hands for vaulting the rail, he gave me only a fleeting smile in welcome, Irwin, the ensign, went silently to his quarters on the boat deck. I was sitting at my desk, just laying out an Italian grammar for study, when I heard angry voices at the bottom of the iron stairs almost directly below my cabin. I heard the captain mounting the stairs, shouting back to someone to "come topside" at once. Then I heard him descending again after a few moments. There was a commotion below, a door banged, and I looked out in time to see the captain vaulting up the steps. His face was white and set. He whipped past my door and dived into his own cabin, slamming the door behind him.

I closed my books and stood uncertainly in my doorway, wondering what on earth was going on. I was about to descend the
steps when Sparks, a tall, handsome youngster, appeared and
motioned me back into the cabin. He sat down and mopped his
forehead, which streamed with perspiration. "Look," he said, holding up his hands, "I'm shaking." We were in an astonishing predicament. It appeared that the ensign had requested that the skipper
show him all coded messages during the voyage, since he, the
ensign, was a communications officer as well as the protection
officer. Matthews, I was told, had answered that he would show
Irwin only those messages which directly concerned him. The
argument had not been settled at the convoy conference, and on
the way out to the ship the two young men had had another
squabble about the matter. Both were very young, ambitious,
acutely conscious of their responsibilities, and jealous of what they
conceived to be their rights and duties. Matthews was an ebullient, two-fisted man; Irwin, although he appeared very quiet, even
timid, was also a man of determination and courage.

After they had returned, unspeaking, from the conference, the
skipper went to the ensign's room and they quarreled again. Then
he had ordered Irwin to come topside. When, instead, he sent word
that the captain could come to see him if he wished to talk,
Matthews had dashed downstairs, burst in, and—according to the
story—smashed Irwin in the jaw. The ensign came to his feet
with a pistol in his hand and gave the captain five seconds to get
topside before he killed him. At this moment the captain was shut
in his own cabin, probably arming himself, while Irwin was arming
his navy crew, who were spreading throughout the ship. One, with
a rifle in his hand, was even standing guard over the galley. Now
some of the merchant crew were going to their own quarters and
slipping pistols into their pockets. This was absurd and mad. It
was also deadly dangerous. One or more murders seemed inevitable
unless something were done, and of course with one stray shot
through the cargo hold we would all be blown into nothingness.
And the *Reed* had to sail at dawn.

I was the only neutral on board, but I had no idea what to
attempt. I didn't know who was right and who was wrong, or
whether this was mutiny or civil war. It grew dark in the passage-
ways, and the only lights were the red lanterns that hung from the
bulkheads. In the dark the silence was ominous. I found myself,
as I had in the moments of crisis aboard the airplane in August,

scribbling notes on the progress of events, a reflex action that gave my hands and mind something to do:

"8:30 P.M.—They say the ensign is in his room with a rifle across his knee challenging all comers. Captain in his cabin also challenging anybody. They say ensign's hand is shaking on the gun and that he will fire on slightest provocation. If either or both have lost their heads it will be bad. . . . Few minutes ago the captain tried to signal with lights from the bridge to the shore, asking for help. Apparently ensign came to bridge and drove captain into his cabin and is now signaling himself. Should I try to talk them into sensible state of mind? Boys don't think it will do slightest good.

"8:45 P.M.—No results from signaling except the answer: 'To whom is this message addressed?' That makes everything lovely. Sparks wants to open up with radio, call for help, but rules forbid it when in convoy position like this. He could get into serious trouble if authorities take a poor view of it. Some of merchant boys determined jump ship if we do not sail. Fed up. . . . I went gingerly down steps to boat deck, glimpsed dark figure which pulled back behind bulkhead corner. As I reached deck, gun shoved in my face. It was the ensign. I so startled could hardly say anything. Finally managed to say I was sorry about this. He says he is too, but says he should have killed skipper, that he would have been in right if he had. Obviously impossible for me to pacify him; he is no longer white and shaking but in a cold fury. . . . Few minutes ago ensign drove captain off bridge again at the point of gun. It is very dark out on open deck, can hear scuffling of navy boys' feet as they patrol with their damned rifles. Moon is becoming full now.

"9:10 P.M.—I went in to see the captain. He seemed to regret that the journalist aboard should know about all this; I said I couldn't help it when I run into a pistol at every corner. Captain denies he hit the ensign. 'This is a plain case of mutiny,' he says. 'The Navy radio operator came to the bridge apparently heading for radio room, and captain ran out, ordered him downstairs. I walked to my cabin, carefully whistling to avoid being mistaken for one of the belligerents. Captain has been peering around bulkhead watching stairs; believe he has a gun all right. When I looked out he whispered: 'You better get inside your room, Mr. Sevareid.' My room is right in no man's land. I am keeping all my lights on to establish my neutrality.

"9:30 P.M.—Sparks has taken the plunge and opened up on the radio asking immediate armed help. Situation more tense than ever. Every time anybody takes a step now somebody challenges in nervous voice: 'Who's that?'

"9:35 P.M.—Can hear code going out on radio, only sound in dark corridor. Sparks has strapped on his gun now. Second mate, who affects a droll view of situation, is rolling the cylinder in his revolver. Don't like all these belligerents in my room. MacDonald, the first mate, is down in the saloon, drinking his nightly coffee, not frightened, just contemptuous of the whole miserable affair. Why in name of Christ don't captain and ensign at least agree to disarm their own men? I should have negotiated that at least. . . . Ensign on bridge again with three armed men. Second mate poked his head out there and said 'Boo!' and almost got shot. He takes less amused view now. Why doesn't that boat come?

"10:10 P.M.—Now a small boat is circling us, carefully playing a searchlight over the deck and on the antiaircraft guns. Maybe they think enemy saboteurs trying to take over the ship or something. I am getting fed up, exhausted. Almost feel like leaving ship if I have a chance.

"10:30 P.M.—The kid deck cadet got to the Coast Guard officer first and led him around deck, up to captain's cabin, avoiding the ensign who back in his own room. Sparks now worried he will lose his license for opening up with war signals. Apparently Navy radio boy tried to break into radio room. Now Sparks hates to sail with *him*. I sat awhile with Matthews. He is tiring out, held his handsome blond head in his hands and said: 'I *never* have trouble the way I have the last few days. I always prided myself on a smooth-running ship. The ensign has nothing at stake. He's a tax collector by trade. I have worked all my life to be a master. I have too much at stake, too much at stake. I should have bluffed him out. I guess I wasn't man enough.' I told him that if he had tried he probably would not be alive. Coast Guard officer down talking with the ensign.

"Midnight—Everyone feeling nervous exhaustion. Some must begin watches in three hours' time. I have been sitting with the captain, we drinking my Portuguese brandy. Helped him steady his nerves. Then Coast Guard officer returned to captain's room. Excellent mediator type, big, slow-talking man, kind you trust at once. Apparently Matthews had charged ensign was insane. The officer says: 'Naturally, the ensign has his side of the story, too.

Don't think he's out of his mind, exactly.' Grins at skipper. 'Maybe he's a little paranoid or whatever it is. I'm afraid there are big gaps in my psychiatric training.' I left them alone.

"1 A.M.—I am going to turn in. Ensign has been taken off the ship and the kid petty officer put in charge of the navy crew. One Navy boy with gun left guarding door to ensign's office which apparently filled with Navy documents he supposed to take overseas. Few minutes ago captain went to the door but was stopped by the guard. Captain in rage at being balked again, boy says: 'I have to take orders from the navy, sir,' sounding as if he almost in tears. Last thing I have heard is the sound of somebody clicking his revolver cylinder. Too tired to care what that means."

When I awoke, it was broad day, the engines were vibrating, the sailors were sitting peacefully on the deck in their shirtsleeves, and the Virginia coast was merely a black hairline on the horizon. The *Reed* occupied the "coffin corner" of the convoy.

There were lovely days in the Gulf Stream, and there were days of heavy seas when the ship, topheavy with its deck cargo and cement gun·emplacements, rolled sickeningly from side to side. On such days there was no repose even inside one's cabin, where everything movable came alive. The ash tray would leap off the desk and plunge into the wastebasket, which would gently capsize, spilling papers, apple peelings, and ashes on the floor. The electric fan on the wall would swing from side to side as though in steady operation; the books would lean this way, then that, and the tinkling bottles in the medicine cabinet would huddle together in one corner, then race in a group for the other corner. The keys hanging on a nail marked a crescent on the wall as they swung, the towels moved out of reach as I stretched my hand toward them, the chair glided noiselessly across the room, and the carpet rolled itself into a neat bundle. Many of the youthful seamen took to their bunks, quite ill.

There was gale in the night, and the mates, wearing life preservers over their oilskins, peered constantly through the spray, not daring to take their eyes from the dim riding light of the preceding ship. Sometimes they would discover that ship off on our side and sometimes directly under our bow, when bells would be rung and frantic orders shouted to avoid collision. In the moments of sheet lightning whitecaps showed on the turbulent sea, and the dark hulks of the ships in convoy seemed like pachyderms moving in a herd, ponderously silent save when one trumpeted huskily in alarm. But in the dawn they were always there, stretching in ragged rows as far as one could see, making the horizon appear an inhabited shoreline with chimneys emitting peaceful smoke.

Reports came that submarines were to be expected. The convoy ahead—the one we had missed because of the delay on the mud bank—was attacked, and the one before that was bombed in the Mediterranean. But during the warm, lazy days it was impossible to feel apprehension; it was hard to realize that blue Teutonic eyes were probably watching us through a periscope, waiting for a ship to fall behind. My cabin with the books, the Italian lessons, the old clothes, became an accepted, permanent background. Dishes rattled below in the galley; one could hear the slapping of playing cards, the laughter of the young boys, and the quiet voice of the captain instructing the deck cadet in navigation. There were nights when we followed a carpet of moonbeams, straight into the full moon ahead. The bow lifted slowly and settled into the heap of pearls, crushing and scattering them with deliberate monotony, and the dark warm water, streaked with phosphorus, gushed and hissed along the steel walls, to be mixed and treated by the propeller at the stern and then spread behind, a coating of thick white paint on the floor of the sea.

Sometimes in the evening I sat in the darkened chart room with the radio earphones on my head. As the moon thinned, the voices of Europe began to reach us across the sea. Big Ben sounded deep and strong in my ears, and when the clear, decent tones of the BBC announcer came, old feelings of respect and love for England returned with a rush. It was the true voice of England; and the voices that followed from the Algiers radio were the true voices of France, rhythmical, somehow artificial, rising and falling in the old oratorical manner, but still France. The endless "press review," repetitious comment about comment as before. Was it still a house of words? Then came the "personal messages," from those fighting on the outside, trying to send their words to those they loved who were still imprisoned in the silent house of France: "Robert is well and happy and embraces Mamma, Papa, and Anna in France. *Courage! Confiance!*" The neutral ether distributed the small cries of encouragement from sea to sea as well as from heart to private heart; shamelessly I eavesdropped, felt the approach of tears, and called myself a fool.

The day came when a seagull appeared, followed by a flying boat which circled out from Casablanca. Around four the next morning the captain urged me out of bed; I stumbled to the bridge to behold the slice of orange moon, resting on a jet-black hump to the right, which was Africa, revealing a low mass to the left which was Europe. Three days later Algiers appeared as a creamy crescent resting in the hollows of soft green hills which gave way to distant peaks tufted with snow.

2

Few wayside cities have lived through such a turbulent cycle in a brief span as had Algiers. It had been in turn a prosperously indolent resort, a refuge for fleeing anti-Fascists, then their prison, a headquarters for French Fascists, a source of wealth for the enemy who impoverished the place, an uneasy nest for spies and agents from both sides, eventually a plotting den for insurgent conspirators, then briefly a beachhead and battleground. Now, shabby, unclean, living from hand to mouth, it was a half-forgotten Allied headquarters far behind the fighting lines, and the government seat of a few young, strong Frenchmen who planned here the resurrection of the motherland. Through it all the natives and the middle-class French colonists had been unmoved from their emotional and political dead center of unbelief. They cared not a whit for the war and very little for France and waited now only for prices to go down, comforts to return, and the strangers to return whence they came.

Young French "drugstore cowboys" were still in evidence with their narrow-brimmed hats, their wide, knotted ties, their gloves with the cuffs turned back, but all the edges were frayed, and the faces were more pinched than ever. The women wore woolen stockings to a point just below the knee; the only ones with silk were the whores of the Aletti Hotel bar, who got two thousand francs from each soldier customer and were the richest wage-earners in the city. People huddled on the café terraces because they had nothing to do, and for the first time in generations one could sit in a French café without ordering anything. In small, cold theaters orchestras played old American hit tunes, the players garbed in soiled white coats, their jowls dark from lack of shaving soap and razors. In the night Allied soldiers sang loudly in the streets, screamed obscenities at the girls, and fought one another. Merchant mariners stole the sheets from the ship bunks and sold them to the natives for a thousand francs apiece with which to buy "champagne"—which was only *vin mousseux*—at three hundred francs the bottle. Or they stuck the money into the brassieres and girdles of the fat and ugly Arab dancers in the smoky, stench-filled Kasbah cellars, where they yelled at the "sketches *inédits*." They staggered back toward their ships at midnight, remembering (if they were not too drunk) to carry pistols in their hands in order to avoid attack by Arab males. (My friend Sparks was slugged and the eighteen-year-old deck cadet suffered a broken skull.)

Above the meaningless tumult and the shabby half-life, in a cold, barren school on the high hill, were the young men who sat in their overcoats and planned the new French Republic. In the anterooms unshaven soldiers scribbled my name in the old-time civil service ledgers, with the same scratchy pens and purple ink. That was depressingly the same—but the faces behind the desks were not, nor the words they said nor the determined purpose in their breasts. I saw many of them: Tixier, Bonnet, Mendes-France, Menthon, Philippe, and the young Plevin who would not forget that I had been the first journalist to come to see him when he arrived in Washington as the first official emissary from De Gaulle in the days when Washington scorned De Gaulle. These men were planning the re-entry to France, laying out plans for the quick establishment of firm justice in each town to avert civil war, the reorganization of the banks and trusts and of the corrupt newspapers which had helped ruin France, the rebuilding of the trade unions, the reconstruction of the factories and railroads. Already they were making long-range plans for a more democratic educational system, with subsidies for the workers' children, for woman suffrage, new electoral laws, and stronger and more stable legislative and executive organs. It was not revolution that they planned; it was merely the tying up of disastrously loose ends, merely calculated progress, which in our time is necessarily in the leftward direction. They told me everything, because, no doubt, they knew my feelings, but they could not always hide their bitterness toward the Americans. For despite De Gaulle's achievement in taking over from the American-made mess of Darlan and Giraud, despite all their intensive planning, they could not get official assurance from the major Allies that it would be their group, and not others with Vichy connections, who would be allowed to establish control

behind the troops. The day for invasion was coming near; if the
Allies entered France and tried to deal with Vichy, there would
be civil war. If they tried to run French affairs themselves, there
would be chaos. It was a shocking situation, and I tried to explain
it as objectively as possible on the radio. I could not feel neutral
inside myself. What was the matter with the American diplomats?
Why this long, miserable history of dealing with the Pétains,
Weygands, Darlans, and Girauds? All the endless, oversubtle
arguments about "practical approach" and "expedients" which had
confused the American people. With very few moments of doubt,
I and my friends had known from that day years before in London, when De Gaulle paraded his handful, that he and his group
were bound to win out in the end, that a liberated France could
accept no others. It was the old phenomenon of men who had
cleverness but not wisdom, who became lost in a labyrinth of
"facts" and "policies," who felt no touch of history's inevitable
movements, who miscalculated the wishes of the ordinary man
because they did not understand him.

Before proceeding to the Italian war fronts I spent a few days
in Cairo, where Lois, one of the first women sent out from the
States on this monumental task, was helping to organize relief
missions for the Balkans under the United Nations Relief and
Rehabilitation Administration. All the Balkan countries were in
political ferment; monarchical and democratic groups were
maneuvering for future power. The high-minded men and women,
who wanted to save the suffering masses of peoples, had no wish
that the food, clothing, and medicine should become a political
weapon for one side or the other. But it was impossible to see how
this could be avoided, and the problem here was another impressive demonstration of the universal fact that politics is life, everywhere in our time, that it is affected by everything and affects
everything, even the hunger of a child. These groups of welfare
people worked strenuously to create a functioning system (Lois's
remarkable energy gave out eventually, and she was hospitalized);
but even an international organization that asks nothing but the
privilege of giving meets with extraordinary difficulties, simply
because it must work through nationals, using the funds, agencies,
and equipment of individuals and institutions which owe national
allegiance only. The painful progress made in Cairo by this group
responding to a higher vision and a new sovereignty provided a
sharp premonition of the obstacles lying in the way of world

government, of the basic readjustment of men's minds that will be required.

If all men are brothers, still all are alone and never to be entirely explored in their separate minds; if all must dwell in this one small house, still each must have his own room inviolate, and cherished private habits and dreams must suffer no rude invasion. We dwelt near the Pyramids, just off the main road in an enclosure of calla lilies, roses, sweet peas, and bougainvillaea. If one stepped through the ivy-clad fence to the rear, he was in the ancient, unchanged land of the Egyptians. A graceful minaret rose from the village of mud walls, the men and women in black gowns squatted in the fields, kneading the lumpy earth as they have done for centuries, while the little barefoot boys tugged at their donkeys and showed their white teeth in greeting. If one looked to the front he saw the stream of rushing limousines, the army trucks of the foreigners, the garish dancing palaces of the foreigners. Each world flowed around and above the other; they had nothing in common, and their inhabitants were eternal strangers. This, surely, was not the way to the world's unity; from this way no common life of understanding would ever spring.

I flew back along the sandy continental rim, past Carthage, over Mount Etna, across the Straits of Messina, skirting eternal Pompeii and Vesuvius to land on the broken airfield of Naples, realizing as I progressed that my memory would be forever caught and confused in a telescoping of history. The original set of images sprang from classic story, the other from present events. Antony at Alexandria was obscured by a British battleship; G.I.s swam off Carthage seeking relaxation—not Matho in search of Salammbô; Ulysses in the Straits was all mixed up with a convoy of Liberty ships trailing fat balloons. It would be like the two pictures of my own native village—the dreamy vision from childhood and the sharp projection of maturity, and certainty would be always blurred by the overlapping montage.

It was mid-March, and a cold wind stole through the glassless windows along the Naples waterfront; the people drew their rags closely about them, pushed unseeing through the masses of Allied soldiery on the Via Roma and grubbed endlessly among the soiled knickknacks on the venders' stands. "A pigsty in Paradise," one colleague called Naples. The sea and snow-topped Vesuvius were clean, the vineyards were orderly and fresh, but in the old city which the war had side-swiped in passing, faces and bare feet

were soiled, even the children appeared grimed and aging, and
only the apples spread before the patient crones were polished
and bright. This crowded ghetto of fair Italy accepted the Allies and
defeat as it had accepted Fascism and victory, crisis and the Nazis
—with a shrug of the shoulders, with hand outstretched. To the
newcomers it offered a view, fish, and disease, and hardly bothered
to make up its mind whether they were liberators or conquerors—
partly because the newcomers themselves did not know, acting one
role one day and the other the next. Climbing the dusty stairs in
the press building I looked for a moment through an open door
into a private apartment. A demobilized Italian soldier, shirtless
and unshaved, wearing the trousers of his once proud uniform,
was practicing on his violin. On the wall hung the oval portrait
of father or grandfather, looking stern, his breast covered with
medals. A young son or brother of the violinist sat on the piano
bench, tapping time with American army shoes to the nostalgic
strains. I was to see another side of Italian manhood later on,
farther north, but at the moment this seemed to tell the whole
story of these modern descendants of the Caesars.

On the day of my arrival a convoy of trucks bumped along the
broken pavements past the park of headless statues. Each truck
was filled with soldiers, and recognizing the red bull insignia on
their sleeves I realized that this was the Thirty-fourth Division,
the men from my native Northwest region, whom I had last seen
in Louisiana engaged in mock warfare. They were on their way
to the ships to be unloaded again on the famous and bloody Anzio
beachhead. They had changed; their faces were empty and their
practiced bodies rolled loosely from side to side, absorbing the jolts.

This was a period of disillusionment with the whole Italian campaign, and a deep cynicism about the competence of the highest-
ranking officers had set in among combat troops. We were stopped
before Cassino, along the Garigliano River line, and after a narrow
escape from being thrust back into the sea at Anzio, we were
stolidly "taking it" while slowly preparing for the big push. The
Salerno landings had been messed up, and the ranking strategists
who had been convinced that the Germans would not put up a
fight for southern Italy found themselves to be tragically mistaken.
They could not seem to understand the psychology of the opposition and, believing that the Germans would pull back to Rome
or beyond, they ordered the Anzio landing, which turned out to
be a bloody ambush for the Allied troops. At the time of my arrival

the army publicity and propaganda machine, now grown to bewildering proportions, was glorifying individual heroes ("Commando Kelly," who dozed in a corner of the broadcast studio, I
took at first to be the kid private who swept up the place) and
otherwise trying to build morale and divert the soldiers' minds.
But conversations with combat men in the bars or rest centers
almost invariably took on a bitter tone as they discussed the crossing of the Rapido River by the Thirty-sixth Division, an action
which the divisional general had pleaded against with tears and
in which many hundreds of men had been mown down without a
chance. Or they told one about the Volturno River action in November, when men of the Thirty-fourth had been stupidly driven
to their death in a night advance through one of the thickest German mine fields ever ventured over. As the mines flashed off, the
Germans poured artillery fire into the flat stretch of ground, and
the men screamed and died. Some went out of their heads and
ran blindly forward shrieking curses upon the enemy, to perish in
shattering explosions. A few men of bravery beyond all words are
said to have led their comrades, crawling on hands and knees so
that they would catch the mine bursts in their bellies and save
those behind them. But—though reporters were not then permitted
to tell this part of it—some two hundred men had refused to enter
the mine field. They were not cowards; they were simply worn
out, and nothing—not even disgrace and imprisonment for years
—seemed so bad to them as what they were ordered to do. There
were investigations, and stony-faced officers who in this modern
age still believe in the "glories" of warfare sentenced some and
threatened others with execution.

None, so far as I know, was ever executed for "cowardice." Although he would not say so himself, I believe the main deterrent
to have been the decent instincts and brilliant legal mind of an
uncle of mine, Lieut. Colonel John Hougen, my mother's brother.
"Uncle John," who had always been something of a hero to my
brothers and me, was a Minnesota lawyer, a tall man with a strong,
handsome face, who had the greatest gift for friendship I think I
have ever known. He had been a trusted confidant of Governor
Floyd Olson, who once offered him an appointment to the United
States Senate. John had refused it, as he had refused the state
attorney-generalship, a full professorship at the University, a federal judgeship, and various other offers, content to roam the north
woods, and happy most of all in his job as attorney and protector

of the Chippewa Indians. He had been judge advocate for the Thirty-fourth Division since before the war began and had borne all the hardships of the front lines despite his fifty years. To him these soldiers remained the innocent sons of the farmers and businessmen he knew, doing their best in a bloody business, and officers told me how his smiling, persuasive manner had saved many youngsters from irreparable injustice at the hands of various little Napoleons. As the turbulent months wore on, I was to become more and more aware of the valuable function of these graying reserve officers—lawyers, doctors, judges, and teachers—who provided a leaven of thoughtful humanitarianism among yeasty professional officers. They remained a civilizing influence in the midst of a brutalizing process.

3

Pious Italians thought it was God's vengeance; some others believed that it was the unprecedented bombing at Cassino which disturbed the deep fissures of the earth beneath Vesuvius; whatever the cause, the result was something never seen before by the oldest inhabitants. It had begun in the late afternoon, but it was not until Naples lay shrouded in its blackout that we really saw the incredible sight. First we became aware of the people on the roof tops and a pink glare between the buildings. When our jeep reached the water-front drive, there it was. You could not see Vesuvius mountain itself; what you saw was a perpendicular river of fire, curving down in the form of an inverted question mark. It seemed to hang in the sky without visible support, unless this might be the great fat mushroom of white smoke spreading out under the stars, to which the golden stream appeared to be attached like a Gargantuan umbilical cord. To the northeast one could see faint flashes of fire. *That* was Cassino and man-made fire, which could not hold a candle to this transaction of the elements.

I set out in the morning with several officers, a truckload of signal corps soldiers, a mile of wire, and a recording machine, in an effort to record the deep coughing of the world's most famous volcano from somewhere near the cone. We passed down the autostrada and began climbing the narrow, rutted road up the mountain, through the sparse villages of stone and stucco. There were patches of green where vegetables grew upon ancient lava which had returned to the earth and become fertile. The fig trees were white with their winter look, but the oranges were already fat among their bright leaves. Peasants toiled in the climbing vineyards to produce the wine called "Lacrima Christi," the "tears of Christ," and they seemed oblivious to the billowing black clouds on the summit. The little boys ran out from their gates shouting *caramelle* or *cigarette.* They were not really expecting candy or tobacco; it was more like shouting "good morning." We jolted upwards and entered a wasteland of frozen black lava which came from centuries past. To our left we could see a long arrow of white smoke slowly moving down the valley. This was the river of lava which burned bright red at night. It was already in the outskirts of the distant, brightly painted town of San Sebastiano, and a tributary of smoking lava was flowing inexorably toward the big country villa of some wealthy family.

We came to a stone house and a chain across the road. A man trotted out, holding up a printed card which informed us that we must take one of the official guides, according to custom. This was a little like holding the concession for the best view of Hades. So a grumbling graybeard, anxious for advance payment, clung to the side of our jeep as we ascended to Hell. We learned that the funicular railway was half buried already, and its station on the top consumed. Soon not even a jeep could go farther, since a stream of lava a hundred yards wide and five feet high had moved across the road. The big black cinders were cold on the top layer, but down inside the clinkers glowed pink, and we breathed sulphurous fumes as we dashed across.

Then it was a steep climb up sandy shale for an hour until we reached part of the 1906 crater and made our own trail over masses of cold lava heaped in a thousand weird shapes. They were like coils of blackened rope or convoluted piles of quickly frozen molasses, intersticed with streamers of dirty snow. We were very near the erupting cone, but the summit was enclosed in smoke and mist. The explosions were almost deafening now. We climbed on, but the old guide remained behind, and between the roarings of Vesuvius we could hear him, almost in tears, shouting: "Gentlemen, no farther, please! I am the responsible. The risk of the life! The risk of the life!" We stopped. We stopped because a boulder suddenly appeared out of the mist high above us, arched in our direction, and fell with a great clumping sound not thirty yards away, scattering a thousand burning fragments like shrapnel.

The mist closed in further, it began to rain, and pellets of hail cut our faces and necks as we vainly sought shelter in the rocks. Men twenty feet away vanished from sight, and one felt alone and awestruck as the mountain coughed and the enormous rock formation shook beneath one's feet. We endured this for an hour, when suddenly there was blue sky, the valley, and the curving harbor of Naples below. But it was the spectacle above which one will never forget. We were perhaps fifteen hundred feet below and away from the rim. There would come first a faint white flash in the sky above the mouth, a reflection of the bursting caldron down inside. Then a mighty roar. Then black smoke billowed high. Then out from the smoke came a geyser of particles, black as bits of mud against the sky, growing in size and turning fiery red as they cascaded down the ravines. To our left, a hundred yards away, was a river of fire into which the crater was vomiting. It moved rapidly down the steep slope, enormous red boulders swimming in what resembled liquid fire. The river itself was strangely quiet, only hissing and rustling like the crepitation in a forest of leaves. We worked for an hour, trying to record the voice of Vesuvius. Then there was a greater explosion than usual, and in a moment two great chunks landed like dud bombs *behind* us, and we departed without standing upon the order of our going.

Down the mountainside curious visitors were loitering among daisies and buttercups, pitching snowballs into the lava river and sticking green twigs into the flow for a light to their cigarettes.

In an hour we came to San Sebastiano, a young city born only in 1886 and already dead now in March, 1944. Her memory will not be that of Pompeii, a classical tragedy, nor her ruins so stately, but San Sebastiano al Vesuvio remained none the less a place of heartbreak. A cold rain was drenching what remained of the town. American military police in white helmets directed a sad traffic at the corner of the Via Luigi Palmieri. The people had given up. Their priests had taken the plaster statues of their saints out of the church and placed them before the advancing river of fire: But the saints, with their raised hands, could not or would not halt the avalanche, which here on the gentler slope had piled up to a height of thirty feet. The people had taken their most precious things—their family portraits, bits of lace, their holy pictures from above their beds—and gone out. They locked their doors behind them, but the lava crept in through the windows and pushed silently against the walls until the houses were ground beneath the consuming flow and disappeared. Now we saw the villagers crouched silently in the American and British trucks, waiting to be taken to safety. Barelegged boys trudged in the cold rain balancing a few precious sticks of firewood on their streaming heads. On the curb sat an old farmer of the village, his shoulders heaving as he cried unashamedly into his hands. Nature would require one hundred years to bring this earth back to fertility.

Little knots of people were looking down a side street, and one knew from that familiar attitude that tragedy was in that direction. The name plate on the salmon-pink house we approached said it was the Villa Sparano, obviously the house of a rich man—what remained of it. The mass of lava had reached to the third story of the one wall left standing. On the garden gate imitation Roman urns teetered on their pedestals. Half the garden remained, the lettuce fresh and green a few feet from the creeping black death, and the peanut plants were flowering from the unseasonable heat of the earth. We had thought that all the town was evacuated. But one of us pushed in the door of the hovel adjoining and stepped quickly back. The face of an old man with terrible sores on his cheeks appeared from the dark interior. We asked him to leave. He replied: "This is my house," and disappeared inside. Not all the ingenuity of modern man and his engineering skill could do anything for San Sebastiano or for the near-by town of Massa di Somma, named after the crater that destroyed Pompeii nearly nineteen hundred years before. The elements are the elements, and already fifteen thousand people, knowing by instinct the inexorability of Nature, had gone away from their homes.

As we stood there in the street of misery someone shouted. The spectacle on the summit of Vesuvius pulled the muscles of the breast and made one gasp for breath. A ball of black smoke, then one of white, both of incredible proportions, puffed up, rising thousands of feet into the blue and then spreading until half the sky was obliterated. The volcano had "blown its top" for fair. No living men, except those who were to look upon Hiroshima in another performance of elemental power, have seen such a thing.

We drove around the mountain to the ruins of Pompeii. British and American soldiers and sailors were strolling through the ancient forum. The guides were hawking their postcards. The place had the peace of dignified death, with the pain long since forgotten. None of the Italians there mentioned the present tragedy. One felt that to them it was only a kind of impertinence.

Later we learned that the area upon which we had been standing to make the recording had fallen into the void with the giant explosion we had witnessed from the village, two hours after leaving the summit. The explosion covered cities on the other side of Italy with ash, and pilots five hundred miles away flew in darkness. Seventy-five medium bombers on a field near Pompeii were ruined by cinders and had to be abandoned.

The recordings that Major Frank Pellegrin (organizer of the expedition) and I sent to New York—the first ever made of Vesuvius's voice—were apparently not of "network quality" and, so far as I know, were never heard by anyone.

4

Across Italy, around the city of Bari, I lived a few days with the Yugoslav Partisans of Marshal Tito, physically the most virile and spiritually the most dedicated people I had ever known, not excepting the Londoners of 1940. I have met no group like them, although friends tell me the Chinese Communists are the same. I had lived my adult life mostly with complicated people; the simplicity of the Partisans was unacceptable to me at first, but in the end one could not doubt it. My "contact" here was Colonel Didier, a tall, broad young Yugoslav with a great shock of black hair, a strong, graven face, the neck of a bull, and the mind of a humanist poet. He was a confidant of Tito, had been in the Spanish Civil War as a journalist, and was now slowly recovering from a bad head wound—a man destined to become a leader of his people. I met a black-eyed boy of twenty, Ante Raspejarac, with a typical, broad Slavic face and close-cropped hair which barely covered a scalp wound. This boy, unknown to the outside world, was already a hero in his army and at that time probably held the greatest individual record of any infantryman in the world. With rifle, pistol, and grenade he alone had accounted for at least three hundred Germans, Italians, and Chetniks. He was a lieutenant and had just crossed from the battle front. He wore a jacket designed like a British battle dress but made by Partisans out of captured German field gray. He lit my cigarette with a brass lighter taken from a dead German, and the pistol he wore was a Beretta taken from a dead Italian. He did not wear his officer's insignia—"That is not important," he said, "except when you are in battle." He was reluctant to speak of his own exploits and talked in strategic terms of the various offensives; here at once was an essential difference between the Partisan and the American or the British soldier. The latter generally thought of a battle as it related to himself; the Partisan thought of the common affair first and his own individuality last.

The women and girls fought as unquestioned equals with the men. They wore the same clothes and lived under the same arduous conditions. I met one girl of eighteen, a breath-takingly beautiful girl with chestnut hair that rippled to her shoulders. She had killed around forty of the enemy herself, and yet in her soft, glowing face there was not the slightest trace of anything hard or coarse. None of the soldiers I saw wore any kind of decoration, the girls used no cosmetics, nobody received any pay, and sex relations were outlawed in the army for the duration. If a man and women were found together they were liable to be shot. They not only accepted these rigorous standards—they took pride in them.

With the blushing young Sanja as my interpreter I went through the crude Partisan hospital at Grumo, organized by the British who received the wounded by ship. One saw no brisk orderlies in white, but young men and women in battle dress carrying tin trays of army food into the wards or helping others on crutches through the halls. There was nothing of the hushed atmosphere of most hospitals; they all talked together and laughed together. We entered a room of wounded girls and women, a room of gray walls bare save for two portraits, one of Tito scowling into the sun, the other of Stalin, Roosevelt, and Churchill. We sat for a moment on the edge of a cot to talk with a girl named Boja. She was eighteen, with silky flaxen hair, a wide white brow, and great brown eyes which seemed startlingly large because her face was so pale and thin. Sanja said: "We are sorry that Boja cannot sit up and talk with you, but you see the bullet hit her in the spine and her legs do not work." She had been a farm girl when the civil war began, and her mother and father were shot. She began carrying a rifle at fifteen. In reply to my questions she said: "Yes, I saw much fighting, but I am ashamed that I have killed only one German for certain. However, he was an officer. He slipped to the ground very easily when my bullet hit him." I asked her to tell me honestly how she felt when she knew she had killed a man. "Oh," she said, her eyes lighting up, "he was a German and I felt very happy."

The girl named Borka was twenty a peasant type with a broad

face and very white teeth. Her hair stuck to her head in tight curls, and her fingernails were cut square like a man's. She had made the attack on the island of Korcula. The Germans were in a church and, as she explained, "it was a necessity to climb up the hill in plain view of the enemy. I regret that I did not get as far as the church because a machine-gun bullet, the soft kind that spreads out, hit my arm and a little in my breast. However, my comrades took the church." I asked what had happened to her and she said: "Oh, I was quite well. I was able to walk from the place, and of course my comrades carried me when I could not walk any more." I asked if she had killed many Germans, and she threw back her head of curls and laughed. "Why, of course I have killed many Germans!" she said.

Across the room a red-cheeked girl, who lay on her back with her arms supported by metal rods, was singing quietly to herself. I wondered whether it was a love song or a dance tune such as an American, British or French girl would have been singing. Sanja called out to her to tell me. The girl was embarrassed and said: "Oh, it is just a song we sing." In a few moments all the girls in the ward began to sing it for me. It began: "Tito our leader, you are a great man because you have so many brigades. Our machine guns shoot their bullets at the enemy. The enemy's mother is weeping. The Partisan's mother is dancing the Kolo."

In a ward full of men and boys the hero was Djuro Miljusevich, a farmer, now regarded with awe even by these incredibly hardy people because he was still alive with twenty-five machine-gun bullet holes in his body. He had been caught and lined up with the other men of his village to be executed. He fell riddled to the ground, and a German executioner, seeing that the man still lived, gave him what was to have been the coup de grâce, a revolver shot below the eye. When the Germans departed, this man crawled to the house of a Partisan's wife, and comrades took care of him. Miljusevich was only embarrassed by large questions concerning the aims of the war in Yugoslavia and said he believed his country would be a democracy and a happy place. There was no need to ask this man or any of the others why they had begun fighting. Their stories were all the same: families burned to death, mothers tortured and raped, whole villages wiped out in barbarous fashion. They required the impulsion of no coherent political philosophy.

We walked across the courtyard where the convalescents stood about listening to the American news from Radio Bari, and into

the tents where they kept the small children. Some of these were
minus an arm or a leg, and one or two were blinded from explosives.
Their childish crayon drawings were pinned to the bulletin board
—not children's pictures of cows or horses or houses with smoke
curling from the chimney, but fierce caricatures of Hitler and the
Yugoslav Quisling leaders. A splendid, handsome lad of ten with an
honest, open face saluted me sharply and clicked the heels of his
hob-nailed boots. Lesa spoke a little English and like the others
wore miniature battle dress. When I asked him how he had lost his
arm he said: "Well, sir, I was a messenger between two parts of
our army. I was on the trail in the mountains, and the boy with me,
who was sixteen years old, said he was going to desert and join
the traitors. I said if you do that I will report it to my comrades. So
he got angry and threw a grenade at me to kill me so I could not
tell about him." I asked: "Was he a friend of yours?" "No, sir,"
Lesa replied with a flash in his eyes. "If he had been my friend he
wouldn't have wanted to be a traitor."

I could not stand very much of this. I thrust my gifts of candy
into the hands of the nurses and groped my way out of the tents.
At the gate I heard a sharp clicking of heels again. Lesa was
saluting with his one arm, and in precise English gravely said:
"Sir, in the name of my comrades I wish to thank you for the
presents you have brought."

Many months later I was relating all this in London to Churchill's close associate, Lord Margesson. "Ah," he exclaimed, poking
an admonitory finger at me, "but it is no different from the Nazis,
the Hitler youth." I could think of little to say in reply. I suppose,
in a way, he was right. I know that I should be appalled to see
my own children become like that. And yet there was in the experience an enthrallment, a glory, that could not be denied.

5

Parents and wives in America thought of their sons and husbands
overseas as soldiers in the war, all of them. But the mechanical
finger of military fate sorted them into hundreds of groups, mysterious and meaningless to civilians, yet known to all men in uniform. They knew who was really a soldier and who was not; and
they knew, if they were of tolerant mind, that those who weren't
could usually not help their situation and often would have traded

places with those who were, to salvage their self-respect. Between those at home and those at the fighting front there was an immeasurable gulf; the first were living better than ever before in their lives by reason of the same thing that made the second live the worst life they had ever known. But even in this war theater the division was essentially the same. For hundreds in the "base areas" were quite safe from danger; they were, many of them, making more money than they had as civilians, inhabiting finer homes, touring picturesque areas, entertaining lavishly and being entertained. One cannot say for certain how much this condition affected the fighting—probably very little; but it represented an enormous drain of the public funds collected to support this most wasteful of armies. And it poisoned the hearts of many men owing a common allegiance. "PBS" (Peninsular Base Section) became a hateful expression to the combat men. Sometimes they came back exhausted from the fronts to Naples on leave only to be arrested for failing to salute some officer on the crowded Via Roma, which was filled with hundreds of officers. Or they would be stopped while an inspection officer yanked open buttons to see whether their undershirts were proper government issue. The sign on Capri which read "PBS Officers Rest Camp" became the subject of jest for thousands. PBS men wore sun-tans while combat men wore olive-drab, and the relationship became so bad that the latter would not pick up any hitch-hiking soldier in tans. The PBS men for the most part could not help it; they hated the situation as much as anybody else. So both sides coalesced to the extent of heaping the blame on the officer ultimately responsible, Major General Arthur Wilson, who himself was doubtless merely trying to enforce "discipline" and impress his superiors with the spick-and-span way in which his base was operated.

I first saw this gentleman when I was standing before the dusty Terminus Hotel in Naples. There was the clamor of many motors, and loud, peremptory shouts, and then ten or fifteen motorcycles whirled around the corner, preceding a limousine. They drew up abruptly and the men leaped to attention to salute the figure who stepped out of the car, flourishing a swagger stick. It was General Wilson, keeping an appointment for lunch. Although he said nothing to me personally, I learned that I had drawn his wrath upon me with a broadcast one day: ". . . The city of Naples, with the warm sea in front and spring flowers behind, shows signs now of becoming the Cairo of this campaign. Naples has not all the luxuries of Cairo, but Naples is acquiring the same state of mind. Weeks go by, and our armies do not advance; and so, inevitably, many soldiers stationed here lose the feeling of fight. They come to accept their routine life. Enlisted men become intimates—almost members—of Italian families. Desk officers keep regular hours, and some come to resent any intrusion of the war which might mean overtime work. Even with the Americans, a curious social hierarchy is developing; invitations to the best villas are cherished things. New dining and dancing clubs open up, each more exclusive than the last. Merchants are gradually breaking out their hidden hoards of liquor, and private cocktail parties begin to flourish. With the top down and a cushion on the seat, the jeep becomes a passable roadster, and the better-dressed girls are beginning to come out of hiding. Orchestras are put together, and suave tail-coated waiters who served the Fascists and Germans are just as suave and elegant now for us. Parties are organized days in advance in the calm certainty that the war will not intrude. . . .''

This was mild compared with some of the attacks, particularly those in the cartoons of that sly, grinning young genius, Bill Mauldin, or in the Associated Press columns of Kenneth Dixon, who wrote: "A poll taken among G.I.s to determine the person they would most like to be alone with on a desert island resulted in a sweeping victory for General Wilson." Dixon related how the soldiers called Wilson the "Oracle of Oran" (where he had lived in splendor with a string of Arab horses) and the "Hero of Naples." In transmission this was garbled and was printed as the "Nero of Naples." The General developed a furious hatred for both Mauldin and Dixon but was never able to stop the shafts of either one, and the cable censors fortunately owed allegiance elsewhere. Gradually I learned that there existed a definite type of high officer whose attention was fixed, not on the primary matter of fighting, but on the secondary matters of speaking, looking, and living in the way the books had taught him a high officer ought to speak, look, and live. Military life, like civilian, was filled with men trying not so much to *do* something as to *be* something.

One could sit in Naples reading Tolstoi on the Napoleonic wars and realize how little the basic human conditions of war has changed in a hundred years. Enlisted men spoke and thought of their officers now exactly as they did then; there were the same tentative relations between professionals and reservists, between wealthy officers and poor ones; there was the same gulf between the life at the front and the life just behind the front. The popular belief that army life was melting all Americans from whatever social strata, of whatever personal interests, into one common amalgam was pure legend. It is true that in the crisis of battle men became as one, but battles are of brief duration, and meanwhile life goes on—each man making it as nearly like the life he had left as he possibly could. The men who had spent their previous lives in pool rooms now spent them in Italian bars. College boys with intellectual interests studied Italian and went to see Italian scholars. Social climbers from New York tried their best to meet the Italian nobility—Fascists or not—and poor boys sat on the doorsteps with poor families. Those who had been crooks and "smart operators" in Chicago manipulated black markets in Italy and organized gangs of Italian thieves. There was one small coterie of men from famous and wealthy American families, who held fairly high rank as officers and whose army tasks were usually obscure—special "aides" or "advisors" to various headquarters. They had as many changes of spotless uniform as they had had of city clothes; somehow champagne and whisky were always around their billets in quantity; they entertained touring movie stars as they had in New York; army cars seemed to be at their disposal whenever they wished them, and they were forever flying on mysterious trips to Cairo or London or Washington.

In Naples the base institutions seemed to expand without limits and to exist merely for their own existence. With each new batch of Red Cross girls, for example, more offices had to be found, more apartments, more cars and drivers, more cooks and servants, then more "personnel" managers, more publicity agents. There were hard-working girls near the front who did a real service, and the rear establishments were indispensable, but the workers in the latter developed their own kind of life, which appeared to have little to do with the war. One would enter the "snack bar" of the Red Cross club and see lonely combat men eating by themselves, while the girls entertained one another off in a corner, planning their dates or the furnishing of their apartments. If one remained long in the base area he could no more escape its mores than a front-line soldier could escape fright and danger. Correspondents were its victims along with everyone else, though we were usually busier than most, and more than once I, with others, went to the front when nothing was happening there, simply to shake off the clutch of these habits and to clear my head.

Only at the front in times of crisis did one find grim purpose, selflessness, and a spirit of exaltation in the mutual high endeavor. A thousand times one asked himself why they were like this. They understood the war's meaning no more than the others—which is to say, hardly at all. Their country, their families were not in any mortal danger now, and yet they plodded on, fighting on in a way the French had not done in 1940 when their country and loved ones *were* in peril. What motivated them? Surely it could be traced to the high school, the "team spirit," the conviction bred in their American bones that one did not let the team down. A pride in their outfits. The sheer American "pride in competence," for in the American tradition to be guilty of incompetence is the one unbearable disgrace. They did not hate the Germans, except at certain times and places, and only then because the Germans were killing their comrades. They did not hate the concept of Fascism because they did not understand it. But they struggled on, climbing the hills, wading the rivers until they dropped, and sometimes, watching them die in ignorant glory, I had to fight and reason away sharp stabs of conscience: "What right have I to live and urge them on in behalf of my beliefs, these children who die not comprehending?" Common sense told one that in this direction lay only failure and the meaningless void, but reason did not always operate as one stood over a broken, sobbing boy. They had been right who said we were intellectually unprepared for war. More than right, for we were spiritually unprepared as well, and we were doing it as a matter of accepted routine. Yet in all honesty, there had been no other choice. What disturbed one now was this: Are we prepared for *victory*?

At their headquarters in Cessa near the front I discovered the new French army. These men had a cold, implacable hatred of the enemy that was almost frightening; they were driven by such a fierce desire to show the world and regain their pride that one knew at once they could be stopped only by death and that in victory they would show no mercy. In the old army of Gamelin, talk about the fighting was forbidden at any officers' *popote*, although they wrangled freely over politics; now they talked only about the fighting, and talk of politics was frowned upon. They did not love Americans; they did not love the British; they were callous and cruel toward the Italians. Yet it was good to be among them now; it was a reassuring vindication of faith in these people. De Gaulle was now the unquestioned *chef*, although they scorned the "discussions" in the Algiers assembly and felt that action on their part was worth a million words in restoring France. As with the Americans, their specific war aim was to get home again; for them home lay just ahead over the mountain ranges. I went so far as to predict on the radio that they would make a sensational fight, and this time I was not wrong.

If there was selflessness at the American front, the struggle was so little in our bones that this spirit could not survive even the fifty-mile difference between front and rear. There ally sneered at ally, group contested with group, antagonisms deepened, and at times it seemed a mystery that the whole thing held together. It had been better when the generous spirit of Eisenhower had been there presiding, but Field Marshal "Jumbo" Wilson, a stuffy, routine-minded officer, was no Eisenhower. The French were completely self-contained, the British Eighth Army felt its desert glory slipping, and General Mark Clark thought and spoke exclusively in terms of his own Fifth Army. (He formed a 'Fifth Army Association" with attractive membership cards for all. He had songs written, such as "My Heart's in the Fifth." One night in the Caserta Palace theater, little mimeographed slips were distributed through the rows of bewildered officer spectators. They contained the words of a song beginning, "Stand up, stand up for General Clark, let's sing the praise of General Clark." They stumbled to their feet and uncertainly followed the words with the aid of their flashlights while the General stood stiffly at attention. Somebody said the tune was that of "Stand Up, Stand Up for Jesus," but that is probably apocryphal.)

Of all the minor antagonisms the most unsolvable was that between the journalists and the army as represented by the public relations organization. It could never be solved because the correspondents were essentially civilians engaged in a competitive enterprise, and they had to work in a milieu that was military and co-operative. The result was a series of unending squabbles. The PRO officers, of course, were subject to discipline, and we were not; they regarded us as unco-operative and quite unmanageable. Some of them resented the fact that we were continuing our careers and making money at it, and more than one of them advocated enrolling all correspondents directly into the army—which would have ended what free reporting did go on. We, on the other hand, resented the cozy, routine life into which some of these officers slipped, spending their time "scrounging" transportation or stoves for themselves, while most of us, working all hours, coming and going, not having access to supplies, trudged for miles for a meal and froze at night. There were, as I recall, four jeeps for some fifty reporters. No headquarters in Naples was quite so clammy, ill-lighted, and unsanitary as the press headquarters.

Some of us doubtless expected too much and were cordially hated for it. The correspondents' most violent dislike was reserved for a certain type of ex-journalist turned officer—frequently because he didn't like his job or his wife and was poor at getting on with either. These men had never been quite happy as journalists. They had spent their time hanging outside politicians' doors or auto-matically taking down somebody else's words, until they came to feel they were carbon copies of human beings. They suffered a fundamental contempt of their profession. To become an army officer was to become a real, living, important person. Naturally, as officers, they regarded the war correspondents with contempt. They would spring to their feet and salute any higher officer who passed their desk, but they kept correspondents waiting in the corridors. They were supposed to represent us to the army—accord-ing to our view of it—but they generally represented the army to us. One young major became the symbol of all our animosities. In the prewar maneuvers he had been a lieutenant, willing to provide the reporters with anything so long as they would write about his division. Now he was more rigid and military than any West Point officer I ever knew. He treated the reporters—some of them gifted and distinguished artists—as though they were his "men," under his command. He would scowl and say: "Lots of these reporters aren't earning their salt," meaning that they were not writing enough pure publicity about the army. Since he so regarded re-porters, he considered it a sacrilege to house correspondents in decent billets which army officers—i.e., real people—might have instead. Wherever we were, though, he managed to commandeer the most comfortable rooms for himself, and even when we walked for want of transport he would keep a private jeep to himself. I think the last time I ever spoke to him was the evening I returned with a British colleague from the front, exhausted and still shaking from a narrow escape, and he rose stiffly to say: "I must reprimand you men. You are late for supper."

There were others, of course, such as Majors Pellegrin and Hotchkiss and Lieutenant Zimmerman, the radio supervisor. They were cheerful, devoted men who worked their hearts out on behalf of the reporters and the public and received little thanks for it. One of the best was Major Jay Vessels of Minneapolis, air force PRO. For a long time, his Naples apartment was home to a large group of reporters, including the well-loved Ernie Pyle. But Jay was too unorthodox for some of his superiors; I remember the time when General Clark's publicity colonel took Vessels aside and reprimanded him for playing poker with an enlisted man. The enlisted man was Bill Mauldin, the greatest cartoonist the war produced.

Few men are able to think of the individuals around them in terms of their meaning in society. This correspondent was merely Joe with the big feet and the ill-fitting uniform; that one was merely Sam, who required a supply of gin every day and who snored at night. Officers and censors could hardly think of Sam and Joe as the instruments by which a sacred democratic principle was being carried out, as the representatives of millions of anxious families who had a right to know what was happening to their sons. If a reporter lost his temper in an argument with censors—as I frequently did—and tried to talk of his duties in these terms, he received a queer look, and when he was gone they laughed and marked him down as a crackpot. I arrived at the fronts with a deep desire to describe it all as it truly was—its glories and brutalities, its achievements and stupidities, its misery and luxury, happiness and heartbreak. I found I could not.

The censors employed a thousand devious arguments to justify their deletions. Sometimes they said a paragraph would hurt the morale of the troops; sometimes they said it would hurt the morale of the "home front"; sometimes they said it would impair a general's prestige with his troops and thus cripple their confidence and efficiency. Once in a while a censor was frank and simply said it would get him into trouble with his superiors—so out it went. But you could not hurt the troops' morale by reflecting in speech or print their hardships, for they knew these all too well already; you could not possibly inform them that their general was guilty of cruel mistakes, for it was their own bodies and lives that he mishandled, and they had no illusions. Indeed, nothing bolstered a soldier's spirit more than evidence that the truth of the situation *was* being frankly told; nothing gave him more confidence than to know that *somebody* was aware of the things that were wrong. Few reporters had any desire to do a "muckraking" job; but it was sometimes trying indeed to fight for hours with the censors, then

have some realistic combat soldier ask: "Why don't you guys tell
the truth once in a while?" I knew that General Marshall and a few
others of authority wanted the story told freely, because they
dreaded having an "All Quiet" mentality sweep the country after
the war. Certainly far more of the truth was told during this war
than during the first one, but not enough of it by any means, and
we knew that there would be many postwar revelations that would
shock the country.

Gradually I was beaten down in my efforts. The loose conspiracy of fear among censors, the calculated policy of the chief
press officers to glorify their generals, and the "mutual protective
association" among the generals themselves suffocated true freedom of expression. And there was the problem of simple propinquity—one had to live with all these men; one ate and traveled
only at their sufferance. Life and work were almost impossible if
one was marked down as a critic. A few reporters worked as
though they were mere army publicity agents. They stuck with
their regional outfits and wrote glowingly of its achievements day
in and day out. Two or three, with squirming eagerness, cultivated individual generals and took pride in becoming their intimates—which debarred them, of course, from ever writing
objectively about those leaders or their commands. One of the
most rigidly honest, most unflaggingly objective journalists, who
never ceased his efforts to free the news, was Edward Kennedy of
the Associated Press. He was the man who was later to be "dis-
graced" for breaking the final surrender story in Paris. Whatever
his technical violation in that episode, I cannot forget that he did
more to hold the military to the letter of the censorship rules, to
make them keep their agreements with the correspondents (which
they frequently violated), than any other journalist I knew.

One was accustomed to being told what one could not write. It
was a surprise to go with the other reporters to Field Marshal
Alexander's headquarters at Caserta and to be told by his staff
officers what one *ought* to write. These men, who were in ultimate
control of the censorship, effectively stopped any slight suggestion that their chief might have made a mistake; they did not hesitate to ask us over and over again to emphasize that their chief
was in personal command of the spring offensive toward Rome.
To many professional British officers the journalist was still a
"pressman," a lower order of human being, who should be kept
in his place generally and summoned when he may be of use to

the higher orders. American officers like Mark Clark were an improvement by one notch. They reasoned this way: treat the correspondents with respect, give them all possible facilities, because after all they get us our personal publicity without which war-making is a dull job, devoid of glamor and recompense.

6

War ripped apart the physical fabric of lovely Italy; Fascism, one saw at once, had done something to the hearts of the people. I could not share the contempt so many Americans felt for the Italians—even those of the wretched south—since, even upon first acquaintance, I sensed a basic decency and friendliness among them. They were hapless and cast down, but their sense of inferiority was not like that of the Germans; it was a thing of the moment, not of the permanently tortured soul. I did not know for sure whether they could really make democracy work, but the honest instinct for it was there, which one could not say for the Germans. The Italians, I thought, had a capacity for contentment; I was not so sure about the Germans. It was to the everlasting credit of the British and American allies that they tried to treat the Italians as "cobelligerents," if not as outright allies. Not all individuals of rank treated them so in their hearts and in their manner toward them, but there were men like Charles Poletti in surprising numbers who sincerely wanted to resurrect these likable and talented people. The Polettis were often scorned by the professional officer as mere "do-gooders," but the truth was that their task, to rebuild the spirits of people, was far more difficult, and perhaps in the end more useful to the world, than the task of fighting the war, supplying the armies, and reconstructing the physical means of daily life.

My most pleasant and instructive hours in southern Italy were passed at Colonel Poletti's villa with him and his assistants, where the talk was free and where men were not afraid to speak in terms of ideals. Already the Allies had made a serious blunder in retaining Marshal Badoglio and in permitting the vicious little king to retain his throne. This was done in the name of efficiency and "expediency," exactly as had happened in the case of Darlan, and yet the results were the opposite of those expected, for it taught the people mistrust of the Allies, and men whose democratic ideals

had survived twenty years of Fascism were afraid to come forward.
Poletti was a man of courage, and he refused to take the easy way
of appointing Fascists to office simply because they were the ones
who possessed the training and experience the army wanted. "The
men we put in now may be the future leaders of Italy," he said
on a broadcast with me. "So we have to be so careful that sometimes it takes weeks to find a man with integrity, democratic principles, and ability. You see, after twenty years of suppression and
fear, something has atrophied—the day-to-day *practice* of liberty
—and, like a convalescent invalid, they don't quite trust their
newfound faculties. As for the people in general, Fascism has made
them distrustful of government. Fascism was a racket for those
in favor. People don't quite know what to make of a government
which is really set up for their own benefit. They are always looking for a joker. It will take years of honest effort to eradicate this
deep suspicion and make them free in their minds."

A few politicians milled around in a clammy Naples hall, representing party fragments, just beginning to talk freely and trying
to find out what was going to happen. But they were minor figures
politically and intellectually. There seemed no one with the capacity for power, at least on this side of Rome. One day with
Don Minifie and Sonya Tamara I drove down the highway through
the orchards of dust-covered apricot and lemon trees to find
Benedetto Croce, the aging philosopher of towering intellect and
a defiance that the Fascists had never been able to break. Our
driver was a stout, self-contained German Communist who had
fought in Spain, then joined the British army. At Sorrento we
found Croce living in the Villa Tremini, once owned by John
Jacob Astor. It was surrounded by thick tropical gardens of blooming flowers where one wandered among friezes taken from Gothic
cathedrals, Greek cornices, and Roman statues.

Croce's charming daughter led us through the cold villa into a
blue-tiled room whose shelves held thousands of books. The old
man was huddled at a desk, a woolen coat draped over his left
shoulder. He was obviously sick and full of aches, and some of
his teeth were gone; but the eyes in his bulbous, ugly face were
darting and alive. We talked a half-hour or so, and he was little
impressed by the Allied announcement that King Victor Em-
manuel had been persuaded to "retire," though not abdicate, leaving the Prince of Piedmont as lieutenant-governor of the realm.
It was the fault of Churchill, who could not visualize an Italy

without the House of Savoy, and of the Communists whose devious policy led them to support the King. Otherwise, Croce felt, the King could have been forced to abdicate months before. Now it was too late, and he feared lest Italy be hampered by this wretched royal house for years to come, its presence dividing the people; for it could not unite them. Croce talked about a revival of humanism, of free inquiry and free thought. He expressed a fear that Communism would replace Fascism in his beloved country; the transition from extreme right to extreme left is easily made; what is difficult is to pause at the middle stages. The doughty apostle of liberalism huddled in the house of the dead capitalist. Outside, the determined young Communist smoked his cigarettes and waited for this talk to end, talk which to him would surely have seemed inane.

Croce hissed at the mention of Mussolini. "Ah, that wretched man!" he said. "Once he said how he despised this man Croce, the so-called great scholar, and said he had never read a thing of mine. The wretched man, however, stole a quotation from one of my books and used it as his original thought." The hiss turned to a chuckle.

The old man coughed and pulled the woolen coat more tightly around his shoulder. At this decisive but uncertain moment of history he was Italy itself, surrounded by mementos of things past, regarding the unchanging blue sea, the dilapidation of the old and lovely hills, trying to call up old passions, guessing wistfully at the future and incapable of present action. The men of the old Italy were dying; where were the men of the new? Did they hide, listening, in cellars and forests far to the north? Did they remember what this old prophet remembered, or would we find them corroded, brutalized after these many years of cruelty and deceit?

The Allied armies waited, contesting now with time. Only the airplanes moved in their formations, preparing the earth behind the enemy lines. The belated spring arrived; the peasants were plowing up the soft, black soil; the snowline moved high on the mountains of frustration, and the roads to the front were arrows of beige-colored dust. Shawled Italian women trudged barefoot, carrying great baskets on their heads; their faces were stolid until a truckload of Italian men in remnants of uniform would pass on the road, and then the women would show their white teeth as they shouted greetings. The gathering engines caused dust to

settle upon new acres of peace and permanence, stippled with
white crosses. These acres contained the bodies of the first conquerors from the New World ever to invade this much violated
land. They lay as dead as Visigoth or Saracen, and in the afternoon
the broken arches of the ancient aqueduct shadowed these acres
with unaltered precision.

Behind the Allied fronts the earth trembled in the night under
the tread of silent convoys. Whole armies switched positions unnoticed by the enemy; the Americans on the central front moved
down to the Tyrrhenian Sea; the French faced impossible peaks
to our right; the British and the Poles looked at Cassino and the
Liri Valley. Each prong of the steel rake was imbedded in position;
very soon the signal would be given, and the rake would move
northward up the length of the peninsula, furrowing the earth,
heaping the mangled houses and bodies together as it moved. It
was May. Everywhere the fields were delicately tinted with
flowers.

Chapter XIII

THE ALLIED COMMANDER-IN-CHIEF invoked the name of God; the German commander invoked the name of Adolf Hitler. The moon was high and full and impartially illuminated both sides of the front, blessing and betraying both defender and attacker. It lighted the way for the men who crawled on their bellies up the Italian drawbridge toward Fortress Europa; it exposed them to Europe's jailers, touching with iridescence coat buckle, water bottle, gun shaft, and wide young eyes. From Cassino to the sea on the central front the soft spring earth shuddered and heaved in grunting convulsions; the venerable olive trees burst their trunks, bent beneath the blasts of air, and then, half erect, exhibited to the moon their leafless limbs, thin and naked as the arms of an obscene hag.

The first blow for the freeing of Europe had fallen in the night, and in the first hour personal friends lay wounded and dead Two divisions of young Americans who had never before seen combat moved forward over the rolling hills at which they had stared for weeks until they knew each tree and stone in this small area of fate, which to them had become all the planet, its beginning and its end. Within twenty-four hours they were veteran soldiers. By the next dawn, fear was a secondary impulse, and they moved like automata, their limbs stiff with chill, their nostrils black with grime, their beards one day dirtier. They smelled the clover and the dead in alternation and were aware of neither.

It seemed to me that I had been living with the war since that month of September five years before; while the faces, the instruments, the talk were all familiar now, still the moving picture of the fight was new to me, for always before I had known only stalemate or retreat. This was victorious attack, and the spectacle was not at all as the military writers had pictured it. Troops did not "sweep ahead," "wave after wave," tanks did not "charge" the enemy, divisions did not "plunge" nor "pour" at or into anything. It was far more the slow, deliberate behavior of a surveying party than the agitation of a football team. One never saw masses of men assaulting the enemy. What one observed, in apparently unrelated patches, was small, loose bodies of men moving down narrow defiles or over steep inclines, going methodically from position to position between long halts, and the only continuous factor was the roaring and crackling of the big guns. One felt baffled at first by the unreality of it all. Unseen groups of men were fighting other men that they rarely saw. They located the enemy by the abstractions of mathematics, an imagined science; they reported the enemy through radio waves that no man could visualize; and they destroyed him most frequently with projectiles no eye could follow. When the target became quiet, that particular fight would be over and they moved ahead to something else. Never were there masses of men in olive drab locked in photogenic combat with masses of men in field gray. It was slow, spasmodic movement from one patch of silence to another.

The men were real, and the results one saw all around were shockingly real. There is an atmosphere at the front, a heightened feeling which can never be transmitted nor described. Until one becomes drugged with exhaustion, every scene is a vivid masterpiece of painting. The tree and the ditch ahead are all the trees and ditches of creation, informed with the distillation of sacred *tree*ness and *ditch*ness. Each common odor goes down to the final nerve endings; each turn of the road is stamped indelibly upon the brain; every unexplored house is bursting with portent; every casual word and gesture bears vibrant meaning; those who live are incredibly alive, and the others are stupefyingly dead. Obscure villages which were meaningless names on the map—Minturno, Castelforte, Santa Maria Infante—soon acquire the significance of one's native town, each street and each corner the custodian of intimate, imperishable acquaintance.

A young German soldier lay sprawled just inside a sagging doorway, his hobnailed boots sticking into the street. Two American soldiers were resting and smoking cigarettes a few feet away, paying the body no attention. "Oh, him?" one of them said in response to a question. "Son of a bitch kept lagging behind the others when we brought them in. We got tired of hurrying him up all the time." Thus casually was deliberate murder announced by boys who a year before had taken no lives but those of squirrel or pheasant. I found that I was not shocked nor indignant; I was merely a little surprised. As weeks went by and this experience was repeated many times, I ceased even to be surprised—only, I could never again bring myself to write or speak with indignation of the Germans' violations of the "rules of warfare."

Not a single tree in the ravine had retained its leaves; it was exactly as though a cyclone had just swept through. We sat down on the gray earth with a young captain from West Point named Aileo. He had had six hours' sleep in the last seventy-two, but he merely relaxed in the sun, closing his eyes and smiling to himself as our great shells chortled over sounding like locomotives at high speed. An indolent cook handed us hot, fresh cherry turnovers with a wink, as if to say: "All the comforts of home." The shells were sending up sudden plumes from an enemy-held castle on the next ridge. No one watched it; everybody was already bored with battle. A young corporal trudged by, lugging his personal equipment and a book. The captain asked: "Corporal, are you happy in the service?" "Yes, sir," said the corporal. "Why?" "Because I found a room to sleep in tonight," the boy replied. Then he looked at the volume he carried, *The Return of the Native.* "Only thing bothering me right now is that character here they call the Reddleman. That guy keeps coming in and out of the story, and he confuses me." Puddles of dust advanced up the road, and a lieutenant with a smug and happy look on his face emerged, leading a dozen German prisoners walking with their fingers locked behind their necks. They were exhausted and without expression. Between victorious youth and defeated youth no manner of human transaction occurred.

Battles were large or small; points at issue were vital or of minor consequence; but always and everywhere procedure and pattern were monotonously the same. German guns betrayed their presence. We called our planes to bomb them, and we concentrated our own artillery, too numerous to be opposed, and they shelled the German guns. Thereupon the infantry flowed slowly ahead. At each strong point or village there were always a few snipers to be blasted out, always mines which exploded a number of vehicles, always booby traps which filled a few rooms with smoke and mortal cries. Bulldozers would clear the rubble, engineers would fill the craters, the medical troops would set up their aid stations, a few half-starved Italian families would be rooted out of evil-smelling cellars, and while silent men hoisted limp bodies into trucks the news would go out to the world that the place was "liberated." This is the way it was, day after day, town after town, as the enemy moved back and the line of corrosion moved northward across the peninsula leaving an ever-growing area of stately Italy in blackened ruins which were final beyond despair.

Columns of infantry emerged from side paths and with a censor —a Minnesota classmate, Arthur Burck, who voluntarily went to the front to see the events he had to judge with the blue pencil— I stepped into line to take part in the occupation of Scauri on the coast. They were bearded and unwashed, and they walked very slowly (the headlines said they were "racing" along the coast), carrying their packs and clusters of bright yellow hand grenades at their belts. They would fight before they slept again, and only those two things were on their minds. You noticed that their bodies were relaxed, but their faces were not. If you grinned at a man, he grinned back at once. I realized suddenly that in a way these men were happier now than during the long months of waiting. At long last they were doing what they had trained themselves to do, and if death was closer now, so was climax and the end to their bestial routine. A boy walking toward his life's crisis would call: "Hey, Mac, how about puttin' my name in the paper?" Another would ask: "When's the war going to end, correspondent?" Another: "What's going on, fella? They never tell us nuthin'." I realized, too, that I was happy to be with them; that, however officers at the rear regarded a reporter, these men at the fighting front were glad to see me. They knew I did not have to be there, and perhaps that made them one small degree less afraid. Certainly the presence of journalists gave them some slight lifting of the heart in the knowledge that they and their work were not obscure and unnoticed, that if they became victims, somebody somewhere would know why and how it happened. Nothing is quite so awful as anonymity.

A German sniper, no more than a boy, stumbled back down the line under guard, his trousers widely ripped so that his buttocks were exposed. There was muttering as he passed, and I wondered that he was still alive. While we talked with a young lieutenant who was still breathing hard from a reconnaissance by armored car out from the town, a pink-cheeked private approached and hesitantly said: "Lieutenant, sir, pardon me. I can't find my officer We've got some civilians in a house back there. What shall we do with them, sir?" The excited, puffing lieutenant snapped out: "If you can spare a guard send them back. If you can't, why, shoot 'em in the back. That's what we always did in my outfit. Don't take no nonsense from 'em." The pink-cheeked boy received the order to commit mass murder, saluted, and trotted off.

The sea lay serene and blue before us. In an orange orchard the birds were singing, and between the thunderous claps from the big guns one could hear their sweet, untroubled notes. Two jeeps halted beside me. One contained General Clark and his aides; the other contained the army photographer who always accompanied the General. Clark said: "Sevareid, aren't you a bit off limits here?" I had the impression he was slightly disgruntled at seeing a reporter at the point of advance before *he* had reached it. He drove slowly on between the two lines of infantry, leaning out now and then to call encouragement and praise to a soldier who would be startled, then draw himself up and walk more stiffly for a few moments. It was good behavior for a general; it was a help. Just outside the town, the General's party halted, and we overtook them on foot. No one could proceed farther on the road without being shot. While Clark looked at a map and pointed toward the hill where the "fire fight" was in furious progress, his photographer scrambled about to snap the pictures. They were always taken of the General's left profile. I noticed that, although an ordinary soldier risked a fine for not wearing his helmet in a combat area, the General was wearing his little overseas cap. When the pictures were finished and he had seen what he wished, he shook hands all around, mounted his jeep, and turned back toward the pacified area. Then he replaced the overseas cap with his steel helmet.

Newly routed civilians, now homeless like the others, with no idea of where they would next sleep or eat, with all their future lives an uncertainty, trudged back from the fighting zone. A dust-covered girl clung desperately to a heavy, squirming burlap sack. The pig inside was squealing faintly. Tears made streaks down the girl's face. No one moved to help her; the thought did not occur to me any more than to the others. There was too much misery, so much that no one could possibly feel sorrow or compassion. We strolled back through the town and came upon a group of filthy, white-faced Italians standing before a ruined house. One merely noted that they had not been shot, after all. The children were the color of paste and looked more dead than alive. The men gestured as we approached, pleaded for food, and showed us how they had eaten grass and roots while they huddled in the cellar. They were in stocking feet, the Germans, they said, having confiscated their shoes.

A few miles up the hills, I knew, the French, who advanced so rapidly that the communiqués could not keep up with them, were taking their towns, running up their flags, talking loudly, and sending up organized cheers. My countrymen around me here were a different kind of conqueror. It was quiet in the town now, and they stood about, a bit awkwardly, wondering what to do. A youngster with fuzz on his chin uttered a low whistle before a tank which was standing foolishly on its nose. One, who looked like a farm boy with great red hands, surveyed a perforated resort hotel. "Ah'll take a room with a southern exposure," he drawled. Conquerors? They had no sense of conquering a country; they were just after the Germans and had to walk over this particular piece of the earth's surface to get at them. Liberators? The Italians were merely harmless creatures who sometimes got in the way. The New World had returned to the Old. America was now in the world. The American Century, perhaps. This was the way it looked.

2

All that the American and British soldiers knew about the history of Anzio-Nettunia was that Nero had been born there and that he had built the original port, whose ruins they glimpsed as they walked from the yawning mouths of their landing craft at the rocky jetty. Many men were apprehensive as they approached the beachhead, for it had an evil name. Soldiers on leave from there had told them frightening stories, and *Life* magazine had informed them that it was unsafe anywhere to pop one's head above ground. This was a considerable exaggeration, for the area was a dozen miles in length and depth, there were many patches of forest, and, while it was true that no spot was immune, still the German guns were miles away and smoke screens and haze generally obscured much of our installation. Fear, of course, is most intense in anticipation and in retrospect; on the spot and during the event men usually manage. I was no different from the other men; on the way to Anzio-Nettunia I was frightened, and when it was all over I wondered how I had survived; but during the violent affair itself I behaved, I thought, in a normal manner and maintained a reasonable poise.

All men are a little afraid, all the time. That is accepted and understood. In places of average danger men are judged and graded only by their poise or lack of it. Because this was not an average place, even these standards of judgment were abolished by mutual understanding. Four of us were trying to play poker by candlelight one night in a villa by the beach. The usual bombing raid made the night horrible, and fragments from shells were banging against our walls. When the "Anzio Express," the 500-pound shell, came in, the villa rocked and the candle flickered out. One of the players, a young press officer, went immediately to the cellar. When we joined him, he said frankly: "Look how my knees are shaking." He did not think himself a coward; neither did we. He had simply been there too many weeks.

Allied army authorities nearly always told the journalists everything. It was a wise method. We did our work more intelligently and reduced to a minimum the errors that embarrassed both generals and reporters. But it also entailed certain risks for the generals. If we were told and asked to publicize the fact that General Alexander was making all decisions, this helped to glorify him, but it also left him no easy way out if the decisions brought poor results. If we were told, as we were, that the whole object of the campaign was to "destroy the German armies in Italy," with Rome a secondary objective, that only complete destruction of the enemy here would aid the coming second front in France, and that merely pushing the Germans back would amount to failure of the Italian mission—then the issue was irrevocably stated, and the commanders would be judged by their own statements and standards.

The night before the assault out from the beachhead was to begin, we were ushered into the illuminated caves, and they told us all their plans. It was the custom of assembled correspondents to rise when a general entered in recognition of his rank. It had always been a voluntary gesture on our part, but in this headquarters the ceremony followed a different pattern. As we sat in the rows of benches, a beefy staff colonel would rush in and bellow: " 'Tenshun!" We were always startled and a little resentful, but we would rise. Just as we got to our feet, General Clark would stride in, cut the air laterally with his palm, and call: "Sit down, gentlemen!" in a tone which indicated that this was all a mistake, we were all men of parts together, and that he was embarrassed by his colonel's unjustified command. We frequently wondered if they rehearsed it beforehand—it went off with such dramatic flourish.

The German radio often called Anzio "a prison camp where the inmates feed themselves." If that is what it was, this would be the greatest jail break in history. We had overwhelming superiority in men, vehicles, guns, tanks, and planes, and we needed them, for the Germans held the arc of hills and we must assault them directly. As Clark outlined the plan, the main impetus of our attack would be straight north to take Cisterna, continue on to cut Highway Six at Valmontone, carry on farther in a straight line to cut other roadways, and thus bottle up the main body of the German army from the Cassino front, which the British and others were pushing back up the Liri Valley. Thus the greater mass of the enemy in Italy would be eliminated at once, Rome could be taken almost at leisure, and the Germans would have to pour immense forces into northern Italy to hold that valuable industrial region—thus aiding the second front—or give up Italy altogether. The attack would begin at dawn. We would be allowed by the censors to say very little about its aims, of course, but it would be all right, the press officers told us, to say that General Clark was in personal command.

At dawn, with John Vandercook and Sedgwick of the *New York Times* I stood on a slight rise in the flat prairie among the tents of a field aid station attached to the First Armored Division. It was chill and cloudy. There were daisies and flowering thistle at our feet, and as we looked at our watches we could hear the meadow larks singing. A veil of fog partly obscured the German hills. At 5:45 the gun flares spurted in clusters from the left, then far to the right, then all around us they sounded, and the earth began a faint trembling. Shells passed over our heads, and our jackets flipped from concussion. The planes began to arrive. Through a break in the clouds we saw their tight formations, the fighter bombers wheeling and darting and disappearing in the curtain dividing the two armies. Around us now sleepy men crawled from their holes in the ditches and grubbed for cigarettes with stiff and dirty hands. They were waiting for the first violated bodies to be passed back into their care. The tanks came clanking up the highway, moving very slowly and well apart, their radio antennae nodding behind like the drooping pennants of armored horse and knight, jolting slowly to take the field. In and out of their ranks courier jeeps scuttled like agitated beetles. The barrage slackened off; it was 6:30, and we knew that up ahead the infantry was moving into battle. It was now irrevocable; the men had been "committed." Now one could only wait and hope; if any prayed he did it unnoticed. We slid down into a ditch and drank coffee with the medics. One man read and reread an old American newspaper that lay on a sandbag. The black headline said "Joan Sobs on Stand," and the story had a Hollywood dateline. Another man studied and restudied a single page in a book on photography. Nothing portentous was said. One remarked: "They can hear this in Rome, maybe." A shell screamed too close overhead, and we slid deeper into the ditch. A lad grinned at us and said: "Are you noivous in the soivice?"

An ambulance jolted off the highway into our camp. The man with the book, who had not yet turned the page, carefully marked his place and got up. Others, with artfully pretended boredom, followed slowly. The soldier lay unmoving on the grass floor of the tent, staring at the roof. Blood was seeping rapidly through the bandage on his head. His helmet lay on the grass beside his litter, the steel bent back from the hole the shell fragment had caused. I bent down to the boy to say: "You're going to be all right." There was only the faintest flicker in his staring eyes; he said nothing. Two men entered, supporting a German prisoner who hopped on one leg. He sat on a chair and smiled as they bandaged his leg, then nodded briskly and hopped out again into the waiting ambulance. Everyone talked now. The man sterilizing instruments began to whistle. Another ambulance bumped into camp. The familiar routine of war and systematized suffering was well under way.

On the exposed tableland one felt unnaturally large and vulnerable, if not expendable. My jeep driver said: "On this road if you smile Jerry can tell if you have brushed your teeth." Upstairs in a bare whitewashed farmhouse room, where the windows rattled from concussion, we found six German soldiers just captured. One's first thought was: "What miserable, harmless-looking creatures they are!" The master race indeed—they were like ragged, muddy children. Yet one did not feel pity; in the light of their domination of European civilization one felt a little frightened, for in their eyes there was no spark of intelligence. The brilliant, Vienna-born New Yorker who questioned them was very young himself, and yet his manner was that of a reproving parent. Alternately he scowled, beamed, scolded, and chuckled, and they reacted precisely like children who knew they had done something wrong but were not quite sure why it was wrong. They would willingly point out on the map one of their gun positions, and the interrogator would wink at me and say in English: "That's what they do. They betray their comrades all the time. In five minutes we will blow that position off the map." One he would handle by a stern stare and sharp orders, saying: "I am now your superior officer. You will answer my questions." Being German, the prisoner saluted nervously and obeyed. To another he would softly say: "How's Major Schmidt? Is he back from the hospital yet? Too bad how he gets dysentery so often." The prisoner would assume that the interrogator knew practically everything anyway, so he was not loth to fill in a few details. The lieutenant shooed the last one away, stretched, grinned at me, and shook his head. "Ah," he said, "it's too bad. But they're just so damn *dumb*."

Major Hotchkiss and I lay along a high bunker bordering a canal, near the front lines. The sun was warm; I felt comfortable and cozy. There was no use denying the truth: I was happy here; I enjoyed it. Enemy shells whined over us searching out targets in our rear. The fat bazooka gunner from the Chicago stockyards said: "What do you think? Will I get the week end in Rome?" His comrade passed around a box of chocolates, a gift from his Rotary club at home. From a field of camouflaged tanks came the clear radio voice of an American girl announcing a song from the musical comedy *Oklahoma!* A bouncing jeep sped back from the lines, carrying a German prisoner, who held on for dear life, his eyes watering in the wind. We drove back, straining a little at each uncertain crossroads. Here and there in the shoulder of the road was a fresh shell hole which had not been there when we had passed through a few minutes before. Black smoke rose from an ammunition dump the Germans had hit. In the First Armored aid station, Lieutenant Hyman of Chicago was reading aloud to fellow officers an episode from Thucydides on the Peloponnesian Wars. He exclaimed: "You see, that's us! There's nothing ever new in war. We're doing the same damn thing!" On the road, among overfilled ambulances, a soldier was riding a farm horse and carrying a banjo in one hand.

Back at the press villa, exhausted reporters, drivers, and press officers, so coated with dust that one could not recognize good friends, slept in the warm sand. I picked up the thread of tactical events and other, more personal items: The young interrogator of prisoners was in the hospital. He had been sitting in the latrine when a shell burst outside. Tom Craig, the artist, a roommate from Naples, was in the hospital; his jeep had crashed into a tank in the blinding dust. John Hartzell, a remarkable Navy photographer whom I had discovered in the front lines after he had shot and captured a dozen Germans, was in the hospital. A grenade. Gregory Duncan, artist for *Stars and Stripes*, was dead. He was an old friend of Frederick Thompson and shared my love for the San Franciscan. Duncan's jeep had struck a fresh shell hole at top speed. He had been sitting here with me the night before, sketching Hartzell as I prepared a broadcast with the latter. With this news, the exhilaration of the day drained out of me at once. Some men became apprehensive for themselves as the missiles came closer. I also became apprehensive as the blows fell among my own friends, coming, it seemed, closer and closer to me by the simple method of elimination.

I could never quite reason out the reactions of soldiers to danger. Men seemed to behave in two completely opposed ways. If somebody related a dramatic occurrence in which he had figured, part of his audience would react by saying something like this: "Aw hell, that ain't nothing like what happened to me on the Volturno. Why, lemme tell you, we was . . ." Those were the men to whom nothing was quite real except as it involved themselves. The other part of the audience would have a feeling of wonder and awe at the story, even though they themselves had had experiences equally astonishing, if not more so. They were the men for whom anything that happened to themselves was not quite real or valid, who could never come to think of themselves as actors in this performance, as the very persons everybody was writing and thinking about. If such men were stationed in the rear, no matter what their tasks, they thought of those at the front as the ones who were really in danger. Those like them at the front line thought of those out on patrol, and as likely as not when they were out on patrol they thought of those immobilized farther back as the men really in danger. As someone else has pointed out, it was the same with the air force. Men on the ground thought of those in the air as "the ones." Those in the air thought of the wounded, and the wounded thought of the dead.

The offensive was going well; after thirty-six hours we had taken more than a thousand prisoners, and the key town of Cisterna seemed certain to fall. But our attention was now fixed on the progress of the Americans from the southern front who had passed Terracina and were moving rapidly up the coast for an inevitable juncture with the Anzio forces. When they met, the beachhead would no longer be a beachhead, and all the allied armies in Italy would have overland connection. In the late night of May 24 I wrote a broadcast script saying that in a matter of hours there would be only one front in Italy. I fell asleep on the floor while awaiting the broadcast time. I awakened because someone was shaking my shoulder. General Clark's Press Colonel was standing over me, shining his torch in my face. "Eric, old boy, I'm sorry to wake you up. I just wondered if you wouldn't do me a favor and change that script to read: 'There will be one *Fifth Army* front in Italy.'"

Somewhere else in this story I have said that most journalistic "scoops" are primarily a matter of blind luck. The incident of the famous join-up at Anzio is not a bad illustration. Most reporters went to sleep that night with one ear listening. We did not expect the juncture until the next afternoon, but one could never tell, and instructions were given to press officers and men to waken us if anything happened early. I chanced to be sleeping apart from the others, in the shell-marked villa where the radio transmitter was set up. Because of a very late broadcast I did not awaken until around ten the next morning. As I was about to leave for the press villa, a young press officer burst in at the door. When he saw me he actually turned pale. "Oh, my God," he stammered, "I forgot you were sleeping here. They all went to the join-up a couple of hours ago." The supreme fact was that the armies had joined; it was of no interest to the world who reported the story and who did not. But journalistic competition is a kind of virus. I was savagely angry, and as my favorite driver, the placid Freddie, drove me at reckless speed across the Mussolini Canal, passing the other reporters already returning with the story, I felt as humiliated as a cub reporter outwitted on his first assignment. The join-up had caught everyone by surprise, and even General Clark, who got there as fast as anyone else, had to re-enact the greeting for the photographers. The Germans had pulled out of the low marshlands along the coast, and the troops from the southern front had simply driven overland without opposition. At a small bridge that was blown, Captain Ben Souza of Honolulu encountered Lieutenant Francis Buckley of Philadelphia strolling up the road. "Where the hell do you think you're going?" the former demanded. Buckley replied: "I've come to make contact with the Anzio forces." Souza said: "Well, you've made it." That was all there was to it. I pieced together the story and drove back to the press camp, where everyone else had finished writing the story—the big news story of the world that day. I felt a dozen pairs of amused eyes upon me as I banged at my typewriter. A few hours later, when some of the men had received telegrams from their home offices, they came up to me and said: "There's something phony going on. How did you beat everybody else on this story? You were the last man out there."

Army authorities had set 2 P.M. as the release time for the first bulletins to go out by wireless to New York and London. It just happened that I had a regularly scheduled broadcast beginning at precisely that moment. When an excited telegram of congratulations reached me from CBS in New York, I felt obliged, more from embarrassment than from modesty, to reply by asking them not to gloat publicly over our scoop. It was all a silly, childish affair, but it was the way news beats very often occur.

The Fifth Army publicity machine promptly issued a statement saying that Anzio was now justified and broadly implying that the commanders responsible for the landing there had been right all along, always knew they were, and that, in fact, the whole operation proved the wisdom of the high command whose subtle methods were frequently misunderstood by grosser minds. If any correspondents sent off the statement I did not observe them.

Military commentators in London and New York were enthusiastically saying that day that "up to a hundred thousand Germans" were trapped in the coastal lowlands by the juncture. I drove that afternoon down to Naples for an overnight stay and it was clear that the Germans had escaped through the hills. We had captured a few dozen. The net result was that the Allies now had a connected front, shipping could be diverted elsewhere, and the advancing southern troops found great stores waiting for them at Anzio. It was all very dramatic, and it seemed like a great victory; in truth, we had merely extricated ourselves from our own stupid mistake, committed when we landed on those beaches in January. Still, it was thrilling to speed down the highway through the reclaimed Pontine Marshes, to hear the shouts of unfeigned joy from the peasants, to see all the girls dressed in their Sunday best for the occasion, to receive the neatly tied bouquets of wild roses they tossed into our jeep. The family group before every farm gate clapped their hands with a formality that made one laugh and yet touched the heart. At one gate a graybearded veteran of the last war, dressed in his old uniform and his medals, made a loud if

somewhat incoherent speech as we paused for water. The feeling
of being a "liberator" was a good feeling indeed; we assumed that
the farmers in this unviolated region were happy because we had
freed them from the Germans. As Terracina came near, we learned
differently. The trudging peasants here did not smile at us; there
were no bouquets nor welcoming speeches. There were only dull
and sullen looks. For Terracina was an awesome shambles, its
buildings spewn into the roadways, its whole skyline ripped away.
There were still dead mules and bodies along the curbs, and a
terrible stench issued from the ruins. So with Fondi; so with
Formia.

These little places were meaningless names to the outside world.
But to us, who had followed the fighting from hill to crossroad,
from hedgerow to street corner, they were areas of the most intense intimacy. To see a building where once we had been sheltered
from mortars, now decapitated and lifeless, was an emotional experience. Part of our lives was left there forever. We drove through
lines of civilians who were filtering back into Scauri; we drove
serenely across a new bridge, where on innumerable occasions we
had hurried over pontoons, through a smoke screen, bent low and
holding tightly to our steel helmets. We smiled foolishly at one
another and sang at the top of our voices. It was all extraordinary
and wonderful.

3

Something happened now to change the whole strategy of the
Fifth Army offensive. We learned that the impetus of the drive
had been radically switched. Although we had taken Cisterna and
were interdicting Highway Six with a constant rain of shells, we
were abandoning the officially stated strategy of continuing north
to cut the remaining German escape roads, the move designed to
bottle up their main forces. We were now to turn west with our
spearheads and try to drive to the left and right of the Alban Hills,
straight for Rome. What had happened? Was the Eighth Army
coming too slowly up the valley to effect a mass capture of the
enemy? Or had orders arrived from some higher authority to get
Rome without delay? It seemed to some of us that, in view of
Alexander's declaration that the aim of the campaign was the

destruction of the enemy in Italy, this was a serious mistake. In a broadcast script I wrote: "There is a question whether the two aims [of getting Rome and of destroying the enemy] are compatible or mutually exclusive." The censors cut this line out. But General Clark, who saw each morning all press and radio copy of significance, reacted strongly to my suggestion. Before all the correspondents he referred to "a broadcast" that suggested that we might be able to capture the bulk of the Germans. "That is sheer nonsense," he asserted with vigor, and with his pointer he indicated various side roads to the north by which, he said, the Germans could easily escape. No amateur could prove otherwise. (Almost nothing can be proved or disproved in the realm of strategy and tactics, for "military science" is not a science at all, but only a rude kind of art.) Yet such a capture had been our unquestioned aim. Now the General spoke in a manner that seemed to deny that the idea had ever entered his head. Some of us remained puzzled and skeptical. What had happened that we must now rush straight for Rome?

Cisterna, like Cassino, will be an event and a name long remembered among Italians. Its appearance, after the storm abated, was much like that of Ypres in the First World War. In places it was difficult to tell where the streets had been. Our military traffic trudged through thick drifts of caramel-colored dust that reached to the hubcaps. It was a slow and silent procession, like a funeral parade. The ruins had the stillness of ancient ruins, but without their dignity. There was a temple, whose roof had fallen in; one could see through the hollow front and out the rear. Across the front was a legend that read: "The Quietness of Christ." A dust cloud drifted away to reveal a buggyload of old men in what had been the central square. They said nothing. They did nothing. They merely sat there and stared with unbelieving eyes. In the little park the palm trees lay blackened and uprooted. Over them a shining white victory statue stood erect on a pedestal. It was the figure of a woman holding aloft a torch in a gesture of triumph. Though her marble head and her torch were gone, in its present attitude of shocked surprise the statue seemed the only vital, living thing within the city.

On Memorial Day the white crosses in what was probably the largest American cemetery in the war at that time were shimmering in the hot morning sun. Detachments from every division assembled with their banners. Thick smoke from our concealment screen drifted across one edge of the field, and one could hear the sound of our guns and the motors of the ambulance planes which lifted away toward Naples every few minutes, bearing the injured. On this day each white cross bore a small American flag fastened above the name plate and the number. A crowd of shirt-sleeved Italian laborers stood by the great mounds of fresh earth where the unfilled graves were ready. The unfilled graves were so neatly aligned, and there were so many of them, waiting. The General spoke of the glorious achievements of the fighting men and the imminent freeing of the first European capital from tyranny. The corps chaplain (the Baptist who kept a neat file of clippings about himself and always had a new story of his exploits for the reporters) announced over the loud speaker that the men who lay dead before us had died in the cause of "true religion." When orators and formations had marched away, I came upon six new bodies stretched in the sun behind the canvas curtains at the field's edge. The burial sergeant was a West Virginia schoolteacher who begged me not to write a story about what he was doing in the war. One of his assistants said: "You get used to it after a while." The sergeant answered: "That isn't true—I never get used to it." He looked at the bodies and went on: "With a thousand, it would be just a problem of sanitation. With six, it seems like a tragedy."

One saw so many dead each day, so many bleeding bodies. I realized that I was becoming a little obsessed with the tragedy of these youngsters, tending to write about death more and more. Sometimes in the long, lovely evenings when we sat by the sea, the old feelings about the death of youth which I had experienced as a college boy began to steal back, unnerving and frightening me. It would not do; one had to shake off these moods. But it was becoming harder and harder to escape them. I realized now with a start that the sight of a dead German boy did not affect me, while the sight of a dead American did. Did this reaction come from the deep-seated national feelings which go back to childhood, or was it due to simple propinquity? I was unsure.

Even to noncombatants in the field like myself the Germans were not quite real any more as human beings, such is the mental derangement of war. Their bodies did not affect me. But when a colleague showed me some letters, written in a girlish scrawl, which he had taken from a dead German boy, I was moved. I saved the letters, which in part went as follows:

Vienna, April 14. Dear Robert: First of all heartiest greetings. Since I don't hear from you I write you a few lines. I hope they will not be unwelcome. I sent an Easter card to your grandmother, and when she answered she enclosed your address with the hint that I should write to you. And now that I have time, I write, as you see. How do you like the army? I would like to see you as a soldier. How are your girls? Do they write to you often? I want to close now with the heartiest regards. Best regards from Mother. —Feli.

The letters became bolder, more intimate:

Vienna, May 1. Dear Robert: I received your dear letter on the 22nd of last month with great joy. . . . I'm enclosing some writing paper to make sure that you write me more. Maybe I'll take a ride to your grandmother this week. Say, dear Robert, what do you mean by telling me that she is not the only one who loves me? I can't imagine who has the courage to love me. I'm sorry that the army doesn't agree with you. . . . I feel sorry for the poor girl you broke off with. Don't you think she feels hurt? Well, what do I care? . . . I close for today with heartiest regards.—Your Feli.

Vienna, May 7. Dearest Robert: . . . Your grandmother worries very much about you. Please write cheerful letters to her. She worries very much about you and more so when you write her that the going is bad.—Your Feli.
P.S. A stolen kiss.

4

The attack toward Rome slowed to a stop, embarrassing for the generals and deadly for the fighting men. It was the bitter situation so familiar in the Italian campaign: the enemy was holding the high ground—in this case the Alban Hills, the last breastworks defending Rome. Clark had sent the First Armored across the flat ground between the hills and the sea. Every vehicle was easily spotted in the enemy's gun sights and within ten minutes we lost twenty-five tanks. The other divisions could get nowhere in the vineyards, which were dominated by the hill city of Velletri, key to the German defense. Hitherto the summer campaign had been a straightaway, bludgeoning business of hammering frontally with

our great superior weight of shells and bombs. I, at least, had never
seen anything subtle or unorthodox attempted at any time. Unorthodox ideas are generally frowned upon in military commands,
and, to be sure, they are usually not worth the risk when one has
overwhelming superiority in everything. But the proposal of Major
General Fred Walker of the Thirty-sixth Division was accepted.
He drew two regiments from in front of Velletri, circled them
around to the right in darkness, and started them climbing the
two-thousand-foot height *behind* Velletri. It was a gamble. If
the Germans could close their lines again, these men would be
lost. If not, the final defenses of the Eternal City were breached.

With that brave and tender-hearted photographer-writer, Carl
Mydans of *Life,* I set out to witness this seemingly impossible feat.
By noon we had found the advance C.P. of the division, which
now consisted of several bearded officers squatting under a railroad
trestle studying a map. General Walker gave me a curt nod and
continued pacing back and forth under the trestle. He was a
solemn, self-contained man, and this was the first time I had ever
observed him in a state of perturbation. A good friend, Lieutenant
Colonel Hal Reese, smiled benignly at me as he drew a map with
his cane in the dirt to indicate the route we would have to follow
in order to mount the hill—"if you get past the snipers." I had
bunked with Reese in the LST that brought his division to the
beach. He was another man like my uncle, a graying businessman
from Philadelphia, who gave a human, civilizing tone to the most
warlike surroundings. He had served closely with Walker in the
first war and had gone into uniform again partly because of their
intimacy.

A husky young major with a full pack hitchhiked a ride with us.
He was John Collings of Detroit, who had just come from the
Pacific and was seeking his new battalion, somewhere up the
mountain. We left the highway, bumped across the rail tracks, and
thumped our tortuous way up a newly cut trail among cornstalks
and vineyards. Only a jeep could do this, but there were sharp
descents and sudden upthrusts where we thought the jeep would
go over on its back. It was very silent. The sun filtered down
through the thick trees. A lone sentry stepped out. "Watch for the
snipers, sir," he said to Collings. Freddie looked back from the
steering wheel, a question on his face. He had orders, as did all
the press drivers, to go only as far as he himself considered safe,
regardless of what the correspondent passengers requested. With

a casual gesture that somehow held the impact of drama, Collings flipped out his pistol, held it cocked in his hand, and, keeping his eyes steadily upon the trees ahead, remarked: "Go ahead, driver. Snipers aren't so bad." A machine gun began to sound near by, like corn popping in a deep kettle. The jeep trudged over ruts and roots, and a party of approaching peasant women carrying great water bottles through which the sun's rays filtered squeezed against the trees to let us pass. They were one of the invariable signs of fighting just ahead.

We emerged again upon the highway. Three soldiers rested in a ditch. "You're visible to the enemy next couple hundred yards," they told us. Implied was: "We are alive by the grace of God; you may die in the next few minutes." The tone was the tone of men saying that it looked like rain. This is the way it was, nearly always, among men in the regions of death. The jeep darted the next stretch and was halted by a soldier who seemed no more than a boy in his teens, the artless, helpless type which ought never to be taken into any army. His eyes were unnaturally large, and his hands were twisting a towel, rapidly, senselessly. "Do you know where the aid station is, sir?" he asked through trembling lips. We thought it was just ahead. "Are you hit?" "No, sir, it's my nerves, I guess." We left him. Though he was a casualty, as surely as any man with a bullet in his head, he could be condemned for desertion.

Another quarter-mile and we could go no farther on the highway. Velletri was invisible, but lay only another thousand yards to the west. Machine guns were sounding again, and it was certain death to proceed. Here now was the cut-off, a narrow "jeepable" trail, mounting sharply between high banks. Freddie would have continued with us, but he had nothing to gain by getting the "story," and it was foolish to risk another man. He stayed at this point with the jeep, which was a mistake. We began hiking upward in the hot sun; we rounded a bend and there were *tanks* chugging up, their massive breadth plugging the whole road cut, scraping down dirt and stones from the banks. Scrambling around the tanks, we found the ubiquitous bulldozer, simply carving the trail into a road, roaring and rearing its ponderous way at a forty-degree angle upward. This was all madly impossible, and yet it was being done.

The men themselves, bearded, silent with fatigue, swung their shovels through the loose dirt and pitched it over the banks. A rifle snapped very close at hand, and we heard the sigh of the bullet this time. A trained soldier is generally more afraid of snipers than of artillery; I found I had the reverse reaction. Heavy shell fire was unnerving to me after a while, and I could hardly bear the sense of helplessness and exposure if it were coming in while I was in a vehicle. Rifle fire, though it might be directed right at me, left me completely calm; and it was reassuring to be standing on my own feet, able to take cover by a simple muscular reflex. Perhaps most amateurs are this way; they react to noise and concussion rather than to the missiles themselves.

A couple more bullets whistled overhead and a party of shovelers stood upright. "Oh-oh," one said. Mechanically, as though they had done it a thousand times, two of them let their shovels fall, slipped their carbines from their backs, and crawled over the bank, disappearing in the direction of the sniper. Now a jeep with the Red Cross marking tilted precariously down the trail. Strapped across the hood was a stretcher with a man upon it. His head was almost covered with bandages, only the eyes, nose, and lips exposed. The lips held a cigarette. When Carl pointed his camera, the boy turned his head toward the lens and, in an unforgettable voice tinged with irony, asked: "Do you want me to *smile?*"

We found ourselves with a rifle company, men I had last visited in the fields before Velletri. They had detrucked in the night, then made a ten-mile hike around Velletri and gone straight up the hill, carrying their heavy mortar shells in their bare hands, clutching them to their stomachs. The weighty metal boxes of rifle ammunition they had strapped to their backs, and they had climbed all night, silently, like Indians, forbidden by Walker to have a cartridge in the chamber of their rifles. He would permit no firing, to avoid alerting the Germans. Only a grenade could be used, if absolutely necessary, for the Germans would easily mistake that for a mortar shell and remain ignorant of its origin. (The Germans were ignorant enough—later we learned that they believed that two companies, not two regiments, had made the infiltration.)

In a sun-speckled grove the men lay sprawled on their backs, oblivious to the traffic's dust or the spasmodic machine-gun fire so close at hand, catching any moment that fortune provided for precious sleep. A soldier walked past, going downhill. He held up his hand to show bandages covering what remained of his thumb. "How's that for a cheap Purple Heart?" he said. No one cared for the medal; what he was saying was: "I'll never have to fight, sleep in mud, and be frightened again." One witness muttered: "He's got the war made." "Lucky bastard," said another. Battalion head-quarters was a farmhouse. Inside, three young officers sat at ease around the kitchen table while the farm wife served them wine. One of the men had flown from Cairo with me. We drank and discussed Cairo cafés, like two casual acquaintances in a smoking car. Outside the door lay a dead German sniper wearing American army boots. A Texas lieutenant jerked his thumb toward the body. "That guy shot two of our medics. He made us sore." The German had violated the "rules of war"—or rather, he had outraged his youthful opponents. When they captured him, they instructed him to turn and run for it. He ran and fell with thirteen tommy-gun bullets in his square body.

We debated whether to try to reach the summit. The way seemed clear, but it was growing late, and we must reach Anzio before dark. In any case, the mountain position was safely established; everything was in order. We said goodbye to Collings and started down. (Two months later Mydans met Collings in Rome and learned that the major had pulled away from the farmhouse in a jeep with four other men. They proceeded upwards a quarter-mile and received a burst of German machine-gun fire. Collings alone survived.)

On the highway, we found Freddie crouched in the ditch, clutching his rifle. Machine-gun bullets had just been whispering around his ears. We wrenched the jeep around and departed at full speed, hanging to our helmets.

In the night the Germans tried a counterattack and failed. Our men clung to the heights and fired remorselessly upon the desperate enemy within Velletri. In the morning General Walker, his tanks, and his men rushed the town, entering upon the highway. Lieutenant Colonel Hal Reese insisted upon walking ahead of the tanks; a shell burst killed him at once. When he was informed, Walker averted his face and said: "I asked him not to go ahead like that. I asked him not to." Why did Reese, who was not a professional soldier, who had everything to live for, who understood prudent behavior, act in this rash manner? I do not know. I do not know what lay behind his serene and gentlemanly countenance. But in his notebook they found that he had written: "I got through the last war all right, but I will not survive this one." It is my impression of men who have lost many comrades and who feel no escape for themselves, that they not only take risks in a fatalistic manner—they welcome them. They seek death.

Rome must now fall. Generals Alexander and Clark would soon receive the key to the city, but surely it was General Walker who turned the key. From him they were really receiving it.

Perhaps it is true that we love best those to whom we give and dislike those who give to us. We were never told the reason, but a few weeks later General Walker, whose love for his division was returned in his men's respect for him, who was at the height of his brilliant combat career, was relieved of his command and sent back to the States.

5

In the morning again we drove around the eastern slopes of the lovely green hills, past mutilated Valmontone (another old city we had shot up to no purpose in our reckless way, for the bridges and skirting roadway were all that we required), and as we progressed it began to dawn upon us that the German defenses were falling apart so fast that we would be into Rome within hours. The air was charged with excitement, with savage triumph and obscene defeat. German vehicles were smouldering at every bend of the road, and dead Germans lay sprawled beside them, their faces thickening with the dust sprayed over them by the ceaseless wheels that passed within inches of the mortifying flesh. Shells were screaming over in both directions, but in the general frenzy not even the civilians paid them much notice. By wrecked gasoline stations, in the front yards of decapitated homes, flushed Americans were shoving newly taken prisoners into line, jerking out the contents of their pockets and jabbing those who hesitated with the butt ends of their rifles. A child was vigorously kicking a dead German officer, until a young woman shoved the child aside and dragged off the man's boots. Infantry of the Third Division were arriving in trucks, and their general, "Iron Mike" O'Daniel, jumped from his jeep before it had stopped and in stentorian voice shouted the orders for their detrucking and deployment. One of our tank destroyers ahead burst into flames, and shells began falling nearer. American officers, throwing themselves down and clutching their helmets, shouted questions at one another about how the race for Rome was progressing. While Mydans remained with his camera —he spent a frightening night under bombs—I turned back to Anzio, impelled by the realization that things were now moving

faster than anyone had expected and that somehow the press installation, the censors, and the radio transmitters must be uprooted
at once and taken to the front lines, or the story of the fall, the
whole impact of the "psychological and political victory" that
Rome was to be, would surely be delayed and half ruined. In the
wrecked villages to the immediate rear, medical aides were pulling
our wounded from their ambulances, shabby civilians were gathering in the rubble-strewn public squares, all looking toward the
capital city, and standing beside their ruined parents the children,
in their innocence of tragedy and death, were clapping their
small and grimy hands as we passed them by.

I was black with a thick covering of grime and dust when I
reached the press villa on the now silent beach. I was exhausted
by the hectic journey and by sheer nervous excitement, and my
hands were trembling when I tried to eat at the mess. It appeared
that no orders whatsoever had been given for uprooting the transmitters—indeed nobody there seemed quite aware of what was
happening; and I fear that I transgressed the limits of dignity
in urging immediate action. But nothing could move until morning. At midnight I did my last broadcast from Anzio and was up
again with the others before dawn. Nearly all the other correspondents had vanished in the night toward the front, and it appeared that I would have to guide the slow caravan with Vaughn
Thomas of the BBC, since no others knew the detours. We moved
with agonizing slowness, and I was certain that I would miss the
entry into the city. Near Valmontone the transmitter van behind
us hesitated at a crossroads, and I ran back a couple of hundred
yards to direct them. Returning to the jeep was one of the most
horrible experiences of my life. Perhaps it was that the breeze
shifted or died; I do not know. But I walked into a veritable lake
of stench. There was not a body in sight; the bodies must have
been dragged into the brush just off the road, but the hot sun was
directly on them. I had smelled the sharp, sweet, gaseous odor of
death before, but nothing like this. It inflamed the nostrils, and
I could even taste it in my mouth. Each breath drew it in deeply.
I began to choke, and water streamed from my eyes. I started to
run blindly up the road, which made me breathe more heavily. All
my insides were convulsed, and I felt vomit in my throat. I was
almost in a fainting condition when I reached the jeep, and I
stayed sick for hours afterwards. The sight of death is nothing like
its smell.

The army had not yet crossed the city limits; German antitank guns were interdicting the highway, delaying us, while the enemy hurriedly pushed the bulk of his troops out of Rome by the northern gates. A few hundred yards from the city limits we turned off into a group of workers' apartment buildings, while an army captain named Wickham, who was something of a technical genius, threw up the antennae in an open field. It was Sunday noon. Rome was just ahead, yet all the city proper was obscured in haze and smoke. Guns and shells sounded loudly near us, and from somewhere in the city came the dull sound of explosions—evidence, we thought, that the Germans were blowing the bridges on the Tiber. We hiked up the road and crouched beside cement ramparts along the trolley line, as far as one could go. There was a curious feeling in the air: a combined spirit of battle and of holiday. Reporters sat typing with their machines balanced on their knees. A dying German lay groaning in the hot sun on a cement driveway by a villa while a group of civilians silently watched him. An old man held a cup of water to his lips with one hand and stroked his hair with the other. People hung out of every window and gathered before every gate. The girls and children tossed flowers at the two lines of slowly walking American soldiers, and bouquets were now displayed on the turrets of our tanks.

Two old women approached me as I was typing. They insisted upon shaking my hand. One held out a blond baby for me to kiss. "Now the war is over, thanks to God," one of them said. The other said: "Last night the Germans were here, and now the *Inglesi*. But war is ugly, is it not?" An elderly gentleman came to his gate and began reciting a speech of Garibaldi's. There was singing on the road, and a wedding party came along, walking toward the rear in the middle of the highway between the two lines of troops. The bride was all in gray with hat to match, and she carried flowers in her arm as though she were stepping down the aisle of a church. One or two of the soldiers threw her a kiss, and a few shouted gratuitous advice. Near the transmitter, a winding column of men and women passed, all of them carrying great bundles on their heads and holding the hands of their children. They were headed south. I asked them their destination. "Cassino," they said. "It is our home."

Rome was falling, and all the world was waiting and watching. It was a day of climax and portent, a day for history. I sat before the microphone at a portable table while shells passed over and the concussion whipped my papers. I could say nothing of consequence. I could only say that Rome was falling and that we were all tired and happy. In a thousand editorial columns, on a thousand public platforms, men far from the scene would utter the big thoughts about this. Here, none among us seemed to have anything to say.

(Up the highway a short distance, a conversation was going on, which was not then publicly recorded, but which also, perhaps, merits a footnote in the history of the war and of the personalities who directed it. Brigadier General Robert Frederick, the young and capable commander of the special "commando" regiment of Americans and Canadians, was watching the progress of his men who led the assault. A jeep drew up, and Major General Keyes, corps commander, descended. "General Frederick," he asked, "what's holding you up here?" Frederick replied: "The Germans, sir." Keyes then asked: "How long will it take you to get across the city limits?" Frederick answered: "The rest of the day. There are a couple of SP guns up there." "That will not do. General Clark must be across the city limits by four o'clock." Frederick asked: "Why?" The corps commander answered: "Because he has to have a photograph taken." Frederick looked at Keyes steadily for a long moment and said: "Tell the General to give me an hour." The guns were silenced, the General and his faithful photographer arrived, and the pictures were taken of the conqueror within his conquered city.)

Around ten o'clock at night I stretched out on a cot in the bare villa the press officers had taken over for us, intending to rest for half an hour. An accumulated weight of weariness, which had been waiting just beyond the nerve ends, suddenly crushed down upon me. There was a flicker of protest from somewhere deep within me, a faint realization that I must get up again; but it blurred out almost as it came, and I passed into unconsciousness. In sleep I was vaguely aware of explosions near by, but I was dreaming that I was deep in a safe shelter, and thus I remained unaware that a German plane had strafed the villa and its garden, its small shells exploding right outside the window by my head. It was six in the morning when I was shaken awake. My colleague, Winston Burdett, was standing over me, his face haggard and his eyes rimmed with red. He had got into the center of Rome at midnight. He had driven around, almost alone, while moonlight bathed the ancient ruins, a few faces peered from the windows, and snipers' shots rang out in the stillness. He came back, wrote one of the most dramatic and beautiful broadcasts I have ever read, and delivered it just before he awakened me. It would have been one of the memorable essays of the war; but the operators at the Naples relay station, doubtless exhausted themselves, had not been monitoring us, and his words were lost.

Early in the morning the big entry by troops and correspondents was made. Many great cities were liberated after Rome, and the spectacle was nearly always the same. But to me this entry was a new thing, and I found myself having to hold tight to my emotions. Everyone was out on the street, thousands upon thousands from the outlying areas walking toward the center of the city. A vast, murmurous sound of human voices flooded everywhere and rose in joyous crescendo at every large avenue we crossed. There was a gladness in all eyes, and now and then, as when a German sniper in his green-daubed cape was marched out of the Colosseum, remembrance of hate contorted the faces, even the young children uttered savage cries, and the fists that had held bundles of flowers were doubled in anger. The Piazza di Venezia was jammed with a monstrous crowd, and our jeep proceeded at a snail's pace, while flowers rained upon our heads, men grabbed and kissed our hands, old women burst into tears, and girls and boys wanted to climb up beside us. One tried to remember that they had been our recent enemy, that they were happy because the war was over for them as much as because we had driven out the Germans, that noncombatants such as I had no right to this adulation. But one tried in vain. I felt wonderfully good, generous, and important. I was a representative of strength, decency, and success, and it was impossible at this moment to recollect that Germans or Fascists had also once received this same outpouring of gratitude.

There was a burst of tommy-gun fire in the police headquarters on the square. Several of us worked our way through the gates of the building just in time to see several tough-looking young men, wearing the banner of their underground political group, dashing down a corridor, firing blindly ahead of them. There was a frightening look in their eyes, an expression of sheer bloodlust and hatred. The rat hunt was on. This was not like war; this was a personal matter, and they were out to kill for the sake of killing. There were more shots, the bullets coming our way, and when the hunters scramb!ed frantically back toward us, we shoved our way out of the building in undignified haste.

We drove slowly on, heading for the *Stampa Estera* building which was to be the press headquarters. The curbs were crowded with cheering people who spilled out into the street. A funny little man wearing a big sign around his neck which bore the word "Akron" scuttled from jeep to jeep, shouting: "Anybody here from Ohio?" A middle-aged woman and her daughter, both well dressed and so obviously American middle-class, caught at our arms and said: "We are from New York. We were caught here when the war began. Oh, we just can't tell you how good it is to see Americans!" The mother dabbed at her eyes with a tiny handkerchief and smiled radiantly through her tears. More vigilantes were in operation at every corner. They were smashing in the plate glass of shops that presumably were owned by Fascists or German sympathizers. A terrified man ran out of one, his hands in the air. He was slugged and kicked and went stumbling through the street with blood running down his face. If this was Europe's vengeance upon its tyrants, I knew I did not like the sight of it. I tried to tell myself that these present victims had done frightful things to countless others, that savage oppression must result in savage release. But it remained a sickening thing to see.

In the *Stampa Estera* building the correspondents were typing madly, shouting for censors, and demanding to know how the copy was to be transmitted to London and New York. Everything was in confusion. All the elaborate army plans for joint broadcasts to the world, to give dramatic effect to the great "psychological victory," had apparently broken down. Nowhere could we find the chief press officer with whom we had signed these agreements after endless discussion at Anzio. While the voice transmitter was still working just out of town for the broadcasters, the portable code transmitter for the press representatives was not working. We were told that a shell from the strafing plane had knocked it out of commission. Jay Vessels had jumped into the breach and arranged to have the copy flown from Anzio to Naples after courier jeep· had raced to the beachhead with it. The press reporters were in a frenzied state of fury. Then the chief public relations officer burst into the room to announce that General Clark would hold a press conference at the Campidoglio building immediately.

The General was lounging against the balustrade that over-

looked the square when we hurried up the outside stairway. There
was a jam of people around him, and already the news-reel men
were grinding away, photographing the lean, smiling victor against
the appropriate background of the great city spread out below.
General Truscott arrived, then General Keyes. They worked their
way to Clark's side and regarded the mob of reporters and photographers with a questioning look in their eyes. General Juin of
the French Corps hastened up the steps and also looked at us
with an expression of bewilderment. Clark shook hands with
them and in a modest drawl said to us: "Well, gentlemen, I didn't
really expect to have a press conference here—I just called a little
meeting with my corps commanders to discuss the situation. However, I'll be glad to answer your questions. This is a great day for
the Fifth Army." That was the immortal remark of Rome's modern-
day conqueror. It was not, apparently, a great day for the world,
for the Allies, for all the suffering people who had desperately
looked toward the time of peace. It was a great day for the Fifth
Army. (Men of the Eighth Army, whose sector did not happen to
include Rome but without whose efforts this day could not have
occurred, did not soon forget the remark.) Then Clark spread a
map on the balustrade, and with the whole mob pressing close
proceeded to point out something or other to his commanders. The
cameras ground, the corps commanders, red with embarrassment,
looked back and forth from us to the map. We pushed down the
steps. A colleague commented: "On this historic occasion I feel
like vomiting."

While the detailed story of the entrance into Rome was being
carried by jeep to Anzio, I drove out to the radio station for a
broadcast which would not begin until two o'clock in the afternoon. On the way I remembered a remark of the radio sergeant
with whom I had lived at Anzio. The other day he had said: "You
know we've got a 284 transmitter mounted in this half-track. The
officers aren't planning to use it because it's too weak, but I've been
tinkering with it and I have an idea I can reach Naples with it."
I hurried the driver on to greater speed and when we reached the
villa sought out the sergeant at once. "Yeah," he said. "We got a
beautiful signal into Naples with this thing. Don't know why nobody's been using it." Back in Rome the reporters were looking
at their watches, estimating how near their copy was to Naples and
wondering what editions they would catch with the delayed account of what was occurring in Rome. I hurriedly typed out several

short dispatches describing the welcome and the condition of the city and its people, had them censored, and tossed them into the half-track. The other radio reporters continued typing around me, oblivious to what I was doing. Within minutes my dispatches were in Naples and clicking into my office in New York. I believe that the tireless Daniel DeLuce of the Associated Press, who had taken no chances but had driven down in the night to Naples, got across a dispatch on the advance midnight entry before mine was transmitted. But I had a clear beat on the story of the grand entry with the details of what had happened in Rome. I knew that some of my hard-boiled competitors from Washington and New York regarded me as a "commentator," who sat at his ease and composed neat, epigrammatical essays on the events they worked so hard to report. However smug and selfish the feeling, it was good to know that I could still beat them on occasion in the rough-and-tumble.

Truckloads of young girls with loud speakers and banners toured the congested streets of Rome calling the people to Saint Peter's at five o'clock. At the appointed hour at least a hundred thousand persons jammed the great square before the cathedral as the ponderous bells opened and closed their black mouths, sending a clangorous peal across the white roofs of the city. The Pope walked out on the balcony—rather, he seemed to flow out—in his shimmering white robes, and when he raised his arms and in melodious Italian offered thanks to his Deity for the sparing of Rome, the mass of humanity knelt in a vast, rippling movement. I was, and am, devoid of any feelings of religious awe toward the Vatican, and I have always felt that as a political force it has inclined toward Fascism. Yet in this spectacle there was a medieval splendor and pageantry which, as theater alone, was profoundly stirring. In its controlled mastery the Pope's eloquence was as beautiful as any I have ever heard, and I was impressed both by his "showmanship" and by his political genius. For, by inference, he took credit for the fact that the city had been spared. As time passed, we were to realize how he had taken energetic advantage of the situation in every respect. He knew the Allies were bound to take Rome and win the war. While he had allowed very few Germans inside the Vatican grounds, we discovered that dozens of escaped Allied fliers and prisoners had found sanctuary there. He had given no general audiences to German soldiers, but every day he received and individually blessed hundreds of Allied troops, tat-

tered and dirty though they might be. Furthermore, the Vatican
at its own expense was keeping some three hundred thousand
Italian refugees alive in Rome, and, when the relief administrators
of Allied Military Government arrived, they simply fitted their
organization in with that of the Vatican. The Pope's prestige in
Italy soared to great heights.

The war correspondents, too, were received in audience. At
least, the audience was intended for the journalists, but a couple
of hundred soldiers, nurses, and hangers-on joined our procession
into the long room and lined the walls with us as he mounted the
dais to speak. In several respects this audience broke with Vatican
tradition. It was the first mass meeting the Pope had ever held
with journalists, and it was surely the first time he ever received
a woman wearing trousers. She was an enormously fat journalist
who was temporarily without other garb. As the Pope came upon
her in the lineup, he retained his remarkable composure and merely
smiled benignly. I suppose also that this was the first occasion when
the Pope's wishes were flouted by visitors within his sanctum:
While he spoke from the dais, the photographers scrambled into
their mad performance. They jumped up beside him and snapped
their shutters. They ran around in front of him, bending low for
"angle shots." They dropped their cameras with a clatter, burst
bulbs, and whispered hoarse curses at one another. One went flat
on his stomach before the august presence to get an even better
angle shot. Several times the Pope waved them away with a brief,
peremptory gesture, without pausing in his English discourse,
and his tail-coated attendants gestured madly at the photographers
while sweat poured down their fiery faces. The cameramen continued their antics quite unabashed. Most of us were stiff with
shame and so distracted that we could not follow his words. In
the immense crowd I found the chief press officer standing next
to me and could not refrain from whispering: "Do you want me
to dateline this story *With the Fifth Army in the Vatican?*" He
shuddered.

Soldiers sometimes discuss their religious beliefs among themselves; observers such as correspondents are rarely included in
this talk. But I had a distinct feeling that some of the devout
Catholic soldiers I knew, for whom the Vatican was the whole
center and meaning of Rome, were bolstered in their feeling about
their Church by the splendor and majesty of the Papacy. I thought
of two Catholics who in southern Italy had confessed to me that

they were shaken by the sight of shabby, unshaven priests begging cigarettes on the curb and even offering to take the men to prostitutes.

Late in the afternoon of the day of liberation I checked in at the luxurious Grand Hotel. The suave clerks were receiving us with complete composure, as if this were all in the day's business, though German officers had that very morning checked out; their names were still fresh on the register. The swank bars of the city were already doing business with the new customers, and one had to fight his way through the street girls on the corners. At midnight I wandered toward my hotel and in the moonlight came upon two tired American paratroopers from Frederick's regiment, who were sitting disconsolately on the curbing. They were lost, had no place to sleep, and were under orders to report to their outfit, somewhere outside the city, by six in the morning. I took them to my room and they stretched out on the floor. We talked a while, and one of them, a brawny St. Louis man who had been a milk-wagon driver, said: "You know, I been reading how the FBI is organizing special squads to take care of us boys when we get home. I got an idea it will be needed, all right. See this pistol? I killed a man this morning, just to get it. Ran into a German officer in a hotel near the edge of town. He surrendered, but he wouldn't give me his pistol. You know, it kind of scares me. It's so easy to kill. It solves all your problems, and there's no questions asked. I think I'm getting the habit." Toward dawn I thought I heard the sound of running water and came full awake to discover that the bathroom faucets, useless after the water supply went down, had started functioning in the night. The two paratroopers were sleeping soundly in an inch of icy water, and the beautiful flooring of inlaid hardwood tiles was ruined. Uncertain of the new conquerors, the management said nothing.

In midmorning of the day following the fall of Rome, the correspondents were working feverishly in the press building when a BBC man ran in and shouted: "Eisenhower has announced the invasion of France! It's official!" Every typewriter stopped. We looked at one another. One or two shrugged their shoulders and went back to work; most of us sat back, pulled out cigarettes, and dropped our half-written stories about Rome to the floor. The "play" had suddenly been taken away from the Italian campaign, and after weeks of worldwide attention we had in a trice become

performers without an audience. To a certain extent all of us confused our own progress with that of the war itself, and we were
now in the position of a troupe of actors who, at the climax of their
play, realize that the spectators have all fled out of the door to
watch a more spectacular performance across the street.

6

It was a proper time to take a rest, and I caught a midnight courier
jeep to Naples, en route for a few days in Cairo. We drove out
along the Appian Way. The concealed moon faintly rimmed the
black clouds as we mounted toward the dark mound of the Alban
Hills. In the direction of the sea there were bomb flashes, sudden
spreading waves of orange light. A motor drummed overhead in
the blackness. We drew to a stop and doused our dim lights. A
flare dangled above, drifting slowly, revealing an old portal of
carved stone beside us and in a field the truncated remains of a
Roman aqueduct. The ominous night closed again over these relics
of serenity and grandeur. We climbed slowly and the cypresses
were outlined in a stately row on a hillside. Unlighted Rome vanished behind, drawing the torn veil of darkness around her, jealous
of her unblemished body, distrustful of her sudden peace. The
guard of famous and well-born villages which Rome had given in
fatal hostage sprawled obscenely upon the slopes. Frascati, Velletri, and the others were dead under the dark moon, their bones
showing ghostly white and their insides emptied in cold heaps
upon the roadway. The clinging odor of death was the only reminder of life.

The hectic headquarters glamor was gone from Naples. The city
appeared suddenly in its natural state: without pretenses, more
shabby than ever, a half-deserted village. The previous vortex of
excited crowds, parties, sex, hatreds, and loves could scarcely even
be recalled. A few soldiers from Rome drifted through, jeered at
the Naples gin and the dusty Terminus hotel, and boasted of the
well-dressed girls and the luxuries of Rome, as though these things
were their personal discovery and private property. The Peninsular Base troops were no longer envied. (When the combat men
reached Rome they had immediately planted a sign at the city
limits: "Rome—Off Limits to PBS Troops." And the base troops

had immediately inserted an entering wedge by sending a van to Rome which stood in the Piazza di Venezia bearing a sign: "Rome Beer Express, compliments of PBS Naples.") On Capri, resting fliers sat on the rocks dressed in wide straw hats and sandals with bright sashes around their brown waists. In the Naples park General Wilson was just opening a new club, "for colonels and generals only." The British had organized an Allied yacht club, using confiscated luxury vessels and army gasoline. I swam off the rocks in the warm blue water and sat in the stillness of Axel Munthe's Capri gardens with Charley Poletti. Sorrento was in flower, the fishermen dozed at their oars, the grapes were growing fat in the sun, and Vesuvius was quiet. Southern Italy was returning to itself. The garish screen was removed, and one could see now the humbleness, the essential peace, the unaltered waking dream of barrenness in beauty.

Italy was eternal because the earth is eternal, and however destructive the modern weapons and engines of man, they merely scratch the earth. It is the things that men build with their hands that war destroys. Across half of Italy our war had already destroyed innumerable and irreplaceable treasures of men's art, some of which had come down from classic Greece. The barbaric Nazi vandals, deliberately involving Europe's ruin in their own, had destroyed precious things like the Naples library specifically *because* they were precious. We had destroyed them simply because we did not care what they were, and it required effort to spare them. Though I thought for a long time, I was unable to find logical reason for some of our methods of waging war. There had been scores of episodes like Cassino or Cisterna. For weeks we would be halted before one of these old cities, and we would shell it without pause until it was rubble. Why? The shelling killed only a very few of the enemy, it wasted countless tons of supplies, and yet in almost every case it was only through the final attack by armor and infantry that the Germans were routed from the rubble, which proved better protection for them than the buildings and which merely impeded the movement of our own vehicles. Shelling upon specific objectives could not be avoided, but this wholesale devastation seemed wanton and senseless to me. Frequently one stood with an artilleryman and listened to remarks like this: "I'm getting tired of seeing that big white building there. Knock the goddam thing down." He did not know, and would not have cared, whether it was an enemy headquarters, a family home, or a famous museum. It had become a kind of obsession to destroy, to fire for the sake of firing.

There were many things that were not clear to me. I wondered whether the abrupt change in the beachhead strategy had been ordered because advance word had come that D-day in France was at hand, and it was considered important to get Rome in advance of the northern invasion. Thousands of Germans had got away to the north of Rome, yet no one could really prove that the first strategy would have meant their certain capture, and it was obvious that we had indeed destroyed a formidable part of two German armies. Yet had we accomplished anything decisive so far, with our enormous investment here of men, planes, ships, tanks, and vehicles, which was so immensely greater than the German budget for Italy? It seemed to me that the Italian campaign was, and had been, little more than a war of attrition, as so much of the First World War had eventually become. In any case, the validity of this campaign now rested upon how many troops it forced the Germans to divert from northern Europe, where the real decision in the war would surely be reached.

After ten days away from Italy, I retraced the battle route to Rome. We passed through endless scenes of a silent, primeval desolation, and it required deliberate mental effort to recall that there had been a reason for what had happened here. It was equally difficult to think that there could be a future for these areas. Nothing remained of all that the hands of men and the workings of the centuries had erected upon these hills and fields; yet the instinct for identity was already drawing human beings back again. They knew their homes were no more than dusty heaps of masonry, and still they returned, drawn by nothing of value, since all was gone, but by the deep, mysterious instinct in all animals that find shelter for the senses in the surroundings of their birth, even though there be no shelter for their bodies. The ones who now returned were the poor, the little people, who had had no country homes nor Roman apartments for retreat, and it would be they who would reconstruct this civilization, treating each lump of soil in their hands, replacing brick upon brick. Skinny horses stumbled in the shafts of rickety carts piled high with rickety chairs and tables; barefooted children led overburdened burros; beside the roadway father and son were trying again to patch a tire that would stand no more. Those who had arrived "home" stood help-less before the dusty piles. They betrayed no signs of resentment, nor even of sorrow; they seemed numbed by a fathomless stupe-faction, their minds faintly stirring to marvel that things could be so much altered. They were taking it as they had taken war and the regime that had produced the war and as they took defeat.

In Rome, which could be articulate because the alteration was not so drastic, the people were finding the first refuge, which is always in talk. They were saying: "When the war is all over, Italy will have nothing but her beauty."

The lazy summer weeks passed, the Allied armies moved very slowly through the northern valleys, and Rome became a city without a character of its own. Its crooks grew rich in the black market, its honest men debased themselves to find food and work, its statesmen were frustrated by lack of real authority, its working class grew desperate because Allied wage rates were smaller than either Fascist or German, its social aristocracy seduced unprin-cipled Allied officers as it had seduced German officers, its real patriots became bitter because they were not allowed to fight, and its young girls prostituted themselves to the Allied soldiery. The middle class resented our presence because it disturbed their com-forts, and proprietors haggled acrimoniously over the prices of apartments we were decent enough to rent, as though we were tourists admitted to Rome by special favor. Wealthy British and American women expatriates, married to Italian aristocrats, com-plained bitterly about the war because they had been obliged to walk to market and dress their own children—"My dear man, you have *no* idea what we went through!" For such as these the war had no meaning, nor had the victory. Italy was either in its death throes or in the labor pains of rebirth, and no two Italians agreed which it was; but whichever it was, the suffering was heavy, both physical and moral, and the effort was exhausting.

On the surface Rome appeared at peace. People took their daily siestas as they always did; on Sundays the church bells rang as they had on other Sundays; and, as always, the marvelous sun-sets burnished the tinted walls. Never before in her history had Rome been taken by such a variety of races and peoples. In the beginning the Americans were the most popular, but in time our rowdy, boisterous men spoiled their chances in Rome as they had done almost everywhere else and were to do in many other places later. Of all the invaders, the Negroes were the best liked because

they were the best behaved and because the Italians like men who
smile easily and have a gentle way with children. When our men
first set foot within Rome they felt some slight wonder and awe
among the fabled monuments; but history was not their strong
point, and they soon found their chief fascination in modern comforts and erotic pleasures. Rome might be eternal, but even in Rome
a soldier felt that *his* life might be short. So one night history lovers
who entered the Colosseum found G.I. loud speakers blaring jazz
music from the center of the arena once hallowed by the blood of
Christian martyrs. Rome became a rear-area city like Naples, and
the perquisites were handed out to officers and enlisted men with
the same injustice. Enlisted men could sleep, read, and swim in
YMCA wholesomeness at the Mussolini Forum on the edge of the
city, while officers drank and fornicated in the luxurious hotels
along the Via Veneto, carefully guarded by military police who,
with a stern devotion to duty, ruthlessly excluded infantry officers
from the air force bordellos and vice versa.

The Eternal City became the unholiest pleasure palace in
Europe. It is not likely that this war had seen anything to compare
with the Hotel Excelsior, once the smartest in Rome, which developed into such a roaring, night-long brothel that decent girls
were forbidden by their mothers even to be seen in the vicinity
and the Vatican finally protested. As time passed, the quality of
the girls frequenting the place gradually went down until they
were almost exclusively common whores from the slummier districts. It was hard for anyone to blame the young officers, who had
come back from the miserable front lines and wanted to make the
most of their precious three days of liberty. There was something
deeply disturbing about the behavior of the women. It was generally true that in the excitement of liberation the local men would
seek emotional release by killing Fascists or demanding to fight
with the allies, while the women could express themselves only by
sexual activity. That was the natural reaction everywhere. But
there was another aspect of the phenomenon that revealed a second
biological instinct: the women did not express themselves with
their own men, the vanquished, but gave themselves at once to the
victors, whatever their nationality, no matter what they had done
to the Italian men or the Italian land. Everywhere in Europe one
saw this expression of women's need to attach themselves to the
stronger party. It seemed a fundamental, universal reaction, but
the consequences were always bad. The deserted Italian swains

became embittered against both the Allied soldiers and their own women, head shavings became fairly frequent events, and once scores of girls who emerged from an Allied dance were set upon by a mob of frustrated Italian men. A famous cartoon showed a Roman man meeting another who had a girl on his arm. "How did you get her?" the former exclaimed. "Oh," the other said, "an American G. I. introduced me to her."

Of all the strange complications that occurred in this whirlpool of sex, the strangest was the case of the American major and the swarthy young whore from the suburbs. The major picked up the girl on the streets, danced with her at the Excelsior, and then took her to his room. He spoke excellent Italian, and in the morning, as they chatted while dressing, he showed her a picture of his mother in New York. She stared at the photograph with a frown and then dug out from her shabby purse a photograph of her own mother. It was the face of a much younger woman, but the resemblance between the two was striking. By comparing notes they discovered that the woman had split with her husband years before and gone from Italy to America, leaving her baby daughter and taking her son along with her—and the major and the whore were brother and sister. There is no doubt that this story was true. I met the girl, and she was not only frank about the whole thing— she was proud of it. After the discovery she and the major had gone hand in hand about Rome, both quite happy.

The Italians became officially our cobelligerents, but only on paper, only in oratory. There were some Allied leaders like Poletti (now governor of Rome) who wanted them to be really so, who knew that what was true of the French was equally true of the Italians: that no outsiders could grant them a new life by dispensation, but that they must accomplish it in the struggle of their own hearts if it was to be a valid and durable thing. Two forces worked against them—the stiff attitude of the British, led by Churchill, who really determined Allied policy in Italy, and the natural impersonality of a vast army. The Allied radio would encourage the Italian Partisans north of the front to risk their lives and kill the Germans, and for these purposes guns and advisors were dropped to them in the hills. When, with their help, the Allied army would capture a locality, the Partisans, as often as not, were disbanded, deprived of their arms, and curtly ordered to go back to being peaceful peasants or mechanics. When stories of their shock and bitterness began to seep back into Rome, General

Alexander had a "certificate" engraved, resembling a high school diploma, which was to be graciously awarded these ragged heroes. When a large group of Partisans reached Rome one day, they were buffeted from one headquarters to another and could not even find a place to sleep until the local Communist party installed them in the poorhouse for the night. A Partisan boy of sixteen, burning with eagerness and high ideals, got in to see Poletti at his office. He described with enthusiasm the accomplishments of his band and asked for more ammunition and trucks to carry on the work, leaving Poletti with a sense of humiliation and shame that he could not help the boy.

It was not only the organized Partisans and the political leaders who had fought Mussolini in Spain and spent many years in exile who were stupefied by their treatment at the hands of the Allies. Ordinary, simple people who had tried to help were equally hurt and outraged by official representatives of the "people's war." There was a village in the Alban Hills where the people had risked their lives and given their precious food over and over again to aid liberated Allied prisoners at the time when Mussolini fell. In their simple, superstitious way they thought that, if they did this, their own sons in Allied prison camps would get better treatment. No delegation, no officer of rank ever came to their village later to thank them. Once an Allied officer had dropped there by parachute, during the fighting, to organize the prisoners. The people hid him in their secret caves, and then he ordered them away as if they were a nuisance to him. It was very hard for them to comprehend that great armies are impersonal things of standardized routine, that their tables of organization include no allotment for a man's beliefs, no recognition for private courage outside the system.

In retrospect now, some of it seems almost humorous; at the time it was anything but that. I felt shocked to go from a conversation with the determined Socialist leader, Pietro Nenni, who had suffered years in exile for this moment of opportunity, to another with the elegant ambassador, who really knew better but who would say with a wave of the hand: "Ah, the Italians are pleasant people, very fine at painting scenery and singing arias, but don't make the mistake, my boy, of taking them seriously." It was a shock to receive a dispatch from Winston Burdett, at the Florence front, which said: "We have visited the estate of the Marchesa Torrigiani, formerly Lucy Davis of Worcester, Boston, and Philadelphia. She spoke to us with feeling of her hardships, with butter and coffee so expensive and as many as nine German officers in her salon at one time. But, she told us, the German commander of Florence was a nice man—he gave her a driving permit. She said the greatest outrage occurred when her chauffeur deserted his post to become a Partisan leader. However, she told the British AMG officer, who gave him a good talking-to. He wants his old job back now that the fighting is over. 'But,' said the Marchesa, with the firmness of a lady whose great-grandfather had had something to do with the Boston Tea Party, 'I'm taking him back on probation only.'"

It seemed to me clear, as clear in Italy as it had been in London during the siege, that under the wide, lateral cover of the war of nationalities a vertical social and political revolution was going on. It seemed to me that this movement had to be helped and not hindered, despite its excesses, if there was ever to be a stable peace for Europeans. But did my own people recognize this, or would they now, forgetting what Europeans had suffered from the tyrants, hinder the natural course of events because they were not always a pretty spectacle? How many were there like the woman journalist who came over from New York and wrote about the "terrible spirit of vengeance," the arrests and shootings "merely because of political differences"? To her, political differences were merely something that led to arguments over tea tables or in radio forums. I advised her to do what I had done—to visit the catacombs, where they had just uncovered the bodies of three hundred and twenty Italian men and boys, put to a horrible death by the Germans in a ten-to-one reprisal against the bomb killing of thirty-two German soldiers in Rome. It had happened in March and had been since then a topic of hushed speculation throughout the city. These victims had had nothing to do with the bomb assault; they were simply suspects languishing in jail, whom the Gestapo routed out in the night, half of them in their underclothes. They were taken in trucks to the cave entrance on the edge of the city and herded inside. They were manacled together in groups of four or five and shot with tommy guns, and they fell upon the writhing bodies of those who had preceded them. Then the entrance was dynamited and the place sealed up. Priests near by said they could hear faint cries from the dying for twenty-four hours afterwards. When I entered the clammy, ghostly subterranean chambers, they were faintly lighted by torches, and we choked on the fumes of chlorine

which were intended to dispel the stench of death but which did
not quite succeed. The victims were just bones now, attached to
ragged, rat-chewed fragments of cloth, and experts were assem-
bling the bones on tables, trying to identify them. This was the result of "political differences" in modern Europe. Vengeance is not
a thing of dignity at any time, nor is it always precisely just, but I
found myself quite incapable of advising the fathers and
brothers of such victims to be gentle with those who had caused
the horrors.

7

August arrived, and the correspondents were assembled to be officially told "the worst-kept secret of the war"—plans for the sea-
borne assault on the southern coast of France. General Alexander's
deputy blandly informed us that the Italian front was not and
would not become a secondary front and that we must not suggest
in our dispatches that it was, because the troops' morale would
be injured thereby. (A gross slander on the intelligence of the
soldiers.) All the French and at least three of the best American
divisions would be taken away for the invasion, but Alexander intended to scrape up every man he could from other theaters of
war. And why? Because he meant to drive ahead in northern Italy,
assaulting the Gothic Line and the other lines until we conquered
the Po Valley. And he did not intend to stop there: he would
carry on, entering Germany from the south—which implied fighting
our way through the Alps in the cold season. Generals relinquish
the glories of the offensive with great reluctance; this seemed madness even to us who were amateur militarists. Already, in summer,
with our full force, the going was extremely slow against the mountain defenses. Unless, by some miraculous luck or some unpredictable alteration in the German character, the reduced Allied
force could make such rapid progress that Hitler would be obliged
to send great numbers of men from northern Europe, the plan
simply made no sense. Surely, we thought, it would be wiser just
to hold in Italy while diverting as many men as possible to a flatter
terrain where decisions could be reached.

(In November, when his assaults had failed, Alexander issued
an astonishing defense of the whole Italian campaign. He said that
the Fifth and Eighth armies could not reasonably be expected to

get the Po Valley before spring unless the enemy made serious mistakes. He said the south-of-France invasion had left him with too little strength, though he had known what he would have before he ordered the offensive continued. He told the world that the objective of the Italian campaign had been to destroy "as much as possible" of the enemy forces (an abridgment of his declaration in May) and to "produce a first-class victory before the second front opened in Normandy." "Rome," he said, "was that victory." He repeated the canard that we had never had more than a "slight" numerical superiority over the Germans at any time in Italy. He meant that the Allies had very few more *divisions* than the Germans, omitting to mention that the numerical strength of the average German division there was one half to two thirds of our own, that our air supremacy was around twenty-to-one, and that our supplies of tanks, artillery, and transport were enormously greater than the Germans'. And, most important of all for the final assessment of the Italian campaign, he admitted that the Germans had diverted only five new divisions into Italy from other areas— one, I believe, coming from Yugoslavia. In May his officers had made it clear that the Italian mission would be a failure if we merely forced a slow German retreat and did not oblige the enemy to divert large forces. So it seemed to me that on their own scales the Italian campaign was weighed and found wanting. It was not due to stupidity on the part of generals or to a lack of valor on the part of fighting men; it was due to the impossible terrain of Italy itself, which made it possible for a third-rate army to hold off a first-rate force with one hand. But Italy's terrain was not an unknown quantity when the original decision to proceed up the peninsula was made. Who made this decision, where and why, has never been explained to the Allied peoples. I have heard it said in high places that the campaign was the "remnant of Churchill's abandoned Balkan strategy." I do not know. I do feel that it was all a frightful waste of lives and machines which could have been put to more fruitful use somewhere else. It was true that we had knocked the remaining Italian Fascists out of the war, got important aid to Tito, and done effective strategic bombing from southern Italy. But surely it made no sense to try to attack beyond Rome; perhaps we would have done as well to stop nearer Naples, on the Volturno line. I felt so strongly about Alexander's statement that I wrote a refutation for the *New Statesman* of London. After much hesitation the editors printed it with their fingers crossed, fully expecting a violent reaction from the War Office. There was never a murmur.)

For four years I had looked forward to re-entering Paris on the day of its liberation. The chance now seemed remote indeed, but at least I could go back to France, find out what had happened to her people, and catch a glimpse of her future, which was bound to determine in large measure the future of all Western European civilization. Only two American radio correspondents would be allowed places in the landing craft for the initial assault. When the slips of paper were drawn from the hat, and I saw that I had won a place, I was as excited as a child who is told after much indecision that he can go on the picnic after all. Then a nervous reaction set in. I had no idea what an attack from the sea was like, and the Germans would surely be ready and waiting. One day my Italian assistant remarked: "Everybody in town is talking about an invasion of southern France. Is it true?" I pleaded ignorance and felt perspiration break out on my face. On the street a drunken paratrooper stopped me while I was talking with some American girls on an entertainment tour. The boy leaned on me, attempted to pat one of the girls, and told us how his outfit had been training near Ostia. "Guess we are going to drop around Marsayles or Toulon or one of them French places," he blurted out, and staggered down the street, no doubt spreading his news everywhere he went.

Geoffrey arrived one day in uniform again, tanned and taut and happy to be back with the New Zealand army. He laughed when I told him my fears, then apologized and said: "I don't mean to make fun of it. I was just thinking how many times I've gone through the same torture. It's always the same with people who feel anything. Once you get moving you will be all right."

I doubted that. At night I could not sleep, but twisted about and called myself a fool for undertaking something I did not have to do. I thought of devices whereby I could get out of it, using my family responsibilities and my previous risks as justification to myself for reneging. I felt what I had felt when Walter Port and I had set out from Norway House into the wilderness of Canada. I knew that this act was not rational, that it was not necessary, but deep in the core of consciousness I knew also that if I backed out I would cripple something within me and that I would bear an inner scar for the rest of my life.

Chapter XIV

I DO NOT RECALL that we saw the moon that night; there must have been clouds, which were also indistinct. But a suffused light lay upon the warm sea and gave shadowy form to the other ships lying around us. The metal protuberances about me, the winches and the guns and the iron ladders, glowed softly in this strange illumination. The forms of the Navy men huddled by the guns were quite dark, but when one of them turned his head the whites of his eyes could be seen. If I stepped in front of the wheelhouse I could just make out the rows of dark blobs on the deck which were the jeeps and other vehicles lashed down, their operators still sleeping somewhere in the deeper shadows beside them. Dawn would be approaching soon; this was the third night and the last.

I had no idea what would happen to us when the light came. Nobody on board this LST had the remotest notion of how it would all go off. All of us had speculated about it considerably over the maps, as we examined the enemy gun positions and studied the alignment of obstacles—the pill boxes, the barbed wire, the mine fields, and the high cement walls which the photographs indicated were there. But that was before we boarded the craft off the slopes of Vesuvius and began the voyage. After we had begun nobody discussed the landing very much, and it was true, as Geoffrey predicted, that at that moment fear, too, had dropped away. What had caused this—whether the spectacle of power that one saw all around him or the immediate sense of strength derived from comradeship with the men—I am not sure. Perhaps it was merely that all possibilities of alternative action were gone, and because of movement itself.

I had anticipated that when this inevitable hour arrived I would surely be very much frightened in the face of the unknown; yet I was not. It was true that I could not sleep, but there was no feeling of weariness in nerves or muscles; indeed I thought I had never felt so relaxed and alert, so calm and integrated. I felt much pleased with myself, with the good company in which I traveled, with the good-natured, efficient way in which everything had been done. I had liked the matter-of-fact way in which the Navy officer had spoken to his assembled men, the brief and undemonstrative meeting at prayer on Sunday morning, even the ragged singing, and the messages of good luck from Field Marshal Wilson and General Alexander, which were sincere and manly and devoid of exclamatory heroics. I was happy to be where I was; I would not have been elsewhere for anything in the world. The others perhaps felt differently about our destination, but for me, to come back to France in this manner with my own countrymen was the reforging of an old, broken link; it was a justification, a reaffirmation of personality, a victory.

I gave up trying to pierce the night with the naked eye in order to see the shore, and stretched out again on the cot behind the wheelhouse. It was some minutes before I realized what it was that I was smelling. I sat up and sniffed deliberately, but that way it did not work. So I relaxed and breathed very lightly again, and was sure of it this time. It made me shiver for a moment and wish to call out to the others who slept. I was smelling the land; I was smelling France. There was no doubt of it. It was a very faint perfume, the smell of a pine forest in the stillness of a dewy morning. There was no hint of death or despair in it; France smelled fresh, clean, and whole.

The dawn came, gray and misty, and we were disappointed to see that there were low clouds over the shoreline, which was almost indistinguishable from the rippling, iron-colored sea. This, we thought, would be bad for the bombers; they would miss many of the mines planted in the sands, which would mean that more mines would be exploded by human bodies. But the bombers came, although we could scarcely see them in the mist, and geysers of smoke precisely stippled the shoreline, with the sound like that of a boy a block away running a stick rapidly along a wooden fence. There was undoubtedly an orderly sequence in all that was done, though to one who merely watched, all that happened came as a sudden surprise, and there seemed no connection between events. There were deep, muffled explosions ahead, and we knew that was the dynamite rending the underwater obstacles. There was a tremendous flaring and a shocking series of reports from the rocket-carrying small boats which went in close and fired point-blank at the beaches and the pillbox defenses. It seemed quite impossible that flesh and blood could stand in the face of that. A cracking explosion to the rear made us turn our heads in time to see black smoke drifting in a huge puff from a long, low battleship. As we watched, flame spurted from the great craft again, there was a rushing of wind over our heads, concussion that tipped our helmets sideways, and again the cracking sound. We did not see where the shells landed, but only heard the dull sound of their explosion coming back later from somewhere inland.

At eight o'clock we knew that the first of the infantry assault waves was on the beach, but we could see and hear nothing of what was going on there. After a while a radio message came to the bridge saying that the first waves were safely ashore with extremely light casualties, due chiefly to mines. The battleships fired some more. Down in the officers' wardroom, the ship's surgeon was clearing the tables and fixing a powerful light bulb in the ceiling, preparing for emergency operations. With the two other radio correspondents on board, Chester Morrison and Vaughn Thomas, I began typing short dispatches which were immediately sent out by key from the transmitter mounted in a van lashed to the deck. Somebody called and pointed. An enemy shell had just fallen into the water close to another LST off our starboard bow. Another shell came in and was equally harmless. These were the only manifestations of resistance we had seen. After a time all firing abruptly ceased. Even the shoreline was quiet. The dust and smoke began to drift away, and we could begin to make out the trees and hills. The silence continued; the enemy was not replying. He could not be waiting for better targets; it was too late for that. It could only mean that the climax had already come and gone. I could not quite believe it could all be over so quickly, so easily as this. But the soldiers on the ship understood, for they had known other landings. Their tense little groups began to break up. They started to talk out loud and to form up for breakfast. Some of them tossed away their lifejackets. A few began reading their French manual; others tied the red-white-and-blue identification bands around their arms. I felt almost disappointed. The soldiers did not.

We grated to a halt in the tiny cove, hardly a hundred yards long, which had been picked for the landing of this part of the Forty-fifth Division. It was one of several, poorly defended, and so small that it had not occurred to the enemy that we would dare attempt a landing upon them. The dry hills beyond the beach and the coastal road were burning in several places, and a pink pleasure villa showed a wide hole where a shell had gone clear through. The road was already choked with traffic, and bands of prisoners, their hands in the air, were marching toward the water line. Already army signposts were stuck in the sand, and soldiers were directing traffic with a wave of the hand. The cement wall, five feet thick and eight feet high, had proved a poor defense. The first waves had surmounted it with ladders, and sappers had blown a great breach in it through which we rolled as easily as if we were entering the gate of a city—or a nation. A few trees were sprawling on the streets of Saint-Maxime, and a few lengths of telegraph line were draped over hedges and fences. Three American Negroes sat in the shade against the stucco wall of a bistro, guarding a batch of prisoners from the master race. A white soldier was stretched out by the road with his shoes off under a bright green beach umbrella. Another was methodically moving through a vineyard filling his helmet with fat, bronze grapes. A girl of about thirteen, wearing an American helmet cocked over her long yellow hair, was trying, between spurts of self-conscious laughter, to pin a bunch of bright flowers to the shirt of a raw-boned infantryman.

There were not many civilians around. They watched us with an intense expression of curiosity, and they smiled easily, but there was no wild demonstration in this place. It was clear: the shock of the battle had stunned them, some of their friends had been killed, and they were just a little disappointed that we were not French. I had never been in this region before, but it was all exactly as it should have been. It was France. The blue berets, the Cinzano signs, the powder-blue denim of the workmen, the faintly sourish smell of wine as one passed the *zincs,* the dusty plane trees, the little formal gardens, the soft, translucent air. The Germans had changed nothing. We passed through the village toward our rendezvous on the hill among the cork and pine trees. I did not feel either tense with excitement or weak with sentiment, as I had anticipated. I felt a lightness in my body and a desire to sit somewhere quietly and let it all come back into focus.

In the morning we were camped among vineyards by the beach, on the bay of Saint-Tropez where black and gray battlecraft of all kinds now replaced the bright-colored fishing and pleasure boats of former summers. Other reporters straggled in, blackened with grime and exhausted from their efforts to get to the transmitter along the single, crowded coastal road. Only we three of the British and American radio had come in with the transmitter, which was the only one the Army provided for the invasion, and there appeared to be some resentment by press reporters that we had got the first stories from the beaches back to Rome and the Allied capitals. Yet it had been clear to them all that there was but one transmitter and but one road, which was certain to be jammed with the traffic of three divisions. When two or three friends flew in from Rome they congratulated me on getting the first dispatch to press headquarters there. What had happened was this: on the ship, after some discussion, Major Pellegrin and Captain Bennett, the censor, agreed that it would make no sense to wait for the "release" time—ten minutes past noon—before opening up with our portable transmitter which filed into Rome. At H-hour, which was 8 A.M., all operational radio silence would naturally be broken, and there could be no more secrecy. It happened that I was the first among the three radio reporters on board to turn in my dispatches, and two hours before release time they were in the hands of the Rome censors, who were so surprised and flustered that they sequestered the copy behind locked doors for some minutes before Winston Burdett was able to lay hands upon it. Of course it could not be dispatched abroad until 12:10, and it had to be shared out to the other radio companies in the "pool" arrangement, anyway, so that the scoop was confined in its effect to the reporters. At 12:10, Morrison began speaking in a "live" broadcast to New York, with Thomas and me ready to follow him. After he had spoken for a minute a fuse blew out, and that was the end of the first direct broadcast made from an invasion craft during the European war. Other reporters of course had flown over by plane and returned immediately to Rome with their bird's-eye-view accounts, but for most of the first day the story of the actual landing was radio's story, and those few remaining die-hards of the press who regard radio news as something unstable and suspect were profoundly annoyed. What was really remarkable was that for the first time Army red tape was cut away for a major event—thanks to Pellegrin and Bennett—and the world heard the news as quickly as it was entitled to hear it.

2

A man whose army and country have suffered defeat is not a complete man afterwards; no matter how healthy his body, he is
always a little sick. The conditions of defeat do not count. No matter if he fought bravely himself, no matter if his army never had
a chance, no matter if he was betrayed by treasonable leaders—
none of this provides him more than a lip-service, and he remains
a cripple. Time will not entirely cure him; and it does not suffice
that others restore his country. He must act again himself if he
would recover. And this is, at bottom, why Frenchmen acted. This
is why they never waited until invading troops insured their lives,
but rose up in every village and city before we arrived, sometimes
days before, and did things that were reckless, sometimes useless,
but always magnificent and of imperishable memory. Sometimes
an Allied officer became deeply annoyed with some rash thing
they had done, not understanding the deep, elemental reason for
its doing. Sometimes an Allied soldier would shake his head with
incredulity to see a French farmer assault a German machine gun
with a single grenade and a pistol, and he would say: "These
Frogs are crazy," not understanding why the farmer had to do
this even if he died in its doing. We were to see these things now
every day, everywhere we went for many weeks, and gradually I
understood clearly, in confirmation of all that I had hoped, that
our invasion was not the liberation of a people any more than it
was the joining of two great armies, one from the outside, wearing
khaki, and the other inside, dressed in berets and blue denim.

In the old resort and fishing town of Saint-Tropez, where some
of our paratroopers had come down by mistake, they found that
the FFI had already killed and captured more than a hundred
Germans and that the German garrison in the old blockhouse on
the hill was hopelessly besieged. They charged the fortress along
with the men and boys of the town, and two youngsters, who had
not known the training of war, but only the disgrace of losing it,
raised their heads too high and were killed. There was a hastily
chalked inscription on the schoolhouse which proclaimed it the
FFI headquarters, and here the village people assembled for the
funeral of the two young heroes. Some were dressed in white tennis slacks, some were fishermen in dungarees, and others wore the
remnants of uniforms that dated from the last war. The local

editor, who was sixty-three, opened his black alpaca coat to show us the three bright yellow grenades attached to the cord he used as a belt. The leader of the FFI for the region was a young architect of thirty, Marc Renaud, a darkly handsome man in fashionable sports shirt and white shorts. He wore a lumpy bandage around his neck where an enemy bullet had wounded him, and the blood was still seeping out. After months of hiding and sabotage by midnight, he was suddenly the hero, the great man of the community, and somehow, even in the dress he wore, he was more dramatically military than any uniformed soldier I had ever seen. His fighters marched and wheeled with briskness if not precision, but it did not occur to anyone to smile at this, or at their fierce expressions, or at the motley collection of weapons they bore. All pretenses were down among Frenchmen and nothing mattered but what each had done, what was in the head and heart. Some British and American flags were brought out that had been hidden in a cellar all these years and were now badly mildewed and wrinkled. It seemed to me that they were displayed at this moment, not as the formal symbols of political alliance, but as the symbols of the eternal brotherhood of all decent, civilized peoples. The two plain wooden coffins were laid gently upon rows of kitchen chairs, while the blackened hands of the fighters carefully placed on them some bunches of flowers from the city park. The bereaved mothers were in black but they wore no veils; and their men supported them by the elbows. One of the fathers was a tall, strong man about forty-five, who had dressed in his officer's uniform. The cap was on his head at the old, jaunty angle, but his open, decent face was working as he remained at attention and struggled with the tears. He had fought the formal war and lost it, and now his son, who had worn knee breeches five years ago, for whose protection he had fought, had died to redeem the father's failure, in the first moment of resurrection and peace. The expression in that man's eyes will remain with me long after the details of his face and figure are forgotten.

A French officer who had come ashore with us spoke briefly in the name of General De Gaulle and his government. He said there could be no courage surpassing this, and he begged the townspeople always to remember that France must pay such a price to buy back her dignity and her pride. When the ceremony was over, the two mothers were clinging to the arms of their husbands with both hands, their faces hidden and their bodies quivering.

The fishermen and the shopkeepers blew loudly into their handkerchiefs as the crowd broke up. The women in white sports
clothing dabbed powder on their faces and slowly wheeled their
bicycles toward the road. A German reconnaissance plane was
drumming faintly very high above, and a few shells went up from
one of the ships lying beyond the fringe of trees in the park. In
the evening enemy bombers came, and two or three in the town
were killed. After that, war did not come near Saint-Tropez again.

Within three days the war seemed very far away from all this
region, so rapidly did our formations penetrate back through the
dry mountains. Along the coast the people were engaged in clearing the debris, caring for their injured and working out their new
order of political and community life. San Raphael was badly
smashed up, and as I drove in, a hidden mine tore another building
apart and killed one of our engineers. Though on the beach itself
the Germans fought with devastating effect, the whole town had
fallen behind them before they knew what was up. In the bistro on
the city square the bartender slid cognac across to us and told us
how it had happened. Every night the underground organization
listened to the BBC, until on the night of the 14th they heard the
announcer say: "Nancy has a stiff neck"—which was the signal that
the next dawn would bring invasion. The families were sent to the
shelters or out into the woods, while the men gathered in the back
rooms with their weapons, which had been kept hidden in separate pieces for this moment. The Germans remained incredibly
ignorant of all that was going on, and, as the first men hit the
beaches, the shopkeepers were upon the Germans' backs.

Before the *mairie* a crowd was gathering, the women in a frenzy
of excitement. A man emerged and placed a chair in the center of
the square. Then the town barber came out from his shop holding
a pair of clippers in the air, which he worked energetically while
grinning on the crowd. An FFI fighter led out the first of the young
women who were to pay the community's penalty for sleeping
with German soldiers. The brunette was defiant and stared back
at the crowd as her hair fell in clusters. The one with chestnut hair
cast down her eyes and brushed off the loose strands from her lap
with trembling fingers. When it was over, the false blonde broke
into sobs and ran through the crowd with tears streaming down her
face. Perhaps this town was an exception, but here there was no
mood of viciousness; the crowd laughed and jeered at the girls
almost, it seemed to me, in good-natured banter. But a young

American soldier pushed angrily away from the crowd and snarled: "That's a lot of ——!" In some towns, American soldiers, who had no conception of what lay behind all this, rescued convicted girls at the point of guns and drove off with them. I spoke for a moment with the tall De Gaulle lieutenant, in temporary charge of the town. "I suppose this looks terrible to some of you people," he said, "our letting them do it. We've got to let them. We can't suppress all this—we can only let them blow off steam and try to keep it under control. You don't know how these people feel. If we clamped the lid on everything, there would be an explosion and we would lose our power to keep order here before we gained it. Some of those girls probably would have been murdered if they hadn't paid the price this way." Through some stroke of fortune they did not deserve, Allied chiefs had finally realized that Americans and Englishmen could not apply military government to the French as they had to the Italians, had wisely left it to the only people who could possibly manage it, and had abandoned all idea of dealing with the Vichyites. Whatever the failures and excesses resulting from this decision, the alternative would unquestionably have been violent civil war and chaos in the midst of the organized fighting.

One morning a French journalist announced "on good authority" that the paratroopers had entered Cannes. It seemed not unlikely at the time, although later we suspected the man had deliberately tricked us, for we observed that he had not followed in that direction but went to a more important scene. Six of us in one jeep—the Army remained incapable of providing a more efficient proportion of vehicles—drove along the rubble-strewn Riviera highway and, after a brief, sentimental reunion between one of our number and two aged innkeepers, we arrived at a battalion headquarters just across the bay from Cannes. The city looked temptingly lovely with the sun on its red roofs and the blue sea tranquil before it, but we were unable to taste its fruits, for the Germans still held us off, and we could proceed no farther without meeting fairly certain destruction. We climbed back up the highway cut into the abrupt cliffs. The jeep made a good deal of noise, and we were talking loudly among ourselves, which is why we heard nothing of a disturbing nature. But as we rounded a bend and came out upon a stretch of road which was in direct view of Cannes, we caught sight of two paratroopers fifty yards ahead. Each man was down on one knee. Instantly the jeep stopped and we were stiff with

apprehension. The men ran headlong towards us, shouting:
"Eighty-eights!" Then I noticed a thin tendril of smoke drifting
along the cliff face just ahead. By extraordinary luck there was a
narrow door cut into the cliff no more than thirty feet away, the
only shelter anywhere in sight. The eight of us were through that
door and flat on our faces in a remarkably short time. As we fell
to the ground the narrow cave reverberated with the scream of an
incoming shell, followed instantly by a shattering explosion just
outside and a little to the side. The cave was a shelter and yet
a trap. There was no way out save by the one door. It was about
twelve feet long and five wide, and had been used as a storage
place for empty wine bottles and other refuse from the villa farther
up the side of the cliff. The walls were straight, and there was
nothing to hide behind save a slight declivity in the west wall,
into which I pressed my face. Should a shell land directly opposite the door our packed bodies would scarcely escape a few fragments, and the concussion in this hollow would be frightful. There
was no other traffic on the road, the jeep and the doorway were
in plain view of the German battery over near Cannes, and there
could be no doubt that they had us in their sights by now and were
firing directly at us. This was a relatively new experience for me,
but a familiar one for the soldiers. To be near shellfire intended for
something or somebody else is distressing enough, but to know
that you are the target is quite another sensation.

We could hear the shells leaving the gun, across the bay, making
a faint *boom*. Then we would press our faces to the wall or the
ground, pulling our helmets tightly down over our heads. I would
close my eyes and grit my teeth. Then the sickening scream and
the explosion again, and I was certain each would be the last sound
I would ever hear. I do not know how many shells came in this
manner—perhaps ten or a dozen. When there was a longer period
of silence than usual, one of the paratroopers peered out the door
and remarked in a casual tone: "The jeep got it." If the jeep was
knocked out, it would mean a walk or a run to the bend of the road,
a good quarter-mile away, and I resolved to remain in the cave
until nightfall if necessary before trying that. After about forty-
five minutes, the silence began to seem durable, and one of the
soldiers slipped out the door, saying: "Think I'll take a look at the
jeep." The two paratroopers worked around the vehicle, lifted
the hood, and one of them even crawled under the jeep. If another
shell came, they would never make it back to the cave; I watched

them with humility and awe. One large fragment had perforated
the hood and cut the ignition wires, but with a strand of wire we
found in the cave the men made a splice and started the motor.
The right rear tire was ripped open, but that repair would have
to wait. At a signal, we all rushed from the cave and threw ourselves upon the jeep. With eight of us aboard it thumped slowly
up the road, and the few minutes that elapsed before we reached
the bend were interminably long. While the tire was being re-
paired we sat by a field aid station, and I clasped my knees with
my arms to conceal the shaking of my legs. The jeep was well
riddled, and the front seat I had occupied before the shells began
bore two large gashes. My typewriter case was perforated, but the
sliver of steel had merely nicked the space bar. My toilet kit was
shredded, and a small bottle of mosquito lotion was now a sticky
mess of powdered glass. When we reached the press camp late
in the evening, there was some official annoyance that we had
"gone and wrecked a jeep."

3

There could be no doubt that this campaign was meticulously
planned and executed with brilliance. From the very beginning,
with the exception of a short delay in the landing of one division
everything progressed on schedule or ahead of schedule. The Allies
had never before had such precise information about the German
defenses and the location, numbers, and condition of their troops.
Heroic men of many nationalities were responsible: the pilot who
flew at two hundred feet along the southern beaches, photographing all the pillboxes—the real ones and the false—and returned
with hundreds of holes in his craft. The British and American men
who landed behind enemy lines in small planes by night over a
period of months. The Frenchmen who had come and gone between these hills and Algiers with such complete information that,
when we landed, all our officers carried maps indicating not only
the location of every farmhouse but the name of the farmer dwelling there, over an area of hundreds of square miles.

Within two days all our invading forces, including the airborne
men in the back country, were linked in one solid front. The movement of the advance was not a wide, sweeping progression, but a
series of quick, deep thrusts. Within a week the total of German

prisoners was running close to twenty thousand, and the Allies had suffered hardly more than a thousand casualties. In all the lower half of France the enemy forces were quickly boxed into separate compartments, and each division faced an almost hopeless choice: either escape, or conduct serious battle. And everywhere, in valleys and hills, inside the cities and towns, the Germans found themselves surrounded by an inner circle of the French underground fighters who gave them no rest and made every house and crossroads a place of peril. Surely modern history reveals no comparable example of a civilian guerrilla army intermeshing with regular troops on such a scale and with such efficiency.

The great armies which had invaded from England were stabbing for the heart of the German defense system, while we in the south were cutting off its feet and legs, and everywhere, even among the most weary and cynical soldiers, there was exhilaration in the rising conviction that the whole body would soon collapse. For the first time in the war, the troops themselves, like the optimistic people at home, began to wager on a quick end to the war. And for the first time in my observation of them they began to *enjoy* the war. The sun was warm and the air like crystal. The fruits were ripening, and the girls were lovely. In every village the welcome was from the heart, and for once civilians were a help instead of a hindrance. The enemy was retreating rapidly or surrendering easily; few of our men were being killed. The soldiers observed that the people were cleaner than the Italians, more straightforward in all relationships, and possessed of a pride and dignity beyond the previous experience of our men. Hundreds of soldiers, particularly the junior officers, began to fall in love with France; I hoped against hope—and against experience and reason —that this marvelous relationship would endure. If we could only keep moving on, avoiding a long stay in any one place, perhaps all this would last.

In battle the men's morale depends very little upon the supply of little comforts; it is a thing of the heart and mind. Never had I seen a greater contrast between opposed troops. The Germans, whose national cult was militarism, were behaving like a rabble of unwilling amateurs. Only occasionally did they stand and fight with determination. They were strong and well fed, and their weapons as excellent as ever. But they felt they had been left in the south as a sacrificial offering. One sensed at once that most of them were already defeated in their minds. Our own men, whose cult was antimilitarism, whose habit it was to identify themselves merely as civilians in different clothes who detested soldiering, now subtly changed. There was a dash and a verve about them that I had rarely observed before, and young boys would frankly say: "In Italy all I used to think about was going home. Now I kind of hate to quit before we get to Berlin." It was as if they had suddenly realized they *were* soldiers by profession, with an honest desire to complete this masterpiece of their skill down to the last detail. As they drove on along the neat highways, through the green, lush valleys, there was an almost festive spirit in the triumphal parade. This was war as it ought to be, the war of pageantry and story. There was little confusion between hero and villain, as in Africa and Italy; the poor and oppressed gave honest thanks for their freedom and plied their liberators with the fruits of their toil; the captive maiden remained fair in the flesh.

When their own French troops began to filter through the valleys, there was a second joyful welcome in every village. The girls tossed flowers again, old men and women tried their best to land the ripe pears inside the passing trucks, and the French soldiers, with a practical instinct, scattered shining cans of rations like bright coins to the scrambling, cheering people. A half-dozen times I watched General "Delattre" pause before a village *mairie*, to be received with kisses and tears, and each time he turned away with tears standing in his own bold eyes. It had been the same for the Americans, everywhere. Even a week after a village was freed, one could drive through it again and find them still lining the curbs, still waving the little flags that sprang by thousands from God knows where, still tossing fruit, still imploring one to stop and drink in their cafés and their homes. I thought how suspicious of foreigners the French countryman had once been, how chary with the intimacy of his family hearth, and it made all this seem doubly marvelous and sincere. Values had changed, I thought, in the hearts of the French. Posturing individuals apart, the French en masse do not affect pretenses; they are anything but a "gay" people at bottom, and only an unregenerate cynic could doubt the heartfelt honesty of their welcome. There was a luminosity in their eyes; it was like the expression of a young boy, long ill, who leaves the sickroom and walks for the first time in the garden and the sun. Sometimes, when an innkeeper or a farm couple learned that Thomas and I were of the Allied radio, they would burst into loud cries, summon the neighbors, and throw their arms about us. They

would tell us of gathering at night, month after month, to listen
to their radios, hidden in back rooms and cellars so the Germans
would not hear. They had probably never heard Thomas or me,
but those distant voices had maintained their hearts in contact
with the world's hope and they treated us as if we were the formal
representatives of the invisible hosts who had reinforced their
patience and steadied their resolve.

Through civilized, settled Provence, through the sun fields of
Van Gogh and the green-and-purple patchwork of Cézanne,
through the formal unity of old Europe spread the brown waves
of the invaders from the New World. Their faces were different,
every one. Their voices rang loudly in tranquillity, and their fearsome engines swelled to mammoth proportions in this garden of
precision. "*Il n'y a pas de mystère en Europe.*" The Old World
has exhausted its reserves of secrecy, every ambition and origin
is charted, every hedge and turning is possessed and known, and
only in the new worlds of America and Russia does mystery remain. Now the contrast never ceased to shock and astound; this
was like a bullfight in an eighteenth-century salon.

There were secret enclaves in Europe's heart, however, which
held a hidden savagery I had first dimly perceived around a guillotine five years before. I was to see it now, nursed by the banked-up
coals of injustice and springing into terrifying flame with the first
wind of freedom. One hot day, after watching the battling inside
Marseille and nervously dodging street-corner bursts of firing between FFI and Darnand's *Milices,* we stopped in a country village where a column of twelve hundred German prisoners were
resting. They had marched from Toulon, guarded by French guerrillas. They had walked all night and throughout the burning day
without a pause or a drink of water. Now they were sprawled along
the roadway that led into the village, flat out on their faces or their
backs. Most were army laborers, not fighters, of middle age, and
their clothes were dusty rags. Some cried and moaned upon the
ground, and some stared at us with unseeing, bloodshot eyes. All
of the village were out, the people crowding near the fountain in
the shady square. Off to one side, I noticed, was a stack of fresh
pine coffins, for French guerrillas whom the Germans had killed
some time before. Now the guerrillas were lining up the prisoners,
four at a time, before the fountain. They shoved and kicked the
wild-eyed men into formation, and then at a signal let them go.
The four would run heavily toward the gurgling fountain, uttering

strange, strangled cries like the baying of stricken cattle. They plunged their heads into the pool, gobbling at the cool water, until the dish-faced Frenchman guarding the fountain would crash his rifle stock against their backs and hit them in the face with his fist to drive them back again. This went on for a long time. Back in the line an old German lay twitching upon the ground, and a guerrilla fired his pistol into the ground close to the man's ear to make him stand up. But the twitching ceased and the man was still. He had died before our eyes. Most of the villagers stared without comment, but a pregnant young woman near me, who held a small child, had tears in her eyes and breathed: "Ahh, this cruelty! It is not necessary that they be so cruel!" Inside the old stone church the priest was stooping to speak with three prisoners who were about to die. Three others, just dead, lay near by. When we turned our vehicle to depart, most of the guerrillas were seated at a long table under the trees, a few feet from the prisoners, pouring out the wine and riotously singing *La Marseillaise* and "Auprès de ma blonde." One could say little in justification. It is true that no French army authorities of the De Gaulle government were in the neighborhood to see that things were conducted otherwise, and obviously some of the worst-behaved of the guerrillas were *maquis de dernière minute*. One could reflect that the Gestapo had never shown any mercy to the patriots of this region. That is all one could say; it was not enough.

4

The Germans' Eleventh Panzer Division was trying to get out of its trap in western France. It moved north up the Rhone Valley, crossing to the east bank in order to avoid the *Maquis* forces in the hills on the western side. This was our chance to destroy them, and the Thirty-sixth Division, commanded by the man who had replaced General Walker, moved in close to the eastern bank, with the Drôme River, which flows westward into the Rhone, as their northern boundary. Then an extraordinary situation developed The Panzers found the Thirty-sixth to their fore, blocking their retreat, and part of the Third Division to their rear. And another force of Germans, north of the Thirty-sixth near Valence, began to exert pressure upon the Thirty-sixth from that direction. It was like a four-decker sandwich. Each inner segment was obliged to fight in two directions, and none of the normal rules of strategy seemed to apply. With four colleagues in a command car I crossed the slim bridge over the Drôme at Crest and entered the large square of rolling hills controlled by the Thirty-sixth. We observed —without comprehending—that an antitank gun was in position by the bridge, pointing down the road toward the near-by Rhone, and that the bridge was wired for demolition. The narrow, winding road became jammed with vehicles as soldiers and machines streamed out of their bivouac areas. Something unusual was afoot, for evening was approaching and this was not normal procedure. The moment we walked into the division C.P., a rambling, concealed farmhouse, we knew that everything was wrong. A surprised lieutenant asked: "How did you guys get in here? Is that bridge at Crest still open?" We assured him it was. "Well, okay, you're in, but I doubt if you'll get out."

Our big guns were sounding very close at hand, and German shells were coming in not far away. Officers were talking in little groups, and a few were sitting on the farmhouse steps, reading a little pamphlet—the army instruction pamphlet on what to do if captured. Finally a friend called us together and said: "Look, here's the situation. We're almost completely surrounded. The whole division. We have moved this C.P. three times in the last twenty-four hours. Our front is too long. It's not holding. They have a lot more tanks than we thought, and they're trying to break through. We have only that road and bridge through Crest—their tanks were only a mile from it when you crossed—and another small back-country road. That's not enough to move the whole division. Anyway, we can't. Our mission is to block the German retreat. I would advise you correspondents to clear out while you have a chance, which means right now."

The whole thing was mad, preposterous. An entire American division, one of our very best, the men who had cracked the defenses of Rome, was threatened with annihilation by frantic, *retreating* Germans. We asked to see the commanding general, and when he stepped out of his van my heart sank. Somehow his appearance and manner were more disturbing than anything indicated on the map. He was dressed only in trousers and undershirt, looking very much unlike a general, and there was perspiration on his face. He was obviously a man who was losing his nerve. He looked at us, counted us off, and said: "Five more men will help.

You may have rifles in your hands before morning." His chief of staff, a small dark colonel, dressed as neatly as if this were any ordinary day, was aware of the effect the General was having upon everybody. He went quietly among the officers and calmly told them not to worry, that everything would be all right. That was merely expressing a hope, but it was also his duty, for once men are beaten in their minds, their bodies have no chance.

We correspondents were in a peculiar position, for we alone had the privilege of deciding our own move. The twenty minutes or so in which we discussed what we should do were among the most distressing of my life. I felt at first that we could not leave—that it would involve an insupportable loss of face and that I would be unable to look these men in the eye again. These were the only reasons for remaining. They were moral reasons. The arguments for departing were rational arguments. We could be of no help. They would never, of course, arm us to fight, which was against all the laws governing correspondents, and if we were captured with arms the Germans would be entitled to shoot us. We could only hang around, depending upon some overworked officer or man to see that our personal needs were cared for. If the headquarters had to move suddenly in the darkness, our big command car and the trailer would be in the way. Already the transport sergeant had twice begged us to move it out somewhere, for the place was jammed with vehicles. We looked at one another in embarrassment for a long time, each of us pulled by conflicting instincts. If this had been our first visit to a critical front, or if the men of the division had been soldiers new to combat themselves, the moral pressures would have conquered. But, like the soldiers around us, we had all acquired something of the veterans' psychology. It is a curious but quite rational thing. By its rules, men who take unnecessary risks are regarded not as heroes but as idiots: their comrades feel not admiration but annoyance, and if the heroics cause them additional risk or trouble, they are likely to detest the hero. If we remained, it was just possible that these officers would like us for it; it was equally likely that they would curse us to themselves as troublesome show-offs. We talked, got it as straight in our heads as we could, then decided to leave—if we could make it.

It was twilight as we drove toward the Drôme, and from every farmhouse, along every footpath we observed the figures of the

French *Maquis,* carrying old rifles and bandoleers, gathering under military orders to counterattack with our soldiers in battalion strength.

The bridge was still intact, and we slept on the ground outside the deadly square. When we returned to the command post early in the morning the whole atmosphere was different. The counterattack had been successful, and the position was restored. Our big guns were able to fire point-blank into the massed German convoys along the river, and after our planes came the resultant spectacle of dead horses and men, of burned-out trucks, tanks, and automobiles was not soon forgotten by those who saw it.

Except for this action and the sieges of Marseille and Toulon, there were few sustained, large-scale battles in the southern campaign, and journalistic colleagues to the north were firmly convinced that we correspondents were having a gay good time, devoid of risk or discomfort. Yet the southern campaign was peculiarly difficult to follow and report, and it entailed a very special kind of risk. The advance troops moved so rapidly in so many directions, the press camp was usually so far behind, that dawn-to-midnight travel was the rule rather than the exception if one was to report the newest developments. After five reporters, led by Edward Kennedy, had made a wide swing through western France up to Paris, performing a useful service in describing this immense area, they were "suspended," and the rest of us were ordered not to "go ahead of the troops." Literally interpreted, this rule would have kept us out of many important areas and cities, freed by the *Maquis* or deserted by the outflanked enemy. So we disregarded the rule and took our chances. There were loose bands of Germans everywhere, some only too anxious to surrender, but others living as bandits in the woods, waylaying food trucks and jeeps by sudden ambush. Travel anywhere was a nervous, exhausting business. One developed a sixth sense that warned of danger. A knot of people at a crossroads, a speeding FFI car, a woman running across a street, faces in the windows instead of crowds in the village square—all these things were instant signs of peril in the neighborhood, and it was fatal to relax one's vigilance very long. Sometimes the very expression in the eyes of a farmer by the roadside would make us halt abruptly or turn up a side road. Several times frantically waving village women prevented us from driving straight into an ambush. Sometimes the desperate Germans were dressed in civilian clothes; sometimes they were riding in sedans with FFI markings; and there was one occasion on which we nearly confronted an ambulance from which German soldiers were firing with tommy guns.

After we left the Thirty-sixth my group decided to take a cut-off, a minor road that wound through high mountains before emerging upon the Route Napoléon near Grenoble. German formations were near by, we knew, but we estimated that they would not be on this road. By midafternoon a misty rain began falling and the light was poor. We encountered no signs that troops of either side had passed through this rugged region, but every village was deserted, and we began to grow apprehensive. We peered ahead through the clouded windshield as we carefully skirted each turning along the sheer canyons. Suddenly our driver drew in his breath with a sighing gasp. Our conversation stopped; our breathing stopped. Emerging from the blackness of a mountain tunnel was a monstrous object moving directly upon us. It was a tank in a place where nobody's tanks should be. In the semidarkness we could not make out its lines very clearly, but there was no mistaking the enormous gun barrel pointed at us. We could only go ahead, since the road was narrow, and on our side of it there was nothing but space. I felt paralyzed in every muscle. The gap was closed, and, as the driver wrenched at the wheel to avoid either collision or a tumble into space, I looked out of the corner of my eyes through an aperture in the command car's curtains. A man with a long-visored cap was peering out of the tank at us. It was several moments before any of us could speak. We never learned whether the tank was ours or German.

5

It was a sunny day when we drove into the magnificent green valley of the Vercors, high in the mountains to the west of Grenoble, an area of plateaux and cultivated fields, as neat, cool, and clean as a vast golf course or park. Frenchmen speak of it now and of all that happened there, the inestimable bravery and the tragedy, almost as Americans speak of Valley Forge. After the events local irregulars of the *Maquis* wore shoulder patches with a Vercors insigne. They are identified with the Vercors just as English soldiers are identified with Dunkirk or Americans with Bastogne and Bataan. Vercors had been one of the great hiding places and rally-

ing points for the *Maquis*. They were organized like an army, with
hospitals, transport and supply services, and military courts; they
had everything except heavy weapons and air support, and for
want of these they were almost entirely wiped out when the Germans sent in two whole divisions to end their ceaseless raiding

The first place we reached after climbing from Grenoble was
the resort town of Villard de Lans. As we entered from one side,
a group of French people came walking in from the other, coming
from La Chapelle farther into the valley. They were led by a dignified man in sport clothes who had been a well-known Paris attorney.
He was the judge advocate for the *Maquis* army in the region. His
wife was a gray-haired women of obvious refinement, her gentle
face seamed with a deep, spiritual weariness. They had just found
the grave of their twenty-year-old son who had fought inside a
house to his last bullet and grenade. When his body was recovered
there were dead Germans on top of him, and beside him was his
young sweetheart who had also fought to the end. We went to the
woman's house and sat about a table while she tried to tell us
the whole story of events in the Vercors. She was a woman of great
inner strength, but every few minutes she became incoherent. She
would lose control, her voice would rise almost to a shout, and
then she would lapse into a kind of dry sobbing. It was impossible
to get the account correctly from her and cruel to continue the
questioning, so we decided to get to La Chapelle ourselves.

Long before we reached our destination we could tell that something terrible had happened along these green slopes. There was no
traffic on the roads. There were no cattle grazing on the hills. Each
time we approached a village we would see two or three furtive
figures disappearing inside or behind the houses. The people had
seen no one from the Allied armies, and they thought we were the
Germans coming back. We would stop in the village square, and
after a few moments they would pour out of the houses, running to
grasp our hands, and the shouting children would clamber over
us as if we were long-lost relatives. Then the beginning of the area
of terror—farmhouses without roofs and blackened on the inside,
civilian cars burned and rusting in the ditches. La Chapelle was
sprawled along the road like all French mountain towns. Of its
ninety houses only four were now intact and whole. All the rest
stood empty, shells and skeletons of houses with nothing inside
but blackened rubble. But already the people were trying to restore
them, and when we stopped, men and women climbed slowly from

their ruins and collected about us. They took us to the back wall of one house where the enemy had lined up the sixteen boys and men, machine-gunned them, and then tossed grenades among their writhing bodies. We could see the whitish marks in the stones of the wall where the bullets had struck. At the base of the wall someone had placed little pots containing flowering geraniums, to hide the discoloration of the flagstones where the blood had dried.

The Abbé Pitavy, village priest, had been present throughout the horror. He was a virile man with decorations for bravery in the first war, but as he described events to us his voice occasionally became thick. He put on steel-rimmed spectacles, took out his notebook, and began to recite the facts. The Germans had come on foot and by glider. Among them were many Cossacks and Ukrainians who had been captured in Russia and were now fighting with the Germans. When they arrived all the real *Maquis* fighters were gone, since they could not stand against such opposition in open battle. While the Abbé stood by his side, the German commander instructed his troops to do what they liked to the town. They went from door to door, stealing the linen and the wines and anything else that struck their fancy. As this went on the Abbé sat on a chair near the officer, who continued to drink claret until he was as drunk as his men.

Then the people remaining in La Chapelle were rounded up in three groups. In one were the women and small children, in another the men from forty to sixty, in the third the boys and men from seventeen to forty. None was a *Maquis* fighter. No names were taken, no questions were asked, for this was pure reprisal and form did not matter. The first two groups were allowed to go home for a few minutes to get a few necessities. A line of the small children passed the line of the third group. Four men stepped out to embrace their own children. This saved the lives of these four fathers, for the officer present shooed them on with the women and children. The other fathers, who had not dared to approach their children, went on with the third group. The first two groups, with the Abbé, were taken into the church. From the windows they saw lines of fire spring up all over the village as the remaining houses began to burn. Then, at ten o'clock at night they heard the bursts of machine-gun fire and the grenades. It was the next afternoon that the Abbé organized the burial of the sixteen bodies, which included those of two Italian dairy workers. In all, twenty-two noncombatants were killed at La Chapelle besides sixty men o;

the *Maquis* who died in battle. A few kilometers down the road at Vaisseux, the dead numbered one hundred and thirty-seven.

All those who remained in La Chapelle stood around us, a few feet from the execution wall, while the Abbé read from his notebook. A woman broke in to tell of young boys who had been hanged, two at a time, from the ends of planks like weights on a scale. There was another story of a three-year-old infant hanged by the arm until it died. Finally, when a farmer interrupted to say that two men had just been found in the woods, hanging head down, the priest looked angry. "Now you did not see these things with your own eyes. Remember that when you speak with these journalists you are telling La Chapelle's story to the whole world. Do not give currency to these reports unless you yourself know that they are true."

A blonde woman who had been listening at the edge of our circle began sobbing aloud. She was Madame Rome. Her husband had been one of the sixteen at the wall. Her sister-in-law, who was the schoolteacher in the next village, was shot by the Germans for refusing to give away names of the actual *Maquis*. The Germans camouflaged her grave so that it would not be proved that they had shot a woman, but the grave was quickly found, and there were bullet holes in the body.

We thought that the Abbé Pitavy was finished now, but he wiped his glasses and took out his notebook again. "There is one more thing of which I must speak," he said. "It concerns the Family Blanc. They were living in a small château near here when the glider troops came. The dead are the mother, Suzanne, an infant of eighteen months, one child of two and one of four years, and the grandmother. Arlette, who was twelve years old, was only wounded. She lay among the bodies of the others for seven days until people came to the house. But I am sorry to tell you that Arlette died four days later."

When we clambered into our car, all the people shook our hands and said: "*Bon courage*" instead of "*Au revoir*," as though we were one with them in suffering. We tried to say something decent, but it was all one could do to form a sentence. With their shovels in their hands they walked slowly and deliberately back into the ruins of what had been their family homes for generations. It seemed so clear that the French had never really been defeated in this war and that they never really could be. On the way we picked up five *Maquis* fighters who clung to the sides of our car for many

miles. They had been artillerymen in the war of 'forty, and were
en route to rejoin the French army. These were the men I had seen
going off to war at the Gare de l'Est, silent and bitter, the men I
had seen by the thousands in that hot, terrible summer four years
before, broken, with the spirit crushed out of them. Now these five
were almost gay; despite their rags and their cheap straw suitcases tied with string, they were men of dignity and power. To me
they symbolized all that men can be and do who have truly learned
what freedom is by losing it. On the lip of a lovely valley they left
us to continue on foot. They paused for a moment at the crest, outlined in the golden sun of evening as sharply as a statuary group.
They waved to us and began running down to the valley, to the
future.

Every day around Grenoble one saw little bands of enemy prisoners straggling in under the guard of FFI guerrillas, who were
as casual as herdsmen driving in sheep. Every day new bodies of
Frenchmen killed by the Gestapo or Darnand's *Milices* were taken
from the Isère or discovered in mass graves back in the mountains.
Germans had killed Frenchmen—but Frenchmen, too, had killed
Frenchmen; and, to complicate the picture of sadism and betrayal,
hundreds of France's former allies had also killed and raped and
looted. These were the Cossacks and Ukrainians, illiterates with
no personal principles nor any allegiance to their own government, who committed many of the most awful atrocities simply
for German money, new boots, and women. Sometimes, later on,
when I mentioned this, ardent friends of the Soviet Government
were indignant and unbelieving, but we saw too many hundreds
of these traitors with our own eyes. Intelligent Frenchmen were
not especially disturbed over the phenomenon, for all the world
knew that Frenchmen, too, had gone under Vichy encouragement
to fight the Russians. In this mixed-up war the same thing had
happened everywhere--with the Italians, the Chinese, the Indians,
the Burmese, the Filipinos, almost every nationality. To my knowledge, the only soldiers who did not desert to the enemy in some
degree were the Americans and the British. Once in France five
Hindu soldiers wearing British battle dress straggled into our press
camp and told us they had just escaped from a German prison
camp. They had been captured in the western desert. A distinguished British journalist looked on with pride and said: "You
see! Despite all the fuss about imperialism and the oppressed Indians, when the test comes they all turn to Mother England." A

couple of days later at the fighting front, an American captain mentioned Indian troops. The journalist said: "You mean those prisoners of war?" The captain eyed him, spat, and replied: "You may call them prisoners, but we're fighting a whole regiment of them across that river." The startled British journalist announced: "I shall make it my duty to report this treason to His Majesty's Government!"

On the door of the Grenoble prefecture was a crudely printed sign reading: "Bring your documents on atrocities to the third floor." On the third floor a staff of men was sorting out photographs of stripped bodies and mass burials (German soldiers had a habit of carrying these revolting pictures in their wallets) and collecting lists of families that had been wiped out. In another office of the prefecture other callers were denouncing French men and women accused of betraying *Maquis* to Vichy or to the Germans. On the day we arrived four hundred and fifty French citizens were behind bars, and the machinery of justice was already in motion. It was clear that for many months, below the surface of the Vichy regime, a second government, in liaison with Algiers, had been in existence in every department, commune, and arrondissement. Its position and its task were peculiarly delicate, for justice and public order are not synonymous, nor can they be always enforced simultaneously. I myself had expected far more disorder, far more savagery between opposed Frenchmen when this moment of revenge and political revolt arrived, and so I remained favorably impressed with most of what I saw. But some of my journalistic colleagues—without, I thought, much regard for what the resistance forces had suffered all these years—were outraged by the beatings and the freehand executions. There could be no doubt that private feuds were being settled in the general uprising, that some of the guerrillas were last-minute *Maquis* and often no better than gangsters. But I was astonished and upset to find many responsible journalists concentrating upon the excesses, informing the world that "bloody civil war raged in France" and that "the mob" had taken charge. Yet it remained exceedingly difficult to draw the fine line between mob justice and the people's justice. A reactionary who cares only for order and not for the kind of order it is could make up his mind at once. A determined revolutionist who takes the large, historical view could do likewise. Liberals like myself were pulled this way and that; we would try to think in terms of history only to be shocked by some bloody spectacle of the moment.

Number 37 Rue Maréchal Pétain, originally an apartment house, had been the Gestapo headquarters for Grenoble. The street was fenced off a block away, first to prevent people in the street from hearing the screams and later to prevent a surprise attack. The French Gestapo of Darnand had set fire to the place just before fleeing, leaving thirty FFI prisoners locked inside. The ground floor now was littered with blackened rubble and filth, and we could see dried blood at the foot of the stairs. Just ahead of me two FFI men with rifles were ushering a captive upstairs. He was, I think, the worst wreck of a living man I have ever seen. He climbed very slowly, with great pain. His eyes were swollen shut, his nose was mashed in, and his bloodied shirt hung in tatters. He had no chin, which was due not to his captors but to nature, and despite his wrecked face one could see that he was a degenerate type. He was accused of having betrayed for money payment thirty-seven members of the FFI to torture and death at the hands of the *Milices*. The Gestapo cells were on the top floor. The doors were thick wooden slabs, and one lifted a little hatch to peer in at the prisoners. They sat on the bare floor of the cells, which were devoid of even a chair. In one was a well-dressed woman of middle age with an impassive face. In another were two old crones, peasant women who, we were told, had also betrayed the *Maquis* for money. Some of the men in the other cells showed marks of beating. In an open room FFI men were taking photographs of a husky, full-faced girl of twenty-five. She had a black eye and her head was shaved. One of the FFI indicated her with a jerk of his thumb, grinned at us, and said: "The first time, she slept with a German for a hundred francs, the second time for fifty, and from then on just for the pleasure." Down a dark, stinking passageway we came to the cellar, which had an earthen floor covered with an inch of filthy water. Behind wooden beams were the crude cells where they had kept the FFI victims for torture in the famous bathtub which everyone in Grenoble had known about. The spectacle of the shining white bathtub sitting in the gloomy cellar was something out of Salvador Dali. Despite all the living examples of cruelty we had seen upstairs, this tub, standing alone, gleaming in the murk, was more ominous, more obscene than anything else.

I was sick at my stomach when we emerged onto the sidewalk. I noticed the name of the street again and could not help contrasting the benign-looking façade of the old Maréchal—all that so many of our diplomats had ever seen—with the true face of Vichy France as true Frenchmen had known it.

In the dismal rain of late afternoon, thousands of Grenoble citizens, holding umbrellas and newspapers over their heads, pushed through the streets toward a factory yard, where the Gestapo used to execute patriots and where six of the *Milices* were now to be shot at the stake. The condemned were very young, from seventeen to twenty-six years old. They had been tried in court, defended by lawyers chosen by the Grenoble bar, judged by men from the liberation committee and the FFI. They had not pleaded innocent, but declared they had been misled by Vichy propaganda. A few others tried with them received prison sentences instead of the death penalty. A vast crowd surged over the factory yard; hundreds were clustered in nearby apartment windows; others stood on the walls; and boys clung halfway up the lampposts. Many women were present, holding small children by the hand or babies cradled in their arms. When the police van arrived and the six who were to die stepped out, a tremendous, awful cry arose from the crowd. The six young men walked firmly to the iron posts, and as their hands were tied behind the shafts they held their bare heads upright, one or two with closed eyes, the others staring over the line of the buildings and the crowd into the lowering clouds. The one nearest me was the youngest, a red-haired college student. He maintained his upward gaze, his face without any definable expression. There was a moment of quiet in which the pattering of the rain was the only sound. There was the jarring, metallic noise of rifle bolts and then the sharp report. The six young men slid slowly to their knees, their heads falling to one side. An officer ran with frantic haste from one to the other, giving the *coup de grâce* with a revolver, and one of the victims was seen to work his mouth as though trying to say something to the executioner. As the last shot was fired, the terrible, savage cry arose again from the crowd. Mothers with babies rushed forward to look on the bodies at close range, and small boys ran from one to the other spitting upon the bodies. The crowd dispersed, men and women laughing and shouting at one another. Barbarous? The scene was barbarous A mob? The people were the citizens of Grenoble, who had always raised families, gone to church, taken pride in their excellent university of higher culture, and done no general hurt to humanity before. Was the important thing the way they had behaved, or *why* they had so behaved?

In the press camp to which we returned, miserable in our sodden clothing, I got into a flaring argument with two well-liked colleagues who were outraged by what they believed was drumhead justice. A few minutes later Norman of the London *Times*, a man who shared my fundamental regard for the French, looked up from his typewriter and said to me: "That was a bad thing we saw tonight." Surprised, I asked him why he felt that way. It appeared that I had missed a brief episode just before the shooting. In the factory yard a loud speaker had announced to the crowd that the national liberation committee realized that the relatively light sentences given the others on trial were not in accordance with the desires of the people, and that henceforth the courts would be revised. I went over to the two journalists to whom I had spoken so violently and apologized, and then walked to my tent in the freezing rain, feeling wretched. I was completely at sea. In a situation like this, where did crowd rule end and the rule of law begin? The liberation committee was playing by ear. But all normal authority was broken down in this upheaval of an outraged nation. To bow to the desires of the populace seemed to invite mob rule. Not to do so seemed certain to prevent any authority from taking hold and to invite chaos again. It was my first experience with a violent changing of the political guard, and all the principles of procedure for social change that I had been taught and believed seemed inapplicable and useless in the face of the reality.

But all that was happening in tortured Europe was surely more than a changing of the guard. Perhaps the institutions of communal life in a country like France would not themselves be very much altered; perhaps they would more closely resemble the past than anything really new. Still, one sensed that something deep and fundamental in the human spirit was being reborn, and rebirth is no less unsavory a spectacle than original delivery. Gitta Sereny, the young Hungarian girl, wrote from New York:

"Europe knows that the future is uncertain. Many of us [the young Europeans] are glad that it is so unpredictable. If we knew with certainty what was coming, if we had to deduce the pattern of the decade to come from the happenings of yesterday and today . . . we would feel as if we had started to draw a breath and

*could not bring it to a close. I think it would frighten and finish us.
For we would be bored. In Europe the word* boredom *has taken
on a deeper meaning; it is the boredom of the end of hope. In our
time we can also call it the boredom of certainty.*

"We in Europe have not really had peace as far as I, one of the
millions now in their twenties, can think back. We led ordinary
lives. Some of us were rich and some poor. We went to schools and
prepared ourselves for the future, but there was no security and
little constructive hope in our lives. . . . None of us was ever
really quite young. Not quite. Not really. We had felt incessantly,
although not always consciously, that we were being held by thin
strings, making movements that were dictated to us. So the day of
the declaration of war, I can see now in retrospect, was almost
like a coming to life for us. . . . Gradually, as countries broke
down, as people died, as bombs fell, gradually we began to live.
Even while we were shaken by the helplessness of the older ones
and the very, very young, our own suffering seemed to give us a
completeness such as we had never known. Now we could act
toward an unknown future, a better future. The great surprise.
We have often been accused of hanging onto the past, but we ourselves have been instrumental in destroying it. In every European
city and in almost every town there is something that is beautiful,
something that is old and noble, the sight of which makes us feel
proud that it belongs to our continent. And yet, when we saw the
Allied bombers overhead, we said aloud: 'Allez-y! allez-y!' If we
were born with a heavy heritage of strife and hate, then in this
war, I believe, we have begun to destroy that, too.*

"For five years we were fighting the most united battle in
Europe's history. Because it was a battle of resistance the unity
was forced upon us, imperfect and defensive. Its reason is already
growing old. The unity can become lost among other forgotten
efforts. Not every young European is ready to go on with it. . . .
Many are strictly nationalistic now, guarded, suspicious. Thousands too, are tired and want peace and nothing but peace. But
there are many others who will go on. In the past five years they
have grown up and become very young. They are hungry and too
tired to rest and momentarily bitter after exultation. But they are
filled with imagination and an almost unbelievably violent spirit
of independence. In the past few years they have gained a self-
respect they have never had before. Their violent intention is to
protect it at all costs, however excessive they may seem to out*

*siders. Boys and girls of student age have had to be fighters, not
students. For five long years Europe has obeyed few laws except
its instincts, and it comes out of its terrible isolation more basically
human than it has ever been before. Europe is cold and hungry,
tired and reborn. The youth of Europe stand in front of the great
surprise."*

6

It was the first of September, the anniversary of the war's beginning. I was thinking of Paris and those old days of peace, which
already belonged to a previous era. For I was embarked on a
search for Gertrude Stein, who had never left France and was
believed to be hiding somewhere near the Alps. The first clue came
in a telegram from Paul White in New York, who answered my
inquiries by giving the address she was known to have had two
years before. As it happened, the address was wrong by about
twelve kilometers, and we would have had to search all day had
it not been that the command car broke down as we headed toward
the upper Rhone, an area we believed no Allied troops had entered. As we fussed helplessly with the engine, a jeep appeared
from the direction of the river, to our great surprise. The jeep
driver worked on our car, and the officer, Lieutenant Colonel Bill
Perry, inspector general of the Forty-fifth, drew me aside. "Good
story down that way," he said, and immediately I was afraid my
little scoop was gone already. Perry had wandered into the area
on an idle visit and as he stopped in the town of Belley, a woman
laden with market bags came up to him and said: "I'm Gertrude
Stein. Who are you?" Perry had spent the night at her house,
which was at Culoz, farther north, and had just left her an hour
before meeting us. He promised to give me a day before telling
the story at headquarters.

The assistant mayor of Culoz directed us to the "Dovecote,"
Miss Stein's small château at the base of a towering, rocky hill.
The same old brown velvet cap hung at the entrance way, but the
poodle that answered the ring was not the same homely little
mutt I remembered from Paris. Gertrude greeted us with a shout
and a bearhug. The iron-gray hair was still closely cropped, and
the small eyes were as direct and searching as before, but she was
just a trifle more bent, a trifle heavier in her walk. Alice B. Toklas

—"Pussy"—was still soft, small, and warmly murmurous, but also a little more bowed. The big Picasso portrait of Gertrude dominated the spacious, sunlit living-room as it had previously dominated the small, dark parlor in Paris. The luncheon she served us was magnificent, the coffee decent, the sugar real. When we offered to give them army rations, Alice said: "Keep it. Just give me one American cigarette and I will be happy." We talked, of course, for hours and hours. Rather, Gertrude talked and we listened, and the process was as agreeable as ever before. She wished to fill in the great gap in the gossip that years of silence had interrupted, to know about Hemingway and Thornton Wilder and Woollcott and a dozen others. She did not know that Woollcott was dead, and when we said we had just seen Hemingway's wife, Alice sniffed and said: "That makes his third wife. Tch, tch, tch."

Germans had been living in Gertrude's house until recently, and it had been Italians the year before—"but of course they don't count," she said. When news came that Turin had been bombed, the Italian officer wept. "Can you imagine it, his asking us for sympathy?" The Italians caught onto their American accents right away and said nothing, but the Germans were too stupid to realize they were dwelling with the enemy, and that the lady of the house was not only a Jewess but also a famous writer whose works were on Goebbels' blacklist. "The German way," said Gertrude, "was to bang on the door and demand this room and this room and say 'no answers, please'—not that anybody would ever try to answer them. They were just unpleasant at times but never really bad while they were here, only they had that terrible key complex. They were always going off with the keys, and then I would have to go to the locksmith again. It was such a bother." One poor German soldier used to knock at the door and politely ask permission to walk in her garden.

She said that not everything about Vichy had been so bad. Many of the lower civil servants, like the mayor of Culoz, were perfectly wonderful. Gertrude had a faint tone of sorrow that Pétain had turned out so miserably, and she said it was when he let the Germans round up the young men for service in Germany that the people really turned against the old man. Laval was unspeakable, and for Darnand's vicious Gestapo not even Gertrude had adequate words. The mayor had always protected her secret from the Germans and so had all the people of the village, who knew perfectly well who and what she was. When the Germans began rounding up enemy aliens, the mayor simply forgot to tell them about the Stein household, because, he said to Gertrude, "you are obviously too old for life in a concentration camp. You would not survive it, so why should I tell them?" He had long, handlebar mustaches and a small, bald head and was straight from comic opera. Yet he was a man of courage and decent feeling. When he came in to meet us it was hard for him to preserve his ramrod dignity and not weep in front of everyone.

As Gertrude described them, the occupying Germans were like a fog—something that was always there but which you walked right through and hardly saw or thought about. She confirmed what I had long suspected: that the Germans could never really understand the French, never really penetrate their subtle psychology, that they were in fact the very last Europeans capable of governing Europe. A German subaltern roomed for months with the French station master and was never aware that the man was chief of all the local *Maquis.* When a new German lieutenant took charge of the village he demanded of the mayor if there were *Maquis* on the mountain behind the village. The mayor assured him there were none, because there was no water on the mountain. "When I go hunting there," he said, "I have to take a bottle of water for my dog." The officer did not believe him, but after his men had spent several days searching the mountain, he said: "You are right. There is no water on the mountain." The mayor said to me: "Of course, I did not tell him that men are not dogs and that men live on wine."

For many months through the winter Gertrude was obliged to walk several miles a day for food, and there was a time when her funds ran perilously low, until a friend from Paris stopped by and bought Cézanne's portrait of his mother from Gertrude. With all the difficulties, the isolation from lifelong friends, these had been the happiest years of her life, she said, and one could only believe her. She felt she had come very close to the ordinary French people and had learned more about them in this sharing of their tribulations than in all her previous thirty years in the country. The village people had learned to share, not only their sorrows, but their little pleasures and their material goods in a way one would not have believed of the parsimonious French. If somebody's rooster disappeared, some villager, no matter how hungry his family might be, was certain to return it before very long. The worst time had come when the Germans began rounding up the boys of twenty, when every family was faced with a terrible decision. Most of the lads preferred to run away into the mountains, where they joined the *Maquis* if they did not die of hunger and exposure. The *Maquis'* secrets were wonderfully well kept, and even Gertrude, who knew every soul in the place, did not know until the dénouement—a pitched battle near her house in which fifty Germans were killed —which men were the *Maquis* leaders.

As she talked of these things, sometimes bursting into the old, gay laughter, sometimes almost in tears, a group of small children banged on her door. They wanted permission to play "*Maquis*" in her grounds. The game consisted in pointing a wooden gun and saying: "Bop, bop, bop—ça y est!"

She told us how so many of the fathers, veterans of the last war, were sick at heart when their youngsters wished to go underground, risking the firing squads. "But," she said, "the children tried to explain to their parents that the old ones did not understand this war, that this was the young ones' war, and that the firing squad meant absolutely nothing to them. Anyway," Gertrude went on, "this war makes a whole lot more sense than the last one, which was very dull. This is a logical war and it is a far more interesting one."

She was just then finishing a new book, begun after France was defeated and her exile commenced. It was a book about all the wars she had known, from reading and in life, and its theme, as far as we could gather, was that wars come because every century tries to destroy itself. Hitler, she said, was essentially a nineteenth-century person, and his war had destroyed the nineteenth century. She had scribbled the book in large, bound ledgers, and since her sprawling handwriting baffles everyone but Alice B. Toklas, she had little fear that the Germans would discover it. When Paris was liberated, Alice began copying on the typewriter "like mad." Gertrude had always said she would end the book with the appearance of the first Americans at her house—"I always knew they would come, I always knew that war correspondents would be here, I never doubted it for one single moment"—and she had kept her promise. She gave the manuscript to Frank Gervasi of *Collier's,* who was with me.

I interrupted her flow of talk about Hitler to remind her of our prewar conversation in which she had asserted that Hitler was not dangerous because he was only a German romanticist, who wanted the feelings of triumph but would never go through the blood bath to get it. Miss Stein hesitated only a moment, then went

on with the thread of her conversation, pretending not to have
heard me.

When she said goodbye to us in the command car and we had
turned away, Private Bill, our hardheaded driver from Boston,
said: "Who 'n hell is that old battle-ax?" We said it was Gertrude
Stein, and he replied: "That beats the — out of me," which is
G.I. for "That's beyond me."

We came to fetch her two days later, to take her the forty miles
to Voiron so that she could broadcast for me to the United States.
This was the farthest she and Alice B. had been from Culoz for at
least two years, and the eyes of these two elderly women shone
like the eyes of children on a picnic. She was, of course, something
of a sensation in the press camp, dampened when the other reporters discovered that we had sent our dispatches about her
forty-eight hours before. Her radio speech, in part, went like this:

*"What a day is today that is what a day it was day before yes-
terday, what a day! I can tell everybody that none of you know
what this native land business is until you have been cut off from
that same native land completely for years. This native land business gets you all right. Day before yesterday was a wonderful day.
First we saw three Americans in a military car and we said are
you Americans and they said yes and we choked and we talked,
and they took us driving in their car, those long-awaited Americans, how long we have waited for them and there they were
Lieutenant Olsen and Privates Landry and Hartze and then we
saw another car of them and these two came home with us, I had
said can't you come home with us we have to have some Americans
in our house and they said they guessed the war could get along
without them for a few hours and they were Colonel Perry and
Private Schmalz and we talked and patted each other in that
pleasant American way and everybody in the village cried out
the Americans have come the Americans have come and indeed the
Americans have come, they have come, they are here God bless
them. Of course I asked each one of them what place they came
from and the words New Hampshire and Chicago and Detroit
and Denver and Delta Colorado were music in our ears. And then
four newspaper men turned up, naturally you don't count newspaper men but how they and we talked we and they and they asked
me to come to Voiron with them to broadcast and here I am.*

". . . You know I thought I really knew France through and

through but I did not realize what it could do what it did in these glorious days. Yes I knew France in the last war in the days of their victories but in this war in the days of defeat they were much greater. I can never be thankful enough that I stayed with them all these dark days, when we had to walk miles to get a little extra butter a little extra flour when everybody somehow managed to feed themselves, when the Maquis under the eyes of the Germans received transported and hid the arms dropped to them by parachutes, we always wanted some of the parachute cloth as a souvenir, one girl in the village made herself a blouse of it.

"It was a wonderful time it was long and it was heartbreaking but every day made it longer and shorter and now thanks to the land of my birth and the land of my adoption we are free, long live France, long live America, long live the United Nations and above all long live liberty, I can tell you that liberty is the most important thing in the world more important than food and clothes more important than anything on this mortal earth, I who spent four years with the French under the German yoke tell you so.

"I am so happy to be talking to America today so happy."

7

In liberated Lyon adventures among the literati continued as well as the usual involuntary exploits of dodging *Maquis* and *Milices* bullets and delayed-action bombs. The Germans were gone, having blown up every one of the lovely white arches across the river, and only a few American troops had entered the city, some of whom were trying to throw a Bailey span across one of the central bridges. These methodical engineers paid little heed to the rifle and pistol shooting going on along both banks, until a few bullets spattered near them. They dropped their tools and let fly with their fifty-caliber machine gun, sending tracers into the great mansard dome of the city hospital, the apex of the city's skyline, from which they believed the attack had come. In a few moments the hospital dome was on fire, and the general confusion was thrice confounded. Nurses and aides rushed in and out of the hospital carrying the charity patients on stretchers. They were laid under the plane trees along the parkway by the river near a stack of fresh coffins destined for dead *Maquis* and *Milices*, while FFI cars spurting tommy-gun fire tore back and forth a few feet from the helpless, wild-eyed patients. It was a mad and memorable scene. Hot coals and burning tiles cascaded down from the roaring fire above, and the immense crowd of spectators heaved this way and that, making way for an occasional captured Darnand man who was shoved along by FFI, his face streaming blood. A few steps away French girls were flirting with casual Americans in a jeep. Tramp fishermen were calmly flicking their lines into the river. On the bridge the gaudily uniformed and perspiring fire chief was politely inquiring of the engineers whether it would be all right if a fire engine were allowed to be first across when the bridge was ready. And the immense curtain of black smoke drifted over the rooftops, screening away half of the agitated city. Later I talked with two FFI men who said they had searched the hospital dome just before the fire and found no snipers there. The skyline of old and lovely Lyon was ruined for no reason whatsoever. It was the crowning touch to the wartime relationship of the Lyon citizenry with America, for the major portion of the damage to the city had been done in May by a "high level" American bombing in which a good many homes were destroyed but almost no military objectives touched.

While spasmodic fusillades continued, the bullets flying across the turbulent river, we crouched on the steps of a dead-end street, keeping our heads below street level. With Newbold Noyes, Jr., a gifted youngster from the *Washington Star*, I was engaged in an anomalous undertaking. Hidden somewhere in the city was Charles Maurras, the brilliant and vitriolic old editor of *Action Française*, the famous Royalist newspaper. Maurras, who in his lust for a rightist counterrevolution had publicly screamed: "Thorez and Blum to the gallows," who had divided and confused thousands of Frenchmen, who helped breach the moral and intellectual gates of France for Hitler's entry. For four years now, under his friend Pétain and under Hitler he had had his uncertain, circumscribed moment of glory and pseudo power. Today marked the violent and ignominious end to all that this wretched man represented. Noyes and I were summoning our reserves of grammatical French and printing in a soiled notebook the questions we wanted the deaf old man to answer in the interview we hoped to achieve, which would probably be Maurras' swan song to the world.

We had got onto his track early in the morning. At the prefecture we inquired about Maurras and learned that men of the FFI had been searching for him for several hours without results. As we

were leaving the prefecture an editor of *La Liberté*, one of the
newly sprouted resistance papers, took me aside and said there
was just a chance that he could put us in touch with somebody
who knew where Maurras was living. Offices of *Action Française*
were locked and shuttered, and we walked a couple of hours
through the city inspecting odd cafés and hangouts with no luck
until we climbed the dark stone steps of what had once been the
mairie and found ourselves in the tawdry rooms of a "press club."
It had been a hangout for hirelings of the Vichy press. Only three
or four men were in the gloomy place when we entered. They
were silently munching a bad lunch of soup and roast potatoes,
regarding us sullenly, while a couple of middle-aged, heavily
painted blondes with gaudy hats whispered together in a corner.
Eventually our man arrived. He was Auphan, who had been chief
assistant to Maurras for years. He was an unhealthily plump, white-
faced man of about forty, whose once-elegant suit was rumpled
and shredding at the cuffs. His polka-dot tie was soiled with grease,
and his long hair was badly in need of trimming. We told him that
we wanted him to take us to Maurras. He drummed his fingers
nervously on the table and fingered his tie, and every time a newcomer entered the door he looked up with a start. He had obviously
not slept for a long time, and we learned that at the moment the
FFI were searching for him. "Let them come," he said. "All right,
let them come. I am not afraid to die"—which was something of
a misstatement. He bustled in and out of the door several times
and at length said he would arrange the interview with Maurras for
late afternoon, on condition that we go in civilian clothes and
promise not to tell the FFI where we had seen Maurras. We could
fulfill the second condition but not the first, and he finally agreed.

When the bridge was ready for vehicles, we left our shelter on
the steps and drove the command car across to pick up Auphan.
He crouched well back in the seat each time we passed a shooting
affair on the corners. After a long, circuitous drive we left the car
and walked several blocks to the apartment. Maurras opened the
door for us, and I found myself looking down upon a very small
very old man with a white goatee and tiny eyes that were fierce despite the film of age. With him was Maurice Pujo, tall and bent and
white-bearded, who had replaced Léon Daudet as co-editor two
years before. Their small parlor was stacked high with musty books
and pamphlets; their Victorian clothes, manner and senile bodies
exuded the odor of decay. I felt that in this obscure room we were

witnessing the last hopeless stand of the embattled literary and journalistic giants of the old European tradition.

Maurras was very deaf, and when we wished to interpellate something we had to shout into his ear. He seemed feeble in body, and his voice lapsed into a whistle in the manner of an aged man, but his mind seemed vigorous still and there was precision and punch in his words. He would peer at the questions on the bit of paper, then raise his head and answer in the formal tones of a schoolmaster or platform speaker. When Carl Mydans thrust his ubiquitous Leica close to the man's face, Maurras would stop speaking and adopt a rigid, pretentious pose, which only added to the mad incongruity of the situation. While he spoke of the "grandeur" of the old monarchical France by which his mind was obsessed in perpetual, physiological nostalgia, the curtainless windows rattled faintly from shots and explosions in the streets, where the new order was being born, an order so hateful to these two old gentlemen who detested democracy and believed in a rule of the élite.

Little of what he said is pertinent now. He defended himself and his paper from the charges of pro-Germanism, of course, and he defended Pétain, saying to us: "You must fix it in your mind that Laval was the French government and Pétain the French state. The government was for the protection of Germany, while the state was for the protection of France." He repeated the aphorism with emphasis, as if an intellectual abstraction could subdue the crowd in the streets. When we asked him what kind of government the country would now have, he replied: "I know what kind I would like, but I am no sorcerer. The art of politics consists in making the necessary possible. Monarchy is indispensable to France. A state like France cannot afford the luxury of a republic, for then all the country's resources are squandered for a party— whichever party happens to be in power. France can stagger along for a while, as a beggar, but she cannot continue as a great nation that way." He said his own plans for his future change every morning but that he himself never changes. "So long as I have a tongue to speak and a hand to write, I shall go on repeating what I have said for fifty years. We are not brutish enough to abandon truth now."

I could not avoid a small, sneaking admiration for the old man's personal courage, or a feeling of stupefaction at this utter refusal to grasp the first principles of what was happening in the modern world and what the peoples of France and Europe required. As twilight began to fill the musty room we took our leave with Auphan, who had grown more composed as he listened to his master. Auphan left us by the river, darting with surprising agility into the shadows of his own house. A little later we learned that an FFI man, carrying a pistol in his hand, had been searching for him.

Our stories apparently caused considerable excitement among French friends in America, some of whom accused me of having interfered, in some manner mysterious to me, with the Lyon police and in their search for Maurras. Later, when I returned to Lyon, there was an equally absurd belief among Maurras' unjailed friends that our interview had been the *cause* of his arrest. Actually, of course, he never had a chance of escape, nor did he wish it, and he was arrested the day after our talk. He was sentenced to spend the rest of his life in jail, which annoyed him profoundly, for the vain old man would have preferred death as a "martyr." A year later Auphan was sentenced to thirty years at hard labor for collaboration with the enemy.

8

The towns and cities fell before the relentless American-French advance, and shortly after we had crossed into the northern zone of the full four-year German occupation, contact was made with the armies which had come down from Normandy. In the suburbs of old Besançon, of Spanish origins, I spent a night in the house of a slaughter-house employee while enemy machine pistols rattled their fire a couple of blocks away. Immediately one sensed a difference between the two occupation zones. The people were thinner here, the bitterness and despair had eaten more deeply into their hearts, and those who had truly resisted seemed harder and stronger. Four long years of hatred and humiliation—and then suddenly, on this day, their masters turned into a desperate rabble, the German soldiers grabbing bicycles, stripping the people of watches and jewelry in the streets, and fleeing toward Belfort, the Rhine, and Germany. A day when most of the people crouched in their cellars, holding their frightened children, while German dynamite collapsed the bridges and smashed the shutters, while dust and smoke rose from the old Roman fortress where our shells remorselessly repeated themselves. Then the waving white undershirt that meant surrender. Then the women collecting in baby buggies what remained of the German food inside the walls. A pair of tired American medics with a stretcher searching the innumerable rooms of the white stone citadel. Small boys waving the black enemy bayonets, keeping time with the *Marseillaise* which sounded from an accordion on a balcony across the street. An impromptu parade of singing students with locked arms who surge through the main streets, while down the side streets stagger minor collaborators, including old women, their heads clipped, their bodies stripped naked. A crashing of broken glass in the square as young men smash up the offices of Doriot's Fascist party. A youth melodramatically draws a dagger across a portrait of Laval, and the crowd screams approbation; though when he does the same with a portrait of Pétain the screams are much less in volume.

The north was different from the south in many ways. The trial had been harder to bear for most, but the long occupation had also meant that more of softer spine had given up, accepted the enemy, and adjusted, in the name of comfort, their own lives to the new conditions. In a better, bourgeois hotel a block away from the mad excitement, we found a few prim, silent men and women who glanced coolly at our muddy boots and addressed themselves again to their soup. For these, any new order was disturbing, even a French one. For one happy night the sweaty, reckless fighters from the other side of the tracks dined and drank in the middle-class cafés, their pistols in their belts. The next night they were gone, and the regular customers, in their usual black serge, with the usual white napkin under the chin, were back in their regular places. What we were seeing was a moral renewal and regeneration through armed rebellion; it was a social revolution only incidentally.

It seemed to me that in what I had seen in Italy and France a basic inference of the formative books was sustained and proved again: that possessions give comfort to the mind as well as to the body, and that men who are comfortable in their minds are not the men who perform the decisive deeds that revitalize and change the course of history. The very pattern of social behavior which had held true in nearly all revolts since the start of the mercantile age was repeated in this rebellion. Whether it was New York City in 1776 or the Haute-Saône in 1944, the story was essentially the same: Most of the aristocracy were contemptuous of the rebellion, as much for its manner as for its aim, while a few aristocrats, whose chief possession—their name—was not at stake, answered a higher claim than that of class and became leaders of the rebellion. The burghers and bourgeoisie took cover, weighed the chances of each side, and in order to save their shops and businesses, did their best to take no risks at all. Men who worked with their hands for somebody else provided the basic stuff of the rebellion, and, in both New York and the Haute-Saône, men who, like the Jews, were morally enslaved regardless of social status, put their hearts and intellects to the revolters' cause. The pattern of reaction was generally the same, despite the differing circumstances, but I thought that perhaps the revolt I was witnessing, however limited, would be the last in the old format. Perhaps it was breaking the mold, for after this it was likely that some of the constituent elements would have been worn away. The aristocracy, already half shadow, would hardly survive the aftermath of this upheaval. It was hard to forecast the fate of the burghers in the interval, but next time—if there were a next time—they could not avoid taking a side; for they would be a side.

It was two or three evenings after Besançon had quieted down, when I was stepping toward the restaurant across from my hotel, that I came upon George Millar. After his disappearance from the western desert into captivity I had come almost to regard him as one who was dead. Here, suddenly, he was striding toward me, more radiantly alive than ever, his incredibly beautiful face blooming like that of a young girl in love. He was dressed immaculately in the uniform of a British captain, his square shoulders squarer and solider than before; and his bearing, his whole being conveyed an impression of personal triumph, of a happy self-mastery that was carried with a simple delight. For some reason, this meeting with Millar in this moment and area of success was for me a confirmation, a re-justification of self and purpose to a higher degree even than the landing in France or, later, the return to liberated Paris. He gave an air of elegance to any type of clothing, and when he was dressed as he was now none would have suspected (nor did I know until later) that just a few hours before he had been surrounded with an American captain in a forest by German soldiers. They had lain for two days in the dripping wood, hardly daring to stretch a muscle for fear of cracking a twig, while the Germans searched for them. In the end they had crept to a road, mounted a motorcycle, and driven at top speed through a party of Germans who were preparing a bridge for demolition. By the time the startled enemy was able to bring a machine gun to bear in their direction, they were around the bend.

Through the next couple of days after our meeting—in my hotel room, in his sumptuous apartment, or while riding in the sleek Citroën, driven by the gaunt giant *Maquisard* who was his devoted slave—we extracted each other's story of the intervening years. He had been captured in the desert by a fluke accident in his first engagement with the tanks, shortly after his meeting with Geoffrey outside of Cairo. He was wounded—"the Germans nursed me as if I were a baby." Treatment in the prison camps of Italy and Germany was not so gentle, however; and he was recaptured on his first two attempts at escape. On the third attempt he made it to Strasbourg, where a young woman tending bar surprised him by whispering frankly: "You are an English prisoner. I represent the underground escape organization here. Come to such-and-such an address tonight." There he lived in security for a few days until the girl's boy friend suspected that she was falling in love with Millar. This resulted one night in Millar's making a dash from the rear door through a hail of pistol shots. To make the whole episode completely cinematic, he had to elude a pack of hounds before he was safe again. He marched directly into the office of the mayor in a small French town, revealed his identity, and demanded clothing and papers that would enable him to pass as a Dutch laborer. The mayor said he did not dare, but offered to take George to lunch at his house. During the luncheon the mayor's determined wife told her husband that unless he gave the Englishman everything he needed she would never speak to him again. Well disguised, he entered Paris, strolled around the *Paris-Soir* building where he and Geoffrey had once had their office, put a few mothballs into his wife's fur coat at the storage company's, and then knocked on the door of their former secretary. Miss Scherbatov confirmed this to me later, saying that when she opened the door she exclaimed: "Cox—yes. Morehead—yes. Millar—never!" But she raised ten thousand francs for him, and after tarrying in France long enough to help the underground blow up a gas works George made it to Madrid where Sir Samuel Hoare passed him on to London. There he was decorated, joined the British "cloak and dagger" sabotage organization, and was dropped behind the German lines into France to help organize and lead the *Maquis*. Eventually he was reporting directly to Churchill and had become a key figure in the operations for eastern France.

Millar's *Maquis* made two attempts to capture Pétain, Laval, and Darnand, in Nancy and Belfort. The German guard was too strong, but they did capture Darnand's chauffeur-secretary and his young mistress. The *Maquis* took them to a deep wood at night where valuable documents were found upon the chauffeur. He and the girl, a *poule de luxe,* were obliged to dig their own graves, and then the man was shot. The girl made a desperate effort to save herself. She declared that she knew nothing of politics, had never understood what Darnand's work had been, and that men were men—she liked *Maquis* as well as *Milices.* So saying, she put her arms around the squat, bald-headed *Maquis* leader. As she did so another *Maquisard* shot off the back of her head.

In a small, tastefully furnished château near Besançon, Millar and I shared with several Frenchmen a rich, creamy, alcoholic "victory dinner" which would have done credit to Maxim's in the prewar years. These were some of the handful of men who had held the resistance movement together in the region through the dark times, who themselves had endured the unrelenting tyranny of terror. One was a soft-spoken, shy diplomat who had resigned from the French embassy in Washington when Laval came to power. The day preceding the dinner he had walked behind the German lines near Belfort disguised as a peasant with wheelbarrow, making precise notes on the strategic bridges. Another was a French colonel whose chief source of pride lay in the fact that neither his motherly, middle-aged wife nor his small son had given him away by so much as a careless word when they were severely interrogated by the Gestapo. The third Frenchman was proprietor of the château, a wealthy Jew who held a commission in the air force and operated an art gallery in the town. In the little room on the second floor where we drank our cocktails he had hidden for three months. Once, when the near-by Germans entered the house, his wife had locked him in the steel safe in the corner. Whenever he had crossed the room he did it on all fours to avoid any possible chance of being glimpsed through the window. His tall, handsome Swiss wife who now sat at the end of the dinner table had herself been questioned repeatedly by the Germans but had never given him away. Nor had any of the servants, of whom he spoke with sudden tears in his eyes. Twice he had been obliged to leave the château for a vital conference, and each time his hired hands had sewn him in a gunny sack and heaved him in and out of the horse cart as though he were a heavy sack of potatoes.

All the intoxication of relief, success, and pride was present at the table. This was a happiness which made men as children; they talked loudly and all at once, they drank far too much, proposed foolish, sentimental toasts, embraced one another and each other's wives. It was all wonderful and never to be forgotten, a moment for the brave heart which life would not repeat. They included me, the onlooker, in their happiness, but along with sharing their spirit I experienced a sense of hopeless envy; I would rather have been one of them than anyone else upon earth. I marveled at George and envied him above all the others, for we had started even and he had done so very much more. I remembered one of the days when we had been playing golf near Paris, and the old woman at the clubhouse refused to believe that he was a journalist of years' practice and not a young student, and how he had blushed with anger, hating in that moment his beautiful girl's face. Now there was a tinge of hardness about him, a certain ruthlessness, and a confident sense of strength; yet when one of the Frenchmen retold one of Millar's deeds, the blush of embarrassment returned for a moment, and he was the same youth I had known. There was only one somber interlude during the meal, when they spoke of two famous French boys who had returned to the underground movement after four years in a German camp. They were welcomed back with joy in the moment of climax at Besançon, but, instead of waiting it out for the security they had earned, they had plunged into the fight again and had been captured a few days before, their car full of fatally incriminating weapons. They would be dead now after unmentionable tortures. With this story the gayety went out of our party for a time, it was like a moment of silent worship.

In the town again Millar frowned and told me he had another mission to perform the next night behind the enemy lines near Belfort. It was the first time I had seen him nervous. This would be his last "job" of the war and it was a "rather nasty one." He never told me its nature. I thought about him constantly, until suddenly he was back, walking into our restaurant, dressed in nondescript civilian pants and jacket, smiling radiantly with all his self-possession again. He changed into uniform and flew off to London and the certainty of life.

I returned to Besançon only once after the fighting had moved to the Vosges and that was to see the legend which had come to life, the man with the improbable nose whom I had last seen strid-

ing with an almost arrogant stiffness before a handful of French
fighting men at the Cenotaph in London four years before. For
two hours most of the population of Besançon waited, jammed
elbow to elbow in the public square, enduring the misery of a
chilling autumn rain. Toward all politics and political men the
French as I had known them before were steeped and soured in
cynicism. I watched the faces near me now as De Gaulle spoke,
and observed an intentness, an almost fanatical look of reverence
such as I had never dreamed to see in France. And De Gaulle
had changed with the assurance of power. He had learned how to
gesture, how to speak confidentially and colloquially to the people.
He told them frankly that France's alliances with other nations
would help her only in the measure that the French people with
their own hearts and hands rebuilt their country and reformed it
materially, morally, and politically. He offered them no easy solu-
tions but only the blood, sweat, toil, and tears that Churchill had
once offered the British, and I believed profoundly that most of
them would accept the offer. He asked them to sing the *Marseillaise* with him, and then he walked slowly down the narrow street,
waving and touching the outstretched hands of hundreds. So it
went, in every city and town, the voice and myth become Gallic
reality. I remembered how, in those other days, no Frenchman
had seemed great to the French. Others had—Roosevelt, Stalin,
even Chamberlain—but never one of their own. Now there was a
great Frenchman, too, and they accepted him as such. Perhaps that
is the final test of greatness—to be so among one's own.

9

October was upon us, the October of eastern France, which is filled
with dull cloud masses, the smell of manure in the villages, and
the freezing rain which never ceases, so that one exists in a perpetual twilight and moves in a sodden morass of wet clothing and
yellow clay. The course of the war changed and with it the spirits
of the soldiers. The parade and pageantry were finished; for the
first time the enemy had beaten us to the high ground with time
enough to organize a stand. His supplies were rushed to him in a
hurry from their near-by sources within the Reich, while ours
moved painfully through the mountains from the southern ports
hundreds of miles away, the frozen drivers falling asleep at their

wheels, frequently to die ignominiously in the mud of the ditches. Tempers grew short, there were long silences in any conversation, the honeymoon with the French civilians ceased by mutual withdrawal, and our men, who had known so much more war than most of those who invaded from England, remembered the Italian winter and began to long again for home. Their accomplishments were solid enough: they had freed one third of continental France, the German Nineteenth Army was virtually extinct, the prisoners ran into scores of thousands, including a dozen generals, and a large French army was daily growing larger. But they had thought the war would have ended by now, and this was all that really counted.

They had believed for so long that it would soon end that they continued to think so, although in their hearts they suspected that great exertions were still required and that there was·yet plenty of time in which one could die. They carried out their orders, but it was done perfunctorily; no one wanted to take an extra risk now when the end must surely come. Caution became not a military virtue, but a danger; and a serious morale problem, on the order of the problem in Italy, seemed in the making. Parents and wives at home became an unwitting threat, for in their well-intended letters they spoke of the war's quick ending and of their joy that their men were still alive. Soldiers themselves began to write to the *Stars and Stripes* voicing the feeling that death now was a waste, and the editors were obliged to suppress their letters. Ernie Pyle's famous last column from Europe in which he confessed his inability to stand the sight of another dead young body was widely read and did no good. Even we correspondents, whose lot could not really be compared to that of the combat soldier, grew morose and more gun-shy than we had ever been. It was another of the times that try men's souls, but there were no words of any modern Thomas Paine to help. Instead the men huddled in their dripping tents and read the leading article in *Time* magazine which informed them that all over America mayors and city councils were making plans for "Victory Day," replete with parades and speeches, special radio programs of professionalized cheer, and a great deal of liquor. I tried to explain how the soldiers felt about all this in a cabled dispatch:

"*. . . Across the road from the tent where this article was read aloud a group of convoy commanders huddled in the cold rain,*

*their numb fingers tracing a well-soaked map. They were trying
to get their big guns and supplies up to a difficult point at the front.
That was the only 'planning' they could do at the moment. At home
in America's cities they plan for the day of victory, and this seems
very strange to us over here. Apparently they must organize the
lifting of a weight from the heart the way one organizes a Chamber of Commerce luncheon. The soldiers do not understand. It will
not be like that with them when it comes. Some of them will probably get drunk in a private, personal way, but I doubt if, when
V-Day comes, many of them will be able to bear any speeches or
any organized noise. At home you look at the calendar, which
cannot resist. Here we look at the next mist-covered, ominous range
of hills where the enemy has his guns. We look at the distant for-
tresses of Belfort and Epinal and at the Rhine. The soldier would
like to say to you: 'To hell with the calendar. It doesn't know anything about it.'*

*"Your map tells you that the going has been rapid, but you seem
to have forgotten that war is still war, that feet still swell in wet
boots, that one can still shiver and ache on the ground all night,
that the stomach still contracts when a shell bursts near by, and
that a dead boy with punctured lungs, with the little rivulet of
blood dried on his chin, remains a sight that does not bring
thoughts of gayety, organized or otherwise. Nobody really wants
to reproach the people at home. They cannot see what the soldier
sees nor feel what he feels. It is only to repeat that the imagination,
no matter how it tries, cannot bridge the gulf between those who
are living more miserably than ever in their lives before and those
who, for the same cause, are living better. We shall see the difference, no doubt, on that Victory Day. The civilians will want to
make noise for once, and the soldiers will want to be quiet for
once. They are so very, very tired of noise."*

I dispatched these words and, as always when I tried to speak
for the fighting men, felt a twinge of regret that I had done so, of
worry lest I had been presumptuous and pious. But it appeared
that there were, after all, many at home who did respond. Later
I learned that some of these words were reprinted in full-page
appeals for war bonds in a number of great cities, and my fundamental belief, so often buffeted these days, in the usefulness of
my trade, was again reinforced.

I had never seen Paris from the air before, and from a distance it appeared something strange and fresh, far-scattered, clean, and neat like a thousand villages of red-tiled roofs beaded together. On the back platform of the rackety bus one was thrown from side to side in the former manner. There was the caramel-colored mass of the Versailles Palace, the square where I had seen the guillotine knife descend, Sèvres and the bridges, and then (because I was riding backward) the city of Paris flowing past me, opening up, expanding like a flower with the tones of autumn inlaid among the petals. Then came the central monuments which before had been so much a part of the city that one had ceased to really see them. The Eiffel Tower was precise and small, the Crillon was chipped with bullet scars, the Chamber of Deputies was blackened, and something was wrong with its roof so that the whole symmetry of the Concorde vista was unnatural and wrong. In the warm intimacy of memory I had come to believe that the very cornices would remember me. But there was never so much as a glance in my direction; Paris was cold, composed, and self-sufficient.

It was really I, of course, who had changed, and this the war had done. Wars bring new eras not only in the affairs of men but in their separate minds. It was a curious thing: though I had been younger before, at the very beginning of life, I had really lived with Paris, known and sensed it through its piled-up past. Its special magic for me had come from all that had gone before. Now suddenly the magic was no longer there; the war had wiped it all out, and five contemporary years had replaced a thousand of the old. A curtain had come down in my mind. I realized that I was looking at Paris now as I would look at Pittsburgh or Kansas City. I was thinking of a present place within its present. There was, strangely, little regret, little nostalgia for a vanished nostalgia, for almost at the same instant I realized something else: that another curtain had gone up, that I was thinking of Paris and its people in terms of their future also, and it occurred to me in surprise and relief that now for the first time it was possible for me, if I wished it, to be a part, to understand. I knew at once that it would be true of London, also, and of all the other places. Now at long last, I really had a chance to become a citizen of the world, if so urgently necessary a thing is truly possible.

Chapter XV

ONE UNDERSTOOD, while still in the Paris-London plane, how it would be, how it must be with London and the English. I remembered how it had been five years before at the airline offices in Paris and around the airport: the English men and women, tense with foreboding, fashionable in clothes from Bond Street and the Faubourg St.-Honoré, smart in their nervous jests about the outbreak of war, suddenly strangers to France toward which they had pretended a literate intimacy, fleeing back to England to be together in crisis, to be English together. The few who were there already in fresh, full-bodied uniforms carried themselves with an air of self-conscious reserve and were stared at as if they were indeed special, romantic pioneers. Now in my plane on this October day of 1944 the special object of attention was the one self conscious civilian in tweeds with a government dispatch case pinned between his knees. Everyone else was in uniform, worn, frayed khaki and blue. Collars were a bit soiled, and pockets were lumpy with cigarette packs, handkerchiefs, and wads of letters in a careless fashion which 1939 would never have tolerated. They slipped immediately into the "bucket seats" with automatic movements and drew the straps with a careless flip of the hands. Few even twisted their heads to look out of the window. Life had become a thing of straps and buckles and printed directions. There was a brown overcast on fresh, ruddy British complexions, there were deeper wrinkles around the eyes which came from strange winds and suns. They dozed or they stared half-unseeing at soiled magazines, passively waiting it out. Life had become a matter of waiting out eternal, repetitive passages from day to night, field to field, continent to continent. The passages had accumulated into five long years, so long that weary men did not know they were weary, could not remember how they had been before nor imagine how they might be again.

Five years. Even the Channel seemed inert, passive. The chasings of foam stretched chalky and soiled like the flaked corrugations of some forgotten rococo bordering. The Channel, which had once boiled with our fears and expectations, seemed desolate and cold; in the middle two lonesome patrol boats kept perfunctory watch, huddled close together, unmoving dark smudges in the scroll-work.

Five years, and the struggle had turned full circle. Allied headquarters had just moved from London to the Continent. I remembered when headquarters was in a group of red-tiled buildings in the little town of La-Ferté-sous-Juarte, near Paris. Then the first headquarters in London—a hasty town council able to do little more than desperately beat back the flames from this last small room in the West. Then the long years when London was the master control panel where the impulses of men's decisions moved the fleets of planes and ships all over the world. Now headquarters was back in Paris, the armies were back again at the Rhine precisely where they had stood in the yellow clay during that first uneasy winter. And London was again a rear area, but no longer casual, no longer full of careless pretenses, no longer ignorantly tolerant of the rest of the world. Londoners had become acquainted in the meantime with the Germans—and the Americans.

London was like the grimy anteroom of a great factory, where people have been working overtime on rush orders too long. London was like a famous hotel, gone seamy and threadbare after an interminable business convention which gave no chance for re-decoration, where the formal politeness of the overworked staff had worn away, and they had become direct, abrupt, and a little testy. London was tired and bored. After knowing the deluge, a few daily bombs, even rocket bombs, were a bore; where every man and woman was a hero, heroism was a bore; where men of all known tongues had swarmed, the lingering Americans were a bore; where war had become the permanent condition of monotonous life, war itself was a bore. For Londoners life had the consistency and taste of the powdered eggs upon which they fed.

The statistics said that seven hundred thousand buildings in Greater London were destroyed or damaged. From an airplane view one would never believe this, for the vast, ugly city seemed there in all its sprawling, overlapping parts. But one had only to stroll a few blocks, following a familiar beat of years ago, and one became aware with a sinking heart of the cumulative enormousness of what had happened. The hotel in whose bright lobby I had been sitting when the bomb hit that night was bricked-up now,

gaunt and blind and dark with grime. The buildings on either side
(we had had offices in both) were hollow shells. At the corner
where I had so many times felt with my hands along the bricks
after emerging from the lighted studios, there was no building at
all. The basement, open to the sky, had been converted into an
emergency water tank. Pagani's, where we used to eat spaghetti,
was a shell; so was the concert hall where we used to see them
queue up as we looked down from our office windows. The stone
synagogue near Murrow's flat had no roof, rear wall, or flooring,
and nothing remained to indicate that it had once been a place of
human assembly and meditation save the tattered paper on the
blackened facing where one could just make out the words:
"Blessed is he whose conscience . . . and who hath not fallen
from faith in the Lord."

This is the way it was everywhere one walked. In every block
and circus, at every turning something was gone, the perspectives
out of joint, the design spoiled, so that the whole effect was wrong,
and London was not quite London. There were no words to describe the effect behind Saint Paul's. Here, for blocks and blocks
there was only space. It was so complete in its emptiness that at
first, even by closing my eyes and thinking hard, I could not bring
back the picture of the old City, its maze of narrow, twisting
streets, its close nesting of the multitude. Once I wandered through
Billingsgate, up the lane Sir Walter Raleigh had climbed from his
ship, and sat awhile in the churchyard of St. Dunstan's-in-the-East.
Only the front of the church remained, bearing still the soaring
and slightly absurd wishbone spires. The rector, a gaunt, lumber-
ing man, asked me "inside," and we sat by a portable stove in the
passageway he had blocked up for a shelter and office. He had
been there some thirty years, and it would take another thirty
years perhaps to rebuild it all. I left him a pound for the fund,
and he inscribed my name in the ledger, painfully moving the pen
with his swollen, chilblained hands. Then we walked along the
river to the Tower, while he talked easily of all that had happened
among these stones. Not of what had happened in the war, but of
all the old things from the time of the Conqueror onward, the
things that were really of consequence and meaning to his mind.
The old man's sense of the continuity of his city was a faith with
him, like his religion, and I was a little humbled by his serene
belief in the future as an integral, accepted part of the past.

London was labeled **among correspondents, among migratory** officers and government officials, as "the most comfortable city in Europe," and indeed, after the Continent, life in London for such as these was warm, well lighted, and easy on the bones. But the articulate who go about the world classifying and labeling, are generally privileged in matters of the flesh. I thought when I arrived that I could never forget the fresh wonder of clean sheets, tea on a tray at waking time, and a tub of hot water; yet, after a few weeks, one found himself irritated that the laundry required two weeks, that the Savoy was likely to serve Spam occasionally, that clothing in the stores was of shoddy stuff, that taxis were hard to find at dinnertime, and that no man could be found to repair the bathroom tap. It is so easy, even on the rim of war, to fall back into the old ways, to forget. In order to remember, one had to walk much by day and by night, to peer behind the façades of skeleton houses in the poor sections, and there to see whole families living out the freezing winter within their tiny, tin-roofed garden shelters which one entered by crawling like an animal. One had to descend the tube stairs at midnight and see again the old men and women, whose faces had taken on the gray color of the cement, the withered, unwanted ones, who, from the habit of fear, sat patiently each night on the edges of narrow wire bunks, waiting for the roaring trains to stop and the crowds to thin away so that they could sleep in tiers like domesticated animals at a public fair.

So that I could remember, an M.P., George Strauss of the Labor Party, took me on his weekly visitation with his constituency of bleak North Lambeth. It was almost like a doctor's office. His woman assistant would open the door, say "Next, please," and the patients would come in. They were women for the most part, with the pale faces of people who have not had much sun in their lives, with the timid, heartbreaking manner of London's very poor. They would sit rigidly on the edge of the chair before Strauss, worn hands gripping shabby pocketbooks as they haltingly explained their troubles. The diaphanous fabric of their pitiful daily lives had been broken by the physical impact of war, and they were bewildered and lost by the manifold wartime rules that each must follow so that all could somehow live, however precariously. The tiny problems loomed enormous before their baffled eyes. Miss Smallbone could not work at her factory job any longer, and the Government were going to send her to scrub floors in Middlesex Hospital. She knew she could not—not when her fractured ankle was scarcely mended. Frail Mrs. Atkinson had been blitzed and

no longer had a washing machine. Did she have the right to take
her laundry to the public washing baths some blocks away, just
out of the district? Sixty-year-old Mr. White was a stocky, determined little man who had been wounded in the last war and very
much resented the fact that the magistrate had fined him four
pounds for being persistently late at his job. He flared up a little,
slapped his knee, and declared: "Well, the only thing I can do is
not do another thing for this country, not a single damn thing."
Young Mr. Tow had been released from his factory job on medical
grounds. He had given up precious clothing coupons for the factory
uniform which they gave him and which he had had to turn in.
He wanted the coupons back, for the winter had come and he had
no coat. Mrs. Morris said she would be eighty if she lived until
April ninth. She was very deaf, but she had come on behalf of two
old neighbors, who had received no coal for the last ten weeks.
One of them was blind, but the "blind visitor" didn't seem to have
done much for them. Mrs. Dixon thought she should be getting a
shilling a day from her soldier son's pay check, but the paymaster
had said it was only sixpence. Snow-haired Mr. Walker could not
find a place to lay his head that night. One woman could not find
the right government office to collect her old-age insurance from
and thus had missed eighteen months of it; and another wondered
if her husband, who was forty-five, shouldn't be sent home from
his overseas army post now to help with the store. Bitter young
Mr. Berkeley had been sent to the coal mines when he had asked
to go into the army, and he was allergic to dust which made him
very ill. He had written a letter to the King about it, saying he
would not return to the mines, and that had landed him in Brixton
Prison from which he had just emerged. . . . That was North
Lambeth on a dull, clammy winter day. That was nearly all London in the sixth year of war for survival. They had survived. They
hated, with the free Englishman's sense of injured personal dignity,
this maze of complexities called "government controls." But always they abided by them in the end, knowing by deep, communal
instinct, however politically unlettered they were, that only by
such means had they survived.

The epic siege of London had been over for months. It had left
its mark on the minds of the people as well as upon the city; it was
easier to start a conversation about the old days of the bombings
than about the sporadic missiles that still arrived. The office girls
would get excited over a disputed point about the blitz of four

years before, but would not raise their eyes from their typewriters now when a rocket exploded somewhere in the city. Two minutes after one exploded above the BBC no one on the street even bothered to look up at the drifting smudge of brown smoke. It was all anticlimax; the drama was ended. I drove one night across the river to the scene of a rocket explosion, where a church had been sheared in half and the parson killed, and a block of flats across the street had dropped its wall. The firemen and first-aid people seemed almost amused that American reporters were there. It seemed to have no relation to the war of the nations. It did not even seem like wanton murder; it was like an accident scene in any city. An ancient, decayed woman shuffled from a blasted doorway clutching a market bag which contained all that remained of her possessions. Painfully she whispered in our ears that she had no kin, but she remembered the address of a woman with whom she had chatted in the food queue. We took her there, and when we left, the two old crones were making tea. She would probably have to live there until she died of natural causes. I did not experience the old rush of blood to the head over another barbarous act of Fascism. There had been too much, too long. The old woman did not represent an innocent victim of modern barbarism; she represented an entry in a ledger in some government bureau.

For years people had talked and written and dreamed of the night when the lights would come on again, the moment of magnificence when black and battered London would suddenly blaze from end to end with glorious light. Now, in the middle of November, the lights did come on—a cautious, conservative glow, in a fraction of London, in one of the city's twenty-seven boroughs. The change was from a faint trickle filtering through tiny holes in the covered street lamps to a dull, confined flood shed modestly downward by a low-power bulb through frosted glass. The government said the lights could go on depending upon the policy and equipment of each borough. Ed Murrow looked at the fitful glow and with a wry smile said: "I guess that's the whole story for all of Europe. The lights are going on again, socially, politically, morally. But just a flicker at a time, with caution, 'depending upon policy and equipment.' Especially equipment."

The sun of Indian summer warmed the golden lanes of Sussex, near the sea. There were hard, red holly berries in the ocean of rust-colored ferns. Branches arbored the neat lane with drooping fans of autumnal leaves, and beside the lane on the tinted glass surface of the pond the white swans slid noiselessly along the fringing shore, green and smooth as a lawn. The country people, bound to and from the Sunday morning service, bicycled sound- lessly by in the old steady manner and unsmilingly touched their caps with the deft, perfunctory movement so well remembered. The fifteenth-century church was there at the edge of the village where the lane turned down. The old, worn stone font was there, the crude frieze remained showing the family of the half-forgotten local squire of long ago, all the ten children, eldest to youngest, kneeling in a terra-cotta row. All of this was England—gone, fin- ished, preposterous, yet enduring, undiminishable, and sanctified. Eternally, serenely England. The bell ropes were tied up neatly in the entrance way. It had not yet been necessary to ring the bells on military orders to signal the enemy's arrival. The small placard remained nailed by the doorway, bearing the printed prayer that begins: "Save our beloved land from invasion, O God."

The local pub was like all of England's country pubs, clean, respectable and quiet and faintly redolent of ale. The old copper mugs were shined for Sunday and hung in proper rows from the varnished pegs. The cluster of bicycles expanded beside the step as middle-aged men, bulky and big-footed in battle dress and black army brogans, gathered for the customary glass which preceded Sunday dinner. They were the local men of the Home Guard, and they had been dressing this way, gathering like this, every Sunday since that summer of the blitz. Heroism had not been exacted of them, but steadfast patience, and this they had duly provided. They were joking a little more heartily this day, and the back- slapping was a little more frequent if equally mild, for the Home Guard was about to "stand down" and disperse; and it was a matter for pleasant jest that the German Home Guard had just been called to formation by Adolf Hitler.

Just off the paving of the Brighton Road were small chunks of cone-shaped concrete with iron rings set in their tops. These were the toy-things of 1940, neatly fashioned, very military, designed to slow up the roaring steel tanks of the Nazis. Through a glade wound a narrow ditch, now half filled and rounded over with grass and fern. It was the ditch they had dug clear across southern Eng- land in those days of bravest innocence. Beside the ditch we could make out a small pillbox of brick over which the green moss had long been creeping. This, too, had been intended to save this island

and this ancient, private, cherished way of life from the Wehrmacht hordes, which had since crumpled great cities, poured across oceans, leveled mountains, and turned to powder the fields and forests of half a continent. Blackbirds hopped along the roof of the pillbox, and a wild-rose bush was growing up before its entrance. I wondered, as I looked at all this, what it reminded me of and from what buried spring of memory came the brief, dull pang in the breast. On the train to London I remembered: it was when I had returned to Velva at the age of twenty and wandered through the woods near the river. I had stumbled into a clearing and recognized in a mouldering depression the outlines of the fortress cave that my gang, the Terrible Five, had dug to repel the imaginary Sioux, and I had experienced desire both to laugh and to cry.

Dakota river. Sussex glade. Moss grows upon them, but none of us can quite forget. They are joined together now in the small, one country of the spirit, ditched across the heart in tender pain, and there they stay, forever barricade against invasion.

2

If the avalanching years of war had exposed the inner core of Britain, they had merely hardened and polished it and diminished it not at all. These years had, however, radically disturbed the topsoil. Contemporary mood and thought were heaped into odd formations, understandable after a time, but grotesque and disturbing at first to the visitor with definite memories of the former landscape. When I had first come to this place before the war, I had sensed a static self-sufficiency, an incurious tolerance of the rest of the world which came, I thought, from an inarticulate assumption that the rest of the world was a kind of background or setting for the British Isles. During the second visit, in the months of Britain's crisis, they found quiet glory in their strength-in-weakness. They were the world's heroes, they were modestly pleased with America's adulation, they were politely hopeful of our help for they understood its role. But they assumed, most of them, that because they led the world in the test of virtue, they would remain its leaders in the test of strength. They had accepted our material aid as the consecrated priest, who stands between his parish and the Devil, accepts the parishioners' contributions which are really for their own salvation. And later, when Americans first arrived in the flesh, they were welcomed to the inner fold with honest relief and genuine hosannahs.

But the wheel of history had continued its inexorable turning, and the British were gradually becoming aware that their whole position in the world was altered; their material, political, and moral authority, while not directly challenged, was being quietly ignored; it was no longer taken very seriously, and the English found themselves forced to the undignified, un-British extremity of having to deliberately voice it in rising tones. For many years they had urged Americans to accept the facts of life and come into the world—and now the Americans and the Russians had done so, and in so doing had created a complete new set of life's facts which the British had hardly expected and were beginning now bitterly to resent. The British—of all people—were themselves losing the cool and rational approach to the manifestations of history and were developing a neurosis akin to that which possessed proud Frenchmen after France went down.

I think I first became aware that intelligent Englishmen had entered the realm of irrationality when I casually suggested, simply as an historical phenomenon of common interest, that after this war the American Navy would be not only the world's largest but the only one with really large-scale battle experience. The friend to whom I made this remark was an enlightened person, normally dispassionate. But I was astounded by his reaction. His face darkened, his hands shook, and he fought the statement in a choked voice, proffering, not counterarguments, but indignation, as if this were a moral issue, as if I had insulted his honor.

Then I began to see it all around me and to understand the scope of this psychological change since those previous days when the cool and witty British lecturers had analyzed American civilization and put it in its proper place, to their own satisfaction, if not to ours. This new thing was everywhere, and an American in London had to be careful indeed what he said or did, even with time-honored friends who shared with him the same basic beliefs and hopes for their common world. Suddenly, it must have seemed to them, they were no longer masters of their own fate; not only their strength and national virtue, but their very institutions and ways of life were exposed to judgment—the judgment of contrast, especially with America. Instead of deploring the fact that their own soldiers were so ill paid, they resented the fact that American soldiers were paid so well; instead of seeking more frequent recognition for their own brave men, they were contemptuous of the medals American heroes wore, as if this were somehow a vulgar offense. America was everywhere: they ate American food, saw American films, operated American machinery and ships, their new temporary housing came from America, and the very labor used to put it up was contributed by American soldiers. Their young women by the thousand were marrying American men and plainly stating their desire to spend their lives in the United States. And, what was most difficult of all to adjust to, the overwhelming majority of troops and weapons now driving back the Germans were American, the top direction of the war was American, and Englishmen were not only no longer the unique heroes of the fight, they were of secondary consequence.

Their reaction was a natural and human one, if "un-British" and a surprise to one who had known them before. To the critics a bad American film was a "typical Hollywood product," while a bad British film was merely an unfortunate effort. Consciously or unconsciously they began to compare everything with an American counterpart. A fine British radio production was compared not with other British productions but with the finest American productions. The Beaverbrooks of London used glaring headlines to demonstrate to the people that the B-29 was not up to the capacity of one of their own heavy bombers. They would make a documentary film of battle like *Left of the Line,* showing exclusively the British army in France, but would utter emotional protests when a *March of Time* documentary on cargo ships showed only the American Merchant Marine. They gave adequate but perfunctory press coverage to the tremendous American effort against the Japanese, but would get out the big type for the British effort in the undecisive theater of Burma. When, later, an American fiction film portrayed only Americans in Burma, the British forced its withdrawal in the thin-skinned manner of the uncertain Argentines. When the Germans broke through in the Battle of the Bulge there was a crescendo of careful but obviously well-organized press criticism of Eisenhower and a determined effort to have Montgomery placed in full ground command. When Montgomery, as a wise precaution, dispatched a small number of British troops to the Meuse as the Germans began this offensive, London news reels of this movement bore the blaring caption: "Montgomery Stops the Rot." It was all as though a desperate, deliberate campaign were under way to convince a shaken people that they were still of consequence.

Churchill and others in the Parliament and press went out of their way whenever there was opportunity, to remind the people of those old days "when we stood alone in this island," in tones that indicated nostalgia for the moment of exclusive glory, now somehow unfairly smothered by an avalanche of strange events and strange men who ignorantly seemed to prefer their own achievements and were no longer awed by the Battle of Britain, El Alamein, or even Dunkirk. It was as if in the British mind the Americans were a kind of mass army of robots, a machine which felt no pain nor sorrow, an unhuman Goliath who happened now to be on the side of England who was David. The American army was a vast organization of thick-skinned football players; theirs was composed of individual Rupert Brookes.

The British neurosis grew out of peculiarly British conditions, but the overt deeds and statements in reaction were not so unlike the deeds and statements of their allies. It was common knowledge that the Russians confined their praise to the Russian army, for state reasons of their own, and the publicity methods of some American military groups and many American editors were only too well known. The British were not without provocation from Americans who beat their own loud drums by instinct and lifelong habit. But the causes were different, and they revealed different historic cycles. The Russians, handicapped by an old inferiority complex, were feeding to their people a sense of equality and power in the world. The Americans were crystallizing a latent sense of superiority to the rest of the world. The British were fighting down a creeping sense of inferiority. The first two showed all the awkward and unpleasant symptoms of new world powers; the third showed all the nervous symptoms of a declining world power. Britain was painfully closing the gap, narrow in physical measurement but psychologically a chasm, between her old position as the smallest of the great powers, to her new one as the greatest of the small powers. She told herself that she was perturbed and hesitant only because of the character of the American successor to whom she was entrusting the baton. He was badly dressed and pretty ignorant about his world. He was loud and loutish and obviously not born to the manner; and furthermore his sense of responsibility was very much to be questioned. This is what she told herself; at bottom she was really upset and angry, not because of the new recipient, but because the baton had to change hands at all. The performance was not a happy thing to see; there is no spectacle more unhappy than that of a strong and noble man, wearied from relentless demands upon him, acting ignobly and knowing that he is doing so, yet unable to control himself.

If this sight was discomfiting to an American who cherished England, the behavior of his own countrymen in the foreign world was equally disturbing. For now, in proper England and subtle France, the American soldiers were behaving as I had seen them behave in India and China and all the other places. Those of us who assumed a basic unity in cultural inheritance and hope with Western Europe seemed to be in an appallingly small minority. Most of our uniformed countrymen reacted as if Britain and France and Belgium were as utterly foreign to them as the Orient, and equally inferior and unimportant. They were learning almost nothing because they did not care to learn. Their education had given them the ability to read and write and follow a map; it had not given them intellectual curiosity. And without this they could not be said to have received any education. What they had received was a kind of cultural manual of arms. True, the average British Tommy abroad absorbed no more than the American G.I., and the average French *poilu* was hardly much better. But the American G.I. was now in the world, with far greater authority behind him than either of the others, and in one function or another he would have to stay if the world was to remain at orderly peace. And the task of these new partners in the game was far more subtle and complex, for they were there not as rulers in the outright imperialistic sense, but as guides, arbiters, and helpers. The task would be extremely difficult, and already our men were creating future obstacles by sowing hatred everywhere they went with their loutish behavior and hasty contempt.

From what reservoir of intelligence and goodwill would we draw a new class of worldly American envoys? How many existed who were cut in the pattern of a John Davies or an Edward Murrow? How many who could give leadership and understanding to the deeply imbedded aspirations of the generality of men? Proconsuls of the military type we had. Watchers and peerers of the FBI type we had in plenty. There were Henry Kaisers to organize and break new economic ground. But where were the Philip Adamses? Where were the devoted, long-staying servants like the doctor at the hospital in Accra? Who would be the American advance guard? I was afraid I knew. It would be not the men broad and humane and patient enough to share the suffering and under-

stand the hopes of others, but the bright, urbane young mercan-
tilists like the Pan American Airways boys, who knew what they
were after and confused America's role with their own. The smooth
boys who could sip a cocktail and sign a contract with equal urbanity and ease. The shrewd young operators like the *Time* and
Fortune boys, with their graceful manner, their gray suits and
brown snap-brim hats—the knowing young men who deprecated
passion, sweat, and high belief, who put quotation marks around
both *liberal* and *reactionary*, as if there were a special, exclusive
chamber of conviction and judgment to which they alone held the
private key. I was afraid that was it. America would enter the
world, led, not by a torch that meant freedom, but by a gold-tipped
fountain pen that meant something else.

Four years before, when we had talked in the darkened rooms
against the shattering explosions outside, we believed we had
caught sight of a new vision for England. We thought that if they
survived by their magnificent, family effort, they would never again
grow so far apart. Under the impact of dire necessity Britain had
taken a great stride toward democratic equality. Even in the most
desperate moment, when survival itself was at issue, they had
begun talking of aims far beyond mere survival, of the "new England" which would break the traditional bonds of class-fear and
give all men the chance for a decent life in dignity and freedom.
It had seemed to us in that moment that the British had supplied
the world struggle with its first articulate and positive meaning.

And now, with the war drawing to its inexorable close, it seemed
to us that Britain was the test of its meaning. If these hopes did
not come to fruition in England, they were not likely to be realized
anywhere else in Europe, and if they were realized in smaller
places the pressure of a still-divided, fundamentally reactionary
England would tend to press down the new men and the new ideals
wherever they arose. The issue seemed in grave doubt. The political leadership of the British people had not really changed. It
was still a joint Tory-Labour Government, but the Tories remained
in real command, many of them the very men who had encouraged
or tolerated Fascism, who bore a heavy guilt for appeasement and
for Spain. The politics of class and party were even now beginning
to stir, as victory and the long-delayed election appeared on the
horizon. The Tories clearly intended no fundamental changes in
the system at home or throughout the Empire; they clearly ex-

pected to remain in power. And it was discouraging to realize that many leaders of the Socialist party also expected the Tories to remain their national masters. It seemed to me that too many Labour men had already been defeated in their minds, that those who represented the trade unions had especially become hardened in their mold as professional loyal-oppositionists, and that they did not believe in political victory because at the bottom of their hearts they did not want it. They were afraid of it. I had fears that a big and important section of the Labour Party was already "doing a Ramsay MacDonald," even before their chance for power was tested.

One night at a small dinner with journalists and government officials a hard-bitten American correspondent curled his lip at me and said: "I remember how you and Scotty Reston and others used to write about the 'New England.' When are you going to learn that your naïve ideals just play into the hands of the realists? Democracy in England! You were fooled by what you saw in the blitz. Listen, I remember the Mississippi floods years ago. When the town was in danger you saw the banker out there on the levee heaving sandbags right alongside the little nigger boy; but when the water went down *he* was still the banker, and *he* was still the little nigger boy." I could make no convincing answer. I was not sure he was right, but I was not yet sure he wasn't. I had a guilty feeling that my whole estimation of these people, of the basic undercurrent of modern history, had been an expression of artless, wishful thinking. Murrow, too, was doubtful about the chances. He was beginning to think he had underestimated the resiliency of the Tories and overestimated the convictions and political courage of the common people.

The issue was defining itself, and the inevitable test would soon come. The Tories were appealing to the fears of the people. They were pointing out that Britain would end the war economically exhausted, that she would have to compete for her livelihood with great, new world powers; therefore nothing radical must be attempted at home which would spoil her aim and diminish her authority in the world of power politics. They gave the impression that the fate and future of Britain depended upon Churchill's personal relationships with a couple of other foreign leaders. They appealed to fears of America's economic competition and Russia's political competition. Britain must not sink to the position of a very junior partner in the grand alliance.

Those of the opposition who did not fear the taking of power the young men like Foote and Strachey and Aneurin Bevan, made their answer. Yes, Britain would indeed sink to a lowly position— if she tried to play the old game of power politics, if she tried to assume that the world was the same world that had existed five years before. But the world was changing rapidly. Great new forces, new men, and new hopes were rising everywhere, from the northernmost tip of Scandinavia to the East Indies. They could not be fought back nor be made to pause. A deep undercurrent of potential unity throughout Europe had been produced by Fascism and resistance: Norway, Sweden, Belgium, France, Italy, and Yugoslavia were going to the left, groping toward a new and better system in men's affairs, and other countries were bound to follow. It would be the end of Britain as a force in the coming world if she tried to hold back, to withdraw from all this and oppose it; it would make every European country a battleground of ideas between Britain and Russia; it would sharply divide Europe; it would destroy the chance for that great dream, the social and economic unity of Europe, and ultimately make war again inevitable. Britain could not turn her back upon history without signing her own death warrant.

Britain now faced the issue she had faced after the overthrow of Napoleon. She must decide to do what Palmerston had done in that fateful time—she must support the new, rising forces in Europe. A new leadership inside Britain could do this, and in the doing Britain could provide the new leadership for all Western Europe. Someone must effect the new synthesis of security and freedom which mankind and the times required. A hundred and fifty years before, it was the French who did it. If it were not Britain this time, it might be France again. But it would be someone; for politics abhors a vacuum. This way Britain could again be great and fulfill, if not a world destiny, at least a European destiny. There was no other way.

Every instinct inside me responded to the arguments of these young men. They were right; they *had* to be right, or there was no hope. No hope, and no sense or meaning in all that I had seen, in all that I had painfully come to believe, no meaning, indeed, in the death of a hundred friends and millions of others, or in my own existence. These young men spoke and wrote with power and passion, and I became excited as an adolescent student when I read and listened. The "intellectuals" in the Socialist movement

of England were not a mere adornment; they were its best elements. They were bringing political journalism to its greatest
flourishing in the English-speaking world. They wrote with the
inspiration of Thomas Paine (another Englishman) and they had
brought about a new age of the political pamphlet, as great, it
seemed to me, as that of the eighteenth century. The "little yellow
books"—"The Trial of Mussolini," "Guilty Men," "Why Not Trust
the Tories?" and the others—were incisive and powerful. They
flooded through the British Isles, and the maddened Tories could
not make answer. Intellectual leadership of Britain was passing
irrevocably to a new type and class of men (or perhaps intellectual
and political leadership were coalescing) and in the stillness of
the weary ruins passion and eloquence were born again. There
was greatness still in England, and this time it had little to do with
robes and titles, Homburg hats, drawling accents, and the gracious,
condescending manner. It had little to do with the one great individual leader.

But to what extent was it taking hold with ordinary men and
women who worked each day too hard to leave repose and
energy for contemplation? There were bad signs. The superficial,
Hearstian journals like the *Daily Express* and the *Daily Mail* still
led in circulation. There were good signs. One night I was mod-
erator of a discussion forum in which Michael Foote and two Tories
from the House of Lords took part. The two noble gentlemen had
wit, and they used it to the best of their ability. They had the
"special charm" which Evelyn Waugh describes as "the great
English blight," which has replaced passion and conviction in a
certain type of Englishman. It was all they had. The young Socialist had little charm, but he had the facts, and he had a burning
eloquence and belief which seared the atmosphere and melted
the gentlemen's arguments to a sticky puddle. He was almost
humorlessly downright in the manner which the English Tories
deprecate as not in the best of taste. They regard it as ungentlemanly
to take serious matters too seriously or to possess too many ready
facts, and it was obvious that they were quite unaware that they
had been totally whipped. But when it was all over, it was Foote
whom the lingering audience swarmed around and plied with
eager questions. The lords drifted gracefully out.

I hunched over the rail in the House of Commons and heard
Churchill defend the startling affair in Greece where British troops
were fighting men of Britain's romantically cherished ally. I

watched the round, glowering head swing slowly from side to side like that of a belligerent bull and listened to the astonishing words of hatred and scorn as he called the Greek Partisans bandits and ruffians and murderers. One could sense the electric thrill of shock that ran through the supercharged assembly, and one left the House a little dazed, feeling that nothing made sense any more. Over our ale and herring in the chop-house across the street an eminent British editor said: "This is it. We've known in our bones that this would come one day. The old Churchill is back—the old Bolshevik-hating, tradition-loving Tory Churchill is back. It's a straight course, after all. Anti-Red in 1919. Pro-Franco, pro-Mussolini, pro-Badoglio, pro-House of Savoy. Mark my words, this is the end of Churchill, the national leader. No matter how much he has done for us, no matter how much the people will still love the old pirate, they won't stand for this. He's lost his halo. He doesn't understand what has been happening in this country." And indeed the reaction all over Britain was one of tremendous indignation. Every other Englishman one talked with felt that he had somehow been personally dishonored. Churchill had made himself the target of a powerful weapon which the years of mass killing had not corroded: the conscience of the British people. Eden sweated hard to repair the breach for government and party, and after a time all feeling seemed to have simmered down. The election was still months away. The outcome was still unpredictable.

3

I could not return to the fighting until Murrow came back from the States. The last winter of battle wore on. Colleagues came back from the front and departed again. Fewer and fewer days would pass without the vast drumming from the Allied bomber fleets overhead which filled the streets of London and made the windows rattle faintly. The final climax on the Continent must soon be reached. I wished to go back to the troops, if even for a short time, but my feeling about my relationship with them had changed. I would not return under the strong impulse which had sent me from Washington to the battlegrounds—the desire to identify myself with them, to truly experience and understand what all these men of my generation were undergoing, to get inside their minds and live there. While with the armies I had awakened almost every day with the feeling: You haven't quite captured it; it still evades you; perhaps today something will happen, some conversation, some exhilarating or critical or saddening experience, and you will begin to see into the thing. But the whole period at the fronts had come and gone, and I never achieved the feeling that I had arrived in the realm of common identity with the soldiers. By now I knew it would never happen, and I thought I knew why. I felt a desire for a kind of confessional. I feared it would seem exhibitionistic, but the impulse was overwhelming, and at the end of a Sunday broadcast, I came out with it:

". . . That is what the war is like, this Sunday afternoon. That is, that's what all those called correspondents or commentators, analysts or observers, will be saying it's like. They believe it, the listeners and readers understand it, and what we say is true enough —but only within our terms of reference, in the unreal language of standard signs and symbols that you and I must use. To the soldier, that isn't what the war was like at all. He knows the real story; he feels it sharply, but he couldn't tell it to you, himself. If I plucked one from his foxhole now and put this microphone before him, he would only stammer and say something like this: 'Well, uh, I was lying there, and, uh, I saw this Jerry coming at me with a bayonet, and uh, well . . .' That's how most of them would talk. I know because I've tried them. If the soldier can't tell you what happened to his stomach at that moment, what went on in his beating heart, why the German's belt buckle looked as big as a shining shield—if he can't tell you, no onlooker ever can.

"The army treats all men alike, but the war does not. Not this war. It's too big and far flung. It has a thousand faces and a hundred climates. It has a fantastic variety of devilish means for testing a boy's brain, for stretching his nerves, for making him ashamed or making him proud, for exposing his heart or for burying his heart. It treats no two exactly alike; and so even two soldiers from the same front sometimes don't understand each what the other is talking about.

"Generals—and journalists—use big, standard words like 'teamwork' or 'soldierly behavior,' which are like interchangeable parts and can be fitted into the machine without thinking. But the soldier's handbook gives little guidance on such matters as how

to learn the patience of a saint, how to quench bitterness when his officers make a costly mistake, or how to master the homesickness that comes at sunset.

"Who is to relate these things, which make up the real but secret story of the war? Who is to reconstruct, in scenes and acts, the drama of that American on the desolate airfield in the Gulf of Aden? The one who sat three hours, unmindful of the crashing heat, his eyes fixed upon a stone. He had been there eighteen months, and he didn't talk to his comrades any more.

"What about the soldier with the child's face, who stumbled from the exploding field near Anzio with not a mark on his body but with his eyes too big, his hands senselessly twisting a towel, and his tongue darting in and out between his teeth?

"What was it that had expanded in the soul of a young man I first knew when he was a press-agent lieutenant three years ago? Then, he was rather silly and talked too much, and his men smiled behind his back: I met him next in a French forest. He had learned control and dignity. He was a major commanding a fighting battalion, and the general was quiet when he spoke.

"There was a regimental colonel at Anzio who received notice one night that he could leave next day for Des Moines, where his business was prosperous and his family large. His division had been decimated, but this man's life was now assured. Why, at dawn, at his regular hour, did he risk the mortar shells and crawl on hands and knees from foxhole to foxhole, not missing one, just to speak a confident word to his men?

"Who could really explain about that young corporal with the radio post deep in the Burma jungle? The one who rose suddenly from his bunk in the night and walked straight into the woods, walking westward.

"Only the soldier really lives the war. The journalist does not. He may share the soldier's outward life and dangers, but he cannot share his inner life because the same moral compulsion does not bear upon him. The observer knows he has alternatives of action; the soldier knows he has none. It is the mere knowing which makes the difference. Their worlds are very far apart, for one is free, the other a slave.

"This war must be seen to be believed, but it must be lived to be understood. We can tell you only of events, of what men do. We cannot really tell you how or why they do it. We can see, and tell

*you, that this war is brutalizing some among your sons and yet
ennobling others. We can tell you very little more.*

"*War happens inside a man. It happens to one man alone. It
can never be communicated. That is the tragedy—and perhaps the
blessing. A thousand ghastly wounds are really only one. A million martyred lives leave an empty place at only one family table.
That is why, at bottom, people can let wars happen, and that is
why nations survive them and carry on. And, I am sorry to say,
that is also why in a certain sense you and your sons from the war
will be forever strangers.*

"*If, by the miracles of art and genius, in later years two or three
among them can open their hearts and the right words come, then
perhaps we shall all know a little of what it was like. And we shall
know, then, that all the present speakers and writers hardly touched
the story.*"

This I delivered, and had the old, uneasy feeling that I had
overstepped and that those who had heard it would squirm with
embarrassment. Again I was to be surprised and gratified—and
puzzled. For this confession of failure, this attempt to explain that
I could not really explain the war, brought a response from ordinary
men and women all over America in a volume which had never
before followed a talk of mine. Hildy, the office secretary, wrote
from New York: "I have never seen such mail on my desk. You must
have reached the hearts of millions."

4

In a few days it would be April again in northern Europe. For a
short while, around midday, the sun felt mellow and warm despite
the wind that poured over our faces as the jeep moved across
France and Belgium. But then the fat, scudding clouds would
imperceptibly change from white to gray and lock together to
form the chill, iron curtain which imprisons the rolling land.
The stately rows of poplars then lose their beauty and stand stark
against the dimming horizon; the canals grow somber and cold;
the village squares become grim and lifeless; the cathedrals appear
grotesque, forbidding, like dark Bastilles of the human spirit.
Northern Europe—serene and lovely and gently finished in the

sun, dark and ominous in cloud, cradle and grave for what is best and worst in us. It is the great blood receptacle of history for all of us who are Occidentals, and it has proved its claim upon us all, whether we come from Dakota or Dungeness.

The jeep proceeded past the milestones of personal memory, markers already grown old, as close to Agincourt or Roman as to World War or me: The village house where the supreme French commander had been sitting that day in 1939. The little white pill-box beside the Meuse where the Belgian soldiers had been eating their lunch and dangling their feet; it was now lifeless as a stone. The row of cement teeth in the Siegfried Line where the two enormous German guards had stamped their heels together and stopped Geoffrey and me from nearing the border. The obstacles now were only the broken dentures of the Reich's decaying jaw-bone, hanging open as if grimacing at the hollow and sightless eyes of the Maginot Line across the vale. The station and square in the middle of Aachen. Where the squad of barrel-chested men in black boots had stamped and turned that January day in '39 there was a heap of plaster and rubble crowned with a slashing of garbage. And standing in the square was the kid brother, a little straighter and more solid than two years before. There was a glinting of moisture in his narrowed eyes, and around the temples his hair was gray.

I re-entered Germany precisely where I had come out of it six years before, when it was throbbing with uncontainable power and life, like a dynamo about to burst of its own combustion. Now the strong, square houses sagged, rent and finished beside the frozen heaps of muck they had spewn out as they collapsed. Great trees lay cloven beside the road. Telephone wires straggled over the chipped stone fences. A few villagers and peasants passed, carrying bundles or pushing carts. Sometimes they looked at us without expression in their heavy faces; mostly they did not look at us. I discovered that I was not wondering what they thought of us; I was vaguely wondering what I thought of them. I had rather supposed, when I anticipated this return, that in my soft-ness I would feel sorry for them, now that they were beaten. It is a trait of my kind that we feel for the underdog in any given situation, no matter what his record. But I felt pity no more than hatred. I merely felt wary toward them, and cold. If I had spoken to one of them I would have spoken stiffly, however absurd that would be. The normal instincts of my kind simply did not break through the crust of feeling toward these people, which six years of emotion, however vicarious, had formed in my mind. I wondered if the war had done something to me, caused a basic alteration in the complex created by early home and religious training. In any case, I thought, I can never again in all my life feel a normal human relationship toward these people. They will always be something special to me. I did not know whether this was stupid and bad of me, or wise and proper; and I found I did not care. It was chill twilight as we poked the jeep through the rows of blank-faced brick cottages around München-Gladbach where we sought the press camp in Goebbels' former château. The ruins did not seem sad but merely ugly. People stood in small groups on the corners. They were always silent as we passed. I saw no smiles at any time. When a dog barked suddenly in the stillness, I jumped and felt a rush of anger and resentment, as if some stupid sniper who didn't know the score had fired at me.

On the twenty-fourth of March I stood with my boots sinking in the soft spring earth and looked through the brush at the Rhine. It did not seem very wide or turbulent here in these flatlands where willows grew and the cows cropped close to the water. It was not so impressive and formidable as its name and its history. But it was the *Rhine*. Because it was that, the Germans crouching across from me had put their faith in it, and their demented leader called upon it in this climactic hour as if it were the protecting almighty Jehovah of his dark religion. Well, Hitler had fed his distorted soul upon illusions; this would be his last illusion. The soft-spoken American general back at Supreme Headquarters had said there was no case of a successful river defense in military history. He was from Kansas, and of course in Kansas the Rhine is just a river. As I looked at the river, it seemed listless and without color; a certain torpid dignity, yes. The thought occurred to me: "It is their Pétain; it is their old Maréchal; and they take the calm façade for omniscience and strength." I could see a German army car whisking behind a clump of houses on the other side and smoke going up from a chimney into the windless sky. They did not have over there the secret knowledge we possessed. They did not know that this was the last day when their endless war would still really be a war. Tomorrow the great German raid against the human race would be all over save for the meaningless odds and ends. The last battle would occur when darkness came this night. The whole situation was selfishly satisfying, and I savored it in my thoughts for a while. I, an ordinary man with a name and origin of which Caesar was ignorant, was standing a couple of hundred yards from his camp, knowing the secret of his fate and the fate of his empire. And he didn't know. I, one of his intended slaves, was so much mightier than he. I, who had never kicked a Jew, or looted a village, or burned a book, or stolen a country, or killed anything larger than a hare, was standing with empty hands looking into his final citadel, possessed of the biggest, brightest fact in this moment of eternity—the fact that the terror and tyranny of our times would come to an end this night. It was a pleasing reverie indeed, full of fancy ornamentation. I thought: "Now that I'm here, I'll represent the whole human race, all the millions of people who haven't done the things Caesar has done."

After a while my feet began to feel damp, and my bones were chilling. I crawled carefully back through the bushes to the road, keeping·my head down so the human race would not get itself exterminated in the moment of its triumph.

The noon hour came and passed. There was sporadic firing here and there, but most of the time there was a deathly stillness around the tiny village. Now and then puffballs of antiaircraft fire appeared in the pale blue sky, and once an Allied plane coasted back over our lines, gradually losing height and streaming bright flame behind it. I was with a battalion of British Commando troops, whose objective was the key town of Wesel, whose small spires we could easily see across the river. I had thought at first I should be with my own people for this final battle, the last fighting I ever expected to see in my life. But after a few minutes of strolling about and talking with the young Englishmen the feeling passed away. I was not thinking of myself as an American and of them as British. I realized again, more acutely than ever before, that these *were* my people. I knew I would have felt the same way had I been with the French, or anybody else on this side. It was extraordinary how the sense of distinction melted away, and there remained only the old difference, that between soldier and looker-on.

An enemy mortar shell, in the manner of mortar shells, exploded without warning fifty yards away, and I heard the whizzing of the particles. I moved over behind the squat brick house, the command post, and sat on my helmet. The Cockney sentryman shifted his rifle and eased his back against the bricks. "I say there, correspondent," he said, "ye wouldn't be Mister Vincent Sheen by off chance, would ye?" I said that Mr. Shean was on his way to Rome or New York or somewhere. "I read his book," said the sentry. He lapsed into silence. The brigadier walked back and forth on the cowpath, clasping and unclasping his hands behind his back. It was that moment, that fretting eternity after all preparations are made and there is nothing one can do. "This waitin'," muttered the sentry. "Worse than waitin' for D-day, to my mind." The river remained silent. Now and then a cock crowed in a barnyard. Music was tinkling from a radio jeep behind the next house.

We ate an early supper, in the one good room of a half-wrecked house. There was tea, and somebody had brought along a bottle of American whisky. None of the young officers talked about the coming operation. One asked if he could leave a letter with some-one who would be on this side of the river tomorrow. A bronzed French captain asked me, if I was returning to Paris, to call up his wife and tell her that he was all right. I said I would, thinking that he was being a little premature. He gave me his name, Lorraine. "We just got married a short while ago," he said. "Her father is Paul-Boncour." I said I knew who he was and that I would probably soon see him at the San Francisco conference where they were going to make a new League. "By the way," the captain went on shyly, "would you mind not saying publicly that I am here? They might try to make me go over with the French army. I'd rather like to stay with these fellows." That was understandable. They had the air of young men to whom war has become a profes-sional business, to be dispatched with efficiency. A batman took the tin plates away. We studied the pictures in *The Tatler* by candlelight. Somebody picked up a German photograph from the dirty floor; it showed a dozen German girls in military uniform posing with a Luftwaffe officer. "A scrummy lot," the men agreed. "That one on the end would do if you were hard up."

We gathered outside when the first of the bombers appeared out of the dusk where the sun had set. Great crumping sounds came from the direction of Wesel, and then clouds of dust and smoke began to drift up from the town, obscuring it. More and more planes came steadily, and the ground was shaking. The concussion was strong enough to whip our trousers even at this distance, and the windows rattled. A momentary sensation of pity for the poor wretches underneath that avalanche swept through me, and, I think, through the others. But only for a mo-ment. The brigadier smiled at a soldier and said: "Corporal Smith,

I don't think you'll find any billets in that town tonight." Suddenly our own batteries opened up behind us, and it was almost impos sible to speak. The twilight deepened, darkness crept rapidly over the flatlands, and the great pall of smoke over Wesel was turning a deep violet color.

Seven o'clock. Eight o'clock. Nine o'clock. The barrage did not cease for so much as ten seconds. It was not night, nor was it day. It was a ghastly mixing and overlapping of unearthly colors which senselessly repeated themselves as flares, spots, waves, sparks, flames, and streamers. It was like standing in the middle of some fantastic factory full of bursting boilers and crashing drop ham- mers, illuminated by blue lamps that flickered, kliegs that blinded you and then suddenly went out, spurting acetylene torches, a hundred flashlights that snapped on and off, golden mouths of furnaces that opened and shut, and great blobs of molten ore that splashed on the ground. The ceaseless racket was maddening. You felt like a migraine victim, with the blood steadily beating in your head, slowly fraying away your nerves. An invisible bridge of steel was arching over the Rhine, and the great moat could do nothing about it. Nobody could do anything about it. I had never before seen such a thing; I had never read or heard of such a thing.

I felt my way into the nave of the small stone Catholic church nearer the river. I bumped into wooden chairs and knocked over a candelabrum as I felt for the steps to the tower. I hated this being alone. I dared not light a match, and so I stumbled up the circular stairway, feeling the clammy stone wall with my hands. There was a wooden ladder, a cruel bump on the head, and then a loft. I stepped on the leg of a sleeping man and heard a soft Scottish curse. Another ladder, another maddening bump, and I was at the observation post. I felt a rat brush my boot. The place was cramped and musty and crisscrossed with giant beams. I peered from a vertical slit in the stones and could see very little. Only the Rhine at my feet, pale and translucent in the moonlight. Across on the other side was only the black rim of the shore. Sud- denly I felt horribly conspicuous and vulnerable. I crawled through the beams again and bumped into a large, soft, human form. A growling American voice asked: "Who're you?" I said: "Sevareid." The voice replied: "Oh. Yeah. Heard of you. I'm Belden." We squeezed, grunting, down the ladders. He said he was representing *Harper's Magazine*. I don't know why, but the mention of *Harper's* struck me as extraordinarily funny at the moment. It was good to have company. All evening I had been saying to myself: "This is the last battle. You are going home. You didn't have to come here. You are a fool." Now I no longer felt like that.

At the outer edge of the village I stood beside a Commando major and watched the assault troops take formation. They had been tucked away somewhere all day and I had not noticed them. Now they appeared in long files, coming out of the woods. There was the sound of creaking boots and straps, the occasional clanking of metal upon metal, and the hoarse muttering of subdued voices. They marched in line right before us, some of their faces blackened with soot so that the whites of their eyes seemed abnormally clear. They were slightly bent under their packs, but they shuffled rapidly, and some were singing in soft cadence as they marched toward the dark hulks of the assault craft assembled in the center of the hamlet. The major beside me had only one eye; he had lost the other during the first Commando raid in Norway, and for months his job had been superintending a Commando rest camp in Wales. He had got two weeks' leave from the job— and this was where he had chosen to spend it. Now and then he reached out and touched a passing soldier; just touched him, saying nothing. He became aware that I was watching this gesture and said: "I get a funny feeling at a time like this." Like me, he had been forbidden by the brigadier to make the crossing, since space in the craft was tight. The major would suddenly start away, walking a few paces beside one of the men. Then he would come back to me and after a few moments of watching would start away beside another man. I thought he was speaking to them now. He did this several times, but always returned to our position. I knew suddenly that I was looking into his open heart and that I understood how he felt. The war had become his very life; these men were all his world. Here with them under the dark moon, in the middle of the hellish noise, in this moment when his comrades prepared to challenge the unknown, he was intensely alive. Elsewhere, he was half-dead. And, I thought, there will be many like this man, many who will remain but half-alive when all this is ended.

The assault craft, which possessed both wheels and fins, rumbled slowly out of the hamlet with their charges, leaving the small square and street empty and defenseless in the ghostly light. The artillery fire was now beyond all belief. All the machine guns in the world opened from our bank of the river, and then the astonishing Oerlikons, the rapid-firing guns, commenced at our backs, flinging cascading streams of red tracers over our heads, with a pounding clatter that made one feel his teeth were coming loose. It was as if some giant were flinging hundreds of lighted Christmas trees with blinding speed just over the low roofs. By now the men would be out into the river, exposed to the enemy, if the enemy remained alive and functioning. We stood in a doorway. Through a lighted crack in a curtain at my rear I could see a mess sergeant chopping up a slab of fresh, raw meat. Two Commandos with blackened faces shoved past me, unspeaking, and returned from the interior carrying a stretcher. There had been mortar shells at the river bank. There was a sudden commotion now in the square by the church, and several horses, crazed by the racket and the fireworks, galloped blindly about, crashing into walls and each other, frantically neighing.

We slipped down the road toward the river a short distance and stretched out on a low bed of barnyard straw, pale and yellow in the increasing moonlight. We could still make out the single fire in Wesel which had been started by the late afternoon bombing. A good marker for the night bombers, now due. The infantrymen would be lying on the ground only fifteen hundred yards from the bomb line, ready to rise and charge the town immediately after the bombs had fallen. At 10:25 the Royal Air Force was there, the Pathfinders dripping slowly descending flares into the target town. And then again the bombing of Wesel. The whole area gleamed and glared with flame, and the sickly-pale river appeared to be blotched with blood spots. The spectacle was elemental, primeval, beyond any human reference. Then silence fell upon us, upon the whole region, and we knew that the men were on their feet, hurrying into the town with the handsome, stocky brigadier at their head. I experienced in this timeless moment no feeling of envy. I did not relate myself to them in any manner. I felt drawn out of myself in a sensation of reverence, of purest worship toward gods who did not inhabit my world.

Inside a smoky control van at the outer edge of the village we hunched together and fixed our eyes on the sergeant major with the headphones clamped to his blond face. He would turn his head slightly and repeat: "No mines on the far shore. Very little small arms fire. Forty prisoners . . . two hundred prisoners . . . a major general killed . . . a colonel captured . . . we have had very few losses." The lieutenant beside me could not arrest a slow grin. "Beyond our wildest hopes," he said. "Never dreamed it."

Now one felt suddenly drained of strength and energy. In the command post village three of us tried to sleep on the littered floor of a small house. Now and then mortar shells came in, and frequently their fragments banged against the thin walls that protected us. Belden began to snore at once, but I could not sleep. I lay in the rubbish, distressingly aware of some rotting thing not far from my nose, waiting for the next mortar explosion. When dawn showed vaguely through the smeared windows we got stiffly to our feet, filthy, and aching in every bone. It was cold outside, and the wet pastures were smoking. The sky was clear and blue except for the gray haze which hung over the spot where Wesel had been. In the dining-room of the previous night, three young officers slept, tipped back in their chairs with their heads against the wall. They looked, now, like exhausted children. The wall picture of the Last Supper was hanging askew. The copy of *The Tatler* lay on the dirty floor.

The enlisted men sat on the stone step in front of their billet and regarded us with dull expressions. A tiny mortar fragment had killed one of their comrades in the night, a few yards from where we had been trying to sleep. The men were saying nothing. One idly nudged with his boot toe a wooden plane fashioned by some German child who had penciled the Luftwaffe markings on its wings. The plane was broken.

The morning wore on, and each time the sound of a plane was heard we got to our feet. Finally at ten o'clock the long files of slow American transport planes and gliders streamed in formation out of the mottled clouds to the west. Effortlessly, white clusters of parachutes blossomed beneath the aerial trains and drifted gently toward earth on the other side of the Rhine. It seemed very unwarlike, rather like a spectacular exercise at a fair. I heard no sound of guns, but there were the puff balls hanging in the air among the planes. The transport planes curved over in our direction after dropping their loads. One near me parted with a wing; the body of the plane plummeted earthward while the wing followed, fluttering and scudding like a big leaf. Another plane was streaming fire from both engines. The flames were beautiful golden ribbons against the blue sky as the plane settled slowly toward the tree line. I sat backwards watching it as my jeep returned toward

Goebbels' castle. Everywhere, in the windows of roadside houses, in the gardens and pastures, British and American soldiers were watching the spectacle, transfixed and solemn. The Battle of the Rhine, the last big battle of Western Europe, was really over. The war was really over. The last scene was so imaginative, so graceful in its blue-and-white setting, rather noble, altogether fine and satisfying. I knew I would never see a battle again. There was relief in the thought, but it was followed by another feeling, which I did not admit to myself for some time—a sneaking sensation of nostalgia and regret.

Even Caesar's brave new world "ends, not with a bang, but a whimper." Inside the citadel the Germans were falling back without much attempt at serious resistance, or surrendering in shuffling, abject masses. I drove across the Rhine into the endless mazes of solid red-brick homes on the outskirts of industrial Duisberg. The aftermath of the climactic battle was neither imaginative nor noble. Defeat had the same smell and look in the Reich that it had anywhere else. Cows and horses lay by the roads, horribly swollen by the gas generated in death. Villagers tugged at the shafts of horse carts that bore the bodies of dead neighbors. We came upon a party of four hundred Italian "slave workers" who were stumbling back into the American lines. Their faces were matted with hair, their eyes bloodshot, and their clothes in utter rags. Some had cloth wound about their feet in place of shoes. Even in the chill air the group gave off a sickening stench as one passed by. When they halted for a brief rest, some would root quickly about in the debris and filth like animals, snatching up cigarette ends, bits of garbage, and pieces of string. This is what it had come to, Hitler's dream of organizing all Europeans into the service of his New Europe.

There was a stirring and gathering of people across the railroad tracks, at the entrance to an enormous slag heap among the coal mines. The Germans had driven long tunnels into the slag heap to be used as shelters, and these had become a prison for seven thousand men, women, and children who were unable to leave during the barrage and the infantry fighting that followed it. They had refused to allow the foreign workers to share the shelter with them; and then, when they tried to emerge prematurely, unable to stand the stench, the crowding, the cold, and hunger, German troops had fired on them to drive them back inside. In the indescribable catacombs sick people had died, their bodies festering beside young women who were giving birth to babies in the soot.

Now our Military Government officers were sorting out the sick and the healthy at the entryway, bringing up water for them and dispatching trucks for bread and meat. The Germans clustered in large groups, watching the Americans' every move and gesture. The women's legs were smeared with coal dust, and their hair straggled down over their unwashed faces while the children blinked their eyes and clung to their mothers' skirts. Despite this familiar situation of misery-and-salvation, a thing I had seen many times before, the relationship here was not the normal one. It was conqueror and conquered, of course, but there was something else besides. You could see it in their eyes. There were the sullen expressions of suspicion which one expected, but there were other expressions which revealed a deep, fixed indignation, which said: "This cannot happen to *us.*" There seemed to be a sheeplike desire to do exactly as they were told, and yet an air of outraged dignity. When their burgomaster announced in a loud voice that the Americans would be unable to move them back into their homes until the next day, a muttering ran through the crowd, there were drooping sneers on the faces of some of the younger men and women, and one white-haired grandmother burst into shrieks of despair and anger. Human misery is human misery, but I could not avoid a sudden feeling of detestation and incredulity. Millions of people in many lands were in this same condition, and worse, because of what the Germans had done. The starving, dehumanized foreign workers were just down the road. The homes of these Germans, as we had verified, were stocked with food, warm clothes, new furniture, and radios. One could tell at once merely by looking into their faces that they had not the faintest sense of having done anything wrong, that they were utterly unable to grasp what had happened to them and their country, that they had been, were now, and would continue to be concerned only with themselves, unable even to imagine the suffering of others.

It could have been self-deception, but I had a profound feeling of having seen at a flash into the minds of a people who were different. As we drove back across the river I realized that a contradiction had been introduced into what had been a basic belief of mine. I had made the assumption most of my friends in college had made: that all peoples are essentially the same, that all are capable of democracy and peace, that given bread and security they will have no desire to aggress upon others, that if all people are given bread and security long enough, wars will be impossible. Now I felt entirely unsure of the economic interpretation of political events. Whatever the overpowering logic of Marx and others, I had an uneasy feeling that the structure broke down where the Germans were concerned. It was difficult to put into words, but somehow they *were* different. They were not quite rational or normal in the realm of human relationships, in the procedures of social existence. There was an inexplicable knot in their souls. Their spirit was an ingrown one, not an outgoing one. Perhaps, as some said there was a loneliness in them, but if so it was a loneliness which neither we nor they could assuage on this world, this side of death. Had the generation of organized breast-beating and mysticism alone done this to them? I was not sure; I was inclined to feel it was a basic and permanent matter, and how outsiders—conquerors or others—were to go about altering this state of affairs I had no idea. The war we had poured upon the country had certainly altered Germany; I had yet to believe that it had altered the Germans.

The war was over in Europe. There would be more fighting and perhaps some drama as the final quarry were run down and the last shots fired; but the thing itself was done, and the rest could be only anticlimax. I found myself empty of all interest in the inevitable and incapable of acting any role, however small, as a conqueror. Nothing truly important or unexpected could happen in Western Europe for a long time to come. Perhaps, had I been a fighting soldier, I would have experienced feelings of triumph. But I suspect that many soldiers, too, felt what I now felt: a kind of dull satisfaction, a weary incapacity for further stimulation, a desire to go home and not have to think about it any more—and a vague wondering whether I could ever cease thinking about it as long as I lived.

It was a soft, murmurous spring evening when I entered the Brussels-Paris train, the old train with the blue *wagon-lit*. And it was then that I was caught unaware and suddenly saw Europe again—the Europe of peace and charm which I had first savored in this small country. The conductor wore the uniform of peace and he tipped his cap. The pullman beds were made up, the sheets were crisp and fresh, and the clean red blankets were turned neatly down. The porter bowed and presented a bottle of Eau Vittel, "for the morning." The train started smoothly, without a jerk, and the passengers leaned out of the lowered windows for last-minute handshakes. The spring air poured cooling over our faces. In the suburbs the lilacs were blooming in the walled gardens. The men and women in the gardens rested on their rakes and hoes, their heads turned as they smiled at us. The children ran to the doorways and waved. And there, for an instant, it all existed again in the tingling blood. The foreignness, the charm and fascination. Old Europe, fresh and forever renewing.

And then it was gone. The shades were lowered. The French officer in my compartment pulled off his muddy boots with a sigh and fished an American army cigarette from his soiled tunic.

It was a warm midnight in Paris when we said goodbye until we would meet again at home. I stood in the shadows by the Crillon as he walked across the Concorde in the direction of his billet. The young one, the kid brother, the gentle one who had liked to putter as a child, who had sat alone in the attic until darkness when the puppy died. In the light of the street lamps I could see the two bars on his shoulder faintly sparkle. The boy from North Dakota with the easy stride, the strong, bony wrists, and the lean, American jaw. America walked easily across the Concorde, the heartpiece of Paris and Europe, his boots adding irremovable impress to the stones which had borne the tumbrils and Adolf Hitler. He walked easily, whistling, in the lilac night, and his long shadow, cast by the cautious lamps, passed over the obelisk Napoleon had brought from Egypt.

5

It was late morning when I awoke in the second-rate Washington hotel. Not many hours before, I had been shivering in a snowstorm on the desolate flats of Iceland. It was morning in April, but already one could feel the pressure of the muggy heat. The bedclothes and the towels were limp, and a cockroach crawled in and out of a rip in the wallpaper which was stained with old sweat. Across the street the sun was bright on an orange-colored filling station, and the Negro attendant was polishing the pumps with slow grace, singing to himself. Women and girls in white dresses passed on clicking heels. They were all moving in the direction of Pennsylvania Avenue. I had heard the news from a young corporal at the barracks in Scotland, when he awakened me with a flashlight to announce that my flight was ready.

I did not go near my old office when I left the hotel; I could not bear the prospect of standing on a street corner with a microphone trying to find public words for such an event as this. It was very still in the side streets, with only a few cars moving and the pedestrians walking steadily without much conversation toward the Avenue. This stillness, this gravity, this suspension of normal human interchange—I had known all this once before: on the day that Floyd Olson was buried. When the caisson passed along, behind the horses, I felt a sharp pang. For the box was so *small*. It was impossible to think that it could contain the majesty, the force, the mountainous serenity. When it had passed down the street I noticed the woman standing next to me and felt a curious hypnosis. She was fashionably dressed in the newest mode of spring. The seams of her stockings were straight, and her black pumps were gleaming. She wore a small blue hat from which a white half-veil was suspended. As I watched she pushed the veil upward with the back of her manicured fingers and dabbed daintily at her eyes with a tiny handkerchief. She was truly suffering, but it took me a moment to understand this, for I could not remember having observed well-dressed grief in a very long time.

On the train moving to the Northwest Country, the old phenomena of America which had absorbed me on each return again had the same effect. The cunning fittings of expressionless aluminum that folded and turned for illumination, for smoking, for sitting or leaning or sleeping. The plump, overwhite faces of the men nestled on the white collars, the fat white hands and the shining shoe leather. The wooden buildings which seemed tentative, temporary. In the early morning the frosty earth gave off steamy exhalations in promise of noonday warmth. The galvanized iron washtubs shone like breastplates hanging to the cow sheds on the side that faced the sun.

Perhaps it was because of the weariness that lies halfway between anxiety and content, but the farms and hamlets in this back country seemed different to me now. Each cluster of buildings radiant in the yellow morning sun was a diadem of peace. The region from which I came was no longer an outland, lost upon the far horizon of the world. It was its own world, and it was one with Provence and Sussex, Punjab and Yunnan. It too possessed no boundary nor circumference, no beginning and no end.

Local boosters called San Francisco the Birthplace of the Future. Indeed, in the city's wide-eyed wonder and bustling energy there was portent, in its keen air was promise. But soon the feeling came over one that we were attending the inquest on a dead era, not the birth of a new one, that this was an ending, not a beginning. The feeling frightened me, and I thought: "Your life has so conditioned you that you can function only in the achieving and are unfitted for the achievement. In your own way you bear the curse of the Commando major: you live only in struggle, and the triumph leaves you bored. You are capable only of the motions of life and not of its substance. Either private seeds or your times have left you rootless, as unfitted for stability as a fish for dry land." Then I began to see that the others around me who came from the war were the same. Long hours of memories were recalled with Bech of Luxembourg, whose long locks were now quite gray; with the Frenchmen from the Algiers hilltop; with Englishmen I had known on battlegrounds; with Didier, the towering Yugoslav, who would begin to talk about the new League and end by staring into his glass and speaking of his martyred wife and the look of death on the Belgrade barricade three blocks from his mother's house. There were no others available, but somehow these men were not the ones to make the future, for they were obsessed with the past. They were prepared more by chastisement than by aspiration, by fear rather than by hope. Nor was I a proper person to observe this contest of words and report its dreams in the hopeful tone the people wished to hear. Final victory in Europe was announced; Hitler's demise was made known. The men from the areas of war observed these events as a formality, with a few quiet toasts among themselves; that was all. I sat before the typewriter and microphone, but there was really nothing to say. Only the most banal words would come.

I left the historic meeting before it ended, accepting the effort but unable to rouse myself for any positive contribution, however small. Perhaps because of weariness my sight was distorted, but it seemed to me that the structure these assembled men would build represented a truce and very little more. It was a mechanism that could help resolve the horizontal clash between the entities of nationalism, but it could not solve the vertical clash between classes of men—the deeply rooted, continuing, unstoppable struggle of men for bread and safety, the tide-flow of aspiration which sought to break down the walls between men, the artificial walls they had accepted so long that many believed them to be a condition of Nature.

Along the California coast south of Monterey the land is primitive and wild. Here men have attempted no conciliation with the elements, and all night the sea hammers at the scarified, ageless rocks. Despite the unceasing struggle of Nature, it is a place of special peace, for it seems out of the world of men; and the contest of Nature, unlike that of men, does not compel the observer toward participation. For he cannot pretend to know its origin or guess at its resolution. In this place a man can rest in the sun, remember without pain how he was wrong and without vanity how he was right. He can feel the tense knots slowly loosen within him and watch his children grow as brown as the dried kelp that garlands the granite rocks.

I was thirty-two. Yet I had a curious feeling of age, as though I had lived through a lifetime, not merely through my youth. In a special but true sense, I had. For the age of man is reckoned in eras as well as in years; and what I had vaguely sensed as a student was true: history has been moving in geometric proportions. History is speeding up, telescoping upon itself, so that the time of one man in life is no longer confined within one era. Already I had lived through an era. Our period of the confused and violent struggle against what we called Fascism had been essentially a negative one, of self-defense. Yet underneath the surface the positive tide-flow of men's aspiration had continued rising. Each epoch gives birth to the next. Of what was to come now I had no clear idea. Those of the extreme right and extreme left who think in stereotypes and categories already professed to know. If those who accuse liberals of confusing indecision with open-mindedness are right, then perhaps the imprecision of my own mind explained my inability to discover precision in the design of the future. Perhaps it was merely the weariness, the almost physical exhaustion which seemed to settle in deeper with each new·effort toward calculation. The idea was a foolish one, but for some time the feeling persisted that not only in terms of history had my life already been lived, but that the intellectual and emotional paralysis of age was already upon me. Like so many others at this moment I was simply tired, tired in a way I had nevei known before.

It had seemed so certain, when the fighting ended, that the great chapter of violent struggle for my time in life was finished and that through the foreseeable future, at least, the affairs of men in the places I had known would follow the broad course we had assumed and understood with only minor turbulence and turnings. There could be no big surprises, either in challenge or in corroboration of our basic estimates. Things would move, but they would move slowly, throttled down by the weariness of men and protected by the certainty of peace. I expected nothing sudden or overt to give cause for rejoicing or alarm. But the night I turned on the radio in the room that faced the sea and heard the results of the British election was a night of surprise and exhilaration. The weariness vanished, my heart pounded with excitement as though the struggle of ideas had become physiological with me. Uncertainty disappeared, replaced by a wonderful, satisfying feeling that all was justified—the concept of the struggle and the war itself—and that I and those like me had been righter than we knew. A hoary mold was broken over night by the will and clear comprehension of ordinary men and women, and a great people in orderly fashion were consciously, deliberately breaking the links which had always chained their greatness. Listening to the story of what the little men in the bowlers and soiled raincoats had accomplished by their union and their common sense, I had the happy feeling of personal confirmation, the healing sensation that the time of violence in which I had lived had proved to be far more than one of negative self-defense. Now it seemed to me that I could see the outlines of the era in which the last half of my life would be lived. It would be an era in which my kind could find that basic adjustment which leads, at long last, to inner peace, in which we could live in decency and work in fruitfulness.

But there came another event, one beyond prediction, which sprang out of minds that lived apart from my world of social context, a development of the secret laboratory and not the public market place or parliament—an unsocial event which yet bore upon society with a depthless profundity, unmatched in immediacy and portent by any social idea with which I had been familiar. I did not hear of the revolutionizing fact until a couple of days after the news had stupefied the literate world. I had wandered into the village and was reaching over the drugstore counter when my eyes fell on the headline that announced the transaction at Hiroshima. It was like a heavy blow on the chest, and the con·

cussion left me in a kind of mental coma for days. It seemed then
for a time that everything was not only uncertain but pointless.
It seemed to me that everything I had learned was junk for the
trash barrel, that everything I had seen was senseless illusion, that
all I had come to believe was hollow mockery, and that all my life
to this point had been lived for nothing.

But there is a blind impetus behind the streams of event and
thought which flow from origins hidden in history's high recesses
which will wash over and around any sudden, arbitrary dam. And
man cannot be reborn in midlife; he will try to reduce and confine
even the most unknowable menace or mystery to the terms of his
own limited reference. Life must go on. Now the issue was
squarely put to me and my generation, whose real trial and test
was now revealed to be not at all accomplished, as I had imagined,
but to lie just ahead. *How* was life to go on?

The issue seemed to be scraped bare of all intervening layers,
the matters with which I had been concerned and which now
appeared in the cold and desperate vision as misleading su-
perfluities. Up to the sixth of August, 1945, we had been trying to
make it possible for men to live better. Now we should have to
try to make it possible for men to live. It seemed to me, in despair
at first, that we were abruptly back to the defensive fight. I was
right back where I had started as a college student, when Fascism
rose and we were obliged to abandon our direct concern with the
struggle for a better life. Again we confronted the great diversion.
But this would be a harder and more portentous diversion than
that against Fascism, for Fascism was an obvious conspiracy of
evil, which all men could see, fear, and unite against, and the
stake was only life-in-reason. Now the enemy was fear itself, and
the stake was life. And the new struggle opened, cruelly, at the
precise moment when men were wearied as they have never been
before.

It seemed almost a grim jest. When my father—and, no doubt,
his father before him—had finished early schooling, an older, admonishing speaker had told them that the present generation of
maturity had failed to make the world a safe and decent one and
that now it was up to them. Men of my father's generation had said
the same thing to me and my classmates. "It is up to you." They
had doubtless said it with tongue in cheek. But since they said it
to us the month of August 1945 had occurred, and in the banal
remark of the wooden high-school stage was now contained the con-

centrated power and prophecy of all the sages in the histories of man. The grimmest jest of all, the final curse, or the supreme challenge. We were *it*.

Men possessed but one immediate bulwark: the weak mechanism of truce contrived at San Francisco, which now assumed the most profound significance, which demanded the aid of all hands to shore up and strengthen it. There was a chance, perhaps, that it could be so infused with the spirit and will of good men that it could become the bridge of law itself, and the one great government of the one small world. But it was not the final answer, for, while it could conceivably establish peace, it could not establish justice—and without justice, as all that I had experienced told me, there could not be peace for long. It was even conceivable that the mechanism could make all men compatriots under the law and loyal to the one authority; but there is such a thing as civil war or revolution, and the dreams and fears of men could yet destroy them.

For if I had learned anything, I had learned the great and obvious fact that the decisive desire of men is not for peace, however deep their longing, but for life in dignity, the sense of which burns, however feebly, in every man, however humble his status or obscure his place upon the earth. If men desired peace above all else, the Spaniards would have accepted Franco without a struggle, the free men of Europe would not have resisted Hitler, who had a formula for peace and came near to realizing it, the Chinese would not have suffered their long and bitter martyrdom, and my own countrymen would have stayed in the homes which they so thoroughly believe are the choicest on this earth. In the war I had known, men had given up their peace for life in dignity, and in many areas, chiefly Europe, had almost lost the civilization which makes their dignity possible at all. But now, since the month of August, the margin was closed. Civilized men could not again trade peace for life in dignity without losing both dignity and life. But as the first months of the new era wore on, it was frighteningly revealed that many men were behaving as if they were still prepared to take the risk. It became clear that even in this era of the last chance, they would take it so long as fear remained in them, so long as their hopes and dreams found no fruition.

The struggle of ideas had begun once more, and if the war had resolved old issues and dampened old hatreds, it had cleared the way for new conflicts and fanned into flames new hatreds which once had only smouldered. The new fires must be controlled. They must not be allowed to spread with senseless terror, like a prairie conflagration which only destroyed and left barrenness behind, but must be channeled in purpose like the fires of a forge which would fashion something enduring in the uses of men.

But the great time-space equation of progress was involved, and the differentials appeared sharper than ever. Only in physics is the world truly one; in the laboratory of the mind and heart it is many worlds. Peoples are differently spaced in the time channel of history, and they come to maturity and wisdom (or weariness and decline) at different moments, so that the problem rests in the fact that separate eras must try to live together within the one. In the free Western world we had understood that nationalism was part of the curse and menace of our time, and we had combined and fought to quell the most violent expression of it the world had known. But because time moves at different rates of speed in different places, we found, when the fight was ended, that while we had learned the lesson and knew we must have done with it, the nationalism of others was only just beginning. It seemed in these first months of the new era that what was occurring was both menacing and paradoxical. For out of the great Slav region of Eastern Europe, the core of organized equalitarianism itself, the articulate drive to break the barriers of privilege and class— which must go down if there was to be peace and dignity in the end—was forming into cadres of nationalisms as it continued its advance, and thus peace and the hopes for order were again pushed into jeopardy.

For liberals like myself, for all the confraternity of men of good-will that I had discovered almost everywhere, the new developments posed inescapably the problem of new adjustments; and the way ahead for such as I appeared obscured in dark uncertainty. Always, we had known that the barriers of class and privilege must be broken down, but we, products of the public school which taught us tolerance, of the Christian Church which taught us mercy, of the long tradition of liberalism which cherished human personality—we were discovering that liberalism was being squeezed away in large areas of the world by the new force which crept from the East, whose profession of identical aim we had taken on trust, but whose way was not the way of tolerance or mercy. In many areas of the Europe I had known, the unmerci-ful way was growing. Liberals had never squarely faced the implications of Communism because there had always seemed to be reason to doubt that its present methods would make impossible of fruition its original hope and aim, and because it had resisted heroically the desperate menace of Facism. We had suspected that there was more truth than falsehood in the Communist interpretation of social history, and we were not certain that the future did not belong to Communism. In any case, we had hoped that the junction of liberalism with Communism around the world —possible now that Fascism was destroyed—would give fiber to the one and tolerance to the other. This might yet prove true, but the first signs denied it and gave grim suggestion of a basic enmity between the two forces which ought to be allies for the cause of decent life in fruitful peace.

There remained only one source of material strength and moral force sufficient to tip the balance and alter the course of events in the only direction that men of goodwill could recognize and follow. This source was my own country. I had left it to seek in other places the mainspring of social action for my time, when America was merely the world's hope, and I had come home again to find America the world's necessity. I had gone out into the world carrying only America's curiosity and had been followed by millions of my countrymen who carried America's bright tools and great muscles, her giant voice and will; and however carelessly the tools had been put to use, however confusing the words of the voice, however unchanneled the will, still the world had heard and seen and felt it all. America was involved in the world, all its little Velvas were in the world, and the world was now in them, and neither the world nor America would ever be the same. There was still time for America to tip the balance and work its fashion upon the future. It could still work greatly to create a world in its own great image, but if the result was to be one to capture the allegiance of the confraternity of goodwill, America would also have to greatly work upon herself. All that America truly meant, all that Americans had perished for, would be devoid of consequence or portent unless the image of society that America showed the world was that of the little Velvas as I had known, remembered and cherished them.

My father wrote: "I have been out into Dakota again. It is as green as a garden now, and everyone seems hopeful. The folks there are about the same."

The folks are about the same—and that is the basic fact and the wonderful hope.

In Velva and everywhere the folks are the same, except for this: that a boy from Velva, who also swam in the brown river and saw the rim of the world along the horizon of the prairie, now lies buried in a place called Anzio of which his sixth-grade geography book showed no pictures.

Index